EU FOREIGN INVESTMENT LAW

EU Foreign Investment Law

ANGELOS DIMOPOULOS

OXFORD
UNIVERSITY PRESS

OXFORD
UNIVERSITY PRESS

Great Clarendon Street, Oxford, OX2 6DP,
United Kingdom

Oxford University Press is a department of the University of Oxford.
It furthers the University's objective of excellence in research, scholarship,
and education by publishing worldwide. Oxford is a registered trade mark of
Oxford University Press in the UK and in certain other countries

First published 2011

Published in the United States of America by Oxford University Press
198 Madison Avenue, New York, NY 10016, United States of America

British Library Cataloguing in Publication Data
Data available

Library of Congress Control Number: 2011943635

ISBN 978-0-19-969860-8

Στους γονείς μου
Ανδρέα και Γεωργία

Preface

Regulation of foreign investment is currently one of the most controversial subjects in EU external relations law. The introduction of foreign direct investment (FDI) in the Lisbon Treaty signalled the initiation of discussions aiming towards a comprehensive EU common external policy in the field of foreign investment. Being still in its infancy, the creation of a comprehensive EU investment policy meets a series of legal and practical challenges. The very existence of an EU investment policy depends on the specific delineation of the scope of EU competence over foreign investment. Its successful materialization rests on the careful determination of the specific objectives and content of EU investment agreements as well as on the clear demarcation of the roles of the EU and its Member States. EU institutions and Member States have to set up an investment policy that guarantees the integration and interaction of Member States' national investment policies with EU policy and addresses their views on the role, scope, and content of international investment law. After all, smooth transition from Member States' investment policies to EU investment policy is necessary to preserve European investors' interests and rights and to soothe the concerns of third countries.

Addressing these challenges, this book is based on the proposition that foreign investment is not an entirely new topic in EU external relations. The EU has long been an international actor gradually affecting the balance of powers and the roles of the EU and its Member States in the field of foreign investment and contributing to the development of international investment law. However, this topic has been until recently largely ignored and unexplored. From this angle, the book views and understands the emerging EU common investment policy as a natural consequence of existing EU policies and international agreements. More importantly, the book pays particular attention to the different origins and content of investment regulation under international law and EU law so far, and it attempts to explain and consolidate the divergent perceptions of foreign investment regulation that exist among international and EU lawyers.

In that regard, this book offers a systematic and detailed analysis of EU foreign investment law. It explores the concept of foreign investment and the aspects of international investment regulation and it facilitates a common understanding of the pertinent EU and international norms. Thereafter, it deals with the core question of the existence of an EU foreign investment policy, which requires a determination of the scope, content, and objectives of EU foreign investment policy. The book offers a detailed analysis of the scope of EU powers in the field of foreign investment, discusses their actual exercise—focusing on the conclusion and content of existing and future EU investment agreements—and explores the objectives and principles of EU foreign investment policy. Thirdly, the book examines the legal effects of EU foreign investment law on both the EU and the international legal order. It addresses the legal ramifications resulting from the nature of

EU investment agreements as instruments of international law, and in particular it explores the scope of the EU's and Member States' international responsibility in the field of foreign investment. Turning to EU law, the book focuses on the effects of EU foreign investment policy on Member States' Bilateral Investment Treaties, as well as on the Member States' obligations to perform and comply with EU investment agreements.

Exploring the existing legal framework on the scope and exercise of EU competence and its legal effects, the book aims to contribute to a better understanding of the legal foundations upon which a comprehensive EU common investment policy is based, addressing doctrinal and practical questions that are of interest to academics, policy makers, and practitioners in the field of EU foreign investment law.

Angelos Dimopoulos

Tilburg
July 2011

Acknowledgements

This book is based on my doctoral thesis, written during my time at the European University Institute in Florence, and re-worked from my current location at the Tilburg Law School. The book would not have been possible without the support of numerous people, to whom I would like to express my sincere gratitude.

First and foremost, I am immensely indebted to my doctoral thesis supervisor, Professor Marise Cremona, for her expert guidance, encouragement, and support. I am deeply grateful to Professor Ulrich Petersmann for his invaluable help and from whom I learned much as his student and research assistant. I also wish to express my sincere gratitude to Professor Eileen Denza and Professor Markus Krajewski, who examined my thesis and shared with me their experience and knowledge in this field. Many thanks are also due to Professors Bruno de Witte, Panos Koutrakos, Petros Mavroidis, Heike Schweitzer, and Karl Sauvant—as well as my fellow researchers in Florence—for their critical and thought-provoking comments which helped to strengthen my arguments and advance my work.

This study would not have been possible without the financial support of the Greek government and the excellent research premises of the European University Institute, Tilburg Law School, Columbia Law School, and Cambridge University, where I spent time working on the book. I am also grateful to the staff at Oxford University Press for their guidance, support, and efficiency in bringing the book to press.

Special words of thanks are due to Patricia for her insightful comments, her encouragement, and her support, which have been the most powerful sources of inspiration and motivation. I am also grateful to my sister and my brother for always being there for me and believing in me. Finally, there are no words sufficient to thank my parents without whose love and unconditional support I would not have been able to accomplish this endeavour; in recognition of my immeasurable gratitude this book is dedicated to them.

Contents

II THE SCOPE, CONTENT, AND OBJECTIVES OF EU FOREIGN INVESTMENT LAW

III THE LEGAL EFFECTS OF EU FOREIGN INVESTMENT LAW

Table of Cases

COURT OF JUSTICE OF THE EUROPEAN UNION

(Alphabetical table)

(Chronological table)

EUROPEAN COMMISSION AND COURT OF HUMAN RIGHTS

INTERNATIONAL COURT OF JUSTICE

WTO PANEL AND APPELLATE BODY REPORTS

INTERNATIONAL INVESTMENT ARBITRAL AWARDS

Table of Treaties and EU Legislative and Policy Instruments

TREATIES BETWEEN THE EU AND THIRD COUNTRIES

OTHER TREATIES

EU REGULATIONS, DIRECTIVES AND DECISIONS

EU POLICY INSTRUMENTS

List of Abbreviations

AB	Appellate Body
ACP	African, Caribbean and Pacific
AG	Advocate General
AJIL	American Journal of International Law
Art.	Article
ASEAN	Association of Southeast Asian Nations
BIT	Bilateral Investment Treaty
BYIL	British Yearbook of International Law
CAP	Common Agricultural Policy
CCP	Common Commercial Policy
Ch	chapter
CIS	Commonwealth of Independent States
CMLR	Common Market Law Review
Columbia JTL	Columbia Journal of Transnational Law
Cornell JIL	Cornell Journal of International Law
CYELS	Cambridge Yearbook of European Law Studies
DARIO	Draft Articles on the International Responsibility of International Organizations
DSU	Dispute Settlement Understanding
EA	Europe Agreement
EC	European Communities
ECHR	European Convention on Human Rights
ECtHR	European Court of Human Rights
ECJ	European Court of Justice
ECR	European Court Reports
ECT	Energy Charter Treaty
EDF	European Development Fund
EEA	European Economic Area
EEC	European Economic Community
EFA Rev	European Foreign Affairs Review
EFTA	European Free Trade Association
EIB	European Investment Bank
EJIL	European Journal of International Law
EL Rev	European Law Review
EMA	Euro-Mediterranean Agreement
EMU	Economic and Monetary Union
ENP	European Neighbourhood Policy
EPA	Economic Partnership Agreement
EU	European Union
EuZW	Europäische Zeitschrift für Wirtschaftsrecht
FDI	Foreign Direct Investment
FEMIP	Facility for Euro-Mediterranean Investment and Partnership
FET	Fair and Equitable Treatment
Fordham Int'l L J	Fordham International Law Journal

FTA	Free Trade Agreement
GATS	General Agreement on Trade in Services
GATT	General Agreement on Tariffs and Trade
GPA	Government Procurement Agreement
GSP	Generalised System of Preferences
Harvard ILJ	Harvard International Law Journal
ICJ	International Court of Justice
ICLQ	International and Comparative Law Quarterly
ICSID	International Centre for Settlement of Investment Disputes
ICSID Rev-FILJ	ICSID Review–Foreign Investment Law Journal
IGC	Intergovernmental Conference
IIA	International Investment Agreement
ILC	International Law Commission
ILM	International Law Materials
IMF	International Monetary Fund
Intl ALR	International Arbitration Law Review
IP	Intellectual Property
ITLOS	International Tribunal for the Law of the Sea
JCMS	Journal of Common Market Studies
JDI	Journal du Droit International
JIEL	Journal of International Economic Law
JWIT	Journal of World Investment and Trade
JWT	Journal of World Trade
LIEI	Legal Issues of Economic Integration
MAI	Multilateral Agreement on Investment
MFN	Most Favoured Nation
MIGA	Multilateral Investment Guarantee Agency
Minnesota JWT	Minnesota Journal of World Trade
MOU	Memorandum of Understanding
NAFTA	North American Free Trade Agreement
NJW	Neue Juristische Wochenschrift
NT	National Treatment
OECD	Organization for Economic Co-operation and Development
OJ	Official Journal
PCA	Partnership and Cooperation Agreement
QMV	Qualified Majority Voting
REIO	Regional Economic Integration Organization
RTA	Regional Trade Agreement
RTD Eur	Revue Trimestrielle de Droit Europeen
SAA	Stabilisation and Association Agreement
SWF	Sovereign Wealth Funds
Syracuse J Int'l L	Syracuse Journal of International Law
TBR	Trade Barriers Regulation
TDCA	Trade Development and Cooperation Agreement
TEC	Treaty Establishing the European Communities
TEU	Treaty on European Union
TFEU	Treaty on Functioning of the European Union
TRIMs	Trade Related Investment Measures
TRIPS	Trade Related Intellectual Property Rights

U Ill L Rev	University of Illinois Law Review
U Pa J Int'l L	University of Pennsylvania Journal of International Law
UN	United Nations
UNCLOS	United Nations Convention on the Law of the Sea
UNCTAD	United Nations Conference on Trade and Development
Virginia JIL	Virginia Journal of International Law
WIR	World Investment Report
WTO	World Trade Organization
YEL	Yearbook of European Law

Introduction

Regulation of foreign investment presents one of the most topical and controversial subjects in the EU's[1] external relations law. The adoption of the Lisbon Treaty and the introduction of EU competence over foreign direct investment (FDI) in Article 207 TFEU has generated broad discussions regarding the scope of the 'new' EU competence and how it affects Member States' foreign investment policies and in particular their Bilateral Investment Treaties (BITs). Of course, the foundations for an active EU role in the field of foreign investment were already laid by the Court of Justice. In 2009 the Court declared that certain provisions of Member States' BITs were incompatible with EU law, indicating that the existing legal framework had to be amended.[2] Following these developments, the European Commission announced its intentions to establish a new EU investment policy,[3] which has been followed by renewed interest by EU institutions and Member States on the future of EU investment policy.

Within this framework, the purpose of this book is to identify whether and to what extent the EU has become an international actor in the field of foreign investment, exploring and critically assessing the legal implications of its action in this field, both internally with regard to relations with the Member States and externally with regard to the developments in international investment law and regulation. As a result, the scope of this work is twofold.

On the one hand, it examines the role of the EU as an international actor in the field of foreign investment from a Union law perspective. Questions relating to the delimitation of EU and Member State competence, the actual exercise of EU and Member State powers, and the substantive content of EU (and supplementary

[1] On 1 December 2009 the Lisbon Treaty entered into force, which resulted in the replacement and succession of the European Communities by the European Union. Following the developments in European law, this book will use the term European Union (EU) for referring to all matters of European law that were previous covered by the EC Treaty and Community law in general, to the extent of course that they remain valid and relevant under the new founding Treaties: the Treaty on European Union (TEU) and the Treaty on the Functioning of the European Union (TFEU). For purposes of legal accuracy, any references made to the European Community (EC), the Treaty establishing the European Communities (TEC), and the old Treaty on European Union (EU Treaty) will concern mainly issues of historical interest or issues under the previous regime that have been changed by the Lisbon Treaty.

[2] Case C-205/06 *Commission v Austria* [2009] ECR I-1301; Case C-249/06 *Commission v Sweden* [2009] ECR I-1335; Case C-118/07 *Commission v Finland* [2009] ECR I-10889.

[3] Communication from the Commission to the Council, the European Parliament, the European Economic and Social Committee and the Committee of the Regions, 'Towards a comprehensive European international investment policy', Brussels 7.7.2010, COM(2010) 343; Proposal for a regulation of the European Parliament and of the Council establishing transitional arrangements for bilateral investment agreements between Member States and third countries, Brussels 7.7.2010, COM(2010) 344.

Member State) action in the field of foreign investment are examined, thus clarifying the international position of the EU and its Member States and the scope of and limitations posed by EU law on their international action. In that respect, this work looks systematically at the entirety of Union law questions posed by the international regulation of foreign investment by the EU and its Member States. Touching on almost all major questions raised in EU external relations law, it is argued that the EU is an important international actor in the field of foreign investment. Its competence over foreign investment, even before the entry into force of the Lisbon Treaty, is much wider than commonly understood; it has already created a significant body of international law by partly exercising its powers, while EU law imposes severe limitations on Member State powers and BITs.

On the other hand, this work examines the influence the EU exerts on international law and the regulation of foreign investment. In determining whether and how the EU affects the development of international investment law and regulation, specific attention is paid to the substantive content and orientation of EU foreign investment regulation, taking a comparative approach to the positions adopted so far by the Member States and other international actors, as well as to the ramifications of EU foreign investment regulation for international law. In that respect, it is suggested that, departing from the traditional BIT model, the EU has so far promoted a shift in regulatory priorities, focusing on liberalization and development. Considering, however, the ongoing attempts to establish a comprehensive EU investment policy—there is still ambiguity about whether and how the EU will balance its objectives of liberalization, protection, and development.

Within this framework, the book is divided into six chapters grouped into three parts.

Part I, which consists of Chapter 1, provides the conceptual and normative framework within which this book is developed. To understand the broader context within which the EU is developing as an international actor in the field of foreign investment, the chapter begins by setting out the international law context within which EU foreign investment law emerged, focusing on the socio-economic reasons requiring international regulation of foreign investment and the historical evolution of international investment law. The second part of Chapter 1 is dedicated to the quest for a definition of foreign investment, aiming to consolidate the divergent definitions found in investment protection and liberalization instruments and, most importantly, in international investment law and EU law. Thirdly, the chapter identifies the regulatory scope and the sources of EU foreign investment law, enabling the systematic examination and understanding of the topic. It presents a thematic categorization of sources of law according to the regulated subject matter, stressing the divergent focus of EU regulation on different aspects of foreign investment. Given the broad spectrum of subject matter that foreign investment regulation covers, the thematic categorization of sources of law also serves a systemic purpose, as the questions dealt with in the following chapters are examined in light of this categorization.

After identification of the conceptual and normative framework of this study, Part II deals with the core question of the existence of an EU foreign investment policy. Understanding the role of the EU as an international actor in the field of foreign investment requires a determination of the scope, content, and objectives of EU foreign investment policy, viewed comparatively to the foreign investment policies followed by other international actors. In that regard, Chapter 2 deals with the determination of EU powers in the field while Chapter 3 discusses the exercise of EU powers in the field of foreign investment, focusing on the conclusion and content of International Investment Agreements concluded by the EU (EU IIAs).[4] This is followed in Chapter 4 by an exploration of the objectives and principles of EU foreign investment policy.

More specifically, Chapter 2 explores the scope of EU competence in the field of foreign investment, striving to put an end to the ambiguity concerning the delimitation of powers between the EU and its Member States. In following the thematic categorization of foreign investment regulation, the scope and nature of EU competence is examined separately for each aspect of foreign investment. In that regard, the coverage of foreign investment by explicit power-conferring provisions in the TFEU is identified and the general rules on EU implied competence are applied, determining the scope of EU competence over foreign investment. The conclusions reached on the scope and nature of EU competence are of utmost significance for assessing the role of the EU as an international actor in this field.

Chapter 3 is dedicated to the exercise of EU competence in practice. Aiming to identify the current state of the art, the chapter begins with a depiction of the internal procedures for the conclusion of an IIA by the EU and goes on to discuss the content of EU IIAs, identifying and analysing their substantive provisions with regard to each aspect of foreign investment. The chapter concentrates on the innovations that existing and future EU IIAs have brought and intend to bring to international investment law in comparison to BITs—highlighting the differences and novelties of EU IIAs in terms of their content.

Chapter 4 turns to a legal assessment of the orientation of EU foreign investment law. It aims to complete the picture on EU foreign investment policy by identifying and analysing the principles and objectives that determine the exercise of EU competence in the field. In that regard, first, it offers an insight into the specific principles and objectives that EU action in the field adheres to and pursues, emphasizing their position within the broader framework of the general objectives of EU external action. Secondly, it considers the application of these principles and objectives in practice, looking at the objectives pursued by existing (and future) EU IIAs and assessing whether the legal mechanisms established in EU IIAs are suitable and sufficient for achieving the envisaged objectives. Bearing in mind the objectives of international investment law and regulation, Chapter 4 complements the analysis in Chapter 3, in that it depicts the novelties and differences of EU IIAs from other international investment law instruments in terms of their orientation.

[4] The term EU IIA is used in reference to all international agreements concluded by the EU which include legally binding provisions on foreign investment. Although none of the Union agreements concluded so far deals exclusively with foreign investment, the term EU IIA is used in order to emphasize their character as investment agreements, which, even marginally in certain cases, touch on the international regulation of foreign investment relations.

Having identified the scope, content, and objectives of EU external action in the field of foreign investment, Part III examines the legal effects of EU foreign investment law. Considering that EU foreign investment regulation impacts on both the EU and the international legal order, Chapter 5 is concerned with the international law effects and Chapter 6 with the EU law effects of EU foreign investment law.

Chapter 5 analyses the international law effects of EU external action in the field of foreign investment, addressing the legal ramifications resulting from the nature of EU IIAs as instruments of international law that affect not only the EU and its Member States, but mainly the contracting third countries. In that respect, the chapter explores, first, the question of the EU's and Member States' international responsibility for the performance of investment obligations undertaken in EU IIAs, taking into account in particular, the nature of EU IIAs as mixed agreements and the international law rules on the responsibility of international organizations. Secondly, Chapter 5 deals with the hierarchy of norms between overlapping IIAs from an international law perspective. It examines separately overlaps between EU IIAs and between EU IIAs and Member State BITs, focusing mainly on the methods used for the avoidance of incompatibilities and the potential for conflicting commitments.

Chapter 6 addresses the Union law effects of EU foreign investment law, by identifying the EU law rights and obligations of EU institutions and Member States arising from the regulation of foreign investment by the EU. In that respect, the scope and extent of Union law obligations to comply and perform EU IIAs is primarily considered, determining the scope of this obligation in the field of foreign investment. The chapter also looks extensively into the scope and application of Union law obligations to respect the primacy and autonomy of Union law in the field of foreign investment regulation. Examining the compatibility of EU IIAs and, more importantly, of Member State BITs with EU law, it identifies the violations of Union law that result from Member State action in the field of foreign investment and assesses the suggested proposals for remedy. The chapter also considers the enforceability of these Union law obligations, focusing on the scope of judicial review of EU and Member State actions in light of EU IIAs and the creation of individual rights.

Finally, the primary conclusions are drawn together with a view to providing some final observations on the role of the EU as an international actor in the field of international law and regulation of foreign investment. Based on the developments of primary EU law and international investment law, forward-looking projections are offered on the development of EU foreign investment law.

PART I

THE CONCEPTUAL AND NORMATIVE FRAMEWORK OF EU FOREIGN INVESTMENT LAW

1

The Origins, Definition, and Scope of EU Foreign Investment Law

Understanding the broader context within which the EU is developing as an international actor in the field of foreign investment, one has to identify the origins and the regulatory scope of EU presence in the field of foreign investment. Considering that foreign investment law has been developed within the realm of public international law, it follows without question that the evolution of the international law and regulation of foreign investment present the relevant context for a proper analysis of EU foreign investment law. In that regard, this chapter begins by setting out the international law context within which EU foreign investment law emerged, looking in particular at the socio-economic reasons that require the international regulation of foreign investment, the historical evolution of international law rules on foreign investment, and the reasons behind the development and evolution of regulation of foreign investment by the EU. Secondly, the chapter determines the term 'foreign investment' in EU external relations with third countries, attempting to consolidate the divergent definitions found in investment protection and liberalization instruments and, most importantly, in international investment law and EU law. Thus, it offers the basis for a common understanding of protection and liberalization norms and for distinguishing foreign investment from other economic activities. Thirdly, a categorization of legal instruments regulating foreign investment is provided, which follows a classification of the different aspects of international investment law, sketching the regulatory characteristics of the different areas of international investment law and how the EU has acted in these areas so far.

1.1 The origins of EU foreign investment law

1.1.1 The rationale behind international regulation of foreign investment

Foreign investment has been a key factor in shaping the world economy since the Second World War. Alongside international trade, foreign investment gradually became a significant vehicle of international business leading to economic wealth and prosperity. The establishment of liberal market economies worldwide, as well as technological breakthroughs during the last two decades, have elevated the importance of foreign investment; foreign direct investment (FDI) flows have grown considerably faster than global trade and domestic production, from $50 billion at the beginning of the 1980s to $1.9 trillion in 2007.[1]

The rising interest in foreign investment was mainly triggered by the widespread conviction that foreign investment contributes to the competitiveness, economic growth, and development of recipient countries. Despite the existence of conflicting

[1] UNCTAD, *World Investment Report (WIR) 2008: Transnational Corporations and the Infrastructure Challenge* (2008), p 1. The global financial crisis resulted in a slowdown of FDI in 2008 and 2009, as global FDI inflows have fallen by 14 per cent to $1.7 trillion in 2008 and by 37 per cent to $1.1 trillion in 2009. However, there were signs of recovery in 2010 and the potential for growth is extremely high for 2011 and 2012. UNCTAD, *WIR 2010: Investing in a Low-Carbon Economy* (2010), p 1.

empirical evidence,[2] a common conclusion reached in the vast majority of scholarly work on this topic is that foreign investment can contribute significantly to the host country's development, adding to its economic wealth and welfare.[3] Foreign investors bring essential economic resources, such as financial capital, advanced technology, and production techniques, production facilities and machinery, and managerial expertise which potentially allow the host economy to raise its level of domestic output, to engage in existing or undertake novel activities more efficiently, and to penetrate international markets, thus earning more tax revenues and foreign exchange and allowing competitive substitution of imports. Moreover, foreign investment is regarded as benefiting domestic firms in the host country by increasing local demand, boosting production, and enhancing the competitiveness and expertise of local suppliers. Furthermore, it can create a positive impact on public welfare, since it offers consumers new products, improved quality, and lower prices, contributes to the amelioration of local infrastructure, and generates employment opportunities and higher labour standards, thus raising standards of living.

Next to the advantages for the recipient country, foreign investment can also have positive externalities for the home, capital-exporting country. The literature is almost unanimous on the positive impact that outward foreign investment can have on the local economy of the home state.[4] Outward investment enables domestic firms to increase their competitiveness worldwide and, thus, contribute to net economic growth of the host country by repatriating the profits from their activities abroad. Furthermore, it allows them to acquire external impetus in research and development and adopt more efficient production methods which, in turn, creates domestic competition and helps to upgrade and restructure domestic industries. In addition, outward investment provides a stimulus for exports which, in its turn, has a positive effect on the domestic labour market and social welfare by increasing the proportion of export-related jobs which provide better wages and benefits.

Nevertheless, the positive impact of foreign investment is not always apparent and there is also a potential for negative effects to arise. Indeed, a critical view of

[2] For an overview of the questions raised and the empirical studies conducted see UNCTAD, *WIR 2006: FDI from Developing and Transition Economies: Implications for Development* (2006), pp 184–94; UNCTAD, *Economic Development in Africa, Rethinking the Role of Foreign Direct Investment* (2005), pp 26–36, 76–82.

[3] For an overview of the literature see T Moran, *Does Foreign Investment promote development?* (2005), chs 1, 2, 12, 14; H Kehal, *Foreign Investment in Developing Countries* (2004); A Bende-Nabende, *Globalisation, FDI, Regional Integration* (2002), pp 128–81; T Moran, *Harnessing Foreign Direct Investment for Development: Policies for Developed and Developing Countries* (2006); J Dunning and S Lundan, *Multinational Enterprises and the Global Economy* (2008), chs 11, 14; K Sauvant and J Weber (eds), *International Investment Agreements: Key Issues Volume III* (2005), ch 27.

[4] T Moran, 'What policies should developing country governments adopt toward outward FDI? Lessons from the experience of developed countries' in Sauvant, Mendoza, and Ince (eds), *The Rise of TNCs from Emerging Markets: Threat or Opportunity?* (2008), ch 13; A Kokko, 'FDI and the structure of home country production in Bora (ed), *Foreign Direct Investment* (2002), pp 152–67; T Kenneth, *Competing for Capital: Europe and North America in a Global Era* (2000), pp 24–33; Sauvant and Weber, above n 3, ch 22.

the contribution of foreign investment to economic growth and development to recipient countries indicates that the effects often depend on the initial conditions prevailing in the host country. Empirical evidence suggests that foreign investment follows development and that its positive effects are significantly greater in countries that are already developed.[5] For example, poor human capital conditions in the recipient country decrease its absorptive capacity to take advantage of the positive spillover effects on technology transfer, entrepreneurship of domestic firms, and other linkages. Moreover, foreign investment may have a negative impact on the growth of the recipient country, for example in countries with imperfect competition conditions it can lead to the creation of foreign-owned monopolies, the crowding-out of domestic firms, and eventually to generation of unemployment. Foreign investment may also potentially cause significant social and environmental harm, leading to a 'race to the bottom', as recipient countries, in their effort to attract foreign investment, may lower, or tolerate the violation of, their environmental, labour, and other social standards.[6] Foreign investment can also have detrimental effects for capital-exporting countries, as it deprives them of capital which—if invested domestically—could boost local entrepreneurship and international competitiveness, and may severely affect employment, in particular in cases of domestic companies transferring their business abroad.[7]

In recognition of the positive effects of foreign investment flows and their potential adverse consequences, most countries have gradually taken action to attract foreign investment, to ensure the benefits arising from foreign investment activity, and to mitigate its potential negative impact. More specifically, in their effort to attract foreign investment, countries have attempted to develop a legal and economic environment conducive to foreign investment and greater capital mobility. While the traditional economic determinants driving foreign investment, which relate mainly to locational resources and assets, market variables, and efficiency considerations, remain relevant, investment decisions seem to be increasingly based on the ability of host states to complement economic factors with an institutional regime that guarantees an open, stable, secure, and investment-friendly climate.[8] The significance of regulation as a basic tool for attracting foreign investment becomes more apparent when investment promotion measures are taken

[5] UNCTAD, *WIR 1999: FDI and the Challenge of Development* (1999), pp 313–28. UNCTAD, *Investment and Technology Policies for Competitiveness: Review of Successful Country Experiences* (2003); UNCTAD, *WIR 2006*, above n 2, pp 2–4, 44–5.

[6] For a brief overview of the potential negative impact of foreign investment see indicatively: Dunning and Lundan, above n 3, chs 10, 17; R Lipsey, 'Home and host country effects of FDI' in Baldwin and Winters (eds), *Challenges to Globalization* (2004), pp 333–82.

[7] S Globerman and D Shapiro, 'Outward FDI and the economic performance of emerging markets' in Sauvant, Mendoza, and Ince (eds), *The Rise of TNCs from Emerging Markets: Threat or Opportunity?* (2008), pp 229–71; Lipsey, above n 6; Moran, above n 3.

[8] On the determinants of foreign investment location see Dunning and Lundan, above n 3, ch 5; UNCTAD, *WIR 1998: Trends and Determinants* (1998), pp 89–96; S Griffith-Jones, *Global Capital Flows* (1998), pp 158–60, 171–5; S Kahai, 'The Role of Foreign Direct Investment and its Determinants' in Kehal (ed) *Foreign Investment in Developing Countries* (2004), pp 36–47.

into consideration.[9] In addition to liberalization and protection measures, many countries facilitate foreign investment by improving the ease with which foreign investors can conduct business and also by offering incentives, such as preferential tax treatment and access to local infrastructure.[10]

Foreign investment regulation plays a significant role in maximizing the positive effects of foreign investment and minimizing its negative ones. In that regard, many countries have utilized a number of measures in order to maximize benefits from foreign investment activity: they have imposed performance requirements and other conditions on foreign investors—for example requiring technology transfers—and they have targeted certain sectors of their economy, thus facilitating inward investment crucial for their development sectors and encouraging outward investment from their most dynamic firms.[11] In pursuit of social and environmental policies concerning, for example, the establishment of minimum standards, governments are able to eradicate potential negative social and environmental effects which foreign investment activity brings about.

Considering the variety of policy measures available, it becomes apparent that measures seeking to maximize benefits of foreign investments may make a given country less attractive as an investment location and vice versa. Reflecting in essence the divergent corporate interests of private investors and the national development interests of states, this tension between policies to attract foreign investment and to maximize its benefits indicates that there is a need for a balanced regulatory framework. The significance of an integrated foreign investment regulatory framework becomes more imminent as potential tensions may also arise from the divergent interests of a country as both a host and as a home country. Lastly, the creation of a balanced regulatory regime also faces the challenges that the emergence of integrated international production systems and the globalizing world economy place on national legislators.[12]

As a response to these challenges, the establishment of a comprehensive and efficient regulatory framework must extend beyond national borders. Reflecting the realities of the global economy that exist beyond national borders and where national economies are interdependent and complementary, there has been a growing trend towards internationalization of foreign investment regulation. Following the global character of foreign investment activity, the internationalization of

[9] The term 'investment promotion' is used in a narrow sense, relating only to the measures that affect the institutional capacity and willingness of host states to promote foreign investment and not to all measures that create favourable determinants for foreign investment, as the latter definition would also include liberalizing and protection measures.

[10] H Loewendahl, 'A framework for FDI promotion' (2001) 10 Transnational Corporations 1; UNCTAD, *WIR 2003: FDI Policies for Development: National and International Perspectives* (2003), pp 123–8; C Oman, *Policy Competition for Foreign Direct Investment: A Study of Competition Among Governments to Attract FDI* (2000), pp 9–22, 113–26.

[11] UNCTAD, *WIR 1999* above n 5, pp 195–228; UNCTAD, *FDI and Performance Requirements: New Evidence from Selected Countries* (2003), pp 1–41; UNCTAD, *WIR 2003*, above n 10, pp 99–154; UNCTAD, *WIR 2002: Transnational Corporations and Export Competitiveness* (2002), pp 221–42; Dunning and Lundan, above n 3, ch 12.

[12] T Agmon, 'Who Gets What: the MNE, the National State and the Distributional Effects of Globalization' (2003) 34 Journal of International Business Studies 416.

foreign investment rules presents an effective means for addressing the problems and the concerns that foreign investment activity raises.[13]

First, the creation of international rules serves the need of foreign investors and policy makers for legal certainty and allows for the depoliticization of disputes arising from national measures affecting foreign investment. Setting common standards for the treatment and especially the protection of foreign investors, international rules minimize the political risks attached to the initiation of business activities beyond national borders. Complemented by an impartial and effective mechanism for the enforcement of these norms, an international regulatory framework enables foreign investors to secure their interests, without requiring them to resort to traditional means of diplomatic protection by their home state, which would inevitably raise political concerns.

In addition, the establishment of international rules serves the need of foreign investors and policy makers for efficient and transparent regulation. The adoption of substantive international rules brings about standardization of the regulatory framework, enhancing its simplicity and, consequently, strengthening the confidence of foreign investors.[14] Besides legal certainty, the establishment of a framework clarifying the relevant national rules enhances the transparency of the national system and adds to its efficient application by national administrations. Furthermore, the internationalization of foreign investment rules provides an opportunity for national policy makers to review and modernize their national legislation, in particular in developing countries lacking the required expertise, which can benefit from the internationalization of foreign investment rules.

In that regard, internationalization of foreign investment rules is in many circumstances an optimal way for balancing the divergent interests of capital-importing/capital-exporting countries and foreign investors. International agreements give an opportunity to all relevant actors to raise concerns and to achieve a political compromise, also enabling countries to raise their own conflicting interests within a broader framework.[15]

1.1.2 The emergence of international norms on foreign investment

The importance of international norms for maximizing benefits from foreign investment was gradually recognized by all countries, which slowly contributed to the development of international investment law. After the Second World War most developed countries took initiatives gradually to liberalize capital transfers and facilitate the establishment of foreign investors in their territory, while at the same time offering various incentives in order to enhance their attractiveness as

[13] J Salacuse and N Sullivan, 'Do BITs Really Work: An Evaluation of Bilateral Investment Treaties and Their Grand Bargain' (2005) 46 Harvard LJ 67, 75–6; Z Elkins, A Guzman, and B Simmons, 'Competing for Capital: The Diffusion of Bilateral Investment Treaties, 1960–2000' (2008) U Ill L Rev 265, 277–9.

[14] Salacuse and Sullivan, above n 13, pp 95–6.

[15] B Hoekman and R Newfarmer, 'Preferential Trade Agreements, Investment Disciplines and Investment Flows' (2005) 5 JWT 949, 949–50.

foreign investment destinations. The establishment of the European Economic Community in 1957 provided the first significant effort to liberalize and regulate foreign investment flows among developed countries, as freedom of capital movement accompanied by freedom of establishment were two of the four fundamental principles on which European integration was initiated. Following the European example, significant steps towards liberalization of capital movements and regulation of foreign investment were taken by most developed countries at a global level in the Organisation for Economic Co-Operation and Development (OECD), which, albeit limited in scope, indicated the trend for liberalization.

The advantageous impact of foreign investment on developing countries has not always been irrefutable. In the aftermath of the Second World War and the colonialist era, many newly independent states agitated for a new world order, which would allow them to control their own economies and put an end to the economic dominance of the former colonial powers. In their effort to put pressure on developed countries, law became a powerful tool as they tried to formulate new doctrines through the use of their numeric strength in the General Assembly of the United Nations. Several resolutions were enacted asserting the doctrine of permanent sovereignty over natural resources and calling for the establishment of a New International Economic Order.[16]

During this period, regulation of foreign investment was considered as being mainly provided for in national law, enabling host states to control all economic activities within their territory. The massive nationalizations that occurred in many developing countries in their attempt to gain control over their vital resources and industries raised the interest in international law norms granting protection to foreign investors. Customary international law on diplomatic protection of aliens, which granted 'prompt, adequate and effective' compensation to foreign investors in cases of expropriation of their property,[17] was fiercely opposed by many developing countries, which questioned the existence and content of customary international law norms of foreign investment. On the other hand, developed countries' efforts to guarantee basic procedural rights for foreign investors met with success and led to the conclusion of the ICSID Convention (Convention on the Settlement

[16] UNGA Resolution 1803 (XVII), Permanent Sovereignty over Natural Resources, adopted on 14 December 1962; UNGA Resolution 3281 (XXIX), Charter of Economic Rights and Duties of States, adopted on 12 December 1974. For general literature on the New International Economic Order (NIEO) see K Hossain (ed), *Legal Aspects of the New International Economic Order* (1980); G White, 'The New International Economic Order: Principles and Trends' in Fox (ed), *International Economic Law and Developing states: An Introduction* (1992); DC Dicke, 'Public International Law and a New International Economic Order' in Sarcevic and van Houtte (eds), *Legal Issues in International Trade* (1990), pp 23–52.

[17] In the early twentieth century the world's principal nations shared the view that investors were entitled to have their property protected by international law and that the taking of an alien's property by a host nation required compensation that was 'prompt and adequate'. The terminology arose in the 1930s in a dispute between Mexico and the United States and became known as the 'Hull rule', in reference to the US Secretary of State who, in an exchange of diplomatic notes, put forward the formulation of the full compensation standard. For contemporaneous literature see CF Amerasinghe, *State Responsibility for Injuries to Aliens* (1964); C Lipson, *Standing Guard, Protecting Foreign Capital in the Nineteenth and Twentieth Centuries* (1985).

of Investment Disputes between States and Nationals of Other States), contributing to the legalization and depoliticization of foreign investment disputes. However, most developing countries were reluctant to conclude international treaties that included substantive norms on foreign investment.[18]

Nonetheless, the ability of developing states to exert their collective influence on shaping the law on foreign investment has shifted dramatically since the late 1980s. The rise of free market economies, the emphasis on foreign investment rules by the World Bank, the acceptance of an open door policy by China, and the dissolution of the Soviet Union have led to the emergence of new market economies and the triumph of liberalism. Developing countries and economies in transition started competing for foreign capital, which was considered vital to support their development. They became eager to negotiate and conclude International Investment Agreements (IIAs) with developed, capital-exporting states, introducing new foreign investment norms.[19] This has led to a massive boom in Bilateral Investment Treaties (BITs) resulting in a colossal and complex network of international agreements, numbering more than 2,600.[20]

This remarkable law-making activity by states—illustrated by the number of IIAs concluded in the last two decades—indicates the increasing significance international investment law has received, becoming one of the most dynamic fields of international law. The prominent interest in foreign investment is reflected in the massive expansion of case law on international investment: there are more than 350 known investment treaty cases, 250 of which have been initiated since 2000.[21] This eagerness by states to regulate foreign investment in international treaties, and the widespread use of these instruments by foreign investors, has generated extensive interest in the role of IIAs, in particular in light of the new challenges raised by the evolving nature and demands of the world economy.

Despite the great number of IIAs, and in particular BITs, international regulation of foreign investment is limited. The vast majority of IIAs are BITs, which leave outside their scope significant regulatory concerns. Recalling past nationalizations, countries were primarily interested in securing protection for their investors in the BITs.

Next to protection-oriented IIAs, there have been other IIAs concluded, such as the OECD Codes of Liberalization of Capital Movements and the Multilateral Investment Guarantee Agency Convention (MIGA), which have a complementary character, aiming to cover specific issues of foreign investment, the international regulation of which was deemed necessary. Combining elements of investment protection and liberalization and linking them with international trade, a growing number of bilateral and regional preferential trade agreements

[18] R Dolzer and C Schreuer, *Principles of International Investment Law* (2008), pp 14–17.

[19] A Guzman, 'Why LDCs Sign Treaties That Hurt Them: Explaining the Popularity of Bilateral Investment Treaties' (1998) 38 Virginia JIL 667; Elkins, Guzman, and Simmons, above n 13, pp 297–9.

[20] UNCTAD, *IIA Monitor No 3 2009*, Recent developments in international investment agreements, available at <http://www.unctad.org/en/docs/webdiaeia20098_en.pdf> (last accessed 30 April 2011).

[21] M Malik, 'Recent developments in international investment agreements: Negotiations and Disputes', IISD Paper (2010).

include comprehensive investment provisions, adding another layer to international regulation of foreign investment. Of course, the proliferation of foreign investment norms included in an indeterminable and unmanageable body of law threatens the long term foundations of international foreign investment law.[22] Although a multilateral agreement on foreign investment was attempted under the auspices of both the OECD[23] and the World Trade Organization (WTO),[24] aiming to establish a globalized legal framework on foreign investment, the international community failed both times to reach a consensus.

The fragmented nature of international regulation of foreign investment is also relevant for assessing the suitability of IIAs to achieve the objectives of foreign investment regulation to attract foreign investment and increase the benefits from it. Despite the widespread belief that BITs advance foreign investment flows, the empirical evidence is controversial on whether, and to what extent, this is true.[25] The existence of controversial evidence does not necessarily question the role of international regulation as a basic determinant of foreign investment flows. Without exaggerating the role of international regulation—since other factors such as the domestic institutional and economic environment or the existence of natural resources and favourable market conditions are important variables of foreign investment flows—the empirical evidence rather indicates that the scope and content of the provisions of IIAs are of utmost importance for assessing their effectiveness as tools for attracting foreign investment.[26]

While not denying the tremendous importance of investment protection norms, due to their focus on protection against expropriation, BITs have been unsuccessful in addressing other, equally important, regulatory determinants of foreign investment, such as market access.[27] Furthermore, while providing general rules

[22] On the debate regarding the effects of the proliferation of norms in international investment law see indicatively K Sauvant (ed), *Appeal Mechanisms in International Investment Disputes* (2008), chs 4, 5, 7, 8.

[23] The most significant effort for the establishment of a multilateral regime on foreign investment has been the negotiation of a Multilateral Agreement on Investment (MAI) under the auspices of UNCTAD during the late 1990s, which ultimately failed. On the MAI negotiations see R Geiger, 'The Multilateral Agreement on Investment' (1998) 31 Cornell JIL 467; G Kelley, 'Multilateral Investment Treaties: A Balanced Approach to Multinational Corporations' (2001) 39 Columbia JTL 483; J Salacuse, 'Towards a Global Treaty on Foreign Investment: the Search for a Grand Bargain' in Horn (ed), *Arbitrating foreign Investment Disputes* (2004), p 80; Sauvant and Weber, above n 3, ch 26.

[24] On the WTO efforts to create an investment discipline see K Kennedy, 'A WTO Agreement on Investment: A Solution in search of a problem?' (2003) 24 U Pa J Int'l L 77; C Correa and N Kumar, *Protecting foreign investment: implications of a WTO regime and policy options* (2003); J Kurtz, 'A general Investment Agreement in the WTO?', 2002 Jean Monnet Working Paper; E Kentin, 'Prospects for Rules on Investment in the new WTO Round' (2002) 29 LIEI 61.

[25] On the impact of IIAs on FDI flows see in particular L Sachs and K Sauvant (eds), *The Impact of Bilateral Investment and Double Taxation Treaties on Foreign Direct Investment Flows* (2009); Salacuse and Sullivan, above n 13; UNCTAD, *WIR 2003,* above n 10, pp 99–145; J Tobin and S Rose-Ackerman, 'Foreign direct investment and the business environment in developing countries: The impact of bilateral investment treaties', Yale Law School Center for Law, Economics and Public Policy Research Paper No 293; E Aisbett, 'Bilateral Investment Treaties and Foreign Direct Investment: Correlation versus Causation', MPRA Paper No 225, March 2007.

[26] Sachs and Sauvant, above n 25.

[27] Griffith-Jones, above n 8, pp 158–60, 171–5.

applicable to all types of investment activity, BITs do not take into account the emerging and evolving characteristics of foreign investment that raise particular regulatory concerns, such as the shift in most investment activities towards services[28] or the role of state-controlled foreign investors.[29]

In addition to their ability to attract foreign investment, BITs have been the subject of even greater scepticism regarding their role in maximizing the benefits from foreign investment activity and contributing to the general development of host countries. In particular, criticism has been focused on the broad scope of protection of investors' property. Protection against expropriation has given rise to challenges of national measures implementing public policies,[30] allowing little room for environmental, public health, human rights, or other development concerns to be taken into consideration.[31] Next to the potential negative effects of BIT provisions on the development of host countries, they remain silent on other important regulatory aspects since they do not address the interaction between investment activity and the achievement of development objectives. Leaving these regulatory concerns to the discretion of national policy makers, BITs fail to recognize that the social development aspects of foreign investment activity obtain an increasingly international character. Considering the international network of production of most foreign investors, international cooperation is required in order to increase their accountability and to set common minimum standards for investors' behaviour.

As a result, foreign investment activity remains high on the agenda of international relations. Many countries are reconsidering the content of their IIAs, a fact reaffirmed by the emergence of new types of IIAs which attempt to incorporate these concerns, while these developments also attract avid scholarly attention.

1.1.3 The evolution and development of EU foreign investment law pre-Lisbon

Parallel to the development of international investment law, increasing emphasis has been placed on foreign investment activity between the EU and third

[28] On the shift towards services and the regulatory concerns that it raises see UNCTAD, *WIR 2004: The Shift Towards Services* (2004), pp 147–80, 208–12.

[29] On the regulatory concerns that arise from the activity of state-controlled foreign investors and, in particular, Sovereign Wealth Funds see OECD, OECD Declaration on Sovereign Wealth Funds and Recipient Country Policies (2008); IMF: International Working Group of Sovereign Wealth Funds, Sovereign Wealth Funds, Generally Accepted Principles and Practices—Santiago Principles (2008).

[30] Eg *Metalclad Corp v United States of Mexico*, ICSID Case No ARB (AF)/97/1, Final Award, 30 August 2000, 5 ICSID Reports 212; *Aguas del Tunari SA v Republic of Bolivia*, ICSID Case No ARB/02/3, Decision on Juirsdiction, 21 October 2005, (2005) 20 ICSID Rev-FILJ 450; *Azurix Corp v Argentine Republic*, ICSID Case No ARB/01/12, Award, 14 July 2006.

[31] On the interaction of international investment law and human rights see P Dupuy, F Francioni, and EU Petersmann (eds), *Human Rights in International Law and Arbitration* (2009). See also A Cosbey et al, *Investment and Sustainable Development: A guide to the Use and Potential of International Investment Agreements* (2004), pp 9–14; L Peterson and K Gray, *International Human Rights in Bilateral Investment Treaties and in Investment Treaty Arbitration* (2005), p 6.

countries. Indeed, the pivotal role of the EU and its Member States in the international economic scene becomes imminently apparent as, excluding intra-EU FDI flows,[32] the EU's share of world FDI outflows was 34 per cent in 2006 while its share of world FDI inflows was around 20 per cent, thus being the largest capital exporter and capital importer in the world.[33] Indicating the establishment of the EU as a major actor in international economic relations, foreign investment is becoming a new field in which the EU asserts new powers and exercises its current ones. Following the developments in the field of international trade, where the EU has substituted the Member States and has become an influential international actor,[34] the growing coverage of foreign investment in EU external relations as well as the demand for Treaty changes that vest the EU with firm powers in this field, affirms the significance that foreign investment is gradually acquiring in EU external relations.

To understand the evolution and development of foreign investment regulation in EU external relations, particular attention should be paid, first, to the internal regime determining foreign investment flows between EU Member States. Even though the examination of EU regulation of intra-EU investments is not the focus of this work, its foundations present the main tools for explaining the EU's policy orientation towards foreign investment regulation with third countries.

While international law and regulation was mainly used for securing foreign investors' property in third countries, Union law's main goal has been to establish a framework allowing free entry and non-discriminatory treatment of European investors. The free movement of capital and the freedom of establishment, which constituted the foundations of the common market, aimed at creating a liberal regime for foreign investments among EEC Member States, where European investors could freely decide on the location of their investment, without discriminating against nationals of other Member States.[35] The process of European integration, which was marked by the creation of the internal market, further led to the formulation of common rules, covering significant aspects of the operation of foreign investment in various sectors. By using the tools of harmonization and mutual recognition, the EU created common norms, facilitating the establishment and operation of foreign investors.

In contrast with international law on foreign investment, the protection of EU investors' property from state intervention has not been an autonomous subject matter of EU law. This does not infer that protection of EU investors' property rights falls outside the scope of Union law. With regard to interventionist measures by the EU legislator, the European Court has acknowledged that there are

[32] Intra-EU FDI flows amounted for more than 70 per cent of total EU FDI flows, thus reflecting the success of European integration and the creation of the common market.

[33] Eurostat, *European Union Foreign Direct Investment Yearbook 2008* (2008), pp 11–14.

[34] On the role of the EU as a major international actor in the field of international trade relations see indicatively AR Young, 'Trade Politics Ain't What it Used to Be: The EU in the Doha Round' (2007) 45 JCMS 789; M Smith and S Woolcock, 'European Commercial Policy: A Leadership Role in the New Millennium?' (1999) 4 EFA Rev 439; L Bartels, 'The Trade and Development Policy of the European Union' (2007) 18 EJIL 715.

[35] See indicatively C Barnard, *The Substantive Law of the EU: The Four Freedoms* (2010), pp 559–91.

principles of Union law that determine the scope of protection of private property rights.[36] EU law has also been relevant in determining national measures interfering with private property, since national measures should not interfere with the fundamental freedoms and should be compatible with EU rules in general.[37] Despite this role of EU law in the protection of EU investors' property within the EU, it is far from establishing a comprehensive legal framework similar to that covering the entry and operation of foreign investment.

Complementing existing Union principles, the Lisbon Treaty introduces a new era for the protection of EU investors' property rights. Article 17 of the Charter on Fundamental Rights—which is a legally binding instrument having the same legal value as the founding Treaties[38]—provides for a right to property and determines the conditions under which deprivation and limitation of private property rights resulting from Union measures are allowed.[39] Besides, the requirement of the Union to accede to the European Convention of Human Rights (ECHR),[40] (which is already binding for all EU Member States),[41] appears to create a legal framework for the protection of intra-EU investments from EU and Member States' interventions.

Despite the creation of a legal framework on intra-EU investments, the EU did not initially appear as a key player in the international community in the field of international regulation of foreign investment. Bearing in mind that the EU is a supranational organization with limited attributable powers,[42] the evolution and development of EU foreign investment policy has been in direct correlation with the existence and exercise of EU competence in the field of foreign investment. Until the entry into force of the Lisbon Treaty, the EC Treaty had never included a legal basis explicitly mentioning foreign investment that would enable the EU to take external action in that field. EU Member States, which were always reluctant to hand over any power over foreign investment issues to the EU, had consistently considered that international foreign investment regulation lay under their exclusive competence and have concluded numerous BITs with third countries. Nevertheless, the EC Treaty included a number of provisions enabling the EC

[36] Case 4/73 *Nold* [1974] ECR 491; Case C-84/95 *Bosphorus* [1996] ECR I-3953. See also Section 2.5.1.

[37] Case 6/64, *Costa v ENEL* [1964] ECR 1251; Case 182/83 *Fearon* [1984] ECR 3677. See also Section 2.5.2.

[38] Art 6(1) TEU.

[39] Art 17 of the Charter provides that:

Everyone has the right to own, use, dispose of and bequeath his or her lawfully acquired possessions. No one may be deprived of his or her possessions, except in the public interest and in the cases and under the conditions provided for by law, subject to fair compensation being paid in good time for their loss. The use of property may be regulated by law in so far as is necessary for the general interest.

[40] Art 6(2) TEU.

[41] For the protection of property rights in the ECHR system see indicatively A Coban, *Protection of Property Rights within the European Convention on Human Rights* (2004); L Sermet, *The European Convention on Human Rights and Property Rights* (1998).

[42] According to the principle of attribution, which is enunciated in Art 5(1) TEU, the EU shall act only within the limits of the competences conferred upon it by the Member States in the Treaties to attain the objectives set out therein.

to take action and conclude international agreements with third countries in the field of foreign investment, such as the provisions on capital movements, establishment, and the Common Commercial Policy (CCP). Building on them and complementing them, the Lisbon Treaty introduces for the first time the concept of foreign investment in primary Union law, as it establishes an express competence over foreign investment, by including it within the scope of the CCP. In particular, Articles 206 and 207 TFEU provide that, 'the Union shall contribute, in the common interest, to the harmonious development of world trade, the progressive abolition of restrictions on international trade and on foreign direct investment' and that, 'the common commercial policy shall be based on uniform principles, particularly with regard to . . . the conclusion of tariff and trade agreements relating to trade in goods and services, and the commercial aspects of intellectual property, foreign direct investment'.

However, the Lisbon Treaty does not introduce foreign investment in EU law for the first time. Based on a patchwork of dispersed and limited competences, the EU had already attempted to formulate its own, distinctive foreign investment policy, 'encroaching' gradually on Member State powers in the field. Using the legal tools available in the EC Treaty, and which are still relevant, the EC formulated a legal framework for foreign investment and concluded IIAs (hereinafter, EU IIAs), focusing initially in areas not covered by Member States', international agreements. Without questioning Member State powers, the Commission considered EC foreign investment policy complementary to that of the Member States', inserting provisions on issues that were not covered under Member State BITs, such as capital movements and investment promotion as a field of development cooperation. After broadening the scope of Community competence, especially in the field of the CCP as well as the exercise of its competence in the internal market, the EC foreign investment policy was gradually expanded in other areas of foreign investment regulation: the EC was a pioneer in the introduction of investment-related norms in multilateral agreements, such as the Agreement on Trade-Related Investment Measures (TRIMs) and the General Agreement on Trade in Services (GATS) in the framework of the WTO.[43] The gradual strengthening of EU external powers was followed by an indirect but continuous questioning of the scope and exercise of Member State powers in the field of foreign investment,[44] indicating the ongoing internal power struggle between the EU and its Member States over foreign investment.

Next to the internal power struggle, the formation of EU foreign investment policy has been influenced by the objectives of EU external relations. The scope and content of foreign investment provisions in Union agreements can be first justified by the specific policy objectives of EU external economic relations. Focusing mainly on liberalization of foreign investment, the EU has aimed to address its interests to provide access for EU nationals to third country markets and to increase

[43] Hoekman and Newfarmer, above n 15, pp 961–6.

[44] The European Commission has insisted on the renegotiation of the BITs between the newly acceded Member States and the United States, while it has brought infringement proceedings against Austria, Sweden, and Finland for having concluded BITs that were incompatible with the EC Treaty. See Section 6.2.2.

competition in the internal market. The opening of third country markets to EU nationals has been explicitly considered a fundamental objective of EU external commercial policy, reflecting the belief that access to third countries' markets will enhance the global competitiveness of European companies, enabling them to survive and achieve greater profits in an increasingly open and competitive global economic environment.[45] Furthermore, the adoption of an open market access regime signifies the end of protectionism by national entrepreneurs, which distorts competition, allowing only for exceptions in sensitive sectors, where state intervention is considered necessary for protecting security or other strategic interests.[46] In recognizing the ever-growing importance of market access as a major regulatory determinant of investment decisions, EU agreements have also attempted to reflect the interests of European investors and to increase the attractiveness of third countries as investment locations.[47]

In addition to the specific external economic policy objectives, it is important to note that EU foreign investment policy has been developed within the broader framework of EU external relations. Instead of international agreements focused on foreign investment, the EU has opted to incorporate foreign investment in broader agreements dealing with a variety of external policy issues, so that regulation of foreign investment has been largely influenced by the general objectives pursued by such agreements. Considering, for example, the orientation of EU external policy with regard to developing countries, which focuses on their development and integration in the world economy,[48] it is understandable that the investment provisions found in the agreements with developing countries place an emphasis on the development aspects of foreign investment regulation.

Within this framework of divergent objectives and ambiguous powers the EU has developed its own model for international regulation of foreign investment. The dynamic, which characterizes the evolution of EU foreign investment law thus far combined with renewed interest in foreign investment brought about by the Lisbon Treaty, indicates that a new, comprehensive EU foreign investment policy is emerging.

1.2 Definition of foreign investment

The importance of a clear definition becomes apparent in light of the wide range of foreign investment definitions that exist under EU and international law; this fact reflects the multiplicity of the sources of law on foreign investment. The different

[45] Commission Communication, Global Europe: Competing in the World, Brussels 4.10.2006, COM(2006) 567.

[46] Ibid, at para 3.1(ii).

[47] S Szepesi, *Comparing EU Free Trade Agreements: Investment*, InBrief 6D of European Centre for Development Policy Management (2004).

[48] On EU external development policy see Joint Statement by the Council and the Representatives of the Governments of the Member States meeting within the Council, the European Parliament and the Commission on European Union Development Policy, The European Consensus, OJ C46/1, Brussels 22.11.2005; K Arts, 'ACP-EU relations in a new era: The Cotonou Agreement' (2003) 40 CMLR 95.

scope and content of foreign investment regulatory instruments impacts on the notion of foreign investment, leading to definitions which have not always been consistent. In fact, there is not even a consensus on the nature of foreign investment, as it has been argued that foreign investment is a thing, namely a subset of assets, as well as an activity which mainly involves the cross-boundary transfer of assets.[49] This semantic diversity is at the heart of the notion of foreign investment, which renders the consolidation and consistent reading of different definitions a difficult task.[50]

The following analysis focuses on the nature and characteristics of investment as well as on the notion of foreignness by examining the meaning of foreign investment, first, under international law and, secondly, in EU law. In order to establish the foundations for the use of the term 'foreign investment' in EU external relations with third countries, the international law definition of foreign investment is examined and then compared with the concept of 'investment' and 'direct investment' under EU law, and, in particular, internal market law. Considering the different origins and definitions provided under international and EU law, the following analysis offers the basis for a common understanding of what constitutes foreign investment as regards EU external relations with third countries.

1.2.1 Definitions of foreign investment in international law

Despite the commonalities of the rationale behind foreign investment regulation in international law, the concept of foreign investment is not consistently defined in the various treaty instruments and in customary international law. In that regard the notion of investment and its characteristics are examined initially, followed by a clarification of the term 'foreign'.

1.2.1.1 The meaning of 'investment'

The concept of foreign investment in international law was initially formulated in the context of the law on state responsibility and consisted basically of the property rights held by aliens.[51] Bearing in mind the protection-oriented nature of international investment law, the notion of investment was described more in terms of the forms that foreign capital took after its entry into the host state rather than in its initial form as capital and thus it was linked with the notion of property. However, the evolution of the concept of property—expanding from physical

[49] N Rubins, 'The notion of Investment in International Investment Arbitration' in Horn (ed), *Arbitrating Foreign Investment Disputes* (2004), p 284; UNCTAD, *World Investment Report 2003, FDI Policies for Development: National and International Perspectives* (2003), pp 99–100; C Leben, 'L'évolution du droit international des Investissments' in *Un accord multilatéral sur l'investissement: d'un forum de négociation à l'autre*, (1999) 10 Journée d'études de la SFDI 1 at 11–17.

[50] D Carreau and P Juillard, *Droit international économique* (2003), p 379; A Bencheneb, 'Sur l'évolution de la notion d'investissement' in Kahn and Leben (eds), *Souveraineté étatique et marches internationaux a la fin du 20eme siècle, Mélanges en l'honneur de Ph Kahn* (2000), pp 182–3; D Müller, 'L'investissement etranger: tentative d'une identification' in Daillier (ed), *Droit de l'économie internationale* (2000), p 645.

[51] I Brownlie, *Principles of Public International Law* (2008), pp 531–3.

property to intangible assets, intellectual property, contractual rights, and many other forms of economic transactions—has rendered this customary international law definition redundant, as it would allow most cross-border economic activities to qualify as foreign investment. Such a broad concept of foreign investment would significantly curtail state sovereignty and domestic control over economic activities, and would also lead to inconsistent overlaps with trade and other forms of cross-boundary economic regulation.

Next to customary international law, IIAs provide valuable guidance for the determination of investment. All BITs, as well as the investment chapters of Free Trade Agreements (FTAs) include analytical definitions of foreign investment, while arbitral practice under the ICSID Convention offers useful and determinative insights into the notion of investment. In addition, investment definitions existing in other instruments such as the MIGA Convention offer an alternative perception of investment, which complements rather than conflicts with the definitions existing in the main foreign investment protection instruments.

All international treaties pertaining to investment promotion and protection provide a definition of investment. In contrast with earlier BITs, which offered a relatively restricted definition, linking the concept of investment to capital or local establishment,[52] modern BITs adopt a broad, descriptive definition. Most identify investment as a subset of assets of economic value, usually by enumerating them in an illustrative or exhaustive list.[53] Typical categories of assets found in most investment treaties include real estate and other direct property rights over tangible assets, shareholdings and other forms of participation in local companies, claims to payment or performance under contracts of a financial value, intellectual property, and other intangible rights and concession agreements. In addition to these, some treaties[54] include further categories of assets, such as licences and permits, and many categories of specific contract rights.

Despite the broad scope of investment, which is sometimes described as including 'every asset',[55] most sophisticated investment treaties limit the scope of investment, especially with regard to contract rights and concessions, requiring that assets need to have certain characteristics to qualify as an investment. For example, the US-Singapore FTA[56] as well as the Draft MAI,[57] provide that assets will not be considered investments, regardless of the form they take, unless they incorporate investment characteristics, which are considered to be the commitment of capital, the expectation of profit, and the assumption of risk. Hence, IIAs tend to conceptualize investment as property in very extensive terms,

[52] Rubins, above n 49, p 292.

[53] Eg NAFTA provides an exhaustive list of assets that can be regarded as investment. On the other hand, most BITs emphasize that the enumerated assets are solely an indicative list of covered assets.

[54] NAFTA Art 139.

[55] ASEAN Agreement for the Promotion and Protection of Investments, Art 13, available at <http://www.aseansec.org/12812.htm> (last accessed 1 May 2011).

[56] US-Singapore FTA, Art 15, note 15–1.

[57] J Karl, 'On the Way to Multilateral Investment Rules: Some Recent Policy Issues' (2002) 17 ICSID Rev-FILJ 293.

distinguishing it, however, in most cases from economic assets of a purely contractual, risk-free nature.[58]

The most salient example that the notion of investment is not a general descriptive term encompassing all types of economic activities, but has an autonomous normative content is the ICSID Convention. Article 25(1) of the ICSID Convention, dealing with jurisdiction *ratione materiae*, provides that 'the jurisdiction of the Centre shall extend to any legal dispute arising directly out of an investment'. Even though the Convention does not provide a definition of investment, its importance for jurisdictional purposes has given rise to extensive discussion on the scope and extent of the notion of investment.

The omission of a specific definition of investment in the Convention is intentional and does not mean that the term is devoid of content. The drafters of the Convention were conscious of the issue,[59] but the lack of consensus on a specific definition, which would allow a dynamic and consistent interpretation, resulted in renouncement of any attempt to define the term.[60] This led to considerable debate among jurists about whether the notion of investment is determined only by the parties,[61] whose consent to arbitration is expressed in most cases via a BIT, or whether it entails a core of elements that characterize investments. The fact that there are boundaries to the definition of investment for the purposes of ICSID jurisdiction has been accepted in arbitral decisions such as *Salini v Morocco*,[62] *Fedax v Venezuela*,[63] *CSOB v Slovak Republic*,[64] *Jan de Nul v Egypt*,[65]

[58] R Echandi, 'A new generation of international investment agreements in the Americas: impact of investor state dispute settlement over investment rulemaking', Fourth Annual Conference of the Euro-Latin Study Network on Integration and Trade (ELSNIT) (2006), pp 13–14.

[59] The first draft of the Convention included a very broad definition: 'any contribution of money or other assets of economic value for an indefinite period, ... or not less than five years'. Washington Convention, First Draft, Art 30, found in 1 Analysis of Documents Concerning the Origin and Formulation of the Convention 116 (1970).

[60] As Delaume, a main negotiator of the Convention explained,

> To give a comprehensive definition ... would have been of limited interest since any such definition would have been too broad to serve a useful purpose and might have arbitrarily limited the scope of the Convention by making it impossible for the parties to refer to the Centre a dispute which would be considered by the parties as a genuine 'investment' dispute'

(G Delaume, 'Convention on the Settlement of Investment Disputes Between States and Nationals of Other States' (1966) 1 International Lawyer 64, 70.)

[61] Eg the Report of the Executive Directors of the World Bank on the ICSID Convention, ((1965) 4 ILM 524) which has been described as the clearest source of the ICSID drafters' legislative intent, as well as early commentators on the Convention, such as M Tupman and A Broches, 'Case Studies in the Jurisdiction of the International Centre for Investment Disputes' ((1986) 35 ICLQ 816) and 'The Convention on the Settlement of Investment Disputes: Some observations on Jurisdiction' ((1966) 5 Columbia JTL 268) adopt this view.

[62] *Salini and Italstradale v Kingdom of Morocco*, ICSID Case No ARB/02/13, Decision on Jurisdiction, 23 July 2001, 42 ILM 609.

[63] *Fedax NV v Venezuela*, ICSID Case No ARB/96/3, Decision on Jurisdiction, 11 July 1997, 37 ILM 1378.

[64] *Ceskoslovenska Obchodni Banca v Slovak Republic*, ICSID Case No ARB/97/4, Decision of the Tribunal on the Further and Partial Objection to Jurisdiction, 1 December 2000, 14 ICSID Review 251.

[65] *Jan de Nul v Arab Republic of Egypt*, ICSID Case No ARB/04/13, Decision on Jurisdiction, 16 June 2006.

and *Malaysian Historical Salvors v Malaysia*,[66] where arbitral tribunals attributed four main characteristics to investment: that it consists of 'contributions', of 'certain duration', that it 'participate in the risks of the transaction', and 'contributes to the economic development' of the host state.[67] These characteristics have also been recognized as inherent characteristics of an investment outside the ICSID framework, namely under a BIT-style broad definition of investment, indicating that the need to distinguish investments from other commercial activities is based on certain characteristics of an investment.[68]

1.2.1.2 Characteristics of investment

The multiplicity and vagueness of definitions of investment in international treaties cannot always provide clear guidance as to which activities qualify. By taking inspiration from ICSID jurisprudence and using it as a benchmark for a theoretical determination of an investment, many academics have supported a definition of investment based on features similar to those found in the *Salini* case.[69] In arbitral practice these criteria have been used in a number of cases, in order to determine whether and to what extent a foreign investment exists for the purposes of ICSID jurisdiction. Although these characteristics of investment are not expressly provided for under most BITs, they are highly relevant for understanding the intrinsic limits of the notion of investment, in particular with regard to the most controversial assets that fall under the broad definition of an investment. In certain cases these characteristics have been named as necessary conditions, so that all must be present in order for an economic activity to qualify.[70] However, most ICSID tribunals have examined them in their totality in order to assess the existence of an investment, so that most tribunals will still examine the nature and degree of their presence in order to determine whether, on a holistic assessment, there is an ICSID investment.[71]

1.2.1.2.1 Commitments of economic value

An investment mainly consists of a commitment of economic value. Recalling the protectionist origins of international investment law, apart from its initial form

[66] *Malaysian Historical Salvors Sdn Bhd v Malaysia*, ICSID Case No ARB/05/10, Award, 17 May 2007.

[67] Most academics have widely supported the objectivist view adopted by ICSID tribunals. For relevant literature see F Yala, 'The notion of Investment in ICSID Case Law: A Drifting Jurisdictional Requirement?' (2005) 22 Journal of International Arbitration 105.

[68] *Romak SA v Republic of Uzbekistan*, PCA Case No AA280, Award, 26 November 2009, paras 206–8, 242; J Ho, 'The meaning of 'Investment' in ICSID arbitrations' (2010) 26 Arbitration International 633, 644–6.

[69] In favour of an 'objective' definition of investment see indicatively C Schreuer, *The ICSID Convention: A Commentary* (2001), pp 140f; M Sornarajah, *The international law on foreign investment* (2010), pp 8–19; E Gaillard, 'Chronique des sentences arbitrales' (1999) JDI 273; R Dolzer and M Stevens, *Bilateral Investment Treaties* (1995), pp 25f; Carreau and Juillard, above n 50, pp 381–4, 387–90; Yala, above n 67, pp 106–10; Rubins, above n 49, pp 297–300.

[70] *Patrick Mitchell v Democratic Republic of Congo*, ICSID Case No ARB/99/7, Decision on the Application for Annulment of the Award, 1 November 2006, para 27; cf *Malaysian Historical Salvors Sdn Bhd v Malaysia*, ICSID Case No ARB/05/10, Decision on the Application for Annulment, 16 April 2009.

[71] *Malaysian Historical Salvors*, above n 66, para 106.

as capital commitment, investment also consists of the specific assets that have entered and/or been created in the host state. Difficulties arise, however, with regard to which assets qualify as investment and how their territorial link to the host state is established.

Following the evolution of the concept of property, the notion of investment expanded gradually to include new forms of property and to match modern, complex economic transactions. Starting with direct rights over tangible assets, such as land, factories, and production facilities, the notion of investment was slowly extended to include intangible assets. Initially, these consisted of contractual rights in pursuance of which the foreign investor took its assets, such as machinery and equipment. The rights associated with the holding of property, such as leases, mortgages and liens, and loans also came to be included. The inclusion of shareholdings and other forms of direct capital participation in the notion of investment was more difficult. After the *Barcelona Traction* case,[72] where the International Court of Justice (ICJ) held that shareholders' rights in a company could not be protected under customary international law, shareholders' rights were directly addressed in BITs and the ICSID Convention,[73] thus leading to their widespread recognition as investments.[74]

At a later stage, intellectual property and other intangible assets were included in the meaning of investment. The widespread need for technology transfer from the foreign investor to a local partner led foreign investors to lobby for their protection and hence the inclusion of intellectual property in the meaning of investment.[75] Although most IIAs include intellectual property in the notion of investment, the content and scope of IP rights which constitute an investment is not entirely straightforward, since intellectual property rights do not exist as such, but are created by the laws of the host state. Therefore, IP rights of foreign investors constitute an investment, as long as they are created according to local laws.

What appears to be more problematic is the consideration of contractual rights as investment. In a historical setting, contractual rights came under the notion of investment in order to protect foreign investors and prevent host states from manipulating the legislation pertinent to the foreign investor's contract.[76] The contracts that have become subject to 'internationalization' are mainly concession agreements and other contracts that foreign investors have concluded with the host state or its agencies. Even though many BITs nowadays provide that rights to performance or payment under contractual agreements are forms of investment, the broad coverage of this category of investment has attracted fierce criticism. It is argued that it transforms every contractual breach into expropriation, thus exceeding by far the sovereign powers that states intended and were willing to sacrifice when concluding

72 *Barcelona Traction* [1970] ICJ Reports 1.

73 The ICSID Convention recognizes indirectly shareholders' rights in that it prescribes in Art 25(2) that a host state can regard a locally incorporated company whose shareholders are foreigners, as a foreign one.

74 See below Section 1.2.1.2.5.

75 Sornarajah, above n 69, pp 12–14.

76 Rubins, above n 49, p 305; Bencheneb, above n 50, pp 191–2.

IIAs.[77] Despite the feeble nature of this argument, since a literal interpretation of the wording of most BITs would seem to indicate the opposite, it provides an initial argument that not all contractual rights always fall under the definition of investment. Hence, even though contractual rights as such should qualify as investment, the subtle delineation between breach of contract and expropriation depends mainly on whether a contractual right also has the other features of an investment.[78]

Finally, another basic category of assets covered under the definition of investment is administrative law rights. Many IIAs[79] include in the scope of investment 'licenses, authorizations, permits and similar rights conferred pursuant to domestic law'. Similar to contractual rights, their internationalization was mainly a result of the need of foreign investors for stability and predictability in all phases of an investment project, while their broad coverage has been criticized for curtailing enormously state sovereignty.[80] To address this problem, the same IIAs that recognize them as investments provide for specific criteria, which in fact incorporate the other features of foreign investment.

Most of the assets described above would easily pass the territoriality test, in that they present commitments which the foreign investor holds in the host country. However, difficulties can arise with regard to certain forms of foreign investment which have a transnational character. In particular, contractual agreements for the provision of services may entail that part of the provided service is performed in another country, thus limiting the territorial link with the host state.[81] The qualification of such services contracts as investments is highly controversial, considering that a strong territorial link between the investment and the host state is justified by the restraint of state sovereignty by international investment regulation as well as the role of investment for the development of the host country.[82]

[77] Sornarajah, above n 69, pp 14–17; Yala, above n 67, pp 110–14.

[78] As the arbitral tribunal in the *Azinian* case noted:

> Labelling is, however, no substitute for analysis. The words 'confiscatory' . . . or 'repudiation' may serve as a way to describe breaches which are to be treated extraordinary, and therefore as acts of expropriation, but they certainly do not indicate on what basis the critical distinction between expropriation and an ordinary breach of contract is to be made.

(*Robert Azinian, Kenneth Davitian and Ellen Baca v United Mexican States*, ICSID (Additional Facility) Case No ARB(AF)/97/2, Award, 1 November 1999, 39 ILM 537, para 90.)

[79] Eg the new model US BIT and the model UK BIT include such rights in the definition of investment.

[80] Sornarajah, above n 69, pp 14–17.

[81] Examples of such services agreements would be all agreements falling under GATS first mode of cross-border supply of services, which occur when the service is delivered within the territory of the host state from the territory of another state.

[82] In the *SGS* cases (*SGS Société Générale de Surveillance SA v Pakistan*, ICSID Case No ARB/01/13, Decision on Jurisdiction, 6 August 2003, 8 ICSID Reports 406; *SGS Société Générale de Surveillance SA v Republic of the Philippines*, ICSID Case No ARB/02/6, Decision on Jurisdiction, 29 January 2004, 8 ICSID Reports 518), it was decided that a contract for the provision of pre-shipment inspection and certification services, which were mainly provided in the territories of the countries of origin of the imported goods, had a substantial link with the host state, since the investor had 'injected' capital in it through expenditure and by establishing liaison offices in the host states, which carried out a significant part of the work. These awards have been criticized for not taking into account investors' costs and expenditure that occurred outside the host state and for not offering clear guidance on the level of territorial link required. Yala, above n 67, pp 114–20; Y Shany,

Relevant to the territorial link between an investment and the host state is the condition provided in many BITs that an investment is protected only if it is in accordance with local laws and regulations. This provision, the rationale of which lies in the preservation of host state control over entry and operation of foreign investment, does not set another substantive condition for the qualification of an economic activity as an investment, in the sense that it constitutes a *renvoi* to domestic law for defining investment. It merely implies that investments which have been established or operate illegally fall outside the scope of the BIT that includes such provision and does not disqualify economic activities from being considered as investments.[83]

The territorial link between an investment and the host state should also be distinguished from cases where an investment has not yet entered the territory of the host state. The actual entry of the investor is relevant mainly for jurisdictional purposes under BITs, which usually offer protection and standards of treatment to investments only after their entry into the host state.[84] However, the inclusion of standards of treatment of foreign investors at the pre-establishment phase in modern IIAs implies that the characteristics of investment are also relevant before the realization of a projected investment, since the latter needs potentially to fulfill the described requirements in order to benefit from pre-establishment treatment provisions.

1.2.1.2.2 Duration

A basic characteristic of foreign investment is the extended duration of an investment project.[85] Presumably this criterion was developed in the framework of investment protection treaties in order to address the desire of host states to encourage long-term inflows of foreign capital on which it could rely for its economic development. Recognizing the significance of long duration for economic development, treaty texts and arbitral practice have emphasized the role of duration as one of the indispensable characteristics of investment.

The Draft ICSID Convention recognized duration as an essential element of the investment definition, as it provided that it should not be less than five years.[86] More recently, many IIAs make explicit or implicit references to the duration of an investment, in particular with regard to certain assets, such as contracts, bonds,

'Contract Claims vs Treaty Claims: Mapping Conflicts between ICSID Decisions on Multisourced Investment Claims' (2005) 99 AJIL 835.

[83] *Salini v Morocco*, above n 62, para 46; *Bayindir v Islamic Republic of Pakistan*, ICSID Case No ARB/03/29, Decision on Jurisdiction, 14 November 2005, paras 108–9; Rubins, above n 49, pp 306–7.

[84] The arbitral award in the *Mihaly v Sri Lanka* case proves that pre-entry costs do not fall under the usual definition of investment that exists in most BITs. *Mihaly International Corporation v Democratic Socialist Republic of Sri Lanka*, ICSID Case No ARB/00/2, Award, 5 March 2002, (2002) 17 ICSID Rev-FILJ 142.

[85] Schreuer, above n 69, pp 140f; Gaillard, above n 69, p 292; Yala, above n 67, p 113; Rubins, above n 49, p 297.

[86] See above n 59; M Endicott, 'The Definition of Investment in ICSID Arbitration: Development Lessons for the WTO?' in Gehring and Cordonier-Segger (eds), *Sustainable Development in World Trade Law* (2005), pp 384–5.

and loans, which can also be short term.[87] In addition, arbitral tribunals have attributed a significant role to the duration of investment, in particular with regard to construction contracts, opining that the minimum length for an investment is two to five years.[88]

Apart from the quantitative dimension of duration of an investment, recent arbitral jurisprudence has put forward a qualitative dimension, which complements the quantitative one and is linked to the other characteristics of investment. More specifically, in *LESI-Dipenta*[89] and in *Malaysian Historical Salvors*,[90] the tribunals linked duration with contribution to development, considering that an investment satisfies the criterion of duration in the qualitative sense, as long as it has a duration that guarantees the economic commitment and contribution of the investor to the development of the host country. However, the addition of a qualitative dimension of duration does not always involve an additional condition, but provides the necessary flexibility for taking into account the development concerns that lie behind the existence of duration as a characteristic of investment.

Consequently, short-term investment projects can qualify as investments if they contribute to development of the host state; however, it would be more difficult to disqualify investments lasting for a sufficient period if they do not contribute to development, given the ambiguous normative content of the latter criterion.[91] As the US Senate rightly stated, 'it is entirely clear from the negotiating history [of the Convention] that the term "investment" in Art. 25(1) does not exclude from its scope an investment simply because it is a short-term investment'.[92] The inclusion of contracts and portfolio investments in the definition under most IIAs proves that short-term projects also qualify as an investment. Nonetheless, it is this inclusion of short-term projects that renders duration in its qualitative sense of greater importance, since duration is very significant in order to distinguish between investments and one-time sales and purchases and temporary commercial credits, which do not fall within the scope of investment.[93]

1.2.1.2.3 Risk assumption and profit expectation

Investments normally display a certain regularity of profit and return, as the expectation of profit is an indispensable aspect of any investment.[94] Due to the expectation of profit, an investment will most probably entail the assumption of some form of risk, in the sense that an investor incurs or shares the industrial risk arising from setting up or operating an investment.[95] Indeed, the existence of risk is the element

[87] Eg NAFTA and the model US BIT refer to the long-term character of these assets in their definition of investment.

[88] *Salini v Morocco*, above n 62, para 54; *Autopista Concesionada de Venezuela, CA v Venezuela*, ICSID Case No ARB/00/5, Award, 23 September 2003, (2001) 16 ICISD Rev-FILJ 469, para 101; *Jan de Nul*, above n 65, paras 93–5.

[89] *Consorzio Groupement LESI and ASTALDI v Algeria (LESI Dipenta)*, ICSID Case No ARB/05/3, Award, 10 January 2005, (2004) 19 ICSID Rev-FILJ 426, para 73.

[90] *Malaysian Historical Salvors*, above n 66, paras 110–11.

[91] See below Section 1.2.1.2.4.

[92] US Senate, 89th Congress, 2d Session, Executive Report No 2, p 15.

[93] Rubins, above n 49, p 297.

[94] *CME Czech Republic BV v Czech Republic*, Separate Opinion of Ian Brownlie, para 34.

[95] Yala, above n 67, p 113; *LESI- Dipenta*, above n 89, para 73.

that necessitates international regulation and protection of the foreign investor, since the returns of a riskless project would be stable in any event and would not require international regulation.

The existence of risk and profit becomes crucial for differentiating investment from mere commercial transactions. Contractual relations that are ephemeral, speculative, in the sense that profit will be realized with little or no sacrifice from the foreign actor, or eminently predictable in outcome, like a sale of goods, do not qualify as investments.[96] Thus, profits should be distinguished from prices and operational risks from contractual breaches.

The application of these criteria becomes more difficult in cases of financial securities or services contracts that usually qualify as investment under the broad definitions given in IIAs. These contracts would not be considered as investments according to traditional views, which claim that risk assumption and profit expectation exist only where profit is generated from the commercial exploitation of an activity and the foreign actor bears the risk of commercial performance.[97] On the contrary, arbitral practice has consistently adopted a liberal approach, interpreting these criteria in less stringent terms. In particular, the credit risk involved in bond purchases[98] and insurance contracts,[99] the risk of premature termination and alteration of a construction contract in conjunction with the risks of potential costs of labour involved,[100] and the commercial risks entailed by inspection services[101] were found to support the conclusion that an investment exists. Despite the criticism that these awards broaden dangerously the scope of investment,[102] it should be noted that they also illustrate the flexibility of the term 'investment', enabling it to encompass new forms of economic transactions, which have similar regulatory needs to classical forms of investment, while they safeguard the basic delineation between commerce and investment.

In this context, the importance of risk for defining investments under the MIGA Convention is limited only for the purposes of that Convention. The importance attached to the specific 'political' risks mentioned in Article 11 of the Convention (currency transfer, expropriation, breach of state contract, and war), as well as the division of investments into eligible, potentially eligible, and not eligible, which is based largely on whether they constitute equity investments, does not offer a definitive proposal for the meaning of investment. The MIGA Convention follows the distinction between political and commercial risks adopted by many IIAs, but instead of distinguishing between the types of risks for determining the scope of protection that is offered, it uses this distinction at the definition level. Given that the MIGA

[96] *Salini v Morocco*, above n 62, para 115; *Joy Mining Machinery Ltd v The Arab Republic of Egypt*, ICSID Case No ARB/03/11, Award on Jurisdiction, 6 August 2004, (2004) 19 ICSID Rev-FILJ 486, paras 53–8; S Manciaux, *Investissements étrangers et arbitrage entre Etats et ressortissants d'autres Etats: 25 années d'activité du CIRDI* (2005), pp 61–4; Rubins, above n 49, p 309.

[97] Yala, above n 67, pp 112–13.

[98] *Fedax v Venezuela*, above n 63, para 40.

[99] *LESI- Dipenta*, above n 89, para 73.

[100] *Salini v Morocco*, above n 62, para 55; *Bayindir*, above n 83, paras 135–6.

[101] *SGS v Philippines*, above n 82, para 105.

[102] Yala, above n 67, pp 113–14.

Convention is concerned only with guaranteeing certain types of risks that foreign investors face, the distinction between political and commercial risks is relevant for defining the scope of its application and is thus inserted at the definition level.[103]

1.2.1.2.4 Contribution to host state development

The last characteristic of investment brings into the definition the justification of foreign investment regulation. As already noted, the contribution of an investment operation to the development of the host country constitutes the basic reason why states are willing to sacrifice their sovereignty, indulge in international negotiations, and accept binding norms that curtail their political flexibility on regulating foreign investments.

The importance attributed to development can be immediately identified in most IIAs. All BITs, the ICSID Convention, NAFTA, as well as other investment treaties emphasize the role of development, providing that the positive impact of foreign investment on the development of the host state is their main objective. In fact, the positioning of development in the Preamble or in the first article of these treaties solidifies the broadly accepted view that contribution to development constitutes an essential characteristic of every economic operation that falls under the scope of investment regulation.[104]

Nonetheless, most IIAs refer to development in very broad terms. The deliberate lack of a definition, which allows for flexibility and enables host states to determine for themselves what they consider beneficial for their development, generates many difficulties with regard to the definition of investment. From this, questions arise: whether only economic or other aspects of development should be taken into account, which criteria should be used for an objective assessment of the contribution to development, and what is the role for internationally accepted parameters of development when the host state does not incorporate them in its policy orientation? These questions are important not only as regards the normative content of the substantive provisions of IIAs on the treatment and protection of foreign investment, but also at the level of definition of an investment.[105]

Contribution to development as a constitutive element of an investment has always attracted less attention than other criteria. Although arbitral jurisprudence has recognized the 'paramount significance' of contribution to development,[106] most tribunals have found it sufficient to make general comments on the contribution to development of specific investment projects, particularly in cases concerning construction contracts, where their contribution to the public infrastructure of the host country is easily discernible.[107]

[103] Carreau and Juillard, above n 50, p 386; Leben, above n 49, pp 14–16.

[104] A Cosbey et al, *A guide to the Use and Potential of International Investment Agreements* (2004), pp 1, 29–30; Endicott, above n 86, p 388; Rubins, above n 49, pp 299–300.

[105] Endicott, above n 86, pp 388–9.

[106] *Joy Mining v Egypt*, above n 96; *Jan de Nul v Egypt*, above n 65, para 92; *Malaysian Historical Salvors*, above n 66, para 123.

[107] *Salini v Morocco*, above n 62; *Bayindir*, above n 83; *Jan de Nul*, above n 65.

Contribution to development was thoroughly discussed in two awards concerning the characterization of a law firm and of a marine salvage contract as investments. In *Mitchell v DRC*[108] the ad hoc annulment Committee considered that the award should be annulled, as it did not justify adequately whether and to what extent the law firm, which was considered as an investment, was contributing to the development of the host country. Even though the annulment Committee did not made a definite ruling on whether the operation of the law firm was linked with the economic development of the DRC, it was the first time that the link between an economic activity and its contribution to development was examined in detail. On the other hand, *Malaysian Historical Salvors*[109] was the first case where an economic activity was found to fall short of satisfying the requirement. The Tribunal found that there was not enough evidence that the marine salvage contract at issue was contributing to the economic development of the host country. However, the award was annulled as the annulment Committee ruled that contribution to development is not a jurisdictional requirement under the ICSID Convention.[110]

Despite the conflicting positions on the importance of contribution to development as a characteristic of an investment, it is obvious that it is no longer a characteristic of foreign investment devoid of any substantive content. Nevertheless, caution is required when development considerations are used for defining investments; rather than excluding certain economic activities from the scope of protection under IIAs, development considerations would be more suitable to be addressed as regards the content and level of protection offered to foreign investors.

1.2.1.2.5 Shareholders' rights and portfolio investment

The protection of shareholders' rights opened up the meaning of investment to all forms of indirect participation in a company and to portfolio investment. Even though these forms of investment were admittedly not included in the notion of investment as a matter of customary international law,[111] they have been gradually included in investment definitions of IIAs, either explicitly or through the broad definition of shareholders' rights.

In contrast with foreign direct investment, where shareholding includes equity securities that guarantee active management or control of the securities' issuer by the investor, portfolio investment represents passive holdings of equity or debt securities, such as bonds, stocks, or other financial assets, none of which entail managerial control over the company.[112] This distinction between foreign direct investment and portfolio investment is largely based on the assumption that direct managerial control of a company is a basic characteristic of investment.[113] It signals the foreign entity's stable

[108] *Mitchell v Congo*, above n 70, paras 34–41.

[109] *Malaysian Historical Salvors*, above n 66, paras 125–45. On a critical reading of the tribunals' decision on the definition of investment see Y. Andreeva, 'Salvaging or Sinking the Investment? *MHS v. Malaysia* revisited', (2008) 7 The Law and Practice of International Courts and Tribunals 161.

[110] *Malaysian Historical Salvors*, Annulment Decision, above n 70.

[111] Sornarajah, above n 69, p 12.

[112] IMF, 2001 Global Portfolio Investment Survey, p 1.

[113] The OECD, UNCTAD, the IMF, and the WTO consider a direct investment to be one in which ownership is at least 10 per cent of the voting securities of an incorporated business enterprise.

involvement in the host state's economy, while portfolio investment can be of limited duration and may not contribute to the development of the host state, as it does not usually lead to technology transfers or other beneficial effects of direct investment.[114]

Nonetheless, opposition to the inclusion of portfolio investment in the notion of investment should be viewed cautiously, since portfolio investment can have all the characteristics of an investment.[115] Managerial control is no longer considered a characteristic of investment,[116] thus incorporating minority shareholdings into the notion of investment. In addition, it is widely accepted that short-term investment is included in the notion of investment[117] and that portfolio investment contributes significantly to the economic development of the host state,[118] albeit not in the traditional form of technology transfer or the creation of employment opportunities. Moreover, the basic reason for excluding portfolio investment from the scope of investment regulation, which was the denial of protection for stock market speculative investments, has lost importance since regulation of foreign investment relating to issues other than their protection refers to both direct and portfolio investments. Therefore, the breadth of investment regulation requires that policy issues, such as protection of portfolio investment, should be addressed as a matter of substance of the regulatory regime and should not create unjustifiable distinctions at the level of the definition of investment.

1.2.1.3 The notion of 'foreign'

Distinguishing international investments from domestic investments, the notion of 'foreignness' has been linked in international law with investors; the perception of investment as a subset of assets can be consistent with the distinction between foreign and domestic investment only if the latter distinction is based on the owner and holder of the assets that qualify as an investment.

In international law the definition of foreign investor has been historically linked to the nationality of the investor. The choice of nationality as the only criterion of foreignness can be traced back to the international law on diplomatic protection, so that the nationality of a person determines whether she and her assets in a state different from the one granting her nationality will be offered protection against the illegal acts of the host state.[119] Furthermore, the vast majority of IIAs choose nationality as the distinctive criterion for determining foreignness, even though they provide for more complex definitions and exceptions to this rule. The determination of an investor's nationality follows the acknowledged rule of customary international law on diplomatic protection; that nationality is determined by the

[114] Sornarajah, above n 20, pp 8–10.

[115] Rubins, above n 1, pp 316–20.

[116] Arbitral practice confirms that non-controlling shareholding constitutes an investment: *CMS Gas Transmission Co v Argentina*, ICSID Case No ARB/01/8, Decision on Jurisdiction, 17 July 2003, 42 ILM 788, paras 62–3; *Enron Corp v Argentina*, ICSID Case No ARB/01/3, Decision on Jurisdiction, 2 August 2004, paras 27–31; *GAMI Investments Inc v Mexico*, UNCITRAL Final Award, 15 November 2004, para 33.

[117] See above Section 1.2.1.2.1.

[118] IMF, *World Economic Outlook 2001: The Information Technology Revolution* (2001), ch 4, pp 141–60.

[119] Carreau and Juillard, above n 50, pp 391–3; Brownlie, above n 51, pp 402–3.

law of the state the nationality of which is claimed.[120] However, the application of this rule becomes complicated with regard to dual nationals and, more importantly, with regard to corporate nationality.

As regards natural persons, the determination of nationality raises difficulties for persons who possess dual nationality. More specifically, there is no consensus whether investments held by persons who are nationals of both the host state and the home state constitute foreign investments. Customary international law on diplomatic protection adopts the test of dominant and effective nationality,[121] thus considering as foreign, dual nationals who have a stronger tie with the home state. The application of this test by the Iran-US Claims Tribunal, which dealt with the heaviest caseload of dual nationals' investment claims, proves its general recognition and importance.[122] However, the criterion of dominant and effective nationality is not universally accepted in all IIAs. The ICSID Convention categorically states that individual investors who are nationals of the host state, even if they possess the nationality of another Contracting State are excluded from the scope of ICSID jurisdiction.[123] On the other hand, many modern BITs provide that natural persons who possess the nationality of both BIT parties can claim treaty protection.[124] Hence, the qualification of investments of dual nationals as foreign remains dependent on the specific legal instrument.

Next to dual nationals, the determination of corporate nationality has been an extremely controversial topic. Local incorporation in the host state as well as the existence of divergent interests among shareholders have become 'hot' issues, since they determine whether a company can benefit from foreign investment rules and which among them are applicable. Taking into account that the majority of foreign investment is carried out by legal persons, the importance of corporate nationality becomes immediately apparent.

The general rule of customary international law on corporate nationality, as stated in *Barcelona Traction*,[125] is very rigid, stating that a corporation has only the nationality of the state in which it is incorporated or in which it has its effective seat. The ICJ aimed to offer legal certainty and exclude the possibility of piercing the corporate veil and look at the nationality of the shareholders, since that would undoubtedly transpire to be complex in cases of multinational corporations.[126] This rule of customary international law, which recognized the criteria of place of incorporation and '*siege social*' that are used in most domestic legislations for

[120] Brownlie, above n 51, pp 383–5.

[121] *ICJ Nottebohm* [1955] ICJ Reports 4. For a discussion of this test see J Schokkaert and Y Heckscher, 'Protected Investors Nationality' (2009) 10 JWIT 699, 703–10.

[122] For a detailed analysis of dual nationality claims by the Iran-US Claims Tribunal see G Aldrich, *The jurisprudence of the Iran-US Claims tribunal* (1996), pp 54–80.

[123] *Champion Trading v Egypt*, ICSID Case No ARB/02/9, Decision on Jurisdiction, 21 October 2003, (2004) 19 ICSID Rev-FILJ 275; Schreuer, above n 69, Art 25, paras 440–7.

[124] Echandi, above n 58, p 8.

[125] *Barcelona Traction*, above n 72.

[126] For literature on the *Barcelona Traction* case see M Burgstaller, 'Nationality of Corporate Investors and International Claims against the Investor's Own State' (2006) 7 JWIT 857; C Staker, 'Diplomatic Protection of Private Business companies' (1990) 61 BYIL 155; G Sacerdoti, 'Barcelona Traction Revisited: Foreign-owned and Controlled Companies in International Law' in Dinstein (ed), *International Law at a Time of Perplexity: Essays in Honor of Shabtai Rosenne* (1989), pp 699ff.

defining corporate nationality, has been accepted and applied in later decisions and awards.[127] However, it has generated fierce criticism and difficulties for the protection of foreign companies, since it neglected shareholder protection and excluded the protection of investments that were locally incorporated mainly because of host state limitations on the entry of foreign investments.

The problems caused by the strict definition of corporate nationality in customary international law have been effectively addressed by most IIAs, which although generally accepting the test provided for in *Barcelona Traction*, combined it with supplementary criteria, thus creating a more flexible definition. Most modern BITs and FTAs as well as the ICSID Convention use a combination of the criteria of place of incorporation and seat of the company for determining corporate nationality.[128]

The exclusion from the notion of foreign investors of companies that are locally incorporated and/or seated but controlled by foreign persons, according to the criteria of incorporation and effective seat, has led to the inclusion of control as a third criterion of corporate nationality. Despite scholarly criticism of using control as a determinant of corporate nationality, since it pierces the corporate veil,[129] most IIAs include it as a determinant due to 'its importance for international development'.[130] However, it is perceived more as an exception to the general criterion of incorporation/effective seat than as an equally applicable test. The ICSID Convention illustrates this approach, as it provides that domestically incorporated companies can be considered foreign nationals when there is foreign control and an agreement that foreign control amounts to foreign nationality. While the existence of an agreement has been broadly interpreted,[131] the element of foreign control appears more complex, since the form and extent of control required differs between IIAs. Even though the majority of a company's capital stock appears a simple and certain criterion, it is not necessarily a reliable indicator of control. Different voting rights, decision-making procedures, and the exercise of management all contribute to a complex picture of control.[132] Despite possible conflicts between IIAs over the extent of the recognition of foreign control—which can lead to jurisdictional difficulties in arbitral proceedings—it is indisputable that

[127] *ELSI Case* [1989] ICJ Reports 1.

[128] *Holiday Inns v Morocco*, ICSID Case No ARB/72/1 (1980) 51 BYIL 123; *Amco Asia Corp v Indonesia*, ICSID Case No ARB/81/1, Award on Jurisdiction, 25 September 1985, 23 ILM 351.

[129] Sornarajah, above n 69, pp 197–201; P Acconci, 'Determining the Internationally Relevant Link between a State and a Corporate Investor—Recent Trends concerning the Application of the Genuine Link Test' (2004) 5 JWIT 139, 143.

[130] *Fedax v Venezuela*, above n 14, paras 21–6. See also *Ronald S Lauder v The Czech Republic*, UNCITRAL Final Award, 3 September 2001, 9 ICSID Reports 66.

[131] ICSID tribunals have found that an implicit agreement suffices. Further, most BITs include an explicit reference that they constitute an agreement for the purposes of ICSID Art 25(2)b. See *Amco v Indonesia*, above n 128; *Cable TV v St Kitts and Nevis*, ICSID Case No ARB/95/2, Award, 13 January 1997, (1998) 13 ICSID Rev-FILJ 328; Schreuer, above n 69, Art 25, paras 507–21, 531–7.

[132] Even though ICSID jurisprudence favours the simplistic equation of control and majority shareholding (*Clockner v Cameroon, LETCO v Liberia*) other IIAs, such as the ECT or the UK Model BIT use all relevant criteria, thus allowing minority shareholding to justify foreign control. See Schreuer, above n 69, Art 25 paras 564–78; Burgstaller, above n 126, pp 866–71; Dolzer and Stevens, above n 69, pp 143–4; Echandi, above n 58, pp 9–11.

foreign control offers an alternative basis for shareholders to profit from international investment regulation.

1.2.1.4 Definition of foreign investment in the OECD and the WTO

In contrast with protection-oriented IIAs, the OECD Codes of Liberalization of Capital Movements and the WTO Agreement view foreign investment from a different perspective, emphasizing—similar to EU law—its aspects relating to the transfer of capital and its initial form as an investment.

More specifically, the OECD Codes of Liberalization of Capital Movements provide in Annex A, a detailed description of the economic activities that constitute capital movements, investments being the most significant among them.[133] Furthermore, although the WTO generally ignores foreign investment, the TRIMs and the GATS agreements contain provisions regulating foreign investment issues.[134] Even though neither of these agreements provides a definition of foreign investment, a broad perception of foreign investment can be extracted from their regulatory scope.

In particular, the TRIMs Agreement, which concerns the treatment of investors after their establishment in the host state, defines direct investment as an undertaking established for a long period and carrying out an economic activity.[135] Thus, the notion of investment is understood in its traditional sense, since only direct investments can be affected by measures imposing trade restrictions such as import and export requirements.[136] A similar definition of foreign investment can be constructed in the framework of the GATS, which conceptualizes trade in services to include direct investment in service sectors as well.[137] While defining services in a very broad manner as 'any service in any sector except services supplied in the exercise of governmental authority', it provides that 'commercial presence' is a mode of supply of trade in services. Article XXVIII provides that commercial presence means 'any type of business or professional establishment, including the constitution, acquisition or maintenance of a juridical person, or the creation or maintenance of a branch or a representative office'. Thus, the GATS recognizes direct investments, in the form of an established enterprise, as a mode of supply of trade in services.[138]

[133] OECD, *Forty Years' Experience with the OECD Code of Liberalisation of Capital Movements* (2002); Carreau and Juillard, above n 50, pp 379–80.

[134] T Brewer and S Young, 'Investment issues at the WTO: the architecture of rules and the settlement of disputes' (1998) 1 JIEL 457; P Gugler and J Chaisse, 'Foreign Investment Issues and WTO Law—Dealing with Fragmentation while waiting for a Multilateral Framework' in Chaisse (ed), *Essays on the Future of the World Trade Organization*, vol I (2008), pp 135–57.

[135] WTO Panel Report, *Indonesia-Autos*, WT/DS 54,59,64/R, Report of 2 July 1998.

[136] P Civello, 'The TRIMS Agreement: A Failed Attempt at Investment Liberalization' (1999) 8 Minnesota JWT 97.

[137] M Koulen, 'Foreign Investment in the WTO' in Nieuwenhuys and Brus (eds), *Multilateral Regulation on Investment* (2001), p 288.

[138] The notions of establishment and services and their relation to foreign investment is analytically explored in Section 1.2.2.

1.2.2 Definition of foreign investment in EU law

Contrary to international law, EU law has not yet provided a clear-cut definition of foreign investment. Until the entry into force of the Lisbon Treaty, the term did not appear in primary EU law, not even with regard to intra-EU investments, while the international agreements concluded by the EU (hereinafter, Union agreements) do not usually contain the term, even though their content relates to foreign investment regulation. However, the Lisbon Treaty introduces for the first time an explicit reference to foreign investment, albeit limiting it only to FDI.

Although Article 207 TFEU presents the first explicit reference to foreign investment in primary EU law, this does not mean that the concept of foreign investment has so far been unknown under EU law. The absence of the term in the EC Treaty as well as in Union agreements can be reasonably explained. As the notion of foreign investment has been mainly linked with instruments of protection, and protection of foreign investment was traditionally considered to fall under the competence of the Member States, those states were reluctant to accept the use of the term foreign investment in Community law, because they were afraid that this could endanger the delineation of competence between them and the EC.[139] In addition, regulation of intra-EU investments was based on a different terminology, thus influencing the language used in the field of foreign investment regulation. Last but not least, the orientation of EU regulation on foreign investment towards entry and establishment of foreign investors rather than their protection has influenced the language used, thus leading to the adoption of terms such as capital movement and establishment, which had already been used internationally in instruments concerning investment liberalization.

The absence of this terminology should not, however, lead to the conclusion that Community law did not regulate foreign investment and did not provide a definition for it. On the contrary, the examination of the scope and content of EU primary and secondary law, as well as those of Union agreements, allow for a definition of foreign investment to be extracted. The explicit reference to FDI in the Lisbon Treaty merely confirms that EU law offers a definition of foreign investment. On the other hand, the limitation of Article 207 TFEU only to foreign *direct* investment complicates the determination of the concept of foreign investment under EU law. Neither portfolio investment nor other forms of foreign investment are explicitly recognized in the TFEU. This does not mean that EU law does not consider them as foreign investment, as the other Treaty rules remain significant for their determination and regulation. The explicit reference to FDI, which is the most important category of foreign investment, indicates rather that the CCP is primarily concerned with foreign direct investment. Subjecting direct investment to different competence and (possibly) substantive rules from other forms of foreign investment, it is first necessary to identify what constitutes FDI under EU law

[139] J Reiter, 'The EU-Mexico Free Trade Agreement: Assessing the EU Approach to Regulatory Issues' in Sampson and Woolcock (eds), *Regionalism, Multilateralism and Economic Integration* (2003), p 90.

and, secondly, to examine whether and where EU law provides rules for other, non-direct forms of foreign investment and for which of them.

1.2.2.1 The notion of foreign direct investment under EU law

The Lisbon Treaty includes an explicit reference to foreign investment under the CCP. It is apparent from the wording of Articles 206 and 207 TFEU that the new competence is limited only to FDI. Before examining the concept of FDI under the Lisbon Treaty, it is necessary first to identify how this term has been interpreted under internal market law. The examination of the concept of direct investment under internal market law is important, not only because it can inform the interpretation of the relevant term under the CCP, as explained below, but also because it assists in the distinction between direct and non-direct foreign investment, given that, under EU law, non-direct foreign investment is defined and regulated under the internal market provisions.[140]

1.2.2.1.1 The notion of direct investment under the capital movement rules

The notion of direct investment is linked in EU law with the definitions of capital, and establishment under the TFEU rules on free movement, since they refer to it directly or indirectly and portray its characteristics. Articles 63 to 66 TFEU provide for complete liberalization of capital movements not only between Member States but also between Member States and third countries. The unified approach towards intra-EU and external capital movements indicates that the notion of capital movement is the same for both categories, even though capital movements to and from third countries are to a certain extent regulated differently from intra-EU capital movements.[141]

Even though the Treaty does not provide any definition of capital movement, clear guidance has been given by the European Court of Justice (ECJ) and the now-expired capital Directive 88/361/EEC.[142] Even though the ECJ has not found it necessary to provide an all-embracing definition of capital movement, it indicated in its early cases of *Casati*[143] and *Luisi and Carbone*[144] that physical transfer of financial assets could be a movement of capital as long as it was 'essentially concerned with the investment of funds'. After the expiration of the Directive the Court endorsed the use of the nomenclature annexed to Directive 88/361 as an indication of which operations constitute capital movement, although it has made clear that the nomenclature is non-exhaustive.[145] In particular, the nomenclature—which is based on the OECD classification of capital movements—classifies capital movements according to the economic nature of the

[140] See Sections 2.3. and 2.4.

[141] Joined Cases C-163, 165 & 250/94 *Sanz de Lera* [1995] ECR I-4821; J Handoll, *Capital, Payments and Money Laundering in the European Union* (2006), p 88.

[142] Directive 88/361/EEC on the implementation of Article 67 of the Treaty [1988] OJ L178/5.

[143] Case 203/80 *Casati* [1981] ECR 2595.

[144] Joined Cases 286/82 & 26/83 *Luisi and Carbone* [1984] ECR 377.

[145] Case C-222/97 *Trummer and Mayer* [1999] ECR I-1678; Case C-367/98 *Commission v Portugal* [2002] ECR I-4731; Case C-463/00 *Commission v Spain* [2003] ECR I-4581; Case C-98/01 *Commission v UK* [2003] ECR I-4641; Case C-174/04 *Commission v Italy* [2005] ECR I-4933.

assets and liabilities concerned, thus demonstrating that the term 'capital' connotes an asset of economic value.

The first and most important category of capital movements indicated in the nomenclature includes movements linked to direct investments. The notion of direct investment, as used, is associated with the establishment of, extension of, or participation in, new or existing undertakings via equity or securities holdings which establish or maintain direct links between the person providing the capital and the undertaking to which the capital is made available in order to carry out an economic activity. Further, the nomenclature recognizes long-term loans that aim to establish or maintain lasting economic links as direct investments, hence acknowledging that long-term financial contracts are of equal significance with the establishment or participation in undertakings. The above definition, which according to the Council has to be understood in its widest sense,[146] makes apparent that the basic characteristics of direct investment are the commitment of capital for carrying out an economic activity, the existence of a lasting link, and in all cases except for long-term loans the managerial control of the undertaking by the person providing the capital.[147] Nevertheless, the ECJ is unclear as to the conditions that identify a long-lasting link and managerial control.[148]

Hence, the notion of direct investment in EU law corresponds to the concept of direct investment, as the latter was described above with regard to international law. Even though both regimes conceptualize investment as an economic asset, EU law defines investment in terms of the form that capital has before and after its transfer across national borders. In particular, it defines as investments the economic assets that are moved from one country, which are usually financial assets, and the form they initially obtain in the host country, which is usually shareholdings.[149] Thus, the property rights acquired by the undertaking controlled by the investor are not included in the notion of investment, not because they do not qualify as investment as such but simply because they fall outside the regulatory scope of the freedom of capital movement.

As noted, the notion of capital includes all types of economic assets that cross national borders as well as all forms that capital takes after its entry into the destination country. For example, the initial capital can consist of a tangible good, such as machinery, the transfer of which is not treated as a movement of goods, but as a capital movement.[150] Moreover, real estate and rights directly linked to it are

[146] Handoll, above n 141, pp 27–8.

[147] Case C-112/05 *Commission v Germany (VW case)* [2007] ECR I-8995, para 18; *Commission v Spain*, above n 100, para 53; *Commission v UK*, above n 145, para 40; *Commission v Italy*, above n 145, para 28. See also S Hindelang, 'The EC Treaty's Freedom of Capital Movement as an Instrument of International Investment Law?' in Reinisch and Knahr (eds), *International Investment Law and Context* (2007), p 47; Von der Groeben and Schwartze, *EU-EG Vertrag, Kommentar* (2004), Art 56 EG, p 1731; S Johannsen, 'Die Kompetenz der Europäischen Union für ausländische Direktinvestitionen nach dem Vertrag von Lissabon' (2009) 90 Beiträge zum Transnationalen Wirtschaftsrecht 1, 11–13.

[148] See below Section 1.2.2.1.2.

[149] W Frenz, *Handbuch Europarecht: Europäische Grundfreiheiten* (2004), p 1031.

[150] The recognition of material goods as capital derives straightforwardly from ECJ jurisprudence; in *Thompson* (Case 7/78 [1978] ECR 2247) the Court distinguished the scope of free movement of goods from that of free movement of payments on the basis of the function and the aim of

also considered investments. In particular, the specific recognition in the nomenclature of acquisition of real property as a category of investment-related capital movements reaffirms its importance,[151] especially when an investment does not occur via establishment of an undertaking.[152]

Finally, it is worth noting that the inclusion of an economic activity in the nomenclature does not mean that it will be treated as a capital movement in all circumstances and thus that the proscribed capital will qualify as an investment.[153] In order to define capital movements, the ECJ distinguished them from payments, which are also transfers of financial assets, because capital payments were subject to different rules from capital movements until the entry into force of the Maastricht Treaty. Although this distinction has been rendered defunct, since Articles 63 to 66 TFEU apply to both capital movements and payments, their differences are important for the determination of the concept of investment in EU law.

In *Luisi and Carbone*[154] the ECJ set out the criteria for distinguishing capital movements from payments, opining that 'capital movements are concerned more with the investment of funds rather than remuneration for a service, while payments actually constitute the consideration for an underlying transaction'. In that respect, the presence of an investment purpose, which exists when the transfer does not constitute remuneration for the provision of services or the price for a sale of goods, determines whether a transfer is a capital movement or a payment.[155] Hence, the ECJ has actually acknowledged in an indirect way that profit expectation and risk assumption are basic characteristics of investments and of capital movements linked to them, since it recognizes that investments must have a profit-making orientation, but it rejects transfers, where profit is eminently predictable in outcome, as in the sales of goods.

1.2.2.1.2 The notion of direct investment under the establishment rules

The examination of the notion of establishment as well as its link to capital movements is essential to determine whether and to what extent these concepts are relevant for the definition of investment in EU law. Even though the relevant chapter

the movement and not according to its material incorporation. This criterion can be used by analogy for distinguishing between free movement of goods and capital. Hence, material goods that are transferred for investment purposes qualify as capital. See S Hindelang, *The Free Movement of Capital and Foreign Direct Investment: the scope of protection in EU Law* (2009), p 47; J Müller, *Kapitalverkehrsfreiheit in der Europäischen Union. Bedeutung, Inhalt und Umfang, Weiterentwicklung, Auswirkung auf Völkerrecht und nationales Recht* (2000), p 192.

[151] Handoll, above n 141, p 28.

[152] Acquisition of real property which is linked with entrepreneurial purposes, and thus with a direct investment, is considered to fall under the category of direct investment, as the nomenclature provides that acquisition of real estate is a separate category of capital movements as long as it is not covered by direct investments. See also Hindelang, above n 150, p 52.

[153] Frenz, above n 149, pp 1032–3; Hindelang, above n 150, pp 54–5; Müller, above n 150, pp 156–60; Von der Groeben and Schwartze, above n 147, p 1732.

[154] *Luisi and Carbone*, above n 144.

[155] The criterion of single-sidedness of the transfer has also been proposed for distinguishing capital movements from payments. However, the use of this criterion can be problematic since certain transfers, eg in the case of investment in real estate, are not actually single-sided, as they arise as a result of the obligation to pay under the selling contract. Müller, above n 150, p 157; J Usher, 'The Evolution of the Free Movement of Capital' (2008) 31 Fordham Int'l LJ 1533, 1539–42.

of the TFEU applies only to intra-EU movements of persons, it is highly relevant for determining direct investment, not only because they have influenced the language and content of EU foreign investment regulation, but also because the TFEU itself uses these terms when it regulates investments to and from third countries—for example in Article 64 TFEU.

The concept of establishment, as described in Article 49 TFEU, includes the setting-up and management of an undertaking (primary establishment) as well as the setting-up of dependent undertakings, such as agencies, branches, or subsidiaries (secondary establishment).[156] Even though the Treaty text refers only to setting up an undertaking, its scope also covers the purchase of existing undertakings as well as cross-border mergers.[157] Furthermore, it is obvious from the definition of establishment that entrepreneurial control is a definitive characteristic of the notion of establishment. As the Court recently stated, the holding must 'confer on the holder definite influence over the company's decisions and allow it to determine the companies' activities'.[158] Nevertheless, the Court does not always provide explicit criteria for identifying when a person exercises managerial control over an establishment. Article 54(2) TFEU makes it explicit that profit expectation is a basic characteristic of establishment, while the Court has repeatedly stressed that the creation of a permanent link with the economy of the destination country is a typical characteristic of an establishment.[159]

Bearing in mind the definition and characteristics of direct investments in the field of capital movements, it is apparent that the notion of establishment includes direct investments, even though its scope extends beyond them, and that direct investments except for long-term loans qualify as establishments. As a result, the notions of both establishment and capital movement are related to a large extent with direct investments, which fall within the scope of the respective Treaty provisions.[160]

[156] The concept of establishment also includes the possibility of self-employed persons to take up and pursue economic activities in a permanent manner in another Member State. However, the activities of self-employed persons do not constitute foreign investments, as there is no separate financier of the activity from another country who exercises entrepreneurial control. Hindelang, above n 147, p 51.

[157] Case C-208/00 *Überseering BV v Nordlic Construction Co (NCC)* [2002] ECR I-9919, para 77; Case C-411/03 *Sevic Systems AG* [2005] ECR I-10805, para 19.

[158] Case C-446/04 *Test Claimants in the FII Litigation v Commissioner of the Inland Revenue* [2006] ECR-I-11753, para 37; for the criteria adopted by the Court to find the necessary degree of control needed to be exercised in order for an undertaking to qualify as an establishment see A Arnull et al, *Wyatt and Dashwood's European Union Law* (2006), pp 841–7.

[159] The existence of a permanent link as an important characteristic of establishment has been emphasized in the Court's case law, due to its importance for distinguishing between establishment and provision of services. In particular, the ECJ has ruled that establishment entails the integration of the established person into the local economy, which is apparent whenever there is a permanent link. Case C-221/89 *Factortame II* [1991] ECR-I 3905, paras 34–6; Case C-55/94 *Gebhard* [1995] ECR I-4165, para 25; Case C-70/95 *Sodemare SA* [1997] ECR I-3395, paras 25–7.

[160] The distinction between establishment and capital movement and the scope of application of the relevant Treaty chapters with regard to foreign investment is examined in Section 2.2.1.2.

1.2.2.1.3 The notion of 'foreign' under internal market law

Under internal market law the term 'foreign' should be defined in such a way as to distinguish investments having an international character from intra-EU investments and domestic investments. Since intra-EU investments also have an element of 'foreignness', the distinction between the criteria used for identifying the intra-EU or international character of an investment is vital.

Similar to international law, the nationality of the investors appears at a first glance to be the distinctive criterion between domestic/intra-EU and international investments. Article 20 TFEU, which establishes EU citizenship, clearly provides that citizens of the Member States are beneficiaries of Union law rights and can rely on the provisions establishing the four fundamental freedoms. However, nationality is not the only criterion determining the application of the fundamental freedoms. EU law also requires the existence of a cross-border element for its provisions to apply.[161]

In determining nationality of natural and legal persons, EU law adopts the generally accepted rules analysed above with regard to international law. More specifically, the nationality of natural persons is determined in accordance with the laws of the Member State of which nationality is claimed, while the determination of corporate nationality, as defined in Article 54 TFEU,[162] is based on the general criterion of place of incorporation and effective seat.[163] However, contrary to international law, managerial control of the legal person does not appear as a third criterion determining corporate nationality. The rejection of managerial control as another complementary criterion for identifying the nationality of a company can be easily explained by the aim and the scope of application of the freedom of establishment: EU law does not intend to exclude third country nationals who incorporate their company in an EU Member State from the scope of the Treaty. Conversely, it does not favour EU nationals who prefer to incorporate in a third country, thus avoiding the regulatory control exercised by the EU and its Member States and abusing the preferential provisions of the TFEU.[164]

Despite the general recognition of nationality as determining the scope of personal application of the Treaty provisions relating to the fundamental freedoms, the TFEU does not always condition free movement on nationality. The applicability

[161] The element of border-crossing is very significant for distinguishing intra-EU and domestic movements of goods, persons, services, and capital. The Treaty text is very clear in Arts 34, 35, 45, and 57 TFEU that the relevant freedoms relate only to 'movements between Member States'. Internal movements are regulated by EU law only insofar as they have been the subject of harmonizing legislation in the framework of the internal market. Frenz, above n 149, pp 54, 106–7.

[162] The definition of corporate nationality appears in the chapter providing for freedom of establishment, while the TFEU limits the scope of this definition only 'for the purposes of this chapter'. Nonetheless, the importance of this definition for all four fundamental freedoms is apparent, since Art 62 TFEU relating to freedom to provide services refers back to Art 54 TFEU, while the lack of a similar reference in the chapters relating to the freedoms of goods and capital can be explained by the inappropriateness of nationality as a criterion determining the scope of application of these freedoms. T Kingreen, *Die Struktur der Grundfreiheiten des Europäischen Gemeinschaftsrechts* (1999), pp 80f.

[163] On the relation of these criteria see C Barnard and S Deakin, 'Market Access and regulatory competition' in Barnard and Scott (eds), *The Law of the Single European Market: Unpacking the Premises* (2002), pp 197–224; P Cabral and P Cunha, 'Presumed Innocent: Companies and the exercise of the Right of Establishment under Community Law' (2000) 25 EL Rev 157.

[164] Frenz, above n 149, pp 764–5.

of the provisions relating to free movement of capital and goods is conditioned only on the notions of capital and goods and does not attribute any importance to the person carrying out the movement.[165] The purpose of this is the free transfer of capital and goods as such. The rationale behind establishing a strong link only with the material character of capital or goods lies in the aim of the internal market, which can only be achieved if trade and investment can be conducted without obstacles.[166] In that respect, free movement of goods and capital differs from the freedoms of establishment and services, which by definition are linked to the persons undertaking the specific activity. In particular with regard to capital movements, nationals of third countries can invoke the Treaty provisions whenever they undertake an intra-EU or an international capital movement.[167]

Therefore, since capital in its fundamental nature is linked only to the territory where it is situated, the element of border crossing becomes the only relevant criterion for distinguishing between domestic and intra-EU capital movements as well as between intra-EU and foreign investments, depending on the national borders across which capital is transferred. The nationality of the investor plays, contrary to international law, an important role, only insofar as an investment falls within the scope of the freedoms of establishment and provision of services.

1.2.2.1.4 The notion of foreign direct investment under the CCP

Even though there is no further clarification of the term in the TFEU, the concept of FDI should be interpreted with regard to EU rules which refer to direct investment and, most importantly, in accordance with the notion of FDI in international law. Similar to the concept of trade in services, which in the framework of the CCP should be interpreted by reference to international trade practice and not to the identically worded Treaty chapter on provision of services,[168] the international law definition is more important for defining FDI within the scope of the CCP. As mentioned, in EU law the term direct investment under the capital movement and establishment rules associate direct investment with the establishment of, or participation in, new or existing undertakings via equity or securities holdings, which is characterized by the existence of a lasting link and managerial control of its activity as well as with long-term loans.[169] The concept of direct investment in EU law corresponds to the concept of direct investment in international law, which emphasizes duration and managerial control as the main elements.[170]

165 Ibid, pp 92, 94, 244–5, 1034; Hindelang, above n 150, pp 60–3.

166 Handoll, above n 141, p 40; Sideek, above n 174, pp 52–3.

167 This conclusion is not contrary to Union citizenship provisions, since they only reaffirm that Union citizens enjoy the rights conferred by primary EU law without excluding third country nationals from enjoying such rights.

168 Opinion 1/2008 [2009] ECR I-11129, paras 119–21. See also Section 2.2.2.2.2.

169 See Section 1.2.1.2.

170 J Ceyssens, 'Towards a common foreign investment policy? Foreign investment in the European constitution' (2005) 32 LIEI 259, 274; M Krajewski, 'External Trade Law and the Constitutional Treaty: Towards a federal and more democratic common Commercial Policy?' (2005) 42 CMLR 91, 112; J Karl, 'The Competence for Foreign Direct Investment' (2003) 4 JWIT 413, 420; C Tietje, 'Die Außenwirtschaftsverfassung der EU nach dem Vertrag von Lissabon' (2009) 93 Beiträge zum Transnationalen Wirtschaftsrecht 1, 15–16; Johannsen, above n 147, p 15.

Of course, the criteria determining managerial control, and thus FDI, remain problematic. First, in order to avoid the uncertainty existing under internal market law as regards the determination of a direct investment, the EU should distinguish the concept of FDI under Article 207 TFEU from the concept of direct investment under internal market law. In this regard, the EU could rely on international instruments to determine the threshold for managerial control, for example to adopt the IMF definition which considers FDI a long-term placement of capital representing control of at least 10 per cent of shares, equity, or voting rights in the undertaking operating in a third country.[171] However, an exact definition of what constitutes FDI, in particular in comparison to portfolio investment, would be unnecessary if the EU opts to regulate FDI and other forms of foreign investment together, including asset-based definitions of foreign investment in its future EU IIAs.[172]

Regarding the determination of foreignness, the nationality of the investor presents the main criterion for the qualification of a direct investment as foreign. Although nationality is not relevant under the capital movement rules, the link to nationality under the EU establishment rules as well as in international law indicates that the determination of a direct investment as foreign under Article 207 TFEU rests on the nationality of the investor, at least insofar as the establishment and operation of a foreign direct investment is concerned. The use of the nationality of the investor as the relevant criterion for including a direct investment in the scope of the capital movement provisions of EU IIAs[173] strengthens the position that nationality should be the relevant criterion for defining FDI in EU external relations.

However, the determination of nationality should not depend on managerial control, but only on place of incorporation and effective seat, abiding by the criteria set in Article 54 TFEU.

1.2.2.2 Defining other (non-direct) forms of foreign investment under EU law

Although (foreign) direct investment is the main form of foreign investment recognized under EU law, other forms of foreign investment are also indirectly defined. In order to identify their main characteristics, it is necessary to locate the relevant TFEU provisions pertinent to their regulation, which provide the appropriate framework for EU external action.

1.2.2.2.1 Portfolio investments

Apart from direct investment and real estate investment, the free movement of capital recognizes other economic assets as capital. The nomenclature under Directive 88/361/EEC defines all operations in equity or debt securities—such as bonds and

[171] S Woolcock and J Kleinheisterkamp, 'The EU approach to international investment policy after the Lisbon Treaty', Study Directorate General for External Policies of the Union (October 2010), pp 11–12.

[172] See Section 3.2.7.1.

[173] See below Section 1.2.2.3.

shares, which are dealt with on the capital or on the money market—as capital movements. Thus, it recognizes portfolio investments as capital, subjecting them to the same regulatory treatment as direct investments.[174] As portfolio investment falls within the scope of the capital movements rules, the general characteristics defining capital movements and, in particular, risk assumption—which is the distinguishing characteristic from capital payments[175]—and the determination of foreignness irrespective of the nationality of the capital holder,[176] are important characteristics of portfolio investments under EU law. Hence, under the capital rules, the distinction between direct investment and portfolio investment is mainly one of concretization of different kinds of investment and not one of differentiation between them.

It is noteworthy that the nomenclature also includes categories of capital movements of personal or commercial character. Personal capital movements—such as gifts, inheritances, and physical transfer of money-credits and financial loans related to commercial transactions or to provision of services, and transfers in performance of insurance contracts, fall within the meaning of regulated capital movements. However, this does not imply that EU law regards capital transferred for these reasons as investment. Transfers of assets for personal or commercial reasons lack the characteristic of profit expectation and risk assumption, which lies at the heart of the notion of investment and differentiates investment from all other economic activities. Hence, even though the notion of capital under the capital movement rules embraces the notion of investment, it is a broader concept and should be distinguished.

1.2.2.2.2 Investment in the form of concession and state contracts

Finally, it is worth examining whether and how EU law regulates contractual commitments that would qualify as foreign investments under international law. In that respect, the freedom to provide services presents the relevant framework internally which also affects the scope for EU action externally.

The freedom to provide services is highly relevant for the definition of investment as many economic operations that consist of services contracts and concession agreements, especially with the public sector, are considered investments in international law. Despite the residual character of the freedom to provide services, its cumulative application by the ECJ, next to the provisions relating to freedoms of establishment and capital movement, renders its examination necessary.[177] At first glance, the notion of services, as articulated in Article 57 TFEU, does not seem to be linked with investments. The definition of services as 'any kind of economic activities which are only temporarily provided for remuneration'[178] appears

[174] Handoll, above n 141, pp 29–31; Hindelang, above n 150, p 69; M Sideek, *European Community Law on the Free Movement of Capital and the EMU* (1999), p 240.

[175] See above Section 1.2.2.1.1.

[176] See above Section 1.2.2.1.3.

[177] Case C-484/93 *Svensson and Gustavsson* [1995] ECR I-3955; H Jarass, 'A Unified Approach to the Fundamental Freedoms' in Andenas and Roth (eds), *Services and Free Movement in EU Law* (2002), p 141.

[178] For an analytical presentation of the definition of services see L Woods, *Free Movement of Goods and Services within the European Community* (2004), pp 157–79.

to exclude investments, since risk assumption and duration do not seem to be characteristics of services. However, the broad interpretation of the requirements of remuneration, which includes any form of economic consideration,[179] and of temporariness, which is used only for contradistinction with the permanent link that characterizes establishment,[180] entails that services contracts of a longer duration which are not offered for predetermined remuneration fall under the scope of the Treaty articles on provision of services.[181]

It is worthy of note that the criterion of risk assumption, which is of particular importance in international law for distinguishing between plain services or goods contracts and investments, is also used in secondary Union law. The Procurement Directive[182] and the Utilities Directive[183] distinguish between concession contracts, where consideration amounts solely to the right to exploit the work or to this right together with payment,[184] and other public work, services, or utilities contracts. Even though bearing the commercial risk is critical only for submitting a public contract under the procurement rules, it proves a useful tool for distinguishing investments from commercial contracts in EU law. As a result, the chapter on provision of services includes a category of investments, namely contracts that have the characteristics of an investment, which are however only a small fraction of the economic activities covered by the relevant Treaty rules.

1.2.2.3 The notion of foreign investment in EU IIAs

Aiming at the liberalization of foreign investment, EU IIAs define foreign investment comparable to primary EU law and the OECD and WTO legal instruments. In order to ensure consistency with primary EU law, most existing Union agreements refer to foreign investment by regulating capital movements, trade in services, and establishment. Nevertheless, future EU IIAs will probably adopt a different approach.[185]

All Union agreements relating to trade and economic cooperation regulate capital movements, even though each provides for a different degree of liberalization.[186] In defining capital movements, they make explicit reference to direct investment, thus emphasizing their importance, while some of them either contain an annex similar to the nomenclatures annexed in the Capital Directive or in the

[179] Case C-263/86 *Humbel* [1988] ECR 5365, paras 16–20.

[180] *Gebhard*, above n 159.

[181] Case C-231/03 *Coname* [2005] ECR-I 7287; Case C-358/00 *Die Deutsche Bibliothek* [2002] ECR-I 4685; Case C-324/98 *Telaustria Verlags* [2000] ECR-I 10745.

[182] Directive 2004/18EC on the coordination of procedures for the award of public works contracts, public supply contracts and public service contracts [2004] OJ L134/114.

[183] Directive 2004/17/EC on coordinating the procurement procedures of entities operating in the water, energy, transport and postal services sectors (Utilities Directive) [2004] OJ L134/1.

[184] Case C-458/03 *Parking Brixen* [2005] ECR I-8612; S Hjelmborg, P Jakobsen, and S Poulsen, *Public Procurement Law—the EU Directive on public contracts* (2006), pp 165–70.

[185] See Section 3.2.7.1.

[186] S Fares, 'Current Payments and Capital Movements in the EU-Mediterranean Association Agreements' (2003) 30 LIEI 15, 20–2.

OECD Codes of Liberalization, or they make explicit reference to them.[187] For example, the EU-Mexico Agreement on Trade in Services[188] stipulates in Article 28.1 that, 'investment... means direct investment, investment in real estate and the purchase and sale of any kind of securities, as defined in the OECD Codes of Liberalisation'.

In addition to capital movements, many Union agreements, especially those which have formed a free trade area between the EU and a third country, refer to establishment as an operation directly linked with foreign investment.[189] However, due to the divergent regulatory scope and the degree of liberalization envisaged in each agreement, different definitions of establishment appear in different EU IIAs, which depart from the notion of establishment as it appears in the TFEU.

More specifically, agreements which adopt a GATS approach to establishment provide a broad definition, very similar to that found in the TFEU, however, excluding from their scope activities undertaken by the self-employed. For example, in the Association Agreement with Chile[190] establishment is defined as 'the constitution, acquisition or maintenance of a legal person' or 'the creation or maintenance of a branch or a representative office' in the territory of one of the parties. However, many EU IIAs and most notably the Partnership and Cooperation Agreements as well as the Association Agreement with Jordan[191] define establishment only as secondary establishment, limiting their scope to the establishment of subsidiaries and branches, thus excluding the right of individuals to set up undertakings.[192] Even in agreements that include a broad definition similar to the one found in primary EU law, such as in the Stabilization and Association Agreements,[193] secondary establishment is the main subject of establishment regulation, thus in essence limiting the scope of establishment to secondary establishment.

Hence, it is obvious that the notion of establishment in EU IIAs is linked to the scope of establishment regulation. The more restrictive definitions of establishment in Union agreements do not imply that the EU adopts a different approach to the definition of establishment in its international agreements. On the contrary, the notion has the main characteristics of establishment that were identified under EU law, and thus covers direct investments. The restrictive definition is primarily

[187] S Bezborodov, 'Freedom of Establishment in the EC Economic Partnership Agreements: in Search of its Direct Effect on Direct Taxation' (2007) 35 International Tax Review 692, 699; B Kiekebeld and D Smit, 'Freedom of establishment and free movement of capital in Association Agreements and direct taxation' (2007) 35 International Tax Review 216, 223–4.

[188] Decision No 2/2001 of the EU-Mexico Joint Council of 27 February 2001 implementing Articles 6, 9, 12(2)(b) and 50 of the Economic Partnership, Political Coordination and Cooperation Agreement [2001] OJ L276/45 (hereinafter, EU-Mexico Services Agreement).

[189] S Szepesi, *Comparing EU Free Trade Agreements: Investment*, InBrief 6D of European Centre for Development Policy Management (2004), pp 5–8.

[190] Agreement establishing an association between the European Community and its Member States, of the one Part, and the Republic of Chile, of the other part [2002] OJ L352, Art 131.

[191] Agreement establishing an association between the European Community and its Member States, of the one Part, and Hashemite Kingdom of Jordan, of the other part [2002] OJ L129/3, Art 32.

[192] S. Bezbodorov, above n 187, p 687.

[193] Eg, see the Stabilisation and Association Agreement between the European Community and its Member States, of the one part, and the Republic of Serbia, of the other part [2008] OJ L119, Arts 52 and 53.

concerned with the types of establishment subject to the establishment rules and the more restrictive scope of establishment regulation, rather than the characteristics of establishment as such. Consequently, it is safe to conclude that for the purposes of foreign investment regulation EU IIAs perceive establishment in a similar way to the TFEU, so that it covers direct investments, even though their regulatory scope differs significantly, covering only certain types of direct investments/establishments.

Furthermore, EU IIAs differ from primary EU law in the sense that they adopt nationality as the criterion for subjecting investments to their regulatory scope. Not only the establishment of an undertaking but also the liberalization of capital movements is dependent on the nationality of the investor. The existence in the chapters regulating capital movements of the provision that, 'The liquidation and transfer abroad of any direct investment made... by Community residents or in the Community by... residents, and of any profits stemming therefrom, shall not be affected by [the provisions restricting capital movement]'[194] entails that nationality determines the foreignness of an investment.

1.2.3 Concluding remarks

Despite the diverging concepts of foreign investment in international and EU law, a consolidated definition can be constructed based on a synthesis of its characteristics which are common under both regimes; differences between definitions should be regarded as non-conflicting accentuations of different features of foreign investment.

Starting with its nature, investment appears to be conceived in EU law, at least within the internal market, as an activity; namely as a transfer of assets or as the establishment of an undertaking, which is contrary to the international law perception of investment as a sum of assets. This observation is incorrect, since European law also conceptualizes investment as an economic asset, illustrated by the concept of direct investment in the framework of capital movement rules, which is affirmed in the Lisbon Treaty. The concept of establishment as the activity relating to the creation, acquisition, or maintenance of an investment, can be regarded as reaffirming the concept of investment as an economic asset. In that respect, investment should be distinguished from the concepts of capital movement and establishment, which actually refer to the activities that have an investment as their main object.

The economic assets that qualify as investments should be defined in broad terms to bridge the differences between instruments of protection and liberalization. As mentioned, EU law defines investment in terms of the form that capital has before and after its transfer across national borders, while international law refers only to assets after establishment in the host country. Nonetheless, the narrower definition given in traditional instruments of international law should not be interpreted as excluding the initial capital from the definition of investment,

194 Eg Art 33(2) of the EU-Israel Agreement (above n 190) and Art 32 of the EU-Mexico Services Agreement (above n 188).

but only as excluding it from its regulatory scope. In fact, the inclusion of pre-entry commitments in many IIAs suggests that investment is understood in international law as also incorporating the initial capital.

With regard to the actual assets that are perceived as an investment, all legal regimes include traditional as well as new forms of property rights—namely shares, real estate, and the rights related to them, and securities and other portfolio investments. Specific mention should be made of the contractual rights included in the definition. European law appears to offer clear and certain criteria for discerning the contractual rights perceived as investments, even though it does not explicitly name them as such, since it distinguishes between concessions and other contracts relating to the provision of goods or services. As international investment arbitration has dealt with this distinction, which is critical in most IIAs, and endorses the rationale behind distinguishing concessions from other contracts, the adoption of similar criteria in international law is desirable.

The lack of reference to IP rights as investment in liberalization instruments does not mean that they are excluded from the notion of investment. On the contrary, their separate regulation, which is also aimed at their protection either by means of harmonizing their treatment or by establishing minimum standards, reaffirms the importance attributed to their regulation. In fact, the detailed rules concerning their creation, their treatment, and their protection prove that, due to their importance, international IP rights have become a distinctive kind of foreign investment, which, albeit falling under the general norms pertaining to foreign investment, are subject to specific regulation.

The convergence of definitions of foreign investment in European and international law becomes apparent when the characteristics of investment are taken into account. Even though liberalization instruments use different terminology, they provide similar and, in certain circumstances, clearer tests for distinguishing investments from other economic operations. The importance attributed to the cross-border element, the lasting link required, and the distinction between capital movements and payments as well as between concession contracts and other contracts confirms that the existence of territorial links, duration, profit expectation, and risk assumption are necessary for the qualification of specific assets as investments.

Nevertheless, contribution to development does not appear to be an autonomous criterion for defining investment in liberalization instruments. This omission should not be regarded as understating the role of development, as they all adhere to the principles and the objectives of sustainable development.[195] Their difference lies in the consideration that investment liberalization always advances economic development, therefore contribution to development constitutes an inherent characteristic of every investment. Instead of disqualifying economic operations that do not promote development of the host state, contribution to development constitutes more of an aspirational goal and an interpretative tool, which runs through

[195] Sustainable development constitutes a basic objective and principle of all liberalization instruments, as is positioned in their Preambles (WTO Agreement, OECD Agreement) or in their first articles (Art 3(5) TEU, Union Agreements).

the entire content of foreign investment regulation and prevents its abuse by foreign investors who may harm local development.[196]

Finally, the nationality of the investor still determines the foreignness of an investment. However, the different importance attributed to managerial control under international and EU law presents a potential threat to a common understanding of foreign investment. While international law considers foreign-controlled undertakings as foreign investment, EU law considers this criterion relevant only for distinguishing direct from other forms of investment and not foreign from domestic or intra-EU investments. Besides, the ambiguity regarding the level of managerial control necessary under EU law may present additional difficulties for EU foreign investment regulation in the future, if FDI is regulated separately from other (non-direct) forms of foreign investment.

1.3 The regulatory scope of EU foreign investment law

The need to elaborate on the regulatory scope of EU foreign investment law becomes immediately apparent from the divergence of the sources of law pertaining to it. Even though the classical distinction between protection and liberalization instruments, as used in the section above, could serve as a basis for classifying the regulatory scope of EU foreign investment law, its importance is gradually diminishing; the constant broadening of the substantive scope of both categories alienates them from their traditional aims, while an increasing number of regulatory instruments include both liberalization and protection norms. In that respect, a thematic classification of sources of law according to the substantive regulated issue is followed, which offers a thorough view of the aspects of foreign investment that are regulated. However, this section does not attempt to analyse the substantive content of EU foreign investment law, it aims only to identify which aspects of foreign investment are regulated, and in which legal instruments, not how they are regulated.[197]

1.3.1 Outward and inward investments

Although foreign investment is usually associated with the host country, where the investment project is accommodated, an essential precondition of foreign investment is that the home country allows for capital to be detached from it in order to be invested in another country and that its nationals can establish an investment in the host country. In that respect, an important aspect of foreign investment regulation pertains to outward investment, namely the conditions under which the home state enables investment in the host state. Outward investment is usually

[196] On the objectives of EU foreign investment regulation and in particular on the role and the importance of sustainable development see the analysis in Chapter 4.

[197] The substantive content of EU foreign investment regulation is considered below in Chapter 3.

regulated alongside inward investment, insofar as entry of foreign investment is concerned. The legal norms regulating capital transfers usually refer to both outward and inward investments, even though they do not always provide the same standards for each.[198] Further, the legal provisions pertaining to establishment are also relevant for determining restrictions of outward investment, even though their primary subject matter is inward investment.[199]

1.3.2 Admission of foreign investment

Admission of foreign investment concerns whether and to what extent a country permits alien investors to make investments in its territory.[200] Under customary international law states enjoy the absolute freedom to regulate the entry of foreign investors in their territory, including the conditions and the extent of carrying out their investment activities, as a prerogative deriving from national sovereignty.[201] However, this discretion enjoyed by host states has been significantly curtailed as a growing number of IIAs include provisions regulating the entry of foreign investments. The ever-growing importance attributed by foreign investors to market access as the major regulatory determinant of the investment location[202] explains the rising willingness of states to enter into international commitments concerning capital movements and the establishment of alien investors.

1.3.2.1 Capital movements

The EU and its Member States have been extremely active in the field of regulation of capital movements to and from third countries. In their effort to promote foreign investment and maximize benefits arising from investment flows, they have been eager to adopt liberalizing regulation: the TFEU provides for liberalization of capital movements between EU Member States and third countries. Even though the EU has maintained certain restrictions and can impose restrictions in exceptional circumstances provided in Articles 64 to 66 TFEU,[203] it is notable that the EU unilaterally liberalized capital movements with third countries and opened

[198] Eg the agreements the EU has concluded with Russia (Agreement on Partnership and Cooperation establishing a partnership between the European Communities and their Member States, of the one part, and the Russian Federation, of the other part [1997] OJ L327) and Jordan (above n 191) envisage in Arts 52 and 49 respectively the possibility of subjecting Russian or Jordanian outward investment to further conditions imposed by domestic laws.

[199] For a discussion of the relevance of establishment rules for outward investments see Kiekebeld and Smit, above n 187, pp 220–3.

[200] A Parra, 'Principles Governing Foreign Investment, as Reflected in National Investment Codes' in Shihata (ed), *Legal treatment of Foreign Investment: The World Bank Guidelines* (1993), p 312.

[201] *Oppenheim's International Law* (eds Jeggins and Watts, 1992), p 522; I Shihata, 'Recent Trends Relating to Entry of Foreign Investment' (1994) 9 ICSID Rev-FILJ 47. I Gomez-Palacio and P Muchlinski, 'Admission and Establishment' in Muchlinski, Ortino, and Schreuer (eds), *Oxford Handbook of International Investment Law* (2008), pp 240–2.

[202] Griffith-Jones, above n 8, pp 171–5; See also Section 1.1.1.

[203] Handoll, above n 141, pp 93–103.

its territory to investors from third countries, without subjecting such preferential treatment to reciprocity.[204]

Most EU Member States are also members of the OECD[205] and thus bound by the OECD Codes of Liberalization of Capital Movements and Current Invisible Operations, which stipulate progressive, non-discriminatory liberalization of capital movements. In particular, they forbid all measures constituting restrictions to capital movements, except under specific circumstances, such as in cases of difficulties concerning the balance of payments. They further oblige Members to list their exceptions, thus adopting a 'top-down' approach on liberalization, and they also provide that these exceptions should apply on a most favoured nation (MFN) basis.[206]

Further, the EU is promoting liberalization of capital movements in its agreements with third countries. Most EU IIAs include provisions liberalizing capital movements thus providing added value to the capital movement rules by allowing free entry of European capital to third states. More specifically, Articles 40 to 45 of the European Economic Area Agreement[207] replicate, with only minor differences, the relevant provisions of the TFEU, while the Association Agreement with Turkey[208] and the Stability and Association Agreements (SAAs) with Balkan countries[209] provide for gradual abolition of all restrictions, aiming at their future accession to the EU. Further, all Euro-Mediterranean Agreements,[210] Partnership and Co-operation Agreements (PCAs),[211] as well as the Association Agreements, which the EU has concluded with Mexico, Chile, Korea, South Africa, and the CARIFORUM states,[212] contain provisions on capital movements which,

204 Sideek, above n 174, pp 231–2.

205 As of 1 May 2011, only 19 EU Member States were also Members of the OECD. However, two of the remaining eight EU Member States, namely Estonia and Slovenia, are invited to open discussions for membership of the Organization, while the remainder (Bulgaria, Cyprus, Latvia, Lithuania, Malta, and Romania) have observer or participant status in many OECD activities.

206 OECD, above n 133.

207 EEA Agreement [1994] OJ L1/3. Members of the EEA are Norway, Iceland, and Liechtenstein.

208 [1973] OJ C113/1.

209 The EU has concluded SAAs with Croatia [2001] OJ L26/3, the Former Yugoslav Republic of Macedonia [2004] OJ L84/13, Albania [2006] OJ L239, Montenegro [2007] OJ L345, Bosnia and Herzegovina [2008] OJ L169/1, and Serbia [2008] OJ L119.

210 The EU has concluded Euro-Mediterranean Association Agreements with Algeria [2005] OJ L265, Egypt [2004] OJ L345/115, Israel [2000] OJ L147/3, Jordan [2002] OJ L129/3, Lebanon [2002] OJ L262/2, Palestine [1997] OJ L187/3, Morocco [2000] OJ L70/2, Tunisia [1998] OJ L97/2, and has concluded negotiations with Syria.

211 The EU has concluded PCAs with Armenia [1999] OJ L239/1, Azerbaijan [1999] OJ L246/46, Georgia [1999] OJ L205/1, Kazakhstan [1999] OJ L196/1, Kyrgyzstan [1999] OJ L196/46, Moldova [1998] OJ L181, Russia [1997] OJ L327, Ukraine [1998] OJ L49, and Uzbekistan [1999] OJ L229/1.

212 Above n 188; above n 190; Agreement on Trade, Development and Co-operation between the European Community and its Member States, of the one Part, and the Republic of South of Africa, of the other part [1999] OJ L311/2; Economic Partnership Agreement between the CARIFORUM States, of the one part, and the European Community and its Member States, of the other Part [2008] OJ L289/3 (the CARIFORUM states are a regional grouping of 15 Caribbean countries, namely Antigua and Barbuda, the Bahamas, Barbados, Belize, Dominica, the Dominican Republic, Grenada, Gyana, Haiti, Jamaica, St Kitts and Nevis, St Lucia, St Vincent and the Grenadines, Suriname, and Trinidad and Tobago).

however, are not uniform, reflecting the different levels of liberalization acceptable to the states concerned.[213] Finally, the Energy Charter Treaty (ECT),[214] which is the most important sectoral investment agreement concluded by the EU and its Member States, guarantees the free transfer of investment-related capital subject to specific limitations.[215]

1.3.2.2 Establishment of foreign investors

Establishment concerns the setting-up and management of a primary or dependent undertaking in the host state. Regulation of establishment aims at the identification and gradual abolition of the domestic regulatory restrictions that impede market access to foreign investors, such as foreign equity ownership limitations, quantitative restrictions, administrative authorizations, and restrictions on the legal form of establishment.[216] In particular, the scope of establishment regulation ranges from transparency provisions, which oblige the host state merely to have a transparent foreign investment regime, thus allowing investors to be aware of the relevant national laws, to provisions offering complete market access, MFN, and national treatment (NT) to foreign investors.[217] Nevertheless, most IIAs regulating establishment provide for gradual liberalization, as they grant MFN and NT to foreign investors, but only with regard to certain types of establishment, or establishment in specific sectors of the economy—usually subjected to specific limitations.

Until the entry into force of the Lisbon Treaty, the EC Treaty did not contain any provisions dealing directly with the establishment of third country nationals. However, based on a patchwork of disperse and limited competences,[218] the EC concluded international agreements that granted market access to third country investors in the EC and to European investors in third countries. The most important agreement among them is the GATS, as it covers investment in all service sectors in WTO Member States. Recognizing commercial presence as a mode of supply of trade in services, the GATS in essence regulates the conditions for entry of foreign investment in service sectors. Another sectoral multilateral agreement concluded by the EU and its Member States containing provisions on the establishment of foreign investors is the ECT, which aspires to gradual liberalization of establishment rules.[219] On a bilateral level, many EU IIAs include provisions

[213] Eg the agreements with Tunisia, Morocco, and Algeria mention full liberalization 'when the time is right' (Art 34), while the agreements with Israel (Art 31), Mexico (Art 28), and Chile (Art 165) provide for complete liberalization, subject to restrictions similar to those found under the TFEU. Bezborodov, above n 187, pp 692–3, 699–700; Fares, above n 186, pp 24–6.

[214] [1998] OJ L69/1.

[215] Art 14 ECT.

[216] UNCTAD, *Admission and Establishment* (1999), pp 1–4.

[217] J Salacuse, 'Towards a Global Treaty on Foreign Investment: the Search for a Grand Bargain' in Horn (ed), *Arbitrating foreign Investment Disputes* (2004), p 73; W Shan, *The legal framework of EU-China investment relations* (2005), pp 116–17.

[218] For a detailed analysis of the scope of EU competence over establishment of foreign investment see Sections 2.2.2. and 2.2.3.

[219] T Wälde, 'The Energy Charter Treaty' in Redgwell (ed), *Energy Law in Europe* (2001), pp 171ff; S Haghighi, *Energy Security, The External Legal Relations of the European Union with major Oil- and Gas- Supplying Countries* (2007), pp 198–203.

on establishment. Following the TFEU, the GATS, or a combination of them as regulatory models, many Union agreements include commitments on establishment of foreign investors, while establishment of foreign investment remains at the forefront of the emerging EU investment policy.[220]

Although establishment of foreign investment has not typically been the subject of any Member State BIT with third countries, certain Member States have undertaken international commitments relating to the establishment of foreign investment. For example, such provisions are included in the OECD Codes of Capital Movements and Invisible Operations which are binding for the majority of EU Member States. The 1986 and 1992 reforms of the OECD Codes added establishment in services and other sectors as another field where the non-discrimination principle applies, thus facilitating establishment of investors of OECD Members in the territory of another OECD Member.[221]

1.3.3 Post-admission treatment and operation of foreign investment

Once a foreign investor is admitted and established in the host country, she is subject to specific legal rules, which determine her entire activities. While national law provides detailed rules as to how foreign and domestic investors may conduct their businesses, international treaties have mainly strived to secure general, abstract standards of treatment, which apply in almost all business affairs relating to the investment—such as its operation, management, maintenance, access to public services and resources, and in general its legal status.[222] On the other hand, certain activities relating to foreign investment, such as taxation,[223] recognition and protection of IP rights,[224] performance requirements, movement of investment-related natural persons and investment guarantee are not only subject to the general standards, but are usually regulated separately, due to their significance for foreign investors.

1.3.3.1 General standards of treatment of foreign investment

Investment-exporting countries have always promoted general standards of treatment in order to enhance the legal protection of investors' property in third countries. In that respect, customary international law was regarded initially as

220 For a detailed analysis of the different establishment provisions found in EU IIAs see Sections 3.2.2. and 3.2.7.2.

221 B Görs, *Internationales Investitionsrecht* (2005), pp 127–31.

222 Shan, above n 217, pp 146–7.

223 Although IIAs do not usually include specific provisions relating to the tax treatment of foreign investments, taxation of foreign investors is the main subject of a considerable number of double taxation treaties, which aim at coordinating different tax regimes and relieving foreign investors from the burden of double taxation. The scope of investment-related taxation norms and their importance for investment regulation however goes beyond the scope of this book.

224 As mentioned, IP rights have become the subject of distinct regulation, which aims at harmonizing their treatment and providing a minimum level of protection. The scope of investment-related IP norms and their importance for investment regulation however goes beyond the scope of this book.

recognizing an international minimum standard for the treatment of foreign investors. However, the existence and the content of this standard as a matter of customary international law generated fierce debate.[225] On the one hand the ICJ rejected that generally accepted rules on the treatment of foreign investment existed internationally because of the 'intense conflicts of systems and interests'.[226] Nonetheless, some IIAs[227] make explicit reference to customary international law standards of treatment, and arbitral tribunals have given meaning to the standards of treatment incorporated in treaties by making reference to general international law standards.[228]

In order to secure and clarify the standards of treatment of foreign investors, most countries have incorporated general standards of treatment in their BITs and IIAs. All BITs that EU Member States have concluded offer to foreign investors MFN, NT, Fair and Equitable Treatment, and Full Protection and Security, or a compilation of these standards.[229] However, the exact scope and content remain ambiguous[230] and they are usually subjected to limitations and other exceptions. Next to BITs, general standards of treatment of foreign investors are also included in the OECD National Treatment Instrument[231] which has been adopted by 24 EU Member States.

General standards of treatment of foreign investment are also included in EU IIAs; all of which provide for the establishment of European investors in third countries and third country investors in the EU and include general standards of treatment of foreign investment at the post-admission stage.[232] However, following the great diversity of establishment provisions found in EU IIAs, general standards of post-admission treatment of foreign investment present significant differences from traditional BITs as, for example, they cover only investments made in accordance with their establishment provisions.[233]

225 For a broad overview of the positions concerning the international minimum standard see Sornarajah, above n 69, pp 349–58; A Adede, 'The Minimum Standards in a World of Disputes' in MacDonald and Johnston (eds), *The Structure and Process of International Law* (1983), pp 1001ff.

226 *Barcelona Traction*, above n 72.

227 Eg Art 1105(1) NAFTA.

228 *Asian Agricultural Products Ltd v Sri Lanka*, ICSID Case No ARB/87/3, Final Award, 27 June 1990, 30 ILM 577.

229 J Schokkaert, 'European Conventional Practice of Protection of Investments Abroad' (2002) 3 JWIT 615, 628–31.

230 Eg the extension of the application of the MFN clause to procedural provisions, the application of the national treatment standard insofar as state subsidies and public procurement is concerned, whether fair and equitable treatment is an independent standard or refers to the international minimum standard are all highly controversial questions. See also Section 3.2.2.4.3.

231 As at 1 May 2011 Bulgaria, Cyprus, and Malta are the only EU Member States not bound by the OECD National Treatment Instrument.

232 See also Section 3.2.2.3.

233 Even though post-establishment treatment is usually reserved for the types of foreign investments in sectors where initial establishment commitments exist, there are also agreements that extend post-establishment treatment to all foreign investment established in the host country. Eg, Art 30 of the Agreement with Jordan offers MFN treatment with regard to the initial establishment of subsidiaries of Jordanian companies in the EU and the better of MFN or NT with regard to the operation of these subsidiaries.

1.3.3.2 Specific issues of foreign investment operation

General standards of treatment and, most notably, NT are not always sufficient to offer foreign investors the desired level of profitability and protection. Therefore, many IIAs explicitly regulate certain aspects of activity, proscribing in many cases specific rights to foreign investors. Performance requirements, repatriation of profits, movement of investment-related natural persons, and guarantee of the investment are discerned, as there are specific treaties devoted to their regulation and they usually receive separate attention in both investment protection and liberalization IIAs.

1.3.3.2.1 Performance requirements

In order to obtain the benefits of foreign investment to the fullest possible extent, many states impose requirements on foreign investors relating to the operation of their business. The most common form of imposed requirements are trade-related performance requirements such as import and export quotas, use of local goods or services, and regulation of production rates. In addition, host states are usually prone to subject the operation of foreign investment to specific rules concerning use of foreign exchange, transfer of technology to local entrepreneurs, monopoly rights, and eligibility for subsidies and grants.[234]

While the NT standard covers many of these aspects, since they do not always apply to domestic entrepreneurs, many IIAs do not provide for unfettered NT and usually exclude, entirely or partially, performance requirements from NT, or contain express provisions for them. However, in sharp contrast with typical North American IIAs, most Member State BITs do not include provisions prohibiting (certain) performance requirements. Thus, Member State BITs leave performance requirements to be regulated at national or international level.[235] Similarly, EU IIAs do not deal with performance requirements as such, referring only in some instances to the relevant multilateral rules.

Except for BITs, performance requirements are also analytically addressed in multilateral IIAs, especially those linked to trade. First and foremost, the TRIMs Agreement deals with certain types of export- and trade-related performance requirements and provides for their phased elimination.[236] Trade-related performance requirements are also addressed in the ECT, which prohibits the imposition of certain performance requirements on foreign investors and requires notification and examination of the legality of others.[237]

1.3.3.2.2 Repatriation of profits

Repatriation of profits constitutes a capital movement which occurs after the establishment of the foreign investor and has a reverse direction, namely from the host

[234] C Correa and N Kumar, *Protecting foreign investment: implications of a WTO regime and policy options* (2003), pp 69–82.

[235] Schokkaert, above n 229, pp 628–9.

[236] P Civello, above n 136; T Brewer and S Young, *The Multilateral Investment System and Multinational Enterprises* (1998), p 123.

[237] Arts 5 and 10(7) and (11) ECT.

state to the home state. Due to its importance for foreign investors, who intend to make profits and repatriate all or a percentage of them to the home state,[238] repatriation of profits is specifically mentioned both in capital movement instruments as well as in BITs. In particular, all BITs that EU Member States have concluded provide for an absolute right of repatriation of profits subject to (only under certain BITs) restrictions imposed under exceptional circumstances. In addition, most EU IIAs make explicit reference to repatriation of profits either by providing for a specific right to repatriation, when liberalization of capital movements is only envisaged,[239] or by subjecting repatriation of profits to existing restrictions, when complete liberalization is foreseen.[240]

1.3.3.2.3 Movement of investment-related natural persons

An important regulatory aspect of the post-admission operation of foreign investment concerns the movement of investment-related natural persons whom foreign investors wish to employ for their activities in the host country. Distinguished from movement of workers, the main characteristic of which is access of natural persons to the labour market of the host state,[241] movement of investment-related natural persons primarily concerns the employment of persons in key positions for the business activities of the foreign investor on a temporary basis. Without affecting national legislation concerning the formalities for entry and residence of third country nationals or national legislation concerning employment conditions, regulation of movement of investment-related natural persons relates essentially to the right of foreign investors to employ third country nationals for a limited period in key positions necessary for the operation of their investment.

Provisions on movement of investment-related natural persons exist primarily in IIAs that regulate the establishment of FDI, indicating that movement of natural persons is primarily linked with the setting-up, management, and operation of FDI. First, it is worth looking at the GATS, which provides that the fourth mode of supply of services concerns the movement of natural persons related to the supply of the service. The EU has in its schedule of commitments defined specific categories of natural persons that fall under the scope of Mode 4 commitments.[242]

Movement of key personnel is also dealt with in the ECT as well as all bilateral EU IIAs which regulate establishment of foreign investors.[243] Certain agreements adopt a GATS approach to the movement of natural persons,[244] while others regulate the movement of key personnel by providing specific definitions of categories

[238] Schokkaert, above n 229, pp 638–9.

[239] Eg Arts 33 and 34 of the Agreements with South Africa and Tunisia respectively. See Fares, above n 186, pp 25–7.

[240] Eg Annex XIV of the EU-Chile Agreement.

[241] C Barnard, above n 35, pp 266–9.

[242] WTO Trade in Services Division, *A handbook on the GATS agreement* (2005), pp 4–5.

[243] See Section 3.2.2.5.2.

[244] Eg Art 101 of the EU-Chile Agreement.

of natural persons who qualify as key personnel and determining, in certain circumstances, the maximum period of stay in the host state.[245]

1.3.3.2.4 Guarantee of foreign investment

Apart from the economic risks that foreign investors assume when they operate an investment project, they are also susceptible to 'political' risks resulting from regulatory measures or political conditions that exist in the host state. In order to be secured from such risks, which can significantly influence the existence and operation of a foreign investment, industrialized states have created guarantee schemes,[246] both on a national and an international level, which undertake to cover entirely or partially the costs incurred by the occurrence of political risk.[247]

Most EU Member States have established national investment guarantee schemes, which protect investments of their nationals. In order to facilitate the function of these schemes, most BITs include subrogation clauses, which enable the home state to succeed to the investor's claims against the host state, thus reaffirming the role of guarantee as a very significant determinant of foreign investment.[248] On the international level, the most important guarantee scheme is MIGA, which offers political risk insurance for investment projects in a broad range of sectors in 143 developing member countries. In particular, it offers guarantees against expropriation, currency transfers, war and civil disturbance, and breach of state contracts, thus providing security to foreign investors against the most important political risks they may face in the host country.[249]

1.3.3.2.5 State contracts and the umbrella clause

Securing the rights of foreign investors deriving from state contracts, many BITs include a catch-all provision, rendering conditions and privileges afforded to foreign investors under (commercial) state contracts within the ambit of Treaty protection. Although the scope of umbrella clauses is rather ambiguous, depending on the wording of each BIT, they result in the internationalization of contractual commitments made by sovereign states.[250] Even though many Member State BITs include umbrella clauses, similar provisions have not yet been inserted in existing EU IIAs. However umbrella clauses will, in all likelihood, be included in future EU IIAs.

[245] Eg Arts 54 and 28 of the Agreements with Croatia and Armenia respectively.

[246] Guarantee schemes differ from private law insurance schemes, which may also cover similar risks, in the sense that they are instituted by governments, they are funded by public resources, and they serve a public interest, as they aim to secure foreign investors from political risk. Carreau and Juillard, above n 50, pp 481–2.

[247] Leben, above n 49, pp 14–16.

[248] Sornarajah, above n 69, p 222; Schokkaert, above n 229, pp 639–40.

[249] On the MIGA Convention see I Shihata, *Multilateral Investment Guarantee Agency and Foreign Investment* (1988).

[250] Sornarajah, above n 69, pp 304, 322.

1.3.4 Protection against expropriation and other political risks

Protection of foreign investment against expropriation has always been considered the core element of international investment law. The extensive nationalizations of the 1970s and the regulatory control of the host country over concessions and other state contracts, especially with regard to natural resources, stirred up the debate about the content of customary international law norms protecting foreign investment and have eventually led to the massive conclusion of BITs, which aimed mainly at offering protection against expropriation. Hence, customary international law and BITs have formed a substantial body of law regulating outright takings of foreign property, determining the legality of such, and providing for compensation; however without always using the same criteria and offering the same solutions.[251]

Even though nationalizations and outright takings of foreign investments have become less frequent in international practice, regulation of expropriation remains important. The evolution of the notion of property, as described above with regard to the definition of investment, as well as the emergence of new forms of takings—broadly defined as 'indirect', 'regulatory', 'creeping', and de facto expropriation—have expanded the regulatory scope of expropriation norms, which are so broadly defined in most BITs to include anything 'tantamount or equivalent' to a taking. In addition, divergent criteria are used for determining compensation, ranging from 'just' to 'prompt, adequate and effective', while the same standards have been contradictorily interpreted and applied in different fora. Next to protection of foreign investment against expropriation; many IIAs provide protection to foreign investors' property against other political risks, such as destruction during war and other national emergencies.

In comparison with all other aspects of foreign investment, protection against expropriation is a field so far excluded from EU foreign investment regulation. Even though the EU arguably has always had the competence to regulate expropriation of foreign investment[252] existing EU IIAs, with the exception of the ECT, stop short of including provisions relating to expropriation and refer to the BITs concluded by its Member States. Nevertheless, protection of foreign investment against expropriation and other political risks constitutes an important element of the emerging comprehensive EU foreign investment policy, indicating that it will be covered in future EU IIAs.[253]

1.3.5 Dispute settlement

IIAs establish mechanisms suitable for the settlement of investment disputes, following the trend of increased judicialization of international economic relations.[254]

[251] For a general overview of expropriation regulation in international investment law see Dolzer and Schreuer, above n 62, ch 14; Sornarajah, above n 69, chs 10, 11.

[252] See Section 2.5.2.

[253] See Section 3.2.7.3.

[254] See EU Petersmann, 'Justice as Conflict Resolution: Proliferation, Fragmentation and Decentralization of Dispute Settlement in International Trade' (2006) 37 U Pa J Int'l L 280.

Following the principle of 'free choice of means'—established in Article 33 UN Charter—states have adopted a different approach on dispute settlement in each legal instrument; ranging from 'political' to adjudicative models and from classical international law interstate settlement procedures to investor-state arbitration.

An institutionalized framework for the political settlement of disputes arising out of the application of foreign investment provisions is established in the majority of EU IIAs: namely the SAAs, the Euro-Med Agreements, the PCAs, and the Trade, Development and Cooperation Agreement with South Africa. Dispute settlement relies essentially on consultation and negotiation and, in cases of disagreement, on arbitration or conciliation. Considering that these agreements do not provide detailed legal rules determining the procedures and lack any reference to compliance procedures, they rely essentially on the 'best efforts' of the parties.[255]

In contrast with the majority of Union agreements, adjudicative or quasi-adjudicative models for the settlement of investment disputes are established in certain EU IIAs that deal specifically with foreign investment, either autonomously or alongside trade. Nevertheless, while IIAs dealing exclusively with investment grant direct rights to foreign investors and allow their participation in the settlement procedure, the inclusion of foreign investment provisions in instruments primarily oriented towards trade regulation infers that the same settlement mechanism, which is open only to state actors, is used for both trade and investment disputes.

The WTO presents the most important multilateral regime dealing with investment regulation and offers a rigorous interstate dispute settlement system characterized by efficiency, effectiveness, and flexibility. Its success is primarily based on the fact that its jurisdiction is compulsory and exclusive, thus obliging its Members to resolve any dispute according to the rules set in the Dispute Settlement Understanding (DSU) and to abide by the outcome reached according to the relevant procedures.[256] In line with the spirit of the WTO dispute settlement, the trade agreements with Mexico, Chile, Korea, and CARIFORUM states initiated a shift in EU bilateral agreements, in the sense that they include more judicialized systems of dispute settlement.[257] Following the WTO model, the agreements provide for compulsory recourse to arbitration, detailed procedures, and enforcement mechanisms—introducing, however, important differentiations from WTO rules.[258] Contrary to the North American Free Trade Agreement (NAFTA), which provides for different dispute settlement mechanisms for trade and investment, existing EU IIAs establish a dispute settlement mechanism applying to all trade and trade-related matters, including foreign investment, thus depriving foreign

[255] ER Robles, 'Political and Quasi-Adjudicative Dispute Settlement Models in European Union Free Trade Agreements', WTO Economic and Research Statistics Division, Staff Working Paper ERSD-2006–09, November 2006, pp 11–21. See also Section 3.2.5.1.

[256] For a detailed presentation of WTO Dispute Settlement see D Palmeter and P Mavroidis, *Dispute Settlement in the World Trade Organization* (2004); Y Guoha, B Mercurio, and L Yongjie, *WTO Dispute Settlement Understanding: A Detailed Interpretation* (2005); EU Petersmann, *The WTO Dispute Settlement System 1995–2003* (2004).

[257] Robles, above n 255, p 28.

[258] See Section 3.2.5.2.

investors from the unique characteristic of international investment law, namely investor-state arbitration.

The main innovation of IIAs in comparison to trade agreements is that besides interstate settlement they provide for dispute resolution between investors and host states, thus granting a right to private parties to pursue their interests directly. Indeed, all BITs that EU Member States have concluded, as well as the ECT, provide for investor-state arbitration, institutionalized or ad hoc, containing rules on conflict of jurisdiction between the available fora, which stipulate that choice of one forum excludes resort to the other.[259] Although, investor-state arbitration has not as yet been a feature of EU IIAs, in its effort to establish a comprehensive investment policy, the Commission intends to incorporate investor-state arbitration in future EU IIAs.[260]

Despite the great diversity of fora provided in BITs for settlement of investment disputes, ICSID arbitration has been the main mechanism used broadly since the emergence of investor-state arbitration. It allows private investors to pursue their interests independently from their home country, thus promoting depoliticization of investment disputes and, thus, rendering interstate arbitration redundant.[261] More specifically, the ICSID Convention presents a specialized forum for investment disputes, as it limits its jurisdiction only to disputes 'arising out of an investment'.[262] Therefore, it constitutes a unique arbitration system as it combines elements of both commercial and interstate arbitration. While it adheres to the basic rule of arbitration that consent of the parties is a *sine qua non* condition of arbitration, it requires double consent of the defendant state party, one of them being the ratification of the ICSID Convention, the other relating to the specific dispute. Further, the Convention determines the applicable law in the absence of agreement of the parties as the national law of the host state and general international law.[263] Moreover, it provides for annulment and legal review of the awards as well as for a strong and efficient implementation mechanism of ICSID awards; it obliges states to treat them as if they were a final judgment of a national court, thus avoiding the restrictions posed by the New York Convention on the Recognition and Enforcement of Foreign Arbitration Awards, most importantly the sovereign immunity of the host state.[264]

Finally, it is notable that national courts play an important role in the settlement of investment disputes. All Member State BITs provide recourse to the national courts of the host state as an alternative for private investors, while some provide for primary exhaustion of local remedies as a basic condition for initiation

[259] Schokkaert, above n 229, pp 640–3; T Wälde, 'Investment Arbitration under the Energy Charter Treaty: An Overview of selected Key Issues based on Recent Litigation Experience' in Horn (ed), *Arbitrating Foreign Investment Disputes* (2004), pp 193ff.

[260] See Section 3.2.7.4.

[261] Echandi, above n 58, pp 5–7.

[262] For a detailed analysis of ICSID dispute settlement see C Schreuer, *The ICSID Convention: A commentary* (2001); M Sornarajah, *Settlement of Investment Disputes* (2000); R Bishop, J Crawford, and W Reisman, *Foreign Investment disputes: Cases, materials and commentary* (2005).

[263] E Gaillard and Y Banifatemi, 'The meaning of "and" in Article 42(1) Second sentence of the Washington Convention: The role of international Law in the ICSID Choice of Law process' (2003) 18 ICSID Rev-FILJ 375.

[264] Sornarajah, above n 69, p 209.

of arbitration proceedings. In addition, national courts of monist states are well equipped to apply and interpret, under certain circumstances, the provisions of international agreements, thus allowing foreign investors to bring claims based on express rights conferred on them by IIAs. Bearing in mind the direct effect of Union agreements, the ECJ acquires a significant role in applying and interpreting their investment provisions when a violation by the EU or its Member States is alleged.[265]

1.3.6 Promotion of foreign investment

In addition to the substantive aspects of foreign investment regulation described above, promotion of foreign investment is an important field, in which both the EU and its Member States are engaged. Most IIAs stress the importance of the creation of an environment favourable to foreign investment and support the stimulation of foreign investment initiatives. Even though the implementation of these policy goals is left to individual states and the provisions relating to promotion of foreign investment are primarily considered to be of an aspirational character, the explicit recognition of promotion of foreign investment alongside its protection emphasizes the importance attributed to foreign investment promotion as an objective of IIAs.

In that respect, the vast majority of Union agreements grant a crucial role to foreign investment promotion. They establish a specific framework for cooperation on investment promotion, providing the strategic instruments and the principles governing them, which are necessary for the implementation of this policy goal. Furthermore, the EU has instituted specific development aid instruments focusing on the promotion of foreign investment in different regions and countries in the world and has granted investment promotion a central role in the general aid instruments established for developing countries. The EU has developed general and specific aid instruments aimed at foreign investment promotion, incorporating investment promotion among the basic objectives of broad aid instruments and adopting special programmes aimed at stimulating private sector development and facilitating a higher level of economic growth.[266]

1.3.7 Concluding remarks

Foreign investment regulation is multifaceted, and norms regulating foreign investment are scattered in diverse legal instruments adopted by the EU or its Member States establishing a complicated framework for multilayered regulation of foreign investment. The multilateral agreements that the EU and its Member States have concluded, like the WTO and the OECD instruments, regulate only a few aspects of foreign investment, while existing EU IIAs provide piecemeal regulation which excludes important areas of investment regulation. Building

[265] See Section 6.1.3.1. [266] See Section 3.2.6.

on Member State BITs, EU IIAs raise the danger of creating a complex system, consisting of overlaps, incoherent rules, and serious gaps.

The proliferation of sources of EU foreign investment law indicates the high potential of overlap between different legal instruments, raising concerns about their hierarchy and compatibility. The parallel regulation of various aspects of foreign investment in multilateral and bilateral EU IIAs as well as in Member State IIAs concluded between the same countries, questions the international law validity and the hierarchy of norms established thereunder. For example, many Union agreements include limitations on capital movements that also apply to repatriations of profits, which are unrestricted under most Member State BITs. Furthermore, the existence of multiple legal instruments requires increased scrutiny of the compatibility between EU and Member State IIAs and primary EU law, as the involvement of various actors blurs the scope of the freedoms and restrictions imposed by the TFEU.

In addition, the diversity of instruments of EU foreign investment law increases the need for coherence in the application, implementation, and interpretation of the relevant rules. Considering the variety of wording used in different rules on the same or similar subject matter, their coherent reading is necessary not only to avoid conflict and ensure compatibility, but also to increase unity in EU foreign investment law—for example the existence of standards such as MFN and NT in all fields of foreign investment regulation dictates a subtle delineation of their content with regard to the various aspects of foreign investment and the different treaty instruments, while the meaning of these standards in foreign investment law should be distinguished from their substantive content when used in the context of other international law fields and, most notably, trade.[267] Moreover, the existence of multiple dispute settlement options brings into international investment law the complexities arising out of the proliferation of settlement mechanisms, such as the dangers of inconsistent decisions and forum shopping.[268]

[267] Eg, the application in foreign investment regulation of the NT standard, which is based on the existence of 'like circumstances', differentiates from its long-settled interpretation in the context of the GATT, since likeness of products is not comparable with likeness of investment projects and their operation. See also Section 3.2.2.4.1.

[268] See Petersmann, above n 254.

PART II

THE SCOPE, CONTENT, AND OBJECTIVES OF EU FOREIGN INVESTMENT LAW

An examination of EU foreign investment regulation is intrinsically linked with the question of the formation of an EU policy on foreign investment. Unlike other fields where common policies have been developed, such as trade policy, until the Lisbon Treaty primary EU law lacked an explicit reference to foreign investment policy, failing to identify its scope, content, and orientation. Although the Lisbon Treaty marks a new era for EU foreign investment regulation, the existence of rules on foreign investment in a variety of EU legal instruments indicates the elements of EU foreign investment policy. Hence, the determination of the scope, content, and orientation of EU foreign investment regulation is essential in order to analyse the extent to which the EU has become an international actor in the field of foreign investment, the characteristics of its action in the international field, and how it is differentiated from other international actors.

Determining the role of the EU as an international actor and whether there is an EU foreign investment policy first begs the question of the exact competences of the EU in the field of foreign investment. Identifying the scope and nature of EU powers in the field is the foundation on which a distinctive policy can be built, thereby indicating the limits of EU external action.

The second question that arises concerns the exercise of EU competence. In order to determine the content of EU regulation of foreign investment and whether it amounts to the coherent exercise of an EU policy, it is necessary to look at how the EU has exercised its powers and, more specifically, whether it has concluded international agreements on foreign investment and the content of their provisions. Assessing the content of Union agreements in the field of foreign investment by comparison to other instruments of international regulation of foreign investment is an indispensable step in the analysis of the role of the EU as an international actor in the field of foreign investment.

Thirdly, an analysis of the content of EU regulation of foreign investment would be incomplete without regard to the principles and policy objectives driving the exercise of EU powers. Considering the legal, economic, and political rationales behind EU regulation of foreign investment as well as their implementation in EU international investment agreements (IIAs) is a prerequisite for a thorough examination of whether a distinctive foreign investment policy has been formed, while it explains the direction of EU foreign investment regulation, particularly if it is viewed comparatively with other IIAs. Following the analysis of the content of EU foreign investment regulation, the objectives and policy goals pursued by the EU are explained and assessed in practice.

2

EU Competence over Foreign Investment

Until the entry into force of the Lisbon Treaty, the scope of EU competence in the field of foreign investment was unclear. The exact delineation of EU competence has been complex and ambiguous given that the EC Treaty did not refer to foreign investment, even with regard to intra-EU investments. But even after Lisbon, which expressly grants competence to the EU over foreign direct investment in Article 207 TFEU, the matter is not entirely unambiguous, as it does not cover all forms of foreign investment, while its link to pre-existing power-conferring provisions of the EU Treaties raises questions.

The ambiguity of the EC Treaty, which gave rise to struggles between the Commission and the Member States concerning the scope of their respective powers over foreign investment, was reflected in practice. All Union agreements, including foreign investment provisions, are mixed agreements, without including a declaration of competence, providing only in a general manner that the EU and its Member States act within the scope of their respective competence.[1] Furthermore, the identification of the legal norms on which foreign investment regulation in these agreements was based also lacks clarity. While earlier EU international investment agreements (IIAs) referenced many relevant Treaty provisions—such as the Energy Charter Treaty (ECT) and the Partnership and Co-operation Agreements (PCAs)[2]—newer agreements, which tended to include investment provisions within the framework of a broader association agreement were based only on Article 310 TEC (now Art 217 TFEU).[3] Nevertheless, there are important exceptions such as the Global Agreement with Mexico which, despite its strong resemblance to some of the association agreements, was adopted under a plurality of legal bases.[4]

Since the Lisbon Treaty, and in light of Article 207 TFEU regarding EU competence over foreign direct investment (FDI), the Commission intends to establish a comprehensive EU investment policy, concluding new generation EU IIAs

[1] J Heliskoski, *Mixed Agreements as a Technique for Organizing the International Relations of the European Community and its Member States* (2001), pp 10–13.

[2] The Energy Charter Treaty was adopted on the basis of Arts 54, 57, 66, 73C, 87, 99, 100, 113, 130S, and 235 EEC Treaty and the PCAs on Arts 44, 47, 55, 57, 71, 80, 93, 94, 133, and 308 TEC.

[3] Art 310 TEC was used as a legal basis for the conclusion of the Stability and Association Agreements (SAAs), the Euro-Mediterranean Agreements, the Agreement with Chile, and the Trade, Development and Cooperation Agreement with South Africa.

[4] The Global Agreement with Mexico was adopted on the basis of Arts 44(2), 47, 55, 57(2), 71, 80(2), 133, and 181 TEC. See also N Maydell, 'The European Community's Minimum Platform on Investment or the Trojan Horse of Investment Competence' in Reinisch and Knahr (eds), *International Investment Law and Context* (2007), p 75.

with third countries.[5] Despite the broad pronouncement of EU competence over investment matters, the Commission has so far avoided clarifying its views with regard to the exact scope of EU competences over foreign investment. In that respect, in order to delimitate EU from Member State competence on foreign investment as well as to clarify and identify the scope of the specific legal bases on foreign investment, it is necessary to examine the different forms of foreign investment separately, examining whether and to what extent the different regulatory aspects of each form of foreign investment fall under EU competence. To examine EU competence for different categories of foreign investment, it is logical to begin with FDI, given its gravity as the most important category of foreign investment. In that regard, EU competence on FDI will be scrutinized to examine whether the EU enjoys competence over admission and post-admission treatment and operation of foreign investment. After that, Union competence to regulate portfolio investment and foreign investment in the form of concession contracts is examined, considering the existence of competence for regulating the conditions for admission and treatment of these forms of investment. Thirdly, the delimitation of EU competence in the common for all categories of foreign investment fields of property expropriation and dispute settlement is analysed—highly ambiguous areas both before and after the entry into force of the Lisbon Treaty. However, before examining in detail the scope of EU competence on foreign investment, it is necessary to establish the legal framework of EU external competences, identifying its main principles and basic characteristics.

2.1 General principles of EU external competence

2.1.1 Existence of EU competence

The EU is based on the principle of attributed powers and therefore any EU action needs a specific legal basis, namely a source of law that confers to it the precise power in question. This principle, which is prescribed in Article 5 TEU, applies both to actions of the EU taken within the internal legal order as well as to EU actions in the sphere of international law.[6]

In the field of EU external competence[7] such attribution is primarily expressed in the provisions of primary EU law. Articles 3 and 4 TFEU provide a list of categories

[5] Commission Communication, Towards a comprehensive European international investment policy, Brussels 7.7.2010, COM(2010) 343 (hereinafter, Investment Policy Communication).

[6] The clearest expression of the principle of attribution of powers in the field of external relations can be found in Opinion 2/94 (*Accession to the ECHR*) [1996] ECR I-1759. On the principle of attribution of powers see A Dashwood, 'The Attribution of External Relations Competence' in Dashwood and Hillion (eds), *The general law of EC external relations* (2000), ch 8.

[7] Due to the various meanings given in the literature to the terms 'external' and 'internal' with regard to EU competence, these terms are used in this book to define whether the scope of EU action extends to relations with third countries and their nationals. In order to distinguish between the types of action taken, namely between secondary EU legislation and international agreements or other international law instruments, the terms 'autonomous measures' and 'international agreements' or 'international law measures' are used respectively.

of EU competences, indicating also the nature of EU competence. The areas in which the EU is endowed with express external competence and are directly or indirectly related to foreign investment have gradually expanded from the Common Commercial Policy (CCP) and Article 217 TFEU on the negotiation and conclusion of Association Agreements to other fields including capital movements, monetary union, development, and economic, financial, and technical cooperation.[8]

Besides its express powers, Union competence to conclude international agreements can be also implied. The existence of EU implied powers, which was recognized by the European Court in its early jurisprudence,[9] is now explicitly addressed in Article 216(1) TFEU. Article 216(1) TFEU, alongside Article 3(2) TFEU, attempts to codify the jurisprudence of the Court of Justice on the existence and exclusivity of implied powers. Considering that the drafters of the Lisbon Treaty aimed to codify the jurisprudence of the Court, it is necessary to examine the development of the Court's case law on implied powers.

According to the Court, implied competence arises initially in cases where the EU has enacted secondary legislation in accordance with primary EU law provisions, within the framework of these provisions.[10] However, even though the existence of secondary legislation can be a valuable indication of the existence of implied powers, it is not an essential precondition for their existence. As the Court has often acknowledged, implied competence arises in all cases where the EU has been conferred power for the purpose of attaining a specific objective and it is necessary to extend that power to action in the international sphere for the attainment of that objective.[11] Despite the obvious importance of the requirement of necessity for the establishment of competence to conclude international agreements, the Court has used vague definitions of 'necessary' in more than one case, without always distinguishing whether necessity is actually a requirement for the existence or for the exclusivity of implied competence.[12] Given that in the majority of the cases the conflict concerned exclusive competence, as only exclusivity could preclude action taken by the Member States, the Court has preferred in most of its judgments to avoid clarifying the doctrine of implied powers, insofar as the difference between existence and exclusivity is concerned; this lack of clarity in the Court's judgments has triggered an extensive and controversial legal debate.[13]

[8] Arts 63, 207, 208, 212, 217, and 219 TFEU.

[9] Case 22/70 *Commission v Council (AETR)* [1971] ECR 263.

[10] Opinion 1/2003 (*Lugano Convention*) [2006] ECR I-1, para 114.

[11] Opinion 2/91 (*re ILO Convention No 170*) [1993] ECR I-106, para 7.

[12] For an overview of the early controversy on necessity see J Bourgeois, 'External Relations Powers of the European Community' (1999) 22 Fordham Int'l LJ 149; M Klamert and N Maydell, 'Lost in Exclusivity: Implied Non-exclusive External Competences in Community Law' (2008) 13 EFA Rev 493, 496–502.

[13] A highly debatable issue was whether necessity in the sense of an 'inextricable link' as the latter test was formulated in Opinions 1/76 ([1977] ECR 741) concerns only exclusivity and does not affect the existence of external competence as such. Even though it has been argued that Opinion 1/76 concerns the existence of EU competence (P Eeckhout, *External relations of the European Union: Legal and constitutional foundations* (2004), pp 65–9, 89–91), it is widely accepted that the inextricable linkage test is only relevant for exclusivity purposes (Dashwood, above n 6, pp 132–6). Further, it is argued that even though the wording of the Court's judgment in the *Open Skies* cases (below n 20, paras 55–7) seems to require the existence of an inextricable link for the recognition

However, in Opinion 1/2003[14] the Court clarified that existence and exclusivity of implied powers are two different stages in the examination of Union implied competence to conclude international agreements. Even though the Court did not enter into an examination of the notion of necessity as a condition for the existence of implied powers, it set the ground for interpreting necessity in accordance with its previous case law, as requiring that a specific action must be necessary to fulfill the objectives of the founding Treaties, as they are specified in the provision chosen as the legal basis for the contested action. The choice of this criterion is in accordance with the logic of *effet utile* underpinning the jurisprudence of the Court, which is centred on the possible use of all types of action in order to achieve the fulfillment of the objectives of the founding Treaties.[15] While the Court is very careful to ensure that competence to conclude international agreements does not override the substantive and institutional limits determining its competence to legislate in a specific area, it recognizes that a power-conferring provision should not be understood as granting only autonomous legislative powers, but as also including the possibility of concluding international agreements and taking international law measures.[16] Hence, as Eeckhout rightly states, the requirement of necessity is 'better understood as establishing general parallelism, by emphasizing that implied external powers are Treaty-based and therefore not confined to areas where the [EU] has already legislated'.[17] Construing the doctrine of implied powers in such a way, fulfills the international legal capacity of the EU and recognizes the practical needs of increasing international legislation.

The recognition of parallelism between international agreements and autonomous legislation as alternative forms of EU action to achieve Union objectives entails that the existence of implied powers is based on the same principles which determine the scope of EU competence to legislate in a specific area of law. However, parallelism should not be read as establishing external competences in all fields where internal competence exists. The doctrine of implied powers cannot

of the existence of implied powers, the Court refers to exclusivity, as it concerns the *a priori*, or otherwise, character of exclusivity and not the existence of implied powers as such. R Holdgaard, 'The European Community's Implied External Competence after the Open Skies cases' (2003) 8 EFA Rev 365, 383–5.

[14] Above n 10, para 115.

[15] P Koutrakos, *EU International Relations Law* (2006), p 124. A different understanding of the Lugano Opinion is put forward (Klamert and Maydell, above n 12, pp 505–7; T Eilmansberger, 'Bilateral Investment Treaties and EU Law' (2009) 46 CMLR 383, 390–1) according to which the term 'necessity' requires that external competences 'facilate' the objectives of the Treaty. If facilitation is understood as 'further[ing] the attainment of internal objectives' (Dashwood, above n 6, pp 136–7), then the existence of external competence is based on the same criteria that determine internal competence (this does not establish parallelism of external and internal powers in the sense of Opinion 1/94, as the authors rightly point out and is explained in the following para). However, if facilitation is perceived as an additional criterion, providing 'a lower threshold test' in comparison to necessity required for exclusivity, it would actually add to the obscurity concerning the existence of external competence, given that, as the authors contemplate, 'unresolved is the question of the exact standard of facilitation to be required for establishing implied non-exclusive competence'.

[16] *AETR* judgment, above n 9, paras 23–7; Dashwood, above n 6, pp 136–7; Eeckhout, above n 13, p 99.

[17] Eeckhout, above n 13, p 99.

be used for extending Union competence beyond that included in primary EU law, so that the EU cannot take action with regard to third countries and their nationals in a specific area of law, if such action is excluded from the scope of the relevant provisions. The rejection of this form of parallelism between external and internal competences was clearly recognized by the Court in Opinion 1/94,[18] which ruled that implied competences exist within the substantive limits set by primary law provisions and emphasized the importance of primary EU law objectives for determining the existence of implied competence.[19]

Turning now to Article 216(1) TFEU, the wording of this provision, in particular when read together with Article 3(2) TFEU, generates questions as to whether it effectively alters the doctrine of implied powers. Indeed, the wording of these provisions is to a large extent identical, establishing similar conditions for existence and for exclusivity of implied competence. This raises the danger of considering implied competence as being always exclusive, which can in turn result either in a narrow definition of existence of implied powers or in a broad definition of exclusive implied powers, which in either case would be inconsistent with the Court's jurisprudence.[20] Nevertheless, Articles 216(1) and 3(2) TFEU can be read in a manner consistent with the evolution of the jurisprudence on implied powers.

First, a proper interpretation of Articles 216(1) and 3(2) TFEU requires considering them in their historical context. Both provisions are identical to provisions included in the Constitutional Treaty, which aimed to codify the existing case law at that time on implied powers.[21] Considering that these provisions predated the clarification of the doctrine of implied powers by Opinion 1/2003, they followed the complex and confusing statements of the Court's jurisprudence until that time. However, using an interpretative technique similar to that used by the Court in Opinion 1/2003—where it clarified the rules on implied competence based on its earlier jurisprudence—Articles 216(1) and 3(2) TFEU can be read to reflect the evolution of the doctrine of implied powers.

As regards the existence of implied powers, Article 216(1) TFEU recognizes that implied powers arise where it is necessary to achieve one of the Union's objectives. This provision can be understood as encapsulating the main condition for the existence of implied powers, interpreted identically to what has been argued above with respect to Opinion 1/2003. On the other hand, the broad reference to Union objectives without any link to the specific objectives of an internal legal basis, can broaden the scope of implied powers, considering that Article 21 TEU encapsulates

[18] Opinion 1/94 [1994] ECR I-5267.

[19] For a detailed analysis of Opinion 1/94 and the rejection of this form of parallelism between external and internal competences, see below Section 2.2.2.1.1.

[20] M Cremona, 'A constitutional basis for Effective External Action? An assessment of the provisions on EU External Action in the Constitutional Treaty', EUI Working Paper 2006/30, pp 10–11.

[21] On the history of Arts I-13(2) and III-323(1) see A Antoniadis, 'The EU's implied competence to conclude international agreements after the Reform Treaty Reformed enough?' in Laursen (ed), *The EU in the Global Political Economy* (2010), pp 79–82.

a general list of objectives of Union external action.[22] Moreover, the fact that Article 216(1) TFEU continues enumerating the existence of Union legislation, which allows the conclusion of international agreements and the possible effect on common rules as circumstances where implied competence exists, complicates the discussion. The fact that the latter situations are more relevant for exclusivity rather than the existence of implied competence, as explained in the section below, can result in a narrower reading of when implied powers are 'necessary' for the conclusion of an international agreement. Avoiding this danger, the existence of Union legislation and the effect on common rules could be regarded as specific situations where Union action is necessary to attain Treaty objectives which are elaborated in Union legislation, rather than as mutually exclusive situations.

In that regard, the recognition of the existence of implied powers expands Union competence on foreign investment substantively. Given the broad scope of foreign investment regulation, which covers not only FDI but also portfolio investment and investment in the form of concession contracts, many provisions of the founding Treaties can offer a legal basis for adopting autonomous legislation as well as concluding an international agreement on different aspects of foreign investment regulation. More specifically, the chapters on the freedoms of establishment and services, on visas and immigration, on competition law, as well as the provisions on harmonization in the internal market need to be specifically examined, due to their direct and indirect linkage with many aspects of foreign investment regulation.

2.1.2 Exclusivity of EU competence

An examination of whether external competence exists is not sufficient, as it is necessary to distinguish whether such competence is exclusive or shared. In fact, both the Court's jurisprudence and the literature place more emphasis on exclusivity, given its practical implications.

Both express as well as implied powers can be exclusive. Insofar as express powers are concerned, primary EU law determines the exclusive nature of EU competences. Under the EC Treaty most provisions usually determined the exclusive—or otherwise—character of the competence attributed to the EU next to their substantive scope. For example, the provisions on development and economic, financial, and technical cooperation confirmed the non-exclusive character of EC competence in that field, establishing shared competence. In other cases however, such as the CCP, the Court established the exclusive character of EC competence and affirmed its character as *a priori* exclusivity, as the Member States were pre-empted from taking any action in the areas covered by the CCP, even with regard to those with which the EU had not yet taken any legislative action.[23] Clarifying the nature

[22] M Cremona, 'External relations and external competence of the European Union: The emergence of an integrated policy' in Craig and de Búrca (eds), *The Evolution of EU Law* (2011), pp 225–6.

[23] Opinion 1/75 [1975] ECR 1355. For an analysis of the *a priori* exclusive character of the CCP, see Koutrakos, above n 15, pp 13–17.

of Union express powers, the Lisbon Treaty indicates in Articles 3 to 6 the nature of EU competence in each field. For example, Article 3(1)(e) TFEU provides that the EU has exclusive competence in the field of the CCP,[24] and Article 4(2)(a) TFEU verifies the shared nature of EU competence in the field of the internal market.

The question of exclusivity of implied powers has been the subject of numerous cases in which the Court had the opportunity to establish criteria for determining the exclusivity of implied competence.[25] Similar to the rules concerning the existence of implied powers, the Lisbon Treaty has attempted to codify in Article 3(2) TFEU the basic rules formed by the Court regarding the criteria that determine the exclusive nature of implied powers.[26]

Starting with the development of the concept of implied exclusive powers, the Court has gradually formulated two different tests for recognizing exclusivity, focusing again on complementarity between competence to take autonomous measures and international action and aiming at limiting exclusivity in cases that would not affect the balance struck internally. Elucidating the main characteristics of the two exclusivity tests, it becomes apparent that their application in the field of foreign investment requires a very careful and detailed examination.

The first type of exclusivity (*AETR* exclusivity) arises in circumstances where common rules have been adopted and exclusivity is necessary to avoid any effect on the common rules which may result from autonomous action taken by Member States.[27] *AETR* exclusivity, which covers areas of law largely covered by Union rules, aims at preserving the effectiveness of the *acquis* and at eliminating the conflicts between Union rules and provisions of national law in the form of an international agreement concluded by the Member States, thus in effect applying the doctrine of supremacy of EU law.[28] Assessing whether common rules can be affected, the Court clarified that Member States cannot enter into international commitments

[24] See below Section 2.2.3.2.

[25] The most important judgments concerning exclusivity of implied powers are found in *AETR*, *Kramer* (Joined Cases 3, 4 & 6/76 [1976] ECR 1279), Opinion 1/76 (above n 13), Opinion 2/91, Opinion 2/92 ([1995] ECR I-521), Opinion 1/94 (above n 18), the *Open Skies* cases (Case C-466/98 *Commission v UK* [2002] ECR I-9427, Case C-467/98 *Commission v Denmark* [2002] ECR I-9519, Case C-468/98 *Commission v Sweden* [2002] ECR I-9575, Case C-469/98 *Commission v Finland* [2002] ECR I-9627, Case C-471/98 *Commission v Belgium* [2002] ECR I-9681, Case C-472/98 *Commission v Luxembourg* [2002] ECR I-9741, Case C-975/98 *Commission v Austria* [2002] ECR I-9797, Case C-976/98 *Commission v Germany* [2002] ECR I-9855) and Opinion 1/2003 (above n 14).

[26] J Wouters, D Coppens, and B de Meester, 'The European Union's External Relations after the Lisbon Treaty' in Griller and Ziller (eds), *The Lisbon Treaty: EU Constitutionalism without a Constitutional Treaty?* (2008), p 169.

[27] The clearest formulation of *AETR*-type exclusivity can be found in Opinion 1/94, paras 76–8 and 96 and in the *Open Skies* cases, paras 104–11. For an analysis of *AETR*-type exclusivity see Koutrakos, above n 15, pp 84–8, 110–12; Eeckhout, above n 13, pp 59–64, 92–4; Holdgaard, above n 13, pp 385–8; D O'Keefe, 'Exclusive, Concurrent and Shared Competence' in Dashwood and Hillion (eds), *The general law of EC external relations* (2000), pp 182–7.

[28] Eeckhout, above n 13, p 99. The type of autonomous action taken by Member States that can affect the *acquis* has been broadly interpreted in the *IMO* case (Case C-45/07 *Commission v Greece* [2009] ECR I-701), as covering not only legally binding commitments undertaken by Member States, but also preparatory measures and proposals that can lead to the adoption of binding for the EU measures by an international organization. For a critical analysis of this judgment see M Cremona, 'Extending the Reach of the AETR Principle: Comment on *Commission v Greece* (C-45/07)' (2009) 34 EL Rev 754.

even if there is no contradiction between these commitments and EU rules. *AETR* exclusivity will arise in particular where there is complete harmonization of a given area of law, where there exists internal legislation relating to treatment of nationals of non-Member States, and finally where the power to negotiate with non-Member States has been conferred to EU institutions. However, the mere distortion of competition and the deflection of the internal market that can result from autonomous action by Member States are not enough in themselves to affect the common rules and render EU competence exclusive.[29] Hence, *AETR* exclusivity arises only in fields where the EU and the Member States enjoy concurrent powers to legislate, after the EU has exercised its powers and has legislated in the field.

The second type of exclusivity (Opinion 1/76 exclusivity) arises when exclusivity is necessary for the attainment of the objectives of the founding Treaties. This type of exclusive implied competence was initially recognized in Opinion 1/76,[30] which found that the EU enjoyed exclusive implied powers to enter into an international agreement, even if no prior internal legislation was adopted, since the international agreement in question was inextricably linked with the objectives of the relevant provision and internal competence could not be effectively exercised without the EU entering an international agreement. This type of exclusivity has generated long and controversial debates, mainly concerning the notion of 'necessary' and whether such exclusivity arises a priori or whether it is the result of the exercise of the EU's competence.[31]

The existence of an inextricable link concerns the inappropriateness of internal legislative measures and the need for international action on behalf of the EU in order to achieve the objectives of a specific primary EU law provision.[32] Hence, the assessment of necessity requires a case-by-case examination of the effectiveness of the available internal legislative measures and whether international action is the only available means for taking action in a specific case. Such a reading of the requirement of necessity is better understood if we consider that Opinion 1/76 exclusivity does not establish a priori exclusivity but arises only at the moment competence is actually exercised.[33] Given that exclusive implied powers arise only in fields where the EU and the Member States have concurrent powers, any doctrine that would grant *a priori* exclusivity only with regard to international action is contrary to the general balance between autonomous legislative measures and action in the international sphere, which has become the main rationale underpinning the Court's decisions in external competence cases.[34]

As a result, Opinion 1/76 is better understood as constituting an alternative form of *AETR* exclusivity, in the sense that Member States are precluded from taking external action where the EU has legislated in the field—the only differences being that EU rules are in the form of international agreements and that

[29] *Open Skies* (*Commission v Denmark*), above n 25, paras 107–12.

[30] Above n 13.

[31] For the divergent Opinions on the scope of Opinion 1/76 exclusivity see A Dashwood, 'The Relationship between the Member States European Union/European Community' (2004) 11 CMLR 355, 372; Eeckhout, above n 13; Koutrakos, above n 15, pp 92–5, 109.

[32] Koutrakos, above n 15, pp 113–14.

[33] Eeckhout, above n 13, pp 90–1.

[34] Ibid, pp 91–2, 99; cf Holdgaard, above n 13, pp 384–6.

exclusivity arises at the moment of the formation of the will of the EU to act in the specific field. Such a reading of exclusivity is consistent with the argument used by the Court that exclusivity arises only in special circumstances, where the alternative option of concerted action by the Member States would not be an alternative means of international action. The preference of concerted Member State action over exclusive Union powers is only an expression of the Court's assessment of the principle of subsidiarity, where the Court can assess *in concreto* whether EU action should be taken in a specific case.

Similar to Article 216(1) TFEU, Article 3(2) TFEU does not fit comfortably with the determination of exclusivity of implied powers by the Court. Despite the broad wording of the provision, which itself carries risk, it can be interpreted consistently with the Court's jurisprudence on exclusive implied competence. Indeed, the third situation in which implied powers are exclusive, namely when common rules are affected, seems to incorporate the *AETR* doctrine.[35] This broad and open-ended provision can be interpreted in light of the Court's jurisprudence on the specific situations where Member State action can affect or alter the scope of common rules. However, such an interpretation would be at odds, given that Article 3(2) TFEU recognizes as an autonomous basis for exclusive implied powers the existence of Union legislation. Elevating the existence of Union legislation to a separate situation that justifies exclusivity can broaden, dangerously, the scope of Union exclusivity: the Union legislature may circumvent the principle of subsidiarity in the area of international agreements, possibly rendering every shared external power exclusive despite the possible effect on common rules.[36] The third situation where exclusivity arises under Article 3(2) TFEU is when EU action is necessary 'to enable the exercise of internal competence'. Although this is broadly worded, it can incorporate the jurisprudence of the Court regarding Opinion 1/76 exclusivity, in that exclusivity arises where internal legislative measures are inappropriate for the exercise of an internal competence. Indeed, the fact that Article 3(2) TFEU refers to necessity in order to exercise internal competence rather than necessity to achieve Union objectives indicates that Article 3(2) TFEU is narrower than Article 216(1) TFEU, so that the existence of implied powers is linked to the scope of internal competences, defined on the basis of the objectives pursued, while exclusivity is linked with the exercise of internal competences. In conclusion, the codification of the doctrine of implied powers in Articles 216(1) and 3(2) TFEU re-opens the debate on the existence and exclusive nature of implied powers. Despite the dangers inherent in the broad wording of these provisions, the fact that they are roughly based on prior case law and aim to codify the law, enable the Court to affirm its current jurisprudence on implied powers and develop it in a way which would be done irrespective of these provisions.

[35] A Dashwood, 'Mixity in the era of the Treaty of Lisbon' in Hillion and Koutrakos (eds), *Mixed Agreements Revisited* (2010), pp 360–2. It has been pointed out that the wording of this provision has an 'editorial mistake' as it provides that exclusivity arises insofar as a Union agreement 'may affect common rules' instead of referring to Member State agreements. R Schütze, 'Lisbon and the federal order of competences: a prospective analysis' (2008) 33 EL Rev 709, 713–14.

[36] Ibid, 712–13.

The recognition of exclusivity under Article 3 TFEU in accordance with the jurisprudence of the Court is limited and leaves a large area of law falling under shared competence. Following the general principles on shared competence in the internal sphere which are codified in Article 2(2) TFEU, shared competence means that both the EU and the Member States can take action in the specific field, subject to the principle of subsidiarity.[37] This means that it is not necessary for the EU to be joined by the Member States when taking external action in a field of shared competence. Nevertheless, the EU cannot obstruct the Member States from taking autonomous action in the international sphere in the respective field.[38] In that sense, shared competence should be distinguished from cases where the EU and the Member States are obliged to act together, either as a result of an explicit provision, such as ex Article 133(6)(b) TEC, or because neither of them enjoys competence with regard to all aspects of the subject matter of the external action at issue.[39] Hence, it is necessary to identify the aspects of foreign investment which fall under shared competence, not only by reference to those which are not subject to exclusivity, but also by reference to the subject matter (if any) that falls entirely outside EU competence.

2.2 EU competence over admission and operation of FDI

The introduction of FDI within the scope of the CCP in the Lisbon Treaty has altered significantly the determination of EU competence over FDI. In contrast with Article 207 TFEU, the EC Treaty lacked a specific reference to FDI, which required a thorough analysis of a number of primary EU law provisions that granted competence to the Community. Taking into account the major changes introduced by the Lisbon Treaty with regard to EU competence over FDI, it is necessary to examine both the pre- and post-Lisbon legal regime. The analysis of EU competence over FDI under the EC Treaty is necessary not only for historical reasons, as existing EU IIAs were concluded on the basis on the EC Treaty, but more importantly for understanding the interaction of the new FDI competence with other primary EU law provisions which still play a significant role in the determination of EU competence over FDI.

Recalling that the main aspects of foreign investment regulation concern the admission of foreign investment, its post-admission treatment, expropriation of foreign investors' property, and dispute settlement, the analysis of EU competence over FDI will be construed in a similar pattern. Initially, EU competence over capital movements as a condition for the admission of FDI will be examined, followed by EU competence over establishment and treatment of FDI, thus considering Union powers over the conditions of initial establishment and post-establishment

[37] P Craig and G de Búrca, *EU Law: Text, Cases, and Materials* (2008), pp 127–37.

[38] O'Keefe, above n 27, pp 197–8.

[39] A Rosas, 'The European Union and Mixed Agreements' in Dashwood and Hillion (eds), *The general law of EC external relations* (2000), pp 203–7; O'Keefe, above n 27, pp 192–4. cf Heliskoski, above n 1, pp 27–46.

treatment of FDI. Thirdly, specific issues relating to the operation of FDI will be analysed, looking at aspects such as performance requirements and movement of key personnel. As the questions of competence over expropriation and dispute settlement are common to all categories and raise broader concerns, they are examined separately with regard to all forms of foreign investment.

2.2.1 Competence over capital movements

2.2.1.1 The scope of the capital movements provisions

Capital movements relating to foreign investment, which form the prerequisite for foreign investment activity in the host country, have traditionally fallen within the regulatory scope of Article 63 TFEU. As already described, Article 63 TFEU has been interpreted to include any capital movement relating to direct investment, in accordance with the nomenclature annexed to the Capital Directive.[40] Given that the freedom of capital movement has been extended since 1992 also to include capital movements between EU Member States and third countries, capital movements relating to inward and outward FDI fall within the scope of the chapter on capital movements.

It is without objection that the EU enjoys express competence with regard to capital movements within the limits described in the relevant chapter.[41] Even though the freedom of capital movements was for many years the poor relation to the other four freedoms, the provisions on free movement of capital gradually acquired similar status, gaining direct effect, as most restrictions allowing Member State regulation in the field were eliminated. As a result the EU has become the prime regulator in the field, allowing Member States to limit free movement of capital only within the framework provided in Articles 64 and 65 TFEU.

The scope of the freedom of capital movements extends to all measures that may affect free movement of capital, so that Member States are precluded from taking any action that may interfere with freedom of capital. Considering that Article 63 TFEU does not distinguish between intra-EU and third country capital movements, the prohibition provided in Article 63 TFEU applies equally to capital movements to and from third countries.[42] Abandoning the previous wording of Article 67 EEC which referred to 'discrimination based on the nationality or on the place of residence of the parties or on the place where such capital is invested', Article 63 TFEU is so broadly construed as not to limit its scope only to discriminatory measures. As the Court has often reiterated,[43] Article 63 TFEU applies to

[40] See Section 1.2.2.1.1.

[41] W Shan, 'Towards a common European Community policy on investment issues' (2001) 2 JWIT 603, 608–9; J Karl, 'The Competence for Foreign Direct Investment' (2004) 5 JWIT 413, 414–15.

[42] S Hindelang, *The Free Movement of Capital and Foreign Direct Investment: the scope of protection in EU Law* (2009), pp 197–200.

[43] Case C-222/97 *Trummer and Mayer* [1999] ECR I-1661; Case C-35/98 *Verkooijen* [2000] ECR I-4071; Case C-367/98 *Commission v Portugal* [2002] ECR I-4731; Case C-483/99 *Commission v France* [2002] ECR I-4781; C-101/05 *Skatteverket v A* [2007] ECR I-11531.

all national measures that are 'liable to dissuade' or 'liable to deter' foreign investors from undertaking a capital movement. Hence, the adoption of an 'adverse effect' test, where any measure is likely to affect capital movements reveals the broad scope of the chapter, which brings within the ambit of EU rules all measures that are directly or indirectly related to capital movements to or from third countries.[44]

Nevertheless, Article 65 TFEU does establish two significant restrictions on freedom of capital movement: allowing Member States to regulate in a rather limited manner issues concerning the tax treatment of capital movements and to set public policy restrictions on the free movement of capital.[45] In accordance with the overall limited interference of EU law with tax measures with regard to the four fundamental freedoms, Article 65(1) TFEU allows Member States to retain, to a significant extent, their right to apply the provisions of their national tax law with regard to capital movements. Secondly, Article 65(1) TFEU includes a standard public policy/security derogation, similar to those found elsewhere in the TFEU, which enables Member States to adopt measures restricting capital movements necessary to prevent infringements of national law or to protect public policy/security needs. However, measures adopted under both derogations are subject to a proportionality test since, according to Article 65(3) TFEU, they 'shall not constitute a means of arbitrary discrimination or a disguised restriction on the free movement of capital'.

However, these restrictions on free movement of capital do not imply that the EU does not have the competence to regulate capital movements in their entirety in its international agreements. Drawing a parallel to the free movement of goods, where the EU enjoys exclusive competence in regulating all aspects of trade in goods with third countries, Member States can still take action and restrict movement of goods to or from third countries on similar grounds,[46] it is arguable that the EU enjoys external competence with regard to the entirety of issues concerning

[44] S Peers, 'Free Movement of Capital: Learning Lessons or Slipping on Split Milk?' in Barnard and Scott (eds), *The Law of the Single European Market* (2002), p 345; C Barnard, *The Substantive Law of the EU: The Four Freedoms* (2010), pp 571–3; W Frenz, *Handbuch Europarecht: Europäische Grundfreiheiten* (2004), pp 1052–64; J Usher, 'Monetary Movements and the Internal Market' in Nic Shuibhne (ed), *Regulating the Internal Market* (2006), pp 193–7; cf Hindelang (above n 42, pp 122–8) and Emch (A Emch, 'News from Luxembourg: Is the New EU Investment Law Taking Shape?' (2008) 9 JWIT 497, 511–14), who argue in favour of a narrower determination of what constitutes a restriction to free movement of capital in line with the *Keck* doctrine, so that a substantial impediment to capital movements is necessary in order for a national measure to breach the freedom of capital movements (Joined Cases C-267 & 268/91 *Keck and Mithouard* [1993] *ECR* I-6097).

[45] On the substantive content of these restrictions concerning especially the scope of their application with regard to capital movements to and from third countries see F Benyon, *Direct Investment, National Champions and EU Treaty Freedoms* (2010), pp 32–8; Usher, above n 44, pp 198–207; Hindelang, above n 42, pp 216–43; Emch, above n 44, pp 514–16.

[46] The *EC-Asbestos* (WTO Appellate Body Report of 12 March 2001, WT/DS135/AB/R) and the *EC-Biotech* (WTO Panel Report of 29 September 2006, WT/DS291, 292, 293/R,) cases in the framework of the General Agreement on Tariffs and Trade (GATT) 1994, which was concluded exclusively by the EU, where only certain Member States imposed a ban on imports from third countries, show that the right of Member States to impose restrictions does not affect the EU's competence to regulate trade in goods in its entirety.

capital movements. As primary EU law guarantees that any restrictions imposed by Member States must abide by the principles of non-discrimination and proportionality, it is obvious that Member State action under Article 65 TFEU does not affect the existence of EU competence, but can influence how it is exercised.

With regard to the exclusive character of EU competence, the EU enjoys shared competence to regulate capital movements related to FDI. EU competence in the field of the substantive freedoms has been traditionally shared between the EU and the Member States,[47] which is now explicitly recognized in Article 4(2)(a) TFEU. Although exclusivity may arise by virtue of the existence of common rules in the field,[48] Member States still largely retain the power to initiate external action in the field of capital movements. However, given the broad coverage of Article 63 TFEU and the limitations on Member State powers provided in Article 65 TFEU, the potential scope and content of Member State action is actually severely limited.

2.2.1.2 The relevance of the capital movements provisions for the establishment of FDI

The chapter on capital movements not only establishes Union competence over capital movements relating to foreign investment, but also has significant implications for the initial establishment of foreign investors. The direct references to the right of establishment in Articles 64(2) and 65(2) TFEU as well as the reference to capital movements in Article 49(b) TFEU reveal the relevance of the freedom of capital movements for the establishment of third country investors in the EU. Of course, the scope of the establishment chapter is clearly limited only to nationals of EU Member States,[49] thus indirectly excluding foreign investors from its scope. However, if conditions of initial establishment are found to fall within the scope of the capital movements chapter, their scope is automatically extended to third country investors, hence establishing EU competence in that area.[50] Hence, the relation between the freedom of capital movements and the freedom of establishment determines whether Article 63 TFEU also expands its scope to the establishment of third country investors.

Indeed, the close link between capital movements related to the establishment of foreign investors and their actual establishment blurs the distinction for the purposes of the application of the different free movement chapters. Article 64(2) TFEU could be interpreted as providing the competence to the EU to take measures concerning the establishment of direct investment. Recognizing the close link between capital movements relating to FDI and establishment, this provision

[47] For a discussion of the scope of exclusivity over the four freedoms see D O'Keefe and P Twomey (eds), *Legal Issues of the Maastricht Treaty* (1994), pp 40–58.

[48] See below Section 2.2.2.2.2.

[49] Art 49 TFEU clearly stipulates that 'Within the framework of the provisions set out below, restrictions on the freedom of establishment of nationals of a Member State in the territory of another Member State shall be prohibited'.

[50] R Torrent, 'Derecho comunitario e Inversiones extranjeras directas: Libre circulacion de los capitales vs Regulacion no discriminatoria del establecimiento. De la golden share a los nuevos Open Skies', (2007) 22 Revista Espanola de Derecho Europeo 283, 307–8.

confers on the Council the power to adopt any measures concerning capital movements to and from third countries involving FDI and establishment.

It could be argued that Article 64(2) TFEU confers on the EU competence over establishment of foreign investors, which is broadly formulated to include all measures that can affect the establishment of foreign investors.[51] However, even if it were considered that Article 64(2) TFEU provided competence to the EU with regard to the establishment of FDI, such competence would be limited. According to Article 65(2) TFEU action taken under Article 64(2) TFEU 'shall be without prejudice to the applicability of restrictions on the right of establishment which are compatible with the Treaties'. As a result, the Member States would be able to maintain the restrictions imposed on the initial establishment of third country investors and even impose further restrictions, as establishment of third country nationals is excluded from the scope of the chapter on establishment.[52] However, once the EU exercises its competence, either by adopting autonomous measures or by concluding an international agreement, then its powers on the specific subject would be rendered exclusive according to the *AETR* principle. However, the Council has not yet used the possibility offered by this provision.

As a result, the correct interpretation of the relation between the provisions on free movement of capital and freedom of establishment, distinguishing the scope of application of the relevant chapters is crucial for the determination of EU competence over establishment of third country investors.

2.2.1.2.1 The jurisprudence of the Court of Justice

The Court does not offer clear guidance as to which Treaty provision applies in cases concerning both freedoms; taking into account the supplementary scope of the freedom of capital movements and the freedom of establishment, (the Court does not distinguish between them in intra-EU cases), considering that examination of a measure under the scope of one usually renders unnecessary the examination of the other. For example, in the field of taxation the court assessed the legality of national measures only with regard to the freedom of capital movements[53] or only with regard to establishment[54] or both freedoms together.[55] In addition, the Court has considered the legality of measures concerning property ownership under both establishment and capital rules, increasingly tending to decide such cases under the capital provisions.[56]

More importantly for foreign investment cases, the Court showed a clear preference for the capital rules in the *Golden Shares* cases.[57] In the late 1990s the

[51] Hindelang, above n 42, pp 301–2; W Shan, *The legal framework of EU-China investment relations* (2005), pp 60–2; Karl, above n 41, p 415; Maydell, above n 4, p 91.

[52] See also below n 75.

[53] *Verkooijen*, above n 43.

[54] Case C-251/98 *Baars* [2000] ECR I-2787; Case C-268/03 *De Baeck v Belgische Staat* [2004] ECR I-5961; Case C-196/04 *Cadbury Schweppes* [2006] ECR I-7995.

[55] Case C-503/99 *Commission v Belgium* [2002] ECR I-4641.

[56] Case C-302/97 *Konle* [1999] ECR I-3099; Case C-423/98 *Albore* [2000] ECR I-5965.

[57] For an overview of the *Golden Shares* litigation see A Arnull et al, *Wyatt and Dashwood's European Union Law* (2006), pp 855–63; Hindelang, above n 42, pp 90–6.

Commission challenged, in most cases successfully, a series of national laws that restricted the rights of shareholders, usually relating to companies with a strong public interest undergoing privatization. The Court ruled that national provisions limiting the right of participation in the management of a company,[58] or requiring prior authorization before the acquisition of shares,[59] fell under the scope of the capital rules, which would determine their legality. The Court in most cases did not examine the provisions on establishment, ruling that restrictions of shareholders' rights also constitute restrictions of the right to establishment, as they are 'a direct consequence of the obstacles to the free movement of capital'.[60] A similar approach was confirmed by the Court in more recent cases, where voting rights limitations were found to infringe the provisions on free movement of capital as they were likely to dissuade direct investors.[61]

The Court, therefore, considered that conditions relating to shareholding rights and not only to the acquisition of shares as such, which actually presents the capital transfer, are subject to the capital movement rules. This implies that all measures that can affect shareholding, which is the basic form of establishment of a foreign investor, fall under the scope of the chapter on capital movements and also apply to third country nationals. As a result, the *Golden Shares* jurisprudence can be logically interpreted as bringing the basic form of establishment of foreign investment, namely shareholding, under the chapter on capital movements and, thus, under EU competence.[62]

Nevertheless, the Court seems to acknowledge the significant implications arising from the parallel application of both freedoms with regard to measures directed towards non-Member States. In a series of mainly tax cases, the Court has adopted a 'centre of gravity' approach, according to which the compatibility of a measure is examined only with regard to the freedom rules that are primarily affected.[63] Emphasizing the purpose and the effect of the national measure in question, the Court has found that if a measure principally affects establishment, namely shareholdings that enable the holder to exercise managerial control, neither the establishment rules apply, as their scope does not cover relations with third countries, nor the capital rules, as their restriction is 'an unavoidable consequence of the freedom of establishment'.[64]

[58] Case C-174/04 *Commission v Italy* [2005] ECR I-4933; Case C 503/99 *Commission v Belgium* [2002] ECR I-4809.

[59] *Commission v Portugal*, above n 43; Case C-463/00 *Commission v Spain* [2003] ECR I-4581; Case C-98/01 *Commission v UK* [2003] ECR I-4581.

[60] *Commission v France*, above n 43.

[61] Case C-112/05 *Commission v Germany (VW case)* [2007] ECR I-8995; Joined Cases C-463/04 & C-464/04 *Federconsumatori* [2007] ECR I-10419; Case C-274/06 *Commission v Spain* [2008] ECR I-26. For a discussion of these cases see Emch, above n 44, pp 498–503; Benyon, above n 45, pp 16–20.

[62] Torrent, above n 50, pp 308–9.

[63] B Kiekebeld and D Smit, 'Freedom of establishment and free movement of capital in Association Agreements and direct taxation' (2007) 35 International Tax Review 216, 225–6.

[64] Case C-492/04 *Lasertec* [2007] ECR I-3775; Case C-102/05 *A&B* [2007] ECR I- 3871; Case C-524/04 *Test Claimants in Thin Cap Group Litigation v Commissioner of the Inland Revenue* [2007] ECR I-2107. The centre of gravity approach was first adopted in Case C-452/04 *Fidium Finanz* [2006] ECR I-9521, which concerned the distinction between capital and services rules. For an

Applying the centre of gravity approach, the Court has in essence refused to apply the capital rules regarding movements that were related to an establishment; that is, direct investment. It refused to consider the validity of national measures that concerned the tax treatment of dividends,[65] on the grounds that the purpose and effect of the measure in question concerned only capital transfers relating to an establishment. In that regard, the adoption of the centre of gravity test by the Court for distinguishing between the respective chapters appears to exclude direct investments in total from the scope of the capital movements provisions. In essence, this test can be interpreted as allowing national legislators to distinguish between direct and portfolio investments and to nullify the effect of free movement of capital in cases of FDI by basing the need for differential treatment on the criterion of managerial control.[66]

However, in more recent cases the Court has adopted a more nuanced approach regarding the relationship between the two chapters. Revising its jurisprudence on the centre of gravity approach, the Court applied the capital rules for determining the legality of national measures that concerned establishment of EU nationals in third countries or establishment of third country nationals in the EU.[67] In determining the criterion according to which national measures related to a direct investment/establishment should also be assessed in light of the capital rules, the Court found that measures of a generic nature that apply both to situations which qualify as establishment and to those which do not are subject to capital movement rules.[68]

This controversial jurisprudence has been criticized for the ambiguous criteria used and for its effects on FDI and the scope of liberalization envisaged by Article 63 TFEU.[69] Even though the Court appears to underline the significance of the distinction between establishment and capital rules, the criteria used for this distinction do not materialize the substantive differences between capital and establishment. In that regard it is necessary to examine also from a theoretical perspective the rules regarding the scope of application of capital and establishment rules and the criterion that can be used for such distinction.

analysis of these cases see S Bezborodov, 'Freedom of Establishment in the EC Economic Partnership Agreements: in Search of its Direct Effect on Direct Taxation' (2007) 35 International Tax Review 658, 675–81; S Hindelang, 'The EC Treaty's freedom of capital movement as an instrument of international investment law?' in Reinisch and Knahr (eds), *International Investment Law and Context* (2007), pp 58–65.

[65] Ibid.

[66] Hindelang, above n 64, pp 58–66; Bezborodov, above n 64, pp 679–81.

[67] Case C-157/05 *Holböck* [2007] ECR I-4051; Case C-446/04 *Test Claimants in the FII Litigation v Commissioner of the Inland Revenue* [2006] ECR-I-11753; Case C-374/04 *Test Claimants in Class IV of the Act Group Litigation v Commissioners of the Inland Revenue* [2006] ECR I-11673; Case C-207/07 *Commission v Spain* [2008] ECR I-111, paras 33–9; Case C-326/07 *Commission v Italy* [2009] ECR I-2291, paras 35–6.

[68] Hindelang, above n 42, pp 105–7; Bezborodov, above n 64, pp 680, 682–3; Kiekebeld and Smit, above n 63, p 226; Benyon, above n 45, pp 75–6.

[69] Hindelang, above n 64, p 43; Hindelang, above n 42, pp 107–8; Bezborodov, above n 64, p 680; D Scharf, 'Die Kapitalverkehrsfreiheit gegenüber Drittstaaten' (2008) 76 Beiträge zum Transnationalen Wirtschaftsrecht 1, 20–3.

2.2.1.2.2 The different scope of application of capital and establishment provisions

It is obvious that the firm distinction between the freedom of establishment and the freedom of capital movements is of major significance, due to the latter's application to third country nationals. In that respect, the *Golden Shares* jurisprudence, as well as the earlier case law of the Court that did not distinguish between the two freedoms, appears to blur the distinction between capital and establishment that is made in primary EU law. If EU law covered the establishment of third country nationals in the EU, it would provide so under the chapter on establishment or it would at least allow for such action to be adopted by means of secondary legislation; as is explicitly provided for under Article 56(2) TFEU which enables the Council to adopt measures extending the freedom to provide services to third country nationals. On the other hand, the exclusion of any measure affecting direct investment from the capital movements rules according to the centre of gravity jurisprudence of the Court runs contrary to the explicit reference to direct investment in the provisions of that chapter. In that regard, the revised centre of gravity test appears to apprehend better that both the chapters on capital and establishment are relevant for direct investments. However, instead of favouring the parallel application of establishment and capital rules with regard to all measures related to a direct investment,[70] it is necessary to distinguish between the issues related to a direct investment which fall under the scope of each chapter.

To understand which aspects of direct investment fall under the scope of freedom of establishment and which under the freedom of capital movements, it is necessary to bear in mind the definitions of capital movement and establishment. As discussed, initial establishment of FDI concerns the setting-up and management of a primary or dependent undertaking in the host state, while regulation of initial establishment aims to identify and determine the domestic regulatory restrictions that impede market access to foreign direct investors.[71] On the other hand, a capital movement is a transfer of assets that is essentially concerned with the investment of funds, so that regulation of capital movements affects the transfer of funds that can be used, among others, for the establishment of an undertaking, that is, a direct investment.[72] Hence, freedom of capital movements does not concern the establishment of an FDI, but only the capital transfers relating to FDI, for example the act of the acquisition of shares or the transfer of dividends. The conditions under which the capital linked with a direct investment can be used, for example shareholders' rights, is the subject matter of the freedom of establishment.[73]

Such an interpretation of the scope of the capital rules is, first, in accordance with the primary law rules concerning the relation of the relevant Treaty

[70] For arguments in favour of the parallel application of both establishment and capital rules, see Hindelang, above n 64, pp 67–71 and references therein.

[71] See Section 1.2.2.1.2.

[72] See Section 1.2.2.1.1.

[73] Torrent, above n 50, pp 303–7; Bezborodov, above n 64, pp 674–5.

chapters and in particular Articles 49(2) TFEU and 65(2) TFEU. At a first glance these two provisions appear to conflict. On the one hand, Article 49(2) TFEU subjects the application of the chapter on establishment to the provisions of the chapter on capital movements, while Article 65(2) TFEU subjects its application to the restrictions on establishment imposed in accordance with the chapter on establishment. Nevertheless, these provisions can be interpreted consistently, so that the capital chapter does not affect measures related to initial establishment of a direct investment. More specifically, Article 65(2) TFEU explicitly provides that the capital movement chapter does not apply to the restrictions on establishment imposed in accordance with the chapter on establishment, such as restrictions on the establishment of third country nationals. The primacy of the establishment chapter is further reinforced in Article 64(2) TFEU which enables the Council to regulate capital movements with third countries. On the contrary, Article 49(2) TFEU does not mean that the freedom of establishment is limited only to certain types of establishment, excluding any conditions of establishment falling under the capital movement chapter. It only requires that liberalization and harmonization of establishment rules shall not in effect nullify any restrictions imposed under the capital movement chapter.[74] Within this framework, the subrogation of Article 49(2) TFEU can be better understood in its historical background, as it existed in the original text of the Treaty of Rome. It served the purpose of safeguarding at the time, the limited, scope of the freedom of capital movements from any effect that measures taken under the much broader freedom of establishment may have on it. However, given the complete liberalization of capital movements, this provision has lost much of its initial significance.[75]

The need for distinction between capital and establishment rules is justified by their nature and objectives: while the freedom of capital movements is based on liberalization achieved at the primary EU law level, leaving almost no scope for national regulation, the freedom of establishment requires a significant amount of regulation, mainly through harmonization or mutual recognition rules.[76] Confirming such interpretation of the capital and establishment rules, legislative

[74] Torrent, above n 50, pp 304–6; Usher, above n 44, pp 200–5.

[75] It is also argued (Hindelang, above n 42, pp 243–7; Frenz, above n 44, pp 1040–2) that these provisions do not determine the scope of application of the chapters on capital and establishment but they apply on the level of the grounds of justification of a measure violating in principle Arts 49 and 63 TFEU, so that a restriction that serves a legitimate interest recognized within the ambit of free movement of capital or the freedom of establishment is justified under both TFEU chapters. However, such an interpretation of Arts 49 and 63 TFEU would be contrary to the rationale behind the scope of these provisions. If it were considered that all measures related to FDI fall under the scope of the capital rules, then, as the freedom of establishment does not apply to third country nationals, it would mean that Member States can retain any restrictions related to the establishment of third country nationals, thus nullifying in essence the inclusion of FDI under the capital rules. Besides, if it were considered that any deviation from free movement of capital rules related to FDI could be based only on grounds of justification provided in the founding Treaties, then the paradox situation would arise, providing less grounds for justification of restrictions on FDI than intra-EU investments.

[76] Torrent, above n 50, p 302.

practice seems to adhere to a distinction between free movement of capital and freedom of establishment. The Capital Directive regulates only transfers of capital assets, referring to foreign investment and establishment for classification purposes only as the destined use of the capital.[77] However, EU legislation concerning establishment conditions and in particular shareholders' rights, such as Directive 2004/25 EC,[78] is based on the provisions relating to establishment.

Consequently, capital rules should be narrowly interpreted as covering only the actual transfers of capital destined for, or resulting from, the establishment of a foreign investor. The conditions of initial establishment are the subject of the establishment provisions which, despite the limitation of their scope to EU nationals and establishment in EU territory, determine the scope of regulation of the initial establishment of direct investment alongside other provisions.[79] Nevertheless, although the provisions on capital movements do not apply with regard to measures affecting market access conditions for the initial establishment of FDI, this does not imply that freedom of capital movements is not applicable in cases of capital transfers related to FDI. National measures that affect capital movements destined for, or resulting from, the operation of a foreign investment must conform to the capital movement rules, irrespective of whether they concern mainly capital movements related to an establishment or portfolio investment.[80]

In that regard, the revised centre of gravity approach provides a useful but not entirely appropriate test for determining the scope of the capital movement provisions with regard to FDI. Focusing on the purpose of the national measure challenged, the Court rightly recognized that the application of the respective chapters depends on the aspects of FDI that are regulated. Hence, capital rules are also applicable to measures of a generic nature that apply both to situations that qualify as establishment and to those that do not. Nevertheless, the Court should go a step further and elaborate on the generic nature of the measures that fall under the capital rules based on the distinction between capital and establishment, so that capital rules cover all measures affecting the transfer of assets related to an FDI and not the conditions of establishment of FDI.

In summary, Articles 63 and 64(2) TFEU can be validly used as legal bases for EU action in the field of FDI. Nevertheless, despite their broad scope, the key provision of Article 65(2) TFEU, which provides that capital rules shall not affect restrictions on establishment which are compatible with the founding Treaties, indicates that national rules concerning the initial establishment of foreign investors fall outside the scope of the chapter on capital movements. However, such a narrow interpretation of the capital movement rules does not imply that capital transfers related to an establishment are excluded from the scope of the capital movement rules.

[77] Ibid, p 303.

[78] OJ L142/2004, 0012–0023.

[79] See below Section 2.2.2.2.1.

[80] Above n 67.

2.2.2 Competence over establishment and post-establishment treatment of FDI under the EC Treaty

EC competence over initial establishment and post-establishment treatment of foreign investment was controversial under the EC Treaty. Given the importance of market access for foreign investors, the Commission often claimed EC competence especially over establishment of third country nationals.[81] This position met with fierce opposition from Member States, which challenged, successfully to a great extent, EC competence on establishment and post-establishment treatment of third country persons. Opinions 1/94 and 2/92[82] dealt extensively with this question, without offering clear delimitation of competence in the field. Furthermore, the changes introduced to the EC Treaty as well as developments in the Court's case law blurred the matter, thereby revealing its complexities.

2.2.2.1 Competence over initial establishment based on Article 133 TEC

The CCP provided the main legal basis used for claiming EC competence over establishment of foreign investors. Given the exclusive character of Community powers under the CCP, its scope with respect to establishment was an issue of great controversy in the 1990s leading to Opinions 1/94 and 2/92 as well as to substantive changes in the EC Treaty text in the Intergovernmental Conferences (IGCs) in Amsterdam and Nice. However, the vagueness of the Court's judgments as well as the complex wording adopted by the Treaty amendments left certain aspects of the matter unclear.

2.2.2.1.1 The traditional scope of the CCP

In the much discussed Opinion 1/94 the Court found that establishment of legal persons under the General Agreement on Trade in Services (GATS) did not fall under the scope of the CCP. Although it accepted that the dynamic character of the CCP, as was profoundly declared in Opinion 1/78,[83] could not exclude as a matter of principle the GATS from the scope of the CCP, it rejected the Commission's view that the GATS and, for our purposes, commercial presence, fell under the scope of the CCP and hence under exclusive Community competence. Pointing out that the Treaty included specific chapters on the free movement of persons, the Court in essence emphasized the structural differences between the four freedoms in the internal sphere and their reflection in external relations.[84] Despite the heavy criticism of the Court's Opinion,[85] it constituted a benchmark for the future development of the CCP, signalling that the CCP cannot be expanded to a Common

[81] The Commission has been the main supporter of EC competence over establishment of third country persons during the Court proceedings in Opinions 1/94 (above n 18) and 2/92 (above n 25).

[82] Above nn 18 and 25. [83] [1978] ECR 2151. [84] Eeckhout, above n 13, p 29.

[85] For a critical analysis of Opinion 1/94 (above n 18) see J Bourgeois, 'The EC in the WTO and Advisory Opinion 1/94: An Echternach Procession' (1995) 32 CMLR 763; M Hilf, 'The ECJ's Opinion 1/94 on the WTO, No Surprise but Wise?' (1995) 6 EJIL 245; T Tridimas, 'The WTO and OECD Opinions' in Dashwood and Hillion (eds), *The general law of EC external relations* (2000), p 48; Koutrakos, above n 15, pp 46–8.

Economic Policy, but should be balanced with the internal aspect of the establishment question.[86]

The same issue was also dealt with in Opinion 2/92, which concerned the treatment accorded to foreign-controlled undertakings established in the territory of OECD Member countries.[87] Although the Court reaffirmed its position on the scope of the CCP concerning establishment in general, it avoided any reference to the distinction between trade in goods and services and it recognized that aspects of the OECD National Treatment Instrument related to international trade and, thus, the CCP.[88]

Both Opinions presented the Court's reluctance to extend, at the time, the notion of international trade to include establishment rules, either in general or only with regard to service sectors. Despite the dynamic interpretation of the CCP in accordance with the evolutionary character of international trade, the Court was not willing to expand the 'traditional' CCP. Considering the *a priori* exclusive character of Community competence under the CCP, as well as the institutional balance struck in Article 133 TEC, which favoured the Commission and excluded the Parliament from decision making, the Court attempted to moderate EC powers in external economic relations: the Community enjoyed exclusive competence under the CCP only to a limited extent, which could not supersede its inherent internal powers.[89]

2.2.2.1.2 The 'new aspects' of the CCP after Nice

Following the strict interpretation of Article 133 TEC and addressing contemporaneous trends in international trade, especially in the framework of the WTO, the IGCs in Amsterdam and Nice expanded the scope of the CCP into the fields of trade in services and trade-related aspects of intellectual property. By adding paragraphs 5 to 7 to Article 133 TEC, the IGCs brought issues of establishment under the auspices of the CCP, providing, however, numerous exceptions and complex procedural rules.

First, Article 133(5)(1) TEC established an express competence for the Community to conclude international agreements in the field of trade in services, subject however to the exceptions provided in Article 133(6) TEC. Even though the Treaty text referred only to services, the term 'trade in services' was not, and after Lisbon is not, limited to services, as defined under the relevant primary EU law chapter, but was much wider as it reflected the similar term found in the WTO Agreements.[90] Hence, Article 133(5)(1) TEC also included the third

[86] Eeckhout, above n 13, p 57.

[87] Opinion 2/92, above n 25, para IV.5.

[88] Opinion 2/92, para IV.9.

[89] Koutrakos, above n 15, p 47.

[90] Opinion 1/2008 [2009] ECR I-11129, para 119; M Cremona, 'Balancing Union and Member State interests: Opinion 1/2008, choice of legal basis and the common commercial policy under the Treaty of Lisbon' (2010) 35 EL Rev 678, 683–4; M Cremona, 'A Policy of Bits and Pieces? The Common Commercial Policy after Nice' (2001) 4 CYELS 61, 69–70. Cf S Griller and B Weidel, *External Economic Relations and Foreign Policy in the European Union* (2002), pp 91–3 who argued that Art 133(5) TEC excluded commercial presence from the scope of the CCP, because the

mode of provision of services, namely commercial presence. This entails that the Community had the power to regulate the establishment of persons who were willing to pursue trade activities in the services sector.

It is obvious from the above definition that the competence established in Article 133(5) TEC did not extend to all sectors of the economy. The Community had the power to regulate the establishment of persons trading in services. Thus, the establishment of foreign investors who wished to set up an undertaking for producing or manufacturing goods or whose business activities did not involve trade was excluded from the scope of the CCP.[91] It is worth noting that while trade in services included the establishment of the trader, the traditional notion of trade in goods, as regulated in Article 133(1)–(4) TEC did not seem to be similarly expanded to include the establishment of traders in goods. This difference reflected WTO law, which provides rules on establishment only in the field of services and can be mainly explained by the fact that, contrary to goods, provision of services usually requires the establishment of a service provider in the territory where the service is offered. Hence, Article 133(5) TEC retained in the field of goods, the classical distinction between investment and trade, albeit recognizing their link in the field of services.

The second major limitation of Community competence on establishment of foreign investors according to Article 133(5)(1) TEC was found in Article 133(6) TEC, which parallelized internal and external powers and curbed Community competence with regard to certain service sectors. The first subparagraph of Article 133(6) TEC established parallelism between internal and external powers, excluding, in particular, competence to harmonize in fields where harmonization was ruled out by the EC Treaty. This limitation was, however, of minor practical significance, as the Treaty explicitly ruled out harmonization in the fields of employment, education, culture, and public health[92]—fields explicitly mentioned in the second subparagraph of Article 133(6) TEC. For these services the Treaty established *a priori* shared competence

Intergovernmental Conference (IGC) deliberately did not include foreign investment in the CCP and that identical terms found in the EC Treaty should be systematically and coherently interpreted. As the Court recognized, the intention of the IGC in Nice was to broaden the scope of the CCP to reflect the WTO. Secondly, the wording of the term 'services' in Art 133 TEC differed from the wording of Art 49 TEC (now Art 56 TFEU), as the former referred to 'trade in services', which is a term found in the GATS and includes commercial presence, while Art 49 TEC concerned the 'provision of services'. In addition, the different interpretation of identical terms found in different Treaty chapters is not contrary to a coherent interpretation of the founding Treaties. The example of the term 'undertaking', the meaning of which differs in the field of freedom of goods from competition rules, shows that different interpretations are necessary when the same term is used in a different context and serves divergent goals. (For an analysis of the different meanings of public undertaking see V Louri, 'Undertaking as a jurisdictional element for the application of EC competition rules' (2002) 29 LIEI 143.)

[91] J Ceyssens, 'Towards a common foreign investment policy?—Foreign investment in the European constitution' (2005) 32 LIEI 259, 260.

[92] Exclusion of harmonization was provided in Arts 129(2), 137(2)(1), 149(4), 150(4), 151(5), 152(4)(c) of the EC Treaty. The Treaty text was clear that only cases where harmonization was ruled out fell outside the scope of Art 133(5)(1) TEC, so that it included fields where the Treaty provided for minimum harmonization. C Hermann, 'Common Commercial Policy after Nice: Sisyphus would have done a better job' (2002) 39 CMLR 7, 22.

between the Community and the Member States, requiring that it had to be exercised jointly.[93] Finally, the third subparagraph of Article 133(6) TEC excluded transport from the scope of the CCP, thus following the reasoning of the Court in Opinion 1/94 that Community competence in transport services is established only within the limits set in the respective chapter.[94]

Differentiating from trade in goods, Community competence over trade in services, including establishment of foreign investors in service sectors, was shared with the Member States.[95] Article 133(5)(4) TEC provided an express derogation from the exclusivity rule, as it grandfathered prior Member States, agreements and reaffirmed also their right insofar as trade in services was concerned to conclude new agreements.[96] Hence, even though the Community had the possibility itself to conclude an international agreement in this field, it was a political question whether the Member States would allow the Community to proceed on its own or demand the conclusion of a mixed agreement, as they were entitled to do.[97] In fact, the insistence of Member States to participate in the conclusion of two WTO GATS-related agreements, namely the Vietnam Accession and the conclusion of the GATS agreements on the granting of compensation for modification and withdrawal of certain commitments following the accession of new Member States to the European Union, led to two Court cases, indicating that Member States were unwilling to recognize EC exclusive competence.

However, once the Community took action in the specific field its competence would be rendered exclusive. The last sentence of Article 133(5)(4) TEC reiterated the basic principle of implied exclusivity in cases of concurrent powers, so that exclusivity could arise only after the Community had legislated in the field.[98] An exception to

[93] Opinion 1/2008, above n 90, paras 133–6, 150. See also Cremona, above n 90, pp 73–4; HG Krenzler and C Pitschas, 'Progress or Stagnation? The Common Commercial Policy After Nice' (2001) 6 EFA Rev 291, 308–9.

[94] Opinion 1/2008, above n 90, para 162.

[95] Opinion of Kokott AG in Case C-13/07 *Commission v Council (Vietnam Accession to the WTO)*, delivered on 26 March 2009, paras 53–66. See also Cremona, above n 90, p 84; Hermann, above n 92, p 19; Krenzler and Pitschas, above n 93, p 306.

[96] It has also been argued that competence under Art 133(5) TEC was exclusive, due to the direct reference to Art 133(1) TEC in the first subpara (M.Krajewski, 'External Trade Law and the Constitutional Treaty: Towards a federal and more democratic common Commercial Policy?' (2005) 42 CMLR 91, 96–7). However, such a reading of Art 133(5)(1) TEC would render subpara 4 void and deprive it of any normative content.

[97] Cremona, above n 90, p 85.

[98] Opinion of Kokott AG, above n 95, paras 75–6. See also Krenzler and Pitschas, above n 93, p 455; Holdgaard, above n 13, p 386. Cf Hermann (above n 92) who argues that the lack of a declaration in the Nice Treaty that express concurrent powers could be rendered exclusive by way of implication, left the question open not only with regard to Art 133 TEC, but all Arts conferring express concurrent powers. Cremona (above n 90) also argued that reading the last subpara of Art 133(5) TEC as incorporating *AETR* exclusivity would result in a denial of the clear wording of the Article that the right of the Member States to conclude agreements shall not be affected by the expansion of Community competence. Even if this provision were interpreted as expressing the duty of cooperation in cases of shared competence, it could not be considered as retaining intact the competence of the Member States in the field and ruling out potential exclusivity. Shared competence existed only insofar as the Community had not adopted internal rules that led to complete harmonization, so that Member States retained their right until the Community decided to harmonize a specific area of law. A different interpretation would be contrary to the principles of

exclusivity was introduced in Article 133(6)(2) TEC, which provided in its last sentence that agreements in the fields of educational, cultural, social, and public health services should be concluded jointly by the Community and the Member States. Given that harmonization in these fields was excluded, this provision actually safeguarded the Community's right to participate in international agreements in these fields, thus establishing mixity in all international agreements in this area.[99]

Finally, it should be noted that according to Article 133(5)(1) TEC, Community competence with regard to trade in services was limited only to the conclusion of international agreements. Contrary to the traditional CCP, Article 133 TEC could not be used for the adoption of autonomous measures, either in the form of substantive rules or in the form of implementing legislation. The Community was bound to use different EC Treaty chapters, leading to a further proliferation of legal bases for taking complete action in the field.[100]

In sum, the CCP, especially after the Nice amendments, conferred on the EC significant powers to regulate the establishment of foreign investors. However, the important limitations of these powers concerning establishment in non-service sectors and in certain service sectors, their non-exclusive character, and the inability to adopt autonomous measures weakened their effectiveness, so that Article 133 TEC was a long way from creating a single legal basis for establishment. Nevertheless, the express recognition of Community powers in the field was the first important step to consider establishment and FDI in general as part of the CCP and to promote its complete inclusion in the Lisbon Treaty.

2.2.2.2 Competence over initial establishment based on implied powers

The incomplete coverage of EC competence over establishment of foreign investment by the CCP was complemented by EC implied powers. In the field of establishment in non-service sectors as well as in the transport sector the existence of implied competence was crucial, while exclusivity of implied competence was a key question concerning establishment in all economic sectors.

2.2.2.2.1 Existence of implied powers

For competence in the field of initial establishment in non-service sectors and in the transport sector, the provisions of the chapter on establishment alongside the provisions on harmonization presented the relevant framework, on which EC implied competence was based.[101] In order to examine the existence of EC

pre-emption and supremacy, which characterized Community action irrespective of whether it is taken in the form of autonomous legislation or an international agreement.

[99] Opinion 1/2008, above n 90, paras 134 and 150. See also M Cremona, 'The External Dimension of the Internal Market' in Barnard and Scott (eds), *The Law of the Single European Market* (2002), pp 377–8; Hermann, above n 92, pp 21–2.

[100] Cremona, above n 90, p 83.

[101] Concerning transport, the Court recognized in the *Open Skies* cases that the chapter on the freedom of establishment applies also to the transport field as, contrary to the chapter on services, there is no Art in primary EU law which precludes its provisions on freedom of establishment from applying to transport. *Open Skies* (*Commission v Denmark*), above n 25, para 123.

competence to regulate the initial establishment of third country nationals in the EU and of EU nationals in third countries, it is essential to analyse the objectives of the relevant Treaty provisions and consider whether regulation of establishment of foreign investors was necessary for the attainment of these objectives.

At first glance, the rules excluded establishment of foreign investment from their scope. Article 43 TEC (now Art 49 TFEU) provided that freedom of establishment concerns the 'establishment of nationals of a Member State in the territory of another Member State'. Despite its clear wording, Article 43 TEC could confer implied competence to the Community regarding the establishment of non-EU nationals in the EU as well as the establishment of EU nationals in third countries.

The use of Article 43 TEC as conferring external competence over establishment of foreign investors was initially recognized by the Court in Opinion 1/94, which, even though it concerned only establishment in service sectors, had greater implications for establishment in all economic fields.[102] It has been widely argued that the Court's rejection of implied powers based on Article 43 TEC was only referring to the exclusive character of implied competence and not to their existence as such.[103] That said, the reference to secondary legislation which included provisions on third country nationals shows that the Court possibly favoured the existence of implied powers and by no means rejected their existence.[104] However, the vagueness of the Court's Opinion on the subject requires a closer view of the objectives of the chapter on establishment.

First, the broad powers granted to the Community to take measures in order to contribute to the completion of the internal market in the field of establishment covered the establishment of third country nationals in the EU. Article 44 TEC (now Art 50 TFEU) set out the basic fields where Community action could be taken in order to attain freedom of establishment, while Article 94 TEC (now Art 115 TFEU) provided for harmonization in the field of establishment. As a result, the Community had the power to set up the regulatory framework for the establishment of EU nationals in the EU in all economic sectors.[105] The proper functioning of such a regulatory framework required, however, that the establishment of third country nationals was also subject to the same rules, otherwise divergent laws in Member States setting out different conditions for third country nationals could impede EC measures from establishing a uniform and complete framework regulating an economic activity.[106] The need for regulation of the establishment conditions of third country nationals in the EU in order to complete the internal market was already proven in practice, as there were many

[102] Opinion 1/94, above n 18, para 81.

[103] For a review of the literature on the issue see Koutrakos, above n 15, pp 106–12.

[104] Cf Eeckhout, (above n 13, p 76), who argues that Opinion 1/94 should be read as referring to the existence of Community powers and not to exclusivity due to the emphasis the Court placed on the wording of Art 43 TEC.

[105] S Weatherill, 'Supply of and demand for internal market regulation: strategies, preferences and interpretation' in Nic Shuibhne (ed), *Regulating the Internal Market* (2006), pp 38–44.

[106] Griller and Weidel, above n 90, p 80.

economic activities—such as financial services—where a uniform and harmonized regulatory framework existed.

Secondly, as regards the establishment of EU nationals in third countries, implied competence could be derived from the need to secure equal and non-discriminatory treatment of EU nationals. Such a competence could be indirectly inferred by the Court's reasoning in the *Open Skies* cases concerning the infringement of Article 43 TEC. Borrowing its reasoning from the case law on double taxation treaties,[107] the Court held that ownership and control clauses found in a bilateral agreement between a Member State and a third country concerning the establishment of their nationals were infringing Article 43 TEC, as they excluded nationals of other Member States from benefits accorded to nationals of the Member State which concluded the agreement, namely preferential market access to a third country.[108] Primarily this case recognized the limitations imposed on Member States concerning the exercise of their competence to include in their international agreements provisions on establishment of their own nationals in third countries.[109] However, its implications were broader, as it recognized that equal treatment of EU nationals in third countries is linked with the objectives of the internal market and could be necessary for the attainment of freedom of establishment. As a result, establishment of EU investors in third countries could come within the scope of Community competence, which could effectively ensure equal and non-discriminatory treatment of Community legal persons.

Furthermore, the extension of Community competence over establishment of foreign investors in non-service sectors was in accordance with the logic underpinning the relationship between internal and external competence. As establishment in service sectors was expressly under Community competence according to Article 133 TEC, there was no reason for distinguishing between services and non-service sectors in the field of establishment. On the contrary, the fact that autonomous measures concerning establishment in the services sector had to be adopted on the basis of the establishment rules, as they were excluded from the scope of the CCP, proves that the chapter on establishment provided the appropriate legal basis for Community action on establishment of foreign investors in general.

2.2.2.2.2 Exclusive character of implied powers

The recognition of the existence of Community competence does not imply its exclusivity. The concrete application of the exclusivity criteria according to the *AETR* judgment and Opinion 1/76 on a case-by-case basis means that a thorough examination of EC exclusive powers over establishment of foreign investors would require a lengthy analysis of the regulatory framework in each economic sector. Considering that this area is now covered by Article 207 TFEU, the following analysis provides a critical consideration of the general application of the exclusivity

[107] Case C-307/97 *Saint-Gobain v Finanzamt Aachen-Innenstadt* [1999] ECR I-6161, para 59 and Case C-55/00 *Gottardo v INPS* [2002] ECR I-413, para 32.

[108] *Commission v Denmark*, above n 25, para 127.

[109] See Section 6.2.2.5.

criteria in the establishment field, providing examples of specific economic sectors and examining its implications in sectors where exclusivity cannot be established.

Opinion 1/76-type exclusivity had limited practical value, as the conditions for its recognition are fulfilled only in exceptional circumstances. The existence of an inextricable link between external international action and Community objectives in a field where the adoption of autonomous measures would appear insufficient is highly unlikely in the field of establishment of foreign investors. The Community objectives to be served concerned the freedoms of EU nationals and the creation of an internal market, which have always been achieved primarily by the adoption of internal legislation. It is difficult to imagine an economic sector that remained unregulated because international action was required.[110]

On the contrary, *AETR*-type exclusivity arose in some instances as certain economic sectors were harmonized and a significant number of references to non-Member State nationals existed in secondary legislation. A prominent example of a field where harmonization was achieved was the area of financial services.[111] Therein existed a complete set of secondary legislation[112] determining the conditions of establishment of financial institutions, which also made extensive references to third country legal persons and the conditions which had to be fulfilled in order for them to become established in the Community. Another example of harmonization existed in the field of telecommunication services, where the EC had created a complete and uniform regulatory framework concerning the establishment and functioning of undertakings active in that field.[113]

2.2.2.3 Competence over post-establishment treatment

In contrast with initial establishment, Community competence to regulate the treatment of FDI after its establishment was based on solid and less controversial foundations. The EC was vested with the power to set out rules concerning the operation of foreign investments established in its territory and to negotiate with third countries both general and specific aspects of post-establishment treatment of EU investments in third countries.

Similar to initial establishment, Community competence to take action concerning general standards of post-establishment treatment of FDI was based both on express and implied powers found in the CCP and the chapter on establishment. These provisions allowed the Community to take measures concerning relevant

[110] The energy sector illustrates an example of an economic sector where cooperation and coordination with third countries is required for its complete regulation, due to its international character and Europe's dependence on energy sources from third countries. However, establishment of private entities wishing to pursue an economic activity in this field is not one of the regulatory issues that can only be resolved by means of international action. On the scope of necessity and exclusive implied powers in the energy sector see S Haghighi, *Energy Security: The External Legal Relations of the European Union with major oil and gas supplying countries* (2007), pp 90–2.

[111] For a more detailed analysis see Cremona, above n 99, pp 367–74.

[112] For a complete list of the regulatory framework of financial services see W Hemetsberger et al, *European Banking and Financial Services Law* (2006), chs A, B, C.

[113] For the degree of harmonization in the field of telecommunications services see I Walden and J Angel, *Telecommunications law and regulation* (2005).

and absolute standards of treatment, including most favoured nation (MFN), national treatment (NT), and fair and equitable treatment (FET).[114] The existence and exclusive character of Community competence over general standards of treatment was the main subject of Opinion 2/92.[115] The Court was presented with the question whether the EC had exclusive competence to participate in the Third Revised Decision of the OECD Council concerning national treatment of foreign investors. It held that the Community had competence to take external action in the field, but such competence was shared with the Member States.

More specifically, the Court initially examined the scope of the CCP, which at the time was not extended to trade in services, and whether it covered all aspects of post-establishment treatment of foreign investors. The Court firmly recognized that Article 133 TEC conferred competence to the Community, as the OECD Decision concerned the conditions for the participation of foreign-controlled undertakings, 'in trade between the Member States and non-member countries, conditions which are the subject of the common commercial policy of the Community'.[116] However, exclusive competence based on Article 133 TEC was rejected, as treatment of foreign investors also concerned 'the participation of foreign-controlled undertakings in intra-Community trade',[117] which was excluded from the scope of the CCP. Hence, the Court accepted that insofar as the operation of foreign investments concerned trade between Member States and non-Member States, the Community was exclusively competent to regulate it.[118]

With regard to the operation of foreign investments concerning intra-Community trade as well as non-trade activities, the Court accepted the existence of Community competence, but ruled out its exclusivity on the ground that 'although the Community has adopted measures capable of serving as a basis for an exclusive external competence . . . it is undisputed that those measures do not cover all the fields of activity to which the Third Decision relates'.[119] Considering that the scope of the Third Decision extended to a great variety of measures such as government procurement, state aids and subsidies, access to local finance, and tax, the Court examined whether the criteria of *AETR*-type exclusivity existed in these fields and found that the degree of harmonization necessary for rendering Community competence exclusive did not exist. Even though the Community did not enjoy exclusive competence, Community law imposed limitations on the exercise of the Member States' concurrent powers.[120]

It should be noted that the Community enjoyed competence not only with regard to national treatment of foreign investors, but also with regard to all general standards of treatment and especially MFN and FET. Even though Opinion 2/92 concerned EC competence to conclude a national treatment instrument, its rationale was applicable to all general standards of treatment. MFN is an expression of the principle of non-discrimination, while FET essentially guarantees substantive

[114] See Sections 1.3.3.1 and 3.2.2.4.
[115] Opinion 2/92, above n 25.
[116] Ibid, para IV 7.
[117] Ibid, para IV 8.
[118] Tridimas, above n 85, pp 56–7.
[119] Opinion 2/92, above n 25, para V 6.
[120] See Sections 6.1.2 and 6.2.2.4.

and procedural fairness in the adoption and application of national measures, which are covered under the scope of the free movement rules.[121]

In summary, the EC enjoyed competence over initial establishment and post-establishment treatment of FDI. However, although the foundations of Community competence were numerous, none were able to support on their own a general Community competence. Furthermore, exclusivity existed only to a limited extent with regard to specific economic sectors, thus allowing Member States to remain active in the field. Despite the possibility of pure Community action in the field, the lack of a clear power-conferring provision and the eagerness of Member States to continue playing an active role resulted in a partial and incomplete picture on EC competence over FDI.

2.2.3 Competence over establishment and post-establishment treatment of FDI after the Lisbon Treaty

The Lisbon Treaty established for the first time an express competence over foreign investment, by including it within the scope of the CCP. Articles 206 and 207 TFEU expand the scope of the CCP providing an explicit reference to FDI and offering clearer wording. Its express inclusion under the CCP empowers the Union to take external action in most fields of FDI regulation and facilitates the exercise of its competence by establishing a specific legal basis for it.

2.2.3.1 The scope of FDI competence

It should be noted that the Lisbon Treaty establishes Union competence only with regard to FDI. As a result, portfolio investment as well as foreign investment in the form of concession contracts are excluded from the scope of the new competence. This exclusion does not mean that the EU does not enjoy competence to take external action in this regard: the express recognition of competence over FDI does not negate EU powers which are conferred on it by virtue of other Treaty provisions.[122] On the contrary, the EU is competent to the extent that the EU Treaties empower the Union to regulate these forms of foreign investment.

Concerning the substantive content of the new competence over FDI, the inclusion of FDI as part of the CCP does not necessarily mean that the EU can take action under Article 207 TFEU with regard to all matters concerning FDI. At first glance, issues related to the admission and post-establishment operation of FDI seem to fall within the scope of Article 207 TFEU. However, as important aspects of FDI regulation are also covered under other TFEU chapters, the scope of FDI competence is determined by assessing its relation with other power-conferring provisions. In addition, Article 207(6) TFEU establishes inherent limits to the scope of Union competence under the CCP, which also apply with regard to FDI.

121 See below Sections 3.2.2.4.2 and 3.2.2.4.3.

122 W Shan and S Zhang, 'The Treaty of Lisbon: Half Way toward a Common Investment Policy' (2010) 21 EJIL 1049, 1064. See also Sections 2.3 and 2.4.

More specifically, issues of initial establishment of foreign investors fall within the scope of FDI competence.[123] Its placement under the CCP, which is based on the principles of uniformity and liberalization, reveals that FDI competence is primarily concerned with market access, hence allowing the EU to take action with regard to conditions of establishment of foreign investors. However, FDI competence overlaps partially with Union competence for trade in services which includes establishment in service sectors. Even though as a matter of principle FDI competence should be considered as embracing establishment in all economic sectors, thus uniting rules on establishment, the distinction between FDI and trade in services competence is of minor practical significance since they are both part of the CCP and are subject to identical rules.

In contrast with initial establishment, it is unclear whether FDI competence encompasses capital movements relating to foreign investment. Article 63 TFEU refers explicitly to capital movements to and from third countries, while Articles 64 to 66 TFEU establish specific rules concerning limitations on capital movements to and from third countries. Indeed, Article 63 TFEU does not provide explicitly for the conclusion of international agreements, while Article 207 TFEU concerns predominantly EU action in the international sphere. Even though it can be argued that the mere fact that measures adopted under the CCP have repercussions for certain economic sectors falling under other chapters it does not constitute a reason to exclude them from the scope of the CCP,[124] this is not the case for FDI-related capital movements. As the Court recognized in Opinion 1/2008, in a context where agreements may cover commitments in many different areas, it is not helpful to think in terms of predominant/incidental purpose.[125] Indeed, IIAs not only have effects on capital movements, but also aim to provide a framework for their liberalization. The jurisprudence on Articles 63 to 66 TFEU is pertinent for FDI-related capital movements, which need to be taken into consideration for the conclusion of future EU IIAs. Thus, FDI-related capital movements should be excluded from the scope of Article 207 TFEU, which indicates that they fall under shared competence.

It is also unclear whether FDI competence includes all aspects of post-establishment treatment of foreign investors. Article 49 TFEU remains the basic provision concerning treatment of EU companies within the EU regardless of their ownership or control. Thus, applying the rationale of Opinion 2/92,[126] the treatment of foreign investors established in the EU according to Article 54 TFEU seems to be excluded from the scope of the CCP. On the other hand, Article 207 TFEU has a much broader scope as it confers powers with regard to all foreign-established

[123] Ceyssens, above n 91, pp 276–7; Krajewski, above n 96, p 114; Karl, above n 41, pp 421, 434; C Tietje, 'Die Außenwirtschaftsverfassung der EU nach dem Vertrag von Lissabon' (2009) 93 Beiträge zum Transnationalen Wirtschaftsrecht 1, 14.

[124] See eg the Court's reasoning in Opinion 1/94 (above n 18, para 29) where it found that the Agreement on Agriculture should be concluded under Art 133 TEC and not under Art 37 TEC on the CAP. See also Ceyssens, above n 91, p 284; S Johannsen, 'Die Kompetenz der Europäischen Union für ausländische Direktinvestitionen nach dem Vertrag von Lissabon' (2009) 90 *Beiträge zum Transnationalen Wirtschaftsrecht* 1, 20–1.

[125] Opinion 1/2008, above n 90, paras 140 and 163.

[126] See Section 2.2.2.3.

persons, irrespective of whether they fulfill the criteria of Article 54 TFEU, thus conferring competence over post-establishment treatment of foreign-owned and/or controlled branches and agencies. Moreover, FDI competence is broader in order to ensure the treatment of EU-controlled or managed undertakings in third countries.[127] Consequently, Articles 207 and 49 TFEU should probably be used jointly for concluding EU IIAs regulating post-establishment treatment of foreign investors, so that aspects of post-establishment treatment of FDI fall under shared competence.

It should further be mentioned that the Lisbon Treaty retains the exclusion of transport services from the scope of the CCP. Following the reasoning of the Court in Opinion 1/94, which was affirmed in Opinion 1/2008, that EU competence with regard to transport services is established only within the limits set in the respective chapter,[128] the Lisbon Treaty provides in Article 207(5) TFEU that, 'the negotiation and conclusion of international agreements in the field of transport shall be subject to Title V of Part Three and to Article 218'. Hence regulation of FDI in the transport sector falls under the shared competence of the EU and its Member States, according to the doctrine of implied powers analyzed above.

The expansion of the CCP to cover FDI has rendered necessary the establishment of an explicit link between the internal market and external action. The need to avoid the paradox of an external competence superseding internal powers, which was expressed in Article 133(6) TEC, is also followed in the Lisbon Treaty, which provides in Article 207(6) TFEU limitations on Union competence in the field of the CCP based on the principle of parallelism. However, the Lisbon Treaty adopts a different approach towards parallelism: Article 207(6) TFEU preserves the powers of Member States in fields excluded entirely from Union interference or from harmonization by means of EU secondary legislation.[129] Paragraph 6 actually precludes the Union from taking action in relation to third countries in fields where its competence in the internal market is limited, thus preserving the competences of Member States insofar as they have retained the power to regulate a specific issue in the internal market.[130] Consequently, when the Union exercises its powers under the CCP, it is subject to the same limitations on its competence that exist in the internal market with regard to the same subject matter. However, this does not mean that the lack of exercise of Union internal competences poses a limitation on the existence or the exercise of external competence. It is remarkable that the requirement of unanimity for the adoption of CCP measures in cases where no internal measures have been adopted has not been incorporated in Article 207(4) TFEU, thus proving that a lack of internal rules presents no impediment to the adoption of external action even at the procedural level.[131] As a result, the Union

[127] Ceyssens, above n 91, p 276; Karl, above n 41, p 421.

[128] Above n 94.

[129] Art 207(6) TFEU provides that the exercise of the competences conferred by this Article in the field of the common commercial policy shall not affect the delimitation of competences between the Union and the Member States, and shall not lead to harmonisation of legislative or regulatory provisions of the Member States insofar as the Treaties exclude such harmonisation.

[130] Ceyssens, above n 91, pp 279–80; Krajewski, above n 96, p 115.

[131] See Shan and Zhang, above n 122, pp 1064–5.

can take action with regard to FDI to the extent that it is competent to legislate in this area of the internal market, even if it has not as yet acted.

Article 207(6) TFEU is of particular importance for determining the scope of FDI competence, indicating one major limitation to the scope of EU powers to regulate admission and treatment of FDI.[132] The second sentence of Article 207(6)(2) TFEU, which provides that the exercise of Union powers is limited in fields where harmonization is excluded, means that the CCP cannot be used for the adoption of Union measures in fields in which other Treaty provisions allow for only limited Union interference. Considering that the Lisbon Treaty kept the exceptions to harmonization provided in the EC Treaty in the fields of employment, social policy, education, culture, and public health,[133] the limitation of Article 207(6) TFEU means that the EU cannot use its FDI competence to adopt measures that would lead to harmonization in these areas. Although the Lisbon Treaty incorporates social, health, education, and cultural services in the general scope of EU competence under Article 207(1) TFEU—doing away with the confusing reference to shared competence in Article 133(6)(2) TEC—the elimination of Article 133(6)(2) TEC does not necessarily mean that these fields are included entirely within the scope of EU competence.

Nevertheless, Article 207(6) TFEU does not limit the scope of EU competence with regard to the general standards of treatment that it can include in its international agreements. Taking into account that in the internal market, primary EU law provides mainly for non-discrimination and market access, but not for FET or other absolute standards of treatment, it is argued that the latter do not fall within the scope of FDI competence.[134] Despite the lack of explicit recognition of these standards in internal market law, it is arguable that similar protection is actually provided to EU nationals in the internal market.[135] Although such standards are not provided as such in EU law, this does not mean that the EU lacks internal, and thereby external, competence to establish them by means of secondary law.

Finally, it is worthy of note that Article 207 TFEU grants the possibility both to conclude international agreements and to adopt autonomous measures with regard to FDI. Contrary to Article 133 TEC, which stipulated that the EC enjoyed competence only to negotiate and conclude international agreements in the field of trade in services, the Lisbon Treaty enables the EU to adopt autonomous measures with regard to all aspects of the CCP. As Article 207(1) TFEU does not distinguish between the different areas of the CCP, Article 207(2) TFEU enables the EU to adopt autonomous measures, both in the form of substantive rules and rules necessary for the implementation of international agreements.[136] Consequently, the Lisbon Treaty puts an end to the need to use different legal bases having different

[132] For the importance of Art 207(6) TFEU in relation to other aspects of FDI regulation see below Sections 2.5 and 2.6.

[133] Exclusion of harmonization is provided in Arts 149(2), 153(2)(a), 165(4), 166(4), 167(5), 168(4) TFEU.

[134] Ceyssens, above n 91.

[135] Shan and Zhang, above n 122, p 1065. See also above n 121.

[136] Krajewski, above n 96, p 107; Ceyssens, above n 91, p 276.

institutional and decision-making rules to adopt autonomous measures with regard to establishment and operation of FDI.

2.2.3.2 The exclusive nature of FDI competence

The most important novelty of the Lisbon Treaty, not only with regard to FDI but also with regard to trade in services and the commercial aspects of intellectual property, is that it provides explicitly for the exclusive character of Union competence in the field. In contrast with the Nice Treaty which distinguished between trade in goods and trade in services and commercial aspects of IP rights, the Lisbon Treaty assimilates all fields of the CCP, in the sense that they all fall under the EU's *a priori* exclusive competence. Article 3(1)(e) TFEU clearly stipulates that the CCP falls under the exclusive competence of the Union, while Article 2(1) TFEU integrates the principle that express powers are of *a priori* exclusive nature. In contrast with the previous regime, exclusivity is not only relevant for the traditional scope of the CCP, but also includes trade in services, IP, and FDI. It is notable that Article 207 TFEU does not include a provision similar to Article 133(5)(4) TEC, which retained the right of the Member States to maintain and conclude agreements with third countries. Article 207 TFEU does not distinguish between the different fields of the CCP in terms of the nature of competence, nor does Article 3 TFEU limit its scope to trade in goods. Furthermore, the fact that there are exceptional rules concerning voting requirements for trade in services, IP, and FDI has no implications for the exclusive character of Union competence.

In addition, the limitation set in Article 207(6) TFEU cannot be interpreted as carving out exclusivity in the fields where the Union does not have exclusive competence in the internal sphere. Paragraph 6 concerns the internal powers of Member States and establishes parallelism by excluding Union exclusive competence in the fields where the Union internally does not enjoy any competence. It cannot be interpreted as establishing shared competence with regard to all fields of the CCP that internally fall under shared competence, nor does it have a 'reverse *AETR* effect', hence leading to exclusivity in the internal market in an area of shared competence. This would contradict the clear recognition of exclusivity in Article 3 TFEU.[137]

However, CCP exclusivity should not be broadly interpreted as affecting the exercise of Member States' internal concurrent powers. Even though measures adopted under the CCP can lead to internal harmonization in a specific field, this does not mean that the EU is exclusively competent to regulate in that field. Exclusivity under the CCP appears only in relations with third countries, in fields where the Union is vested with the power to take measures internally and to the extent that harmonization achieved through the adoption of such measures is allowed.[138]

[137] M Krajewski, 'The Reform of the Common Commercial Policy' in Biondi and Eeckhout (eds), *European Union Law after the Treaty of Lisbon* (2011, forthcoming).

[138] Cremona, above n 20, p 32.

Hence, the EU is vested with exclusive competence regarding the majority of aspects relating to the admission and treatment of FDI. Considering, however, that the scope of FDI competence does not cover capital movements, post-establishment treatment of foreign nationals established in the EU in accordance with Article 54 TFEU, and transport services, regulation of FDI with regard to these issues falls under the shared competence of the EU and its Member States.

2.2.4 Competence over specific issues relating to the operation of FDI

In addition to competence over treatment of FDI, the EU is also vested with competence over specific issues that relate to the operation of FDI and constitute the subject of international regulation of foreign investment. In that regard, the EU has competence to regulate performance requirements and the movement of third country natural persons related to the operation of a foreign investment.

2.2.4.1 Competence over performance requirements

Regulation of performance requirements falls to a large extent under the exclusive competence of the EU. EU express and implied powers cover different forms of performance requirements that may be imposed upon FDI concerning its establishment and operation in the host country. The CCP, the Monetary Policy, and competition rules provide the necessary legal bases for EU action, restricting the scope and exercise of the powers of Member States in these areas.

The first and most important category of performance requirements, namely trade-related performance requirements, falls within the scope of Article 207 TFEU and thus under EU exclusive competence. Trade-related performance requirements, such as import and export quotas, the use of local goods or services, and the regulation of production rates, are issues regulated in the Agreement on Trade-Related Investment Measures (TRIMs), which is part of the WTO Multilateral Agreement on Trade in Goods. As the Court manifestly declared in Opinion 1/94 that the EU is exclusively competent to conclude this agreement,[139] it is inferred that the EU enjoys exclusive competence to regulate the imposition of trade-related performance requirements.[140]

The EU also enjoys exclusive competence with regard to performance requirements concerning foreign exchange. Article 207 TFEU presents the main power-conferring provision, given that the regulation of foreign exchange performance requirements related to FDI will usually have minor repercussions for EU foreign exchange rules. Nevertheless, to the extent that measures adopted under the CCP have significant repercussions on foreign exchange policy,[141] EU competence is based on the TFEU provisions on monetary policy, which grant exclusive competence to the EU to conduct foreign exchange operations and to regulate monetary policy. More specifically, Article 219 TFEU grants to the EU the express power

[139] Opinion 1/94, above n 18, para 34.
[140] Shan, above n 41, p 618; Karl, above n 41, p 418.
[141] See also above Section 2.2.3.1 regarding the relation of Arts 207 and 63 TFEU.

to negotiate and conclude agreements concerning monetary or foreign exchange regime matters (including investment-related foreign exchange matters), which according to Article 3(1)(c) TFEU is exclusive.[142] However, EU competence is effectively limited only to Eurozone Member States, as the other Member States do not yet participate completely to the Economic and Monetary Union or have obtained a derogation from the application of that Treaty chapter.[143]

The last important category of performance requirements over which the EU enjoys competence is competition-related performance requirements, concerning mainly monopoly and exclusive distribution restrictions, technology transfer agreements, and state aids and subsidies. Again, Article 207 TFEU presents the main legal basis for the regulation of competition-related performance requirements in EU external relations. Nevertheless, to the extent that a measure not only incidentally affects competition rules, EU action with regard to competition-related performance requirements has to be based on the provisions on competition policy. Articles 101, 102, and 106 TFEU provide a complete regulatory framework for the conduct of undertakings which have been granted special or exclusive rights, regardless of whether they are foreign-owned or controlled, insofar as their conduct can affect trade between Member States.[144] Hence, these provisions grant competence to the EU which, according to Article 3(1)(b) TFEU, is exclusive, to regulate the anti-competitive conduct of third country investors established in the EU, as long as there is an effect on the internal market. Indeed, the EU has itself concluded international agreements which regulate not only the conduct of third country undertakings affecting the internal market, but also the conduct of EU undertakings affecting the third country.[145] Given, however, that it is widely considered that the EU does not have the competence to regulate the conduct of its undertakings having an effect in third countries or a purely national effect,[146] it is arguable that the competence to include monopoly and exclusive distribution-related performance requirements in an international agreement is jointly shared by the EU and the Member States.

With regard to technology transfer, the EU has established to a great extent harmonization of rules on technology transfers,[147] thus arguably acquiring *AETR*-type

[142] R-M Lastra, *Legal Foundations of International Monetary Stability* (2006), pp 284–6.

[143] Regarding the Member States that do not yet participate in the Eurozone, they are required to coordinate their foreign exchange policies with Eurozone countries, so that the exercise of their competence on foreign exchange matters is subject to limitations arising out of their duty of cooperation. J de la Rochére, 'EMU: Constitutional Aspects and External Representation' (2002) 19 YEL 427; C Hermann, 'Monetary Sovereignty over the Euro and External Relations of the Euro Area: Competences, Procedures and Practice' (2002) 7 EFA Rev 1, 9–11.

[144] For an overview of the applicable scope of these provisions see J Mestmäcker, *EG-Wettbewerbsrecht: Kommentar*, Band I (2007), pp 651–83.

[145] Competition rules exist eg in Arts 32–38 of the Agreement with Turkey (Decision No 1/95 of the EC-Turkey Association Council of 22 December 1995 on implementing the final phase of the Customs Union [1996] OJ L35/1, in Art 70 of the SAA with Croatia, and finally in Art 23 of the EU-Switzerland FTA ([1972] OJ L300/189), which is a pure Union agreement.

[146] Mestmäcker, above n 144, Band I, pp 103–27.

[147] Commission Regulation (EC) No 772/2004 of 27 April 2004 ([2004] OJ L123/11) provides the regulatory framework for technology transfer agreements in the EU. For its content see C Ritter, 'The New Technology Transfer Block Exemption under EC Competition Law' (2004) 31 LIEI 161.

exclusive competence. Finally, most forms of state aids fall under the strict control of the EU in accordance with Articles 107 to 109 TFEU and a series of secondary legislation.[148] Even though there has not as yet been complete harmonization of rules on state aids, the EU is competent to set the general rules concerning access of foreign investors to state aids, whereas Member State competence is severely limited by the extended scope of EU rules.[149]

2.2.4.2 Competence over investment-related movement of natural persons

An important regulatory aspect of the operation of foreign investment concerns the movement of third country natural persons whom foreign investors wish to employ in the host country. Movement of natural persons concerns the movement of key personnel, namely persons employed in key positions for the business activities of the foreign investor, and movement of workers, while short-term stays, which are mainly important for setting up a foreign investment, are distinguished from long-term stays.[150]

Primary EU law includes a number of provisions relevant for investment-related movement of third country nationals. First, the chapter on freedom, security, and justice provides for broad EU competence to regulate immigration and visas for non-EU nationals, thus covering significant aspects of investment-related movement of natural persons. Additionally, Article 207 TFEU establishes EU competence over trade in services and FDI, including movement of specific categories of natural persons for a limited period. Finally, Article 153 TFEU confers power to the EU to regulate the 'conditions of employment' of third country nationals legally residing in EU territory.

Considering first long-term movement of natural persons, which is atypical of IIAs, Article 79(2)(a) TFEU empowers the EU to regulate the conditions of entry of third country nationals for paid employment, including visas, residence, and work permits.[151] Even though the EU has not yet legislated in the field, there are current proposals concerning the conditions for long-term entry and residence of third country nationals in the EU.[152]

As IIAs are more prone to include provisions regarding short-term movement of natural persons, it is more important to examine EU competence regarding the conditions for entry and work of third country nationals for a limited period.

[148] For a detailed analysis of the EU state aid system see Mestmäcker, above n 144, Band I, pp 834–1111.

[149] Karl, above n 41, p 419.

[150] See Section 1.3.3.2.3.

[151] For an analysis of the scope of EU competence on issues of workers' immigration see S Peers, *EU Justice and Home Affairs Law* (2006), pp 187–9 and 222–4.

[152] The Commission has announced two proposals for Directives, the first 'on a single application procedure for a single permit for third-country nationals to reside and work in the territory of a Member State and on a common set of rights for third-country workers legally residing in a Member State' (COM(2007) 0638 final, 23 October 2007) and the second on the conditions of entry and residence of third-country nationals for the purposes of highly qualified employment (COM(2007) 0637 final, 23 October 2007). See also S Peers, 'EU Justice and Home Affairs Law' in Craig and de Búrca (eds), *The Evolution of EU Law* (2011), pp 290–1.

Article 77(2)(a) TFEU enables the EU to adopt legislation and by implication to conclude international agreements concerning the visa and residence status for short-term stays of third country nationals. With regard to the exclusive character of EU competence over short-term visa and residence policy, the Schengen *acquis* as well as the development of a common visa policy through a series of secondary legislation have gradually conferred *AETR*-type exclusive competence with regard to certain aspects of short-term visa policy.[153]

Concerning the conditions for entry of third country nationals for work purposes for a short term, it is important to underline that movement of investment-related personnel for a limited time does not concern access to the internal labour market, nor does it grant rights to natural persons for entry and residence in the host country. Rather, movement of natural persons for a limited period is linked with the right of the foreign investor to establish and operate in the host state. In the internal market, the Court and subsequently the legislature have recognized the right of service providers to transfer their employees who are legally employed in one Member State to the territory of another Member State for a short period, in order to exercise their freedom to provide services.[154] By analogy, short-term movement of third country nationals is related to the right of foreign investors to establish and operate in the host state, to the extent that such a right has been conferred to foreign investors. This was already recognized in the Europe agreements[155] and is currently regulated in the SAAs which provide explicitly that beneficiaries of the right of establishment have the right to employ third country nationals who are considered key personnel for a limited period.[156] Furthermore, the intention of the Commission to propose secondary legislation concerning movement of key personnel, which is excluded from the scope of the proposed Directives on conditions of entry and residence for third country nationals,[157] illustrates that movement of investment-related natural persons is linked with the right of establishment of the foreign investor. Hence, EU competence with regard to establishment and post-establishment treatment of foreign investors covers also movement of investment-related personnel for a limited period.

In that respect, Article 207 TFEU confers on the EU exclusive competence to regulate short stays of key personnel. As establishment of FDI is at the core of the FDI competence, it follows that Article 207 TFEU allows the EU to take external

[153] On the extent of harmonization concerning the uniform visa regime and the implications for external competence see Peers, above n 151, pp 151–68 and 176–8.

[154] The two most prominent cases are Case C-43/93 *Van der Elst v OMI* [1994] ECR I-3803 and Case C-113/89 *Rush Portuguesa* [1990] ECR I-1417. The jurisprudence of the Court on posted workers was adopted by the legislature in Directive 96/71 EC on Posted Workers in the framework of provision of services ([1997] OJ L18/1).

[155] Art 52 of the Europe Agreement with Poland (OJ L348/1).

[156] Eg Art 54 of the SAA with Croatia.

[157] Arts 3(2)(c) and 3(2)(f) of the proposed Directives COM/638 and COM/637 (above n 152) provide that third country nationals, 'entering a Member State under commitments contained in an international agreement facilitating the entry and temporary stay of certain categories of trade and investment-related natural persons' are excluded from the scope of the Directive as they will be subject to specific rules.

action concerning short-term stays of key personnel. Also, the inclusion of trade in services within the scope of the CCP has expanded EU competence, as the notion of trade in services in the CCP is based on the WTO GATS model, which provides that the fourth mode of trade in services concerns the short-term movement of key personnel. However, in accordance with paragraph 6, EU competence under Article 207 TFEU is not extended to investment-related immigration, or to the visa regime of key personnel, so that EU external action in these fields should be based on Articles 77 and 78 TFEU.

With regard to the conditions of employment of third country nationals transferred for a short stay, the EU has joint competence with the Member States to legislate. In accordance with the 'posted workers' case law and Directive 96/71 EC,[158] Member States are not precluded from insisting that their mandatory labour legislation, for example on minimum wages, is extended to those workers. However, Article 153 TFEU confers expressly to the EU authority to take measures affecting 'the conditions of employment of third country nationals'.

As a result, the EU is vested with powers to enter into international agreements concerning the entry, residence, and employment of investment-related personnel, both for a long- and short-term period. Considering that international regulation of foreign investment is mainly focused on the short-term movement of natural persons and in particular of key personnel rather than workers, Article 207 TFEU provides a sufficient legal basis conferring exclusive competence to the EU to conclude IIAs that provide for short-term movement of investment-related key personnel.

2.2.4.3 Competence over investment guarantee

Subrogation clauses present a basic provision of most IIAs, as they enable host states to succeed to foreign investor's claims against a host state. As discussed, subrogation clauses are directly linked with national investment guarantee schemes, which provide guarantees to local entrepreneurs investing in third countries against 'political' risks.[159] Primary EU law enables the EU to include subrogation clauses in EU IIAs, linked either with an EU-wide investment guarantee scheme or with existing national guarantee schemes.

The EU is empowered to establish an EU-wide investment guarantee scheme. Similar to the establishment of other EU financial instruments targeted at outward investments, such as the European Investment Bank (EIB) Investment Facility for outward investment in African, Caribbean and Pacific (ACP) countries,[160] the EU has the competence to set up a broad EU-wide guarantee scheme, offering political risk insurance for investment projects in a broad range of sectors in third countries. Although the establishment of an EU-wide guarantee scheme is legally possible, either under the aegis of the EIB or as an independent financial instrument adopted under Articles 207 and 352 TFEU, the Commission has indicated

[158] Above n 154. [159] See Section 1.3.3.2.4.

[160] For an analysis of the Investment Facility see European Investment Bank, *Investment Facility Annual Report* (2009).

its eagerness to retain national investment promotion schemes targeted at outward investments.[161]

Irrespective of whether investment guarantee schemes are EU-wide or national, the EU can include subrogation clauses in future EU IIAs, providing for subrogation by operation of law and incorporating the right of sovereign insurers to take up investor's claims against host states. Considering that subrogation is a procedural mechanism that concerns the transfer of any associated rights and duties which arise in respect of an insurance claim, EU competence to include subrogation clauses depends on whether the EU has competence over the substantive provision that is the subject of the claim. Hence, to the extent that the EU has competence over the different areas of foreign investment regulation, it can include subrogation clauses in its IIAs.

2.3 EU competence over portfolio investment

Unlike FDI, primary EU law does not confer express powers to the EU with regard to portfolio investment. However, the delimitation of EU competence in this field does not appear as complex as in the case of FDI, since portfolio investment is not linked with establishment and does not raise any of the specific issues of post-establishment treatment concerning performance requirements or the movement of natural persons. As the main regulatory aspects of portfolio investment concern the movement of capital and the participation of foreign investors in the capital market of the host state, the EU enjoys competence to regulate.[162]

The existence of EU competence to regulate is based on the provisions on capital movements. As the notion of capital is extended to portfolio investment,[163] the chapter on capital movements confers, to the same extent as for FDI, competence to the EU to take external action in the field. Given that a capital movement is a transfer of assets essentially concerned with the investment of funds and Article 63 TFEU covers all measures likely to affect capital movements,[164] the EU has broad competence to regulate portfolio investment. Although Member States can still adopt measures within the limits provided in Article 65 TFEU, these limitations do not affect the scope and existence of EU powers but, rather, may influence the actual exercise of EU competence.[165]

As the EU shares competence with the Member States in the field of capital movements, Member States are not precluded, as a matter of principle, from taking external action to regulate portfolio investment. Nevertheless, it is arguable that the EU enjoys, to a certain extent, exclusive implied powers to take action in

[161] Investment Policy Communication, p 6.

[162] Investment Policy Communication, p 8; Shan and Zhang, above n 122, p 1064; Ceyssens, above n 91, p 275; S Hindelang and N Maydell, 'The EU's Common Investment Policy—Connecting the Dots' in Bungeberg Griebel and Hindelang (eds), *International Investment Law and EU Law* (2011), p 1.

[163] See Section 1.2.2.2.1.

[164] See Section 2.2.1.1.

[165] Ibid.

this area. Applying the criteria of *AETR*-type exclusivity, it appears that the field of capital market regulation is an area of law 'largely covered by Union rules', where harmonization has been achieved.[166] More specifically, the series of company law and capital market Directives, such as the Stock Exchange Law Directive,[167] the UCITS Directives,[168] and the Markets in Financial Instruments Directive[169] establish a harmonized regulatory framework for portfolio investment and make explicit references to relations with third countries, aiming at securing and enhancing transparency and investor protection, regardless of the nationality of the investor. Nevertheless, considering the broad scope of regulatory measures that can affect portfolio investment, Member States still hold powers in this field.

Consequently, regulation of portfolio investment falls under EU competence and the EU can take action in the international arena for the access and treatment of European investors in third countries as well as those of third country investors in the EU. Nevertheless, such competence is shared with the Member States, which, subject to the limitations imposed by primary and secondary EU law, can also take external action in the field of portfolio investment.

2.4 EU competence over foreign investment in the form of concession contracts and state contracts

Next to EU competence over FDI and portfolio investment, it is also necessary to examine EU competence over the most controversial category of foreign investment, namely concession contracts, as well as EU competence over (commercial) state contracts, which allow the EU to include umbrella clauses in EU IIAs. For both categories EU competence is based on a plurality of primary EU law provisions, similar to those which were relevant for FDI under the EC Treaty. Article 63 TFEU establishes EU competence in the field of capital movements, which is however of less importance in the field of concession and state contracts; Article 207 TFEU confers broad competence to the EU in the field of trade in services, which is important for contracts in service sectors; and Article 56 TFEU serves as a basis for implied EU powers, which are important for concession and state contracts in non-service sectors.

[166] On the scope of harmonization of capital markets law see Von der Groeben and Schwartze, *EU-EG Vertrag, Kommentar* (2004), Art 56 EGV, pp 1756–62.

[167] Directive 2001/34/EC on the admission of securities to official stock exchange listing and on information to be published on those securities [2001] OJ L184/1.

[168] Directive 85/611/EEC on the coordination of laws, regulations and administrative provisions relating to undertakings for collective investment in transferable securities (UCITS) [1985] OJ L375/3; Directive 2001/108/EC amending Council Directive 85/611/EEC on the coordination of laws, regulations and administrative provisions relating to undertakings for collective investment in transferable securities (UCITS), with regard to investments of UCITS [2002] OJ L41/35.

[169] Directive 2004/39/EC on markets in financial instruments amending Council Directives 85/611/EEC and 93/6/EEC and Directive 2000/12/EC of the European Parliament and of the Council and repealing Council Directive 93/22/EEC [2004] OJ L145/1.

The chapter on free movement of capital confers competence to the EU to regulate inward and outward capital movements of foreign investors necessary for the execution of concession and state contracts. Given that the notion of capital includes all types of economic assets that cross national borders, freedom of capital movements is of particular importance for the movement of tangible goods, such as machinery, which can be crucial for the execution of many contracts.[170]

Concerning admission and treatment of foreign investments in the form of concession or state contracts, Article 207 TFEU vests the EU with broad powers to regulate contracts in service sectors. The fact that the Court in the *MOU* case[171] ruled out competence based on the CCP provisions on the ground that procurement of services involved the movement of persons which fell outside the scope of the CCP, should be read in the context of Opinion 1/94 which examined the scope of the CCP prior to the changes brought about by the Nice Treaty. The inclusion of trade in services within the scope of the CCP has expanded EU competence over admission and treatment of foreign nationals operating in service sectors, thus including foreign investors who conclude contracts for the procurement of services.[172] In practice, Article 207 TFEU has been used for the conclusion of public procurement agreements with third countries, and most importantly the WTO Government Procurement Agreement, which concern, inter alia, concession contracts with public entities for the provision of services.[173] Considering that after the entry into force of the Lisbon Treaty Article 207 TFEU confers exclusive competence to the EU in the field of trade in services, the conclusion can be drawn that the EU holds exclusive powers to regulate foreign investment in the form of services contracts.[174]

EU powers to regulate foreign investment in the form of concession or state contracts in non-service sectors are based on the chapter on the freedom to provide services in accordance with the doctrine of implied powers. Even though Article 56(1) TFEU limits its scope to nationals of EU Member States providing a service in another EU Member State, it is strongly arguable that the TFEU provisions establish EU competence over the provision of services in the EU by foreign

[170] See Section 1.2.2.1.1.

[171] Case C-360/93 *European Parliament v Council* [1996] ECR I-1195.

[172] S Arrowsmith, *The Law of Public and Utilities Procurement* (2005), pp 1316–17.

[173] Art 207 TFEU has been used as the legal basis for the procurement agreements with the EEA countries, Chile, Mexico, Israel, Korea, Switzerland, and the United States. For a detailed analysis of their provisions see Arrowsmith, above n 172, pp 1340–51.

[174] Even under the EC Treaty, it was argued that the EU enjoyed exclusive competence over public concession contracts in service sectors. The conclusion of the WTO Government Procurement Agreement had given rise to a long debate between Member States, many of which considered that there was no need to ratify it, as the EU enjoyed exclusive competence or exercised its concurrent powers to conclude it itself. (For a discussion of the different arguments raised by the Member States with regard to the conclusion and ratification of the GPA, see M Dischendorfer, *Implementation and Legal Effects of the WTO Agreement on Government Procurement in the European Community* (2002), pp 74–5 and 99–101.) Following this practice, the EU has itself concluded procurement agreements with third countries, thus extending its exclusive competence in the field of public concession contracts.

nationals and the provision of services in third countries by EU nationals.[175] The existence of EU competence is based on reasoning comparable to that which determined Community competence over establishment of FDI by virtue of the chapter on establishment. The power to set up the regulatory framework for the provision of services in all economic sectors, which necessitates the regulation of provision of services by third country nationals, as well as the need to grant EU nationals equal treatment insofar as they provide services in third countries, confers competence on the EU to regulate admission and treatment of foreign service providers,[176] thus including foreign investors having concession contracts for providing a particular service.

In examining the nature of EU competence flowing from these provisions, the distinction between private and public contracts, namely whether contracts are concluded between a foreign investor and the host state or between a foreign investor and a private person, is necessary for determining the exclusive character of EU competence. First, with regard to public contracts, concession and commercial, it is highly arguable that the EU enjoys exclusive competence to regulate entry and treatment of foreign investors. *AETR*-type exclusivity appears to cover public works and utilities concessions, which are covered by the respective Directives and have been completely harmonized.[177] With regard to private concession contracts, *AETR* exclusivity appears to be precluded, as there has not yet been any harmonization of the regulatory framework on private concession contracts. Internal market regulation in the field of free movement of services is mainly directed at removing obstacles to cross-border movement and at guaranteeing market access, instead of regulating each specific economic sector.[178] Nevertheless, in the economic sectors where harmonization has been achieved, such as in the financial services sector, there are common rules on the supply of services,[179] thus conferring exclusive competence to the EU to regulate private concession contracts in specific economic sectors.

[175] Although Art 56(2) TFEU confers competence to the EU regarding third country nationals providing services in the EU, this provision is expressly limited to third country nationals who are established in the EU, thus covering only a minor category of foreign investors who wish to provide services in the EU.

[176] See Section 2.2.2.2 on harmonization and regulation in the field of free movement of services, see L Woods, *Free Movement of Goods and Services within the European Community* (2004), pp 258–77.

[177] Directive 2004/18/EC on the coordination of procedures for the award of public works contracts, public supply contracts and public service contracts (Public Sectors Directive) [2004] OJ L134/1; Directive 2004/17/EC coordinating the procurement procedures of entities operating in the water, energy, transport and postal services sectors (Utilities Directive) [2004] OJ L134/1. Despite the great degree of harmonization established by these Directives, it is argued by Arrowsmith (above n 172) that *AETR*-type exclusivity is precluded, as measures relating to external relations in procurement will not and cannot necessarily affect or alter the internal EU procurement regime, as 'the effect of external measures is often simply to affect the extent of competition from third countries in the different national markets'. However, this argument seems to neglect the basic rule formed by the Court that, in areas of complete harmonization, common rules are affected, even where there is no contradiction between international action taken by the Member States and internal market rules.

[178] Woods, above n 176, pp 274–5.

[179] Cremona, above n 99, p 374.

Finally, it is worth considering that concession and state contracts are, in many instances, linked with performance requirements and movement of natural persons. Similar to FDI, the EU is vested with powers, which are in many instances exclusive, to regulate these specific issues of the operation of foreign investors.[180]

As a result, the EU can undertake international action to regulate entry and treatment of foreign investment in the form of concession contracts, as well as to include umbrella clauses in EU IIAs, which may render claims arising out of commercial state contracts into claims under EU IIAs. However, EU competence is only partly exclusive, thus Member States are not precluded from undertaking international commitments in the field.

2.5 EU competence to regulate protection of foreign investment against expropriation and other political risks

Protection of foreign investment against expropriation and other political risks has so far been completely excluded from Union agreements dealing with foreign investment, as this field has been widely considered to fall under the exclusive competence of the Member States. Both during the negotiations for the ECT, as well as during the negotiations for the Multilateral Agreement on Investment (MAI), the participation of the Member States was considered necessary for the conclusion of those agreements, as they included provisions on expropriation. On the other hand, Union agreements with extensive investment provisions, such as the ones with Chile, Korea, and CARIFORUM states, despite the fact that they are mixed agreements, avoid any reference to protection of foreign investment against expropriation and other political risks. They explicitly provide that the Bilateral Investment Treaties (BITs) concluded by the Member States are safeguarded, thus expressing the political unwillingness of the Member States to hand over any competence to the EU, so that protection from expropriation remains an issue that each Member State can determine separately. Within this framework, the Commission intends to include provisions on the protection of foreign investment against expropriation and other political risks in future EU IIAs, thus indicating its preparedness to assert EU competence over this aspect of regulation.[181]

2.5.1 The scope of Member State exclusive competence under Article 345 TFEU

The exclusive competence of Member States over property protection has been supported not only on the basis that there is no provision in primary EU law granting powers to the EU to regulate expropriation, but also on the fact that the TFEU expressly precludes the EU from taking any measures that can 'prejudice the rules

[180] See above Section 2.2.4.
[181] Investment Policy Communication, pp 8–9.

in Member States governing the system of property ownership'.[182] It has been argued that Article 345 TFEU expressly prohibits the adoption of EU measures that can interfere with the property system of the Member States, while the system of property ownership is considered to include all norms that regulate the existence of rights and obligations linked with property, the limitations of these rights, and in particular the conditions for the conversion of private property to public property.[183] Such a broad interpretation of Article 345 TFEU would entail that all rules concerning the rights of property owners in cases of expropriation or other political risk, especially with regard to the legality of the expropriation and the amount of compensation, fall within the scope of Article 345 TFEU and as a result under the exclusive competence of the Member States.[184]

However, the Court's jurisprudence on Article 345 TFEU seems to favour a much narrower interpretation. From its early jurisprudence the Court pointed out that the Member States do not enjoy complete autonomy in the field of property regulation, as their property rules, especially concerning expropriation, must not interfere with the fundamental freedoms. In *Costa v ENEL*[185] and in *Fearon*[186] the Court clearly stated that Article 345 TFEU does not preclude the application of EU rules in the field of property protection, so that any national measures affecting property must comply with the principle of non-discrimination. Further, in the *Golden Shares* cases[187] the Court reiterated its conviction that Article 345 TFEU cannot be used by the Member States for justifying a violation of the capital rules.

The narrow scope of Article 345 TFEU has been firmly recognized in the field of intellectual property, where the Court found that national rules on IP have a great impact on the exercise of the free movement of goods and competition rules.[188] Initially, the Court formulated the theory of core rights, according to which rules concerning the existence of IP rights could not infringe EU rules, while the exercise of those rights may do in certain circumstances, so that the exercise of IP rights can be the subject of EU rules.[189] In a second stage, the Court considered that EU rules can also interfere with the core substance of IP rights, so that regulation of IP rights concerning not only their exercise but also their existence can be adopted at EU level, especially by means of harmonization.[190] The theoretical recognition of EU competence to regulate the entire regime of intellectual property was also affirmed in practice, as the EU has adopted significant pieces of legislation harmonizing trade mark rights and IP rights for computer software.[191] Following these developments, the Lisbon Treaty establishes in Article 118 TFEU a specific legal

[182] For an overview of the opinions raised see Shan and Zhang, above n 122, pp 1060–4.

[183] Von der Groeben and Schwartze, *EU-EG Vertrag Kommentar* (2004), Art 295 EGV, above n 166, p 1527; H Rittstieg, 'Grundgesetz und Eigentumsordnung' (1982) NJW 721.

[184] Ibid. [185] Case 6/64 [1964] ECR 1251. [186] Case 182/83 [1984] ECR 3677.

[187] See above n 57. [188] Case C-30/90 *Commission v UK* [1992] ECR I-892.

[189] Case 24/67 *Parke Davis v Probel* [1968] ECR 55. For an analysis of the existence versus exercise doctrine see Mestmäcker, above n 144, Band II, pp 15–43.

[190] Case C-350/92 *Spain v Council* [1995] ECR I-1985.

[191] Directive 89/104/EEC on the approximation of the Laws of the Member States Relating to Trade Marks [1989] OJ L40/1; Directive 91/250/EEC on the legal protection of computer programs [1991] OJ L122/42.

basis for the creation of European IP rights, aiming to provide 'uniform protection of intellectual property rights throughout the Union', thus recognizing that the EU has explicit competence to regulate not only the exercise but also the existence of IP norms in the EU.

The extensive scope of EU competence in the field of intellectual property demonstrates that Article 345 TFEU does not exclude EU action affecting the existence and exercise of property rights. The rationale behind the narrow interpretation of Article 345 TFEU in the field of intellectual property can be applied to all other forms of property, given that IP rights constitute a form of property rights that are as equally protected as traditional property rights and are recognized as falling within the scope of the right to property in national, European, and international law.[192] Consequently, Article 345 TFEU should be narrowly interpreted as not hindering the EU from taking measures to regulate protection against expropriation and other political risks. In that respect, it is supported by certain authors that Article 345 TFEU has only a declaratory function[193] or that it is 'exhausted' at the moment of acceding to the EU in the sense that any changes in the property regime cannot be a condition for accession to the EU.[194] However, such an interpretation of Article 345 TFEU would deprive it of any normative content and cannot explain the fact that it has not been removed from primary EU law.

The drafting history of Article 345 TFEU clearly shows that its purpose was to prevent EU interference in decisions concerning the public or private character of property.[195] The Member States kept their competences with regard to the characterization of property as private or public and the right to change the property status from private to public or vice versa. Hence, Article 345 TFEU is essentially concerned with the right of Member States to decide on nationalization of private property and privatization of public property.[196] However, the clear recognition of EU competence in the field of property law requires that Article 345 TFEU is narrowly interpreted to concern only questions of nationalization or privatization, so that any other interference with the property regime is not excluded from the scope of EU action.

Such a narrow interpretation of Article 345 TFEU entails that the EU is not excluded by virtue of Article 345 TFEU from regulating the protection of foreign investment against expropriation and other political risks. First, as Article 345 TFEU is only concerned with nationalizations and privatizations, limitations on property rights that result from other causes, such as armed conflict, are excluded from the scope of Article 345 TFEU. More importantly, indirect or regulatory

[192] A Coban, *Protection of Property rights within the European Convention of Human Rights* (2004), ch 2.

[193] I Pernice, *Grundrechtsgehalte im Europäischen Gemeinschaftsrecht* (1979), p 181.

[194] R Riegel, 'Die Einwirkung des europäischen Gemeinschaftsrechts auf die Eigentumsordnung der Mitgliedstaaten' (1979) 25 Recht der Internationalen Wirtschaft 744, 745–6.

[195] For a discussion of the drafting history of Art 345 TFEU see C von Milczewski, *Der grundrechtliche Schutz des Eigentums im Europäischen Gemeinschaftsrecht* (1994), pp 23–30.

[196] Ibid; R Kovar, 'Nationalisations—privatisations et droit communautaire' in Schwartze (ed), *Discretionary Powers of the Member States in the Field of Economic Policies and their Limits under the EEC Treaty* (1988), pp 99–102.

expropriations, which concern indirect interferences with property rights, are also excluded from the scope of Article 345 TFEU. This provision concerns only outright taking of property, thus not excluding EU action with regard to the most common form of expropriation of foreign investment namely indirect expropriation. In addition, even with regard to direct expropriations it can be validly argued that Article 345 TFEU does not exclude EU action. Article 345 TFEU concerns only the existence of the right of Member States to decide whether to privatize or nationalize property.[197] The conditions under which nationalization or privatization occurs are subject to EU rules, as *Fearon* and the *Golden Shares* cases manifestly proved.[198] Given that regulation of expropriation in IIAs does not prohibit expropriation as such, but rather sets conditions under which an expropriation is legal, international investment law does not affect the existence of this sovereign right, but determines the limits of the exercise of this right. As a result, Article 345 TFEU does not preclude the EU from regulating the legality of an expropriation and the right to compensation for the affected private person.

2.5.2 Competence based on Article 207 TFEU

As the EU is not precluded from regulating the conditions of expropriation of foreign investors' property as a matter of principle, it is necessary to examine whether the adoption of concrete measures is supported by primary EU law. In that respect Articles 207, 114, 115, and 352 TFEU can serve as a legal basis for taking external action in the field—Article 207 TFEU with regard to FDI and the other provisions with regard to other forms of foreign investment.

Starting with the scope of Article 207 TFEU, it is arguable that it brings protection against expropriation under EU competence, thus covering the most important aspect of foreign investment regulation which so far remains entirely outside the scope of EU regulation. The broad pronouncement of FDI competence under Article 207 TFEU indicates that it covers all aspects of FDI regulation, including protection of FDI against expropriation.[199] Nevertheless, the exclusion of investment protection from the scope of the CCP is strongly advocated, based on the trade character of the CCP and on the limitation of Union competence in the field of the CCP according to Article 207(6) TFEU,[200] which is important if investment protection were to be considered as excluded from the scope of internal Union powers.

With regard to the trade orientation of the CCP, it is argued that the CCP cannot extend to measures of investment protection, as this goes far beyond the 'traditional' character of the CCP which concerns market access and abolition of

[197] Von Milczewski, above n 195, pp 29–30.

[198] Kovar, above n 196, pp 102–3.

[199] M Bungenberg, 'The Division of Competences Between the EU and its Member States in the Area of Investment Policies' in Bungeberg Griebel and Hindelang (eds), *International Investment Law and EU Law* (2011), pp 36–7; C Hermann, 'Die Zukunft der mitgliedstaatlichen Investitionspolitik nach dem Vertrag von Lissabon' (2010) 77 EuZW 207, 211.

[200] See above Section 2.2.3.1.

restrictions, hence covering only issues of establishment and post-establishment treatment.[201] Article 206 TFEU provides that, 'the Union shall contribute, in the common interest, to... the progressive abolition of restrictions on foreign direct investment', thus not including FDI protection in its scope. However, this argument does not take into consideration that the CCP has been expanded beyond trade, not only by the inclusion of foreign investment, but also by the inclusion of the commercial aspects of intellectual property, which are mainly related to property protection and limitations rather than liberalization. In that regard, the concept of restrictions on FDI mentioned in Article 206 TFEU can be interpreted as including restrictions on property protection, similar to the property protection restrictions abolished by the Agreement on Trade-related Aspects of Intellectual Property Rights (TRIPS). The fact that Article 207 TFEU does not distinguish between trade in goods and the other fields of the CCP, as did Article 133 TEC, illustrates that the Lisbon Treaty is moving further away from the traditional trade orientation of the CCP and is expanding towards all commercial fields.[202]

In considering the limitations imposed by Article 207(6) TFEU, it becomes obvious that EU competence to regulate expropriation of FDI is directly linked to the internal market provisions that determine EU competence to regulate expropriation of other forms of foreign investment. Hence, it would reasonable to exclude protection against expropriation from the scope of the new FDI competence, if Article 345 TFEU were interpreted as safeguarding the powers of Member States with regard to the entirety of the issues affecting their property regime.[203] Moreover, if internal harmonization of rules on expropriation were to be excluded from the scope of Articles 114, 115, and 352 TFEU then, again, the principle of parallelism affirmed in Article 207(6) TFEU would exclude investment protection from the scope of the CCP. However, if internal harmonization can be achieved, the CCP can be used for regulating protection against expropriation. The fact that the internal power has not as yet been used does not mean that external competence does not exist, as this would negate the foundations of the principle of parallelism which determines the scope of EU external competence.[204] It is remarkable that the requirement of unanimity for the adoption of external action in cases where no internal measures have been adopted was not included in Article 207(4) TFEU, thus proving that the lack of internal rules is no impediment for the adoption of external action, even at a procedural level. As a result, it is also necessary to examine, for the purposes of Article 207 TFEU, the internal market provisions that confer powers to the EU to regulate the protection of foreign investors' property against expropriation and other political risks in the EU and EU investors' property in third countries. Hence, to the extent that the EU can harmonize conditions on expropriation internally, Article 207 TFEU is the appropriate legal basis

[201] Krajewski, above n 96, p 114.

[202] Shan and Zhang, above n 122, pp 1060–1; Ceyssens, above n 91, pp 278–9; Karl, above n 41, p 421.

[203] Tietje, above n 123, pp 14–15; Johannsen, above n 124, p 16.

[204] Shan and Zhang, above n 122, pp 1062–3. Cf Ceyssens, above n 91, p 281.

for including in EU IIAs provisions on protection of FDI against expropriation and other political risks.

2.5.3 Competence based on Articles 114, 115, and 352 TFEU

Considering the relevance of Articles 114, 115, and 352 TFEU for the regulation of expropriation of foreign investment, it is necessary to distinguish limitations on private property resulting from actions of EU organs and expropriation resulting from Member State measures, as indirect expropriation can be the result of both national and EU measures. As regards interferences with private property rights resulting from EU measures, the Court has acknowledged the existence of principles of Union law that determine the scope of protection of private property. Despite the lack of specific rules, the Court recognized in *Nold*[205] and *Bosphorus*[206] that there are general principles of EU law that safeguard property rights and determine the conditions under which these rights can be limited. Drawing inspiration from the common constitutional traditions of the Member States and the European Convention on the Protection of Human Rights (ECHR), the Court found that EU law can pose limitations on property rights and affect their exercise. It is noteworthy that the application of the EU principles on protection of property rights is not limited to EU nationals, but applies to all persons with property rights in the territory of any EU Member State, as the Court clearly recognized in the *Bosphorus* case.[207] Consequently, the existence of EU rules determining the limitations of private property rights implies that the EU has created a legal framework, which can potentially apply to cases concerning the conditions for indirect expropriation of foreign investors' property resulting from EU measures. In that respect, the existence of internal rules entails that external action concerning indirect expropriation of foreign investments as a result of EU measures can also be taken.

The recognition of the EU law principles that determine private property limitations resulting from EU measures was also solidified after the Lisbon Treaty and the adoption of the Charter on Fundamental Rights as a legally binding instrument having the same legal value as the Treaties.[208] Article 17 of the Charter provides for a right to property and determines the conditions under which deprivation and limitation of private property rights are allowed.[209] Even though it is explicitly recognized that the Charter 'does not extend the field of application of Union law beyond the powers of the Union or establish any new power or task for the Union',[210] the fact that it recognizes that EU law can affect the property ownership system of the Member States and sets limits to the exercise of Union powers, shows that the EU can legislate on limitations of private property rights resulting from EU measures, including conditions of expropriation.

205 Case 4/73 *Nold* [1974] ECR 491.
206 Case C-84/95 *Bosphorus* [1996] ECR I-3953.
207 Ibid, para 19. 208 Art 6(1) TEU.
209 On Art 17 of the Charter see Section 1.1.3, n 39.
210 Art 51(2) of the Charter.

Due to the lack of a specific legal basis enabling such action, Article 352 TFEU empowers the EU to regulate in this field. The conclusion of an IIA regulating indirect expropriation as a result of EU measures could be considered 'necessary for attaining one of the Union objectives in the course of the operation of the common market'. The protection of property rights is one of the basic objectives of Union action, as it is firmly recognized in the Court's jurisprudence, and in particular in Opinion 2/92,[211] while regulation of expropriation is directly linked with the operation of the common market as limitations to property rights can have a major impact on the exercise of the fundamental freedoms.[212] Hence, Article 352 TFEU is the appropriate legal basis for including provisions on protection of non-FDI from (indirect) expropriation resulting from Union measures.

In contrast with EU measures affecting private property rights, EU competence to regulate the conditions of expropriation of private property resulting from national measures, is unclear from the outset. As the Court's judgments in *Costa v ENEL* and *Fearon* illustrated, national expropriation measures must be compatible with primary EU law provisions, thus obliging Member States to regulate expropriation in compatibility with EU rules. Such an obligation, however, is far from establishing EU competence to determine the conditions of legality and compensation in cases of expropriation or other political risks resulting from national measures. Such a competence requires that the EU is vested with powers to harmonize national laws concerning conditions of expropriation.

The EU has not as yet taken any action to harmonize national laws on expropriation, even with regard to intra-EU investments. The existence and validity of national laws and Member State competence to determine conditions of expropriation were recognized early on during the French nationalization cases in the 1980s[213] and more recently in the *Eastern Sugar* arbitration, where both the Tribunal and the Commission recognized that expropriation conditions is a field not covered by EU law.[214] However, the absence of EU action in the field so far does not mean that the EU lacks competence to do so. Given that norms on property protection and conditions of expropriation exist in national constitutions as well as in the 1st Protocol to the ECHR, the hesitance of the EU to legislate in this field is primarily linked with political reasons and does not affect EU competence.

Harmonization of national laws concerning conditions on limitations of private property could be primarily achieved in the framework of the internal market by virtue of Articles 114 and 115 TFEU. As already argued, limitations on private property can have an immense effect on the exercise of the fundamental freedoms. Establishing a common framework for defining the legality of private

[211] Above n 25.

[212] On the recognition of human rights protection as an objective of primary EU law and its link to the operation of the internal market, as an element of Art 352 TFEU see Cremona, above n 22, pp 223–4; A Arnull, 'Left to its own Devices? Opinion 2/94 and the Protection of Fundamental Rights in the European Union' in Dashwood and Hillion (eds), *The general law of EC external relations* (2000), ch 5.

[213] Kovar, above n 196, pp 98–9 and in particular nn 3 and 4.

[214] *Eastern Sugar BV v Czech Republic*, ICC Partial Award and Partial Dissenting Opinion, 27 March 2007.

property expropriations, including the determination of compensation, would ensure that the limitations on free movement would not be exceeded. In addition, the fact that harmonization of intellectual property rights is considered necessary for the completion of the internal market indicates that conditions of expropriation can also be the subject of internal market harmonizing legislation. The fact that the Lisbon Treaty establishes a specific legal basis for the creation of European IP rights[215] shows that property protection is a field inextricably linked with the operation of the internal market. Hence, the imperative of the completion of the internal market arguably allows the EU to harmonize rules on expropriation of property located in Member State territory regardless of the nationality of the property owner, thus including foreign investors. As a result, Articles 114 and 115 TFEU enable the EU to determine the conditions for limitations of non-FDI property rights, even when they result from purely national measures, such as tax, social security measures, etc.

With regard to expropriation of property owned by EU nationals in third countries, external EU competence derives from the principle of non-discrimination and the need for the completion of the internal market. Article 18 TFEU provides for non-discrimination of EU nationals, which extends to their treatment in third countries, as discussed in the field of initial establishment and post-establishment treatment.[216] Therefore, as long as the completion of the internal market necessitates the existence of common rules on the conditions for private property limitations, the principle of non-discrimination extends the scope of EU competence to conclude international agreements concerning the conditions of expropriation of EU nationals' property. Even though the need for common rules applied to expropriation of EU nationals' property in third countries has not as yet appeared, the creation of an internal harmonized framework on expropriation would also solidify the need for common standards applied to EU nationals abroad.

Consequently, the conclusion of an IIA including provisions on expropriation would actually result in harmonization of national expropriation rules of non-FDI investments and would ensure the non-discriminatory treatment of EU nationals in third countries in the field of property protection. Therefore, Articles 308, 114, and 115 TFEU[217] provide shared competence for the inclusion of expropriation provisions of non-FDI forms of foreign investment in an EU IIA.

In summary, there is no valid ground for excluding property protection against expropriation or other political risks from the scope of EU competence. Article 345 TFEU should be narrowly interpreted so that it precludes EU action only if the latter interferes with the existence of the right of Member States to determine whether and when expropriation measures should be adopted. However, the conditions concerning the legality of property limitations resulting from expropriation, including the determination of compensation, can be the subject of EU action, both when expropriation results from EU or national measures. Article 207 TFEU

[215] See Section 2.5.1.

[216] See Section 2.2.2.2.1.

[217] See also Case C-317/04 *European Parliament v Council (PNR Case)* [2006] ECR I-4721.

empowers the EU with exclusive competence to regulate property protection of FDI; Article 352 TFEU covers protection of the other forms of foreign investment from Union measures; and Articles 114 and 115 TFEU enable the EU to include provisions on protection of the other forms of foreign investment against expropriation and other political risks from pure national measures.

2.6 EU competence to regulate settlement of investment disputes

The examination of EU competence to include provisions for the settlement of investment disputes in an international agreement requires specific attention, given the importance of dispute settlements as an indispensable part of IIAs. The determination of competence becomes more significant, as most IIAs provide not only for interstate dispute settlement, but also allow individuals to raise claims and initiate a dispute concerning the application of the agreement.

As a general rule, EU competence to enter into an international agreement containing provisions for the settlement of disputes arising out of its application is a self-evident implication of its legal personality. The recognition of the EU as subject of international law in Article 47 TEU entails that, to the extent that the EU can undertake binding commitments in the sphere of international law according to its attributed powers, it is subject to international law rules on responsibility and dispute settlement.[218] The existence of EU competence to subject itself to internationally agreed mechanisms of dispute settlement has been explicitly recognized by the Court in Opinion 1/91,[219] which was further clarified in Opinions 1/00 and 1/09,[220] emphasizing the link between dispute settlement and the autonomy of the EU legal order.

More specifically, the EU can conclude international agreements providing for compulsory dispute settlement systems that grant access to individual claims and deliver binding decisions. As the Court clearly contemplated,

> *where an international agreement provides for its own system of courts, including a court with jurisdiction to settle disputes between the Contracting Parties to the agreement, and, as a result, to interpret its provisions, the decisions of that court will be binding on the [EU] institutions... An international agreement providing for such a system of courts is in principle compatible with [EU] law.*[221]

Hence, the EU is in principle competent to include in its international agreements provisions on both interstate and investor-state dispute settlement, which establish ad hoc or institutionalized arbitration as a means of dispute settlement. This primary conclusion is also supported by current practice, as the EU has concluded important international agreements through rigorous dispute settlement systems, such as

[218] Von der Groeben and Schwartze, above n 183, p 1249; Koutrakos, above n 15, p 8.

[219] Opinion 1/91 *(EEA Agreement)* [1991] ECR I-6079.

[220] Opinion 1/00 *(Common Aviation Area)* [2002] ECR I-3493; Opinion 1/09 *(European Patent Court)* [2011] ECR I-0000.

[221] Opinion 1/91, above n 219, para 3.

the European Economic Area (EEA) Agreement, the WTO Agreement, and more importantly the ECT, which provides specifically for investor-state arbitration.[222]

However, EU competence to enter into an international agreement establishing a compulsory system of dispute settlement is subject to specific conditions. As the Court firmly established in Opinions 1/91, 1/92, 2/94, and 1/00 the EU enjoys such competence as long as the dispute settlement system established does not affect the autonomy of EU law and does not alter the institutional regime created by primary EU law.[223] Examining the competence of the EU to enter into the EEA Agreement, the ECHR, and the European Common Aviation Agreement, which establish a court with compulsory jurisdiction over issues arising out of their application and interpretation, the Court emphasized the need for preservation of its own role as the sole competent forum for questions of EU law. In particular, the Court was concerned with the situations when a third court could offer a binding interpretation of EU rules, when it could decide on the delimitation of competences between Member States and the EU, and when it could affect the powers of EU institutions.[224]

First, the systems for settlement of investment disputes found in different IIAs do not seem to threaten the jurisdiction of the Court of Justice to interpret EU law. IIAs cannot affect the application and interpretation of EU law rules, as neither homogenous interpretation is required, as in the EEA Agreement, the EU does not attach to IIAs any significance for the formulation of internal rules and principles, as it does in the case of the ECHR, nor do EU IIAs allow arbitral tribunals to interpret and apply future EU regulation, as in the case of the European Patent Court.[225] Even where similar or identical wording to EU law is chosen, the application and interpretation of an IIA by an investment tribunal does not affect the autonomy of EU law, as it is well established in case law that provisions of Union agreements that

[222] The question of EU competence to accede in an IIA is different from the question concerning the eligibility of the EU as a supranational organization to conclude an international agreement as a matter of international law. Eg, accession of the EU to the ICSID Convention is currently impossible, as Art 67 of the Convention allows only states to accede to the Convention. See Section 3.2.7.5.

[223] I Govaere, 'Beware the Trojan Horse: Dispute Settlement in (mixed) Agreements and the Autonomy of the EU Legal Order' in Hillion and Koutrakos (eds), *Mixed Agreements Revisited* (2010), p 192; B Brandtner, 'The "Drama" of the EEA: Comments on Opinions 1/91 and 1/92' (1992) 3 EJIL 309.

[224] Govaere, above n 223, p 192.

[225] In Opinion 1/91 the Court ruled that the autonomy of EU law was undermined, because the EEA Court could apply and interpret the EEA provisions without paying attention to future developments of the case law of the Court of Justice. In this way, it deprived the Court of Justice from its power to determine questions of EU law, as the EEA Agreement intended to ensure homogeneity of EEA and EU law and as a result bound the Court of Justice to follow future case law of the EEA Court. In contrast with the clarity of its analysis in Opinion 1/91, the Court rejected in Opinion 2/94 EU competence on these grounds only indirectly. It considered that accession to the ECHR would bring a modification of the system for protection of human rights in the EU with equally fundamental institutional implications for the EU and the Member States. Hence, it is argued that the Court recognized that the potential scope of jurisdiction of the ECtHR could include competence questions and that its decisions would affect the interpretation of the EU law guarantees of fundamental rights. For an analysis of these Opinions see Brandtner, above n 223, p 300; Arnull, above n 212.

are identically or similarly worded to corresponding EU law provisions should not necessarily be interpreted identically.[226]

Secondly, questions concerning the delimitation of EU competence from Member State competence can be excluded from the scope of dispute settlement under IIAs. These questions arise mainly in cases of mixed agreements, where an IIA is concluded jointly by the Member States and the EU. Indeed, questions of competence as well as disputes between Member States have arisen in practice under the UN Convention on the Law of the Sea and the WTO Agreements.[227] However, the existence of such difficulties is related in particular to the effects of an international agreement, without prejudicing the jurisdiction of the Court of Justice and hence EU competence to conclude an international agreement that includes dispute settlement provisions.[228] In addition, the EU has in practice used various mechanisms—such as declarations of competence and 'disconnection clauses'[229]—which enable it to overcome any difficulties and to ensure that proceedings initiated by non-Member States and their nationals are correctly addressed to Member States and/or the EU as appropriate and that the compulsory jurisdiction of the Court is not affected.

Thirdly, dispute settlement systems under IIAs cannot affect, in most instances, the powers of EU institutions and in particular the power of the European Court of Justice (ECJ) to provide binding rulings and to review the legality of acts of Union institutions.[230] Indeed, the binding nature of ECJ rulings could be undermined only if third countries accepted the jurisdiction of the ECJ as the appropriate forum for settling their investment disputes,[231] which is unlikely to arise in the framework of EU IIAs. As regards the exclusive power of the ECJ to review the legality of acts of Union institutions, this requirement does not mean that Union acts cannot be challenged in front of international dispute settlement bodies, but rather that Union measures can only be invalidated by the ECJ. In other words, if an international dispute settlement body finds that a Union measure violates an EU IIA, the autonomy of EU law requires that the measure is not directly invalidated, but it is for the Union legal system to take the appropriate measures to conform to the EU's international obligations.[232] Considering that compensation is the most

[226] Eg Case 270/80 *Polydor* [1982] ECR 329 and Case 104/81 *Hauptzollamt Mainz v Kupferberg* [1982] ECR 3641. See also Govaere, above n 223, pp 197–8. For an analysis of the interpretation of Union agreements see Section 3.2.2.4.

[227] The most salient example is the *MOX Plant* case, where two Member States were parties in a dispute before the International Tribunal for the Law of the Sea (ITLOS), which subsequently led to a court ruling on the same subject matter (Case C-459/03 *Commission v Ireland* [2006] ECR I-4635). In the framework of the WTO the disputes concerning the application of the TRIPS Agreement were initiated against individual Member States, which reached a settlement before the establishment of a panel. See also Section 6.3.2.

[228] A Rosas, 'The European Union and Mixed Agreements' in Dashwood and Hillion (eds), *The general law of EC external relations* (2000), pp 212–13. Govaere, above n 223, p 194. See also below Section 6.3.2.

[229] For the scope and necessity of declarations of competence and disconnection clauses in mixed agreements see Sections 5.1.1 and 6.3.2 respectively.

[230] Opinion 1/00, above n 220, paras 18–21.

[231] Govaere, above n 223, p 195.

[232] Ibid.

common remedy provided in dispute settlement under IIAs,[233] it is obvious that the obligation to pay compensation does not directly affect the validity of challenged EU measures. On the other hand, in cases where restitution or specific performance is required, the awards of arbitral tribunals can review in a binding manner the validity of EU measures to the extent that they are directly enforced in the EU legal order. This is particularly problematic for awards made by the International Centre for Settlement of Investment Disputes (ICSID), considering the strong and efficient implementation mechanism of ICSID awards, which avoid the restrictions posed by the New York Convention on the Recognition and Enforcement of Foreign Arbitration Awards.[234] Hence, if the EU accedes to the ICSID Convention, as is currently envisaged,[235] it has to guarantee in future EU IIAs that ICSID awards demanding specific performance in the form of the annulment of an EU measure will not be directly enforceable in the EU.

As a result, the EU enjoys the competence to enter into IIAs providing for inter-state and investor-state dispute settlement. Nevertheless, this does not mean that its competence is expanded to substantive issues that fall under the exclusive jurisdiction of the ECJ. It is necessary to ensure that a Union agreement cannot confer to an investment tribunal or court the power to adjudicate disputes that can result in a binding interpretation of EU law or affect the delimitation of competences and the powers of EU institutions.

2.7 EU competence to regulate foreign investment in association and cooperation agreements

Regulation of foreign investment is not only the subject of investment-oriented international agreements, but can be part of a broader agreement which may expand to other domains beyond trade and investment. In practice, the EU has concluded a large number of association and cooperation agreements that include provisions on foreign investment, indicating that the EU can regulate foreign investment in the framework of broad association and cooperation agreements. In that respect, a complete and thorough examination of EU competence over foreign investment requires an analysis of the treaty provisions conferring on the EU powers to conclude association agreements as well as development and technical cooperation agreements.

2.7.1 Competence to conclude association agreements

Article 217 TFEU confers on the EU broad competence to conclude association agreements with third countries, which involve 'reciprocal rights and obligations, common action and special procedures'. The vague wording of Article 217 TFEU can actually cover many international agreements, as the concept of association

[233] R Dolzer and C Schreuer, *Principles of International Investment Law* (2008), pp 271–2.
[234] See Section 1.3.5. [235] See Section 3.2.7.4.

and the range of subject matter of the agreement are not defined.[236] The flexibility granted by the Treaty to the EU institutions with regard to the type and subject matter of the agreement appears to allow the EU to regulate foreign investment in its entirety as part of an association agreement under a single legal basis. The fact that the majority of existing EU IIAs were concluded as association agreements illustrates clearly the importance of Article 217 TFEU for EU foreign investment regulation.

The broad scope of Article 217 TFEU was affirmed by the Court in the *Demirel* case,[237] which established very lax criteria for the determination of which agreements can be considered as association agreements and, more importantly, which subject matter can be covered under an association agreement. In particular, the Court considered that association agreements were not only agreements aiming at future accession, but more generally all agreements that created special and privileged links to the EU and required the associated country to take part, to a certain extent, in the Union system.[238] Furthermore, with regard to the covered subject matter, the Court ruled that an association agreement could include commitments towards third countries in all fields covered by primary EU law, thus expanding EU external competence to fields in which the EU has only internal powers. Relations with third countries are omitted from the scope of Treaty provisions.[239]

The expansive interpretation of Article 217 TFEU by the Court empowers the EU to include foreign investment in its entirety in bilateral, regional, and even multilateral agreements. First, the test of a special link which requires the associated country to take part in the Union system is easily passed by all agreements that include foreign investment as part of enhanced economic cooperation. Given that foreign investment is increasingly regulated alongside trade and other economic policy fields as well as social and political cooperation, Article 217 TFEU provides the appropriate legal basis for the conclusion of a broad range of Union agreements with third countries.[240] However, purely foreign investment agreements, having similar content to current BITs, as well as purely economic agreements, fall outside the scope of Article 217 TFEU, as they do not offer the close link to the Union system envisaged by the Court.

With regard to the content of association agreements, Article 217 TFEU provides wide competences to regulate foreign investment. Because it covers all fields found in primary EU law and it is not necessary that relations with third countries fall under the scope of specific Treaty chapters, association agreements can cover all aspects of foreign investment regulation. Similar to the recognition of EU competence to regulate movement of workers with a third country in the *Demirel* case, the EU can regulate establishment of third country nationals and

[236] Eeckhout, above n 13, p 103.

[237] Case 12/86 *Demirel v Stadt Schwäbisch Gmünd* [1987] ECR 3719.

[238] Ibid, para 9; S Peers, 'EC Frameworks of International Relations: Co-operation, Partnership and Association' in Dashwood and Hillion (eds), *The general law of EC external relations* (2000), pp 169–70.

[239] Eeckhout, above n 13, p 105.

[240] For a categorization of the types of association agreements see D Hanf and P Dengler, 'Accords d'Association' (2004) 1 College of Europe Research Paper in Law; Peers, above n 238, p 169.

the provision of services by them, thus being able to regulate the establishment and post-establishment treatment of foreign investors with regard to all categories of foreign investment. Furthermore, it can include provisions on expropriation, on the basis of the objectives and principles of Union law, that can be used for regulating protection of European investors against expropriation in EU law.

As a result, Article 217 TFEU offers the most far-reaching provision granting competence to the EU to regulate foreign investment. Even though the use of association agreements renders void the need for multiple legal bases and precludes the procedural and institutional problems that arise, association agreements are not always the most suitable form for regulating foreign investment. Specific agreements dealing with foreign investment (or trade as well) are excluded from the scope of Article 217 TFEU, while other provisions, such as Article 207 TFEU, offer procedural and institutional advantages for the negotiation and conclusion of those agreements.

2.7.2 Competence to conclude development and technical cooperation agreements

Development cooperation agreements as well as agreements on economic, financial, and technical cooperation provide an alternative framework for the conclusion of agreements that may contain provisions relating to foreign investment. The strong link between foreign investment promotion and protection and economic development, as well as the emphasis on technical cooperation for improving foreign investment flows, illustrate the potential for using Articles 211 and 212(3) TFEU for concluding international agreements pertaining to foreign investment. However, development and technical cooperation agreements are not suitable for regulating substantive questions of foreign investment.

As a matter of principle, agreements pertaining to foreign investment can fall under the scope of Article 211 TFEU: as long as an IIA pursues the objectives of development cooperation, it can be concluded on the basis of that article.[241] This is so, even if the agreement includes measures on other subject matter, as the characterization of an agreement has to be determined with regard to its essential object and not in terms of individual clauses.[242] However, typical IIAs would not qualify as development agreements; especially since their primary objective is to regulate foreign investment as an economic activity and not as a means of contributing to development.[243] This does not imply that development agreements cannot provide

[241] The broad interpretation of the objectives of development agreements was first adopted by the Court in Case C-268/94 *Portugal v Council* [1996] ECR I-6177. For an overview of the case see S Peers, 'Fragmentation or Evasion in the Community's Development Policy? The impact of Portugal v Council' in Dashwood and Hillion (eds), *The general law of EC external relations* (2000), ch 7.

[242] *Portugal v Council*, above n 241, paras 35–9.

[243] In cases of agreements pursuing more than one objective the choice of legal basis rests on the principal aim and object of the agreement. See in particular the Court's judgments in Opinion 2/00 *(Cartagena Protocol)* [2001] ECR I-9713 and *Parliament v Council*, above n 217. See also below Section 3.1.2.1.

a general framework for cooperation in foreign investment matters; it is simply that regulation of foreign investment cannot be the prime objective.

Furthermore, even though a development agreement can include provisions on foreign investment, its content cannot be expanded to regulate substantive aspects of foreign investment. As the Court has already noted, development cooperation agreements cannot impose extensive obligations concerning the specific subject matter included in the agreement, as they are mainly concerned with establishing the framework for cooperation on specific matters.[244] In that regard, Article 211 TFEU would be suitable for the conclusion of an international agreement establishing a general framework for cooperation on foreign investment promotion and protection, without containing any specific legally binding provisions on establishment, treatment, or protection of foreign investors.

Finally, Article 212 TFEU offers another possibility to conclude international agreements pertaining to foreign investment promotion and regulation—it can be primarily used for concluding cooperation agreements with third countries which do not pursue development objectives.[245] However, the positioning of Article 212 TFEU after development cooperation as well as its wording, which resembles that used in Articles 208 and 211 TFEU, indicates that Article 212 TFEU can be used primarily for establishing a general framework for cooperation, without entering into questions of substantive regulation of the specific matters regulated.[246] In that regard, economic, financial, and technical cooperation agreements can provide specific tools and measures that are considered useful for establishing an institutional, regulatory, and infrastructural regime favourable to foreign investment.

2.8 Conclusions

The determination of the scope of EU competence over foreign investment is not an easy task. Foreign investment regulation touches upon different areas of law and encompasses different forms of economic activity. Foreign direct investment, portfolio investment, and concession contracts are only the most common forms of foreign investment, while admission, treatment, and protection of foreign investment relate to completely different normative frameworks. However, foreign investment is a field falling under EU competence, albeit not always exclusive. Until the entry into force of the Lisbon Treaty, EC powers were dispersed and incomplete, impeding the Community from taking external action to regulate foreign investment in

[244] *Portugal v Council*, above n 241, para 45.

[245] Case C-155/07 *Parliament v Council* [2008] ECR I-8103, paras 45–6; in addition, Art 212 TFEU can be used for concluding international agreements pertaining to cooperation in only one specific field. The adoption of the Cultural Diversity Convention on the basis of Art 212 TFEU (Council Decision 2006/515 on the conclusion of the Convention on the Protection and Promotion of the Diversity of Cultural Expressions [2006] OJ L201/15) indicates that this provision can be also used for 'single issue' agreements.

[246] B Martenczuk, 'Cooperation with Developing Countries and Other Third Countries: Elements of a Community Foreign Policy' in Griller and Weidel (eds), *External Economic Relations and Foreign Policy in the European Union*, (2002), pp 406–7.

its entirety. The Lisbon Treaty introduced an explicit reference to foreign investment in Article 207 TFEU, which confers exclusive powers on the EU to regulate FDI. However, primary EU law does not provide a single legal basis for concluding a comprehensive IIA, so that different provisions are relevant for determining the scope of EU competence. Of course, Article 217 TFEU can be used for regulating foreign investment in its entirety; however, the requirement for establishing an association as well as the need for a broader economic, political, and social cooperation framework are non-existent in most IIAs.

Within this patchwork of distinct regulatory concerns and economic activities, the TFEU places greater emphasis on admission and operation of foreign investment. Aiming at liberalization and market access, which have been the main tools for economic integration in the internal market, primary EU law empowers the EU to take external action concerning the admission and operation of foreign investment.

Article 63 TFEU provides for liberalization of capital movements to and from third countries, establishing EU competence which is shared with the Member States. However, the concept of capital movements as well as its relation to the establishment rules of the Treaty indicate that its scope is limited only to portfolio investment and, with regard to FDI, to the actual transfer of assets destined to be used for the initial establishment of FDI, and not to the conditions of initial establishment as such. Although there are certain common rules, portfolio investment and capital transfers related to FDI are an area of shared competence.

Initial establishment–as well as operation of–FDI fall under Article 207 TFEU, which establishes exclusive EU powers and covers issues of initial establishment and partially post-establishment treatment of FDI. Complementing Article 207 TFEU, the TFEU provisions on establishment confer implied powers to the EU with regard to FDI in the transport sector and the operation of foreign-controlled investors that are established in the EU according to Article 54 TFEU. However, such competence is shared with the Member States and exclusivity arises only if the criteria of *AETR* exclusivity are fulfilled. On a similar basis, Article 207 TFEU as well as the provisions on the freedom to provide services are relevant for regulating foreign investment in the form of concession contracts and 'commercial' state contracts.

Performance requirements, investment-related movement of natural persons, and investment guarantee, which are important aspects of foreign investment regulation, present the best example of how foreign investment regulation touches on many areas of law. EU competence to regulate them is primarily based on the specific Treaty provisions dealing with the subject matter. Article 207 TFEU confers exclusive competence with regard to trade-related performance requirements, Article 219 TFEU also confers exclusive competence for foreign exchange performance requirements, but only with regard to Eurozone Member States, and the provisions on competition policy provide competence for including monopoly and state aid rules in an IIA. Articles 79(2)(a) and 77(2)(a) TFEU confer non-exclusive competence to the EU to regulate aspects of investment-related movement of natural persons, which are complemented by Article 207 TFEU insofar as temporary movement of key personnel is concerned.

Protection of foreign investment against expropriation and other political risks is the most widely disputed field of foreign investment regulation in terms of EU competence. Protection of foreign investors' property is neither excluded from EU law nor is it a field where positive action by the EU is not permitted. Article 345 TFEU, which preserves the property ownership system of the Member States, has been interpreted very narrowly, so that its scope concerns only the right of Member States to nationalize private property or privatize public property. It reserves for the Member States only the power to decide if expropriation occurs and not the conditions under which such private property limitations take place. The latter, which is the subject of foreign investment regulation, does not fall within the scope of Article 345 TFEU. On the contrary, the EU has the right to determine the conditions of indirect expropriation of foreign investment resulting from EU measures, while it can also harmonize Member State law on the conditions of expropriation resulting from national measures. Harmonization of the exercise of property rights can be regarded as necessary for the attainment of the objectives of the internal market. As a result, the EU has competence, albeit not exclusive, to include provisions on the protection of foreign investment against expropriation or other political risks in its IIAs.

It is also worth noting that investor-state dispute settlement, which is the most salient feature of IIAs, can be included in IIAs concluded by the EU. As long as investor-state arbitration respects the principles of autonomy of EU law and the jurisdiction of the Court of Justice, the EU has the competence to provide for extensive dispute settlement provisions in its IIAs.

As a result, it is obvious that the EU has competence over the entirety of issues of foreign investment regulation. Article 207 TFEU presents the most important provision, conferring exclusive powers to the EU with regard to many regulatory aspects of foreign investment. However, not all aspects of foreign investment regulation fall under exclusive EU competence. The existence of shared competence in the field of foreign investment indicates that Member States can be actively involved in the formation and conclusion of IIAs in the future. Although the conclusion of pure EU investment agreements is legally possible, the conclusion of future EU IIAs as mixed agreements is also legally possible and, as discussed in the following chapters, even more desirable and realistic, given the political hurdles that exclusion of Member States from external action in the field of foreign investment would create.

3

Conclusion and Content of EU International Investment Agreements

The existence of EU competence in the field of foreign investment would be insufficient, if it were not exercised. The broadening of the scope of EU competence after the Lisbon Treaty and the clear expression of EU institutions to exercise EU competence raises a number of questions regarding the conclusion and content of future EU investment agreements. Nevertheless, future EU international investment agreements (IIAs) would not be the first time that the EU has created international rules on foreign investment. Based on the broad scope of its competence, the EU has already exercised its powers and concluded international agreements relating to foreign investment with third countries.

Provisions on foreign investment are included in the vast majority of the association and cooperation agreements that the EU has concluded with third countries as well as in sectoral and multilateral Union agreements. By examining the exercise of EU competence in the field of foreign investment thus far, this chapter looks first at the conclusion of EU IIAs. Bearing in mind that the rules determining the conclusion of Union agreements differ according to the specific legal basis used, the first section of this chapter takes an instrument-based approach, examining the internal procedures for the conclusion of an IIA by the EU, identifying the different procedural requirements to be fulfilled according to the plurality of legal bases available, and the methods adopted in practice in order to tackle the choice and combination of legal bases as well as the involvement of Member States. Secondly, the scope and content of EU IIAs are explored, adopting a subject-based analysis. The chapter looks separately at each aspect of foreign investment regulation: the provisions of EU IIAs on capital movements, establishment, post-establishment treatment and operation, protection against expropriation, dispute settlement, and investment promotion are identified and grouped in accordance with the breadth of their scope. By analysing the substantive provisions of EU IIAs on foreign investment, emphasis is placed on the influence that EU law, WTO law, and international investment law have exerted on their formation, application, and interpretation. Understanding whether and to what extent EU IIAs borrow elements from the intra-EU investment regime, the General Agreement on Trade in Services

(GATS) and traditional Bilateral Investment Treaties (BITs) and how they combine them, helps to discern the innovations that EU IIAs have brought to international investment law so far, and how these regulatory approaches may affect the content of future EU IIAs.

3.1 Conclusion of EU IIAs

An examination of the procedures and actors involved in the conclusion of EU IIAs has significant institutional and constitutional implications, as it sketches the institutional balance, the legitimacy, and the degree of involvement of Member States in the formation of EU foreign investment policy.[1] In comparison to other Union agreements, the identification of the role granted to EU institutions and Member States presents additional difficulties for EU IIAs. The plurality of primary EU law provisions conferring competence to the EU in the field of foreign investment, in particular under the EC Treaty, which have been used for the conclusion of all EU IIAs so far, complicates the determination not only of the scope and nature of EU competence, but also of the internal procedures for its exercise. Applying the general rules on the conclusion of Union agreements, the need arises first to identify the different voting requirements and the role assigned to EU institutions, in particular the European Parliament, in each power-conferring provision. The procedural implications that arise from the choice of a specific provision as a legal basis thus require an examination of the choice and combinations of legal bases. Adding to the complexities concerning the conclusion of EU IIAs, in practice all existing EU IIAs have been concluded as mixed agreements. Given that, under the EC Treaty foreign investment was a field of shared competence and that investment provisions are included in agreements dealing with a variety of other subject matter, Member States have been directly involved in the conclusion of EU IIAs. However, the conferral of express exclusive competence over foreign direct investment (FDI) in the Lisbon Treaty significantly affects the current legal framework, predicating the conclusion of EU IIAs in the future. The regulatory framework determining the conclusion of EU IIAs is significantly affected by the changes brought by the Lisbon Treaty, which is expected to influence current practice regarding the conclusion of EU IIAs as mixed association agreements. Enhancing parallelism between internal and external powers in this regard and offering a significant role to the Parliament, the Lisbon Treaty adds to the simplification of the procedures for the conclusion of EU IIAs, brings legitimacy in the formation of EU foreign investment policy, and solidifies the effectiveness of its application.

[1] P Koutrakos, 'Legal Basis and Delimitation of Competence in EU External Relations' in Cremona and de Witte (eds), *EU Foreign Relations Law: Constitutional Fundamentals* (2008), pp 171–2; P Eeckhout, *External relations of the European Union: legal and constitutional foundations* (2004), pp 169–70.

3.1.1 Procedural requirements for the conclusion of EU IIAs

The conclusion of EU IIAs follows the general rules that determine the conclusion of international agreements by the EU. The basic legal framework determining the internal procedural requirements that have to be fulfilled regarding the conclusion of international agreements is laid down in Article 218 TFEU. Without affecting the application of the relevant international law rules on the conclusion of international agreements by international organizations,[2] Article 218 TFEU applies to all international contractual commitments undertaken by the EU that have binding legal effect.[3] It is a procedural provision in that it regulates the functions and powers that every EU institution has in the process of concluding an international agreement. Assigning different roles to the EU institutions in the treaty-making process, generally follows the rules for the adoption of internal legislation. The Commission is vested with powers to initiate and conduct negotiations with third parties while the Council and, to a certain extent, the European Parliament form the decision-making body.

However, Article 218 TFEU provides for significant exceptions by creating general links with the procedural characteristics of the substantive power-conferring provisions. Among them, Article 207 TFEU stands out, as the Common Commercial Policy (CCP) has always presented an indispensable legal basis for the conclusion of EU IIAs covering establishment and post-establishment treatment and operation of foreign investment. Considering that the exercise of the CCP is largely conducted through the conclusion of international agreements, Article 207 TFEU distinguishes itself from other substantive power-conferring provisions, as it provides autonomous rules for the negotiation and conclusion of EU IIAs. The importance of the CCP for the conclusion of EU IIAs has been solidified since the Lisbon Treaty—unless investment provisions are included in association agreements, Article 207 TFEU becomes an indispensable legal basis for the conclusion of EU IIAs, which should be complemented by other provisions to the extent that other forms of foreign investment are covered.

In that regard, a combined examination of Articles 218 and 207 TFEU is necessary to identify the procedural rules that affect the conclusion of EU IIAs.

3.1.1.1 Negotiation of EU IIAs

The TFEU grants to the Commission the prerogative to initiate external action and to carry out negotiations with third countries, after having obtained a mandate by the Council. Articles 218(2)–(4) and 207(3) TFEU provide clear wording on the demarcation of the tasks of EU institutions and the order of the steps that

[2] Eeckhout, above n 1, p 175.

[3] Opinion 1/75 [1975] ECR 1355; Case C-327/91 *France v Commission* [1994] ECR I-3641, paras 14–15; Opinion 2/92 (*OECD National Treatment*) [1995] ECR I-521, para II.1. A Rosas, 'The European Union and Mixed Agreements' in Dashwood and Hillion (eds), *The General Law of EC External Relations* (2000), pp 216–17.

need to be taken during the negotiation stage.[4] More specifically, Article 218(2) TFEU grants the prerogative of proposal to the Commission, which may suggest negotiations on a specific topic with a specific country. Based on the Commission's recommendation, the Council, deciding in accordance with the voting requirements applicable for the conclusion of an agreement on the proposed topic, may authorize the Commission to open negotiations on the proposed agreement. The Council's decision grants a negotiating mandate to the Commission, providing general guidelines for the Commission's conduct of the negotiations. Similar to Article 218 TFEU, Article 207(3)(2) TFEU offers to the Commission the privilege to make recommendations for the negotiation and conclusion of an international agreement and to carry out negotiations with third countries, after a mandate to open negotiations is granted by the Council. Although the Commission is free to conduct negotiations within the mandate granted to it, the Council may be actively involved in the negotiations by appointing a special committee to consult and assist the Commission in the negotiations.

The Lisbon Treaty introduces a new relevant actor, granting a formal role to the Parliament at the stage of negotiations of international agreements. Article 218(10) TFEU establishes the right of the Parliament to be fully informed at all stages of the procedure, which is of particular importance for the negotiation of international agreements. A legal obligation on the Commission to inform the Parliament at the stage of negotiations is also included in Article 207(3) TFEU, thus solidifying the right of the Parliament in the field of the CCP.[5] However, this change in essence only recognized the role that the Parliament held at the stage of the negotiations of international agreements under the previous regime, as the Commission was committed by an inter-institutional agreement[6] to forward relevant information on the negotiation process to the Parliament.[7] Although the assignment of a formal role to the Parliament increases legitimacy at the negotiation stage of international agreements, the Lisbon Treaty does not grant a decisive role to the Parliament. Contrary to the conclusion stage of an international agreement, where its consent is required in many instances, the Parliament does not have to give its consent to

[4] J Wouters, D Coppens, and B DeMeester, 'The European Union's External Relations after the Lisbon Treaty' in Griller and Ziller (eds), *The Lisbon Treaty: EU Constitutionalism without a Constitutional Treaty?* (2008), p 182.

[5] M Krajewski, 'External Trade Law and the Constitutional Treaty: Towards a federal and more democratic common Commercial Policy?' (2005) 42 CMLR 91, 123. Wouters, Coppens, and DeMeester, above n 4, p 184.

[6] European Parliament—Rules of Procedure, 15th edn (February 2003) [2003] OJ L61, Art 97 and Annex XIII; Framework Agreement on the relations between European Parliament and the Commission, para 15 [2003] OJ L61/1. On the scope of the inter-institutional agreements see A de Walsche, 'La procédure de conclusion des accords internationaux' in Dony and Louis (eds), *Commentaire J Mégret Relations extérieures* (2005), pp 96–106; R Passos, 'Mixed Agreements from the Perspective of the European Parliament' in Hillion and Koutrakos (eds), *Mixed Agreements Revisited* (2010), pp 272–80.

[7] On the negotiations of international agreements according to Art 218 TFEU see G Zagel, 'Art 300 TEC' in Herzog, Campbell, and Zagel (eds), *Smit and Herzog Law of the European Union: A Commentary* (2005), pp 423–6; Eeckhout, above n 1, pp 170–5; Von der Groeben and Schwartze, *EU-EG Vertrag, Kommentar* (2004), Art 300 EGV, pp 1583–4.

the decision on opening negotiations or defining the negotiation mandate, even if the agreement covers a field where internally its consent is required.[8]

Finally, if an EU IIA concerns monetary and/or foreign-exchange regime matters, then Article 219(3) TFEU establishes an additional institutional actor, assigning a formal role to the European Central Bank (ECB), which must be consulted during the negotiations and the conclusion of agreements concerning monetary and/or foreign-exchange matters.[9]

3.1.1.2 Conclusion of EU IIAs: decision-making in the Council

The signature and conclusion of international agreements is entrusted primarily to the Council, but requiring the assent of the Parliament in many instances. Adopting a decision (or rarely a regulation) which states inter alia the reasons, the legal basis, and the scope of an international agreement, the Council expresses the consent of the EU to be bound by an international agreement.[10] With regard to the voting requirements in order to adopt the decision, Article 218(8) TFEU states that the Council shall act by qualified majority, so that qualified majority voting (QMV) is the basic rule for the conclusion of international agreements under Article 218(8) TFEU. In addition, Article 207(4)(1) TFEU provides that the negotiation and conclusion of international agreements in the field of the CCP are subject to QMV, establishing for the first time a common procedure for all aspects of the CCP without distinguishing between goods, services, FDI, and commercial aspects of IP.

However, Articles 218 and 207 TFEU provide derogations from QMV, requiring that the Council acts unanimously in certain instances. The most important exception relating to the conclusion of EU IIAs concerns the conclusion of association agreements under Article 217 TFEU. Article 218(8) TFEU provides explicitly that the conclusion of association agreements is subject to unanimous voting in the Council. Considering that most EU IIAs that have been concluded were based on former Article 310 TEC (now Art 217 TFEU), the importance of this exception to the QMV rule is highly significant for EU foreign investment regulation.

Secondly, both Articles 218 and 207 TFEU provide that unanimity is required for the negotiation and conclusion of international agreements, insofar as unanimity is required for the adoption of internal rules. This exception to the QMV rule, which confirms the existence of parallelism between internal and external powers at the procedural level as well,[11] is of utmost importance for the conclusion of EU

[8] Wouters, Coppens, and DeMeester, above n 4, p 186.

[9] C Hermann, 'Monetary Sovereignty over the Euro and External Relations of the Euro Area: Competences, Procedures and Practice' (2002) 7 EFA Rev 1, 9–11.

[10] Eeckhout, above n 1, pp 175–6.

[11] J Ceyssens, 'Towards a common foreign investment policy?—Foreign investment in the European constitution' (2005) 32 LIEI 259, 284–5; Krajewski, above n 5, pp 119–20; P-C Müller-Graff, 'The Common Commercial Policy Enhanced by the Reform Treaty of Lisbon?' in Dashwood and Maresceau (eds), *Law and Practice of EU External Relations* (2008), p 200; C Tietje, 'Die Außenwirtschaftsverfassung der EU nach dem Vertrag von Lissabon' (2009) 93 Beiträge zum Transnationalen Wirtschaftsrecht 1, 10. See also Section 2.1.1.

IIAs, since many of the substantive provisions conferring power to the EU over foreign investment require unanimity for the adoption of secondary legislation. In examining the different procedural requirements that are required under the substantive power conferring provisions, it is easy to identify the instances where decision making in the Council requires unanimity.

Starting with the provisions on capital movements, the adoption of secondary legislation in that field does not require, as a rule, unanimity in the Council. EU legislation affecting capital movements to and from third countries, in particular legislation that abolishes the restrictions allowed under Article 64(1) TFEU, are adopted under the QMV rule. Nevertheless, unanimity is required when an EU measure results in a limitation of the existing level of liberalization.[12] Hence, the conclusion of EU IIAs that include provisions on capital movements follows the QMV rule, unless the EU IIA provisions provide for additional restrictions to capital movements in comparison to the existing level of liberalization, where decision making in the Council is subject to unanimity.

Regarding EU IIAs that include provisions on the establishment and operation of foreign investment, the QMV rule applies insofar as they are based on the primary EU law provisions on establishment. Since the adoption of secondary legislation, in particular according to Article 50 TFEU, follows the ordinary legislative procedure described in Article 294 TFEU,[13] there is no need for unanimity in the Council when concluding an EU IIA on this legal basis. The QMV rule also applies when an EU IIA includes provisions on foreign investment in the form of concession contracts or on specific aspects of post-establishment operation of foreign investment, since Article 59 TFEU does not require unanimity for the adoption of secondary legislation. In addition, the conclusion of an EU IIA including provisions on investment promotion or establishing a general framework for cooperation on foreign investment matters based on Articles 209 and 212 TFEU follows the QMV rule set in Article 218 TFEU.[14]

However, the conclusion of an EU IIA including provisions on the protection of foreign investment against expropriation would require unanimity. As the adoption of internal legislation on expropriation of non-direct investment would be based on Articles 115 and/or 352 TFEU,[15] the conclusion of an EU IIA including provisions on expropriation would require unanimous voting in the Council, since both provisions require that the Council acts unanimously for the adoption of internal legislation after consulting the Parliament. As a result, the conclusion of an EU IIA requires unanimity if it restricts liberalization of capital movements and/or results in harmonization in the internal market, in particular by including provisions on the protection of foreign investors against expropriation.

Thirdly, an additional derogation from the QMV rule relevant for the conclusion of EU IIAs is provided in paragraph (4)(3) of Article 207 TFEU which

[12] J Handoll, *Capital, Payments and Money Laundering in the European Union* (2006), pp 146–7; Von der Groeben and Schwartze, *EU-EG Vertrag, Kommentar* (2004), Art 57 EGV, pp 1769–70.

[13] Art 294 TFEU, which establishes the ordinary procedure for internal decision making, provides for QMV in the Council, and requires the assent of the Parliament.

[14] Eeckhout, above n 1, p 118.

[15] See Section 2.5.3.

requires unanimity for the conclusion of EU IIAs covering cultural and audio-visual services 'where these agreements risk prejudicing the Union's cultural and linguistic diversity' and social, education, and health services 'where these risk seriously disturbing the national organization of such services and prejudicing the responsibility of Member States to deliver them.' Although this provision to a large extent resembles the unanimity rule provided in Article 133(6) TEC with regard to the same service sectors,[16] it is less broad as it does not require unanimity whenever FDI in these service sectors is concerned. It is only where the conclusion of an international agreement poses risks to the cultural and linguistic diversity and the national organization and delivery of these services that unanimity is required. Consequently, this provision requires a risk assessment whenever FDI in these service sectors is involved. However, the Treaty does not lay down the means for how such risk assessment should be conducted, nor does it establish the minimum levels of risk that should exist in order for unanimity to apply.[17] Arguably, this ambiguity may result in the application of the unanimity rule in all cases concerning FDI in these service sectors, thus recognizing the concerns of a number of Member States which insisted on the inclusion of subparagraph 3 in the final text of Article 207(4) TFEU.[18]

Fourthly, it should be noted that Article 207 TFEU does away with the provision according to which unanimity is required for the negotiation and conclusion of commercial policy agreements on subject matter on which internal powers have not been yet exercised. Article 133(5)(2) TEC required unanimity also for the negotiation and conclusion of international agreements on subject matter for which internal powers had not been yet exercised. This provision created much ambiguity regarding the determination of the internal rules necessary for avoiding unanimity and the assessment of the extent to which they should cover the topic of the proposed agreement.[19] Abolishing this derogation from the QMV rule, the Lisbon Treaty establishes complete parallelism between internal and external competences

[16] C Hermann, 'Common Commercial Policy after Nice: Sisyphus would have done a better job' (2002) 39 CMLR 7, 24.

[17] Krajewski, above n 5, p 122; Wouters, Coppens, and DeMeester, above n 4, pp 184–5.

[18] M Krajewski, 'The Reform of the Common Commercial Policy' in Biondi and Eeckhout (eds), *European Union Law after the Treaty of Lisbon* (2011, forthcoming).

[19] Considering that a broad interpretation of the unanimity requirement would allow Member States to block international agreements on a matter even though they could not obstruct the adoption of internal legislation in that field, it was convincingly argued that the requirement of unanimity should have been narrowly interpreted, because otherwise the QMV rule would have been rendered void and the exception of Art 133(5)(2) TEC would become the rule. Hermann, above n 16, pp 23–4; HG Krenzler and C Pitschas, 'Progress or Stagnation? The Common Commercial Policy After Nice' (2001) 6 EFA Rev 291, 305–6. Cremona (M Cremona, 'A Policy of Bits and Pieces? The Common Commercial Policy after Nice' (2001) 4 CYELS 61, 77) argues that the logic behind this restriction is that it potentially raises controversies internally with regard to whether they should be adopted by QMV and should be subject to unanimity in external relations, as 'an internal QMV "mistake" is easier to rectify than an international contractual commitment'. This argument actually speaks in favour of a narrow interpretation of the unanimity rule where no internal legislation exists, so that unanimity is required only in controversial fields, where no internal legislation exists.

and avoids the ambiguities raised with regard to the scope and extent of internal rules that had to exist in order for QMV to apply.[20]

Lastly, it should be noted that Article 207 TFEU, unlike Article 133(6) TEC, does not make any reference to horizontal agreements, namely agreements that also 'concern' areas covered by the unanimity rule, as mentioned above. However, the lack of a provision requiring unanimity in such cases should not be interpreted as abandoning the need for unanimity when such is required for the adoption of one part of an international agreement according to subparagraphs 2 and 3 of Article 207(4) TFEU, as it would be practically impossible to apply a predominant purpose analysis in such cases. In that regard, unanimity is required not only in cases where the subject matter requiring unanimity forms a substantial part of the proposed agreement but also in cases where it is ancillary to the main subject matter of the agreement.[21]

As a result, it appears that unanimity has been and will remain the primary rule for conclusion of EU IIAs in the future. This is so, not only because the EU favours the inclusion of investment provisions in association agreements, but also in cases of the conclusion of purely foreign investment agreements. The inclusion of provisions on expropriation in EU IIAs would require a unanimous decision of the Council, as it would bring harmonization of internal rules on the protection of property. Additionally, even if expropriation remained outside the scope of EU IIAs, the existence of provisions on establishment and treatment of FDI in cultural, audiovisual, social, education, and health services, which are part of all EU IIAs so far, require unanimity.

3.1.1.3 Conclusion of EU IIAs: the role of the Parliament

Turning to the role of the European Parliament, it is necessary to distinguish between the previous EU constitutional regime that has so far determined the conclusion of EU IIAs and the changes brought about by the Lisbon Treaty, which affects the institutional balance struck under the EC Treaty, as it provides a more active role for the Parliament. Article 300(3) TEC provided for the limited involvement of the Parliament in the conclusion of EU IIAs, while Article 133 TEC did not formally recognize any role for the Parliament, excluding in practice the CCP from the supervisory, consultative, and legislative role of the European Parliament.[22] Although the minimal role of the Parliament could be justified by the practical concerns that the conclusion of international agreements raise, since after the adoption of the text of an international agreement there is in principle

[20] Krajewski, above n 5, p 121.

[21] Opinion 1/2008 [2009] ECR I-11129, paras 141–2; M Cremona, 'Balancing Union and Member State interests: Opinion 1/2008, choice of legal basis and the common commercial policy under the Treaty of Lisbon' (2010) 35 EL Rev 678, 691; See also the Opinion of AG Kokott in Case C-13/07 *Commission v Council (Vietnam Accession to the WTO)*, delivered on 26 March 2009, where she argues that any agreement even marginally covering the services covered under Art 133(6) TEC is subject to unanimous voting in the Council (paras 116–20, 134).

[22] D Thym, 'Parliamentary Involvement in European International Relations' in Cremona and de Witte (eds), *EU Foreign Relations Law: Constitutional Fundamentals* (2008), pp 214–15.

no more possibility to change or amend it, this position has been subject to severe criticism for upsetting the inter-institutional balance and affecting the legitimacy of international agreements.[23] Taking these concerns into account, Article 207 alongside Article 218 TFEU render the Parliament a co-legislator in the field of foreign investment, following the trend of granting a wider role to the Parliament and enhancing the legitimacy of external relations.[24]

More specifically, Article 218(6) TFEU provides that the conclusion of international agreements requires, as a rule, that the Parliament is only consulted, without requiring the Council to follow its opinion. However, this rule is not absolute, as Article 218(6)(2)(a) TFEU identifies the specific instances under which the assent of the Parliament is necessary. First, the assent of the Parliament is needed for the conclusion of association agreements according to Article 217 TFEU, thus establishing an explicit derogation for all EU IIAs adopted on that specific legal basis. The broad scope of competence conferred on the EU under Article 217 TFEU, which enables it to include a variety of provisions having significant institutional, budgetary, and regulatory implications, justifies the involvement of the Parliament and the need for consensus in the Council.[25]

Secondly, the assent of the Parliament is required for the agreements that provide for cooperation procedures with the other party to the agreement through the establishment of an institutional framework. Considering that most international agreements establish some type of institutional framework, this requirement should be interpreted as applying to agreements that create independent institutions, such as international organizations, which provide decision-making bodies with a power to take legally binding decisions.[26]

Thirdly, the Parliament must consent to the conclusion of agreements having important budgetary implications for the EU.[27] In that regard, the consent of the Parliament can be necessary for the conclusion of EU IIAs, in particular if they provide for financial aid as a means of investment promotion and/or assign the management of such aid to institutions established under the agreement.

Fourthly, the last indent of Article 218(6)(2)(a) TFEU provides that the consent of the Parliament is necessary for the conclusion of international agreements that cover 'fields to which either the ordinary legislative procedure applies, or the special

[23] Thym,, above n 22, pp 228–31; R Bieber, 'Democratic Control of International Relations of the European Union' in Cannizzaro (ed), *The European Union as an actor in international relations* (2002), p 105.

[24] M Cremona, 'The Draft Constitutional Treaty: External Relations and External Action' (2003) 40 CMLR 1348, 1364.

[25] S Peers, 'EC Frameworks of International Relations: Co-operation, Partnership and Association' in Dashwood and Hillion (eds), *The general law of EC external relations* (2000), pp 169–70; Von der Groeben and Schwartze, *EU-EG Vertrag, Kommentar* (2004), Art 310 EGV, pp 1765–6.

[26] F Hoffmeister, 'Outsider or Frontrunner? Recent Developments under International and European Law on the Status of the European Union in International Organizations and Treaty Bodies' (2007) 44 EFA Rev 41, 62–5; Thym, above n 22, pp 212–13.

[27] The criteria for determining the financial importance of an agreement are the duration of the financial obligations, and the comparison of the financial obligations arising from the agreement to the overall EU spending for external operations in the field covered. Case C-189/97 *European Parliament v Council* [1999] ECR I-4741, paras 26–34; Eeckhout, above n 1, pp 178–9.

legislative procedure where consent by the European Parliament is required'. This provision substituted the narrower exception provided in Article 300(3) TEC, according to which agreements that amended an act of internal Community legislation adopted under the co-decision procedure required the assent of the Parliament.[28] In that regard, Article 218 TFEU expands the legislative role of the Parliament from agreements requiring the amendment of pre-existing legislation to any agreement covering a field where its consent is required. Considering that Articles 64, 50, 59, 209, and 212 TFEU, which are relevant for the conclusion of EU IIAs,[29] provide for the adoption of internal legislation according to the ordinary legislative procedure, the conclusion of EU IIAs including provisions on portfolio investment, investment in the form of concession contracts, and investment promotion requires the assent of Parliament.

In examining the fields where the consent of the Parliament is necessary for the adoption of internal legislation, it is striking that the Lisbon Treaty introduces a radical change to decision-making rules in the field of the CCP, as the Parliament acquires an indispensable role in its formation and implementation.[30] According to Article 207(2) TFEU the CCP is a field where the ordinary legislative procedure applies for the adoption of autonomous legislation, requiring the consent of the Parliament.[31] That consent is necessary not only for the adoption of autonomous measures, but also for the negotiation and conclusion of international agreements.[32] Article 207(3) TFEU refers back to Article 218 TFEU, which applies to trade agreements to the extent that Article 207 TFEU does not provide specific rules. Given that Article 207 TFEU provides detailed rules concerning only decision making in the Council, Article 218(6) TFEU on the role of the Parliament applies also to commercial policy agreements.[33] The application of Article 218(6) TFEU is further supported by the fact that this paragraph does not

[28] This exception rendered the position of the Parliament in internal legislative procedures relevant for the conclusion of international agreements, to the extent that secondary legislation had been adopted and it had to be amended in order to be compatible with the provision of the international agreement. Thym, above n 22, pp 208–9.

[29] See above Section 3.1.1.2.

[30] Under the EC Treaty, the only provision that could potentially establish a role for the Parliament in the field of the CCP would appear to be the reference to Art 300 TEC in Art 133(6)(2) TEC, which introduced a potential role for consultations with the Parliament in agreements concerning cultural, educational, and public health issues. Hermann, above n 16, p 25; I Bosse-Platiére, 'Le Parlement européen et les relations extérieures de la Communauté européenne après le Traite de Nice' (2002) 39 RTD Eur 527, 533.

[31] Krajewski, above n 5, p 123; M Cremona, 'A Constitutional Basis for Effective External Action? An assessment of the provisions on EU External Action in the Constitutional Treaty', EUI Working Paper 2006/30, p 30; P Koutrakos, *EU International Relations Law* (2006), p 150.

[32] It is argued that the consent of the Parliament is required only for the conclusion of international agreements that need to be implemented by secondary legislation, the adoption of which requires the consent of the Parliament (Krajewski, above n 18). However, the wording of Art 218(6)(v) TFEU demands the consent of the Parliament where an international agreement covers fields where the ordinary legislative procedure applies, irrespective of whether internal legislation is adopted or has to be adopted to implement the international agreement.

[33] Krajewski, above n 5, pp 122–4.

contain an explicit derogation for commercial policy agreements from its scope, as did Article 300(3) TEC.[34]

In summary, the Parliament has already had a significant role in the conclusion of EU IIAs, which is significantly strengthened by the Lisbon Treaty, so that its assent will be required for their conclusion in the future. The inclusion of foreign investment provisions in association agreements, which is the case for the vast majority of EU IIAs, has been the main mechanism for securing the role of the Parliament in EU foreign investment regulation thus far. The expansion of the role of the Parliament after the Lisbon Treaty in Articles 218(6) and 207 TFEU requires in essence the involvement of the Parliament in the conclusion of all future EU IIAs.

3.1.2 Conclusion of EU IIAs in practice

3.1.2.1 The choice of legal basis

The diversity of the procedural requirements in the various power-conferring provisions indicates that the choice of legal basis has significant implications for the conclusion of an EU IIA. It affects the institutional balance by determining the role of each institution 'in the institutional structure of the [Union] and the accomplishment of the tasks entrusted to the [Union]'.[35] In addition, it serves as an indicator of the scope and nature of EU competence, determining the international posture of the EU and the degree of involvement of Member States in the formation of an EU foreign investment policy.[36] In that regard, the choice of an appropriate legal basis becomes more important in cases where the scope of an international agreement could justify the use of more than one provision as a legal basis.

Recognizing these concerns, the European Court has insisted that the choice of a legal basis must rest on objective factors, amenable to judicial review.[37] Ensuring the application of a correct institutional balance and demarcating the scope and (exclusive) nature of EU competence, the Court adopted an aim and content test

[34] It could be argued that the requirement for the consent of the Parliament in the entire field of the CCP breaks the institutional balance between internal and external competences of the Union, as in the internal market, there are still areas to which the ordinary legislative procedure does not apply and decision making is assigned only to the Council. Eg, Art 115 TFEU on approximation of laws relating to the movement of persons, thus including establishment, grants only a consultative role to the Parliament. Nevertheless, this derogation from parallelism appears necessary in order to ensure the effective application of the CCP, as a common approach to decision making can lead to the avoidance of inter-institutional conflict. Also, the enhancement of democratic legitimacy of external economic relations beyond the degree of internal democratic legitimacy should be viewed positively, as it demonstrates the need for a more active role of the Parliament in economic affairs and external relations.

[35] Case C-70/88 *European Parliament v Council* [1990] ECR I-2041, para 21.

[36] Koutrakos, above n 1, pp 172–4; M Cremona, 'Defining Competence in EU External Relations: Lessons from the Treaty Reform Process' in Dashwood and Maresceau (eds), *Law and Practice of EU External Relations* (2008), pp 39–40.

[37] Case C-54/86 *Commission v Council (GSP)* [1987] ECR I-01493; Case C-300/89 *Commission v Council (Titanium dioxide)* [1991] ECR I-1689.

in order to define the proper legal basis.[38] In cases where an EU measure has more than one purpose or a dual component, the Court has found that if one of those is identifiable as the main or predominant purpose or component, whereas the other is merely incidental, an EU act must be based only on the one required by the main or predominant purpose or component. However, if it is established that the act simultaneously pursues a number of objectives or has several diverse but linked components, without one being secondary and indirect in relation to the other, such an act will have to be founded on the various corresponding legal bases.[39]

Applying the criteria of aim and content to EU IIAs, it is difficult to determine *in abstracto* the appropriate legal basis for their conclusion. As discussed below,[40] EU IIAs vary significantly in terms of content, as they regulate different aspects of foreign investment. More importantly, all EU IIAs concluded so far do not deal exclusively with foreign investment, as it is only one of the subject matter covered. But even if foreign investment were the only subject matter of a Union agreement, it would be difficult to choose only one legal basis between the relevant substantive provisions. Considering the diversity of the EC Treaty power-conferring provisions, each of them carried equal weight in terms of fulfilling the general objective of regulating foreign investment or covering the 'main' aspects of foreign investment regulation.[41]

The lack of a specific provision covering at least the most significant aspects of foreign investment required the use of multiple legal bases for the conclusion of EU IIAs. Indeed, to the extent that an EU IIA covered a specific aspect of foreign investment, all relevant EC Treaty provisions were used together as legal bases. For example, the Partnership and Co-operation Agreement (PCA) with Armenia was concluded on the basis of Articles 44, 47, 55, 57, 71, 80, 93, 94, 133, and 308 TEC,[42] and for the conclusion of the Energy Charter Treaty (ECT) Articles 44, 47, 55, 57, 83, 93, 94, 133, 175, and 308 TEC were used as legal bases.[43] These agreements illustrate that, although foreign investment regulation may not have been the main objective or content of a Union agreement, the relevant EC Treaty provisions had to be included as a legal basis for the conclusion of Union agreements that included legally binding obligations on foreign investment matters.

[38] See Opinion 2/00 (*Carthagena Protocol on Biodiversity*) [2001] ECR I-9713; Case C-281/01 *Commission v Council (the Energy Star Agreement)* [2002] ECR I-12049; Case C-94/03 *Commission v Council (Rotterdam Convention)* [2006] ECR I-1; Joined Cases C-317/04 & C-318/*04 European Parliament v Council (PNR)* [2006] ECR I-4721. For an analysis of these cases and the importance of the choice of legal basis see Koutrakos, above n 1, pp 176–85.

[39] Case C-411/06 *Commission v European Parliament and Council (Waste Shipments)* [2009] ECR I-7585, paras 45–6; Case C-178/03 *Commission v European Parliament and Council* [2006] ECR I-107, paras 35 and 47.

[40] See below section 3.2.

[41] Opinion 1/2008, above n 21, para 140; Cremona, above n 21, p 688.

[42] 1999/602/EC, ECSC, Euratom: Council and Commission Decision of 31 May 1999 on the conclusion of the Partnership and Cooperation Agreement between the European Communities and their Member States, of the one part, and the Republic of Armenia, of the other part, [1999] OJ L239/1.

[43] 98/181/EC, ECSC, Euratom: Council and Commission Decision of 23 September 1997 on the conclusion, by the European Communities, of the Energy Charter Treaty and the Energy Charter Protocol on energy efficiency and related environmental aspects [1998] OJ L069/1.

The use of multiple legal bases has significant implications on the procedural requirements for the conclusion of EU IIAs. Recourse to more than one legal basis is possible only if the decision-making procedures laid down in various provisions are not incompatible with each other, in particular if they do not undermine the role of the Parliament.[44] As a result, depending on the scope of the investment provisions, the conclusion of EU IIAs requires in most instances unanimity in the Council as well as the assent of the Parliament.

The only instance where the conclusion of an EU IIA had a single legal basis was the inclusion of foreign investment provisions in association agreements. Indeed, the vast majority of EU IIAs were concluded on the basis of Article 310 TEC (now Art 217 TFEU), incorporating aspects of foreign investment regulation within their content. Aiming to cover most aspects of external economic relations, association agreements have included provisions on foreign investment alongside international trade and other economic regulation.

3.1.2.2 EU IIAs as mixed agreements

Alongside the choice of legal basis, an important concern for the conclusion of EU IIAs has been the degree of direct involvement of Member States. As discussed, foreign investment was, and still remains, a field of shared competence, so that Member States can be autonomously involved in the conclusion of IIAs with third countries. Exercising their powers, Member States have been eager to participate directly alongside the EU in the conclusion of international agreements with third countries, which take the form of mixed agreements. Indeed, all EU IIAs concluded so far are mixed agreements.

Of course, mixity is not a unique characteristic of EU IIAs, as it follows a long-established practice in EU external relations.[45] In fact, the mixed character of EU IIAs does not result only from the existence of investment provisions: direct involvement by the Member States can be better explained if it is taken into account that all EU IIAs cover other subject matter as well, which fall under either the exclusive or concurrent competence of Member States. Nevertheless, the conclusion of EU IIAs as mixed agreements has significant implications not only for their negotiation and conclusion, but more importantly for their application and implementation. The inclusion of foreign investment provisions in mixed agreements generates a number of international and EU law questions stemming from the lack of precise determination on the part of the actor exercising its competence.[46]

In considering the implications of the mixed procedure on the negotiation and conclusion of EU IIAs, the difficulties arising from the need for coherence

[44] *Commission v Council (Rotterdam Convention)*, above n 38, para 52.

[45] On the origins and development of mixed agreements see J Heliskoski, *Mixed Agreements as a technique for organizing the international relations of the European Community and its Member States* (2001), pp 27–69; A Rosas, 'The European Union and Mixed Agreements' in Dashwood and Hillion (eds), *The general law of EC external relations* (2000), ch 13.

[46] On the international and EU law issues that arise from the mixed nature of EU IIAs regarding the application and implementation of foreign investment provisions see Sections 5.1, 6.1, and 6.3.

and coordination should be noted. The involvement of a plurality of actors threatens the unity and the efficiency of the external representation of the EU and its Member States as well as the internal delimitation and balance of power.[47] The need to tackle these concerns reveals the fundamental role of the duty of cooperation, which determines the procedural obligations of EU institutions and Member States at the stage of negotiation and conclusion of mixed agreements.[48]

3.1.2.3 Conclusion of EU IIAs after the Lisbon Treaty

Following the 'silence' of the EC Treaty, the Lisbon Treaty also omits to deal with questions regarding the choice of legal basis and mixed agreements.[49] However, the substantial changes to the scope and nature of EU competence over foreign investment will definitely have an impact on the conclusion of EU IIAs in the future.

More specifically, the inclusion of FDI under the CCP may minimize the need for using multiple legal bases in order to conclude an EU IIA. To the extent that EU IIAs are covering only FDI, Article 207 TFEU will be the relevant legal basis. Given, however, that a complete legal framework on foreign investment also covers the other forms of foreign investment, even if the main focus is on FDI, the use of multiple legal bases will still be necessary for the conclusion of EU IIAs. As the Court reasoned in Opinion 1/2008, it would be difficult to use a predominant/incidental purpose analysis, due to its crucial implications for Member State participation in future EU IIAs and given that such reasoning would contravene the explicit boundaries on competences set out in the Treaties.[50] In addition, the continuance of the current practice of including foreign investment provisions in association or cooperation agreements dealing with a variety of other subject matter will entail the use of Article 217 TFEU or multiple legal bases.

As for the involvement of Member States, the exclusive nature of FDI competence under the CCP indicates that Member States will have a minor role in the conclusion of EU IIAs. However, the existence of shared competence over the other forms of foreign investment will enable Member States to preserve mixity for the conclusion of EU IIAs. Also, the conclusion of EU IIAs as mixed agreements will continue as long as foreign investment is included within broader association and cooperation agreements. Nevertheless, even in such cases the legal effects of mixity on the FDI provisions will be different due to the exclusive nature of EU competence.

[47] For a detailed analysis see Heliskoski, above n 45, pp 78–86, 95–100; F Hoffmeister, 'Curse or Blessing? Mixed Agreements in the Recent Practice of the European Union and its Member States' in Hillion and Koutrakos (eds), *Mixed Agreements Revisited* (2010), pp 253–67.

[48] M Cremona, 'Defending the Community Interest: the Duties of Cooperation and Compliance' in Cremona and de Witte (eds), *EU Foreign Relations Law - Constitutional Fundamentals* (2008), pp 158–61; Heliskoski, above n 45, pp 61–7.

[49] Cremona, above n 36, p 41.

[50] Cremona, above n 21, pp 688–90.

3.2 Scope and content of EU IIAs

Foreign investment provisions are included in a significant number of Union agreements that differ in nature and scope, which is reflected in the different manner in which they approach foreign investment. Taking a glance at existing EU IIAs, it is necessary to distinguish the GATS, the ECT, and the European Economic Area (EEA) Agreement, because these have been adopted in an entirely different context in comparison to bilateral EU IIAs and they influence, to a large extent, the scope and content of the latter. Acknowledging these differences and taking them into account, this chapter examines all EU IIAs together, aiming to underscore their common characteristics and their differences. Without undermining the different value and importance of the GATS, the ECT, and the EEA Agreement, this chapter focuses on the normative value of their investment provisions, which are viewed comparatively with the investment provisions found in bilateral EU IIAs.

Within this context, EU IIAs appear to present a unique model of international regulation of foreign investment which departs from the traditional BIT or IIA form. In fact, the scope and content of most EU IIAs is better understood if it is viewed under the prism of the influence exerted on its formation by primary EU law, WTO law, and international investment law, in particular BITs, and the effects that the latter have on the application and interpretation of EU IIA investment provisions. In that respect, a thorough analysis of the substantive rules of EU IIAs primarily requires the identification of the different types and content of EU IIA provisions regarding each aspect of foreign investment regulation.

Nevertheless, future EU IIAs may follow an entirely different pattern than existing EU IIAs. Bearing in mind the broad scope of EU competence over foreign investment after Lisbon and, more importantly, the clear intention of the Commission to transform the EU into the main player in the field of foreign investment, it remains to be seen whether the EU will promote the insertion in future EU IIAs of more traditional BIT-oriented provisions and how it will attempt to integrate them with the existing models of regulation of foreign investment that it has developed in agreements with third countries.

3.2.1 EU IIA provisions on capital movements

Regulation of capital movements is a key subject of most Union agreements. Legally binding commitments on capital movements are found in the EEA Agreement, the Stability and Association Agreements (SAAs), all Euro-Mediterranean Agreements (EMAs) and PCAs, in the Association Agreements with Mexico, Chile, South Africa, and the CARIFORUM states, Korea, and in the ECT.[51] Reflecting the belief that free movement of capital constitutes a prerequisite for an increase of foreign investment flows, these EU IIAs provide widely for liberalization of capital movements, focusing primarily on those related to foreign investment. Creating

[51] See Section 1.3.2.1.

international obligations in a field of foreign investment covered only partially by BITs, EU IIAs express the willingness of the EU to export its economic liberalization model. They reaffirm the openness of the EU towards capital movements to and from third countries, as expressed in Article 63 TFEU, and complement it with binding commitments from third countries, thus offering added value to the EU's unilateral liberalization of capital movements, which is not subject to reciprocity.[52]

3.2.1.1 Determining capital movements: exclusion of portfolio investment

Despite the common reference to capital movements in all EU IIAs, the determination of the transactions covered varies between agreements. Many restrict the definition of capital movements, thus differentiating themselves from the broad notion adopted in EU law.[53] For foreign investment, it is important to note that all agreements cover capital transfers related to direct investments, while a number of agreements also expand their coverage to portfolio investment.

More specifically, all the above-mentioned EU IIAs ensure that capital movements related to direct investment are liberalized, subject to certain restrictions. While only a few agreements include a general reference to capital movements—also encompassing movements relating to direct investment[54]—most refer explicitly to direct investment,[55] mainly in order to limit the scope of liberalization, which may otherwise cover portfolio investment and capital movements related to personal or other business activities. It is notable that all agreements granting establishment rights provide explicitly that freedom of capital is ensured not only for direct investments made in accordance with national laws but also for those made in accordance with their establishment provisions.

Considering the type of capital movements covered, EU IIAs make explicit reference only to 'the liquidation or repatriation of [direct] investments and of any profit stemming therefrom'. This does not mean that other types of capital movements are not covered: drawing parallels with BIT language, they simply indicate the most important and ambiguous types of capital movements covered under liberalization rules. For example, the PCA with Russia goes further, indicating that capital movement rules also include, 'any compensation payments arising from measures such as expropriation, nationalization or measures of equivalent effect'.[56]

[52] M Sideek, *European Community Law on the Free Movement of Capital and the EMU* (1999), pp 231–2.

[53] See Section 1.2.2.3.

[54] Art 40 of the EEA Agreement and Arts 31, 49, and 31 of the EMAs with Israel, Jordan, and Lebanon respectively.

[55] Arts 61(1), 60(1),63(1) 63(1), and 59(1) of the SAAs with Albania, Croatia, Montenegro, Serbia, and the Former Yugoslav Republic of Macedonia; Arts 39, 32, 34, 28, and 32 of the EMAs with Algeria, Egypt, Morocco, Palestine, and Tunisia; Arts 41, 41, 41, 41, 41, 47, 52, 48, and 40 of the PCAs with Armenia, Azerbaijan, Georgia, Kazakhstan, Kyrgyzstan, Moldova, Russia, Ukraine, and Uzbekistan; Arts 8.2(1), 123(1), 165, and 33(1) of the agreements with Korea, the CARIFORUM states, Chile, and South Africa; Art 32 of the EU-Mexico Services Agreement.

[56] Art 52 of the PCA with Russia.

An exception to the general reference to capital movements is found in the ECT, which adopts more traditional language. Article 14(1) ECT provides a right of free transfers related to investment, similar to that found under numerous BITs. Without referring to capital movements, it includes an indicative list of types of transfers subject to liberalization—including, among others, initial capital, returns, liquidation of assets, repatriation of profits, and compensation payments. This extensive enumeration, which coincides with the types of capital movements covered under bilateral EU IIAs, indicates that EU IIAs cover the same subject matter as BIT provisions on transfer of assets, albeit in a different manner, as in each type of provision there are different restrictions.

Contrary to direct investments, portfolio investment does not fall under the scope of most EU IIAs. With the exception of the ECT, which includes portfolio investment under its definition of investment[57] as it adopts a broad definition of investment according to international investment law,[58] most bilateral EU IIAs do not cover this area. It is only the EEA Agreement, the Free Trade Agreement (FTA) with Korea,[59] the EMAs with Israel, Jordan, and Lebanon,[60] and the SAA with Montenegro[61] that liberalize portfolio investment, by including portfolio investment in the scope of their capital movement provisions. In addition, all SAAs, with the exception of the agreement with Montenegro, provide for the future liberalization of capital movements relating to portfolio investment after a transitional period.[62] However, the remaining agreements do not extend their scope to portfolio investment, including, at best, a call to the parties' best endeavours for future expansion of their liberalizing provisions to capital movements related to portfolio investment.[63]

3.2.1.2 Scope of liberalization of capital movements

All EU IIAs provide for the liberalization of capital movements relating to foreign investment. However, liberalization is subject to specific exceptions serving economic, monetary, and the broader public interests of the parties. A first significant exception, common to a large number of agreements, restricts free movement only to EU capital, thus allowing EU counterparties to impose further restrictions on their outward investment to EU countries. Aiming at retaining domestic capital, so as to stimulate domestic investments and avoid potential negative consequences arising from capital exports,[64] the EMAs with Algeria, Morocco, Palestine, and

[57] Art 1(6) ECT. [58] See Section 1.2.1.2.5.

[59] Art 8.2(2) and (3) provide for free movement of capital relating to non-direct investment according to the laws of the host country as well as for a standstill and rollback clause, prohibiting the introduction of new restrictions.

[60] See above n 54.

[61] Art 63(4).

[62] Arts 61(2), 60(2), 63(4), and 59(2) of the SAAs with Albania, Croatia, Serbia, and the Former Yugoslav Republic of Macedonia.

[63] Eg Art 52(8) of the PCA with Russia.

[64] S Fares, 'Current Payments and Capital Movements in the EU-Mediterranean Association Agreements' (2003) 30 LIEI 15, 21–4; B Kiekebeld and D Smit, 'Freedom of establishment and free movement of capital in Association Agreements and direct taxation' (2007) 35 International Tax Review 216, 224.

Tunisia, the PCAs with Azerbaijan and Russia, as well as the ECT enable these countries to control outward investments.[65] However, this restriction applies only to residents of these countries and does not cover capital movements relating to investments made by EU nationals established in those countries, for whom the general rules of free movement apply. The aim of this provision is to reassure European investors that their invested capital can be freely repatriated and reinvested, which would otherwise frustrate the right of EU investors to freely transfer capital related to the investment.

Secondly, the EMAs with Jordan, Israel, and Lebanon as well as the PCA with Russia include a standstill clause, providing that the contracting parties have the right to maintain existing restrictions, without however being able to introduce new ones.[66] Starting with the PCA provision, the standstill clause—which became applicable five years after the entry into force of the agreement—presents the next step towards the progressive liberalization of capital movements. Its importance for foreign investment lies mainly in the prohibition of further restrictions on outward investments and portfolio investment by the Russian Federation, thus leading gradually to complete liberalization. While having a similar rationale, the existence of this restriction in the EMAs is mainly of considerable importance for non-direct investment-related capital movements. Since these agreements cover all capital movements, the insertion of a standstill clause was considered necessary in order to preserve the broader public policy interests of the parties and prepare their adaptation to a regime of complete liberalization.[67]

Thirdly, most EU IIAs enable the parties to adopt restrictive measures justified by public policy, public security, or public health reasons[68] and exclude from the scope of their capital movement rules any measures covered under double taxation agreements.[69] Without duplicating the wording of Article 65 TFEU, they establish a similar regime, safeguarding the exceptions to free movement of capital enunciated in that provision.[70]

Fourthly, most EU IIAs provide that the contracting parties have the right to restrict capital movements in exceptional circumstances, which pose serious difficulties for the operation of the exchange rate or monetary policy or to the balance of

[65] Arts 39, 34, 28, and 32 of the EMAs with Algeria, Morocco, Palestine, and Tunisia; Arts 41(3) and 52(3) of the PCAs with Azerbaijan and Russia and Note 3 of Annex 2 to the ECT.

[66] Arts 33,50, 33, and 52(5) of the agreements with Israel, Jordan, Lebanon, and Russia.

[67] Fares, above n 64, pp 25–6.

[68] Arts 63, 62, 65, 65, and 61 of the SAAs with Albania, Croatia, Montenegro, Serbia, and the Former Yugoslav Republic of Macedonia; Arts 34, 34, 34, 34, 35, 40, 46, 41, and 33 of the PCAs with Armenia, Azerbaijan, Georgia, Kazakhstan, Kyrgyzstan, Moldova, Russia, Ukraine, and Uzbekistan; Arts 8.3(a), 225, 194, and 52 of the agreements with Korea, the CARIFORUM states, Chile, and Mexico.

[69] Arts 66, 65, 68, and 64 of the SAAs with Albania, Croatia, Serbia, and the Former Yugoslav Republic of Macedonia; Arts 39, 39, 39, 39, 40, 45, 49, 46, and 38 of the PCAs with Armenia, Azerbaijan, Georgia, Kyrgyzstan, Moldova, Russia, Ukraine, and Uzbekistan; Arts 226, 196, 54, and 225, 194, 52 of the agreements with the CARIFORUM states, Chile, Mexico, and South Africa.

[70] On the scope of these exceptions see below Section 3.2.2.6.

payments.[71] Safeguard measures can be taken only in exceptional circumstances, when they are necessary, for a specific period and if they are in accordance with the GATS and/or IMF rules. However, it is noteworthy that the ECT as well as all EMAs, except those with Israel and Jordan, do not include a safeguard clause. Considering that safeguard provisions in EU IIAs follow broadly the pattern of Article 66 TFEU, the lack of such a restriction on capital movements questions the compatibility of these agreements with primary EU law.[72] Finally, almost all EU IIAs[73] allow for restriction of capital transfers for national and/or international security reasons. In accordance with Article 75 TFEU, which gives the Council and Member States the right, in cases of urgency, to restrict free movement of capital with third countries, EU IIAs safeguard this political restriction.

As a result, it is obvious that only the first and second restrictions present obstacles to complete liberalization. Acknowledging the economic concerns of its counterparties, the EU has achieved partial liberalization of capital inflows and outflows from its counterparties. In contrast, the safeguard, tax, and national and international security exceptions are based on a different rationale. They apply only in exceptional circumstances that require limited intervention to free movement rules. These are necessary in order to internationally secure the right of the EU to adopt measures in accordance with Articles 65, 66 and 75 TFEU.

3.2.1.3 Compatibility of capital movement provisions of EU IIAs with primary EU law

The liberalization of capital movements in EU IIAs does not, in practice, add to the level of liberalization committed by the EU, which has unilaterally liberalized capital movements by virtue of Article 63 TFEU. In fact, EU IIAs take into account the primary EU law provisions on capital movements, reflecting to a large extent the scope and exceptions to free movement of capital to and from third countries.

More specifically, EU IIAs abide by the general rule of free movement of capital, as formulated in Article 63 TFEU. There is no EU IIA provision that imposes an obligation on the EU to restrict capital movements to or from EU counterparties, which would be in direct conflict with Article 63 TFEU. Neither do issues of incompatibility arise for those EU IIAs that limit their scope only to capital movements related to direct investment. The fact that an international agreement creates an international

[71] Art 43 of the EEA Agreement; Arts 61(4), 60(4), 63(6), 63(6), and 59(4) of the SAAs with Albania, Croatia, Montenegro, Serbia, and the Former Yugoslav Republic of Macedonia; Arts 34, and 51–2 of the EMAs with Israel and Jordan; Arts 41(6), 41(7), 41(6,) 41(6), 42(6), 47(6), 52(6), 48(6), and 40(6) of the PCAs with Armenia, Azerbaijan, Georgia, Kazakhstan, Kyrgyzstan, Moldova, Russia, Ukraine, and Uzbekistan; Arts 8.4, 124, 166, 30–1, and 34 of the agreements with Korea, the CARIFORUM states, Chile, Mexico, and South Africa.

[72] See below Section 3.2.1.3.

[73] Arts 124, 118, 127, 127, and 116 of the SAAs with Albania, Croatia, Montenegro, Serbia, and the Former Yugoslav Republic of Macedonia; Arts 103, 85, 100, 78, 85, 89, 70, and 89 of the EMAs with Algeria, Egypt, Jordan, Israel, Lebanon, Morocco, Palestinian Territories, and Tunisia; Arts 87, 90, 90, 90, 84, 91, 99, 94, and 87 of the PCAs with Armenia, Azerbaijan, Georgia, Kazakhstan, Kyrgyzstan, Moldova, Russia, Ukraine, and Uzbekistan; Arts 15.9, 225, 194, and 54 of the agreements with Korea, the CARIFORUM states, Chile, and Mexico.

obligation for the EU that is narrower than its internal Union law obligation does not necessarily indicate incompatibility. A conflict arises only to the extent that the narrower scope of the international obligation does not permit the realization of its internal law obligation. In fact, the reference to direct investment is safeguarding the scope of liberalization envisaged in primary EU law. As Article 64(1) TFEU reserves the right to maintain limitations existing as of 31 December 1993 (and 31 December 1999 for Bulgaria, Estonia, and Hungary), and given that no such limitations existed regarding direct investment, a general reference to all capital movements in EU IIAs has to be complemented by a standstill clause. In cases of complete liberalization of capital movements, EU IIAs are compatible with the TFEU only if they provide that the contracting parties have the right to maintain existing restrictions—this is necessary in order to guarantee the remaining restrictions that affect non-direct investment-related capital movements.[74]

However, incompatibilities with primary EU law arise regarding exceptions to freedom of capital movements under Articles 65, 66, and 75 TFEU. As analysed above, the majority of EU IIAs include exceptions and restrictions to the free movement of capital for direct taxation, public policy, and security reasons and the adoption of safeguard measures or economic sanctions, thus mirroring the exceptions to free movement of capital provided in Articles 65, 66, and 75 TFEU.[75] Nevertheless, the lack of such exceptions and restrictions in certain agreements[76] indicates the latter's incompatibility with the TFEU. The international commitment assumed by the EU in these EU IIAs to liberalize capital movements extends beyond the limits imposed by primary EU law, which reserves the right of the EU and its Member States to impose limitations in certain circumstances.[77]

The existence of such incompatibilities with primary EU law impacts on the validity of the relevant EU IIAs as a matter of Union law. Although the existence of a conflict between the substantive provisions of an EU IIA and the capital movement provisions does not affect their international law validity, so that an EU IIA continues to create binding obligations for the parties,[78] it violates the primacy of EU law. Union agreements are, of course, sources of EU law that are placed higher than secondary law in the hierarchy of EU law norms, but they are subordinate to the provisions of the founding EU Treaties.[79] As legal instruments adopted by EU institutions, Union agreements have to respect the principle of attribution of EU

[74] Eg the EMAs with Israel, Jordan, and Lebanon that cover all capital movements include this restriction.

[75] See above Section 3.2.1.2.

[76] Eg provisions excluding direct taxation from the scope of the capital movement rules and allowing the adoption of safeguard measures are missing from the EMAs with Algeria, Egypt, Morocco, Palestinian Territories, and Tunisia.

[77] The existence of a conflict between the primary EU law capital movements provisions and the provisions of an international agreement (concluded by the Member States) that liberalize capital movements without providing for exceptions that satisfy the limitations inserted in Arts 65–66 and 75 TFEU has been confirmed by the Court in Case C-205/06,*Commission v Austria* [2009] ECR I-1301; Case C-249/06 *Commission v Sweden* [2009] ECR I-1335; and Case C-118/07 *Commission v Finland* [2009] ECR I-10889. See Section 6.2.2.1.

[78] Case C-327/91 *France v Commission* [1994] ECR I-3641. See also Section 6.3.1.

[79] Case C-61/94 *Commission v Germany* [1996] ECR I-3989, para 52.

powers and the primacy of the founding Treaties.[80] In addition, it would be inconsistent to require the compatibility of Member State international agreements with primary EU law and not require the same from Union agreements.[81]

Similar to Articles 65, 66, and 75 TFEU, an incompatibility appears to arise as a result of the lack in all EU IIAs of a provision reserving the right of the Council to adopt measures that constitute a step back in liberalization according to Article 64(2) TFEU. Nevertheless, this does not mean that all EU IIAs are incompatible with the TFEU. Were such a restriction necessary in order to ensure compatibility with Article 64(2) TFEU, it would in essence frustrate the binding commitment on liberalization of capital movements assumed by the EU, which would be able to render its commitment void at any given point in the future. Contrary to Articles 65, 66, and 75 TFEU, which provide for exceptions and restrictions to capital movements intrinsic to the scope of the free movement of capital, Article 64(2) TFEU merely enables the EU to re-determine the degree of liberalization permitted. Next to the first paragraph of Article 64 TFEU, the provision of the following paragraph determines alongside Article 63 TFEU the initial scope of free movement of capital.[82] In that respect, the conclusion of an IIA determining the degree of liberalization of capital movements with regard to a specific country constitutes in essence an exercise of the EU's right to determine the degree of liberalization of capital movements to and from that country, precluding its reassessment for the duration of the IIA.

3.2.2 EU IIA provisions on establishment and post-establishment treatment of FDI

3.2.2.1 The main characteristics of EU IIAs distinguishing them from BITs

Provisions on establishment and post-establishment treatment of FDI are included in the majority of EU IIAs. The GATS and the ECT, as well as most bilateral EU IIAs, namely the EEA Agreement, all SAAs, all PCAs, the EMAs with Jordan and Algeria, and the Association Agreements with Korea, the CARIFORUM states, Chile, and Mexico include substantive provisions on establishment and post-establishment treatment of FDI. With the exception of the ECT, which follows the structure of BITs, EU IIAs have certain characteristics that differentiate them from traditional BITs. First, EU IIAs present a strong link between establishment and post-establishment treatment of foreign investment. Contrary to Member State BITs, which provide standards of treatment of foreign investors at the post-establishment phase without granting any rights for admission and establishment

[80] On the limits imposed on the powers of EU institutions by the principle of attribution and the primacy of the founding Treaties see Section 6.3.1.

[81] On the compatibility of Member State agreements with primary EU law see Section 6.2.

[82] Handoll, above n 12, p 147; S Hindelang, *The Free Movement of Capital and Foreign Direct Investment: the scope of protection in EU Law* (2009), pp 300–1; D Scharf, 'Die Kapitalverkehrsfreiheit gegenüber Drittstaaten' (2008) 76 Beiträge zum Transnationalen Wirtschaftsrecht 1, 10–11.

of FDI,[83] EU IIAs seem to condition the regulation of post-establishment treatment on the existence of provisions on establishment, since post-establishment treatment standards are offered only in the EU IIAs which provide for admission of foreign investment. Nevertheless, this does not necessarily mean that the scope of post-establishment treatment of FDI is identical to the scope of establishment provisions. Although EU IIAs make use of the same non-discrimination standards of treatment for the establishment and post-establishment treatment of FDI—namely, most favoured nation (MFN) and national treatment (NT)—many agreements provide for different standards of treatment at each stage.

Secondly, EU IIAs regulate admission and post-admission treatment of FDI separately from other forms of investment—namely portfolio investment and investment in the form of concession contracts. Instead of providing general standards applying to all types of foreign investment, EU IIAs regulate independently the admission and treatment of direct investment through establishment, considering portfolio investment under the capital movements rules and investment in the form of concession contracts under the cross-border supply of services rules.[84] Although this distinction may be justified with regard to the admission of foreign investment, since the admission of direct investment poses additional regulatory concerns in comparison to short-term investments,[85] such differentiation is more difficult to comprehend with regard to the post-admission treatment of foreign investment, where similar regulatory concerns exist.

Thirdly, EU IIAs provide for different standards of treatment of foreign investment in comparison to BITs. Using language based on the non-discrimination principle, EU IIAs depart from traditional BIT language which formally vests foreign investors with other additional standards. Despite the lack of identical wording in BITs, a common standard provided in the vast majority of BITs is fair and equitable treatment (FET), while many agreements provide additional standards, such as those of Full Protection and Security and protection against arbitrary and discriminatory measures.[86] The lack of such standards of treatment, and most importantly of FET, in EU IIAs appears to be limiting the scope of treatment offered to foreign investors thereunder.

Understanding the different structure of foreign investment regulation adopted by EU IIAs, it is crucial to bear in mind that existing EU IIAs are based on primary EU law and the GATS, which serve as regulatory models. Primary EU law covers investment under the respective chapters on capital movements, establishment, and services, the GATS distinguishes between commercial presence and cross-border

[83] I Gomez-Palacio and P Muchlinski, 'Admission and Establishment' in Muchlinski, Ortino, and Schreuer (eds), *Oxford Handbook of International Investment Law* (2008), pp 240–2.

[84] See also below Section 3.2.3.

[85] As discussed (Section 1.3.2.2), regulation of establishment deals with the way the activity of an investor will take place, considering foreign equity ownership limitations, quantitative restrictions, administrative authorizations, and restrictions on the legal form of an investment, whereas portfolio investment and investment in the form of concession contracts do not raise such concerns. Gomez-Palacio and Muchlinski, above n 83, pp 230–2.

[86] For an enumeration of the different standards of treatment provided in BITs see R Dolzer and C Schreuer, *Principles of International Investment Law* (2008), ch 7.

supply of services, while both regulate establishment and post-establishment treatment of direct investment.[87] Additionally, neither the TFEU nor the GATS use other standards of treatment beyond MFN and NT. Borrowing heavily from them, as will be explained below, EU IIAs have formulated their own distinctive model of FDI regulation that departs substantially from the typical BIT and IIA provisions on admission and treatment of foreign investment.

Finally, it should be pointed out that establishment and post-establishment regulation of foreign investment depends ultimately on the definition of establishment, and not all EU IIAs adopt the same definition. While certain agreements, such as the EEA Agreement, the GATS, and the agreements with Korea, Chile, Mexico, and the CARIFORUM states refer to the setting up and management of a primary undertaking or a secondary undertaking in the form of a juridical person or a branch or representative office by natural or juridical persons, the SAAs, the PCAs, as well as the EMAs with Jordan and Algeria, regulate only secondary establishment, namely the setting up of subsidiaries and branches or representative offices by juridical persons.[88]

Hence, an examination of the EU IIA provisions on the establishment and post-establishment treatment of FDI requires initially a determination of their specific scope; secondly, a critical assessment of the different standards of treatment included therein; and, thirdly, the examination of specific issues relating to establishment, such as the movement of key personnel.

3.2.2.2 The scope of EU IIA provisions on establishment of FDI

As establishment of foreign investors is the main condition for admission of FDI, many countries have been reluctant to take up legally binding commitments in this field. Following the controlled entry model adopted in the overwhelming majority of Member State BITs, certain EU IIAs preserve the sovereign right of the parties to determine the establishment of foreign investors in their territory, containing only aspirational provisions calling for future liberalization of investment conditions. For example, the ECT requires that the parties shall endeavour to provide NT for the establishment of foreign investors. Nevertheless, it introduces a standstill and rollback clause, requiring the contracting parties to avoid introducing new restrictions concerning the entry of foreign investment and progressively to reduce remaining restrictions.[89] However, a significant number of EU IIAs include substantive provisions on establishment.

Due to the diversity of the goals envisaged in each agreement, EU IIAs adopt different models of establishment regulation. Being mainly influenced by EU law, which provides an absolute right to establishment covering all economic activities and requiring non-discrimination, and the GATS, which covers establishment

[87] L van den Hende, 'Free Movement of Services and the Right of Establishment in a Pan-Euro-Mediterranean Economic Area: Between EU Membership and the GATS' in Maresceau and Lannon (eds), *The EU's Enlargement and Mediterranean Strategies* (2001), p 171. See also Sections 1.2.2.1.2 and 1.2.1.4.

[88] See Section 1.2.2.3.

[89] Art 10(3), (6) ECT.

only in the service sectors in which the parties have committed to liberalize conditions of entry, EU IIAs create their own diversified regulatory models.

Categorizing the different EU IIAs, the GATS should be examined first, as it has the broadest coverage of member countries and has served as a model for other EU IIAs.[90] Its importance for foreign investment stems from the fact that it defines trade in services to also include investment in service sectors, through the definition of commercial presence.[91] More specifically, the GATS gives the opportunity to WTO members to make specific commitments to provide market access to foreign investors in service sectors, indicating any possible limitations, and it grants national treatment for the establishment of foreign investment in the sectors where market access commitments are undertaken. It adopts a 'bottom-up' or 'positive list' approach on liberalization, where each member indicates in its schedule of commitments the level of liberalization desired.[92] In addition, irrespective of the level of market access commitments undertaken by the parties, GATS establishes a general MFN obligation, requiring that unless a specific exception is listed, 'each Member shall accord immediately and unconditionally to services and service suppliers of any other Member treatment no less favorable than that it accords to like services and service suppliers of any other country.'[93]

An entirely different approach to establishment regulation is adopted by the EEA Agreement. Article 31 of the EEA Agreement provides in absolute terms a right to establishment, prohibiting restrictions on the establishment of EU nationals in European Free Trade Association (EFTA) countries and vice versa. Adopting almost identical wording to Articles 49, 51, 52, and 54 TFEU, the chapter on establishment of the EEA Agreement provides for complete market access and non-discrimination of foreign investors at the establishment stage of foreign investment.[94]

Drawing on EU law and the EEA Agreement, the SAAs include provisions on establishment, granting broad market access rights to foreign investors. With the exception of the transport sector, all SAAs grant to the parties' companies MFN treatment or NT, whichever is more favourable, regarding their establishment in the territory of the other party.[95] It is important to note that SAAs provide

[90] On the influence of the GATS as a model for agreements on trade and investment in services sectors see M Roy, J Marchetti, and H Lim, *Services liberalization in the new generation of Preferential Trade Agreements (PTAs): How much further than the GATS?*, WTO Working Paper ERSD-2006–07.

[91] See Section 1.2.1.4.

[92] On GATS regulation of establishment see P Delimatsis and M Molinuevo, 'Art XVI GATS' in Wolfrum, Stoll, and Feinäugle (eds), *WTO Trade in Services* (2008), pp 367–95; L van den Hende and H Smith, 'GATS Art XVI and National Regulatory Sovereignty: What Lessons to Draw from US Gambling?' in Alexander and Andenas (eds), *The World Trade Organization and Trade in Services* (2008), pp 461- 80; M Koulen, 'Foreign Investment in the WTO' in Nieuwenhuys and Brus (eds), *Multilateral Regulation on Investment* (2001), p 288; T Brewer and S Young, 'Investment issues at the WTO: the architecture of rules and the settlement of Disputes' (1998) 1 JIEL 457.

[93] Art II GATS.

[94] S Norberg et al, *EEA Law: A Commentary on the EEA Agreement* (1993), pp 427–41.

[95] Arts 50, 49, 53, 53, and 48 of the agreements with Albania, Croatia, Montenegro, Serbia, and the Former Yugoslav Republic of Macedonia respectively.

(apart from general transitional periods, within which their provisions must be realized),[96] for specific transitional periods regarding the establishment of EU companies, within which EU counterparties may adopt restrictive measures that are proportional and non-discriminatory among EU companies, in order to avoid a drastic reduction of the nationally controlled market share in a given industry or to help industries facing serious problems and infant industries to develop.[97]

The next group of agreements conferring extensive market access rights, albeit non-reciprocal and subject to certain exceptions, are the PCAs, apart from the agreement with Russia, and the EMA with Jordan. Similar to the SAAs, they provide for MFN treatment or NT, whichever is more favourable, regarding the establishment of EU companies in the territory of the other party. However, MFN and NT are not absolute, as market access commitments are subject to specific restrictions in specific sectors, which are listed in the annexes to the agreements. More importantly, the scope of liberalization is further limited as the EU offers only MFN treatment to the companies of the other party.[98] MFN liberalization is offered to both third country and EU companies in the PCA with Russia, which, contrary to the other PCAs, ensures strict reciprocity of obligations.[99]

The lack of reciprocity in these EU IIAs is understood if the difference in the level of market access committed internationally by the parties, in particular in the GATS, is taken into account. Bearing in mind that the parties to these EU IIAs were not WTO parties at the time of concluding the bilateral EU IIAs, these agreements in essence extended the application of the EU's GATS commitments to the non-WTO party, ensuring liberalization on the part of the EU's counterparties. The link between the scope of liberalization with the GATS is further enhanced as all these EU IIAs provide that on accession of these countries to the WTO, the treatment granted thereunder should not be more favourable than the parties' GATS commitments.[100] Nevertheless, the scope of liberalization in these IIAs goes far beyond the GATS, as these agreements also include commitments in non-service sectors, and adopt a negative list approach to liberalization, which requires the parties to ensure full market access unless a specific limitation is listed.

A similar but more limited approach to liberalization of establishment conditions linked with a country's accession to the WTO is provided in the EMA with Algeria; this extends the scope of EU GATS commitments to Algerian nationals and offers MFN treatment for the establishment of EU nationals in Algeria.[101]

[96] Arts 8, 5, 8, 8, and 5 of the agreements with Albania, Croatia, Montenegro, Serbia, and the Former Yugoslav Republic of Macedonia respectively.

[97] Arts 56, 55, and 54 of the agreements with Albania, Croatia, and the Former Yugoslav Republic of Macedonia respectively. See also van den Hende, above n 87, p 176.

[98] Art 30 of the EMA with Jordan and Arts 23, 23, 23, 23, 23, 24, 25, and 22 of the PCAs with Armenia, Azerbaijan, Georgia, Kazakhstan, Kyrgyzstan, Moldova, Ukraine, and Uzbekistan.

[99] Art 28 of the PCA with Russia. Van den Hende, above n 87, p 181.

[100] As at 1 May 2011, only Jordan, Armenia, Georgia, Kyrgyzstan, Moldova, and Ukraine have become Members of the WTO and, thus, the scope of liberalization envisaged under the bilateral EU IIAs is confined to the parties' GATS commitments. See also Section 5.2.1.1.

[101] Arts 30 and 32 of the EMA with Algeria.

However, commitments on establishment are undertaken only in service sectors. Hence, after the accession of Algeria in the WTO, the parties' commitments on the liberalization of establishment conditions will become redundant.

Another set of EU IIAs heavily influenced by the GATS model are the agreements with Mexico and Chile. Both agreements include an extensive set of provisions on trade in services, largely following the wording of the GATS provisions. The agreement with Mexico offers MFN treatment for the establishment of foreign investors in service sectors, while both agreements offer market access and NT in accordance with the schedules annexed to these agreements, thus adopting a positive list approach.[102] In contrast with the EMA with Algeria, their added value consists of the specific commitments undertaken by the parties in most service sectors, where no liberalization has been committed so far on the multilateral level, while they also include specific rules on key service sectors, such as telecommunications and financial services. Additionally, the agreement with Chile includes a specific chapter on establishment in non-service sectors which provides for NT of foreign investors in the specific sectors where the parties have undertaken commitments, adopting a positive list approach to liberalization.[103]

Lastly, establishment provisions are adopted in the EPA with the CARIFORUM states and the FTA with Korea. Using a GATS-type approach to liberalization, they provide for MFN treatment of foreign investors and include schedules with market access and NT commitments, where the parties have indicated the sectors where establishment has been liberalized, subject to specific restrictions in each sector.[104] The sectoral coverage is not only limited to services, but covers all industrial sectors.

The above overview of establishment provisions in EU IIAs indicates the plurality of models of establishment regulation adopted by the EU in its agreements with third countries. According to the specific objectives pursued by each agreement and in light of the particular political considerations that led to the conclusion of each EU IIA,[105] they provide for different levels of liberalization and follow different models: agreements having integration objectives, such as the EEA Agreement and the SAAs, provide for extensive liberalization, largely following the primary EU law provisions. Agreements aiming at enhanced cooperation with neighbouring countries, such as the PCAs, promote full liberalization subject to specific exceptions and restrictions (negative list approach), while association agreements with third countries aim largely at providing added value to the degree of liberalization offered by the GATS (positive list approach). Understanding the divergence between EU IIAs, their evolution over time should also be considered. This is particularly obvious in the agreements with Mexico, Chile, the CARIFORUM states,

[102] Arts 4–6 and 97–8 of the agreements with Mexico and Chile.
[103] Art 132 of the EU-Chile agreement.
[104] Arts 67 and 70 of the EPA with the CARIFORUM States and 7.11. and 7.14 of the FTA with Korea.
[105] See Section 4.1.3.3.2.

and Korea, the different structure of which largely indicates the gradual formulation of innovative rules based on the GATS.[106]

In any event, EU IIAs depart significantly not only from Member State BITs with third countries, which do not touch on establishment of foreign investment, but also from IIAs concluded by other international actors that include provisions on admission and establishment of foreign investment. In contrast with BITs—most notably those by the United States and Canada, which almost exclusively adopt the full liberalization model, by extending MFN and NT at the establishment phase usually followed by a negative list[107]—EU IIAs make full use of the entire spectrum of available regulatory models, resulting in new models, such as that adopted in the EPA with the CARIFORUM states. However, it is doubtful whether these regulatory models will influence future agreements concluded in the post-Lisbon era.

3.2.2.3 The scope of EU IIA provisions on post-establishment treatment of FDI

The scope of post-establishment treatment of FDI in EU IIAs is significantly affected by the scope of the establishment provisions. This is primarily illustrated in the sectoral coverage of EU IIAs, since post-establishment treatment is granted only for investments in the sectors covered by each EU IIA. Hence, the GATS, the EMA with Algeria, and the agreement with Mexico limit the scope of their post-establishment provisions to foreign investment in service sectors, while the ECT covers post-establishment treatment in the energy sector.

Nevertheless, there are fewer divergences between EU IIAs regarding their standards and scope of post-establishment treatment. Again, the GATS and EU law present the main regulatory models on which other EU IIAs were based. Starting with the EEA Agreement, its scope of post-establishment treatment of foreign investment is completely influenced by primary EU law. Article 31(2) of the EEA Agreement prohibits any discrimination on the basis of nationality regarding the operation of foreign investors. Continuing with the GATS, Article XVII grants NT to service suppliers that have established a commercial presence with regard to all measures affecting their operations. However, NT is granted only to foreign investments in the sectors where market access commitments were undertaken by the parties, and it is subject to specific limitations listed in the parties' schedules of commitments.[108] Considering that the establishment of foreign investors in sectors where no market access commitments are undertaken may be possible under national law, since market access commitments do not prohibit host states from unilaterally liberalizing establishment in other service sectors, the conclusion can be drawn that the GATS excludes foreign investors who are active in service sectors that are not in the host country's schedule of commitments from the scope of its post-establishment treatment.

[106] P Sauve and N Ward, 'Services and Investment in the EC-CARIFORUM Economic Partnership Agreement Innovation in Rule Design and Implications for Africa' ECIPE (2009), pp 6–7.

[107] On the scope of BITs including liberalizing provisions see T Pollan, *Legal Framework for the Admission of FDI* (2006), pp 77–85.

[108] Van den Hende and Smith, above n 92, pp 471–3; Brewer and Young, above n 92, pp 460–1.

A similar approach to post-establishment treatment of foreign investment is adopted in the agreements with Mexico, Chile, the CARIFORUM states, and Korea. These provide for NT of foreign investors that have been established in the sectors where market access commitments are undertaken by the parties;[109] hence, foreign investors established in other sectors do not enjoy the preferential treatment granted by these agreements. Nevertheless, the scope of this exception is not as broad as under the GATS. Considering, first, that the agreements with Chile, the CARIFORUM states, and Korea extend their coverage beyond service sectors and, secondly, that all three agreements have far-reaching liberalization commitments,[110] almost all economic sectors fall within the scope of the provisions on post-establishment treatment.

A different regulatory model on post-establishment treatment of FDI is offered in the SAAs, the PCAs, and the EMAs with Jordan and Algeria. In light of the broad scope of their establishment provisions, these agreements provide standards of treatment regarding the operation of any foreign investment established in the host country, irrespective of whether such establishment benefitted from the parties' commitments on establishment. However, bearing in mind that these EU IIAs cover only secondary establishment, they distinguish between different forms of establishment, offering, to a large extent, different standards of treatment to subsidiaries from branches or agencies of foreign companies.

More specifically, the coverage of post-establishment treatment of foreign investment is extensive in the SAAs, as they aim at the gradual economic integration of the western Balkan countries in the internal market. They provide for MFN or NT, whichever is better, for both subsidiaries and branches of companies of the parties, allowing for exceptions to liberalization on the same grounds that justify limitations on establishment.[111] In contrast, a distinction in the treatment of subsidiaries and branches of foreign investors regarding their operations is provided in the PCAs and the EMA with Jordan. While these EU IIAs provide for MFN or NT, whichever is more suitable, of subsidiaries and branches of EU companies established in the territory of the EU's counterparty, they offer NT only to subsidiaries of companies of EU counterparties, subject to certain limitations listed as annexes to the agreements, while branches of companies of EU counterparties are offered MFN treatment.[112] Similar to establishment regulation, the PCA with Russia presents an exception to other agreements, as it is based on strict reciprocity,

[109] Arts 6 and 7 of the EU-Mexico Services Agreement, Arts 98 and 132 of the EU-Chile Agreement, Art 68 of the EPA with the CARIFORUM states and Art 7.12 of the FTA with Korea.

[110] Sauve and Ward, above n 106, p 21; B Hoekman and R Newfarmer, 'Preferential Trade Agreements, Investment Disciplines and Investment Flows' (2005) 5 JWT 949, 957–60.

[111] Arts 50, 49, 53, 53, and 48 of the agreements with Albania, Croatia, Montenegro, Serbia, and the Former Yugoslav Republic of Macedonia respectively.

[112] An exception to this rule is presented in the PCA with Kyrgyzstan, which provides for MFN treatment of subsidiaries of EU companies established in Kyrgyzstan. Art 30 of the EMA with Jordan and Arts 23, 23, 23, 23, 23, 24, 25, and 22 of the PCAs with Armenia, Azerbaijan, Georgia, Kazakhstan, Kyrgyzstan, Moldova Ukraine, and Uzbekistan. See also S Bezborodov, 'Freedom of Establishment in the EC Economic Partnership Agreements: in Search of its Direct Effect on Direct Taxation' (2007) 35 International Tax Review 692, 699.

thus providing for NT regarding the operation of subsidiaries of EU and Russian companies in Russia and the EU respectively and MFN treatment regarding the operation of branches of EU and Russian companies.[113] Finally, the EMA with Algeria provides for MFN and NT of EU companies established in Algeria.[114]

Illustrating the differences in post-establishment regulation that EU IIAs present in comparison to BITs, it is essential to describe the provisions of the ECT; the only EU IIA that follows a typical BIT approach to post-establishment treatment of foreign investment. In light of the broad definition of investment in Article 1 ECT, Article 10(7) confers MFN or NT, whichever is more favourable, regarding the operations of a foreign investor, while paragraph 1 of the same article confers to foreign investment FET, constant protection and security, and the treatment required by international law.[115] In that regard, these provisions indicate the importance that additional standards have in determining the substantive scope of treatment conferred to foreign investment at the post-establishment stage.

3.2.2.4 Standards of treatment of foreign investment

EU IIAs regulate the establishment and operation of FDI providing for MFN and NT. These two standards of treatment of foreign investment, which are based on the principle of non-discrimination on grounds of nationality, are widely used in international trade and investment agreements, as well as in EU law, requiring a certain conduct by a host state regarding the treatment within its own borders of goods, services, and investors originating from outside its borders.[116] Despite the common origin and nature of non-discrimination standards of treatment, their formulation, application, and interpretation varies considerably between trade and investment treaties, while differences exist further between different trade or investment regimes, such as EU law and the WTO. Bearing in mind the influences of primary EU law, the WTO and other IIAs on the scope of the foreign investment provisions of EU IIAs, the application and interpretation of the MFN and NT standards in EU IIAs needs to be further explored.

It is notable that EU IIAs, with the exception of the ECT, do not make any reference to other standards of treatment widely used in BITs and IIAs, most

[113] Art 28 of the PCA with Russia.

[114] Art 33 of the EMA with Algeria.

[115] S Haghighi, *Energy Security: The External Legal Relations of the European Union with Major Oil and Gas Supplying Countries* (2006), pp 201–2. For a detailed description of the standards of treatment provided under the ECT see C Schreuer, 'Fair and Equitable Treatment (FET): interactions with other standards' in Coop and Ribeiro (eds), *Investment Protection and the Energy Charter Treaty* (2008), p 63.

[116] On the principle of non-discrimination in EU law, international trade law, and international investment law see indicatively C Hilson, 'Discrimination in Community Free Movement Law' (1999) 24 EL Rev 445; C Barnard, 'Fitting the Remaining Pieces into the Goods and Persons Jigsaw' (2001) 26 EL Rev 35; T Cottier and P Mavroidis (eds), *Regulatory Barriers and the Principle of Non-Discrimination in World Trade Law* (2000); F Ortino, 'Non-Discriminatory Treatment in Investment Disputes' in Dupuy, Francioni, and Petersmann (eds), *Human Rights in International Investment Law and Investor-State Arbitration* (2009), pp 344f.

importantly the FET standard. Providing only for non-discrimination standards, EU IIAs appear to exclude from their scope the protection offered to foreign investment and investors by other standards of treatment, such as the FET or the Full Protection and Security standard. Nevertheless, in considering the protective scope of these standards of treatment it is worth examining whether EU IIAs, despite the lack of an explicit provision, grant to foreign investment and investors an equivalent level of treatment.

3.2.2.4.1 The principle of non-discrimination and NT

(i) Differences between IIAs, EU law, and the GATS

The principle of non-discrimination on grounds of nationality is premised on the idea that a state has to treat foreign investors at least as well as it treats its own investors (NT) or investors from other third countries (MFN treatment). As this requires the identification of a comparator in order to determine the level of treatment offered to foreign investors, it establishes 'relative' standards of treatment. In that respect, the MFN and NT standards differ from 'absolute' standards of treatment, such as the FET standard or the prohibition of any restrictions that have an adverse effect on the establishment and operation of foreign investment. The latter guarantees a specific minimum level of treatment, the determination of which does not have to depend on the treatment afforded to domestic or other third country investors.[117]

The 'relative' character of the non-discrimination principle indicates that the determination of whether a national measure violates the NT or the MFN standard requires a comparison between foreign investments/investors and national or other third country investments/investors. Such an assessment rests first on the comparability of investments/investors, which is more commonly referred to as 'likeness' and, secondly, on the existence of less favorable treatment. It is also necessary to examine, either in light of these two tests or as a separate test, whether and under what conditions various policy reasons justify a discriminatory measure.

Despite the common features of the principle of non-discrimination, its application and interpretation varies across legal instruments in the different legal regimes of trade and investment. Reflecting, to a large extent, the different goals and objectives pursued, the tests for identifying a violation of the non-discrimination standards have obtained distinct characteristics, leading to substantial differentiations among legal regimes.[118] Without entering into a detailed analysis of the application of non-discrimination standards in those regimes,

[117] T Grierson-Weiler and I Laird, 'Standards of Treatment' in Muchlinski, Ortino, and Schreuer (eds), *Oxford Handbook of International Investment Law* (2008), pp 261–4; F Ortino, 'From Non-Discrimination to Reasonableness: A Paradigm Shift in International Economic Law?', Jean Monnet Working Papers 1/2005 NYU School of Law, pp 6–8.

[118] On the different objectives of trade and investment regulation and how these are reflected in the scope and interpretation of the national treatment provisions in the WTO agreements and BITs see N DiMascio and J Pauwelyn, 'Non-discrimination in Trade and Investment Treaties: Worlds Apart or Two Sides of the Same Coin?' (2008) 102 AJIL 48.

it is important to highlight the diversity between traditional IIAs, the WTO agreements, and EU law.

Starting with the concept of likeness, the question arises whether the analysis should focus only on the nature and extent of a competitive relationship between the comparable investments/investors or whether it should be expanded to cover the aim of the alleged discriminatory measure. Under BITs and traditional IIAs, likeness has been linked with the determination of a competitive relationship between investors, which has been interpreted both too narrowly and too broadly,[119] but also with the existence of factors that justify deviation in the treatment, as discussed below. The concept of likeness has received more attention in the WTO, both in the General Agreement on Tariffs and Trade (GATT) and, more importantly for foreign investment, in the GATS. Using the same paradigm for both agreements, WTO jurisprudence has rejected an 'aims and effects' test for determining likeness, highlighting that likeness is concerned with competitive relationships between and among products/services and not with the purposes and market effects of the contested measure.[120] Similarly, the application of the non-discrimination principle in EU law depends on the competitive relationship of the comparable persons.[121]

As regards 'less favorable treatment', there exists significant convergence between the legal instruments. All regimes recognize that discrimination can be the result not only of discriminatory language (de jure discrimination), but also from origin-neutral measures having a 'detrimental impact' or 'adverse effect' on foreign investors (de facto discrimination).[122] It is important to highlight that, in order for de facto discrimination to exist under WTO and EU law, the 'adverse effects' have to be linked with the nationality of the investor, so that disadvantages unrelated to the foreign origin of an investment/investor do not amount to de facto

[119] *SD Myers, Inc v Canada*, First Partial Award, 13 November 2000, para 251; *ADF Group Inc v United States of America*, ICSID Case No ARB(AF)/00/1, Final Award, 9 January 2003, para 64; *Occidental Exploration and Production Co v Ecuador*, LCIA Case No UN3467, Award, 1 July 2004. See also Ortino, above n 116, pp 354–6; Grierson-Weiler and Laird, above n 117, pp 291–3; DiMascio and Pauwelyn, above n 118, pp 72–6.

[120] The rejection of the 'aims and effects' test in the field of trade in goods was manifestly declared in the *EC-Asbestos* case (WTO Appellate Body Report, *European Communities—Measures Affecting Asbestos and Asbestos-Containing Products*, WT/DS/AB/135, paras 101–2). In favour of a similar reading of likeness in the GATS see *EC-Bananas III* (*European Communities—Regime for the Importation, Sale and Distribution of Bananas*, WT/DS/AB/158, para 241); J Pauwelyn, 'The unbearable lightness of likeness' in Panizzon, Pohl, and Sauve (eds), *GATS and the Regulation of International Trade in Services* (2008), pp 358–69. Cf M Cossy, 'Some thoughts on the concept of "likeness" in the GATS' in Panizzon, Pohl, and Sauve (eds), *GATS and the Regulation of International Trade in Services* (2008), pp 327–55, who are in favour of the re-introduction of an improved aims and effects test for determining likeness under the GATS.

[121] See eg Joined Cases C-259, 331 & 332/91 *Pilar Allué and Carmel Mary Coonan and others v Università degli studi di Venezia and Università degli studi di Parma* [1993] ECR I-4309. W Frenz, *Handbuch Europarecht: Europäische Grundfreiheiten* (2004), pp 56–8.

[122] For an overview of the jurisprudence see Ortino, above n 117, pp 19–22; F Ortino, 'The Principle of Non-Discrimination and its Exceptions in GATS: Selected Legal Issues' in Alexander and Andenas (eds), *The World Trade Organization and Trade in Services* (2008), pp 177–80; G Davies, *Nationality Discrimination in the European Internal Market* (2003), pp 10–11.

discrimination.[123] However, there are divergences in the determination of de facto discrimination between IIAs, on the one hand, and WTO and EU law, on the other—the most important being that nationality discrimination is established in IIAs simply by showing that a foreign investor has been treated less favorably than at least one domestic investor,[124] while WTO and EU law require a broader nationality imbalance taking into account foreign and domestic investors as a whole.[125]

The most important difference between the WTO agreements and EU law, on the one hand, and IIAs, on the other, is the relation between discrimination and public policy justification. Primary EU law and the WTO contain specific lists with exceptions that can justify discriminatory measures,[126] containing an exclusive list of public policy grounds that justify discriminatory measures and indicating the 'necessity test' to be applied in each case. On the contrary, most BITs lack general exception provisions, so that tribunals have given relevance to public policy justifications interpreting the 'in like circumstances' language as a de facto public policy justification mechanism.[127] Although this interpretative approach enables investment tribunals to take into account public policy justifications that are a necessary step for assessing the discriminatory character of a national measure, it entails greater dangers as it does not offer any guidance to arbitral tribunals as to the degree of deference they should grant national legislators for adopting measures serving public policy goals, while it dilutes the distinction between the stages for the assessment of non-discrimination.

Having sketched the main differences in the application of the non-discrimination principle in EU law, the WTO agreements, and traditional IIAs, it is obvious that IIAs depart from the standards set out in the former regimes. Of course, non-discrimination standards of treatment under IIAs have not been the subject of extensive jurisprudence and detailed analysis, as in EU and WTO law, while the lack of a single international legal instrument on foreign investment impedes the formation of consistent jurisprudence, in a similar manner to the development and evolution of EU and WTO law. Nevertheless, despite the potential for a convergence of the criteria and methods of interpretation used in the different legal regimes, at present non-discrimination standards are applied and interpreted differently in IIAs in comparison to WTO and EU law.

(ii) Primary EU law and the GATS as regulatory models

Turning now to the regulatory model, according to which non-discrimination standards in EU IIAs should be applied and interpreted, it is quite apparent that the GATS and the TFEU provisions on establishment provide, once again, the

[123] WTO Panel Report, Case WT/DS/139/142/R *Canada—Certain Measures Affecting the Automotive Industry*, para 10.300; Case 251/83 *Haug-Adrion v Frankfurter Versicherungs-AG* [1984] ECR 4277, paras 15–16.

[124] *Pope and Talbot, Inc v The Government of Canada*, UNCITRAL, Award on the Merits of Phase 2, 10 April 2001, paras 44–79. See DiMascio and Pauwelyn,, above n 118, pp 70–1.

[125] *EC-Asbestos*, above n 120, para 100; Pauwelyn, above n 120, pp 360–1.

[126] Eg Art 52 TFEU and Art XIV GATS. See also below Section 3.2.2.6.

[127] Ortino, above n 117, pp 28–32; Grierson-Weiler and Laird, above n 117, pp 295–9.

relevant context. Apart from the fact that the scope of regulation of establishment and operation of foreign investment in EU IIAs follows the structure of the GATS and the TFEU,[128] the language on non-discrimination resembles the wording used in these instruments. More specifically, EU IIAs lack any reference to 'like circumstances', which has been the main thrust for determining likeness and justification of discriminatory measures on policy grounds under IIAs, while they provide for general exceptions similar to Article XIV GATS and Article 54 TFEU.[129]

Despite the commonalities concerning the application of the non-discrimination principle in Articles II and XVII GATS and Article 49 TFEU, it is necessary to distinguish further between these provisions. Aside from the specific differences pertaining to the interpretation of non-discrimination, a close examination is necessary mainly because the TFEU also provides protection against non-discriminatory measures that may hinder the freedom of establishment in the same article. Following *Cassis de Dijon*[130] and *Keck*[131] in the field of trade in goods and *Gebhard*[132] in the field of freedom of establishment, the Court of Justice established distinctive criteria for determining the legality of measures which, irrespective of their non-discriminatory character, affect the market access rights conferred by primary EU law. In contrast, rules concerning the legality of non-discriminatory measures that affect market access are dealt with in the GATS under a different heading, namely that of domestic regulation.[133]

In considering whether the interpretation of the non-discrimination principle in EU IIAs should follow the interpretation of the corresponding TFEU provisions or that of the GATS, the jurisprudence of the Court of Justice offers valuable assistance. Within its jurisdiction to apply and interpret Union agreements that have direct effect,[134] the European Court of Justice (ECJ) identified general principles determining the interpretation of Union agreements, in particular in cases of interpretation identical to the provisions of primary EU law. Although the Court has not had the opportunity to interpret provisions regarding the establishment and operation of foreign investors, its decisions regarding the application of provisions of Union agreements in the fields of free movement of goods, workers, and establishment of self-employed persons offer valuable guidance for the interpretation of the establishment provisions of EU IIAs.

Referring to Article 31 of the Vienna Convention on the Law of Treaties, the Court pointed out that a provision in a Union agreement should be interpreted in accordance with the language used in the context of a specific provision in the light of its object and purpose.[135] Although the Court's jurisprudence seems to be based

[128] See above Sections 3.2.2.2 and 3.2.2.3.
[129] See below Section 3.2.2.6.
[130] *Case* 120/78 *Cassis de Dijon* [1979] *ECR* 649.
[131] Joined Cases C-267 & 268/91 *Keck and Mithouard* [1993] *ECR* I-6097.
[132] Case C-551/94 *Gebhard v Consiglio dell'Ordine degli Avvocati di Milano* [1995] *ECR* I-4165.
[133] See also below Section 3.2.2.4.3.
[134] See Section 6.1.3.
[135] Case C-312/91 *Metalsa* [1993] ECR I-3751, para 12; Case C-416/96 *El-Yassini* [1999] ECR I-1209, para 47, with references to Opinion 1/91(*EEA Agreement*) [1991] ECR I-6079, para 14.

on a case-by-case analysis of the relevant provisions,[136] some general remarks can be extracted. Despite the emphasis placed on the objectives and purpose of an agreement, the decision of whether to follow the interpretation of a corresponding primary EU law provision depends rather on the language and the nature of the provision of the Union agreement. The Court seems to adopt an identical interpretation to the relevant EU law provision for determining the ordinary meaning of identical concepts used in Union agreements—such as non-discrimination—irrespective of whether they are found in agreements aiming at closer integration and eventually accession or merely at the establishment of cooperation.[137] On the other hand, the Court has refused to provide identical interpretations of provisions of Union agreements that are linguistically similar or identical to a primary EU law provision, to the extent that the latter has been interpreted in such a way that it grants additional rights that are corollary to the main right secured under a provision.[138]

As a result, it is necessary to examine the language used in EU IIAs. In that respect, the EU IIAs with Chile, Mexico, the CARIFORUM states, and Korea seem to differentiate substantially from the TFEU provisions on establishment. In fact, they are almost identical to Articles II and XVII GATS on MFN and NT. Considering that these EU IIAs follow GATS as a regulatory model not only linguistically but also in terms of scope and structure, the interpretation of their provisions on establishment should follow the GATS/WTO jurisprudence.

The question of interpretation of the establishment provisions of the SAAs, PCAs, and EMAs is different. Bearing in mind that the structure of these EU IIAs provisions follows the TFEU chapter on establishment and that their purpose is to achieve closer economic integration through the establishment of an association or cooperation, it could be argued that the non-discrimination principle enshrined in these EU IIAs should be interpreted in light of the application of the non-discrimination principle under Article 49 TFEU. However, these EU IIAs adopt their own distinctive wording in their provisions on establishment that differs from Article 49 TFEU. Instead of 'prohibiting restrictions on the freedom of establishment', they 'grant treatment no less favorable than that accorded to its own nationals/any third country for the establishment/in respect of the operation of companies [of the other Party]'. The difference in language from Article 49 TFEU indicates that, although the concept of non-discrimination found in the establishment provisions of the SAAs, the PCAs, and the EMAs should be interpreted in

[136] C Caddous, 'Effects of International Agreements in the EU Legal Order' in Cremona and de Witte (eds), *EU Foreign Relations Law—Constitutional Fundamentals* (2008), p 312.

[137] Case C-162/00 *Pokzeptowicz-Meyer* [2002] ECR I-1049; Case C-438/00 *Kolpak* [2003] ECR I-4135; Case C-265/03 *Simutenkov* [2005] ECR I-2579; Case C-171/01 *Wählergruppe Gemeinsam* [2003] ECR I-4301; Case C-136/03 *Dörr and Ünal* [2005] ECR I-4759. For an analysis of these cases see F Jacobs, 'Direct effect and interpretation of international agreements in the recent case law of the European Court of Justice' in Dashwood and Maresceau (eds), *Law and Practice of EU External Relations* (2008), pp 23–31.

[138] Case C-63/99 *Gloszczuk* [2001] ECR I-6369; Case C-235/99 *Kondova* [2001] ECR I-6427; Case C-257/99 *Barkoci and Malik* [2001] ECR I-6557; Case C-416/96 *El-Yassini* [1999] ECR I-1209; Case C-97/05 *Gattoussi* [2006] ECR I-11917. For an analysis of these cases see ibid.

light of its normative content under Article 49 TFEU, the establishment provisions of these EU IIAs should not be interpreted to cover the protection afforded against non-discriminatory barriers to market access under Article 49 TFEU.

Consequently, EU IIAs, with the exception of the ECT, differ from other IIAs with regard to the application and interpretation of the non-discrimination standards found in their investment provisions. EU law and the GATS again present the guiding instruments, the interpretation of which is crucial for the determination of the scope of the MFN and NT standards in EU IIAs. Nevertheless, to the extent that identical interpretation to the primary EU law non-discrimination standard is concerned, this does not mean that the EU IIA establishment provisions also provide protection against non-discriminatory measures that affect the market access rights of foreign investors.

3.2.2.4.2 MFN treatment

The general rules determining the application and interpretation of non-discrimination standards in EU IIAs also apply, of course, with regard to the standard of MFN treatment. However, the determination of the scope of application of MFN treatment presents certain particularities, especially when compared to the other non-discrimination standard, NT. MFN treatment requires a comparison to the treatment granted to foreign investors from third countries, which can result not only from national regulation, but also from international agreements concluded between the host country and third countries. Hence, it is important to examine whether and to what extent MFN treatment covers advantages offered to third country investors under other international agreements.

The determination of the scope of the MFN standard under EU IIAs raises the question whether it covers all substantive and procedural advantages offered to third country investors under other IIAs concluded by the host country. The importance of determining the coverage of the MFN standard in EU IIAs becomes immediately apparent, when it is taken into consideration that the IIAs concluded by EU Member States and EU counterparties with third countries, mainly BITs, grant substantive and procedural advantages that are not offered under most EU IIAs, namely protection against expropriation and investor-state arbitration.[139] Hence, if the scope of the MFN provision of EU IIAs were interpreted broadly to cover all investment advantages offered under other IIAs the parties have concluded, it would in essence provide the foreign investors of the parties with the opportunity to initiate investor-state arbitration based on the EU IIAs, claiming not only a breach of the provisions of an EU IIA, but also of any substantive provision included in the parties' BITs.

A broad reading of the scope of the MFN standard would be favoured at first glance from the use of indeterminate and unconditional language in EU IIAs.

[139] The ECT presents an exception in that respect, where the scope of the MFN clause follows the general considerations on the scope of the MFN clause in BITs. For an analysis of the MFN clause in Art 10(7) ECT see P Friedland, 'The scope of Most Favored Nation treatment under the Energy Charter Treaty' in Coop and Ribeiro (eds), *Investment Protection and the Energy Charter Treaty* (2008), pp 111–14. See also below Sections 3.2.4 and 3.2.5.3.

The GATS, as well as the agreements with Mexico and the CARIFORUM states make reference to measures affecting commercial presence,[140] while the SAAs, the PCAs, and the EMAs with Algeria and Jordan grant MFN treatment 'for the establishment' and 'in respect of the operations' of foreign investors. Were such a broad interpretation of measures affecting commercial presence and/or the operation of foreign investors to be adopted, the MFN clause of these EU IIAs would bring investment protection and investor-state arbitration within their scope, since such measures affect the operations of foreign investors.[141]

However, such a broad reading of the MFN standard goes against the basic rule of *ejusdem generis* which requires that an MFN clause can only operate in respect of the same matter and cannot be extended to matters different from those envisaged by the basic treaty. Investment tribunals have been cautious in determining the scope of the MFN clause, so that even in cases where a broad interpretation of the clause was adopted, this standard could not be interpreted to apply to terms that the parties understood to be the fundamental conditions of their consent to be bound by an IIA.[142] Thus, the insertion of an MFN provision cannot compensate for the lack of consent of the parties to include in EU IIAs provisions, such as on protection against expropriation or investor-state arbitration, which are fundamental provisions of other IIAs. This principle is explicitly recognized in the FTA with Korea, which states that the MFN treatment 'does not extend to the investment protection provisions not covered by this Chapter, including provisions relating to investor-state dispute settlement procedures'.[143] In addition, the existing controversy on whether an MFN provision covers only substantive contingencies or can be extended to the procedural provisions of a BIT,[144] which present a core element of an IIA, indicates that the scope of the MFN provision is limited and in any event cannot be expanded to matters not covered under an IIA. Hence, considering that protection against expropriation and investor-state arbitration have been explicitly left outside the scope of EU IIAs, except for the ECT, the MFN clause cannot be

140 The GATS provides in Art II:1 that the scope of MFN treatment extends to 'any measure covered by this Agreement', referring to Art I:1 which states that the GATS 'applies to measures affecting trade in services', thus commercial presence.

141 For the dangers related to such broad reading of the MFN clause see A Falsafi, 'Regional Trade and Investment Agreements: Liberalizing Investment in a Preferential Climate' (2008) 36 Syracuse J Int'l L 43, 75–9; A Wimmer, 'The Impact of the General Agreement on Trade in Services on the OECD Multilateral Agreement on Investment' (1996) 19 World Competition 109.

142 For a detailed discussion of the limits posed on the scope of MFN clauses by virtue of the *ejusdem generis* rule see *Emilio Augustín Maffezini v Spain*, ICSID Case No ARB/97/7, Decision on Jurisdiction, 25 January 2000, 5 ICSID Reports 396, paras 38–56. S Alexandrov, 'Application of the MFN-clause in investment treaties: Replies to two questions' (2004) 1 Transnational Dispute Management; Falsafi, above n 141, pp 79–81.

143 Art 7.14 of the FTA with Korea, fn 18.

144 For a review of the case law on the scope of MFN clauses under IIAs see indicatively P Acconci, 'Most-Favoured-Nation Treatment' in Muchlinski, Ortino, and Schreuer (eds), *Oxford Handbook of International Investment Law* (2008), pp 381–401; R Dolzer and T Myers, 'After *Tecmed*: Most-Favoured-Nation Clauses in Investment Protection Agreements' (2004) 19 ICSID Rev-FILJ 49; S Fietta, 'Most Favoured Nation Treatment and Dispute Resolution under Bilateral Investment Treaties: a Turning Point?' (2005) 8 Intl ALR 131; Falsafi, above n 141, pp 67–70.

an indirect way to introduce these aspects of foreign investment regulation within their ambit.

To determine the scope of MFN standards in EU IIAs in relation to advantages provided under other international agreements, it is necessary to look also at the exceptions to MFN treatment. As will be addressed below, EU IIAs provide for general exceptions from their scope;[145] however, they also include specific exceptions from the scope of the MFN standard. A first important exception from the scope of MFN treatment in all EU IIAs concerns any tax advantages that are granted under a double taxation agreement with a third country.[146] Safeguarding the integrity of double taxation treaties, EU IIAs justify any discriminatory measures that are taken in accordance with the provisions of double taxation treaties.

Secondly, most EU IIAs provide an exception from the scope of MFN treatment for the treatment provided to third country nationals by virtue of an agreement establishing a regional economic integration organization (REIO). GATS Article V presents the most prominent exception to MFN treatment accorded in GATS Article II, granting a conditional right for WTO members to enter into an agreement liberalizing trade in services among themselves, without extending such beneficial treatment to other WTO members. More specifically, GATS Article V exempts from the scope of the MFN clause treatment accorded under agreements on trade in services that aim at economic integration. It requires that such agreements satisfy two sets of substantive requirements concerning internal and external trade similar to those found in Article XXIV of the General Agreement on Tariffs and Trade (GATT). With respect to the internal trade requirement, GATS Article V:1 requires that trade agreements in services have substantial sectoral coverage and eliminate substantially all discrimination, while GATS Article V:4 aims at minimizing the trade diversion effects of agreements in services by prohibiting the overall level of barriers to trade in services within the respective sectors or subsectors being raised in respect of any WTO member outside a given regional agreement. Nevertheless, Article V is distinctive from GATT Article XXIV, in that it provides for flexibility concerning the degree and the time frame of liberalization, in particular in cases where developing countries are members of a Regional Trade Agreement (RTA) in services.[147] Identical exceptions to the scope of MFN treatment are provided under most EU IIAs. Making an explicit reference to GATS Article V, the majority of EU IIAs exclude better treatment provided under other

[145] See below Section 3.2.2.6.

[146] Arts 66, 65, 68, 68, and 64 of the SAAs with Albania, Croatia, Montenegro, Serbia, and the Former Yugoslav Republic of Macedonia; Arts 103 and 100 of the EMAs with Algeria and Jordan; Arts 39, 39, 39, 39, 39, 40, 45, 49, 46, and 38 of the PCAs with Armenia, Azerbaijan, Georgia, Kazakhstan, Kyrgyzstan, Moldova, Russia, Ukraine, and Uzbekistan; Arts 7.8(3)(b), 70(3), 196, and 54 of the agreements with Korea, the CARIFORUM states, Chile, and Mexico.

[147] For a detailed analysis of Art V GATS see T Cottier and M Molinuevo, 'Art V GATS' in Wolfrum, Stoll, and Feinäugle (eds), *WTO Trade in Services* (2008), pp 125–50; SM Stephenson, 'GATS and Regional Integration' in Sauve and Stern (eds), *GATS 2000: New Directions in Services Liberalization* (2000), p 509.

bilateral EU IIAs that satisfy the conditions set out in GATS Article V from the scope of their MFN clause.[148]

An exception from the scope of MFN treatment for REIOs concluded by the parties is also provided in the EPA with the CARIFORUM states, the FTA with Korea, and the ECT.[149] Without referring to the GATS or duplicating its language, these agreements seem to establish lower standards that need to be achieved in order for a REIO to be excluded from the scope of MFN treatment. Although their internal trade requirement of 'providing for the absence or elimination of substantially all discrimination'[150] and 'creating an internal market'[151] imposes similar conditions to GATS Article V in order for REIOs to be exempt from the scope of the MFN provisions, they do not include an external trade requirement for the minimization of trade diversion effects. Nevertheless, the REIO exception from MFN treatment in these EU IIAs is narrower than most BITs and IIAs, which usually contain a broad REIO exception, without defining what constitutes an REIO.[152]

It should also be pointed out that a REIO clause is omitted from the SAAs. Considering, however, that these agreements aim at the future accession of the western Balkan countries to the EU and, thus, in the EU internal market, an exception from the scope of their MFN provisions for agreements concluded with third countries by either the EU or any of the western Balkan countries would be in direct contrast with the aim of full integration in the EU internal market and the incorporation of the *acquis* in the internal legal order of those countries.

Consequently, the determination of the scope and the exceptions to MFN treatment under existing EU IIAs seems to raise different concerns than under traditional IIAs. The debate whether MFN treatment covers only substantive or also procedural provisions cannot be introduced in EU IIAs, as it would breach the *ejusdem generis* rule. On the other hand, the scope of the exceptions to MFN treatment, in particular treatment provided under REIOs, has been the subject of extensive and elaborate regulation in EU IIAs, mainly in GATS Article V, while it is only a secondary issue in BITs.

3.2.2.4.3 FET and additional standards?

Existing EU IIAs lack an explicit reference to 'absolute' standards of treatment, such as FET or Full Protection and Security, which are provided in BITs and traditional IIAs. Despite the long-standing tradition and greater importance of

[148] Arts 30(3) and 45 of the EMAs with Algeria and Jordan; Arts 38, 38, 38, 38, 38, 39, 44, 44, 45, and 37 of the PCAs with Armenia, Azerbaijan, Georgia, Kazakhstan, Kyrgyzstan, Moldova, Russia, Ukraine, and Uzbekistan; Art 5(2) of the agreement with Mexico.

[149] Arts 70(2), 7.8(2), and 24(4) respectively. It should be noted that the ECT also includes a special exception from the scope of MFN treatment for international agreements concerning economic cooperation between states that were constituent parts of the former Soviet Union pending the establishment of their mutual economic relations on a definitive basis.

[150] Art 25(2) ECT.

[151] Art 70(2) of the EPA with the CARIFORUM states.

[152] OECD, *The REIO Exception in MFN Treatment Clauses* (2004), pp 10–15, 44–7; Falsafi, above n 141, pp 59–66.

'absolute' standards of treatment for investment agreements, EU IIAs, again with the exception of the ECT, seem to ignore them. However, this does not mean that EU IIAs do not offer, to a certain extent, a similar level of protection to foreign investments and investors. Instead of reaching a generalized, superficial conclusion on the lack of 'absolute' treatment standards, it is necessary to examine the protective scope of these standards under traditional IIAs and whether other provisions in EU IIAs offer similar protection.

'Absolute' standards of treatment provide protection of foreign investment against national measures irrespective of their discriminatory character. In that regard, customary international law has been initially regarded as recognizing an International Minimum Standard for the treatment of foreign investors, which has evolved through treaty practice to the modern FET standard.[153] Without entering into a detailed analysis of the scope and content of the International Minimum Standard and the FET standard and their relation, which varies across different instruments depending on their formulation and interpretation,[154] the FET standard has been considered as an expression of the principle of good faith, protecting foreign investors from abusive conduct by host states, ensuring the application of regulatory fairness and transparency, and safeguarding legitimate expectations of investors.[155] In that respect the FET standard has been interpreted, among others, as protecting foreign investors from (a) arbitrary, unjust, and discriminatory measures irrespective of the intent of the host state,[156] (b) the lack of due process and/or of procedural fairness,[157] (c) the inability or failure of host states to create and apply a transparent and predictable regulatory environment,[158] and (d) the frustration of investors' legitimate expectations that were created by the conduct of the host state and were significant in the initial decision to invest.[159]

Protection against arbitrary measures and a guarantee of substantive and procedural fairness and transparency in the adoption and application of national

[153] On the history of the international minimum standard and the FET standard see I Tudor, *The Fair and Equitable Treatment Standard in the International Law of Foreign Investment* (2008), pp 1–4.

[154] On the typology of FET clauses in IIAs see ibid, ch 1.

[155] This categorization of the content of the FET standard is followed in Grierson-Weiler and Laird, above n 117, p 272. See also Dolzer and Schreuer, above n 86, pp 133–48.

[156] *Ronald S Lauder v The Czech Republic*, UNCITRAL Final Award, 3 September 2001, 9 ICSID Reports 66; *MTD Equity Sdn Bhd and MTD Chile SA v Chile*, ICSID Case No ARB/01/7, Award, 25 May 2004.

[157] *Loewen Group Inc and Raymond Loewen v United States of America*, ICSID Case No ARB(AF)/98/3, 26, Award, 26 June 2003, 42 ILM 811; *Robert Azinian, Kenneth Davitian and Ellen Baca v United Mexican States*, ICSID (Additional Facility) Case No ARB(AF)/97/2, Award, 1 November 1999, 39 ILM 537.

[158] *Metalclad Corp v United States of Mexico*, ICSID Case No ARB (AF)/97/1, Final Award, 30 August 2000, 5 ICSID Reports 212; *GAMI Investments Inc v United Mexican States*, UNCITRAL, Final Award, 15 November 2004, 44 ILM 545; *Técnicas Medioambientales Tecmed, SA v United Mexican States*, ICSID Case No ARB(AF)/00/2, Award, 29 May 2003, 43 ILM 133.

[159] *International Thunderbird Gaming v Mexico*, UNCITRAL, Award, 26 January 2006; *Saluka Investments BV (The Netherlands) v The Czech Republic*, UNCITRAL, Partial Award, 17 March 2006; *Waste Management Inc v United Mexican States*, ICSID Case No ARB(AF)/00/3, Award, 30 April 2004, 43 ILM 967.

measures are also provided under EU IIAs, albeit under a different heading. The GATS, which serves as the most prominent example, establishes in Article VI under the heading of domestic regulation, obligations for WTO members, which aim to sanction regulatory behaviour with an unduly trade-distortive effect.[160] The first three paragraphs of Article VI introduce into the GATS the concept of procedural due process, requiring that the administration of measures of general application affecting trade in services is reasonable, objective, and impartial and that there are appropriate remedies and appropriate mechanisms for the consideration and review of administrative decisions applying measures that affect trade in services. Furthermore, Article VI:4 provides for the negotiation of future disciplines relating to qualifications, licensing, and technical standards, indicating that the adoption of measures affecting trade in services should abide by the principles of transparency, proportionality, and non-arbitrariness. In addition, paragraph 5 requires that, until the conclusion of negotiations according to paragraph 4, the application of existing regulation should meet these standards of substantive fairness and transparency.[161]

Reading GATS Article VI under the prism of a FET analysis, it becomes obvious that both set out conditions for the legality of the conduct of national authorities that can affect foreign investors. Albeit in a more limited and less flexible manner, the GATS requires in essence procedural fairness and substantive fairness and transparency in the application of existing regulation, providing for the creation of future disciplines which, similar to the Agreement on Technical Barriers to Trade (TBT Agreement) and the Agreement on the Application of Sanitary and Phytosanitary Measures (SPS Agreement) in the field of trade in goods, will establish criteria of substantive fairness for the adoption of national regulatory measures.[162] Consequently, GATS Article VI offers, to a certain extent, protection to foreign investors against the same forms of conduct of national authorities provided by the FET standard.

Nevertheless, there is a significant difference between the FET standard and domestic regulation. Similar to EU law and the TBT and SPS disciplines,[163] domestic regulation under GATS aims to eliminate barriers to market access, providing a mechanism for bettering those non-discriminatory regulations that are inequitable, excessively interventionist, or more trade-restrictive than necessary to

[160] P Delimatsis, 'Due Process and "Good" Regulation Embedded in the GATS—Disciplining Regulatory Behaviour in Services through Art VI GATS' (2007) 10 JIEL 13, 17.

[161] For a description of the obligations established under Art VI GATS see ibid, pp 19–48; J Wouters and D Coppens, 'GATS and Domestic Regulation: Balancing the Right to Regulate and Trade Liberalization' in Alexander and Andenas (eds), *The World Trade Organization and Trade in Services* (2008), pp 207–63; M Krajewski, 'Art VI GATS' in Wolfrum, Stoll, and Feinäugle (eds), *WTO Trade in Services* (2008), pp 165–95.

[162] Ortino, above n 117, pp 37–47.

[163] For a comparative overview of the role of domestic regulation in the field of trade in goods in the WTO and EU law see F Ortino, *Basic Legal Instruments for the Liberalization of Trade: a comparative analysis of EC and WTO Law* (2004), ch 4; J Scott, 'Mandatory or Imperative Requirements in the EU and the WTO' in Barnard and Scott (eds), *The Law of the Single European Market: Unpacking the Premises* (2002), pp 269; G de Búrca, 'Unpacking the concept of discrimination in EC and international trade law' in Barnard and Scott (eds), *The Law of the Single European Market: Unpacking the Premises* (2002), pp 181f.

achieve a legitimate objective. As a result, contrary to the FET standard which guarantees protection to each individual investor, domestic regulation obligations do not cover measures addressing specific situations but apply only to measures that affect an unidentified number of economic operators, thus hindering the realization of the market access commitments of the violating party.[164]

In contrast with the GATS, most bilateral EU IIAs do not include provisions establishing obligations such as those described under GATS Article VI. The FTA with Korea establishes an obligation on host countries to guarantee substantive and procedural fairness in the administration of national laws affecting foreign investors, but only where authorization is required for the establishment of a foreign investor.[165] Only the agreement with Chile provides for an obligation on substantive fairness, similar to the one established under GATS Article VI:5,[166] while the EPA with the CARIFORUM states establishes an obligation for procedural fairness in the application of domestic regulation.[167] In respect of the remaining EU IIAs, although they may provide for approximation of laws,[168] mutual recognition,[169] or a standstill clause concerning non-discriminatory restrictions to market access,[170] they retain the right of host states to regulate the operation of foreign investment without providing any criteria controlling the adoption and application of domestic regulation.[171] The absence of domestic regulation provisions in bilateral EU IIAs can be explained in light of the harmonizing effects that domestic regulation provisions have. Although regulatory harmonization may be desirable in a multilateral context, such as the WTO, the adoption of common standards at a bilateral level could potentially lead to the multiplication of regulatory regimes imposing different standards. Also, the imposition of additional obligations could deprive countries party to a bilateral agreement from the advantages of regulatory competition, which is higher in an area where multilateral rules do not yet exist.[172]

As a result, most EU IIAs do not afford foreign investors absolute standards of treatment that require substantive and procedural fairness and transparency in the adoption and application of national measures. Nevertheless, the discipline of domestic regulation under the GATS offers, protection against such conduct, albeit in a different context and with a different purpose, which usually underlies most bilateral EU IIAs concluded with WTO members, setting a different example for future EU IIAs as to how they should regulate absolute standards of treatment.

[164] Delimatsis, above n 160, p 20.
[165] Art 7.22 of the FTA with Korea.
[166] Art 102 of the EU-Chile Agreement.
[167] Art 87 of the EPA with the CARIFORUM states.
[168] Eg Art 70 of the SAA with Albania.
[169] Eg Art 9 of the EU-Mexico Services agreement.
[170] Eg Art 29 of the PCA with Armenia.
[171] Eg Art 51(1) of the SAA with Albania states that 'each Party may regulate the establishment and operation of companies and nationals on its territory, insofar as these regulations do not discriminate against companies and nationals of the other Party in comparison with its own companies and nationals.'
[172] C Arup, 'Services and Investment in Free Trade Agreements: Liberalization, Regulation and Law' in Buckley, Lo, and Boulle (eds), *Challenges to Multilateral Trade The Impact of Bilateral, Preferential and Regional Agreements* (2008), pp 180–1.

3.2.2.5 EU IIA provisions on specific issues relating to the operation of FDI

Next to the general standards of treatment of foreign direct investment, EU IIAs contain provisions on specific issues relating to the operation of foreign investment. A significant number of EU IIAs contain provisions on performance requirements and movement of natural persons related to an investment, while the EPA with the CARIFORUM states includes novelty provisions regarding investors behaviour and the maintenance of standards, which were further elaborated in the FTA with Korea. Similar to general standards of treatment, the influence of EU law and GATS in these fields is apparent, distinguishing EU IIAs from BITs and other IIAs. Bearing in mind the broader framework within which EU IIAs deal with foreign investment, they present their own unique regulatory model, adding to the diversity of regulatory approaches on these issues.

3.2.2.5.1 EU IIA provisions on performance requirements

Similar to Member State BITs, which do not provide any prohibition on performance requirements, EU IIAs do not include a specific provision on performance requirements in their respective chapters relating to foreign investment. Adopting the view that the imposition of performance requirements lies in the discretion of national regulators,[173] EU IIAs do not include an outright prohibition of performance requirements. Nevertheless, certain types of performance requirements are dealt with indirectly in separate chapters of EU IIAs.

While considering that all EU IIAs that include foreign investment provisions also include rules for trade liberalization, a first category of performance requirements that is regulated in EU IIAs is trade-related performance requirements. By prohibiting quantitative restrictions to trade, EU IIAs prohibit in essence the imposition of trade-related performance requirements, such as foreign exchange balancing, import-export balancing, and export restrictions. For the remaining trade-related performance requirements, their imposition on foreign investors is subject to the general standards of MFN and NT. EU IIAs guarantee non-discrimination in the application of performance requirements, to the extent of course that performance requirements are not listed as exceptions to MFN or NT. These rules are explicitly incorporated in the Agreement on Trade-Related Investment Measures (TRIMs), which presents the most important multilateral agreement on performance requirements,[174] as well as in the ECT,[175] while for the remaining EU IIAs they can be indirectly derived from the provision prohibiting quantitative restrictions and the scope of the MFN and NT provisions.

In relation to non-trade-related performance requirements, in particular those linked to subsidies, technology transfer, and monopoly rights, EU IIAs generally do not include specific provisions restricting their imposition on foreign investors.

[173] See Section 4.2.2.2.

[174] P Civello, 'The TRIMS Agreement: A Failed Attempt at Investment Liberalization' (1999) 8 Minnesota JWT 97; T Brewer and S Young, *The Multilateral Investment System and Multinational Enterprises* (1998), p 123.

[175] Arts 5 and 10(7), (11) ECT.

To the extent that such matters are subject to the MFN and NT standards,[176] EU IIAs provide general rules that apply to both domestic and foreign investors,[177] or leave these matters to the discretion of national regulators.

3.2.2.5.2 EU IIA provisions on movement of investment-related natural persons

Movement of investment related natural persons is an important aspect of post-establishment operation of foreign investment regulated in all EU IIAs. Considering that the employment of certain natural persons is necessary for the successful operation of a business undertaking, especially during its initial stages, EU IIAs establish a specific right for foreign investors to employ foreign nationals, usually only with regard to key positions for the business activities of the foreign investor and on a temporary basis.[178] The particular weight that EU IIAs attribute to the right of foreign investors to employ foreign nationals under certain conditions is in sharp contrast to many Member State BITs and most IIAs concluded by other international actors. The latter leave this issue to the national regulator, providing at best an obligation for host countries not to use nationality as a condition for the appointment of natural persons in senior management positions.[179]

To determine the right of foreign investors to employ foreign natural persons, EU IIAs have followed distinctive models. Again, GATS presents a regulatory model that has influenced other EU IIAs. Providing that the fourth mode of supply of services concerns the movement of natural persons related to the supply of the service, the GATS establishes a broad framework, within which WTO members can undertake commitments, defining the categories and the circumstances under which natural persons can be employed in the territory of another member country. Bearing in mind the broad scope of mode 4, which covers all natural persons related to a commercial presence as well as self-employed natural persons, most WTO members have distinguished between different categories of natural persons, undertaking distinct commitments for each category in each service sector. Indicatively, in its schedule of commitments the EU has identified three main categories of natural persons—namely intra-corporate transferees, contractual service suppliers, and independent professionals—taking commitments mainly in the first two categories.[180] A similar approach to the movement of investment-related natural persons is adopted in the

[176] Eg the EPA with the CARIFORUM states in Art 60 excludes subsidies from the scope of the treatment standards of foreign investment.

[177] Eg technology transfer agreements and subsidies are usually regulated in competition law provisions, such as Arts 126, 129, and 142 of the EPA with the CARIFORUM states.

[178] See Section 1.3.3.2.3.

[179] Eg Art 9 of the US Model BIT provides that:

1. Neither Party may require that an enterprise of that Party that is a covered investment appoint to senior management positions natural persons of any particular nationality.
2. A Party may require that a majority of the board of directors, or any committee thereof, of an enterprise of that Party that is a covered investment, be of a particular nationality, or resident in the territory of the Party, provided that the requirement does not materially impair the ability of the investor to exercise control over its investment.

[180] WTO Trade in Services Division, *A handbook on the GATS agreement* (2005), pp 4–5; R Chanda, 'Movement of natural persons and the GATS' (2001) 24 World Economy 631.

Agreements with Mexico and Chile, which replicate the GATS language with regard to the movement of natural persons, including, however, more extensive commitments by the parties.

The movement of investment-related natural persons is regulated with more precision in the SAAs, the PCAs, the EMAs with Algeria and Jordan, the FTA with Korea, and the EPA with the CARIFORUM states.[181] Instead of including a general reference to natural persons, these EU IIAs determine the specific categories of natural persons, establishing the specific conditions under which a foreign investor can employ foreign nationals for the operation of its business activities in the host country. More specifically, these agreements enable foreign investors to employ on a temporary basis 'key personnel' necessary for the establishment and management of the undertaking established in the host country. As key personnel qualify persons holding senior management positions or uncommon knowledge essential for the operations of the foreign investor, these EU IIAs limit in essence the scope of movement of investment-related natural persons to intra-corporate transferees. Furthermore, it is worth noting that the FTA with Korea and the EPA with the CARIFORUM states expand the categories of investment-related natural persons, as in addition to intra-corporate transferees, they enable the movement of natural persons from the parent company to its subsidiary in the host state for career development purposes (graduate trainees).[182]

To examine the extent of the right of foreign investors to employ foreign nationals related to their investment in the host country, it is necessary to distinguish EU IIAs from primary EU law and the EEA Agreement, where the movement of natural persons related to an establishment has a broader scope. In addition to the exception of self-employed persons from the scope of EU IIA provisions on establishment, movement of investment-related natural persons is exclusively limited to key personnel. Contrary to the internal market, where service providers have the right to transfer their employees who are legally employed in one Member State to the territory of another Member State for a short-term period in order to exercise their freedom to provide services,[183] EU IIAs do not cover all employees of the foreign investor, and in particular workers. The limited scope of the right of foreign investors to employ only key personnel is explicitly recognized in the PCAs, which exclude from their scope the right of established foreign investors to employ posted workers, even if this is only on a temporary basis.[184]

[181] Arts 55, 54, 58, 58, and 53 of the SAAs with Albania, Croatia, Montenegro, Serbia, and the Former Yugoslav Republic of Macedonia; Arts 28, 28, 28, 28, 28, 34, 32, 35, and 27 of the PCAs with Armenia, Azerbaijan, Georgia, Kazakhstan, Kyrgyzstan, Moldova, Russia, Ukraine, and Uzbekistan; Arts 33 and 34 of the EMAs with Algeria and Jordan; Arts 7.17–7.19. of the FTA with Korea; Arts 80 and 81 of the EPA with the CARIFORUM states.

[182] Arts 7.18 and 80–1 of the FTA with Korea and the EPA with the CARIFORUM states respectively. See B Hoekman and C Özden, 'The Euro-Mediterranean Partnership: Trade in Services- An alternative to Migration?', World Bank Policy Research Working Paper 5049 (September 2009), pp 17–20.

[183] See Directive 96/71/EC on Posted Workers in the framework of provision of services [1997] OJ L18/1. See also Case C-43/93 *Van der Elst v OMI* [1994] ECR I-3803 and Case C-113/89 *Rush Portuguesa* [1990] ECR I-1417. Van den Hende, above n 87, p 176.

[184] Arts 40, 40, 40, 40, 41, 46, 50, 47, and 39 of the PCAs with Armenia, Azerbaijan, Georgia, Kazakhstan, Kyrgyzstan, Moldova, Russia, Ukraine, and Uzbekistan.

3.2.2.5.3 Maintenance of standards and investors' behaviour

The EPA with the CARIFORUM states as well as the FTA with Korea include innovative provisions regarding the operation of foreign investment. More specifically, Articles 72 and 73 of the EPA as well as chapter 13 of the FTA with Korea, elaborating and reorganizing the relevant provisions of the EPA, introduce obligations for the host state that are not linked with rights of foreign investors, but rather aim to set up minimum rules for their conduct. Building on current BIT provisions that concern the relationship between foreign investment and labour or environmental standards,[185] the provisions on investors' behaviour and maintenance of standards oblige the parties to take all appropriate measures to ensure that foreign investment activity conforms to a number of standards.

More specifically, Article 72 of the EPA with the CARIFORUM states sets out the basic obligations of foreign investors, which are inherently linked with the establishment of minimum labour and environmental standards. It provides that the Parties 'shall take... measures as may be necessary to ensure' that bribery of officials by foreign investors is forbidden, that core labour standards as required by the ILO Declaration on Fundamental Principles and Rights of Work (1998) are respected, and that international environmental or labour obligations arising from agreements signed by the parties are not breached by investors' activities. The use of imperative language emphasizes that the EPA not only recognizes the right of the parties to pursue policies that ensure these standards, but it also imposes an obligation on them to take the appropriate and necessary measures. By linking minimum labour and environmental standards to international law instruments binding on the parties, it enables these considerations to be taken into account in determining foreign investors' rights and obligations.

The FTA with Korea adopts a more elaborate approach, placing similar obligations on the parties under the broader framework of the relationship between trade and sustainable development. Recognizing that 'economic development, social development and environmental protection are interdependent',[186] it stresses the obligation on both parties to adopt high levels of protection of labour and environmental standards. Articles 13.4 and 13.5 reaffirm the commitments of the parties under international labour and environmental agreements and the obligation of the parties effectively to implement them, and express the willingness of the parties to cooperate further in order to promote internationally set labour and environmental goals.

Hence, these agreements take a step further than any other IIA by incorporating, in legally binding instruments, certain principles of corporate social responsibility which up until then were adopted by investors on a voluntary basis.[187] Without

[185] Eg Arts 12 and 13 of the US Model BIT and Art 1114 of the NAFTA.

[186] Art 13.1(2) of the FTA with Korea.

[187] Voluntary codes of corporate social responsibility represented by eg the UN Code of Conduct for Transnational Corporations (1986) and the OECD Guidelines for Multinational Corporations (1972 as amended in 2001). For a discussion of voluntary codes see F McLeay, 'Corporate Codes of Conduct and the Human Rights Accountability of Transnational Corporations: a Small Piece of a Larger Puzzle' in DeSchutter (ed), *Transnational Corporations and Human Rights* (2006), pp 219–41.

imposing direct obligations on private individuals, which would be controversial under public international law,[188] the EPA with the CARIFORUM states and the FTA with Korea are carefully drafted to introduce basic limits on foreign investment activity.

The establishment of minimum labour and environmental standards is complemented by provisions requiring the maintenance of existing standards. Both agreements provide that the parties shall ensure that FDI is not encouraged by lowering domestic environmental and labour standards or laws.[189] Even though similar provisions are found in other IIAs, such as Article 1114 NAFTA, these EU IIAs present significant innovations. They adopt clearer and much stronger wording by not appealing to the parties' 'best efforts', and instead obliging them to avoid lowering their national standards.[190] Moreover, it is noteworthy that the EPA broadens the scope of public policy concerns linked with foreign investment, including, next to environmental and labour standards, social, health and cultural concerns, which were not replicated in the FTA with Korea.[191]

3.2.2.6 Exceptions and limitations to establishment and post-establishment treatment

Addressing public policy considerations, all EU IIAs provide for general exceptions and limitations on the scope of establishment and post-establishment treatment of FDI. They provide that their establishment provisions do not apply to activities related to the exercise of official authority and to measures covered within the scope of double taxation agreements. Furthermore, they enable host states to adopt, under certain conditions, measures pursuing specific public policy objectives that would otherwise be considered to infringe the investment provisions of the agreements.

By introducing exceptions and limitations to the scope of establishment and post-establishment treatment of FDI, EU IIAs broadly follow the language of the relevant provisions of the TFEU and the GATS. More specifically, Article XIV GATS as well as Articles 7.50, 225, 135, and 27 of the agreements with Korea, the CARIFORUM states, Chile, and Mexico respectively, which were based on the GATS, provide a general exception from the application of the investment provisions. These provisions allow the parties to adopt proportionate and non-arbitrary measures necessary to protect and secure public morals, the public order, human, animal, or plant life or health, exhaustible natural resources, national cultural

[188] O de Schutter, 'The Challenge of Imposing Human Rights Norms on Corporate Actors' in de Schutter (ed), *Transnational Corporations and Human Rights* (2006), pp 1–43.

[189] Arts 73 and 13.7. of the EPA with the CARIFORUM states and the FTA with Korea respectively. Similar provisions are found in Arts 188 and 193 of the EPA with the CARIFORUM states, which reiterate the obligation of the parties not to lower the standards of their domestic environmental, health, social, and labour legislation in order to encourage foreign investment.

[190] Eg contrary to Art 1114 NAFTA which uses words such as 'it is inappropriate' and 'should not', the EPA and the FTA include the term 'shall'. J Vandenberghe, 'On Carrots and Sticks: The Social Dimension of EU Trade Policy' (2008) 13 EFA Rev 561, 575–6.

[191] On the implications of the introduction of these provisions for the orientation of EU foreign investment policy, see Section 4.2.1.3.

treasures, and other public policy objectives. Adopting a similar wording to GATT Article XX, these EU IIAs extend the scope of that exception to investment provisions, thus allowing the parties to invoke its application for derogating from rules on foreign investment.[192] In that regard, GATT Article XX gains particular importance for the interpretation of these provisions.[193] A similar general exception, albeit offering limited grounds for justification and not applying to expropriation, is provided in Article 24 ECT.

Different language is adopted in the remaining EU IIAs that regulate establishment and post-establishment treatment of foreign investment, which are inspired by EU law. More specifically, they provide that establishment rules shall apply subject to limitations that are justified on grounds of public policy, public security, or public health.[194] The adoption of almost identical wording to Article 52 TFEU indicates that the legality of limitations to establishment rules in these EU IIAs should be interpreted by reference to the meaning of identical or similar terms in Union law. For example, as the Court has already ruled in the *Nazli*[195] and *Jany*[196] cases, the exception of public policy under the association agreements with Turkey and Poland should be interpreted in light of the corresponding term in EU law.[197]

In addition to public policy, public security, and public health, all EU IIAs, including those with Chile, Mexico, and the CARIFORUM states, provide that their provisions do not apply to activities related to the exercise of official authority.[198] Mirroring the first paragraph of Article 51 TFEU, EU IIAs safeguard the exception of public authority activities from the scope of standards of treatment offered to foreign investors, which similar to the public policy, public security, and public health exception, should be interpreted by analogy to Article 51 TFEU.[199]

When comparing the scope of the exceptions to establishment and post-establishment treatment of foreign investment under EU IIAs with BITs and other IIAs, it is immediately apparent that public policy considerations have a different position in the assessment of the legality of a national measure. While EU IIAs provide an explicit exception from the scope of treatment standards, BITs

[192] T Cottier, P Delimatsis, and N Diebold, 'Art XIV GATS' in Wolfrum, Stoll, and Feinäugle (eds), *WTO- Trade in Services* (2008), pp 292–3; Ortino, above n 122, pp 186–93.

[193] On the interpretation of Art XX GATT see indicatively P Mavroidis, *Trade in Goods* (2007), pp 254–86.

[194] Arts 63, 62, 65, 65, and 61 of the SAAs with Albania, Croatia, Montenegro, Serbia, and the Former Yugoslav Republic of Macedonia; Arts 35 and 41 of the EMAs with Algeria and Jordan; Arts 34, 34, 34, 34, 35, 40, 46, 41, and 33 of the PCAs with Armenia, Azerbaijan, Georgia, Kazakhstan, Kyrgyzstan, Moldova, Russia, Ukraine, and Uzbekistan.

[195] Case C-340/97 *Nazli* [2000] ECR I-957, paras 56–61.

[196] Case C-268/99 *Jany and Others* [2001] ECR I-8615, paras 58–61.

[197] On the scope of the public policy, public security, and public health exception provided in Art 53 TFEU see indicatively Frenz, above n 121, pp 840–68.

[198] Arts 63, 62, 65, 65, and 61 of the SAAs with Albania, Croatia, Montenegro, Serbia, and the Former Yugoslav Republic of Macedonia; Arts 35 and 41 of the EMAs with Algeria and Jordan; Arts 34, 34, 34, 34, 35, 40, 46, 41, and 33 of the PCAs with Armenia, Azerbaijan, Georgia, Kazakhstan, Kyrgyzstan, Moldova, Russia, Ukraine, and Uzbekistan. Arts 224, 135, and 27 of the agreements with the CARIFORUM states, Chile, and Mexico.

[199] On the interpretation of the official authority exception see Case 2/74 *Reyners v Belgium* [1974] ECR 63, paras 43–53; see also P Craig and G de Búrca, *EU Law: Texts, Cases, and Materials* (2008), pp 795–8.

have been interpreted to incorporate public policy considerations in the concept of 'like circumstances'. As already argued, this interpretative approach to the scope of standards of treatment does not offer any guidance to arbitral tribunals as to the degree of deference that they should grant national legislators for adopting measures serving public policy goals and dilutes the concept of non-discrimination.[200] This difference is more striking for the ECT which, in contrast to other EU IIAs, follows a more traditional regulatory model, being closer to BITs than the GATS or EU law.

3.2.2.7 Compatibility of establishment and post-establishment provisions of EU IIAs with primary EU law

Regulation of establishment and post-establishment treatment and operation of foreign investment in EU IIAs also raises concerns regarding their compatibility with primary EU law. EU IIAs have to be evaluated in light of primary EU law provisions on the CCP and freedom of establishment, which grant competence to the EU in the field of establishment and operation of foreign investment.

Starting with the provisions on the CCP, the TFEU provides limited assistance in terms of the principles to which it adheres and the objectives it is bound to pursue, granting policy makers a great degree of flexibility when they determine the substantive content of international agreements adopted under Article 207 TFEU. Articles 206 and 207 TFEU identify, albeit in an indirect way, uniformity and liberalization as the guiding principles and objectives determining the exercise of EU powers in the field of the CCP.[201] However, as will be addressed in Chapter 4, the principle of uniformity has only instrumental value, as it determines the areas of the CCP where common rules must be adopted, while it remains 'neutral' with regard to the substantive orientation of the CCP, without imposing an obligation for equal treatment of third countries or for full liberalization of market conditions. Furthermore, prior to the entry into force of the Lisbon Treaty liberalization constituted only an aspirational objective which offers guidance to the political institutions in the formation of the CCP. Whereas the Lisbon Treaty arguably introduces an obligation on EU institutions to respect the existing level of liberalization and refrain from introducing more restrictive measures.[202] However, given that all existing EU IIAs, with the exception of the FTA with Korea, were concluded prior to the entry into force of the Lisbon Treaty, the standstill obligation introduced under Article 206 TFEU applies only for future EU IIAs. As a result, the conformity of EU IIAs with the provisions of the CCP raises questions concerning the observance of competence and procedural limitations rather than substantive content.

Turning to the TFEU provisions on establishment, these impose certain limitations by which EU IIAs have to abide. Of course, contrary to capital movements, the TFEU rules on establishment do not directly address the establishment

[200] See above Section 3.2.2.4.1.

[201] M Cremona, 'The External Dimension of the Internal Market' in Barnard and Scott (eds), *The Law of the Single European Market* (2002), pp 354–5.

[202] See Section 4.1.1.1.

of third country nationals in the EU or that of EU nationals in third countries. Nevertheless, as Article 49 TFEU confers implied external competence to the EU, the latter should respect the directions and limitations provided in the exercise of its competence via the conclusion of international agreements. More specifically, similar to the compatibility issues of EU IIAs with capital movement rules, EU IIAs have to respect the exceptions and restrictions to the free movement rules envisaged in Articles 51 and 52 TFEU. As mentioned, all EU IIAs include provisions that justify derogations from non-discrimination standards regarding the exercise of official authority and for public policy, public security, and public health reasons.

In addition to the restrictions on the scope of establishment and post-establishment treatment regulation, the compatibility of EU IIAs with primary EU law should also be examined in the light of the principle of equal treatment of EU nationals. EU institutions should respect the principle of non-discrimination when they conclude international agreements with third countries, so that any advantage thereby granted would be offered to all EU nationals.[203] The principle of equal treatment of all EU nationals, which is of particular importance for assessing the compatibility of Member State agreements with primary EU law,[204] is also relevant for assessing the compatibility of EU IIAs with EU law. While considering that the determination of EU corporate nationality is based on the general criteria of place of incorporation and effective seat, irrespective of ownership or control of the legal person,[205] the treatment of foreign-owned or-controlled EU companies under EU IIAs raises questions of compatibility.

More specifically, incompatibilities can arise to the extent that EU IIAs result in unequal treatment of foreign-controlled EU companies in EU Member States or in third countries. As regards equal treatment of EU companies in EU Member States, the danger of incompatibility arises to the extent that EU IIAs do not grant equal treatment to undertakings owned or controlled by nationals of the EU counterparty that satisfy the conditions set out in Article 54 TFEU. Almost all EU IIAs offer NT to subsidiaries of EU counterparties' companies, thus they abide by the principle of equal treatment, since subsidiaries present the only form of secondary establishment that satisfies the conditions set out in Article 54 TFEU for acquiring EU nationality. Nevertheless, confusion arises from the definition of legal person under the EU-Korea FTA. For the purposes of establishment, a juridical person of a party is also the one controlled or owned by a natural or juridical person of that party,[206] thus this provision seems to imply that a juridical person established in the EU according to Article 54 TFEU, which is owned or controlled by Korean nationals, is considered under the agreement only a Korean juridical person. In such case, any deviation from national treatment of Korean-controlled EU juridical persons would amount to a violation of Article 49 TFEU.

[203] M Cremona, 'Neutrality or Discrimination? The WTO, the EU and External Trade' in de Búrca and Scott (eds), *The EU and the WTO Legal and Constitutional Issues* (2001), pp 159–60.

[204] See Sections 6.2.2.4 and 6.2.2.5.

[205] See Section 1.2.2.1.2.

[206] Art 7.2(f)(ii).

Furthermore, insofar as equal treatment of EU companies in third countries is concerned, the fact that all EU IIAs provide a definition of 'EU company' in accordance with Article 54 TFEU indicates that all EU companies receive equal treatment in the territory of a third country.[207]

3.2.3 EU IIA provisions on foreign investment in the form of concession contracts

Following the distinction between the different forms of foreign investment adopted in the TFEU, EU IIAs deal with foreign investment in the form of concession contracts in their chapter on provision of services. Contrary to BITs, which provide the same rules of treatment for all forms of foreign investment, as they include a broad asset-based definition of foreign investment, EU IIAs, with the exception of the ECT, regulate foreign investment in the form of concession contracts separately under their provisions on cross-border supply of services, which cover a wide range of economic activities, including this category of foreign investment.[208]

Despite the distinction between FDI and foreign investment in the form of concession contracts, EU IIAs approach the different categories of foreign investment in a similar manner. Provisions on the cross-border supply of services exist in all agreements that regulate admission and treatment of FDI. EU IIAs regulate the admission and treatment of foreign investment in the form of concession contracts by establishing general standards of treatment based on the principle of non-discrimination, using the GATS and EU law as regulatory models.

More specifically, the GATS as well as the agreements with Mexico and Chile regulate foreign investment in the form of concession contracts as covered under the first mode of supply of services, namely cross-border supply of services.[209] As the GATS and the agreements with Mexico and Chile provide general rules applicable to all modes of supply of services, these EU IIAs provide the same standards of treatment applicable to FDI regarding the admission and post-admission treatment of foreign investment in the form of concession contracts. However, as these agreements adopt a 'positive list' approach to liberalization,[210] differences exist with regard to the scope of commitments undertaken by the parties for each mode of supply of services in every sector.

A separate set of provisions dedicated to cross-border supply of services which, in essence, replicates the provisions on FDI, exists in the FTA with Korea, the EPA with the CARIFORUM states, and the EMA with Algeria. Providing for MFN treatment and including schedules with market access and NT commitments, the admission and post-admission treatment of foreign investment in the form of concession

[207] See Section 1.2.2.3.

[208] See Section 1.2.2.2.2.

[209] The concept of cross-border supply of services comprises the supply of services from the territory of one state to the territory of another state, thus covering concession contracts, where the service supplier remains in the home country without establishing a commercial presence or moving natural persons, but the service itself is only provided in the host country.

[210] See above Sections 3.2.2.2 and 3.2.2.3.

contracts in the agreements with Korea and the CARIFORUM states is regulated in a similar manner to the regulation of commercial presence.[211] Furthermore, similar to commercial presence provisions, the EMA with Algeria establishes an MFN obligation for the cross-border supply of services by EU nationals in Algeria, while extending the scope of the EU's GATS commitments to Algeria.[212]

Similar to FDI regulation, the chapter on cross-border supply of services in the EEA Agreement, the SAAs, the PCAs, and the EMA with Jordan is based on TFEU provisions, and in particular the chapter on provision of services. Nevertheless, the scope of liberalization is not as extensive as in the field of establishment. With the exception of the EEA Agreement—which establishes an absolute prohibition of restrictions on the freedom to provide services, adopting similar wording to the TFEU[213]—this group of EU IIAs does not include far-reaching commitments. All PCAs, except for the agreement with Russia, and the EMA with Jordan, provide for the future progressive liberalization of cross-border supply of services, including only certain commitments in the sector of maritime transport.[214] In addition to maritime transport, the PCA with Russia provides for MFN treatment with regard to the cross-border supply of services in specific sectors,[215] while the SAAs include a standstill and rollback provision, prohibiting the introduction of more restrictive measures and requiring the gradual abolishment of all restrictions.[216] These EU IIAs do not offer substantial liberalization, leading to an important differentiation in the treatment of FDI and foreign investment in the form of concession contracts.

The scope of liberalization and the interpretation of the EU IIAs provisions on cross-border supply of services should be determined by reference to their provisions on establishment and operation of FDI. Liberalization is subject to the same exceptions applicable to establishment provisions, thus the scope of the MFN and NT standards should be interpreted by reference to the GATS and primary EU law, depending on the agreement, while the rules on performance requirements and key personnel apply also with regard to foreign investment in the form of concession contracts. It should be noted that the movement of natural persons related to foreign investment in the form of concession contracts acquires an additional dimension in comparison to FDI, as it concerns not only intra-corporate transferees but also business service sellers, contractual service suppliers, and independent professionals who supply services in the host state. The importance of these two specific categories of natural persons for the cross-border supply of services is emphasized

[211] Arts 75–9 and 7.5–7.8. of the EPA with the CARIFORUM states and the FTA with Korea respectively.

[212] Art 31 of the EMA with Algeria.

[213] Arts 36–9 of the EEA Agreement. For an analysis of the services provisions of the EEA Agreement see Norberg, above n 94, pp 447–53.

[214] Arts 30, 30, 30, 30, 30, 30, 36, 37, and 29 of the PCAs with Armenia, Azerbaijan, Georgia, Kazakhstan, Kyrgyzstan, Moldova, Ukraine, and Uzbekistan; Art 37 of the EMA with Jordan.

[215] Art 36 of the PCA with Russia.

[216] Arts 57–8, 56–7, 59–60, 59–60, and 55–6 of the SAAs with Albania, Croatia, Montenegro, Serbia, and the Former Yugoslav Republic of Macedonia.

in a number of EU IIAs that make an explicit reference to movement of natural persons related to the negotiation and/or execution of services contracts.[217]

Finally, it should be pointed out that the EU IIAs that include provisions on cross-border supply of services are compatible with primary EU law. Similar to the issues raised regarding the compatibility of their establishment provisions, EU IIAs respect the few directions imposed by the CCP provisions, while safeguarding the limitations and exceptions established in the chapter on provision of services, which are identical to those provided in the chapter on establishment.[218]

3.2.4 EU IIA provisions on investment protection against expropriation

Protection of foreign investments against expropriation is a subject not covered in EU IIAs. Ambiguity over the scope of EU competence to regulate the conditions for expropriation of foreign investment,[219] as well as a lack of political will to incorporate the traditional, core aspect of international regulation of foreign investment in EU IIAs, which would bring about significant legal and political effects on Member State BITs and foreign investment policy in general,[220] has so far hindered the creation of a complete regulatory framework on foreign investment in existing EU IIAs. Nevertheless, as explained below, protection of foreign investment against expropriation lies within the scope of future EU IIAs according to the intentions of the Commission.[221]

Protection against expropriation of foreign investment is regulated in the ECT, which is the only EU IIA that follows the widely used regulatory model of BITs. Article 13 prohibits the nationalization, expropriation, and any other measure having equivalent effect, unless such measure is justified by public interest, is non-discriminatory, is carried out under due process of law, and, more importantly, is accompanied by the payment of prompt, adequate, and effective compensation, amounting to the fair market value of the expropriated investment.

Hence, Article 13 ECT mirrors the provisions on expropriation found under BITs, which present the relevant framework for its application and interpretation. Without entering into a detailed analysis of expropriation regulation under the ECT, it seems that interpretation questions such as the meaning of de facto and regulatory expropriation, and the assessment of compensation, should be examined in light of the relevant arbitral jurisprudence on these matters under BITs and other IIAs.[222] Indeed, recent arbitral awards interpreting Article 13 ECT have

[217] Eg Art 83 of the EPA with the CARIFORUM states, Arts 7.19 and 7.20 of the FTA with Korea, Arts 57, 56, 59, and 55 of the SAAs with Albania, Croatia, Serbia, and the Former Yugoslav Republic of Macedonia and Art 37 of the PCA with Russia.

[218] Art 62 TFEU refers back to Arts 51–4 TFEU.

[219] See Section 2.5.

[220] See Section 1.1.3.

[221] See below Section 3.2.7.

[222] C Schreuer, 'The Concept of Expropriation under the ECT and other Investment Protection Treaties' in Ribeiro (ed), *Investment Arbitration and the Energy Charter Treaty* (2006), pp 108f; T Wälde, 'Investment Arbitration under the Energy Charter Treaty: An Overview of Selected Key Issues based on Recent Litigation Experience' in Horn (ed), *Arbitrating Foreign Investment Disputes* (2004) pp 223–6.

been based on BIT jurisprudence regarding the scope of de facto and regulatory expropriation,[223] thus reflecting the belief that the ECT provisions on expropriation belong systematically to the traditional BITs.

3.2.5 EU IIA provisions on dispute settlement

Recognizing the prominent role of dispute settlement in foreign investment regulation, all EU IIAs provide for the settlement of disputes arising out of the application of their foreign investment provisions. However, the dispute settlement mechanisms provided in existing EU IIAs depart significantly from the well-established model of investor-state arbitration that has become an essential characteristic of BITs and IIAs in general. The close link between EU IIA foreign investment provisions within EU law and the use of the GATS as a regulatory model, which influences the substantive content of EU IIAs, also affect the choice of legal means for the resolution of disputes arising out of their application. The vast majority of EU IIAs adopt the traditional 'diplomatic' model of settlement for all disputes arising out of the application of their provisions, while a few of the latest agreements present a shift of EU preferences, by establishing more judicialized mechanisms. A notable exception to these models is the EEA Agreement, where the resolution of disputes has been vested with the EFTA Court, the establishment and functioning of which illustrates a successful example of advanced market integration both at the substantive and procedural level.[224]

3.2.5.1 Political settlement of investment disputes

An institutionalized framework for the political settlement of disputes arising out of the application of provisions on foreign investment is established in the SAAs, the EMAs, and the PCAs. These establish a single, loose mechanism for the settlement of any dispute relating to their provisions, thus also covering foreign investment disputes.

To briefly describe the dispute resolution mechanism established in these EU IIAs, dispute settlement relies essentially on consultations and negotiations. The agreements provide in very general terms that disputes should be resolved by a joint political organ established by the agreement, usually named the Association Council or Committee, and in cases of disagreement by arbitration or conciliation.[225] That said, arbitration presents an alternative only insofar as there is consensus, as each party can block the adoption of a decision by the political

[223] *Plama v Bulgaria*, ICSID Case No ARB/03/24, Award, 27 August 2008, pp 58–60; *Nykomb Synergetics Technology Holding AB, Sweden ('Nycomb) v The Republic of Latvia*, Award, 16 December 2003, p 33; *Petrobart Ltd (Gibraltar) v Kyrgyzstan*, Award, 29 March 2005, p 77.

[224] For an evaluation of the work of the EFTA Court see C Baudenbacher, 'The EFTA Court Ten Years on' in Baudenbacher, Tresselt, and Örlygsson (eds), *The EFTA Court Ten Years On* (2005), pp 13–51.

[225] Eg Art 86 of the PCA with Armenia and Art 97 of the EMA with Jordan.

organ, as well as the establishment of an arbitration panel.[226] Additionally, the agreements do not provide detailed legal rules determining the procedures, and lack any reference to compliance procedures. For these reasons, the agreements include a self-help provision allowing the parties to adopt 'any appropriate measures', if they consider that the other party has failed to fulfill its obligations under the relevant agreement, without, however, conditioning unilateral measures to prior recourse to dispute settlement and without defining the limits on the measures that can be adopted.[227]

In order to understand the choice of political settlement of disputes in these agreements, the broad scope of EU IIAs should be taken into account. As these Union agreements do not limit themselves to economic cooperation but regulate foreign investment alongside trade and other matters aiming at political, economic, and social integration, a legalized framework for the settlement of all disputes arising out of the application of the agreement was deemed unsuitable, in particular for non-economic provisions.

The choice of a more judicialized system for the settlement of disputes arising out of the trade and investment provisions of an international agreement is, of course, less contentious. Nevertheless, the preference for diplomatic means for settlement of trade and investment disputes in these EU IIAs can be explained by the evolution of dispute settlement provisions in Union agreements. Following the tradition established by the Association Agreements concluded in the 1970s, when there was limited experience, even in the international context of the GATT, with legal adjudication as an instrument for solving trade and investment disputes, these EU IIAs expressed the considerations existing at the time of their conclusion that recourse to legal adjudication could be potentially disruptive to important bilateral relationships.[228]

More importantly, the EU's hesitancy in adopting legal adjudication methods for resolving trade and economic disputes can also be explained by the fact that the EU wanted to avoid the application of EU law by external adjudicatory bodies. As discussed, the trade and investment provisions of these EU IIAs are modelled on primary EU law, so that their provisions have to be applied and interpreted in many instances similarly to TFEU provisions. Due to the close link between the *acquis* and the economic provisions of EU IIAs, the influence exerted by one legal system on the other can be inverse. Hence, the application and interpretation of EU IIAs by arbitral tribunals that are not subject to the control of the Court of Justice could undermine the autonomy of EU law and the role of the Court.[229]

[226] ER Robles, 'Political and Quasi-Adjudicative Dispute Settlement Models in European Union Free Trade Agreements', WTO Economic and Research Statistics Division, Staff Working Paper ERSD-2006-09, November 2006, pp 11–21.

[227] Ibid.

[228] IG Bercero, 'Dispute Settlement in European Union Free Trade Agreements: Lesson Learned?' in Bartels and Ortino (eds), *Regional Trade Agreements and the WTO System* (2006), pp 389–90.

[229] Ibid.

3.2.5.2 Interstate dispute settlement

Dissatisfaction with the effectiveness of the diplomatic model of dispute settlement has led to the use of legal adjudication for settlement of investment disputes. Bearing in mind the successful use of interstate dispute settlement mechanisms for the resolution of trade disputes, an increasing number of EU IIAs provide interstate dispute settlement systems that apply not only to purely trade disputes but also to disputes concerning the application of the provisions on foreign investment. The expansion of the scope of interstate dispute settlement systems to cover foreign investment disputes presents certain peculiarities, in particular if it is compared to the model of investor-state arbitration, which has been widely used in BITs and most IIAs. However, before examining the basic characteristics of interstate dispute settlement which are pertinent to the settlement of investment disputes, it is necessary to describe briefly the models of interstate dispute settlement established in EU IIAs.

The WTO dispute settlement system presents the most prominent example of a quasi-adjudicatory interstate dispute settlement mechanism applied for resolving foreign investment disputes that arise from the application of the GATS. As mentioned above,[230] the WTO dispute settlement system is highly effective, which results primarily from the fact that its jurisdiction is obligatory, compelling states to resolve any dispute according to the rules set in the Dispute Settlement Understanding (DSU) and to abide by the outcome reached according to the relevant procedures.[231] After an initial consultation, parties have the right to have a Panel established, which delivers its report based on detailed procedural rules, while the Panel's conclusions are subject to judicial review by the Appellate Body (AB). Further, automatic adoption of Panel and AB reports is provided and 'prompt compliance' with Panel/AB Reports is requested, which is guaranteed by efficient enforcement procedures.

With regard to bilateral EU IIAs, the Trade, Development and Cooperation Agreement (TDCA) with South Africa presented a first timid step towards a more judicialized dispute settlement system. Ensuring the establishment of an arbitration panel even in cases where there is no consensus, providing detailed rules on arbitration procedure, and binding the parties to implement arbitral decisions, this EU IIA introduced important adjudicative elements.[232] Nevertheless, it was the agreements with Mexico and Chile that introduced for the first time adjudicative or quasi-adjudicative models for settlement of investment disputes, while this trend has been affirmed by the EPA with the CARIFORUM states and the FTA with Korea.

[230] See section 1.3.5.

[231] The DSU does not provide any explicit rules on the obligatory jurisdiction of the WTO system, but the latter can be implied by Art 1, which specifies the coverage of the DSU, 3.1 in which members affirm their adherence to the principles of dispute settlement and Art 23 in which members accept to settle any disputes according to the rules contained in the DSU.

[232] Bercero, above n 228, p 391.

Following the GATS as a regulatory model in terms of their substantive provisions on foreign investment, the agreements with Mexico, Chile, the CARIFORUM states, and Korea are also in line with the spirit of the WTO dispute settlement system. Adopting the WTO model, these EU IIAs provide for compulsory recourse to arbitration, detailed procedures, and enforcement mechanisms.[233] However, they introduce important differentiations from WTO rules. On the one hand, they go beyond them, as they ameliorate procedural efficiency and compliance by providing for shorter time frames and rules on sequencing of compliance procedures.[234] In addition, they enhance transparency by allowing public hearings and guaranteeing the admissibility of *amicus curiae*.[235] On the other hand, the agreements with Mexico, Chile, Korea and the CARIFORUM states present deficiencies in comparison to WTO rules, as they lack a system of checks and balances similar to the AB, while in the Agreement with Chile the adoption of Panel reports can be blocked if there is no consensus between the parties.[236]

The extension of interstate dispute settlement under these EU IIAs to cover foreign investment disputes marks a significant departure of EU IIAs from BITs and other IIAs. Contrary to IIAs, such as the North American Free Trade Agreement (NAFTA), which include both trade and foreign investment provisions and different dispute settlement mechanisms for trade and investment, the WTO and more explicitly the agreements with Mexico, Chile, Korea, and the CARIFORUM states do not contain rules specifically pertaining to the settlement of investment disputes.[237] In sharp contrast to BITs and IIAs that grant direct rights to foreign investors and allow their participation in the settlement procedure, these EU IIAs establish only one dispute settlement mechanism applying to all trade and trade-related matters, including foreign investment, thus applying all elements of interstate dispute settlement to investment disputes. This has significant implications for the legal standing and remedies offered to private individuals.

More specifically, private individuals are prevented from initiating or participating in a dispute. Being given only the possibility of submitting *amicus curiae* briefs,

[233] Arts 181–9 and Annex XV of the agreement with Chile, Arts 37–43 of the EU-Mexico Services Agreement, Arts 206–23 of the EPA with the CARIFORUM states, Arts 14.4–14.17 of the FTA with Korea.

[234] Eg the timeframe for the issuance of a final report is four to six months under the agreement with Mexico, three to five months under the agreement with Chile and three to four months under the FTA with Korea, in comparison to six months provided under the DSU. Regarding the sequence of compliance proceedings, the agreements deal with the problems created by the application of Arts 21 and 22 DSU, providing that retaliation is allowed only if the panel rules that the measures taken to comply with the initial panel report are still in breach of the IIA provisions and that, if compliance is achieved after concessions have been suspended, there is a procedure allowing for the lifting of sanctions. For a detailed analysis see Bercero, above n 228, pp 396–9; M Karli, 'Assessing the Development Friendliness of Dispute Settlement Mechanisms in the Economic Partnership Agreements', Occasional Paper European Studies Centre, University of Oxford (August 2008), pp 23–4, 29–30.

[235] Eg Arts 35–7 of Annex XV of the EU-Chile Agreement, Art 14.15 of the FTA with Korea, and Art 217 of the EPA with the CARIFORUM states. See also Bercero, above n 228, pp 387–9; Karli, above n 234, pp 31–2.

[236] Art 185 of the EU-Chile Agreement. See also Robles, above n 226, pp 29–30.

[237] Hoekman and Newfarmer, above n 110, pp 954–6.

they need to convince their home states to put forward their claim and initiate interstate settlement proceedings. Nonetheless, internal legal orders, recognizing the need for private traders and investors to pursue their legitimate interests, may provide for private actors' participation in the initiation and management of a dispute. In the EU, European companies and individuals can use the mechanism established under the Trade Barriers Regulation (TBR),[238] which was devised to facilitate complaints by private persons regarding trade obstacles encountered in third countries. However, the TBR does not allow for effective indirect participation of private persons in interstate arbitration, as it grants a wide margin of appreciation to the Commission and the Council on whether a complaint should be initiated, which is only partially scrutinized under legal review by the ECJ.[239]

Furthermore, private investors cannot benefit directly from the remedies provided by these EU IIAs. In accordance with the interstate character of dispute settlement, the basic remedy offered is withdrawal of inconsistent provisions. Compensation can be granted only if the immediate withdrawal of the measure is impracticable and only as a temporary measure, while suspension of concessions or other obligations on a discriminatory basis vis-à-vis the other party is viewed only as a last resort.[240] Private investors' damages are not taken into account nor does compensation present a possible remedy, thus diminishing the effectiveness of foreign investment dispute settlement. Hence, the WTO as well as the bilateral EU IIAs with Chile, Mexico, Korea, and the CARIFORUM states draw away from the model of investor-state arbitration, which has been successfully adopted by most international investment treaties, as it allows private investors to pursue their interests independently from their home country, promoting depoliticization of investment disputes.[241]

3.2.5.3 Investor-state arbitration

Departing from the model of political or interstate dispute settlement, the ECT is so far the only EU IIA that largely follows the dispute settlement systems set in BITs. Next to interstate dispute settlement, it also provides for investor-state dispute settlement, thus granting a right to private investors to pursue their interests directly and resolve their disputes with a sovereign state. Although bilateral EU IIAs

[238] Council Regulation 2641/84/EEC on the strengthening of the common commercial policy with regard in particular to protection against illicit commercial practices [1984] OJ L252.

[239] Case C-69/89 *Nakajima* [1991] ECR I-2069; Case C-70/87 *Fediol IV* [1989] ECR 1781; R MacLean and B Volpi, *EU Trade Barrier Regulation: Tackling Unfair Foreign Trade Practices* (2000), Ch 9; S Billiet, 'The EC and WTO Dispute Settlement: the Initiation of Trade Disputes by the EC' (2005) 10 EFA Rev 203, 208–12.

[240] For a detailed analysis of the remedies offered in the WTO Dispute Settlement, which were largely replicated in the agreements with Chile, Mexico, Korea, and the CARIFORUM states see Y Guohua, B Mercurio, and L Yongjie, *WTO Dispute Settlement: Understanding A Detailed Interpretation* (2005), 235–41, 255–66.

[241] R Echandi, A New Generation of International Investment Agreements in the Americas: Impact of Investor State Dispute Settlement over Investment Rulemaking, Fourth Annual Conference of the Euro-Latin Study Network on Integration and Trade (2006), 5–7.

do not yet allow investor-state arbitration, it is the intention of the Commission to include such provisions in future EU IIAs.[242]

As regards the ECT, Article 27 ECT provides for interstate ad hoc arbitration. As with most BITs, it enables the parties to the agreement to initiate arbitration proceedings against another party for a violation of the treaty provisions.[243] Similar to the other EU IIAs based on the WTO DSU, the ECT ensures the establishment of a Panel and the rendering of an award, granting flexibility to the parties regarding the procedure to be followed. However, it differentiates considerably from dispute settlement under the WTO and the other EU IIAs in that it remains silent on the question of enforcement of awards, which largely follows the rules set out in the New York Convention on the Recognition and Enforcement of Foreign Arbitration Awards.

Article 26 ECT establishes rules for the settlement of investment disputes between a foreign investor and a contracting party. Investors can raise a claim before the courts and tribunals of a contracting party regarding violation of the ECT investment provisions, or in accordance with a previously existing settlement procedure, or, most importantly, by initiating investor-state arbitration.[244] Similar to BITs, investor-state arbitration can be carried out either through the International Centre for Settlement of Investment Disputes (ICSID), or ad hoc arbitration established under UNCITRAL rules or under the Arbitration Institute of the Stockholm Chamber of Commerce.[245] The ECT grants flexibility to foreign investors to choose between the available fora as, contrary to some BITs, it does not require foreign investors to exhaust local remedies before resorting to investor-state arbitration.[246] The ECT, like most BITs, contains rules on conflict of jurisdiction between the available fora. Generally, it is clear that investors cannot switch to international arbitration during litigation in another setting. However, unless the contracting parties make use of the opt-out provided in Article 26(3)(b)(i) ECT, which provides that the parties do not grant their consent to arbitration where an investor has used another dispute settlement option, private investors have the right to resubmit the same dispute to a different forum, even if it has previously been settled in another.[247]

242 See below Section 3.2.7.

243 On interstate dispute settlement under BITs see M Sornarajah, *The International Law on Foreign Investment* (2010), pp 221–2.

244 On investment dispute resolution under the ECT see J Blanch, A Moody, and N Lawn, 'Access to dispute resolution mechanisms under Art 26 of the Energy Charter Treaty' in Coop and Ribeiro (eds), *Investment Protection and the Energy Charter Treaty* (2008), pp 1–15; P Pinsolle, 'The Dispute Resolution Provisions of the Energy Charter Treaty' (2007) 10 Intl ALR 74.

245 Art 26(4) ECT.

246 Art 23(3)(a) ECT provides that the parties give their unconditional consent to international arbitration. Haghighi, above n 115, p 207; Wälde, above n 222, pp 218–21.

247 Many contracting parties, among which the EU, have opted out and do not allow foreign investors to resubmit a dispute to international arbitration that has already been settled in another forum.

3.2.6 EU IIA provisions on investment promotion

Finally, the regulatory framework that EU IIAs establish in respect of promotion of foreign investment should be reviewed. Similar to BITs, which are instruments on the 'promotion and protection of foreign investment', EU IIAs acknowledge the pivotal role of foreign investment for economic integration, stressing the importance of the creation of an environment favourable to foreign investment and supporting the stimulation of foreign investment initiatives. However, the inclusion of legally binding provisions on investment promotion presents an important innovation in comparison to most BITs; the latter include mainly 'best efforts' provisions, focusing on transparency of national laws and regulations, and rarely provide for general or specific investment promotion measures and policy frameworks that home and host states should adopt in order to promote foreign investment flows.[248]

Bilateral EU IIAs recognize the significance of foreign investment promotion and establish a framework for cooperation. Depending on the broader aims envisaged by each agreement, investment promotion is integrated in their provisions on economic and/or development cooperation, constituting primarily an autonomous cooperation field. Cooperation aims at the establishment of a clear and transparent institutional regime that enables easier and better access to information on foreign investment opportunities and regulation as well as the creation of a legal environment conducive to investment protection and liberalization.[249]

In order to achieve these goals of investment promotion, many EU IIAs, in particular those concluded with developing countries, provide primary, but not exclusive, tools to this end. More specifically, they include a commitment on the part of the EU and its Member States for financial support and technical assistance, training, and capacity building, which aim to establish mechanisms for promotion of investment and enhance the capacities of investment promotion agencies in host countries. For example, the Economic Partnership Agreement (EPA) links development cooperation with the EU instruments for financial and technical assistance,[250] such as the European Development Fund (EDF),[251] so that the CARIFORUM states can use the instruments of EU development aid for promoting foreign investment. Also, the EPA provides a general framework

[248] UNCTAD, *Investment Promotion Provisions in International Investment Agreements* (2008), pp 13–14.

[249] Arts 91, 85, 93, 93, and 84 of the SAAs with Albania, Croatia, Montenegro, Serbia, and the Former Yugoslav Republic of Macedonia; Arts 53, 46, 67, 47, 50, 39, and 50 of the EMAs with Algeria, Egypt, Jordan, Lebanon, Morocco, the Palestinian Territories, and Tunisia; Arts 47, 47, 47, 47, 47, 53, 58, 54, and 46 of the PCAs with Armenia, Azerbaijan, Georgia, Kazakhstan, Kyrgyzstan, Moldova, Russia, Ukraine, and Uzbekistan; Arts 21, 121, 52, and 33 of the Agreements with Chile, the CARIFORUM states, Mexico, and South Africa.

[250] Art 7(3) of the EPA with the CARIFORUM states.

[251] For an overview of the EDF structure and scheme see O Babarinde and G Faber, 'From Lomé to Cotonou: Business as usual?' (2004) 9 EFA Rev 27, 33–5, 38–42. For an analysis of its current implementation and allocation of funds see Commission Communication, Regional Integration for Development in ACP Countries, Brussels 1.10.2008, SEC(2008) 2538.

for cooperation, indicating the priorities and tools that can be used for promoting foreign investment in the framework of development cooperation.[252]

Albeit not directly related to the content of EU IIAs, it is worth pointing out that in line with its obligations under EU IIAs the EU has instituted specific development aid instruments focusing on the promotion of foreign investment in different regions and countries. For example, with regard to Mediterranean countries, the EU has developed general and specific aid instruments that aim at foreign investment promotion in the Mediterranean region. The MEDA programme, which is the main instrument of financial and technical assistance to most countries engaged in the Euro-Mediterranean Partnership, incorporates investment promotion among its basic objectives and offers a coherent framework for the distribution of financial resources and technical support.[253] In addition, the Facility for Euro-Mediterranean Investment and Partnership (FEMIP) is a special programme aimed at stimulating private sector development in the Mediterranean region and facilitating a higher level of economic growth, by granting loans and technical assistance for investment projects in the region.[254]

3.2.7 The content of future EU IIAs

The scope and content of foreign investment regulation in existing EU IIAs illustrate that they depart from the traditional model of international regulation of foreign investment. In order to complement them and address foreign investment in a unified and comprehensive way, the EU intends to develop a new model for foreign investment regulation in future EU IIAs, covering many aspects outside the scope of existing EU IIAs.[255] Indeed, the EU purports to develop a common international investment policy which will 'seek to integrate investment liberalization and investment protection'.[256] However, the creation of a broad common investment policy raises a number of questions regarding its substance. Considering that current EU agreements differentiate substantially in terms of content from the standards provided in other IIAs, and in particular BITs, it is necessary to highlight the potential choices and hazards that the drafting of future investment agreements may bring about.

[252] Art 121 of the EPA with the CARIFORUM states. D te Velde and S Bilal, 'Foreign Direct Investment in the Cotonou Agreement: Building on Private Sector Initiatives' in Babarinde and Faber (eds), *The European Union and Developing Countries The Cotonou Agreement* (2005), pp 211–14; Sauve and Ward, above n 106, pp 44–7.

[253] P Holden, 'The European Community's MEDA Aid Programme: A strategic instrument of civilian power?' (2003) 8 EFA Rev 347.

[254] Commission Communication, Assessment of the Facility for Euro-Mediterranean Investment and Partnership (FEMIP) and Future Options, Brussels 17.10.2006, COM(2006) 592.

[255] Commission Communication, Towards a Comprehensive European International Investment Policy, Brussels 7.7.2010, COM(2010) 343 (hereinafter, Investment Policy Communication); Council of the European Union, Conclusions on a Comprehensive European International Investment Policy, Luxembourg 25.10.2010 (hereinafter, Council Conclusions on Investment Policy); European Parliament Resolution of 6 April 2011 on the Future European International Investment Policy (2010/2203INI) (hereinafter, Parliament Investment Resolution).

[256] Investment Policy Communication, p 5.

3.2.7.1 Defining foreign investment

First, there is ambiguity about whether the EU will promote a broad definition of foreign investment, similar to that found under most IIAs, or whether it will distinguish between the different forms of foreign investment. Although it is clear from the outset that future EU IIAs will cover both FDI and portfolio investment,[257] this does not indicate whether a broad asset-based definition of foreign investment or a specific, detailed description of the different forms of foreign investment will be used. Although this choice may not impact the breadth of activities covered under future EU IIAs, the choice of the definition will impact on the scope of protection given to the different forms of foreign investment. Considering that existing EU IIAs regulate separately the different forms of foreign investment, the adoption of a broad definition will necessarily require a departure from the substantive standards offered under existing EU IIAs. On the other hand, the distinction between the different forms of foreign investment may result in a narrow definition, excluding certain activities that would qualify as investments under traditional BITs, and it may produce legal uncertainty whether an investment is direct or non-direct.

Current practice suggests that a detailed definition, enumerating the different forms of foreign investment and determining their characteristics is based on existing patterns. The extensive definitions on (direct) investment, capital movements, and cross-border supply of services provided in the FTA with Korea, which was concluded after the Lisbon Treaty entered into force, indicate the willingness of the EU to differentiate between the different forms of foreign investment, including specific definitions affecting the scope of each set of rules. A distinction between the different forms of foreign investment is also favoured by the Parliament, which has pointed out to the Commission the different nature of EU competence over FDI and other forms of foreign investment, which may in essence affect the scope of future EU IIAs.[258]

On the other hand, it is precisely the ambiguity of the concept of foreign direct investment and the different nature of EU competence which may result in a broad asset-based definition. Avoiding questions of competence and guaranteeing broad protection of foreign investors, EU institutions may ultimately opt for a broad asset-based definition of foreign investment, which would also be easier to negotiate with third countries. In any event, the choice of the appropriate definition is directly linked with the actual standards of treatment offered to the different forms of foreign investment.

What is more problematic is how future EU IIAs will determine foreign nationality. Bearing in mind that primary EU law requires the consideration of foreign-controlled entities established in accordance with Article 54 TFEU as EU nationals, future EU IIAs should avoid including the control criterion in their definitions of foreign investment, so as not to raise issues of incompatibility similar to the ones raised by the FTA with Korea.

[257] Ibid, p 8; Parliament Investment Resolution, para 11.
[258] Parliament Investment Resolution, para 11.

3.2.7.2 *Admission and operation of foreign investment*

Turning to the conditions for the admission and treatment of foreign investment, EU institutions recognize the importance of provisions on admission of foreign investment for increasing investment inflows and outflows and hence the competitiveness of the EU.[259] Therefore, it is expected that EU agreements will continue to place particular emphasis on market access commitments;[260] however, it is still unclear whether the EU will continue to follow an adapted GATS model to regulate admission and post-admission treatment of foreign investment, as it has done in the agreements with the CARIFORUM states and Korea, or whether it will adopt the general non-discrimination language existing in many BITs, covering equally pre- and post-admission treatment.

The emphasis on competitiveness and growth in the past, which is also pertinent to current investment policy,[261] indicates that it is highly unlikely that the EU will discontinue its current practice. Liberalizing foreign investment based on specific market access and national treatment commitments allows the EU to address the interests of EU investors in third countries in accordance with the criteria of current and potential investment flows.[262] In that respect, it should be expected that regulation of admission of foreign investment will follow current practice, distinguishing between the different forms of foreign investment.[263] More importantly, the choice of adherence to the existing model, rather than the adoption of broad non-discrimination standards as provided in BITs, is directly linked with the substantive scope of protection provided to foreign investors. As explained above, the NT standard is subject to different interpretations under BITs and EU IIAs.[264] This is particularly relevant regarding the exceptions to NT, especially in light of the exceptions mandated under primary EU law.[265] Moreover, the clarifications on the scope of MFN treatment under existing EU IIAs, which make specific exceptions for MFN treatment and delimitate the scope of this standard, are more suitable to address the different commitments made by EU Member States in different sectors and allow for closer cooperation agreements with certain countries.[266] Hence, the achievement of EU investment policy objectives would be better served if admission of foreign investment was based on the model developed in existing EU IIAs.

On the other hand, a departure from the existing model of regulation of post-establishment treatment seems more probable. Considering first that existing EU IIAs limit the scope of non-discrimination standards only to investments made

[259] Investment Policy Communication, p 8.

[260] Ibid, p 5; Parliament Investment Resolution, para 21.

[261] See Section 4.1.1.3.

[262] Ibid.

[263] Cf S Woolcock and J Kleinheisterkamp, 'The EU approach to international investment policy after the Lisbon Treaty', Study Directorate General for External Policies of the Union (October 2010), pp 32–3, who argues that the EU should adopt a NAFTA model regarding admission of foreign investment, thus offering NT regarding pre-establishment and include exceptions to that list.

[264] See above Section 3.2.2.4.1.

[265] See above Sections 3.2.1.3, 3.2.2.7, and 6.3.1. Cf Woolcock and Kleinheisterkamp, above n 263, p 33, who only mention the limitations under the chapter of free movement of capital, without taking into consideration the limitations existing under the other free movement chapters.

[266] See above Section 3.2.2.4.2; Woolcock and Kleinheisterkamp, above n 263, p 34.

in accordance with their admission provisions, they leave outside their protective scope foreign investments made in areas were the parties decided not to make binding commitments. Moreover, while the distinction between the different forms of foreign investment seems necessary as regards admission of foreign investment, there are no valid reasons for distinguishing between the different forms of foreign investment as regards their post-admission treatment and operation.[267] Nevertheless, the adoption of common non-discrimination standards does not necessarily entail that the scope of non-discriminatory standards of treatment will depart from existing EU IIAs. Considering the exceptions mandated by the TFEU regarding the exercise of official authority, public policy, public security, and public health, it seems that future EU IIAs would have to provide a broad exception from non-discriminatory treatment on those grounds.

More importantly, EU institutions clearly have the intention of broadening the scope of treatment offered to foreign investments by providing absolute standards of treatment. Building on existing Member State BITs, EU IIAs will incorporate at least the additional standard of FET.[268] However, the question arises as to how the EU will attempt to define absolute standards of treatment and in particular FET. Considering that there is no consensus on the customary international law content of the term,[269] it is unclear whether the EU will attempt to bind the treatment offered in its agreements to the international minimum standard or whether it will attempt to provide a more specific definition of the term.[270]

More specifically, a narrow definition of FET amounting only to the international minimum standard would reduce the competitive position of EU investors in third countries, disadvantaging them in comparison to other investors who enjoy broader protection. On the other hand, a broad definition of FET would raise the risk of incompatibilities with EU law as regards the treatment of foreign investors in the EU, given that there are EU law principles protecting legitimate expectations, procedural and substantive fairness, and against arbitrary and/or non-transparent treatment.[271] Additionally, in accordance with the call for protecting the EU's right to regulate and promote legal certainty,[272] a detailed definition of FET mirroring internal EU standards would be optimal, but would be difficult to negotiate. Moreover, it is undisputable that the FET standard should also be subject to the same exceptions as the relative standards, at least those mandated by primary EU law.[273]

Moreover, the Commission intends to include an 'umbrella clause' in future EU IIAs, thus offering treaty protection to contractual rights offered by states to foreign investors.[274] Although the EU has competence to regulate 'commercial' state contracts,[275] the drafting of future umbrella clauses needs careful consideration to take into account existing rules of secondary EU law on public procurement, as

[267] See Sections 1.3.2 and 1.3.3.1.
[268] Investment Policy Communication, p 8; Parliament Investment Resolution, para 19.
[269] See Section 3.2.2.4.3.
[270] Woolcock and Kleinheisterkamp, above n 263, pp 35–6.
[271] See T Tridimas, *The General Principles of EU Law* (2006), Ch 6; Section 3.2.2.4.3, n 163.
[272] Parliament Investment Resolution, paras 24–5.
[273] See also Section 6.3.1.
[274] Investment Policy Communication, p 8.
[275] See Section 2.4.

well as the lack of clarity under international law, as to the scope of 'commercial' state contracts covered under umbrella clauses.

As regards the operation of foreign investment, there seems to be no reason for discontinuing the existing practice of regulating the movement of key personnel, which adds to the scope of protection offered by traditional BITs. In addition, future EU IIAs will address labour, environmental, health, and other policy objectives. The Investment Policy Communication clearly states that the Union's investment policy will be consistent with other policies,[276] thus it could be expected that provisions on maintenance of standards and adoption of international standards, similar to the ones included in the agreements with Korea and the CARIFORUM states will be included in future EU IIAs. Nevertheless, as discussed below, it is unclear how such provisions will be balanced with investment protection norms.

3.2.7.3 Protection against expropriation and other risks

In substantive terms, the most important new element of future EU IIAs is that they will include provisions on protection of foreign investors against expropriation and other political risks. Although the Commission recognizes the importance of expropriation provisions for a complete regulatory framework on foreign investment,[277] the controversial and ambiguous content of investment protection provisions found in different BITs requires further consideration from the EU as to the scope and content of expropriation provisions. Given the large diversity of provisions on expropriation found in BITs, the scope of protection against indirect expropriation under future EU IIAs and the balance between investment protection against the pursuance of regulatory public goals requires careful consideration.[278]

In that respect, the Investment Policy Communication indicates that there may not be a standard provision on expropriation, as it highlights that the robustness of the investment protection provisions included in future EU IIAs will also depend on the 'political, institutional and economic climate of partner countries'.[279] In that respect the EU retains its flexibility to adjust the degree of investment protection with regard to different countries, thus increasing its negotiating leverage.

Secondly, the determination of the scope of expropriation provisions will need to be compatible with primary EU law and in particular the provisions of the Charter on Fundamental Rights. As discussed,[280] Article 17 of the Charter provides a right to property, determining the conditions under which deprivation and limitation of private property rights are allowed. Although Article 17 is broadly formulated, future EU IIAs should be carefully drafted to avoid even potential conflicts between the Charter and the interpretation of expropriation provisions by investment tribunals.[281]

276 Investment Policy Communication, p 9.
277 Ibid, p 8.
278 Woolcock and Kleinheisterkamp, above n 263, p 38.
279 Ibid, p 9.
280 See Sections 2.5.2 and 2.5.3.
281 See also Section 6.3.1.

Drafting the provisions on expropriation in light of the wording of the Charter would actually require a careful determination of the right to regulate, which is particularly emphasized by the Parliament.[282] In that respect, a general provision that non-discriminatory and transparent measures that aim to achieve legitimate public policy objectives—such as the protection of public health, national security, the environment, and workers' and consumers' rights—do not amount to indirect expropriation, as long as they are proportionate, would sufficiently clarify the rules, protect the right to regulate, and achieve coherence with the Charter.

3.2.7.4 Dispute settlement

By complementing existing EU IIAs, EU institutions underscore the importance of dispute settlement. Recognizing that investor-state arbitration is a key characteristic of investment regulation, they aim to incorporate investor-state arbitration provisions in future EU IIAs.[283] More importantly, the Commission has already indicated the basic principles that will guide the negotiation of future EU IIAs. By aiming to enhance transparency and legal certainty, the EU will attempt to increase the openness of arbitral proceedings, especially via allowing *amicus curiae* briefs, and it will attempt to enhance consistency and predictability in arbitral proceedings.[284] In addition, EU institutions are aware of the difficulties that arise from the fact that the EU is not a party to the ICSID Convention—which is open only to states—indicating the willingness of the EU to accede to the ICSID Convention after amending it to allow for REIOs to be party to it.[285] In light of the inherent difficulties that the amendment of the ICSID Convention presents, given that the consent of 157 countries that are signatories to ICSID is required, EU IIAs should, in the medium term, refer to other arbitration rules, such as UNCITRAL or the ICSID Additional Facility Rules. However, non-ICSID arbitration does not offer the advantages of the ICSID Convention, which provides a self-contained system of arbitration, fully autonomous and independent of any national legal systems, including the system prevailing at the place of an arbitration conducted under the Convention.

Nevertheless, the Commission is unclear as to the scope of investor-state arbitration and whether it will present an alternative to interstate dispute settlement with regard to disputes concerning all provisions of future EU IIAs. Providing that 'future EU agreements including investment protection should include investor-state dispute settlement',[286] it is unclear whether investor-state arbitration will be an alternative for investors in cases of violations of the investment liberalization provisions. Considering, however, that most IIAs including provisions on admission of foreign investment do not exclude them from the scope of

[282] Parliament Investment Resolution, paras 23–6.

[283] Investment Policy Communication, p 9; Parliament Investment Resolution, para 32.

[284] Investment Policy Communication, p 10; Parliament Investment Resolution, para.31. For a detailed analysis of ways to enhance transparency and avoid forum-shopping see Woolcock and Kleinheisterkamp, above n 263, pp 45–9.

[285] Investment Policy Communication, p 10; Parliament Investment Resolution, para.33.

[286] Investment Policy Communication, p 10.

investor-state arbitration and bearing in mind the deficiencies of the interstate dispute settlement system discussed above,[287] EU IIAs should allow for investor-state arbitration for the majority of their provisions. A significant exception from the scope of investor-state arbitration would probably be claims for violation of the provisions on adoption and maintenance of labour, environmental, and other standards. In the FTA with Korea these provisions are excluded from interstate dispute settlement and they are subject to a unique consultation and arbitration system, therefore it should be expected that similar provisions in future EU IIAs will be excluded from dispute settlement.

Finally, future EU IIAs will have to address the question of international responsibility of the EU and its Member States. As discussed in Chapter 5, the fact that future EU IIAs will probably be concluded as mixed agreements will require the inclusion of specific provisions as to the entity undertaking responsibility and participating in dispute settlement.[288]

3.2.7.5 Balancing investment and public policy considerations

The recognition of public policy considerations as grounds limiting the scope of protection of foreign investors' rights is evident both in investment liberalization and protection provisions. As noted above, primary EU law requires the insertion of certain exceptions to the scope of investment provisions, while additional exceptions may be necessary in order to balance public interests of the EU and its Member States. Indeed, the Investment Policy Communication highlights the importance of consistency of future EU IIAs with other Union policies including protection of the environment, labour standards, health standards, consumer protection, etc.[289] In that regard, future EU IIAs may include separate lists of exceptions for admission, treatment, and protection of foreign investment, addressing in each case the specific requirements of primary EU law and EU public policy interests. On the other hand, the EU could develop an all-inclusive exception provision—promoting provisions similar to the ones found in the FTA with Korea and the EPA with the CARIFORUM states—identifying the carve-outs from the scope of EU IIAs provisions. Indeed, specifying the public policy grounds that can justify limitations to investors' admission, treatment, and protection rights in a similar manner, and determining the conditions under which such limitations can be imposed would address the concerns of the Parliament regarding the right of the EU (and third countries) to regulate.

3.2.7.6 Investment promotion

Finally, it is indisputable that future EU IIAs will aim at investment promotion, especially in developing countries. Nevertheless, it is unclear and doubtful whether, and to what extent, future EU IIAs will include legally binding obligations that will

[287] See above Section 3.2.5.2.
[288] See Section 5.1.4.
[289] Investment Policy Communication, p 9.

actively promote sustainable investment and ensure their development orientation. Although preambular references regarding the linkages between investment and development will almost certainly appear, as explained in Chapter 4, it is unclear whether the concerns and suggestions put forward by the Parliament, which can contribute to a more development-friendly investment policy, will materialize in specific provisions under future EU IIAs.[290]

3.2.8 Concluding remarks

The scope and content of foreign investment regulation in existing EU IIAs illustrates that they depart from the traditional model of international regulation of foreign investment, as they are distinctive from BITs and other IIAs. Although the conclusion of a traditional IIA by the EU would not meet any legal hurdles, as the analysis of EU competence and the conclusion of the ECT by the EU demonstrate in theory and in practice, EU IIAs have so far excluded from their scope investor-state arbitration and protection of foreign investment against expropriation. Reflecting political considerations on the limitations of EU competence in the field of foreign investment, as well as on the objectives of EU external action, EU IIAs have focused on admission and treatment of foreign investment, following largely the GATS and the EU internal market provisions as a model for regulation of foreign investment. Completing these gaps, future EU IIAs will attempt to provide more comprehensive regulation of foreign investment. However, taking into account the development of EU IIAs so far and the different context in which they arose, the determination of the content of future EU IIAs raises a number of questions and dangers both for foreign investors and for the EU legal order.

So far, primary EU law and the GATS have exerted significant influence on the structure, scope, and content of EU IIAs. EU IIAs cover the same aspects of foreign investment regulation as primary EU law and the GATS, they have comparable structure, and are similar, or even to a certain extent identical, in content. In that respect, with regard to the EU IIAs based on EU law, it can be contended that they do nothing more than expand selective aspects of the intra-EU investment regime to third countries with which the EU aims to establish closer economic relations. Depending on the degree of economic integration the parties aim to achieve, the more (or fewer) elements of the intra-EU regime are reflected in an EU IIA. As for EU IIAs based on the GATS, it can be contended that they merely present a commitment to a higher level of liberalization than that achieved under the WTO. These EU IIAs reflect the willingness of the parties to benefit mutually from further liberalization, which seems rather impossible to achieve at the multilateral level in the near future.

However, perceiving EU IIAs as a mere duplication of primary EU law or the GATS does not do them justice. EU IIAs have sufficient original elements that can justify their characterization as an innovative model for international regulation of foreign investment. Using elements from both primary EU law and the GATS,

[290] See Sections 4.1.2.2, 4.1.3.4, and 4.2.2.

they create their own distinctive characteristics in terms of scope, structure, and content. The new EU IIAs with the CARIFORUM states and Korea are a good example: although they are seemingly based on the GATS, their scope is extended to cover investment beyond service sectors. They distinguish between the different modes for supply of services in terms of structure, and include original provisions, such as those on investors' behaviour and maintenance of standards, as well as detailed provisions on issues that are deemed of greater importance, such as movement of investment-related natural persons.

In light of the unique model of foreign investment regulation in existing EU IIAs, the intention to 'marry' them with traditional BITs presents a number of difficulties. Investment liberalization has been regulated differently in traditional BITs, so that policy makers will need to choose between two separate regulatory models. As regards investment protection, future EU IIAs will have to ensure compatibility with primary EU law, which includes specific norms on this subject matter that were developed in a different context and have been subject to different interpretation than IIAs.

4

The Principles and Objectives of EU Foreign Investment Law

The exercise of EU competence over foreign investment through the conclusion of EU international investment agreements (IIAs) is directed by specific principles and objectives on which the formation of EU foreign investment regulation is based. The EU's decisions whether and to what extent it may exercise its competence and, more importantly, how to exercise its powers in terms of the substantive content of EU IIAs can be better understood and explained in light of the objectives and principles to which EU foreign investment regulation adheres. The examination of the general legal, political, and economic framework within which the principles and objectives of EU foreign investment regulation have been developed as well as their specific implementation in EU IIAs complements the technical analysis of the exercise of EU competence in the field of foreign investment in Chapter 3. In addition, discussion of the principles and objectives of EU foreign investment regulation sheds light on the future direction of EU policy on foreign investment, indicating the characteristics of a future distinctive and autonomous EU foreign investment policy.

The determination of the principles and objectives of EU foreign investment law is founded on primary EU law. According to the principle of attribution—which is declared in Article 5 TEU—'the Union shall act only within the limits of the competences conferred upon it by the Member States in the Treaties to attain the objectives set out therein', indicating that the scope and exercise of EU competence in all fields is directly linked with the pursuance of the specific objectives set out in the founding Treaties.[1] Building on the principle of attribution, the founding Treaties provide the general objectives which EU action serves, elaborating on them in specific provisions dealing with a particular field of action. Of considerable importance for foreign investment is also that the founding Treaties provide for principles and objectives pertinent to the entire area of EU external relations, establishing a legal framework for the orientation of EU external action. Within the context set by primary EU law rules and based on the objectives inscribed therein, EU institutions have declared the policy goals of EU external action in the field of foreign investment and have formulated specific aims that are pursued by EU foreign investment regulation.[2]

[1] K Lenaerts and E de Smijter, 'The European Union as an Actor under International Law' (2000) 19 YEL 95.

[2] Commission Communication, Towards a Comprehensive European International Investment Policy, Brussels 7.7.2010, COM(2010) 343, (hereinafter, Investment Policy Communication); Council of the European Union, Conclusions on a Comprehensive European International Investment Policy, Luxembourg 25.10.2010 (hereinafter, Council Conclusions on Investment

The determination of the principles and objectives of EU foreign investment regulation based only on primary EU law and policy documents is incomplete. Complementing the theoretical framework provided by primary rules and policy instruments, the determination of the principles and objectives of EU IIAs indicates the practical orientation of EU foreign investment law. External EU action plays a central role in implementing the Treaty-mandated and political objectives of foreign investment regulation, indicating the degree of consistency between policy making and practice. In fact, it is the EU IIAs that indicate the actual objectives of EU foreign investment regulation.

In that respect, this chapter first examines the legal and political framework within which the objectives of EU foreign investment law are determined. It looks at the directions provided by primary EU law to political institutions for forming EU foreign investment law and the limits posed on their discretion, as well as actual determination of the objectives of EU foreign investment law by EU political institutions. Focusing on the interaction between different objectives and the need for consistent and coherent application, the objectives of EU foreign investment law are viewed comparatively to those pursued through other instruments of international investment law and the policy objectives adopted by other international actors. Secondly, the actual implementation of the objectives of EU foreign investment law in EU IIAs is examined, considering not only the link between the declared objectives and the Treaty-mandated and politically determined objectives, but also the effectiveness and suitability of EU IIA provisions to achieve these aims.

4.1 The legal and political framework determining the objectives of EU foreign investment law

Unlike other fields of external EU action where the goals pursued are set out explicitly in a Treaty provision and further elaborated by EU institutions,[3] the identification of specific objectives and principles of EU foreign investment law presents greater difficulties. Until the entry into force of the Lisbon Treaty, the EC Treaty did not provide for a foreign investment policy and EC external action in the field of foreign investment was based on a plurality of Treaty provisions, so that Community action in the field of foreign investment served the specific goals

Policy); European Parliament Resolution of 6 April 2011 on the future European international investment policy (2010/2203INI)) (hereinafter, Parliament Investment Resolution).

[3] Eg, Art 208 TFEU sets out the specific objectives that EU action in the field of development cooperation shall pursue, whilst the main policy orientation of the EU in this field is reflected in a series of EU documents. Joint Statement by the Council and the Representatives of the Governments of the Member States meeting within the Council, the European Parliament and the Commission on European Union Development Policy, 'The European Consensus', OJ C46/1, Brussels 22.11.2005 (hereinafter, European Consensus on Development). See also Commission Communication, Towards a Global Partnership for Sustainable Development, Brussels 13.2.2002, COM(2002) 82.

pronounced in each power-conferring provision. But even after the introduction of foreign direct investment (FDI) competence under Article 207 TFEU, other primary law provisions remain relevant for the formation of EU foreign investment regulation, which is reflected at the level of objectives pursued by EU external action in this field.

In that respect, the principles and objectives of the Common Commercial Policy (CCP) are highly important for determining the objectives of EU foreign investment law, to the extent of course that they affect the exercise of EU competence in the areas of the CCP related to foreign investment, namely in the areas of trade in services and FDI. Parallel to the CCP principles and objectives, EU foreign investment law is premised on the objectives served in the internal market. Focusing on the objectives pursued with regard to the external aspects of the internal market, it is important to examine how the internal market objectives are linked with and affect the exercise of implied powers on foreign investment.

Under the EC Treaty, the formation of a unified EU foreign investment policy was missing, at least on a formal level. Although the Commission had developed a Minimum Platform on Investment for EU Free Trade Agreements, which was used as a basis for negotiations on foreign investment in practically all EU bilateral trade negotiations,[4] EU institutions had not officially adopted policy instruments identifying the scope and goals of EC action in the field of foreign investment. The main policy instruments dealing with foreign investment related to the CCP and the external aspects of the internal market, ascribing largely to the same general objectives that determine trade policy.

After the entry into force of the Lisbon Treaty, the principles and objectives of EU foreign investment policy have become clearer. The intention of the Commission to create a comprehensive European international investment policy has shed light on how EU institutions perceive that the specific objectives of the CCP and the internal market, as well as broader EU external relations objectives, affect the orientation of EU foreign investment policy. However, the views of the Commission are not entirely shared by other EU institutions and, in particular, the Parliament, which as a new actor under the CCP, raises different priorities for EU investment policy.

Furthermore, EU foreign investment regulation is affected by broader objectives that are not directly relevant for foreign investment regulation but which influence its orientation. Among them, the objectives in the field of development and technical cooperation with third countries are of particular importance, as they play

[4] The Minimum Platform on Investment has not been made public by EU institutions. Considering that it would 'prejudice the EU's position in its current trade negotiations but would also have an adverse effect in future negotiations', the Council has refused to grant public access. See Reply adopted by the Council to Confirmatory Application 15//01/09, made by email on 20 May 2009, pursuant to Art 7(2) of Regulation (EC) No 1049/2001, for public access to document 15375/06, Brussels 4.6.2009. For a description of the scope and content of the Minimum Platform on Investment see N Maydell, 'The European Community's Minimum Platform on Investment or the Trojan Horse of Investment Competence' in Reinisch and Knahr (eds), *International Investment Law and Context* (2007), pp 75–9.

a major role in the formation of EU foreign investment law. Complementing the specific principles and objectives and tying them together, EU foreign investment law, as with all other fields where the EU undertakes external action, abides by general principles and objectives of constitutional value. Given the plurality of objectives that EU action in the field of foreign investment pursues, they aim to ensure a balance between different objectives and to guarantee coherence and consistency in the formation and application of EU foreign investment law.

To systematize the examination of the objectives pursued, it is necessary to look first at the specific investment-related goals of EU action. Secondly, other objectives of EU external action and their importance for foreign investment regulation have to be identified, focusing mainly on development policy. Thirdly, the interaction between the various objectives has to be explored, identifying how foreign investment objectives are accommodated within the broader framework of EU external action.

4.1.1 Investment-related objectives of EU foreign investment law

In determining the specific investment-related objectives of EU foreign investment regulation, the prominent role of the CCP becomes immediately apparent. Next to the wide scope of EU competence over foreign investment that the CCP provides, even after the Lisbon Treaty, its value for identifying the principles and objectives of EU foreign investment regulation is greater, as it has been traditionally used as the main tool for propelling EU external policy priorities, extending in many instances beyond pure trade considerations. Since the establishment of the European Economic Community (EEC) but also after the gradual expansion of Community and Union powers in other fields of external relations, the CCP has been an area of greater importance for the formation of EU external economic action, not only because of the wide scope and nature of EU competence in the field, but also because of its suitability for promoting and integrating a variety of policy objectives in international relations with third countries.

In addition to the CCP principles and objectives, the orientation of EU foreign investment regulation is confined within the legal framework set by the internal market provisions that confer competence on foreign investment. Indeed, the scope and exercise of EU competence over foreign investment is affected by the principles and objectives that determine EU action in the internal market. However, since regulation of foreign investment is based only on the external competences provided by these provisions regarding third country nationals, the latter are not always subject to the same principles and objectives that determine intra-EU investment regulation adopted on the basis of those provisions.

Within the framework established by the CCP and the internal market, a number of EU policy documents dealing with foreign investment have been adopted, presenting the goals and priorities of EU action in the field. The Commission, the Council, and the Parliament have expressed their views on the future European international investment policy indicating, not always along the same lines, how they view the main objectives of EU action in the field of foreign investment and the tools for their achievement. In addition, the Commission Communications on

Global Europe[5] and on Trade, Growth, and World Affairs[6] present key instruments in that respect, setting out the main objectives of EU policy in external economic relations with third countries, including foreign investment. As a follow up, the Commission Working Paper on the external aspects of the single market provides further guidance for the determination of EU foreign investment regulation, identifying the challenges that globalization and interaction with third countries present to the single market.[7]

In order to tackle successfully the challenges posed by globalization, all policy documents identify that the principal goal of EU investment policy should be the enhancement and expansion of EU global competitiveness, which requires competitive and open markets both within the EU and in third countries. Contributing to the objective of smart, sustainable, and inclusive growth—set out in the Europe 2020 Strategy[8]—regulatory concerns play an important rôle, aiming at openness through the removal of regulatory barriers and enhanced regulatory cooperation with third countries, adopting best practices followed elsewhere.[9] In addition to openness, the objectives of economic growth and competitiveness are directly linked in the field of foreign investment, with the existence of a stable, sound, and predictable environment, which assures investors that they can operate in an open and properly and fairly regulated business environment.[10] In that respect, the policy instruments adopted after the Lisbon Treaty indicate explicitly that investment protection is an important objective of EU foreign investment law. Moreover, as the enhancement of competitiveness and openness may have a disruptive impact for certain aspects of economic activity within the EU, social justice goals present an equally important objective of EU foreign investment policy, by aiming to ensure that European citizens fully reap the benefits of competitiveness and openness, while supporting green and sustainable growth.[11]

In examining these strategic goals in light of their relevance for EU action, it is important first to analyse their strong correlation to the primary EU law-mandated objectives. The focus on competitiveness, market openness, and a stable investment environment is better understood when viewed in light of the binding and non-binding objectives of foreign investment law found in the EU Treaties, in particular in the CCP and internal market provisions. Furthermore, the objectives of EU foreign investment law have to be examined in light of the general objectives of international regulation of foreign investment, indicating the role of the EU as a

[5] Commission Communication, Global Europe: Competing in the World, Brussels 4.10.2006, COM(2006) 567 (hereinafter, Global Europe Strategy).

[6] Commission Communication, Trade, Growth and World Affairs, Brussels 9.11.2010, COM(2010) 612 (hereinafter, Trade Strategy).

[7] Commission Staff Working Paper, The External Dimension of the Single Market Review, Brussels 20.11.2007, COM(2007) 1519 (hereinafter, External Single Market Strategy).

[8] Commission Communication, Europe 2020: A Strategy for Smart, Sustainable and Inclusive Growth, Brussels 3.3.2010, COM(2010) 2020 (hereinafter, Europe 2020 Strategy)

[9] Investment Policy Communication, pp 4–5; Council Conclusions on Investment Policy, paras 6–7, 13; Parliament Investment Resolution, para 15; Trade Strategy, pp 6–7; Global Europe Strategy, p 3.

[10] Investment Policy Communication, pp 4–5.

[11] Parliament Investment Resolution, paras 3, 6–7; Trade Strategy, pp 6–7; External Single Market Strategy, p 3.

global actor in the field of foreign investment and its differences from other international actors.

4.1.1.1 The primary EU law-mandated objectives of the CCP

Bearing in mind the importance of the CCP, it may be expected that it is the most clearly defined EU policy in terms of the principles it adheres to and the objectives it is bound to pursue. However, the EC Treaty has to a large extent been historically silent with regard to the orientation of the CCP, as it provided limited guidance for identifying the principles and objectives of the CCP, thus granting policy makers a large degree of flexibility. More specifically, Articles 131 and 133 TEC provided that the CCP was 'based on uniform principles' and 'aims to contribute to the harmonious development of world trade, the progressive abolition of restrictions on international trade and the lowering of standards'. Hence, the EC Treaty text identified, albeit in an indirect way, uniformity and liberalization as the guiding principles and objectives determining the exercise of Community powers in the field. Building on the EC Treaty provisions, Articles 206 and 207 TFEU retain the role of uniformity and liberalization as the main objectives of the CCP. However, the Lisbon Treaty impacts on the role of these principles and objectives regarding the orientation of the EU action in the field of foreign investment, in particular since Article 206 TFEU offers a different role for the objective of liberalization.

4.1.1.1.1 The principle of uniformity and the objective of equal treatment

The principle of uniformity has been a major characteristic of the CCP throughout its evolution, reflecting in external relations the interests of the EU and the needs of the internal market. Aiming to protect the unity of the common market by avoiding distortion in competition and risks of trade deflection that could arise if Member States pursued individual external trade policies, the principle of uniformity requires the adoption of common rules throughout the EU in the field of the CCP.[12] In fact, the exclusive nature of EU competence in the field of trade in goods arose as a result of the application of the principle of uniformity.[13]

However, the role of uniformity for foreign investment is not as important as in the field of trade in goods. Uniformity is an imperative only in areas of the internal market that have been fully harmonized so that common external rules are necessary for the proper functioning of the internal market.[14] In the areas of the internal market where there are deviations from the establishment of common rules, uniformity no longer presents an imperative for the CCP, allowing for flexibility and

[12] M Cremona, 'The external dimension of the internal market' in Barnard and Scott (eds), *The Law of the Single European Market* (2002), pp 354–8; G Marin Duran, 'Development-based differentiation in the European Community's external trade policy: selected issues under Community and International Trade Law', EUI Thesis, Florence, 2008, pp 25–6; P Eeckhout, *External relations of the European Union: legal and constitutional foundations* (2004), pp 349–50.

[13] Opinion 1/75 [1975] ECR 1355; Case 41/76 *Donckerwolke* [1976] ECR 1921.

[14] Cremona, above n 12, pp 359–70; Eeckhout, above n 12, pp 350–1; Marin Duran, above n 12, pp 23–4.

differentiation in Member State trade policies regarding third countries.[15] Hence, in the areas of services and establishment of FDI, where full harmonization exists only to a limited extent in specific economic sectors with regard to specific economic activities,[16] uniformity plays only a subsidiary role. The preference granted to the techniques of mutual recognition and minimum harmonization in these areas indicates that common rules are necessary only to the extent that a minimum level of common standards exists internally in the same area of law.[17]

After the entry into force of the Lisbon Treaty, the principle of uniformity remained at the heart of the CCP rendering the creation of uniform rules in the areas which have been harmonized in the internal market mandatory.[18] However, the requirement of uniformity obtains further importance in light of the explicit recognition of the exclusive nature of Union competence in the field of the CCP. Of course, the exclusive nature of Union competence does not render the creation of uniform rules in the field of FDI mandatory. Similar to the current exceptions to uniformity with regard to trade in goods, which has already been a field of exclusive EU competence, the creation of uniform rules in other areas of the CCP is necessary only to the extent that internal harmonization has been achieved. Even though the Member States can no longer directly impose in these areas of law, different rules concerning third countries and their nationals, the Union, as the single actor in the field, may recognize the different national interests and reflect the policy choices taken by the Member States. Consequently, uniformity remains a powerful negotiating tool for the Union, the use of which lies at the discretion of the relevant Union institutions. However, the exclusion of the Member States as co-decision makers of the CCP changes the actors to whom the exercise of this discretion is addressed.

Furthermore, it should be pointed out that the link between the CCP and the internal market does not imply that the application of the principle of uniformity requires that the CCP aims for the achievement of the same objectives existing in the internal market. Uniformity is only an 'instrumental' principle, determining the form of the measures adopted under the CCP and not its substantive orientation. More specifically, the application of uniformity does not require that the CCP should be based on the principles of non-discrimination and elimination of all trade barriers, which are the main objectives pursued in the internal market.[19] The European Court has clearly recognized that there is 'no general principle obliging the Community, in its external relations, to accord to non-member countries equal treatment in all respects'.[20] As a result, the EU can discriminate not only between

[15] Eg in the field of trade in goods, different national standards apply to imports from third countries insofar as their taxation is concerned, to the extent that indirect taxation of EU products is subject to different national rules determining the tax amount. Case C-228/90 *Simba SpA* [1992] ECR I-3713.

[16] See also Section 2.2.2.2.2.

[17] Cremona, above n 12, p 374.

[18] Art 207 TFEU reiterates in its first sentence that 'the Common Commercial Policy shall be based on uniform principles'.

[19] See below Section 4.1.1.2.

[20] Case 52/81 *Offene Handelsgesellschaft in Firma Werner Faust v Commission* [1982] ECR 3745, para 25. See also Case C-280/93 *Germany v Council (Bananas I)* [1994] ECR I-4973; Case C-122/95 *Germany v Council (Bananas II)* [1998] ECR I-1023; Joined Cases C-364 & 465/95 *T.Port GmbH*

its own and third country investors, but also between third countries themselves, based on the common EU interest.[21]

However, the lack of an obligation of non-discrimination does not mean that the discriminatory treatment of third country investors is always allowed. First, primary EU law requires the equal treatment of third country investors with EU nationals, insofar as such equal treatment is necessary for the proper operation of the internal market.[22] Secondly and most importantly, obligations of equal treatment of third country nationals are located outside primary EU law, in WTO law and in other bilateral Union agreements. However, in such cases equal treatment is a result of international law obligations of the EU, which are freely adopted in the framework of the CCP in accordance with the policy priorities set by the EU political institutions.

As a result, the principle of uniformity has only instrumental value, determining the areas of the CCP where common rules must be adopted. Given that in the field of foreign investment internal common rules present only a small fraction, uniformity is no longer an imperative, but merely a tool that can be used by EU institutions in negotiations with third countries in order to pursue the realization of an emerging common EU interest.[23] Furthermore, it is important to highlight that the principle of uniformity is 'neutral' with regard to the substantive orientation of the CCP. It does not impose an obligation of equal treatment of third country investors or of full liberalization of market conditions, similar to the internal market objectives, but grants almost absolute discretion to the empowered EU institutions to pursue the objectives that, in their view, serve the common EU interest in the best way.

Exercising the discretion provided under primary EU law, the political institutions seem to promote the adoption of common rules in the field of foreign investment. The importance attributed to preserving the 'right policies at home' which are 'underpinned by effective and transparent rules'[24] indicates that EU institutions aim to strengthen the internal regulatory framework on foreign investment from third countries via the adoption of transparent and effective common rules.

4.1.1.1.2 The objective of liberalization under the EC Treaty

The only substantive objective that is provided in primary EU law and can have an impact on the content of the CCP is trade liberalization. Article 206 TFEU, similar to Article 131 TEC, clearly recognizes that the CCP aims at liberalization of world trade through the progressive abolition of trade restrictions. However, the normative value of the objective of liberalization has changed drastically with the Lisbon Treaty.

& Co v Hauptzollamt Hamburg-Jona [1998] ECR I-1023; For an analysis of these cases see S Peers, 'Constitutional Principles and International Trade' (1999) 24 EL Rev 185.

[21] M Cremona, 'Neutrality or Discrimination? The WTO, the EU and External Trade' in G de Búrca and Scott (eds), *The EU and the WTO: Legal and Constitutional Issues* (2001), pp 165–72.

[22] See below Section 4.1.1.2.

[23] Cremona, above n 12, p 374.

[24] Global Europe Strategy, p 3.

In the EC Treaty liberalization was only an aspirational aim, unlike the legally binding obligation of creating uniform rules.[25] Article 131 TEC did not in itself impose an obligation on the Community either to liberalize trade unilaterally or to mirror internal trade liberalization at the external level.[26] The Court verified the non-binding nature of the liberalization objective, emphasizing that it establishes an objective rather than imposing an obligation.[27] It lay in the discretion of the political institutions to assess whether and to what extent CCP measures achieve liberalization of trade.[28]

Hence, liberalization constituted only an aspirational objective which offered guidance to the political institutions in the formation of all aspects of the CCP. The aspirational character of the liberalization objective meant that other policy objectives could influence the content of foreign investment regulation adopted under the CCP, while liberalization did not take precedence over them. Lacking a definition of the type of trade measures falling within the scope of the CCP, the Court endorsed a broad and instrumental approach to the concept of the CCP, so that any type of trade measures would fall within the CCP's scope.[29] In particular at the time when the EEC Treaty lacked specific provisions granting competence to the Community in specific fields, such as environmental protection or development cooperation, the CCP was used for the adoption of trade measures pursuing objectives other than regulating trade flows and trade restrictions.[30]

Of course, the introduction of specific legal bases granting competence to the Community to take external action in specific fields had a significant impact on the use of the CCP for pursuing non-trade objectives. For example, the introduction of Article 301 TEC on trade sanctions, Article 175 TEC on environmental protection, and Article 178 TEC on development cooperation led to numerous legal battles concerning the choice of the proper legal basis for the adoption of a specific measure.[31] Although the Court focused on the procedural issues concerning the choice and combination of legal bases, it recognized the need to use the

[25] The aspirational character of the principle of liberalization becomes evident if it is read in its historical context. The CCP was necessary for the functioning of the EEC as a customs union, which would operate within the framework of GATT 1947. Taking into account Member States' pre-existing commitments, the drafters of the EEC Treaty incorporated the principle of liberalization into the CCP expressing their obligation to comply with the requirement of the GATT that the formation of a customs union shall not lead on the whole to further restrictions on trade with third countries. Also, the aspirational character of the objective of liberalization under the EC Treaty is enhanced when the wording of Art 131 TEC is compared with the wording of other provisions that stated in a mandatory manner the objectives of specific policy fields, such as Art 33 TEC on the Common Agricultural Policy and Art 177 TEC on development policy, or the internal market and the GATT, where trade liberalization is an imperative. See Cremona, above n 12, p 381.

[26] Case 51/75 *EMI Records Ltd v CBS United Kingdom Ltd* [1976] ECR 811.

[27] Case C-150/94 *United Kingdom v Council (Chinese Toys)* [1998] ECR I-7235, para 67; Case 112/80 *Firma Anton Dürbeck v Hauptzollamt Frankfurt* [1982] ECR 1251, para 44.

[28] Cremona, above n 12, pp 382–4.

[29] See Opinion 1/78 [1978] ECR 2151; Opinion 1/75, above n 13; Case C-54/86 *Commission v Council (GSP)* [1987] ECR I-01493.

[30] Eg Art 133 TEC had been used as a legal basis for the conclusion of the Energy Star Agreement, which concerns the coordination of energy-efficient labelling programmes for office equipment, thus also pursuing an environmental protection objective.

[31] See Section 3.1.2.1.

CCP for the adoption of trade measures pursuing objectives found elsewhere in the EC Treaty.[32] However, the Court avoided interfering with the substantive policy choices taken by the legislative and executive organs of the Community, clarifying the interaction between trade and non-trade objectives, their legal value, and whether, how, and by whom they should be prioritized.

Consequently, the EC Treaty did not provide substantive guidance for the orientation of the CCP and, thus, EU foreign investment regulation in service sectors. Liberalization was the main trade-related objective to be pursued; however, it provided only one possible policy orientation, the specific application of which lay in the hands of the EU institutions, which had to assess in any case whether a liberalizing policy would advance the Community interest. It is precisely the determination of the 'Community interest' by the relevant institutions that affected the orientation of the CCP, which may have pursued other trade or non-trade objectives that better served the Community interest.

Indeed, the dominant role of the objective of liberalization under the EC Treaty was reflected in EU policy making. The emphasis placed on market access and openness—both in third countries and also on the part of the EU—indicated the willingness of EU institutions at that time to abide by the objective of liberalization, fulfilling their non-binding commitment to promote liberalization under Article 131 TEC. However, liberalization has not been the only objective pursued. EU institutions have placed equal emphasis on competitiveness, which requires in certain cases limitations on liberalization to the extent that the competitive position of EU investors is threatened by complete liberalization. In addition, the role attributed to social justice objectives, as being equal to competitiveness and openness, indicated the importance of specific non-trade objectives for EU foreign investment regulation.[33]

4.1.1.1.3 The objective of liberalization under the TFEU

The most important change brought by the Lisbon Treaty to the orientation of the CCP concerns the role of liberalization as an aspirational objective. Although Article 206 TFEU defines liberalization in the same terms as Article 133 TEC it substitutes the words 'aims to contribute' with stronger language, providing that the Union 'shall contribute' to trade liberalization. The change of verb indicates that the drafters of the Lisbon Treaty intended to modify the aspirational character of the liberalization objective.[34] The linguistic difference between 'aim' and 'shall' indicates that trade and FDI liberalization is no longer a non-binding objective, the pursuance of which rests in the hands of the political organs of the Union, but Union institutions are bound to formulate the CCP in a way that has positive effects on trade and FDI liberalization. The mandatory nature of the objective of liberalization becomes obvious if Article 206 TFEU is compared with other

[32] See above n 29. [33] Global Europe Strategy, p 4.

[34] M Cremona, A Constitutional Basis for Effective External Action? An Assessment of the Provisions on EU External Action in the Constitutional Treaty, EUI Working Paper Law No 2006/30, p 29.

provisions of the founding Treaties which have similar wording in respect to the objectives of specific Union policy fields. The objective of promoting democracy and the rule of law and respect for human rights under Article 177(2) TEC, which provided identical wording ('shall contribute'), has been considered mandatory by the Court.[35]

However, Article 206 TFEU does not require full liberalization of trade and FDI conditions similar to the internal market, nor does it oblige the Union to proceed with unilateral liberalization of FDI conditions. A careful reading of Article 206 TFEU indicates that the Union is committed to contributing to the gradual liberalization of FDI. The Treaty text is clear that the Union is committed to the 'progressive abolition of restrictions' and the development of 'harmonious world trade conditions'. Of course, this does not mean that the mandatory objective of liberalization is deprived of any normative value. On the contrary, the reference to contribution to gradual liberalization could be interpreted as binding the existing level of liberalization and prohibiting the adoption of new restrictive measures. Such an interpretation would not only give value to the mandatory nature of the objective of liberalization, but would also respect the wording of Article 206 TFEU, which views liberalization as the progressive abolition of restrictions. The requirement that existing restrictions have to be gradually abolished indicates that *a contrario* a step back in liberalization is not permitted, as that would contravene the mandatory objective of pursuing further liberalization.[36] However, restrictive measures could be adopted if they contribute to the general objectives of EU external relations.[37]

Consequently, the Lisbon Treaty emphasizes the commitment of the EU as a major global economic actor to the principle of liberalization, by rendering it a mandatory objective of its CCP. However, the binding nature of the objective of liberalization does not imply that the Union institutions lose their discretion for the determination of the extent and means of liberalization. The CCP retains its flexibility, allowing the political organs to determine whether, when, and to what extent liberalizing measures advance the Union interest.[38] However, the margin of appreciation given to the political institutions is limited, as the Lisbon Treaty appears to oblige them to avoid taking any restrictive measures affecting the existing level of liberalization.

Indeed, the value attributed to liberalization in the Lisbon Treaty is reflected in the Trade Strategy and investment policy documents. Market openness in the EU and in third countries is a key goal, aiming to ensure openness for attracting

[35] Case C-268/94 *Portugal v Council* [1996] ECR I-6177.

[36] It has been argued the such a reading of the binding objective of liberalization is too strict, as the removal of existing tariff concessions or market access commitments is a particular trade policy instrument that can contribute to liberalization in the long run, eg in the case of removal of EU GATS concessions as a result of the 2004 enlargement (M Krajewski, 'The Reform of the Common Commercial Policy' in Biondi and Eeckhout (eds), *European Union Law after the Treaty of Lisbon* (2011, forthcoming). However, Art 206 TFEU expresses clearly the objective of liberalization as 'progressive abolition of restrictions'.

[37] See Section 4.1.3.2.

[38] See Section 4.1.3.1.

investment in the EU and to promote openness of third country markets to accommodate the interests of EU investors. Moreover, the importance attributed to liberalization becomes obvious from the prioritization of future negotiations and partnerships with countries with the best potential to promote the EU's competitive interests.[39]

4.1.1.2 The primary EU law-mandated objectives of the internal market

In contrast to the CCP provisions that refer only to the objective of trade liberalization, the internal market provisions conferring competence over foreign investment pursue a variety of objectives. The establishment of an internal market requires, among other things, the abolition of obstacles to the free movement of persons, services, and capital,[40] mainly through the liberalization of market access conditions and the prohibition of discrimination between EU nationals, the guarantee of competition in the internal market through the prevention, restriction, or distortion of competitive conditions,[41] and the approximation of national laws that directly affect the establishment or operation of the internal market.[42] Considering the wide scope of the internal market, which covers virtually all fields of economic activity, it is reasonable that the adoption of measures contributing to its establishment and smooth operation pursue in parallel a wider set of objectives, such as health, safety, environmental, and consumer protection,[43] covering in essence the entire list of objectives of EU action listed in Article 3 TEU.[44]

Within this broader framework of objectives that EU action in the field of the internal market is bound to pursue, there are two principal objectives that guide the adoption of EU measures in the field of foreign investment. The objectives of liberalization and non-discrimination are more than general objectives, the pursuance of which rests at the discretion of EU institutions, which assess and balance them in light of the circumstances leading to the adoption of a specific measure. They are mandatory, imposing an obligation on political institutions to respect and promote them in the formation and application of EU foreign investment regulation.

Before examining these internal market objectives, it is necessary to point out the role of uniformity in the field of foreign investment regulation under the internal market provisions. Indeed, the principle of uniformity has been central to the formation of the internal market.[45] However, similar to the CCP, the requirement of uniformity is not very strong. Primary law prohibits restrictions to the free movement of capital to and from third countries and to the establishment of

[39] Investment Policy Communication, pp 6–7; Council Conclusions on Investment Policy, paras 6–7, 13; Trade Strategy, pp 10–11. See also S Woolcock and J Kleinheisterkamp, 'The EU approach to international investment policy after the Lisbon Treaty', Study Directorate General for External Policies of the Union (October 2010), pp 20–30.

[40] Arts 4(2)(a) and 26 TFEU.

[41] Art 3(1)(b) TFEU.

[42] Arts 114 and 115 TFEU.

[43] Art 114(3) TFEU.

[44] P Craig and G de Búrca, *EU Law: Texts, Cases, and Materials* (2008), pp 626–8.

[45] For a thorough analysis on the role of uniformity in the internal market see G de Búrca and J Scott (eds), *Constitutional Change in the EU: From Uniformity to Flexibility?* (2000); B de Witte, D Hanf, and E Vos (eds), *The Many Faces of Differentiation in EU Law* (2001).

foreign-controlled EU nationals in another EU Member State,[46] thus leading to negative integration. However, these provisions set the foundations for the establishment of a common regime for capital movements and establishment of foreign investors that applies across the EU. Although the adoption of common rules does not present an imperative, uniformity is a significant tool at the disposal of political institutions, which can be used for furthering the interests of both the EU and the Member States in the field of foreign investment.

Turning to the mandatory internal market objectives, the mandatory nature of the objective of liberalization is explicit in the field of capital movements. Article 63 TFEU dictates the full liberalization of capital movements to and from third countries, prohibiting all measures that may interfere and have an adverse effect on capital movements by foreign investors. As a result, EU foreign investment regulation has to respect liberalization of capital movements and shall not restrict capital movements to or from EU counterparties. Nevertheless, primary EU law provides for exceptions from liberalization, such as in Articles 64, 66, and 75 TFEU.[47]

Although liberalization also constitutes an imperative in the fields of the other basic freedoms, it does not cover foreign investors. Liberalization concerns only the establishment and the provision of services by EU nationals in the territory of another EU Member State excluding from its scope third country nationals. Hence, liberalization presents only an aspirational objective which, alongside other objectives, must be taken into account by EU institutions in determining the content of EU foreign investment regulation.

In addition to liberalization, the internal market has been based on the principle of non-discrimination, which has been used as a minimum guarantee for market openness and undistorted competition.[48] However, similar to liberalization, the principle of non-discrimination aims to ensure the removal of *internal* barriers to free movement, and it does not establish a general principle obliging the EU to accord equal treatment to non-member countries or their nationals.[49] This does not mean that the principle of equal treatment plays only a marginal role in the formation of EU foreign investment regulation. First, equal treatment between third country investors or in comparison to EU investors is mandatory in the field of capital movements, where the prohibition of any restriction to free movement inescapably covers the prohibition of discriminatory treatment.[50] In addition, equal treatment of third country investors is mandatory in cases where they are established in the EU in accordance with Article 54 TFEU, as third

[46] See also Sections 2.2.1.1 and 6.2.2.4.

[47] See also Section 3.2.1.3. On the scope of the exceptions provided in Arts 64(1), 66, and 75 TEU see S Hindelang, *The Free Movement of Capital and Foreign Direct Investment: the scope of protection in EU law* (2009), pp 275–98, 305–26.

[48] G More, 'The Principle of Equal Treatment: From Market Unifier to Fundamental Right?' in Craig and de Búrca (eds), *The Evolution of EU Law* (1999), p 517; J Wouters, 'Constitutional Limits of Differentiation: the Principle of Equality' in de Witte, Hanf, and Vos (eds), *The Many Faces of Differentiation in EU Law* (2001), p 181.

[49] *Offene Handelsgesellschaft in Firma Werner Faust v Commission,* above n 20; See also Marin Duran, above n 12, pp 37–9.

[50] C Barnard, *The Substantive Law of the EU: The Four Freedoms* (2010), pp 571–3.

country nationals are considered EU nationals for the purposes of EU law and, thus, are eligible for equal treatment.[51] Also, the principle of equal treatment of EU nationals plays an additional role in EU foreign investment regulation. As equal treatment of EU nationals extends to their treatment in third countries,[52] to the extent that the EU negotiates a bilateral agreement with a third country, EU institutions are bound to ensure the equal treatment of all EU investors regarding their establishment, treatment, and protection in third countries.

Viewing together the principles and objectives guiding the formation of EU foreign investment regulation based on internal market provisions, the role of liberalization and non-discrimination becomes apparent. Examining whether there is an imperative for liberalization and non-discrimination, it is necessary to distinguish between the different power-conferring provisions. While in the field of capital movements the imperative for liberalization and non-discrimination is stronger, in the fields of establishment and services these principles and objectives become mandatory only to a limited extent.

The prioritization of the objectives of liberalization and equal treatment as required by primary EU law is incorporated in EU policy-making documents. The EU recognizes the importance of liberalization in the field of capital movements and highlights the importance for the proper application of its internal rules, including those on equal treatment.[53] In addition, it places particular emphasis on the benefits of foreign investment activity for EU citizens, providing the necessary flexibility for EU institutions to accommodate important internal market objectives in their external action, such as the promotion of labour standards and job growth, environmental, and consumer interests.[54]

4.1.1.3 The investment policy objectives in light of the general objectives of international regulation of foreign investment

The strategic goals of EU action in the field of foreign investment show that the EU integrates in its policies the main socio-economic rationales that drive the international regulation of foreign investment.[55] First, recognizing the benefits of investment inflows for host countries, the EU aims to attract foreign investment to the EU. In that respect, the strengthening of competitiveness internally is important, as the single market remains the EU's main competitive advantage in

[51] As Art 54 TFEU considers that companies that are incorporated or have their effective seat in an EU Member State as EU nationals, irrespective of their ownership or control, foreign investors which are established in the EU territory are considered EU nationals. See also Sections 6.2.2.4 and 1.2.2.1.2.

[52] Following the jurisprudence of the Court in the *Open Skies* cases, the principle of equal treatment enunciated in Art 18 TFEU is considered to cover not only the advantages that a Member State grants to its own nationals, but also the advantages that a third country offers to the nationals of a specific Member State via a bilateral agreement. See also Sections 2.2.2.2.1 and 6.2.2.5.

[53] Investment Policy Communication, p 9; Global Europe Strategy, p 3.

[54] Trade Strategy, p 8; External Single Market Strategy, pp 5–7, 13.

[55] See Section 1.1.1.

attracting FDI.[56] In addition, the attractiveness of the EU as a destination for foreign investment is pursued through the openness of the European market to third country investors, as it 'exposes the domestic economy to creative competitive pressures, spurring and rewarding innovation, providing access to new technologies, and increasing incentives for investment.'[57]

Next to the goal of attracting foreign investment, the EU institutions place emphasis on the effort to gain benefits from investment inflows and mitigate the negative effects of investment outflows. Within the broader contours of the CCP, the Commission recognizes in its Strategy papers that EU action in the field of foreign investment shall lead to 'inclusive growth' thus fostering consumers' economic interests without affecting labour, safety, health, environmental, and other standards.[58] Regarding the mitigation of negative effects from investment outflows, the Commission underlines the importance of social justice and cohesion, providing opportunities, such as the European Globalization Adjustment Fund, to the affected sectors, regions, and workforce to adapt to the new globalized competitive environment.[59] Despite the prominence given to internal social justice objectives within the CCP, their role is not highlighted under the Commission's Investment Policy Communication. On the contrary, the Parliament emphasizes the importance of securing benefits from inward investment, indicating the importance of guaranteeing the right of host states to regulate, in particular in sensitive sectors.[60]

In addition to the interests of the EU as a capital-importing bloc, the EU institutions provide equal, or even greater, consideration to the interests of European investors and the EU as capital exporter. In order to attain this objective of international regulation of foreign investment, the Commission underlines the objectives of market openness and, since 2010, investment protection.

Opening third country markets to EU investors reinforces the competitive position of EU industry, enabling it to enhance production and lower costs.[61] The Commission highlights the significance of the ability to invest freely in third markets, which is necessary to sustain domestic political support for EU openness, thus highlighting the importance of reciprocity in foreign investment regulation.[62] Placing emphasis on coherence and transparency regarding the internal rule-making process, and promoting supervisory and regulatory convergence and equivalence, the Commission indicates its willingness to achieve its investment goals in the field of foreign investment.[63]

[56] Investment Policy Communication, pp 3–4; Woolcock and Kleinheisterkamp, above n 39, p 17; External Single Market Strategy, p 5.

[57] Global Europe Strategy, p 4.

[58] Trade Strategy, p 8; External Single Market Strategy, p 7.

[59] Trade Strategy, p 8; Global Europe Strategy, pp 4–5.

[60] Parliament Investment Resolution, paras 6, 23–6.

[61] Investment Policy Communication, p 3; Woolcock and Kleinheisterkamp, above n 39, pp 16–17.

[62] Trade Strategy, p 6

[63] Trade Strategy, p 7; External Single Market Strategy, pp 9–12. On the role of the EU as a rule generator see M Cremona, 'The Union as a Global Actor: Roles, Models and Identities' (2004) 41 CMLR 553, 557–8.

Until 2010 investment protection, accompanied by a rigorous dispute settlement system, was excluded from the objectives of EU action in the field of foreign investment. However, the Investment Policy Communication identifies, for the first time, the importance of investment protection norms and investor-state arbitration for guaranteeing an environment favourable to foreign investment.[64] Aiming to establish a comprehensive investment policy, EU institutions identify the 'gaps' in existing Member State BITs, which do not focus on admission of foreign investment, indicating that future EU IIAs will address both liberalization and protection of foreign investment, which will not only increase EU leverage as an international actor, but can lead to overall better competitive conditions for all EU investors abroad.[65]

Establishing a comprehensive EU investment policy requires, of course, a significant rebalancing of the roles of the EU and its Members States in the international arena. So far, the EU has held only a secondary role, adding to Member States' autonomous policy in the field. Recognizing the need for smooth transition from Member State to EU investment policy, which is important for the viability of EU investment policy,[66] the EU sets out its short-term and long-term priorities regarding the negotiation of new, comprehensive EU IIAs. As discussed above, EU institutions aim to determine the objectives to be pursued in each specific negotiating context, thus providing the flexibility necessary to accomplish the maximum benefits for EU competitiveness.

More specifically, the Investment Policy Communication indicates first that the actual trade and investment flows are important determinants for EU investment negotiations. However, recognizing the growth prospects and potential of other markets, the Commission highlights that 'the Union should go where its investors would like to go'. Thirdly, the Commission indicates the 'robustness' of investor protection and the existence of a certain and sound environment as an important determinant of priority countries for future negotiations.[67] When considering the choice of the specific objectives, it becomes obvious that the Commission places greater emphasis on liberalization than on investment protection. Prioritizing countries where a sufficient investment protection environment exists, the Commission highlights the importance of market openness as its main goal of foreign investment policy, focusing on neglected aspects of foreign investment regulation, which constantly increase in importance for states and investors. Along similar lines, the Council emphasizes the importance of economic climate, market potential, and strategic importance for the EU as the main determinants for EU investment negotiations.[68]

[64] Investment Policy Communication, pp 4, 6.

[65] Woolcock and Kleinheisterkamp, above n 39, p 19.

[66] The question of the objectives of EU policy regarding the transition from Member States to EU investment policy is discussed below in Chapter 6, as it is better understood after the question on the compatibility of Member State BITs with EU law is discussed.

[67] Investment Policy Communication, pp 4, 6.

[68] Council Conclusions on Investment Policy, para 12. Parliament Investment Resolution, para 36.

Within this framework, the Commission identifies Canada, Mercosur, India, and Singapore as the first countries where negotiations should begin, continuing in the medium term with China and Russia.[69] Indeed, applying the criteria identified by the Commission in practice, the conclusion can be drawn that the prioritization of negotiating partners matches the criteria identified in the Investment Policy Communication.[70]

4.1.1.4 *A policy preference towards multilateralism?*

In promoting international regulation of foreign investment, it is crucial to highlight the stance adopted by the EU towards multilateralism, on the one hand, and bilateralism and regionalism, on the other. In the field of trade policy the EU has always been a proponent of multilateralism, supporting the creation of a global rule-based system for trade and contributing to its success. At the same time, trade provisions have been inserted in a significant number of bilateral and regional agreements that were considered necessary for enhancing regional, neighbourhood, or development objectives of EU external relations.[71] Although the EU has insisted on the consistency of its bilateral and regional agreements with multilateral WTO rules,[72] the unavoidable effect of the so-called 'spaghetti bowl' of regional Free Trade Agreements (FTAs) has become the subject of significant criticism for its complexity and the threats it poses to the existence and effectiveness of the multilateral system.[73] Following the current stalemate of the multilateral negotiations in the WTO, the EU has been more eager to negotiate FTAs with many of its important trading partners.[74] This pragmatic approach towards further trade liberalization based on pure trade interests beyond regional or development policies indicates a significant turn in the orientation of EU external trade policy, questioning the core of the EU's commitment towards multilateralism.[75]

[69] Investment Policy Communication, p 7.

[70] For an extensive analysis of the criteria see Woolcock and Kleinheisterkamp, above n 39, pp 21–30.

[71] For an analysis of the EU's commitment towards multilateralism see G Glania and J Matthes, *Multilateralism or Regionalism? Trade Policy Options for the European Union* (2005).

[72] The need for consistency of FTAs with WTO norms is emphasized in the Global Europe Strategy (p 8).

[73] On the effects of bilateral agreements on multilateral trade see indicatively J Bhagwati and A Panagariya, 'Preferential Trade Areas and Multilateralism; Strangers, Friends, or Foes?' in Bhagwati and Panagariya (eds), *The Economics of Preferential Trade Agreements* (1996), pp 1–78; T Geiger and D Kennedy (eds), *Regional Trade Blocs, Multilateralism, and the GATT: Complementary Paths to Free Trade?* (1996).

[74] The Trade Strategy (p 10) indicates Gulf countries, Mercosur, India, Russia, and Singapore as the main target countries for concluding FTAs in the short term. See also PJ Lloyd and D MacLaren 'The EU's New Trade Strategy and Regionalisation in the World Economy' (2006) 61 Aussenwirtschaft 423.

[75] S Woolcock, 'European Union Policy towards Free Trade Agreements', ECIPE Working Paper No 3/2007 (2007). The United States follows a similar approach, favouring the model of 'competitive liberalization', which highlights the benefits of bilateral trade liberalization. See J Schott, 'Free Trade Agreements: Boon or Bane of the World Trading System?' in Schott (ed), *Free Trade Agreements: US Strategies and Priorities* (2004), pp 3–20.

These basic parameters of EU external trade policy have also been instrumental for the orientation of EU policy in the field of foreign investment. Nevertheless, the commitment towards multilateralism followed by the adoption of bilateral and regional agreements and the promotion of further bilateralism raise different concerns in the field of foreign investment. As discussed above, foreign investment has always been a field of bilateral relations, since more than 2,500 IIAs exist, whereas international efforts for the creation of a multilateral discipline on foreign investment have failed.[76] Both in the negotiations for the Multilateral Agreement on Investment (MAI) and in the WTO, the EU was one of the main supporters of the creation of multilateral rules on investment, thus affirming its commitment towards a global rule-based system in a field traditionally seen as one of bilateral relations.[77] Following the collapse of the multilateral negotiations, the adoption of investment rules in bilateral agreements has become a priority for EU negotiators, who have gradually inserted provisions on foreign investment in Union agreements. Indeed, considering the lack of a multilateral framework, the adoption of investment rules on a bilateral level serves the economic and broader regional interests of the EU (and its counterparties). Although the introduction of foreign investment provisions in bilateral agreements that are not currently on the WTO agenda can be regarded as an attempt to by-pass the WTO, in essence it contributes to the enhancement of the multilateral system, as regional agreements work as a laboratory for future multilateral investment disciplines, providing the EU with the opportunity to shape future investment rules.[78]

The position of EU institutions towards multilateral and/or bilateral agreements on foreign investment can also be viewed through the prism of the internal struggle for competence with the Member States. The strong support towards investment regulation under the Organisation for Economic Co-Operation and Development (OECD) and WTO auspices was not only inspired by the commitment of the EU towards multilateral rule-based systems of regulation, but was equally based on the belief that it would help the EU to become the principal actor in the field of foreign investment, similar to the way that the General Agreement on Tariffs and Trade (GATT) and the WTO helped the EU to strip Member States of their powers in the field of external trade.[79]

[76] See Section 1.1.2.

[77] The active involvement of the EU in the MAI negotiations is proved by the working papers that it submitted during the negotiations: Communication made by the European Communities and its Member States, Concept papers on Transparency (WT/WGTI/W/110), Definition of investment (WT/WGTI/W/115), Non-discrimination (WT/WGTI/W/122), Modalities for pre-establishment (WT/WGTI/W/121), Consultation and the Settlement of Disputes between Members (WT/WGTI/W/141), Balance-of-payments safeguards (WT/WGTI/W/153).

[78] For an analysis of the benefits of regionalism for multilateralism see C Fink and M Jansen, 'Services Provisions in Regional Trade Agreements: stumbling blocks or building blocks for multilateral liberalization' in Baldwin and Low (eds), *Multilateralizing Regionalism: Challenges for the Global Trading System* (2009), ch 6.

[79] The court judgments in *International Fruit Company* (Cases 22–24/72 [1972] ECR 1219) and Opinion 1/94 ([1994] ECR I-5267) reaffirmed the scope of EU competence over external trade in goods establishing at the same time the role of the EU as the single international actor in the framework of GATT 1947 and GATT 1994.

Within this framework, the Commission focuses on bilateralism and regionalism indicating squarely that bilateral negotiations remain its key focus. However, the Investment Policy Communication is reminiscent of the efforts for the establishment of a multilateral investment regime, indicating that 'the feasibility of a multilateral initiative could be further considered in the long term'.[80] The Commission adopts a pragmatic approach in order best to promote its investment objectives, recognizing that available resources should in the short and medium term be focused only on the conclusion of bilateral agreements.

4.1.2 Linking foreign investment and development objectives

Development objectives play a crucial role in the formation of EU foreign investment regulation. The value of the legal framework on development cooperation becomes apparent due to the central role of development in the definition and content of foreign investment regulation. The contribution to the development of the host country is an essential characteristic of the definition of investment.[81] Also, international regulation of foreign investment is premised on the idea that it can maximize the positive effects of foreign investment; the most important of which is that it can advance the development of the recipient country.[82] In addition, development objectives acquire a role for EU foreign investment regulation through the use of Article 217 TFEU. Bearing in mind that most EU IIAs have been concluded on the basis of that provision,[83] the use of this multi-purpose and flexible legal instrument, which provides no indication regarding the principal objectives and substantive scope of associations, allows EU institutions to pursue a variety of EU external relations objectives according to political choices and priorities.[84] In that regard, it is necessary to examine the primary EU law provisions on development cooperation and their link to foreign investment, complemented by an analysis of the incorporation of development objectives in the EU's general policy objectives regarding foreign investment regulation.

4.1.2.1 The primary EU law provisions on development cooperation

Continuing the examination of the primary EU law-mandated objectives of EU foreign investment regulation, it is necessary to examine the objectives pursued in the remaining power-conferring provisions apart from the CCP and the internal market provisions. Among them, the provisions on development and technical cooperation are of greater significance for EU external action in the field of foreign investment. Although the scope of competence over foreign investment conferred by these provisions is secondary in comparison to the CCP and the internal market provisions, their importance for the orientation of EU foreign investment regulation is immense.

80 Investment Policy Communication, p 7.
81 See Section 1.2.1.2.4.
82 Section 1.1.1.
83 See Section 3.1.2.1.
84 Eeckhout, above n 12, p 105.

The significance of development objectives for EU foreign investment regulation is emphasized in primary EU law. Article 208(1)(b) TFEU requires that 'the Union shall take account of the objectives of development cooperation in the policies that it implements which are likely to affect developing countries'. Article 208(1)(b) TFEU, like other policy integration provisions,[85] calls for 'developmental mainstreaming'[86] of all policies likely to affect developing countries, thus covering at least foreign investment regulation directed towards developing countries. Given that development goals can already be pursued in the exercise of EU external powers under the CCP or the internal market provisions, Article 208(1)(b) TFEU recognizes formally that other EU measures may have a developmental dimension, requiring in fact the specific consideration and the systemic integration of the development objectives provided in Article 208 TFEU in other fields of EU action. Although Article 208(1)(b) TFEU does not oblige EU institutions to enter into a balancing of development objectives with other objectives that are legitimately pursued, it obliges them to take development goals into account in the formation of other EU policies that affect developing countries, including EU foreign investment policy.[87]

Turning to the objectives of development cooperation, the Lisbon Treaty has changed the emphasis on the main objectives of EU external action in the field of development cooperation requiring, thus, an examination of the previous regime, which has influenced EU policy so far, and of the new provisions. Under the EC Treaty Article 177(1) set out three specific objectives of development cooperation: reduction of poverty; sustainable economic and social development of developing countries, in particular of the most disadvantaged ones; and smooth and gradual integration of developing countries into the world economy. In addition, Article 177(2) TEC required that EC development policy contributed to the general objective of promoting democracy and the rule of law and that of respecting human rights and fundamental freedoms and Article 177(3) TEC obliged the EC and its Member States to comply with their international commitments and take account of the objectives that had been approved in the context of international organizations.

The language used in Article 177 TEC indicated, first, the broad scope of the development objectives, which granted considerable discretion to the EU institutions to decide on the appropriate types and content of measures for their implementation. However, Article 177 TEC contributed to the clarification of EC development goals and set common objectives, which went beyond economic growth, covering social development, eradication of poverty, promotion and respect

[85] Other policy integration provisions in primary EU law are Art 11 TFEU on environmental protection, Art 8 TFEU on gender equality, Art 147(2) TFEU on employment, Art 167(4) TFEU on cultural diversity, Art 168(1) TFEU on public health, Art 169(2) TFEU on consumer protection, and Art 174 TFEU on economic and social cohesion. On the role of Art 11 TFEU in EU external relations see G Marin Duran and E Morgera, 'Towards Environmental Integration in EC External Relations? A comparative analysis of selected Association Agreements' (2006) 6 Yearbook of European Environmental Law 179.

[86] Marin Duran, above n 12, p 66.

[87] Ibid, pp 67–8.

for democracy, and the rule of law and human rights.[88] Additionally, the reference to the most disadvantaged developing countries could be understood as encouraging flexibility and differentiation in EC development policy.[89] The importance of the objectives listed in Article 177 TEC was recognized by the Court in *Portugal v Council*,[90] which stressed the mandatory nature of the objectives of Article 177(2) TEC and consequently of all objectives found in Article 177 TEC, providing flexibility to EU institutions to pursue ancillary objectives and to choose adequate and appropriate measures in order to pursue them.[91]

Retaining the mandatory nature of development cooperation goals, Article 208 TFEU adopts different wording, shifting the emphasis of development cooperation towards poverty reduction and eradication, which is its 'primary goal'. However, this does not mean that sustainable economic and social development, integration of the developing countries into the world economy, and promotion of democracy, rule of law, and respect for human rights are no longer objectives of development cooperation. The latter have become general objectives of EU external action, incorporated in Article 21(2) TEU, so that they are to be taken into account by all other policies, including development cooperation and, more importantly for foreign investment, the CCP.[92]

Finally, reference should be made to Article 212 TFEU, which provides a legal basis for economic, technical, and financial cooperation with third non-developing countries. In regard to the objectives EU action has pursued under this provision, Article 212(1) TFEU provides a link to EU development objectives, so that EU action has to be consistent with the development objectives listed thereunder. In that respect, the EU objectives are also pertinent for the adoption of measures affecting countries that have, to a certain extent, similar economic, social, or structural characteristics with developing countries. Nevertheless, Article 212 TFEU is broadly formulated, allowing for the pursuance of other legitimate objectives of EU external relations.[93]

Consequently, development objectives play a significant role in EU foreign investment regulation, despite the marginal role of the primary EU law provisions on development for determining EU competence over foreign investment. The importance of development considerations for international regulation of foreign investment is mainly highlighted in Article 208(1)(b) TFEU, which requires that

[88] K Arts, 'EU Development Cooperation: From Model to Symbol' in Arts and Dickson (eds), *EU Development Cooperation: From Model to Symbol* (2004), pp 1–17; R Williams, 'Community Development Cooperation Law, Sustainable Development, and the Convention on Europe—From Dislocation to Consistency?' (2005) 4 Oxford Yearbook of European Environmental Law 303; B Martenczuk, 'Cooperation with Developing Countries and Other Third Countries: Elements of a Community Foreign Policy' in Griller and Weidel (eds), *External Economic Relations and Foreign Policy in the European Union*, (2002), pp 392–4.

[89] On differentiation in EU development policy see Marin Duran, above n 12, ch 5.

[90] *Portugal v Council*, above n 35.

[91] For a discussion of the case see S Peers, 'Fragmentation or Evasion in the Community's Development Policy? The Impact of Portugal v Council' in Dashwood and Hillion (eds), *The General Law of EC External Relations* (2000), ch 7.

[92] See below Section 4.1.3.2.

[93] Martenczuk, above n 88, pp 406–10.

the mandatory development objectives are incorporated in other external policies affecting developing countries. However, EU law grants a great degree of flexibility to political institutions for determining the appropriate means for the achievement of the stated development goals.

4.1.2.2 The role of development objectives in EU policy making in the field of foreign investment

The pursuance of the primary EU law-mandated objectives of development cooperation are, to a certain extent, incorporated in the policy objectives pursued by EU policy in the field of foreign investment. The significance of development objectives in the field of trade and foreign investment is highlighted in development policy instruments, which require in general the pursuance of development objectives in the field of the CCP as part of their policy coherence.[94] More importantly, development objectives are inserted in the specific policy instruments dealing with foreign investment.

The development objectives pursued by EU action in the field of foreign investment are recognized by the Commission policy documents and more prominently by the Parliament. Although the Commission is primarily concerned with guaranteeing benefits for the EU and its investors, it also underlines the importance of market openness and competitiveness for the development of third countries. Nevertheless, despite the importance of development considerations for EU external relations, the specific policy objectives of EU foreign investment policy, as set by the Commission, seem to grant only a secondary role to development objectives. On the other hand, the European Parliament stresses particularly the development aspects of future EU investment policy, proposing many audacious solutions.

By endorsing a liberal approach towards outwards investment, the Commission aims to offer open and competitive market conditions in the EU, which can help developing countries to benefit from exporting capital.[95] Also, the EU promotes openness of third country markets, with the intention that this will attract foreign investment in developing countries, promoting economic and social development and their integration in the world economy.[96] Nevertheless, the development impact of openness is only considered secondarily, given that the degree of openness pursued with regard to each third country depends on the positive impact on EU competitiveness. Recognizing, though, that complete liberalization on the part of developing countries may not be desirable from the beginning, the EU institutions and current practice allow for asymmetry, assuming a greater level of openness than that required by its developing counterparties.[97]

[94] See above n 3.

[95] Investment Policy Communication, pp 6, 9; Trade Strategy, p 8; Global Europe Strategy, p 5. See also below Section 4.2.2.

[96] Ibid.

[97] Parliament Investment Resolution, para 26. A good example of asymmetric commitments is the EPA with the CARIFORUM states. See P Cardwell and D French, 'Liberalizing Investment in the CARIFORUM-EU Economic Partnership Agreement: EU Priorities, Regional Agendas and Developmental Hegemony' in CordonierSegger, Gehring, and Newcombe (eds), *Sustainable*

Moreover, the promotion of development objectives should be reflected in the determination of the proposed tools and measures for implementing EU external policies. However, according to the Commission, development considerations seem to be relevant only when the relevant measures promote EU competitiveness and the interests of European investors. For example, in the field of regulatory cooperation, the Commission underlines the need for technical assistance for developing countries in order to advance structural reforms and the creation of an institutional environment favourable for foreign investment, encouraging for instance the training of foreign regulators.[98] More importantly, the EU emphasizes the need for linkages between foreign investment and international standards, fostering the global convergence of minimum regulatory standards, such as health or labour standards, which can promote economic and social development in third countries.[99] However, these efforts aim primarily to ensure better treatment of EU investors and to maintain high internal standards, rather than contributing to sustainable development goals. Conversely, the Parliament stresses adequate and appropriate tools for materializing the development aspects of foreign investment activity and emphasizes the need to provide support to developing countries to strengthen their productivity, encourage transfer of technology, and promote FDI in areas other than natural resources thus boosting local economic development.[100]

In addition, EU development policy distinguishes between third countries, adopting a differentiated approach towards developing countries, and even further differentiating between developing countries depending on their specific development needs. As the European Consensus on Development asserts, the

> implementation of the [Union] development cooperation is necessarily country or region-specific, 'tailor-made' to each partner country or region, based on the country's own needs, strategies, priorities and assets. Differentiation is a necessity, given the diversity of partners and challenges.[101]

Following the modalities for differentiation in the field of trade, where the EU has actively promoted differentiation either in the framework of the WTO or through the adoption of autonomous measures, such as the Generalized System of Preferences (GSP) scheme,[102] differentiation is also important in the field of foreign investment. Indeed, the Commission highlights that 'a one-size-fits-all model

Development in World Investment Law (2011), pp 445–6. On asymmetry in external trade relations see M Cremona, 'Flexible Models: External Policy and the European Economic Constitution' in de Búrca and Scott (eds), *Constitutional Change in the EU: From Uniformity to Flexibility?* (2000), pp 74–82.

[98] External Single Market Strategy, p 10.

[99] Trade Strategy, p 7; Woolcock and Kleinheisterkamp, above n 39, pp 50–1.

[100] Parliament Investment Resolution, paras 38–9.

[101] European Consensus on Development, para. 57.

[102] For an analysis of development differentiation in the field of trade policy see Marin Duran, above n 12, chs 4 and 5.

for investment agreements with third countries would necessarily be neither feasible nor desirable'.[103]

Nevertheless, according to the Commission, the prioritization of negotiations with third countries rests only on their positive impact on EU competitiveness, neglecting the development concerns of developing countries. Also, differentiation between third countries depends inter alia 'on the political, institutional and economic climate of our partner countries', thus excluding development needs from the main conditions for differentiation in EU foreign investment policy.[104] On the contrary, the Parliament stresses the importance of development concerns for differentiation in EU investment policy.[105]

Finally, EU action in the field of foreign investment has to be directly linked with the broader development objective of promoting democracy and the rule of law, as well as respect for human rights. The formation of an EU policy 'on Human Rights, Democracy and Development',[106] which was a result of the ever-growing importance attributed to human rights and development in EU external relations requires that EU action in the field of trade and investment not only takes account of such concerns, but that it also actively promotes democracy, the rule of law, and human rights. To highlight the role of democracy and human rights, the EU has insisted on the use of conditionality in autonomous measures and international agreements, leading to the insertion of conditionality clauses in instruments granting financial and technical aid to third countries, as well as international agreements under the form of essential elements clauses.[107] Nevertheless, the insertion of conditionality clauses in future EU IIAs is not an objective of EU foreign investment policy. Taking a different direction, the promotion of respect for human rights and the rule of law is viewed from the perspective of investors, considering how their conduct can be conducive to the promotion of these objectives.[108]

Focusing on the OECD Guidelines for Multinational Enterprises, as 'an important instrument to help balance the rights and responsibilities of investors', the Investment Policy Communication seems to prioritize the development of non-binding standards of corporate social responsibility rather than contributing to the insertion of legally binding provisions in EU IIAs. Whereas, the Parliament emphasizes the importance of creating legally binding obligations so that foreign investors respect at least human rights and anti-corruption standards.[109]

103 Investment Policy Communication, p 6.

104 Ibid, p 7.

105 Parliament Investment Resolution, para 26.

106 Commission Communication, Human Rights, Democracy and Development Cooperation Policy, Brussels 25.3.1991, SEC(91) 61; Resolution of the Council and of the Member States Meeting in the Council on Human Rights, *Democracy and Development*, 28.11.1991, Bull EC 11-1991, 122.

107 For the use of conditionality in internal instruments and international agreements see Cremona, above n 97, pp 70–4; L Bartels, *Human Rights Conditionality in the EU's International Agreements* (2005); M Cremona, 'Variable Geometry and the Setting of Membership Conditionalities: an EU Perspective' in Clapham, Mills, Morner, and Sidiropoulos (eds), *Regional Integration in Southern Africa: Comparative International Experiences*, (2000), pp 193–222. See also below Section 4.2.3.

108 Investment Policy Communication, p 9; Woolcock and Kleinheisterkamp, above n 39, p 52.

109 Parliament Investment Resolution, para 37. See also Section 4.2.3.

The objectives of EU foreign investment policy seem to depart from its existing policy orientation. Taking the African, Caribbean, and Pacific (ACP) countries as an example, the lack of specific policy proposals to incorporate development considerations in investment agreements with ACP countries indicates a lack of coherence between EU policies. The EU-ACP development cooperation framework, as formulated after the Cotonou Agreement which set the policy framework for the negotiation of the European Partnership Agreements (EPAs) with ACP countries, presents a prominent example, requiring the incorporation of development considerations into EU foreign investment policy. The Cotonou Agreement sharpened the role of sustainable development as a key, general objective, while poverty eradication, environment, and institutional development have been labelled 'thematic and cross-cutting issues' and are supposed to be taken into account systematically at all levels of EU-ACP development cooperation.[110] The Agreement provided for specific policies and measures to be adopted to achieve this goal, focusing, among others, on investment promotion through the offer of financial and technical aid,[111] and requiring that the negotiation of EPAs focus on development-oriented regulation of foreign investment.[112] However, the materialization of these objectives via future EU IIAs with ACP countries is at odds, if the Commission's perception of EU foreign investment policy is followed.

4.1.3 Integrating the objectives of EU foreign investment law in the broader EU external relations

In order to accommodate the wide range of objectives and principles that either can or must be taken into consideration in the formation of EU foreign investment regulation, it is necessary to ensure their coherent and consistent application. Similar to other fields of EU action where a plurality of objectives is pursued,[113] coherence and consistency are essential for EU action in the field of foreign investment.[114] In addition, reliance on multiple Treaty provisions renders EU foreign investment regulation a unique field of EU action, as it raises broader coherence

[110] K Arts, 'ACP-EU relations in a new era: The Cotonou Agreement' (2003) 40 CMLR 95, 98–9.

[111] Arts 74–8 of the Cotonou Agreement. See also Joint Report ACP–EU Negotiations on EPAs, 6th ACP–EC Ambassadorial level meeting, ACP House, Brussels, 4 July 2003, p 11, Joint Report of the Third dedicated session on the Development Dimension of EPAs, pp 4–5.

[112] Art 21 of the Cotonou Agreement; D te Velde and S Bilal, 'Foreign Direct Investment in the Cotonou Agreement: Building on Private Sector Initiatives' in Babarinde and Faber (eds), *The European Union and Developing Countries The Cotonou Agreement* (2005), pp 211–14.

[113] The internal market presents the best example of a field where a variety of objectives are pursued that are different in nature and purpose.

[114] The notion of coherence and consistency in the founding Treaties have been the subject of considerable debate in the literature due to their ambiguity. Recognizing their distinctive normative content (Case C-266/03 *Commission v Luxembourg*, [2005] ECR I-4805, para 60; Case C-433/03 *Commission v Germany* [2005] ECR I-6985, para 66), the position largely adopted in the literature is followed that consistency requires the avoidance of contradictions, while the notion of coherence is broader, requiring unity and synergy. For a discussion of the relevant positions see C Hillion, 'Tous pour un, un pour tous! Coherence in the External Relations of the European Union' in Cremona (ed), *New Developments in EU External Relations* (2008), pp 12–17.

questions between different policy fields. The adoption of EU action on foreign investment touches different policies not only because a specific measure *can* be adopted in the framework of more than one policy, but also because the adoption of specific measures sometimes *has to* be based on two or more policies. Hence, it is necessary to examine the primary EU law rules that aim to ensure coherence and consistency in EU action in the field of foreign investment, looking also at how EU institutions have attempted to incorporate this in their policy instruments. At this point it should be noted that the Lisbon Treaty introduced significant changes, creating in Articles 3(5) and 21 TEU a common framework for EU external action, thus subjecting all fields of formerly EC and EU external action to the same common values, principles, and objectives. In that regard, the general rules of primary EU law ensuring coherence and consistency in EU external action are examined, followed by an analysis of the changes that the Lisbon Treaty introduced in this field and, finally, by an examination of the actual integration of EU foreign investment policy objectives into the broader framework of EU external relations.

4.1.3.1 Primary EU law rules ensuring coherence and consistency in pursuance of the objectives of EU foreign investment law

The need for coherence and consistency at these various levels was always recognized in the founding Treaties. The role for coherence and consistency is initially and explicitly stressed in Article 7 TFEU, which recognizes that 'The Union shall ensure consistency between its policies and activities, taking all of its objectives into account and in accordance with the principle of conferral of powers'. In addition, Article 21(3)(2) TEU underlines the importance of coherence and consistency in EU external relations assigning this role to the Council, the Commission, and a new institutional position, the High Representative for Foreign Affairs and Security Policy.[115] Article 7 TFEU indicates the multiple dimensions of coherence and consistency, which derive not only from the harmonious integration and interaction of the different policy fields (horizontal coherence), but also from the cooperation of the EU institutions between themselves (institutional coherence) and with the Member States, which are entrusted with the task of ensuring coherence in EU action (vertical coherence).[116]

Within this broader framework, EU law has always provided general principles, which are valuable for ensuring coherence and consistency in the formation of EU foreign investment regulation as well as its integration within EU external relations.

[115] The principles of consistency and coherence are fundamental for the broader framework of EU external relations, in particular for EU action in the field of the Common Foreign and Security Policy. See S Nutall, 'Coherence and Consistency' in Hill and Smith (eds), *International Relations and the European Union* (2005), p 91; C Tietje, 'The Concept of Coherence in the Treaty on European Union and the Common Foreign and Security Policy' (1997) EFA Rev 211; P Gauttier, 'Horizontal Coherence and the External Competences of the European Union' (2004) 10 European Law Journal 23; R Wessel, 'The Inside Looking Out: Consistency and Delimitation in EU External Relations' (2000) 37 CMLR 1135.

[116] M Cremona, 'Coherence through Law: What difference will the Treaty of Lisbon Make' (2008) 3 Hamburg Review of Social Sciences 11, 14–16; Hillion, above n 114, p 17.

First, in terms of horizontal coherence, EU law provides tools for the avoidance of conflict and contradiction between different policies and the balancing of the different objectives that EU foreign investment regulation pursues. They are valuable for the orientation of EU foreign investment law, in particular for balancing mandatory objectives between them as well as with the general objectives of external relations. For example, the principle of proportionality can be of particular assistance to the avoidance of conflict and the achievement of unity.[117] In the field of the internal market, the balance between liberalization, which is the primary objective pursued, and other legitimate objectives is based on a proportionality test, so that trade-restrictive measures suitable for ensuring the achievement of the objective do not go beyond what is necessary to attain the objective.[118] In that regard, proportionality can also be used in external relations, where mandatory objectives conflict.

In addition, EU rules contribute to coherence and consistency in fields where broad discretion is granted to political institutions, not only by preventing conflict, but mainly by providing direction to the political institutions whether to exercise EU competence and how to balance and prioritize the different objectives pursued. For example, ensuring consistency in EU external action, the choice of objectives is inextricably linked with the choice of the appropriate legal basis.[119] The use of the proper legal basis contributes to the avoidance of conflict and contradiction in EU external action by imposing limits on the scope and types of action that can be undertaken under each power-conferring provision, distinguishing between the different fields of action.

Secondly, primary EU law provides for institutional guarantees of consistency and coherence, assigning specific roles and tasks to EU political institutions, demanding cooperation between them as well as with the Member States, which share (some) powers with the EU in the field of foreign investment and, thus, remain an important actor. It is worth highlighting, in brief, that Article 4(3) TEU places great emphasis on consistency in EU external relations, assigning this role primarily to the Council and the Commission, which have traditionally been the guardians of unity and consistency in EU external relations.[120] In addition,

[117] On the role of proportionality as a general principle guiding the exercise of EU competences see T Tridimas, *The General Principles of EU Law* (2006), pp 175–92; B de Witte, 'Institutional Principles: A Special Category of General Principles of EC Law' in Bernitz and Nergelius (eds), *General Principles of European Community Law* (2000), pp 148–50.

[118] On the role of proportionality for determining the legality of EU action see Craig and de Búrca, above n 44, pp 548–9. See in particular *Viking* (Case C-438/05 *International Transport Workers' Federation and Finnish Seamen's Union v Viking Line* [2007] ECR I-10779) and *Laval* (Case C-341/05 *Laval v Svenska Byggnadsarbetareförbundet* [2007] ECR I-11767), where the Court of Justice entered into a balancing exercise between internal market free movement provisions and social policy objectives, underlining the role of proportionality as an important step in determining the legitimacy of a measure pursuing a social policy objective that is restrictive of free movement rights. For a discussion of the role of proportionality in these cases see A Davies, 'One Step Forward Two Steps Back? The Viking and Laval Cases in the ECJ' (2008) 37 Industrial Law Journal 126.

[119] See Section 3.1.2.1.

[120] Case C–65/93 *European Parliament v Council* [1995] ECR I–643, para 23. See also M Cremona, 'Defending the Community Interest: the Duties of Cooperation and Compliance' in Cremona and de Witte (eds), *EU Foreign Relations Law- Constitutional Fundamentals* (2008), pp 157–8.

Article 4(3) TEU requires close cooperation between EU institutions and Member States, imposing a variety of procedural obligations relating to cooperation and consultation between the two.[121] Finally, the enhancement of coherence provisions in the Lisbon Treaty should be borne in mind. In addition, the TEU entrusts the European Council to 'identify the strategic interests and objectives of the Union',[122] thus contributing to coherence and consistency.[123]

As a final point, consideration should be given to the role assigned to the Court of Justice for ensuring coherence and consistency in the formation of EU foreign investment regulation and its integration within EU external relations, balancing between different conflicting objectives and ensuring inter-institutional synergy and cooperation between the EU institutions and Member States. However, in light of the broad discretion granted to the political institutions to determine how and whether a policy objective can be pursued, the Court has been particularly hesitant to interfere with the policy options of EU institutions in external relations.[124]

4.1.3.2 *The general values, principles, and objectives of EU external action after Lisbon*

One of the principal changes brought about by the Lisbon Treaty in the field of EU external relations was the creation of a common framework of principles, objectives, and values for Union external action. Seeking to integrate the different Union external policies and enhance their consistent and effective application, the drafters of the Lisbon Treaty favoured the incorporation of specific principles, values, and objectives of EU external relations in primary law, establishing a common set of rules guiding the Union's external policy making.[125]

Principles and objectives of EU external action appear very early in the Treaties, indicating the significance of creating a common framework for external relations.[126] Article 3 TEU includes among the values and general objectives of the EU a paragraph summarizing the main principles and objectives of EU external relations. Based on Article 3(5) TEU, Article 21 TEU presents the general framework of principles and objectives that determine EU external action. Retaining to a large

[121] Eg Member States have an obligation to consult the institutions when they negotiate bilateral agreements on foreign investment, even if the EU has not yet exercised its powers, since 'there is a start of a concerted [EU] action at international level': Cremona, above n 120, pp 158–67; see also Sections 6.1 and 6.2.

[122] Art 22 TEU.

[123] Cremona, above n 116, pp 30–1, 33–4.

[124] Eg in *Portugal v Council* (above n 35) the Court of Justice found that the essential element clause served the mandatory objective of respect for human rights and democratic principles and did not 'go beyond' that objective. However, the Court did not deal with the question whether the essential elements clause was an adequate, well-suited, or necessary measure for achieving this objective.

[125] M Cremona, 'The Draft Constitutional Treaty: External Relations and External Action' (2003) 47 CMLR 1347, 1347–50.

[126] For the constitutional role of general principles and objectives as values in EU external relations see M Cremona, 'Values in the EU Constitution: The External Dimension', Workshop on Values in the EU Constitution, EUI Florence, 2003.

extent the text of the Constitutional Treaty, Article 21 TEU provides in its first paragraph the principles on which external action is based, in its second paragraph the objectives it pursues, and in the third the rules determining the application of these principles and objectives.[127] The creation of this 'quasi-constitutional' framework of EU external action significantly influences the exercise of Union competence in the field of foreign investment, offering a clear list of legitimate objectives and enhancing coherence and consistency in EU external relations.

Regarding the general objectives stated in Articles 3(5) and 21 TEU, a first reading of these provisions reveals that the list of principles and objectives of EU external action in reality incorporates existing principles and objectives found in specific policy fields, rendering them overarching objectives of constitutional significance.[128]

When considering the importance of the CCP for foreign investment regulation, it is important to highlight, first, the recognition of trade liberalization as a general objective of EU external relations. Articles 3(5) and 21 TEU provide that the Union shall contribute to 'free and fair trade' and pursue the 'integration of all countries into the world economy, including through the progressive abolition of restrictions on international trade'. A careful reading of these provisions indicates that the general trade objectives are not only limited to trade liberalization, which is the only objective provided in Article 206 TFEU, but include other trade-related objectives. As Article 21(2)(e) TEU indicates, trade liberalization is linked with the broader objective of integrating third countries into the world economy. Trade liberalization as such is not an objective of EU external action of constitutional significance, rather, it presents the basic tool for the pursuance of a broader development objective. The link between liberalization and economic as well as social development is further strengthened in Article 3(5) TEU. The reference to free and fair trade indicates that pursuance of free trade, namely full liberalization of trade conditions, is only one side of the trade policy objectives, which is complemented by fair trade. Although fair trade can be perceived as 'equitable trade', namely trade linked with social and labour goals aiming at a fairer distribution of trade profits, it can also be linked with social development objectives both with respect to internal producers/service providers and third countries' nationals, adding another dimension to the objective of liberalization in the founding Treaties.[129]

[127] In contrast with the Constitutional Treaty, which provided for a single chapter on EU external relations, the Lisbon Treaty places the general principles and objectives of EU external action in the TEU just before the provisions on the CFSP, whereas the rest of the Union external policies are found in the TFEU. However, despite the abandonment of the single chapter structure of the Constitutional Treaty, the Lisbon Treaty retained the substantive link between general principles and objectives and all fields of EU external relations. It is worth noting that Art 21(2) TEU emphasizes that the objectives it states apply 'in all fields of international relations' while Art 205 TFEU makes a direct reference to the TEU general provisions on external action, establishing an express link between Art 21 TEU and the external policies found in the TFEU.

[128] Cremona, above n 34, p 5; Cremona, above n 125, p 1349.

[129] As the European Commission has put it 'The objective of fair trade is to ensure that producers receive a price which reflects an adequate return on their input of skill, labour and resources, and a share of the total profit commensurate with their input' (Commission Communication, Fair Trade,

Turning to the specific non-trade principles and objectives provided in Article 21 TEU, their recognition is of great value for EU foreign investment regulation, illustrating the broader objectives that need to be accommodated under Union action in this field. In that respect, the objective of promoting democracy, rule of law, and respect for human rights is of greater importance for foreign investment law, as it legitimizes the current practice of inserting positive and negative conditionality clauses in trade agreements and granting trade preferences to countries adhering to these objectives.[130] Furthermore, the reference to the Union's security and integrity as well as to the preservation of international peace and security is highly relevant for EU foreign investment law.[131] In addition, Article 21 TEU incorporates environmental protection and development cooperation within the fundamental objectives of EU external action, rendering the principles enshrined in Articles 11 and 208(1)(b) TFEU of general, fundamental value. Finally, Article 21 TEU identifies multilateralism and good governance as basic objectives of EU external action, indicating that the Union shall be committed to multilateral investment negotiations, shall participate actively in institutions such as the WTO, and shall promote and contribute to their effective operation.

The recognition of the aforementioned principles and objectives as general objectives suggests that the principles and objectives of EU external action are not only aspirational but oblige the Union to act within the framework they create. Their mandatory nature, which renders them probably justiciable, is softened, however, by their broad formulation. The Union is, for example, required to 'consolidate and promote' democracy, respect for human rights, and good governance, to 'foster' sustainable development' and to 'help develop' environmental protection measures. Hence, the Lisbon Treaty leaves a great degree of discretion to the policy-making institutions to assess when, whether, and how these objectives can be pursued.[132]

At this point, it has to be underlined that the danger of conflicting mandatory objectives has increased since the Lisbon Treaty. Considering the strengthening of the commitment to liberalization in the framework of the CCP and bearing in mind that the CCP does not have a provision similar to Articles 51, 52, 64(2), and 65 TFEU—which allow exceptions to liberalization—the adoption of restrictive measures that pursue general objectives contradicts the objective of liberalization and, thus, appears to be prohibited. However, such an interpretation would negate the explicit recognition of the general objectives in Articles 3 and 21 TEU and Articles 205 and 207 TFEU. In that regard, the pursuance of the specific objectives provided in Articles 3 and 21 TEU should lead to the adoption of restrictive measures, without however legitimizing purely protectionist measures. Bearing in mind

Brussels, 29.11.1999, COM(1999) 619, p 4). On the concept of fair trade in EU external relations see M Cremona, 'Free and Fair Trade' (forthcoming).

[130] On the pursuance of the objectives of human rights and democracy through trade conditionality see Bartels, above n 107.

[131] For an overview of the relation between trade and foreign policy see Eeckhout, above n 12, pp 422–64.

[132] Cremona, above n 34, pp 5–6.

the role of the principle of proportionality in balancing conflicting objectives, it is arguable that, in order for a restrictive investment measure to be legitimate, it is necessary not only to pursue a general objective envisaged in Article 21 TEU, but also it must not go beyond what is necessary to attain that objective.[133]

As a result, the Lisbon Treaty marks a new era for the orientation of EU foreign investment regulation. It strengthens the commitment of the EU towards gradual FDI liberalization, signalling at the same time the transformation of EU action in the field of foreign investment into an integrated part of EU external relations, characterized by common values which guarantee unity and consistency in the exercise of Union powers.

4.1.3.3 Linking foreign investment with broader EU external relations policy objectives

Following the requirement for coherence and consistency in EU external relations, EU institutions have incorporated further objectives in the policy framework on foreign investment and foreign investment objectives in other external relations policies. The EU has placed considerable emphasis on the development aspects of foreign investment regulation. In addition, the EU has focused its attention on the national and international security aspects of its policy orientation in the field of foreign investment. Finally, foreign investment objectives have been specified and adapted in order to contribute to the broader policy objectives that the EU is pursuing with regard to each third country.

4.1.3.3.1 The link between investment and security objectives

As national and international security concerns gain increased significance in EU external relations, it is necessary to look at how they are linked with the objectives of foreign investment regulation. The pursuance of market openness and liberalization can lead to regulatory regimes that can be exploited and misused by private actors, posing dangers to the EU's internal security interests as well as to international security.[134] More specifically, internal and international security objectives become relevant for foreign investment regulation in the framework of EU counter-terrorism policy.[135] Free movement of capital rules can be abused so as to facilitate terrorist financing, thus necessitating the existence of screening mechanisms and regulatory cooperation, which, however, can be considered as restrictions to free movement. Incorporating these security objectives in foreign investment regulation, the EU has made use of the security exceptions provided in Articles 65 and 75 TFEU and has taken action in order to prevent the financing of terrorism and organized crime.[136]

Furthermore, liberalization of capital movements and foreign investment conditions can threaten national security when market openness is exploited by sovereign

[133] Krajewski, above n 36.

[134] Investment Policy Communication, pp 3–4; Parliament Investment Resolution, para 26.

[135] Council of the European Union, The European Union Counter Terrorism Strategy, Brussels 1.12.2005.

[136] Directive 2005/60/EC on the prevention of the use of the financial system for the purpose of money laundering and terrorist financing [2005] OJ L309/15.

states, which, by using investment vehicles, aim to obtain political influence in strategic sectors, such as energy or defence. The emergence in particular of Sovereign Wealth Funds (SWFs) as powerful investors which can acquire the control of companies operating in sectors that are strategic for the EU and/or its Member States, has alerted policy players worldwide, not least the European Commission. In order to face the dangers posed to national security by the operations of SWFs the Commission has issued a communication calling for a common strategy towards SWFs.[137] Without nullifying liberalization of capital movements and market access conditions, the Commission proposes the creation of a common European regulatory framework regarding exceptions to free movement of capital according to Article 65 TFEU. It calls for regulatory cooperation both at the EU and at the international level aiming for the adoption of a code of conduct ensuring transparency and that the basic motives for the investment of these SWFs become clear and that the funds themselves apply good corporate governance.[138]

4.1.3.3.2 The link between investment and political objectives

A comprehensive understanding of the policy framework determining EU action in the field of foreign investment must take into consideration the political objectives pursued with regard to each third country. Differentiation in EU external relations is also reflected in the field of foreign investment, where the broader objectives of market competitiveness, openness, and development are adapted to meet the political goals of the EU. The EU demonstrates flexibility, promoting different levels of market liberalization with regard to each of its trade and investment partners and using different legal mechanisms for achieving its objectives.

First, the objective of foreign investment regulation with regard to candidate and potential candidate countries for accession to the EU is influenced by the EU enlargement policy. Both during the previous enlargement as well as under the current enlargement policy with western Balkan countries, the EU integrates investment objectives in its policy, adapting them to the specific demands of a potential accession to the EU. Aiming at their future integration in the internal market and the approximation of their regulatory framework with the *acquis*, the EU promotes complete liberalization of investments and market openness, similar to the internal market. In parallel, the EU supports the economic and social development of these countries, promoting gradual liberalization that meets the needs of candidate states and devoting substantial resources for financial and technical assistance. Additionally, the EU promotes the establishment of a national regulatory framework on company law, taxation, competition law, and state aids, which are indispensable elements of a regulatory environment favourable to foreign investment.[139] Equally strong investment objectives are pursued in the similar,

[137] Commission Communication, A Common European Approach to Sovereign Wealth Funds, Brussels 27.2.2008, COM(2008) 115,.

[138] For an analysis of the Commission's position on SWFs see P Gugler and J Chaisse, 'Sovereign Wealth Funds in the European Union: General Trust Despite Concerns', NCCR Working Paper 2009/4, January 2009.

[139] On the importance of the objectives of economic development and integration of western Balkan countries in the internal market see Commission Communication, The Western Balkans and European Integration, Brussels 21.5.2003, COM(2003) 285.

albeit different, context of EU relations with European Free Trade Association (EFTA) countries, with which a level of economic integration equivalent to the single market is pursued.

Secondly, investment objectives are adapted to the objectives of regional cooperation in the framework of the European Neighbourhood Policy (ENP).[140] The ENP, as well as its predecessors, the Euro-Mediterranean Partnership (EMP)[141] and the regional policy on relations with the Commonwealth of Independent States (CIS) countries,[142] have influenced the objectives of foreign investment regulation. Placing particular emphasis on sustainable development and the enhancement of economic cooperation and integration, the EU has acknowledged the pivotal role of foreign investment for the achievement of these objectives. Stressing the importance of the creation of an environment favourable to foreign investment and supporting the stimulation of foreign investment initiatives in the region, the EU has emphasized primarily the role of instruments of foreign investment promotion and regulatory reform, envisaging complete liberalization in the future.[143]

Thirdly, it is notable that even with regard to countries with which the EU bases its foreign investment policy orientation on a stronger commercially driven basis, political objectives still play an important role. For example, acknowledging the influence of the United States on the formation of international regulatory models for foreign investment, the Commission places higher emphasis on transatlantic regulatory cooperation, aiming to strengthen its position as an international actor.[144] Another example of political objectives inserted into EU foreign investment policy is the EU's trade and investment relations with China. The Commission, recognizing the opportunities and dangers posed by inward and outward foreign investment to and from China, pursues the establishment of a 'stronger global partnership' based not only on trade and investment, but also on the sustainability, safety, health, and environmental aspects and impacts of its economic relations with China.[145]

[140] Commission Communication, A Strong European Neighbourhood Policy, Brussels 5.12.2007, COM(2007) 774; Commission Communication, Wider Europe Neighborhood: A New Framework for Relations with our Eastern and Southern Neighbours, Brussels 11.3.2003, COM(2003) 104; Commission Communication, European Neighbourhood Policy—Strategy Paper, Brussels 12.5.2004, COM(2004) 373.

[141] The EMP was initiated in 1995 with the adoption of the Barcelona Declaration (Barcelona Declaration and Work Program (1996) 1 EFA Rev 125).

[142] Commission Communication, Eastern Partnership, Brussels 3.12.2008, COM(2008) 823; Commission Communication, Agenda 2000: For a Stronger and Wider Europe, Brussels, 15.07.1997, COM(1997) 2000.

[143] B Gavin, 'Trade and Investment in Wider Europe: EU Neighborhood Policy for Enhanced Regional Integration' (2003) 4 JWIT 893, 898–903.

[144] Trade Strategy, p 11. P Mavroidis, 'Transatlantic Regulatory Cooperation: Exclusive Club or "Open Regionalism"' in Bermann, Herdegan and Lindseth (eds), *Transatlantic Regulatory Cooperation: Legal Problems and Political Prospects* (2001), p 263.

[145] Commission working document accompanying COM(2006) 631 final, Closer Partners, Growing Responsibilities A policy paper on EU-China trade and investment: Competition and Partnership, Brussels 24.10.2006, COM(2006) 632 final. R Leal Arcas, 'EU Relations with China and Russia: How to Approach New Superpowers in Trade Matters' (2009) 4 Journal of International Commercial Law and Technology 1, 42–5.

4.1.3.4 Is EU investment policy coherent?

The development of EU investment policy before the entry into force of the Lisbon Treaty indicates that EU political institutions managed to sufficiently integrate investment objectives with broader EU external relations objectives. The approach to investment liberalization took cognizance of the broader political, security, and development objectives of EU external relations, adjusting the envisaged degree of liberalization according to the specific goals pursued with regard to different groups of countries. Although the linkages between investment liberalization and development policy were not always very extensive, the EU actively promoted development policy objectives through its investment policy.

Conversely, the Investment Policy Communication casts doubts and entails dangers for the coherence of the future EU investment policy, in particular in light of the common values, principles, and objectives of EU external relations adopted after Lisbon. Although it recognizes the importance of consistency and the role of common principles and objectives,[146] the substantive elements of the emergent EU investment policy seem to undermine non-economic objectives, considering them only secondarily and to the extent that they are compatible with the objective of promoting EU competitiveness.[147] Bearing in mind the pre-Lisbon objectives of EU investment policy, the change of orientation is clearly visible with regard to investment liberalization, as development, accession, and neighbourhood objectives do not materialize in specific commitments on how the goals of EU investment policy will be pursued in the future.

On the other hand, the Parliament's stance on the future EU investment policy reflects a more coherent approach. Linking foreign investment with external policies—in particular development policies—as well as internal policies, the Parliament aims to set limits on the rights of foreign investors and create new obligations for them, signalling that the introduction of the EU as a new international actor in the field of foreign investment drastically affects the landscape of international investment law, bringing more balance between the objectives envisaged by international regulation of foreign investment and the objectives pursued in practice.

Nevertheless, the pursuance of such wide development-oriented EU foreign investment policy may not be the most appropriate option under the current economic and political situation. As the Parliament emphasizes, the Commission should 'bear in mind the lessons learnt on a multilateral, plurilateral and bilateral level, in particular regarding the failure of OECD negotiations on a Multilateral Agreement on Investment'.[148] Considering that the MAI failed (also) because of the high expectations that an investment instrument would incorporate and address non-economic objectives, the insistence on including broad and far-reaching development-oriented provisions in future EU IIAs may drastically impede the capacity of the EU to succeed in concluding IIAs. In addition, the

[146] Investment Policy Communication, p 9.
[147] See Section 4.1.2.2.
[148] Parliament Investment Resolution, para 8.

existence of fragile links between investment and other EU external policies does not necessarily lead to the pursuance of conflicting policies. Bearing in mind the broad discretion enjoyed by EU institutions as regards the appropriate means for the pursuance of external relations goals,[149] the promotion of economic objectives giving less value to development considerations may be more realistic in light of the global economic and political situation in the post-financial crisis era.

4.2 The objectives of EU foreign investment law in practice: the objectives of EU IIAs

In order to implement the political and Treaty-mandated objectives of foreign investment regulation, external EU action plays a central role. As argued,[150] the establishment of international rules is necessary in order to achieve regulatory goals in the field of foreign investment. Of course, certain objectives can be better served by internal regulation; for example, the internal market and competition law are essential for achieving and guaranteeing the competitiveness of the internal market, which presents a key factor for attracting foreign investment in the EU. However, the majority of regulatory objectives in the field of foreign investment can be better served via the existence of international treaty rules. These can be much more effective than internal legislation, for example in achieving market openness, and can create common ground rules for internal action, for example for minimizing the negative effects of foreign investment activity through the establishment of common standards. Consequently, EU IIAs are at the heart of EU policy on foreign investment, being the main regulatory instruments charged with the task of achieving the EU foreign investment policy objectives.

Ensuring consistency between policy making and practice, existing EU IIAs reflect partially the investment policy goals set out by the EU. EU IIAs represent a shift in regulatory priorities from most other IIAs and in particular Bilateral Investment Treaties (BITs). Instead of focusing on investment protection, EU IIAs first emphasize market openness and competitiveness, aiming to address the economic interests of EU investors in third countries and of the EU as an investment recipient state. In addition, EU IIAs link foreign investment with development objectives, aiming to promote the interests of developing countries as investment exporting and importing states, attempting to balance any negative effects that market openness may have on their economy. Finally, EU IIAs aim to incorporate in their investment provisions the broader political goals pursued in EU external relations both in general and with regard to each third country, intending to reflect policy coherence at the practical level as well.

At this point it is necessary to distinguish the Energy Charter Treaty (ECT) from all other EU IIAs, as it presents the only EU IIA so far that ascribes to the traditional objectives of international regulation of foreign investment.

[149] See Section 4.1.3.2.
[150] See Section 1.1.1.

Following the patterns of most IIAs, the investment chapter of the ECT aims to ensure the creation of a level playing field for energy sector investments focusing on the protection of foreign energy investments based on the principle of non-discrimination.[151] Considering that investment protection is a new objective of EU foreign investment regulation, it is worth examining the ECT as an example of how EU investment policy objectives can be implemented through the conclusion of more 'traditional' investment agreements and how these objectives will be pursued in future EU IIAs.

Viewing EU IIAs through the prism of their relation to the policy objectives of EU external action in the field of foreign investment requires an analysis of their scope and content from a different perspective than that followed in Chapter 3. First, it is necessary to identify the specific objectives of EU IIAs and analyse whether and to what extent they reflect the political determination of EU foreign investment policy objectives. However, a mere examination of the provisions determining the objectives of EU IIAs is not sufficient to demonstrate how EU IIAs incorporate foreign investment policy objectives. The substantive content of EU IIAs also needs to be scrutinized, exploring the suitability and effectiveness of the specific provisions of EU IIAs in achieving the declared objectives.

4.2.1 The investment-related objectives of EU IIAs

4.2.1.1 The objectives of market openness and competitiveness

The objectives of market openness and competitiveness play a central role in almost all EU IIAs. Starting with the multilateral EU IIAs, liberalization of market access conditions is an aspirational objective explicitly stated in the Preamble of the ECT, while in the General Agreement on Trade in Services (GATS) the role of liberalization as the main means for establishing a multilateral framework of principles and rules for trade in services is clearly defined at the beginning of the Preamble. Furthermore, all bilateral EU IIAs clearly state in their first provisions that one of the main objectives that the association, which they establish, pursues is the promotion of economic relations with the EU, including foreign investment. Of course, bilateral EU IIAs not only create a framework for trade and investment regulation; following the long-standing tradition of EU Association Agreements, the EU has been promoting the model of a broad association addressing political, social, and economic considerations under a single agreement, thus contributing to the coherence and effectiveness of EU bilateral relationships with third countries.[152] Within this broader framework, economic cooperation has become the backbone of the association agreement and trade and investment liberalization has gradually become the dominant characteristic of bilateral EU IIAs.

[151] Energy Charter Secretariat, *The Energy Charter Treaty and Related Documents* (2004), p 14.

[152] S Peers, 'EC Frameworks of International Relations: Co-operation, Partnership and Association' in Dashwood and Hillion (eds), *The General Law of EC External Relations* (2000), pp 175–6.

Reflecting the different scope of economic integration aspired by each agreement, the objective of achieving closer economic relations with the EU is expressed differently in each EU IIA. For example, the Stability and Association Agreements (SAAs) aim to 'promote harmonious economic relations and gradually develop a free trade area' with the EU;[153] the Euro-Mediterranean Agreements (EMAs) aim to 'establish conditions for the progressive liberalisation of trade in goods, services and capital';[154] the Partnership and Co-operation Agreements (PCAs) aim to 'promote trade and investment and harmonious economic relations between the Parties';[155] the agreement with Chile aims at 'the expansion and diversification of the Parties' bilateral trade relation';[156] and the EPA with the CARIFORUM states aims at 'establishing and implementing an effective, predictable and transparent regulatory framework for trade and investment between the Parties' through the 'progressive, reciprocal and asymmetric liberalisation of investment and trade in services'.[157] In clarifying the type of economic cooperation envisaged, these provisions indicate clearly that trade and investment liberalization present the main elements on which economic relations with the EU are based.

The role of liberalization, market access, and competitiveness as a main objective of EU IIAs is not only reflected in their Preamble and general provisions, but also acquires specific expression in their substantive provisions. As already analytically described in Chapter 3, EU IIAs contain legally binding commitments by the parties to liberalize the conditions for admission of foreign investment and to promote competitiveness by ensuring equal treatment. Incorporating the objectives of openness and competitiveness in the field of foreign investment, the substantive provisions of EU IIAs not only satisfy the primary EU law-mandated objectives,[158] but they go far beyond the necessary degree of liberalization, addressing the interests of foreign investors and investment-recipient countries.

With regard to the interests of foreign investors, EU IIAs recognize the ever-increasing importance of market access as a major regulatory determinant of investment decisions.[159] Liberalizing the conditions for entry of foreign investment and regulating important aspects of its operation, such as employment of key personnel, EU IIAs aim to increase the attractiveness of countries as investment locations, thus shaping foreign investors' preferences. In addition, the emphasis placed on liberalization also reflects the interests of the EU in providing access to its Member States' nationals to third country markets and to increase competition in the internal market. The opening of third country markets to EU nationals can enhance the global competitiveness of European companies, enabling them to survive and achieve greater profits in an increasingly open and competitive global economic environment. Furthermore, the adoption of an open market access

153 Eg Art 1(2) of the SAA with Albania.
154 Eg Art 1(2) of the PCA with Armenia.
155 Eg Art 1(2) of the EMA with Egypt.
156 Art 2(4)(d) of the Agreement with Chile.
157 Arts 1(b) and 60(1) of the EPA with the CARIFORUM states.
158 See above Sections 4.1.1, 3.2.1.3, and 3.2.2.7.
159 S Szepesi, *Comparing EU Free Trade Agreements: Investment*, InBrief 6D of European Centre for Development Policy Management (2004).

regime signifies the end of protectionism of national entrepreneurs, which distorts competition, allowing only for exceptions in sensitive sectors, where state intervention is considered necessary for protecting security or other strategic interests.[160]

The substantive provisions of EU IIAs also demonstrate the adaptation of the objective of investment liberalization to the political objectives of the EU with regard to each of its trading and investment partners. The degree of market liberalization varies between the agreements in accordance with the level of economic integration pursued. In that respect, many EU IIAs achieve in practice the declared objectives of economic cooperation and integration. The SAAs are an illustrative example, as they promote complete liberalization of investment conditions aiming at the future adoption of the *acquis* by the EU's partners, thus implementing the goals of the Stabilization and Association process.[161] Nevertheless, other EU IIAs do not transpose sufficiently in legally binding commitments the declared political objectives: the most prominent example is the EMAs, where the absence of substantive liberalization in the field of foreign investment indicates their failure to achieve the level of regional economic integration envisaged in the EMP, and has actually been one of the reasons leading to proposals for their substitution by a new regulatory framework, the so-called Mediterranean Union.[162]

4.2.1.2 The objectives of investment protection

With the exception of the ECT, EU IIAs have not so far actively pursued the objective of investment protection, which was pursued by Member States' national investment policies. Existing EU IIAs preserved the status of Member State BITs, safeguarding the rights of foreign investors under them.[163] Aiming to establish a comprehensive EU investment policy, investment protection is considered as a core objective of future EU IIAs,[164] and to that end in order to provide a stable and safe environment for investment, the EU intends to include in future EU IIAs provisions offering to foreign investors fair and equal treatment (FET), guaranteeing their protection against expropriation and enabling them to resolve their disputes with expediency under investor-state arbitration.[165] Materializing the objective of investment protection, the EU will address the interests of EU investors, offering comprehensive, common standards for the protection of their property abroad. It can also enhance the attractiveness of EU Member States as investment

[160] Woolcock and Kleinheisterkamp, above n 39, pp 16–18. See also Section 4.2.1.3.

[161] R Petrov, 'Exporting the *Acquis Communautaire* into the Legal Systems of Third Countries' (2008) 13 EFA Rev 33, 39–41. See above Section 4.1.3.3.2.

[162] On the political proposals for the creation of a Union for the Mediterranean and the reasons that led to its proposal see F Liberti, 'The European Union and the South Mediterranean Partners: *L'Union pour la Méditerranée*, a French Attempt to Refocus the EU Engagement toward the South' in Delocour and Tulmets (eds), *Pioneer Europe? Testing EU Foreign Policy in the Neighbourhood* (2008), pp 93f; M Reiterer, 'From the (French) Mediterranean Union to the (European) Barcelona Process: The 'Union for the Mediterranean' as part of the European Neighbourhood Policy' (2009) 14 EFA Rev 313.

[163] See Section 5.2.2.

[164] Investment Policy Communication, p 4.

[165] See Section 3.2.7.

recipient countries through the establishment of common EU standards, applicable throughout the EU and subject to the scrutiny and control of EU authorities.

4.2.1.3 Investment objectives and public policy considerations

Existing EU IIAs take note of the negative effects that liberalization may bring about and aim to maximize the benefits from investment inflows and mitigate the negative effects of investment outflows. Ascribing to the goals of social justice and cohesion and the protection of consumers' economic interests, existing EU IIAs incorporate exceptions and limitations to liberalization that serve public policy interests. It is worth pointing out that the public policy goals served by the investment provisions of EU IIAs not only aim to 'shield' the European internal market and EU nationals, but also have a strong development dimension, contributing equally, at least in most EU IIAs, to the protection of public interests in third countries, which can be threatened by the use of the liberalizing provisions by European investors in order to enter and operate in their market.

First of all, EU IIAs include a variety of exceptions that enable host countries to raise their development concerns and pursue public policies in conformity with their foreign investment commitments. As discussed in Chapter 3, certain EU IIAs that follow the GATS example, provide a general exception from the application of their investment provisions, allowing the parties to adopt proportionate and non-discriminatory measures necessary to protect and secure public morals, the public order, human, animal, or plant life or health, exhaustible natural resources, national cultural treasures, and other public policy objectives. Additionally, the remaining EU IIAs introduce limitations to liberalization, which are justified on grounds of public policy, public security, or public health.[166] As a result, these exception mechanisms give host countries the opportunity effectively to pursue public policies without infringing the liberalizing provisions of EU IIAs, granting great leverage to host countries to construe and implement national policies beneficial for their development.

At this point it is important to consider the importance that the public security exception obtains in light of growing security concerns that foreign investment activity by state-controlled entities such as SWFs raise.[167] The broad formulation of the national and international security exceptions in EU IIAs grant an opportunity to the parties to control, in accordance with the criteria set out in these provisions, the admission and operation of foreign investment by state-controlled entities and protect their security interests without violating their market access commitments.

Furthermore, the achievement of public policy objectives is also pursued through minimum standards provisions. In that respect the EPA with the CARIFORUM states and the FTA with Korea are unique, as their innovative provisions on the promotion of international labour and environmental rules and maintenance of standards establish legally binding commitments for the parties to incorporate

[166] See Section 3.2.2.6. [167] See above Section 4.1.3.3.1.

minimum standards and retain their labour, health, environmental, and cultural standards.[168] Introducing limits to foreign investment activity, these innovative provisions aim to guarantee that foreign investment will not impact negatively on the consumer, economic, and social interests of civil society, granting flexibility to the host states to adjust their regulatory regime according to their particular needs.

Despite the importance and innovative content of these provisions of EU IIAs, they do not seem to address fully the public policy concerns of host states. EU IIAs do not include the proper mechanisms for ensuring that civil society can effectively raise public policy concerns, which has to rely on home or host state action. For example, if the provisions of the EPA with the CARIFORUM states on investors' behaviour and maintenance of standards are breached, the persons directly affected are not provided with any means for demanding enforcement of the provisions, as such violations may be economically beneficial for both the host and the home state and its investors. Also, the adoption of such standards may be economically burdensome for developing host countries and instead of contributing to their development may impede economic progress. Moreover, the general exceptions raise similar concerns to those raised in the framework of the WTO concerning the interaction between trade and the pursuance of national public interests.[169] Considering national preferences and public policies as exceptions to liberalization minimizes the discretion enjoyed by national governments to determine and pursue their national public policy interests. EU IIAs adopt the traditional trade approach regarding the relation between foreign investment and public interest, granting, on the one hand, deference to national governments to determine their public policies, but subjecting them to the scrutiny of dispute settlement bodies in accordance with overarching international norms, on the other hand.

However, the question of the proper balance between investment objectives and public policy considerations obtains a new dimension in light of the additional objective of investment protection and the possible reorientation of investment liberalization provisions that will be pursued in future EU IIAs. As regards liberalization and post-admission treatment provisions in future EU IIAs, the adoption of a traditional model of investment regulation can minimize even further the existing potential for public policy exceptions, the determination of which falls largely within the discretion of arbitral tribunals.[170] Nevertheless, the need for limitations to the scope of liberalization and post-admission treatment provisions according to primary EU law indicates that the existing leeway for pursuing public policy objectives will continue.

More importantly, the scope and content of public policy exceptions to future EU IIA provisions on FET and protection against (indirect) expropriation will indicate

[168] J Vandenberghe, 'On Carrots and Sticks: The Social Dimension of EU Trade Policy' (2008) 13 EFA Rev 561, 578–9. See also Section 3.2.2.5.3.

[169] For an overview of the debate on trade and development in the WTO see M Gehring and M-C Cordonier Segger, *Sustainable Development in World Trade Law* (2005) and in particular chs 3, 5, and 6.

[170] See Sections 3.2.2.4.1 and 3.2.2.6.

the degree of adherence of the EU to a balance between investment objectives and public policy considerations. As discussed above,[171] consistency with primary EU law requires either a narrow or a detailed determination of the scope of investment protection provisions, granting the possibility to (supra)national regulators to adopt restrictive measures that are justified under certain public policy objectives. In addition, the reference in EU policy documents to specific public policy goals, such as the protection of the environment, decent work, consumer protection, and cultural diversity,[172] indicates the willingness of the Commission to carve out exceptions from investment protection for the pursuance of public policy objectives. But even if the Commission is successful in promoting public policy exceptions to investment protection provisions in future EU IIAs, it would not address the criticism raised against existing EU IIAs, that they exclude affected stakeholders from dispute settlement and that they limit excessively the discretion enjoyed by (supra)national governments to determine and pursue their public policy interests.

4.2.2 The development objectives of the investment provisions of EU IIAs

Having established that EU IIAs aim to increase foreign investment flows and ensure benefits from foreign investment activity for host countries, albeit not always successfully, it is necessary to examine whether and to what extent they pursue development objectives. In that respect, the effects of the general development objectives of EU IIAs are explored initially, after which the development dimension of the substantive provisions that liberalize and protect foreign investment is considered, followed by an analysis of the development orientation of the rules on investment promotion.

4.2.2.1 Sustainable development as an objective of EU IIAs

Contribution to the sustainable economic, social, and environmental development of EU counterparties is a principal objective of many EU IIAs[173] as well as of the Cotonou Agreement which provides the general framework under which EPAs with ACP countries function. It is worth noting that in the EPA the role of sustainable development as an objective is emphasized as 'to be applied and integrated at every level of their economic partnership'.[174] Hence, sustainable development is a basic principle which runs through the entire content of these agreements, and as all policies and strategies aim to serve sustainable development goals, it has a

[171] See Section 3.2.7.3 and 3.2.7.5.

[172] Investment Policy Communication, p 9; Parliament Investment Resolution, para 25.

[173] All EMAs, as well as the Trade, Development and Cooperation Agreement (TDCA) with South Africa, the Agreements with Chile and Korea, and the EPA with the CARIFORUM states explicitly acknowledge that support of the economic and social development of the parties is a main objective of the agreement.

[174] Art 3 of the EPA with the CARIFORUM states.

considerable impact on the application and interpretation of foreign investment provisions.[175]

Even though EU IIAs do not offer a definition of sustainable development, it is without doubt that the term 'sustainable development' has a specific normative content. Both in international as well as in European law, the concept of sustainable development is linked with a substantive body of legal norms that generate rights and obligations for states (in international and EU law) and for citizens (in EU law). According to the 2002 New Delhi Declaration on the Principles of International Law Related to Sustainable Development[176] and the European Consensus, which imprint the objectives and principles of sustainable development as a legal concept, many common features can be distinguished. In broad terms, sustainable development incorporates the economic, social, and environmental dimensions of development, emphasizing the need for their integration and inter-relationship. Eradication of poverty, accompanied by good governance and protection of human rights are basic objectives, common for all actors, who, however, have different responsibilities. Developing countries are responsible for creating a domestic environment conducive to their development, while the developed world, including the EU, bears the burden of contributing to the reduction of unsustainable patterns of production and to capacity building in developing countries. The EU commitment to development is implemented by delivering effective financial and technical aid to developing countries, which targets liberalization of trade and investment, supporting environmental protection and sustainable management of natural resources, promoting democracy, human rights, and good governance and enhancing social cohesion and employment opportunities.[177]

The recognition of sustainable development as an objective of EU IIAs with a specific normative content has important implications for their investment regime. According to public international law, the objectives of international treaties such as EU IIAs establish a relevant context for the interpretation of the other provisions of the treaty,[178] hence investment provisions as well. As a result, the EU IIAs that make explicit reference to sustainable development require that regulation of foreign investment contributes to the sustainable development of EU counterparties.

Nevertheless, the recognition of sustainable development as a general objective of many EU IIAs does not seem suitable or sufficient to address effectively the development concerns that foreign investment regulation raises and to guarantee the development orientation of foreign investment. Given that the development

[175] J Nwobike, 'The Emerging Trade Regime under the Cotonou Agreement: Its Human Rights Implications' (2006) 40 JWT 291, 300–1.

[176] International Law Association 2002 New Delhi Declaration on the Principles of International Law Related to Sustainable Development.

[177] On the clarity of the normative content of sustainable development in international and EU law see MC Cordonier-Segger and A Khalfan, *Sustainable Development Law: Principles, Practices and Prospects* (2004), ch 3; N Schrijver and F Weiss, *International Law and Sustainable Development* (2004).

[178] Art 31(1) of the Vienna Convention on the Law of Treaties (VCLT) states that '[a] treaty shall be interpreted in good faith in accordance with the ordinary meaning to be given to the terms of the treaty in their context and in the light of its object and purpose'.

effects of foreign investment activity cannot be practically judged *in abstracto* and *a priori*, excluding foreign investors from the beneficial scope of foreign investment provisions, the objective of sustainable development obtains an important role only *ex post facto*, in cases where the actual impact of foreign investment activity on development is questioned under dispute settlement proceedings. But even in such cases, the contested and vague nature and normative content of sustainable development may discourage dispute settlement bodies from using it to restrict the scope of the substantive provisions of EU IIAs.

4.2.2.2 The development orientation of the substantive provisions of EU IIAs

The development needs and concerns of host states are better incorporated in the substantive provisions concerning entry and operation of foreign investment. Starting with the provisions on capital movements, EU IIAs promote the liberalization of capital movements related to foreign investment, thus reflecting the belief that the free movement of capital is a prerequisite for an increase of foreign investment flows and, consequently, economic growth of third countries. However, as mentioned in Chapter 3, EU IIAs allow for exceptions to the liberalization of capital movements.[179] The safeguard, public policy, and security exceptions to capital movements are, of course, necessary in order to achieve compatibility with primary EU law, but they also reflect the belief that specific public interests may result in a legitimate restriction of capital movements. Also, a significant number of EU IIAs enable EU counterparties to maintain restrictions on outward investment, which are considered necessary for boosting the local economy of developing countries by stimulating domestic investments and avoiding the negative development consequences arising from capital exports.[180] Nevertheless, many, and especially, more recent EU IIAs lack such exceptions, questioning their development orientation. In fact, they endorse a liberal approach towards outward investment from developing countries, considering that liberalization can result in benefits for developing countries similar to those enjoyed by developed countries. Given that the number of globally competitive firms from developing countries is constantly increasing, it is argued that it can be in the interest of developing countries to allow them to invest abroad, resulting in positive externalities for the home state.[181]

The development dimension of liberalizing provisions is further illustrated in the provisions dealing with admission and treatment of foreign investment. This is particularly illustrated in the agreements with Mexico, Chile, and the CARIFORUM states, which, by following the example of the GATS, require that the parties make market access and national treatment (NT) commitments, determining for themselves the sectors and the forms of entry and operation of foreign investment that

[179] See Section 3.2.1.2.

[180] Such restrictions are provided in the EMAs with Algeria, Morocco, and Tunisia, the PCAs with Azerbaijan and Russia, and the ECT. See Section 3.2.1.2.

[181] For an analysis of the policy concerns on outward investment from developing countries see T Moran, 'What policies should developing country governments adopt toward outward FDI? Lessons from the experience of developed countries' in Sauvant, Mendoza, and Ince (eds), *The Rise of TNCs from Emerging Markets: Threat or Opportunity?* (2008), ch 13.

are liberalized. They adopt a 'positive list' approach to liberalization and aim at the gradual liberalization of investment rules, thus enabling EU counterparties to set their priorities and promote their development policies.[182] Regarding the remaining EU IIAs that adopt a 'negative list' approach to liberalization, their development orientation is directly linked with the objective of economic integration that they promote, expressing the idea that regional integration can advance their economic development and foster political and social development.

Of course, the EU's position towards admission and treatment of foreign investment is subject to criticism, as it could be argued that it creates an inflexible liberal regime, which does not take into account the changing priorities of developing countries,[183] or that it encourages protectionism in sectors where liberalization can produce positive effects. In order to address these criticisms, EU IIAs offer a 'procedural' solution, as they provide an institutional framework for addressing such policy concerns, which can eventually lead to informed changes in the list of each party's commitments. Every EU IIA includes institutional provisions establishing a number of specific institutions which are assigned the task, among others, of assessing the impact of liberalizing foreign investment commitments.[184] Nevertheless, these mechanisms have not so far been used to address any need for correction of the schedules of commitments of developing countries.

The development orientation of the liberalizing provisions of EU IIAs is also strengthened by the fact that EU IIAs do not include a general prohibition on performance requirements, but include them in their scheme with regard to entry and treatment of foreign investment. Recognizing that host countries may acquire significant benefits from the imposition of trade, competition, and other performance requirements,[185] EU IIAs enable host states to make qualified market access and NT commitments, thus being able to target foreign investment activities that can contribute to their economic development.

Moreover, the promotion of regional economic integration that certain EU IIAs promote, contributes to the development effect of foreign investment liberalization. The role of regional trade liberalization and economic integration is highlighted in particular in the EPA with the CARIFORUM states, which indicates also its importance for future EPAs with other ACP countries. The EPA sets the foundation for the achievement of regional integration among the CARIFORUM states, which is considered 'a mechanism for enabling these States to achieve greater economic opportunities, enhanced political stability and to foster their effective integration into the world economy'.[186] As a result, the creation of larger markets will provide great business opportunities and generate more foreign investment, addressing an

[182] Te Velde and Bilal, above n 112, pp 215–16. [183] Nwobike, above n 175, pp 312–13.

[184] Eg Art 230.3(a) of the EPA with the CARIFORUM states assigns to the CARIFORUM-EC Trade and Development Committee the task of monitoring and assessing the implementation of the agreement on sustainable development, assisting the Joint CARIFORUM-EC Council in taking binding decisions concerning the operation and implementation of the agreement.

[185] On the benefits that performance requirements may have on host state development see UNCTAD, *FDI and Performance Requirements: New Evidence from Selected Countries* (2003).

[186] Art 4 of the EPA with the CARIFORUM states.

important economic determinant of market-seeking foreign investors. Even though regional integration may initially lead to winners and losers within a region due to inter- and intra-regional capital flows, thus depriving certain countries of foreign and domestic capital,[187] it is expected that any losses suffered by certain countries will only be short term, as financial and technical aid can help them transform their economy with competitive economies of scale.[188]

Nevertheless, the potential for a development dimension of the substantive provisions of future EU IIAs is less clear. As was argued, the Commission seems to undermine non-economic objectives, considering them only secondarily and to the extent that they are compatible with the objective of promoting EU competitiveness.[189] Even if the guiding principles suggested by the Parliament were taken into consideration, this would in all likelihood result in an approach similar to existing EU IIAs as regards exceptions to capital movements, market access via a positive list, performance requirements, and regional integration; however, the development aspects of future EU IIAs may be undermined by the extensive negotiating leverage of the EU, which can result in broad concessions by developing countries.[190] In addition, the development dimension of investment protection provisions in future EU IIAs, even for if norms were subject to significant exceptions for certain public policies,[191] would in fact dictate the orientation of national development policies, requiring their conformity to those exceptions provided in EU IIAs.

4.2.2.3 The development dimension of the investment promotion provisions of EU IIAs

Finally, the inclusion of investment promotion provisions in many EU IIAs strengthens their orientation towards sustainable development. As discussed in Chapter 3, most EU IIAs provide for technical and financial assistance to EU counterparties intending to help them to improve their regulatory regimes and enhance their institutional capacity to attract and benefit from foreign investment. Hence, EU IIAs address the potential lack of financial and human resources on the part of developing countries, and establish a firm commitment on the part of the EU for development aid.

[187] G Faber, 'Economic Partnership Agreements and Regional Integration' in Babarinde and Faber (eds), *The European Union and Developing Countries The Cotonou Agreement* (2005), pp 92–4; G Thallinger, 'From Apology to Utopia: EU-ACP Economic Partnership Agreements Oscillating between WTO Conformity and Sustainability' (2007) 12 EFA Rev 499, 503–4.

[188] P Sauvé and N Ward, 'Services and Investment in the EC-CARIFORUM Economic Partnership Agreement Innovation in Rule Design and Implications for Africa' ECIPE (2009), p 57; Faber, above n 187, pp 88–91.

[189] See Section 4.1.2.2.

[190] On the effects of EU negotiating leverage with ACP countries that led to the conclusion of the EPA with the CARIFORUM states see Cardwell and French, above n 97, pp 439–41.

[191] See Section 4.2.1.3.

Taking into account the criticism that development aid has not, as yet, proved helpful and sustainable in the long term,[192] EU IIAs include a number of mechanisms aiming to ensure the effectiveness of investment promotion as part of development cooperation. First, EU IIAs establish an institutional framework which is responsible, among other things, for monitoring development cooperation and making recommendations concerning new cooperation priorities.[193] Secondly, EU IIAs generally grant the flexibility to host states to determine for themselves the specific investment promotion measures they deem suitable and necessary. Without entering into the detailed regulation of the measures that EU counterparties should adopt in order to attract and benefit from foreign investment, such as investment incentives or specific performance requirements targeted at specific foreign investment activities, EU IIAs provide only a general framework for cooperation. Finally, EU IIAs, through their link to EU development cooperation policy, promote outward investment from EU nationals to third countries. For example, the European Development Fund (EDF) includes a specific instrument focused on promotion of foreign investment in the ACP countries, namely the Investment Facility, which provides venture capital, ordinary loans, guarantees, and interest subsidies for investment projects in ACP countries, financing high-quality and productive infrastructure.[194]

4.2.3 The political objectives of the investment provisions of EU IIAs

Except for the GATS and the ECT, most bilateral EU IIAs are not simple trade and investment agreements, as they also promote political and social cooperation, establishing a multilevel association between the EU and third countries. Contributing to the coherence of EU external relations, political principles and objectives that go beyond pure economic considerations are a vital element of bilateral EU IIAs, significantly affecting their economic provisions.

The main political objective introduced in bilateral EU IIAs that can have a significant impact on their investment provisions is the recognition of respect for human rights, democracy, and good governance as basic principles and an essential element of the agreements. Following the adoption of various human rights clauses in EU Association Agreements in the early 1990s,[195] a standardized clause has gradually developed, which the EU has successfully integrated in all its international agreements. All EU IIAs, but for the FTA with Korea, provide, under their principles, that 'respect for democratic principles and fundamental human rights... inspires the domestic and external policies of the [parties] and constitutes

[192] For an analysis of the policy implications arising from the inclusion of promotion provisions in IIAs see UNCTAD, *Investment Promotion Provisions in International Investment Agreements* (2008), pp 7–12 and 65–8.

[193] Eg Art 230(3) of the EPA with the CARIFORUM states.

[194] For an analysis of the Investment Facility see European Investment Bank, *Investment Facility Annual Report* (2009).

[195] For the history, development, and typology of human rights clauses in EU FTAs see E Fierro, *The EU's Approach to Human Rights Conditionality in Practice* (2003), pp 213–43.

an essential element of this Agreement'. The essential elements clause is complemented in most EU IIAs by a non-execution clause, completing its effectiveness by offering the possibility to the parties to take appropriate unilateral measures if the other party fails to fulfill an obligation under the agreement. Considering that violation of the essential elements clauses is a 'material breach' of the agreement or a case of 'special urgency',[196] the non-execution clause allows for immediate action to be taken, bypassing the dispute settlement mechanism established in the agreement.[197]

The recognition of respect for human rights, democracy, and the rule of law as an essential element of bilateral EU IIAs significantly affects the investment regime established therein in multiple ways. Essential elements clauses establish a strict obligation to respect human rights, the rule of law, and democracy,[198] incorporating the EU's human rights policy into its international agreements.[199] As a result, the parties can resort to unilateral measures if they observe a violation of human rights and can suspend the application of EU IIA provisions. The parties can take measures varying from the suspension of technical and financial cooperation provisions, which are vital for economic development, thus coercing their counterpart to respect human rights, to suspension of trade and investment commitments, thus blocking the function of the EU IIA.[200] Hence, human rights violations which are linked directly with foreign investment activity can be addressed by sanctioning the host state for not efficiently protecting human rights in its territory.

Furthermore, the threat of suspension of favourable provisions can also act preventatively; it discourages developing countries from lowering or waiving their human rights obligations in order to encourage foreign investment and it deters investors from 'violating' human rights in the course of their activities in the host country, as the suspension of trade and investment provisions would result in the

[196] Non-execution clauses can be found in all bilateral EU IIAs (but for the FTA with Korea). Nevertheless, a declaration that violation of the essential elements clause is a case of special urgency or a material breach, usually called as a Czech/Slovak declaration, is missing from Euro-Mediterranean Agreements (except for the agreement with Egypt).

[197] For an analysis of the suspension mechanism under human rights clauses see A Rosas, 'Human Rights in the External Trade Policy of the European Union' in *World Trade and the Protection of Human Rights: Human Rights in Face of Global Economic Challenges* (2001), p 193; M Cremona, 'Human Rights and Democracy Clauses in the EC's Trade Agreements' in Emiliou and O'Keefe (eds), *The European Union and World Trade Law* (1996), p 62.

[198] Essential elements clauses introduce an autonomous and binding obligation of the parties to respect and promote human rights. Since non-execution clauses allow for self-help measures only in cases of violations of parties' obligations under the agreements and the violation of the essential elements clause is considered as a material breach (violation) of the agreement giving rise to self-help measures, the conclusion can be drawn that essential elements clauses oblige the parties to respect human rights. Also, the obligation to respect and promote human rights is usually linked to international human rights instruments, such as the Universal Declaration on Human Rights and/or the Helsinki Final Act and the Charter of Paris. For an analysis of the obligations established by essential elements clauses see Bartels, above n 107, pp 93–106.

[199] For a critical analysis of the legal principles defining the EU's human rights policy see P Leino, 'European Universalism? The EU and Human Rights Conditionality' (2005) 24 YEL 329; cf DC Horng, 'The Human Rights Clause in the European Union's External Trade and Development Agreements' (2003) 9 European Law Journal 677.

[200] On the nature of the measures that can be taken and their limitations see Bartels, above n 107, pp 110–20.

loss of preferential treatment on which their establishment was based. In addition, the obligation to respect human rights may play a decisive role in the settlement of investment disputes. A harmonious interpretation of the essential elements clause and the provisions on foreign investment is required, since both include binding obligations on the parties and therefore must be consistently interpreted, without the one frustrating the fulfilment of the other.[201]

However, the use of the essential elements clauses raises similar concerns to those regarding the effectiveness of the development dimension of EU IIAs. Human rights conditionality is a political mechanism used by the EU to 'sanction' third countries for severe violations of human rights and does not present a legal instrument allowing for an automatic response to specific human rights violations resulting from foreign investment activity. In fact, even in flagrant cases of violations of human rights, the suspension mechanism has rarely been used.[202] The unsuitability of the suspension mechanism for addressing development concerns of investment activity is also illustrated by the fact that the investment activity that could raise human rights concerns is based on the provisions of EU IIAs, the inclusion of which the EU has strongly supported and insisted on. Thus, the imposition of sanctions would condemn a developing country for actions by foreign investors, instead of contributing to the amelioration of human rights, democracy, and governance conditions in the host state.

Nevertheless, human rights conditionality will no longer be an element of future EU IIAs. The lack of a conditionality clause in the FTA with Korea indicates the willingness of the EU to draw away from provisions that can complicate negotiations, especially with important negotiating partners. This tendency is confirmed in the EU investment policy documents which make no reference to conditionality clauses, but rather link the promotion of respect for human rights and the rule of law with the adoption in the framework of the OECD of standards of corporate social responsibility.[203]

Although conditionality clauses were not an appropriate means to address the human rights implications of foreign investment activity, they presented at least a legally binding obligation for host states to promote those basic values. If the Commission's proposals materialize, this would in essence reduce the human rights aspects of investment activity to a mere best efforts obligation to contribute to the development of the OECD guidelines. Conversely, the Parliament's proposal to introduce human rights obligations in future EU IIAs, allows the EU investment policy to devise another legally binding mechanism for ensuring that foreign investment activity does not result in violations of human rights. Only in that way would the EU be able to effectively integrate human rights concerns with foreign investment policy and adhere to the fundamental values it proclaims to pursue in its external relations.

[201] Art 31(1) VCLT, above n 178. See also I Sinclair, *The Vienna Convention on the Law of the Treaties* (1984), pp 130f.

[202] For an overview of the practical application of human rights clauses see Bartels, above n 107, pp 35–40.

[203] Investment Policy Communication, p 9. See also Section 4.1.2.2.

4.3 Conclusions

Reviewing the different levels of EU foreign investment regulation, the consistency in terms of the objectives pursued is striking. The objectives of EU action in the field of foreign investment that are provided in primary EU law are preserved, expanded, and further explained in EU policy instruments which are further implemented by EU IIAs.

Indeed, market openness and competitiveness have been and remain the main objectives of the EU in the field of foreign investment. The founding Treaties clearly offer a central role for liberalization, rendering it mandatory in certain circumstances and urging the EU institutions to promote liberalization in EU external relations, while they promote the enhancement of competitiveness by promoting common standards and, to a certain extent, equal treatment. The objectives of liberalization and competitiveness are clearly declared as the main aims of EU action in the field of foreign investment by EU policy makers. Taking into consideration the demand for increasing investment flows, EU policy makers affirm the creation of a favourable regulatory environment as the main objective of foreign investment action, providing for investment liberalization and, since 2010, also for investment protection. Following these objectives, existing EU IIAs provide mainly a framework on entry and operation of foreign investment, while rigorous investment protection provisions will be included in future EU IIAs.

Of course, market access and competitiveness are not the only objectives pursued by the EU in the field of foreign investment. Foreign investment touches on a variety of other EU external relations objectives, among which development cooperation stands out. The objectives of development cooperation proclaimed in general terms in primary EU law are taken into consideration by EU policy instruments and are incorporated in EU IIAs. Considering the broad discretion enjoyed by EU institutions in determining the appropriate means for the pursuance of development objectives, EU policy instruments and EU IIAs recognize development and public policy considerations as their objectives, but grant them only a secondary role. Nevertheless, the EU manages to offer a more nuanced balance between the divergent interests of foreign investors and home and host states in comparison to most BITs. The EU has established a framework that aims to guarantee the development orientation and effectiveness of foreign investment provisions, placing, for example, special weight on investment promotion and the need for host countries to be able to maintain and pursue their national interests consistently with their investment obligations. In that respect, the formation of a new, comprehensive investment policy presents an excellent opportunity for the EU to reaffirm its commitment to public policy and development objectives, introducing innovative provisions in future EU IIAs, incorporating (at least) to a certain extent the suggestions put forward by the Parliament.

In order to avoid any conflicts in which the pursuance of the above-mentioned, seemingly divergent, objectives may result, the EU places particular emphasis on consistency and coherence. Making use of the tools provided in EU law, EU institutions insist on consistency and coherence, aiming to bridge and integrate the various objectives of foreign investment regulation. The effort to ensure coherence and consistency is further reflected in EU IIAs, which attempt to balance, for example, liberalization and public policy objectives. Although in practice the links between investment and other EU external policies are fragile, the EU has so far managed to avoid conflicting policies. Despite the fact that market access and competitiveness may in the end outweigh all other objectives of EU foreign investment policy, this policy orientation is premised on realism, at least not impairing the pursuance of other objectives of EU external relations.

PART III

THE LEGAL EFFECTS OF EU FOREIGN INVESTMENT LAW

Having discussed the scope, content, and orientation of EU IIA provisions dealing with foreign investment and after their critical examination, it is necessary to examine how they are integrated in the international and EU legal order. Similar to other Union agreements, EU IIAs are and will probably be mixed agreements and arise in a field already covered by international commitments entered into by individual Member States. This raises complicated questions concerning the international responsibility of the EU and its Member States, the validity and compatibility of prior IIAs, the implementation and interpretation of EU IIAs, and the creation of individual rights. Without entering into the general debate concerning the legal effects of Union agreements, this Part focuses on the legal ramifications of the investment provisions found in Union agreements in light of existing and future IIAs.

A systematic analysis and evaluation of the legal effects of EU IIAs requires a distinction between international law effects and EU law effects, rendering clearer the demarcation of the bearers, the nature and the content of rights and obligations. In that regard, Chapter 5 analyses the international law effects of EU IIAs, considering in particular the question of international responsibility of the EU and its Member States under current and future EU IIAs and the international law relation and compatibility between EU IIAs and Member State IIAs. Chapter 6 deals to a certain extent with similar questions, viewing them from an EU law perspective. More specifically, the EU law responsibility of the EU institutions and of the Member States for the performance of EU IIAs is examined, followed by the compatibility of Member State BITs and EU IIAs with EU law.

5

International Law Effects of EU IIAs

The effects of EU international investment agreements (IIAs) in the international legal order are considered first, since they address the nature of EU IIAs as instruments of international law and concern not only the EU and its Member States, but also the contracting third countries. The need for legal certainty with regard to the international contractual commitments of the EU and its Member States towards third countries[1] presents the main thrust for delimitating the international law rights and obligations of the EU and its Member States, arising from both EU IIAs and other IIAs entered into by Member States. Existing EU IIAs do not offer clear-cut answers, as they are all mixed agreements and do not always indicate explicitly whether and how they affect previous Member State BITs. In that regard, the international responsibility of the EU and its Member States for the performance of EU IIAs is examined, taking into consideration the scope of EU competence in the field of foreign investment and the nature of existing and future EU IIAs as mixed agreements. The second section of this chapter deals with the hierarchy of norms between overlapping IIAs from an international law perspective, examining, separately, overlaps between EU IIAs and between EU and Member State IIAs, focusing mainly on the methods used for the avoidance of incompatibilities and the potential for conflicting commitments.

5.1 Distinguishing between the international obligations and responsibility of the EU and its Member States

5.1.1 Setting out the *problematique*

The exact delimitation of the EU's and Member States' international responsibility for the performance of their international law obligations arising from EU IIAs presents similar difficulties to mixed agreements. International law rules determining the treaty-making capacity of international organizations and the allocation of obligations found in agreements concluded by both the international organization and its Member States are rather obscure and cannot easily accommodate the concerns arising from the *sui generis* status of the EU as an international organization and the practice of mixed agreements. The ambiguity of international law rules becomes greater where the responsibility for the breach of the obligations found in a mixed agreement is concerned, as it depends not only on the apportionment of the obligations to the international organization and/or its Member States, but also on the attribution of the conduct violating the obligations to the international organization or its Member States.

Starting with the broader question on the apportionment of the international law obligations arising out of EU IIAs, it is a well-established rule of general international law that international organizations are subjects of international law and

[1] J Heliskoski, *Mixed Agreements as a Technique for Organizing the International Relations of the European Community and its Member States* (2001), pp 14–18.

have the legal capacity to enter into international commitments.[2] This is affirmed in the Vienna Convention on the Law of Treaties between States and International Organizations and between International Organizations of 1986[3] (hereinafter, Vienna Convention/VCLT) and in particular in Article 6, which provides that international organizations have the capacity to enter into commitments to the extent that this is allowed according to their internal rules. Within this framework, the international legal personality of the EU and its capacity to act within its sphere of competences is widely recognized.[4] The explicit declaration of EU legal personality in Article 47 TEU, which replaced Article 281 TEC, has been widely accepted in international practice, as proved by the vast number of bilateral and multilateral international agreements that the EU has concluded.

However, problems arise from the limited legal capacity of international organizations; according to Article 6 of the Vienna Convention they can only act within the scope of their competences.[5] This limitation generates concerns not only with regard to the validity of international agreements concluded by international organizations acting *ultra vires*, but, more importantly for the EU, with regard to the delimitation of the obligations undertaken by the international organization in agreements concluded by both the international organization and its Member States. Even though the validity of *ultra vires* acts is dealt with in Articles 27 and 46 of the Vienna Convention, international law does not provide clear rules for delineating the obligations assumed by an international organization and its Member States in cases of mixed agreements.

Addressing the need for demarcation of the field of international obligations of the EU and its Member States in cases of mixed agreements, a number of solutions have either been used in practice or proposed in theory, without however being able to provide clear rules. A first instrument, used in practice, for resolving the problem has been the annexation of declarations of competence in mixed agreements, indicating to third countries the distribution of competence between the EU and its Member States and, consequently the obligations assumed by each party, responding to the need of third countries for legal certainty.[6] However, declarations of competence have not proved very useful, as they are usually only indicative, unable to address the delimitation of competences in fields of shared competence and the

[2] *Reparation for Injuries Suffered in the Service of the United Nations* [1949] ICJ Rep 174.

[3] 1155 UNTS 331. Even though the Vienna Convention has never come into force, it is generally recognized as codifying principles of customary international law. E Steinberger, 'The WTO Treaty as a Mixed Agreement: Problems with the EC's and the EC Member States' Membership of the WTO' (2006) 17 EJIL 843.

[4] On the EU's legal personality and capacity see J Klabbers, *An Introduction to International Institutional Law* (2002), p 42; P Lachmann, 'International Legal Personality of the EC: Capacity and Competence' (1984) 10 LIEI 5.

[5] It is argued that the due to the degree of European integration and the distinctive features of the EU in comparison to other international organizations, the EU should be treated as a subject of international law similar to states. However, the limited legal capacity of the EU, which is one of the main characteristics that distinguish states from international organizations, is affirmed by the principle of conferral, which is manifestly declared in Art 5(2) TEU and widely accepted by the Court.

[6] Opinion 2/2000 (*Cartagena Protocol*) [2001] ECR I-9713. On the relevance of competence considerations for determining international responsibility see below Section 5.1.2.

evolving character of EU competence in a given field.[7] As a result of the unsatisfactory solutions offered by declarations of competence, existing EU IIAs do not include declarations of competence indicating which investment-related obligations are assumed by the EU and which are the responsibility of the Member States.

Apart from declarations of competence, some mixed agreements include less sophisticated arrangements for addressing the need of third parties for legal certainty. The Energy Charter Treaty (ECT) is a prominent example of this category of mixed agreements, as it contains a declaration of the EU and its Member States providing a procedural solution[8] for cases of investor-state dispute settlement where the EU or one of its Member States is involved.[9] Even though such arrangements provide practical solutions to the determination of the EU's and Member States' international responsibility, they do not provide any criteria for a definitive answer to the problem, as they merely internalize the question of demarcation, without allowing third countries to know beforehand the contracting party assuming an obligation.

EU IIAs may not provide any indication as to the apportionment of obligations between the EU and its Member States. The proposition for joint and several responsibility of the EU and its Member States in cases of mixed agreements that do not address apportionment has been proposed in theory[10] and in the case law of the Court of Justice.[11] However, a broad adoption of the principle of joint responsibility undermines both the rationale behind the adoption of mixed agreements, namely the division of powers, and the existence of limitations vis-à-vis the powers of the EU and its Member States to enter into treaties,[12] as well as its explicit acknowledgement by third countries.[13] Therefore, an analysis of the question of apportionment for the specific obligations found in EU IIAs is necessary according to the relevant international law rules, in particular the Vienna Convention and the ILC Draft Articles on the International Responsibility of International Organizations (hereinafter, DARIO).[14]

[7] For a criticism of declarations of competence see Heliskoski, above n 1, pp 161–6; M Cremona, 'External Relations of the EU and the Member States: Competence, Mixed Agreements, International Responsibility and Effects of International Law', EUI Working Paper No 2006/22, p 21; M Björklund, 'Responsibility in the EC for mixed agreements—Should Non-Member Countries care?' (2001) 70 Nordic Journal of International Law 373, 376–82 and references therein.

[8] On the proceduralization of the question of international responsibility for the performance of mixed agreements see Heliskoski, above n 1, pp 161–6.

[9] See below Section 5.1.2.

[10] A Rosas, 'Mixed Union - Mixed Agreements' in Koskenniemi (ed), *International Law Aspects of the European Union* (1998), pp 125–49; C Tomuschat, 'The International Responsibility of the European Union' in Cannizzaro (ed), *The European Union as an Actor in International Relations* (2002), pp 184–5; I Macleod et al, *The External Relations of the European Communities* (1996), pp 158–60.

[11] Case C-316/91 *European Parliament v EDF* [1994] ECR I-625, para 29; see also the Opinion of AG Jacobs in Case C-316/91 *Parlaiment v Council* [1994] ECR I-624, para 69 and the Opinion of AG Tesauro in Case C-53/96 *Hermes International v FHT Marketing* [1998] ECR I-3603, paras 13–14.

[12] Heliskoski, above n 1, pp 141–53.

[13] E Neframi, 'International Responsibility of the European Community and of the Member States under Mixed Agreements' in Cannizzaro (ed), *The European Union as an Actor in International Relations* (2002), p 200.

[14] The ILC Draft Articles on the International Responsibility of International Organizations has not been yet finalized and therefore it does not constitute yet, as such, a binding instrument of

Apportionment of the obligations arising out of EU IIAs is not the only question concerning international responsibility that raises problems. Difficulties also appear with regard to the second condition that needs to be satisfied in order for international responsibility to arise, namely attribution of the conduct breaching an obligation to the EU or its Member States. The DARIO contains a number of provisions determining when and to what extent illegal conduct is attributable to an international organization, and it contains provisions determining when an international organization is responsible despite the lack of attribution, bearing in mind that the Member States of an international organization are responsible for the conduct of the latter.[15] Given that the EU differs substantially from other international organizations in that the implementation of EU obligations rests on both the EU and its Member States,[16] it appears necessary to examine when and to what extent a breach of an EU IIA is attributable to the EU, to a Member State, or to both. The importance of the question of attribution becomes more relevant in determining international responsibility for breach of expropriation provisions, which is currently a question only under the ECT.

The question of international responsibility of the EU and its Member States will acquire further importance in the light of the Lisbon Treaty. EU exclusive competence in the field of the Common Commercial Policy (CCP) renders necessary a re-examination of the apportionment question for existing EU IIAs, while the question of international responsibility under future EU IIAs, which will include provisions on expropriation, raises both doctrinal and practical concerns.

5.1.2 International obligations arising out of EU IIAs

As mentioned above, there are currently no EU IIAs containing a declaration of competence determining which investment-related obligations are undertaken by the EU and which are the responsibility of Member States. A large number of EU IIAs—such as the WTO Agreement, the Stability and Association Agreements (SAAs), the Euro-Mediterranean Agreements (EMAs), and the Trade, Development and Cooperation Agreement (TDCA) with South Africa—do not provide any indication with regard to the extent to which the EU undertakes the international law obligations contained therein, usually making reference to the EU and its Member States as a single contracting party.[17] However, a significant number of EU IIAs includes clauses, both general and investment-specific, that

international law. Given, however, that its provisions are drafted on the basis of the ILC Articles on the International Responsibility of States, its provisions will henceforth be mentioned as reflecting the developments in international law on the responsibility of international organizations.

[15] Arts 5–8, 13–18, and 57–62 DARIO respectively.

[16] Art 216(2) TFEU provides that 'agreements concluded by the Union are binding upon the institutions of the Union and on its Member States'. Thus, Member States are bound under 'internal' EU law to comply with international treaties concluded by the EU. Case C-13/00 *Commission v Ireland* [2002] ECR I-2943, paras 15, 21; Case C-459/03 *Commission v Ireland (Sellafield)* [2006] ECR I-4635, paras 80–5.

[17] Eg all bilateral agreements provide that they are concluded by the EU and its Member States, of the one part, and the third country, of the other part.

link the assumption of obligations with the respective competences of the EU and its Member States.

5.1.2.1 Distinguishing between EU IIAs that include references to the division of competence and those that do not

A common feature of some EU IIAs is the existence of a general clause linking the assumption of obligations with the division of competences between the EU and its Member States. This is achieved by determining the term 'parties', so that '[it] shall mean the [EU] or its Member States or the [EU] and its Member States, within their respective areas of competence as derived from the [founding Treaties]'.[18] The relevance of the division of competences between the EU and its Member States for the determination of the obligations assumed by each actor is also evident in all Partnership and Co-operation Agreements (PCAs). They include a general clause concerning their relation to prior agreements entered into by individual Member States, providing different rules for obligations in areas falling within EU competence and obligations falling within Member State competences.[19]

In addition, all PCAs as well as the IIAs with Mexico and Chile also render the division of competences important for the determination of some investment-related obligations. The provisions on investment promotion and protection found in these agreements include an explicit reference to the boundaries of EU and Member State powers, stipulating that the parties shall act within the scope of their own competence.[20] It is notable that these provisions do not render the division of competences relevant for the allocation of all investment-related obligations found in those EU IIAs. On the contrary, they are limited to the provisions establishing a framework for cooperation in the fields of investment promotion and protection, without touching the core investment-related obligations concerning capital movements, and establishment and operation of foreign investment.[21]

Despite the explicit recognition of the division of competences in both general and investment-specific clauses, these provisions are far from distinguishing the obligations assumed by the EU from those assumed by the Member States. Unlike declarations of competence, they do not identify the specific areas falling within EU or Member State competence, nor do they indicate the nature of the respective competences as exclusive

[18] Arts 197 and 233 of the EU-Chile Agreement and the EPA with the CARIFORUM states respectively.

[19] Eg Art 97 of the PCA with Armenia provides

> This Agreement shall not, until equivalent rights for individuals and economic operators have been achieved hereunder, affect rights assured to them through agreements binding one or more Member States, on the one hand, and Armenia, on the other, except in areas falling within Community competence and without prejudice to the obligations of Member States resulting from this Agreement in areas falling within their competence.

On the importance of this provision for the relation between the PCAs and prior Member State BITs see below Section 5.2.2.2.

[20] Art 21 of the EU-Chile Agreement, Arts 33 and 34 of the EU-Mexico Services Agreement, Arts 47, 48, 49, 46, 47, 53, 58, 54, and 46 of the PCAs with Armenia, Azerbaijan, Georgia, Kazakhstan, Kyrgyzstan, Moldova, Russia, Ukraine, and Uzbekistan respectively.

[21] See also Sections 3.2.1 and 3.2.2.

or shared. Nevertheless, these provisions reflect the need for separate responsibility of the EU and its Member States, in accordance with their respective competences, and make this evident to third parties.[22] The division of competence acquires an international law dimension, as third parties acknowledge that the EU and its Member States assume only the obligations that fall within their respective competence.

Similar to the agreements containing a clause on the division of competences, it is argued that division of competences is also relevant for mixed agreements that do not make any reference to it.[23] As AG Mischo has put it,

> the fact that the EC and its Member States had recourse to the formula of a mixed agreement announces to third parties that the agreement does not fall wholly within the competence of the Community and that the EC is only assuming responsibility for the performance of the obligations which fall within its competence.[24]

This position indicates that division of competences is relevant for the determination of the responsibility of the EU and its Member States, irrespective of whether it has been explicitly declared to third countries, as the EU is an international organization of limited legal capacity and according to international law can only assume obligations that fall within its attributed powers.

Accepting that the division of competences is relevant for the determination of international responsibility does not necessarily mean that joint responsibility is ruled out. Given the lack of a declaration of competence, a separation of the obligations established in EU IIAs in accordance with the division of powers, as the latter is set out in primary EU law, is not a task entrusted to third parties not belonging to the Union legal order. Apart from the fact that such interpretation would severely undermine the autonomy of Union law,[25] it is not founded on international law.

5.1.2.2 Union, Member State, or joint and several responsibility?

The acknowledgement of the limited competences of the EU as an international organization and, thus, its limited responsibility should be read in light of the provisions of the Vienna Convention regarding the internal rules of states and international organizations. Article 27 provides that a state or an international organization 'may not invoke their internal rules as justification for their failure to perform a treaty', while Article 46 provides that a State or an international organization

> may not invoke the fact that its consent to be bound by a treaty has been expressed in violation of a provision of its internal law regarding competence to conclude treaties as invalidating its consent unless that violation was manifest and concerned a rule of its internal law of fundamental importance.

[22] P Kuijper and E Paasivirta, 'Further Exploring International Responsibility: The European Community and the ILC's project on responsibility of international organizations' (2004) 1 International Organizations Law Review 111, 119.

[23] Heliskoski, above n 1, pp 141–53; Björklund, above n 7, p 400.

[24] Opinion of AG Mischo in Case C-13/00 *Commission v Ireland* [2002] ECR I-2943, paras 29, 30.

[25] Heliskoski, above n 1, pp 18–21; I Govaere, 'Beware of the Trojan Horse: Dispute Settlement in (Mixed) Agreements and the Autonomy of the EU Legal Order' in Hillion and Koutrakos (eds), *Mixed Agreements Revisited* (2010), pp 193–4.

These provisions indicate that the division of competence is primarily an internal question that does not affect the validity of the obligations entered into by the EU and its Member States. To the extent that their consent to be bound by a treaty is not partial, which can be the case in agreements including a declaration of competence, legal certainty requires that both the EU and its Member States assume full rights and obligations over the whole breadth of the agreement.[26] The only exception to this rule, which incorporates the principle of the limited responsibility of international organizations, is the existence of a manifest violation of competence rules which is of fundamental importance. As a result, the Vienna Convention, balancing the concerns for legal certainty and limited legal capacity of international organizations, links the existence of limited responsibility with the division of competences only to the extent that there is a clear lack of competence to assume an obligation, and this is objectively evident in accordance with normal state practice and good faith.[27]

Turning to the question of whether apportioning the entirety of the investment-related obligations found in EU IIAs to both the EU and its Member States is a manifest violation of competence rules, it is necessary to look at the division of powers in the area of foreign investment. As discussed in Chapter 2, the delimitation of EU and Member State competence is not straightforward. Until the entry into force of the Lisbon Treaty, the EC enjoyed competence in all areas of foreign investment, but its competence was not *a priori* exclusive. As a result, almost all investment-related provisions found in existing EU IIAs fell at the time of their conclusion—which is the critical time for determining international responsibility—within the scope of the EU's and the Member States' shared competence. The recognition of EU exclusive competence over foreign direct investment (FDI), which arguably encompasses almost all aspects of FDI regulation,[28] requires, however, a new reading of the rules on international responsibility, especially regarding future EU IIAs.

As to the apportionment of investment obligations under future EU IIAs, the recognition of EU exclusive competence over FDI indicates that only the EU will bear responsibility for the violation of provisions on FDI, except for capital transfers and FDI in transport services. Irrespective of whether future EU IIAs are concluded as pure Union agreements or as mixed agreements, it will be evident to third countries that FDI is a field of *a priori* exclusive EU competence and, therefore, the EU is the only responsible actor for the performance and violations of the investment obligations.[29] Similar to the General Agreement on Tariffs and Trade (GATT) 1994, which evidently falls under the scope of EU competence, in cases of actions brought against individual Member States, Member States could successfully invoke Article 46 of the Vienna Convention and escape responsibility for violation of FDI provisions resulting from their own or EU conduct.[30] However, given that there is still shared competence over

[26] A Bleckmann, 'The Mixed Agreements of the EEC in Public International Law' in O'Keefe and Schermers (eds), *Mixed Agreements* (1983), p159; Björklund, above n 7, p 388.

[27] Steinberger, above n 3, pp 844–5; Björklund, above n 7, pp 389–91.

[28] See Section 2.2.3.1.

[29] F Hoffmeister, 'Litigating against the European Union and Its Member States—Who Responds under the ILC's Draft Arts on International Responsibility of International Organizations?' (2010) 21 EJIL 723, 743.

[30] Steinberger, above n 3, p 856.

the other forms of foreign investment, capital transfers and FDI in transport services, this indicates that there may be scope for Member States' international responsibility under future EU IIAs concluded as mixed agreements, requiring further explanation of the question of apportionment in fields of shared competence.

As regards existing EU IIAs, the recognition of EU exclusive competence over FDI does not affect the determination of international responsibility of the EU and its Member States. It is true that the explicit recognition of EU exclusive competence indicates that only the EU will be able to take action and perform the FDI-related obligations of EU IIAs. However, as the recognition of EU exclusive competence arises after the assumption of obligations by the Member States, the consent of the Member States to be bound by all obligations cannot be altered *ex post facto*[31] and, consequently, apportionment of FDI obligations has to be determined on the basis of shared competence.[32]

Thus, in areas of shared competence, which affect all existing EU IIAs and the non-FDI provisions of future EU IIAs, the question of apportionment of international obligations is still pertinent. The question of whether there has been a manifest violation of competence rules depends primarily on the determination of the actor that exercised its (shared) competence at the time of the conclusion of the agreement. Some authors hold that in mixed agreements the EU is engaged only to the extent of its exclusive competence, so that commitments in fields of shared competence are undertaken by the Member States,[33] while other authors are more favourable to the exercise of shared competence by the EU.[34] The Court offers little guidance, as it accepted that the EU may exercise its shared competence,[35] and linked the actual exercise of shared competence with the legal basis used for the adoption of the mixed agreement.[36] For EU IIAs adopted on the basis of Article 217 TFEU,[37] which is a broad competence-conferring provision, it is actually difficult to distinguish in which of these EU IIAs and to what extent the EU has exercised its powers and assumed investment-related obligations. As for the EU IIAs, the adoption of which is based on articles conferring shared competence to the EU and its Member States, it is also difficult to extract definitive answers, since the legal basis is only one indication of the exercise of shared competence, which also

[31] M Villiger, *Commentary on the 1969 Vienna Convention on the Law of Treaties* (2009), p 589.

[32] However, it is possible that the EU will assume international responsibility for any violation of existing EU IIAs in the future. The assumption of EU's international responsibility under the GATT 1947 presents a good example. While the EU was not even a contracting party of the GATT 1947, the *ex post* transfer of exclusive competence in the field of trade in goods from the Member States to the EU led to the de facto recognition of the EU as the single responsible actor. Even though Member States were still theoretically responsible, third countries have never brought any case against individual Member States, nor have Member States initiated a case by themselves. J Heliskoski, 'Joint Competence of the European Community and its Member States and the Dispute Settlement Practice of the World Trade Organization' (1999) 2 CYELS 61.

[33] Heliskoski, above n 1, pp 46–7.

[34] A Rosas, 'International Dispute Settlement: EU Practices and Procedures' (2003) 46 German Yearbook of International Law 284; Opinion of AG Maduro in Case C-459/03 *Commission v Ireland (Sellafield)* [2006] ECR I-4635, para 33. See also Cremona above n 7, pp 17–18.

[35] Case C-239/03 *Commission v France (Etang de Berre)* [2004] ECR I-9325, para 30.

[36] Case C-459/03 *Commission v Ireland (Sellafield)*, above n 16, paras 96–7.

[37] See Section 2.7.1.

rests on other factors. This difficulty in determining whether the EU or its Member States have exercised their shared competence actually indicates that, irrespective of the answer, apportioning investment-related obligations of existing EU IIAs or non-FDI obligations of future EU IIAs to both the EU and the Member States does not constitute a manifest violation of competence rules.[38]

The same conclusion can also be reached with regard to apportionment of obligations falling in areas of implied exclusive competence at the time of the conclusion of an EU IIA. Despite the existence of *AETR* exclusive competence covering a substantial part of the area, it cannot be argued that Member States are not responsible for performing the obligations falling under implied exclusive competence. Although *AETR* exclusivity is a fundamental rule of EU law, which third states should take into account when concluding mixed agreements, the specific application of this principle in the field of foreign investment has been largely unmanageable and unpredictable. In addition, EU competence in a specific field of shared competence can be rendered exclusive during the lifecycle of an international agreement, as a result of the adoption of internal rules after the conclusion of the international agreement. Consequently, the division of competences based on the existence of *AETR* exclusive competence is too complicated and, hence, the violation of this rule would not be manifest, in the sense of being objectively evident to third parties.[39]

The equal apportionment of obligations in areas of shared competence between the EU and its Member States is also recognized, albeit rather secondarily and superficially, in the reports of the International Law Commission (ILC) and its Special Rapporteur on the responsibility of international organizations.[40] Professor Gaja explicitly acknowledges that obligations found in mixed agreements without a declaration of competence are equally binding on both the EU and its Member States.[41] In addition, by making an explicit reference to the *EDF* case,[42] the ILC recognizes the importance of that judgment as setting a general principle of international law and attaches specific weight to legal certainty, which was the main rationale for the adoption of joint and several responsibility by the Court of Justice. Additionally, the report of the Special Rapporteur confirms the rule that the assumption of obligations beyond EU competences are binding.[43]

As a result, it is safe to conclude that the investment-related obligations of existing EU IIAs are apportioned to both the EU and its Member States. On the other hand, the recognition of EU exclusive competence over FDI indicates that under

[38] Björklund, above n 7, pp 393–5 and references therein; P Eeckhout, 'The EU and its Member States in the WTO—Issues of Responsibility' in Bartels and Ortino (eds), *Regional Trade Agreements and the WTO System* (2006), p 464. Neframi, above n 13, p 200.

[39] Steinberger, above n 3, p 848.

[40] Commentary on the ILC Draft Articles, Official Records of the General Assembly, 61st Session, Supplement No 10 (A/64/10) (2009) (hereinafter, ILC Commentary 2009), p 144; Second Report of the Special Rapporteur on the Responsibility of International Organizations, 2 April 2004, UN Doc A/CN.4/541 (hereinafter, 2nd Report).

[41] Ibid, para 8.

[42] Above n 11.

[43] 2nd Report, above n 40, paras 25 and 52.

future EU IIAs joint and several responsibility will apply for non-FDI obligations, capital transfers and FDI in transport services, while FDI-related obligations will be apportioned only to the EU.

5.1.3 Attribution of wrongful conduct breaching obligations under EU IIAs

Having already established who is responsible for performing investment-related obligations found under EU IIAs, it is necessary to examine who is responsible in the event of their violation. According to international law, international responsibility is born where there is a breach of an international obligation attributable to a state or an international organization.[44] The application of these principles in cases of breach of mixed agreements causes difficulties, as both the EU and the Member States can act in order to fulfil their obligations and therefore can be the authors of a wrongful act. However, even though a violation of an investment-related obligation can be the result of either EU or Member State acts, this does not necessarily mean that the wrongful act is attributable only to its author, nor does it exclude the possibility of joint responsibility despite the lack of attribution. Therefore, a systematic analysis of the question of attribution requires a separate examination of the responsibility of the EU and of the Member States both for wrongful acts of which they are authors and for wrongful acts conducted by the other.

5.1.3.1 EU responsibility for the conduct of EU organs

A breach of the investment-related obligations found in EU IIAs can, first, be the result of the conduct of an EU organ. It is not difficult to imagine a case where the enactment of legislation by the EU would be contrary to its commitments undertaken under an EU IIA. For example, the issuance of a Directive or a Regulation prohibiting foreign investors from the CARIFORUM states from obtaining control of activities in the field of manufacturing would violate Article 67 of the Economic Partnership Agreement (EPA) with the CARIFORUM states, which in conjunction with the commitments listed in Annex IV of that Agreement ensures full market access to foreign investors in the respective field.

In such cases, the conduct of the EU organs issuing this illegal legislation is attributable to the EU. According to Article 5 DARIO, which mirrors Article 5 of the ILC Articles on the International Responsibility of States, the international organization is responsible for the conduct of its organs, just as the conduct of state organs is normally attributed to the state to which they belong.[45] Consequently, the EU is responsible for the wrongful acts of its organs, without however excluding potential Member State responsibility for the same conduct.

[44] Art 4 DARIO.

[45] See also the ILC Commentary 2009, above n 40, pp 60–3; Commentary on the ILC Draft Articles, Official Records of the General Assembly, 56th Session, Supplement No 10 (A/59/10) (2004) (hereinafter, ILC Commentary 2004) ch IV, pp 104–9.

It is important to note that a wrongful act of an international organization can exist not only in an act, but also in an omission.[46] Therefore, an omission by EU organs can be wrongful conduct attributed to the EU, in particular where the EU has undertaken an obligation of result, namely an obligation to take positive action.[47] For example, the omission to enact legislation in order to remove barriers to the establishment of foreign investors which are prohibited by an EU IIA would constitute a wrongful act attributed to the EU. Given, however, that the implementation of the EU's international obligations rests on both the EU and its Member States,[48] an omission on the part of the EU does not always lead to its international responsibility. The existence of a wrongful act in such cases depends also on the conduct of Member States, which can take the positive action required for the fulfilment of the EU's international obligations.

5.1.3.2 EU responsibility for the conduct of Member State organs

Wrongful conduct can also be the result of action taken by Member States. More specifically, states can enact their own legislation, which may breach the obligations assumed under EU IIAs. In the field of foreign investment, Member States' legislation is enacted mainly in areas where the EU has not exercised its competence or in order to implement EU legislation. Furthermore, wrongful conduct of Member State organs can also exist in cases where the EU has enacted directly applicable legislation, since they are in most cases the organs entrusted with the actual enforcement of EU law. As a result, there are four different scenarios where the conduct of Member State organs can violate the obligations assumed under EU IIAs, namely where (a) a Member State organ enforces EU legislation that breaches EU IIAs, (b) a Member State organ 'incorrectly' enforces correct EU legislation in a manner that violates the provisions of an EU IIA, (c) EU legislation grants discretion to the Member States concerning its implementation and a Member State organ enacts and enforces implementing legislation that violates the provisions of an EU IIA, and (d) there is no EU legislation and a Member State organ enacts and/or enforces national legislation violating the provisions of an EU IIA.[49]

5.1.3.2.1 Are Member State organs EU organs?

Examining whether the conduct of Member State organs in the above scenarios is attributable to the EU and, more generally, whether the EU bears international responsibility, it is necessary to examine first if Member State organs are acting as EU organs in these circumstances. From a pure EU law point of view, this appears to be correct, at least in scenarios (a) and (b), where Member State organs

[46] ILC Commentary 2009, above n 40, p 78; Third Report of the Special Rapporteur on responsibility of international organizations, UN Doc A/CN.4/553, 13 May 2005 (hereinafter, 3rd Report), para 8. Hoffmeister, above n 29, p 730.

[47] A Conze, *Die Völkerrechtliche Haftung der Europäischen Gemeinschaft* (1987), p 56; Eeckhout, above n 38, p 463.

[48] See above n 16.

[49] See also Steinberger, above n 3, p 850.

act as executive organs.[50] However, from the viewpoint of international law, the characterization of Member State organs as EU organs does not fit comfortably with the definition of organs in accordance with Article 5 DARIO.[51]

A different way of attributing the conduct of Member State organs to the EU is to consider Member State organs as de facto EU organs. Indeed, support for the recognition of Member State organs as EU organs can be found in the case law of the WTO, where Member State organs enforcing EU law were recognized as acting 'de facto as organs of the Community, for which the Community would be responsible under WTO law and international law in general'.[52] The conduct of Member State organs has led to the recognition of EU international responsibility in three more WTO cases, where Member States acted as executive organs enforcing EU legislation and implementing EU legislation in a manner violating WTO law.[53] However, in the latter cases the Panels avoided issuing explicit findings as to whether the conduct of Member State organs was attributed to the EU, or whether EU international responsibility was born as the result of the explicit adoption of the conduct of Member States by the EU.[54]

On the other hand, viewing Member State organs as EU executive organs met with considerable scepticism in other international fora and, in particular, in the European Court of Human Rights (ECtHR).[55] Even in cases where Member State organs applied and implemented EU law, the Court attributed the conduct to the Member State concerned.[56] Considering that the EU was not a party to the European Convention on Human Rights (ECHR), the hostility of the ECtHR to attribute Member State conduct to the EU is understandable, given its willingness

[50] Kuijper and Paasivirta, above n 22, pp 126–7; Eeckhout, above n 38, p 461.

[51] P Klein, *La responsabilité des organisations internationales dans les ordres juridiques internes et en droit des gens* (1998), p 385.

[52] WTO Panel Report, Case WT/DS174/R *European Communities—Protection of Trademarks and Geographical Indications for Agricultural Products and Foodstuffs*. See also WTO Panel Report, Case WT/DS315/R *European Communities—Selected Customs Matters*.

[53] WTO Panel and Appellate Body Reports, Cases WT/DS26/R, WT/DS48/AB/R, WT/DS68/R *European Communities—Measures Concerning Meat and Meat Products (Hormones)*; WTO Panel Reports, Cases WT/DS62/R, WT/DS67/R, WT/DS68/R *European Communities—Customs Classification of certain computer equipment (LAN)*; WTO Panel Report, Cases WT/DS291/R, WT/DS292/R, WT/DS293/R *European Communities—Measures Affecting the Approval and Marketing of Biotech Products* (*EC-Biotech*).

[54] Hoffmeister, above n 29, pp 731–4, 737–8. It is notable that the ILC considers that in the above cases the EU's responsibility was based on the adoption of the Member State conduct by the EU rather than on the recognition of Member State organs as EU organs (ILC Commentary 2004, above n 45, pp 120–1).

[55] See eg Case 175/84, *Krohn v Commission* [1986] ECR 753, 768; *M & Co v Germany*, Decision of 9 February 1990 of the European Commission of Human Rights on Application No 13258/87, *Decisions and Reports*, vol 64, p 138; *Bosphorus Hava Yollari Tuzirm ve Ticaret Anonim Sirketi v Ireland* [GC], Application No 45036/98, § 137, ECHR 2005-VI, paras 137, 151–7; Joined Cases C-402/05 P & C-415/05 *Yassin Abdullah Kadi and Al Barakaat International Foundation v Council of the European Union* [2008] ECR I-6351.

[56] Seventh Report of the Special Rapporteur on the Responsibility of International Organizations, 27 March 2009, UN Doc A/CN.4/610 (hereinafter, 7th Report), para 31.

to affirm its jurisdiction and achieve its mission, namely to provide effective human rights protection.[57]

In light of the above conflicting examples, the consideration of Member State organs as EU organs appears to be contrary to the determination of de facto organs of international organizations under Article 6 DARIO. This provision states that the conduct of a state organ is attributable to an international organization if it is placed 'at the disposal of' the international organization and the latter exercises 'effective control' over that conduct. Taking a closer look at the ILC commentaries, it becomes clear that they do not address under this article the question of attribution to a Regional Economic Integration Organization (REIO), such as the EU, of the acts of the organs of its Member States, in particular of the acts taken in order to implement, apply, and enforce obligations assumed by the REIO.[58] Referring only to military and peacekeeping operations, this provision seems to be designed to apply only in situations regarding the attribution of the conduct of armed forces.[59]

In fact, the ILC Commission rejected the EU proposal of adding a rule on attribution so that, when implementing a binding act of the EU or 'other potentially similar organizations', the conduct of the organ of a Member State would be attributed to that international organization.[60] Article 6 DARIO is inappropriate for transforming Member State organs into EU organs, even in cases where they act as executive organs of the EU, as they remain under the effective control of the state to which they belong.[61] As Professor Gaja puts it 'Member States are generally free to provide for implementation in the way they prefer, through State organs that remain under the State's control'.[62] However, this position does not rule out EU international responsibility for acts of Member State organs, which is based on different grounds.

5.1.3.2.2 EU responsibility as corollary to Member States' responsibility

Although Member State organs cannot be considered de facto EU organs under Article 6 DARIO, there are other provisions that can be used for holding the EU responsible for the conduct of Member State organs. First, Article 8 DARIO provides that

> conduct which is not attributable to an international organization under the preceding draft articles shall nevertheless be considered an act of that international organization under international law if and to the extent that the organization acknowledges and adopts the conduct in question as its own.

[57] Hoffmeister, above n 29, pp 734–5; P Kuijper, 'International Responsibility for EU Mixed Agreements' in Hillion and Koutrakos (eds), *Mixed Agreements Revisited* (2010), pp 211–12.

[58] Hoffmeister, above n 29, pp 726–7; Kuijper and Paasivirta, above n 22, p 127.

[59] ILC Commentary 2009, above n 40, pp 64–71; ILC Commentary 2004, above n 45, pp 109–15.

[60] Seventh Report of the Special Rapporteur on the Responsibility of International Organizations, 27 March 2009, UN Doc A/CN.4/610 (hereinafter, 7th Report), paras 31–3.

[61] 2nd Report, above n 40, p 6 fn 18 and references therein.

[62] 3rd Report, above n 46, para 12.

In that regard, the EU can assume responsibility for the acts of Member State organs under all circumstances. For example, the eagerness of the EU to assume responsibility for the acts of Member State organs in WTO proceedings provided an alternative basis for establishing EU responsibility.[63]

Secondly, the EU bears responsibility for their conduct if it directs and controls a Member State in the commission of an internationally wrongful act. Article 14 DARIO incorporates the principle that an international organization is responsible for acts of state organs when the latter are under the direction and control of the international organization. A first reading of this rule raises similar concerns to Article 6 DARIO, as it requires in essence the existence of factual effective control over the conduct of Member State organs.[64] However, as the ILC Commission points out,

> in the relations between an international organization and its member States the concept of 'direction and control' could conceivably be extended so as to encompass cases in which an international organization takes a decision binding its members. The assumption is that the State or international organization which is the addressee of the decision is not given discretion to carry out conduct that, while complying with the decision, would not constitute an internationally wrongful act.[65]

Hence, it is necessary to examine whether and to what extent the EU 'directs and controls' Member State organs in the scenarios sketched above, in order to determine to what extent it bears responsibility for their conduct. Starting with scenarios (c) and (d), where the EU has not taken any action to comply with its international obligations or has left a wide margin of discretion to the Member States, the requirement of a binding decision that leaves no discretion to the addressee state seems to exclude EU international responsibility for the conduct of Member State organs. Of course, in such cases the EU avails itself of the control mechanism established in Article 216(2) TFEU, which, reinforced by Article 4(3) TFEU, establishes an obligation for Member States to take all measures necessary for the effective implementation of EU international obligations, encompassing all obligations under a mixed agreement.[66] However, this control mechanism comes into play only when a wrongful act has been committed by Member State organs. Granting wide discretion to the Member States to decide in the first place how they can implement the EU's international obligations, it does not satisfy the criteria set out in Article 14 DARIO.

On the contrary, the EU appears to direct and control the conduct of Member State organs enforcing EU legislation. Under scenarios (a) and (b), the EU is actually providing specific orders to Member State organs, which the latter have to follow, without having any discretion.[67] Support for this argument can also be found in the jurisprudence of the Court of Justice concerning non-contractual liability of the

[63] ILC Commentary 2009, above n 40, p 77.

[64] Commentary on the ILC Draft Articles, Official Records of the General Assembly, 57th Session, Supplement No 10 (A/60/10) (2005), pp 97–8.

[65] ILC Commentary 2009, above n 40, pp 87–8.

[66] See Section 6.1.1.1.

[67] Hoffmeister, above n 29, pp 740–1.

EU, where the margin of discretion left to Member State authorities is the decisive criterion for determining whether the EU is liable for their acts.[68]

Thirdly, and more importantly, international responsibility of the EU for acts of its Member State organs can be founded on Article 16 DARIO. This provision stipulates that an international organization incurs responsibility if it adopts a legally binding decision requiring its member states to commit an act that would be internationally wrongful if committed by the former organization or if it authorizes or recommends such an act and the member states actually commit it. This provision, which was adopted in order to avoid an international organization circumventing its international obligations by granting authority to its member states to take action violating its international obligations,[69] can be used for holding the EU responsible for the conduct of its Member State organs under all relevant scenarios. More specifically, under scenario (a), the EU is responsible as it adopts a legally binding decision requiring the Member States to adopt this conduct. Under scenarios (b) and (c) the EU explicitly authorizes Member States to take action in order to implement its international obligations, while the fact that the EU may not have the intention of circumventing its obligations is irrelevant for establishing its responsibility.[70] The same is also true under scenario (d) despite the lack of a specific decision, as Article 216(2) TFEU presents a general obligation and authorization to the Member States to take action in order to implement the EU's international obligations.[71]

As a result, the conduct of Member State organs can lead to EU international responsibility in particular in cases where these organs have limited discretion in implementing and enforcing EU legislation. However, this does not mean that the conduct of Member State organs rules out Member States' international responsibility. Considering that Member State organs should not be automatically perceived as EU organs, their wrongful conduct is attributed primarily to the Member State and the international responsibility of the EU is born as a result of its control exercised over Member State organs.[72]

5.1.3.2.3 Establishing EU responsibility for Member State conduct when acting within the scope of EU law

Articles 8, 14, and 16 DARIO do not present the only means for holding the EU responsible for the conduct of Member State organs. In fact, the DARIO contains other provisions which are better suited to justify the assumption of responsibility

[68] Case C-282/90 *Industrie en Handelsordneming Vreugdenhil BV v Commission* [1992] ECR I-1937, para 15. See also Kuijper and Paasivirta, above n 22, p 136.

[69] ILC Commentary 2009, above n 40, p 90.

[70] Ibid, p 91.

[71] 3rd Report, above n 46, paras 13–15, 36; Steinberger, above n 3, pp 853–4.

[72] Art 18 DARIO explicitly provides that 'this Chapter is without prejudice to the international responsibility of the State or international organization which commits the act in question, or of any other State or international organization'. In addition, even if wrongful conduct by a Member State is adopted by the EU, this does not mean that the EU assumes entirely the responsibility for the unlawful act of the Member State. As the ILC Commentary on the Responsibility of States (Commentaries on the ILC Draft Articles on Responsibility of States for Internationally Wrongful Acts, Official Records of the General Assembly, 56th Session, Supplement No 10 (A/56/10) (2004)) provides, 'such an assumption of responsibility would have to go further and amount to an agreement to indemnify for the wrongful act of another'.

by an international organization for the conduct of its Member State organs. Avoiding the imposition of joint responsibility on the EU and its Member States—which would result from Articles 8, 14, and 16 DARIO—Article 63 DARIO provides the opportunity to attribute Member State conduct to the EU, when the former act within the scope of Union law.

Article 63 DARIO provides that special rules relating to international responsibility may supplement more general rules or even replace them. Bringing an example of a *lex specialis* the ILC Commission makes an explicit reference to EU responsibility for the conduct of Member State organs, when they implement binding acts of EU law.[73] Without clarifying the extent to which this rule applies, whether it covers all types of Member State acts and if it supplements or replaces the general rules on attribution, the ILC Commission appears to recognize an additional legal norm that can be used for establishing EU responsibility for the wrongful conduct of Member State organs.

Indeed, Article 63 DARIO can be used to render the internal rules of an international organization relevant for determining attribution.[74] In that sense, Article 63 DARIO would render the EU solely responsible for the acts of Member State organs under scenarios (a) and (b), when enforcing or implementing Union law, given that under EU law they act as agents of the Union. Moreover, Article 63 DARIO can be used to render the EU internationally responsible for the conduct of Member States under scenarios (c) and (d). EU law ultimately requires that Member States act in accordance with the Union's international obligations (Art 216(2) TFEU), when they exercise their discretion. Thus to the extent that the Union has entered into an international obligation, Article 63 DARIO can justify EU international responsibility for Member State acts.

As a result, the EU can be held responsible for the wrongful conduct of its Member States violating its obligations under EU IIAs. Whether international responsibility should be based on Articles 8, 14, and 16 or 63 DARIO is contentious, revealing the inability of international rules at this stage to accommodate the realities arising from the existence of REIOs. The refusal to construe specific rules determining the attribution of Member State acts to an REIO has led to the devise of mechanisms for international responsibility beyond the principle of attribution, which is the backbone of the system of international responsibility.[75] Nevertheless, irrespective of the dogmatic inconsistencies of the system, international law provides sufficient rules for establishing the EU's international responsibility for wrongful acts of its Member State organs.

5.1.3.3 *Member States' responsibility for the conduct of their organs*

The establishment of EU's responsibility for wrongful acts violating EU IIAs does not rule out international responsibility on the part of the Member States. Starting with Member States' responsibility for the conduct of their own organs, the existence of Member States' responsibility is founded on the premises that an act of a state organ

[73] ILC Commentary 2009, above n 40, pp 178–9.
[74] Hoffmeister, above n 29, pp 729–30; Kuijper, above n 57, pp 222–3.
[75] Eeckhout, above n 38, pp 462–3.

is generally attributed to that state.[76] This is also true when Member States act in the framework of Union law in order to fulfil international obligations assumed by both themselves and the EU. As argued above, it is strongly advocated that the conduct of Member State organs, even when implementing or enforcing EU international obligations is attributable to the Member States, which primarily bear the responsibility for wrongful acts of their organs. This would be particularly so if one accepts that EU responsibility for the conduct of Member State organs is based on Articles 8, 14, and 16 DARIO, as the existence of the EU's international responsibility in these cases does not prejudice the simultaneous responsibility of the Member States.

However, the recognition of Member State organs as EU organs under Article 63 DARIO, especially where they enforce EU law, carves out an exception to the international responsibility of Member States. Nevertheless, it would be more difficult to use Article 63 DARIO to exclude Member States' responsibility in cases where they have significant discretion to act. In addition, as the ILC explicitly recognizes, 'dual or even multiple attribution of conduct cannot be excluded'.[77] Thus, in areas where Member State organs act with discretion, fulfilling not only EU obligations under EU IIAs, but also obligations assumed by the Member States, their conduct should be attributed to both the EU and the Member States, thus giving rise to Member States' international responsibility.[78]

5.1.3.4 Member States' responsibility for the conduct of EU organs

Establishing Member States' responsibility for the conduct of EU organs raises similar problems to those concerning EU responsibility for the conduct of Member State organs. Holding Member States responsible for the conduct of EU organs, either on the basis of direct attribution or because Member States direct and control EU organs, requires that Member States exercise effective control over the conduct of EU organs. However, the criteria of effective control do not seem to be fulfilled under these circumstances. Member States can only exercise minimal *ex post* control over the conduct of EU organs, as they cannot force EU organs to comply with their international obligations, unless the latter have direct effect under Union law.[79] More importantly, Member States cannot be considered to exercise *ex ante* control over the conduct of EU organs, in particular because of their participation in EU decision making.[80] As Professor Gaja puts it,

> the role that a member State may have within the organs of an international organization would not justify attribution of responsibility to the State for the conduct of the organization: this would be tantamount to denying the separate legal personality of the organization.[81]

[76] Art 4 of the ILC Draft Articles on the Responsibility of States.

[77] ILC Commentary 2004, above n 45, p 101.

[78] Steinberger, above n 3, p 857.

[79] In the infamous *Bananas* cases the ECJ held Member States cannot bring an action according to Art 263 TFEU (ex Art 230 TEC) to force the EU to comply with its WTO obligations, because the latter did not have direct effect (Case C-280/93 *Germany v Council* [1994] ECR I-4973). See also Section 6.1.3.1.

[80] ILC Commentary 2009, above n 40, pp 164, 166.

[81] Fourth Report of the Special Rapporteur on responsibility of international organizations, UN Doc A/CN.4/564/Add.1, 12 April 2006 (hereinafter, 4th Report), para 67. See also Kuijper, above n 57, pp 219, 223.

Nevertheless, Article 60 DARIO devises a mechanism similar to Article 16, which establishes the international responsibility of Member States for the conduct of organs of international organizations of which they are members. Aiming to prevent states from circumventing their international obligations by conferring competence to an international organization which then adopts wrongful conduct, the DARIO recognizes that states cannot evade their international law obligations by availing themselves of the separate legal personality of an international organization of which they are a member.[82] More specifically, Article 60 DARIO sets out three conditions that need to be fulfilled so that the international responsibility of Member States is established: first, an international organization must have competence in relation to the subject matter of an international obligation of a state; secondly, the international organization must commit an act that, if committed by the state, would have constituted a breach of the obligation; and thirdly, there must be a significant link between the conduct of the Member State seeking to avoid compliance and that of the international organization in the sense that the act of the international organization has to be prompted by the Member State. An assessment of a specific intent on the part of the Member State of circumventing an international obligation is not required.[83] This view has also been affirmed in practice, in particular in the field of human rights, where the ECtHR has held Member States responsible for EU acts violating the human rights obligations of the Member States.[84]

Although Article 60 DARIO may be particularly important and necessary to prevent the circumvention of Member States' international responsibility under international organizations where the EU is not a party and, thus, has not assumed any relevant obligations, its relevance is less apparent in cases where the EU is also a party, such as under mixed agreements.[85] Additionally, it would be extremely difficult in the case of EU IIAs to satisfy the last criterion under Article 60 DARIO, proving that an EU act has been prompted by a specific or a number of Member States, given the sophistication in decision making and independence of EU institutions.

Consequently, it is arguable that as a matter of principle Member States should not bear international responsibility for violations of obligations under EU IIAs, when they result from acts of EU organs. Article 60 DARIO, which provides the conditions under which states are responsible for the acts of international organizations, is primarily important for cases where the EU acts in areas where only the Member States have entered into international obligations; besides it would

[82] ILC Commentary 2009, above n 40, pp 167–8; Commentary on the ILC Draft Articles, Official Records of the General Assembly, 61th Session, Supplement No 10 (A/61/10) (2006), pp 283–4.

[83] ILC Commentary 2009, above n 40, pp 169–70. The reservations expressed regarding the broad scope of Art 60 led to the introduction of the third condition requiring a link between the conduct of the Member State and the international organization. See 7th Report, above n 60, paras 77–83.

[84] *Matthews v United Kingdom* [*GC*], Application No 24833/94, §§ 26–35, ECHR 1999-I, paras 26–35; *Bosphorus v Ireland*, above n 55; for an overview of the cases and relevant literature see 4th Report, above n 81, paras 68–73.

[85] Kuijper, above n 57, pp 219–21; Kuijper and Paasivirta, above n 22, pp 131–2.

be difficult to establish a 'significant link' between an EU act and the conduct of specific Member States.

5.1.4 Revisiting the rules: international responsibility under EU IIAs

The international responsibility of the EU and its Member States for violations of EU IIAs rests on a combined reading of the rules on apportionment of obligations under EU IIAs and attribution of the conduct of EU and Member State organs. In that regard, the division of competences on foreign investment between the EU and its Member States after the Lisbon Treaty and the DARIO can be coherently read to determine the actor(s) bearing international responsibility for the violation of existing and future EU IIAs.

On the one hand, in areas of EU *a priori* exclusive competence, only the EU should be internationally responsible for any violation resulting from EU or Member State conduct. This rule is particularly important for the FDI provisions of future EU IIAs, the violation of which will result only in EU international responsibility. Of course, the recognition of EU exclusive responsibility in cases of violations of FDI obligations poses questions, in particular as regards international responsibility for expropriations resulting from Member State measures. As the EU can regulate only the conditions under which nationalization or privatization occurs and not the right of Member States to nationalize private property, either directly or indirectly,[86] a Member State will still be able to expropriate foreign investments. Given that investment obligations will be assumed only by the EU because of its exclusive competence, it is questionable whether the EU bears responsibility for acts of expropriation by Member States, which it cannot hinder.

Nevertheless, holding the EU responsible for expropriations resulting from Member State measures is compatible with international responsibility rules. Starting from the determination of the obligation that is violated, it should be highlighted that IIAs do not restrict the right of states to expropriate private property as such, but set conditions concerning the legality of an expropriation and the right of the foreign investor to compensation.[87] Given that the EU has exclusive competence to set such conditions for expropriations resulting not only from its own measures but also from measures adopted by Member States, it is obvious that, while Member States will be able to decide whether an expropriation of foreign investment occurs, they must comply with EU law rules determining the legality and compensation for acts amounting to expropriation of foreign investments. Hence, the conduct of Member States will amount to a violation of an EU IIA only if it applies EU law that violates the standards set in the IIA (scenarios (a) and (c), or, if EU law is compatible with the IIA, to the extent that it violates EU law (scenarios (b) and (c)). Although Member States may enjoy certain discretion in the application of the EU IIAs norms, they fall under strict EU normative control, thus according to Article 63 DARIO Member State conduct should result only in EU responsibility.

[86] See Sections 2.5.2 and 2.5.3. [87] See Section 1.3.4.

On the other hand, in areas of shared competence, even if EU competence is rendered subsequently exclusive by virtue of an *AETR*-effect, the question of international responsibility is highly dependent on attribution. This is important for determining responsibility under existing EU IIAs, as well as for the violation of the non-FDI, capital transfers and FDI in transport services provisions of future EU IIAs. As international obligations under EU IIAs are equally apportioned to the EU and its Member States in areas of shared competence, the attribution of the conduct violating an EU IIA determines international responsibility. As a result, if the violation of an EU IIA provision falling under shared competence results from the conduct of EU organs, only the EU should be held responsible, as Article 60 DARIO is unsuitable for EU IIAs. However, if the violation results from the conduct of Member State organs, then both the EU and the Member States should be responsible: the EU's responsibility resting on Articles 63, 14, and 16 DARIO and the Member States' responsibility on Article 4 of the ILC Draft Articles on the Responsibility of States. Considering how the EU and its Member States are responsible, the Court of Justice favours the existence of joint and severable responsibility, enabling third countries to choose either to seek remedies from the EU and its Member States together, or the party of their choice for the whole of the damages suffered.[88] From the point of view of international law,[89] the fact that both the EU's and Member States' responsibility arise under mixed agreements from one single act violating an obligation that both the EU and the Member States bear equally, indicates that responsibility cannot be apportioned between them and that each of them is fully liable to the injured party.[90]

The recognition of EU responsibility for violation of EU IIA provisions falling under EU exclusive competence and joint and several responsibility for Member State conduct violating EU IIAs provisions under shared competence raises a number of practical and moral hazard concerns.

As regards joint and several responsibility, it raises practical concerns with regard to the remedies offered to third countries. Considering that retaliation and compensation are possible remedies offered under certain EU IIAs in particular circumstances,[91] it appears harsh to be able to impose them on individual Member States for implementing or enforcing a defaulting EU act. Given the magnitude of the internal market, any default on the part of the EU could potentially cause significant damages to a third state and result in compensation or retaliation, which would be insurmountable for a single Member State to offer. Besides, the possibility of joint and several responsibility, in particular in cases of retaliation, enables a third country to target specific Member States and their investors and deprive

[88] Above n 11.

[89] Under public international law there is no recognition of a general rule of joint and several responsibility in all cases where wrongful conduct is attributable to more than one actor; however joint and several responsibility is not excluded, depending on the circumstances. Commentaries on Responsibility of States, above n 58, p 125. J Noyes and B Smith, 'State Responsibility and the Principle of Joint and Several Liability' (1988) 13 Yale Journal of International Law 225.

[90] See Art 47 of the ILC Draft Articles. ILC Commentary 2009, above n 40, p 144; 2nd Report, above n 40, para 8; Steinberger, above n 3, pp 860–1.

[91] See Section 3.2.5.2.

them of significant benefits accrued by them under an EU IIA.[92] For example, a third country could target the Member State, the investors of which are benefitting the most from market access commitments, and suspend all benefits they are enjoying under the EU IIA, whereas if retaliation was taken at the EU level, retaliation would amount to the suspension of limited commitments.

So far, these dangers have not materialized. With regard to trade in the framework of the WTO, the EU has always appeared eager to assume responsibility for its acts and also for the acts of its Member States, and it has managed to avoid rulings against individual Member States.[93] Despite the theoretical recognition of joint and several responsibility, it can be expected that in practice the EU will be eager to assume responsibility for violations of all investment obligations under existing and future EU IIAs.

More important concerns are raised with regard to EU's responsibility for Member State acts. It entails the moral hazard that Member States may act in violation of their obligations under EU IIAs, knowing that compensation or retaliation for their acts can be partly assumed by the EU and (indirectly) by the other Member States. This danger will be more acute under future EU IIAs including expropriation provisions. Considering that only the EU will be responsible for such acts raises the moral danger that Member States would violate expropriation rules, knowing that they will not be held responsible. Of course, moral hazard arguments are minimized, given that the EU can bring infringement proceedings against Member States according to Articles 258 and 260 TFEU and require that they comply with EU and IIA law. However, these provisions are unsuitable to require from Member States the compensation that has to be paid by the EU to a foreign investor. In addition, these provisions do not tackle the practical problems that arise from the lack of responsibility of Member States towards third countries. While the EU may bring infringement proceedings against Member States, it will be 'forced' to support the legality of the wrongful conduct of Member States in dispute settlement proceedings against foreign investors. Apart from the inherent conflict of interests which the EU has to support in different fora, the exclusion of Member States from dispute settlement proceedings against foreign investors weakens any possible justification of their wrongful conduct.

It is notable that similar problems were raised in the *EC-Biotech* case,[94] where the EU was internationally accountable for the conduct of Member States, which it considered conflicted with its international obligations.[95] This case demonstrated the preparedness of the EU to assume responsibility for acts taken by Member States serving national regulatory interests, similar to those that can lead to the adoption of expropriatory measures. Despite the fact that the EU did not bring

[92] For a discussion of the relevant dangers in the WTO framework see M Footer, 'The EU and the WTO Global Trading System' in Laurent and Maresceau (eds), *The State of the European Union: Deepening and Widening* (1998), pp 323–4.

[93] Heliskoski, above n 1, pp 209–38; Rosas, above n 34.

[94] Above n 53.

[95] S Poli, 'The EC's Implementation of the WTO Ruling in the Biotech Dispute' (2007) 32 EL Rev 705.

infringement proceedings against the concerned Member States, this does not mean that the EU will not take action against Member States in the future, particularly in cases where the EU will be held liable to compensate a foreign investor.

The existence of practical and moral hazard concerns should not necessarily lead to a limitation of the EU's international responsibility, being complemented by Member States' responsibility. Except for the fact that recognition of Member States' responsibility would contravene the exclusive nature of EU competence and, thus, international law rules on division of obligations, EU law can create appropriate tools to minimize the negative effects. Indeed, the Commission indicates its aim to be internationally responsible not only for EU acts, but also for Member State acts affecting investments that fall within the scope of future EU IIAs, thus covering violations of FDI and non-FDI related provisions.[96] Recognizing that investor-state arbitration may have significant financial consequences for the EU, the Commission indicates that existing and new instruments can be used, which will assist in better management of international responsibility under EU IIAs.

Guaranteeing the rights of foreign investors and promoting legal certainty, future EU IIAs may opt first for the 'proceduralization' of responsibility questions. A number of mixed agreements include provisions which, while safeguarding legal certainty by allowing third countries to initiate proceedings against the EU, or Member States, or both, create a procedural framework which enables the EU and its Member States to determine themselves the question of who is internationally responsible in a given case.[97] The ECT presents a successful example of such a procedural mechanism. Pursuant to Article 26(3)(b)(ii) ECT, which provides for investor-state arbitration in cases of violation of its investment provisions,[98] the EU and its Member States have deposited a declaration according to which the EU and its Member States, on a request by a private investor, must determine within 30 days who is responsible in a given case and will be a respondent party to arbitration proceedings.[99] The fact that a procedural solution was deemed appropriate in

[96] Commission Communication, Towards a Comprehensive European International Investment Policy, Brussels 7.7.2010, COM(2010) 343, p 10.

[97] Hoffmeister, above n 29, p 744; Heliskoski, above n 1, pp 161–6, 244–8.

[98] See Section 3.2.4.

[99] The text of the declaration provides:

> The European Communities are a regional economic integration organization within the meaning of the Energy Charter Treaty. The Communities exercise the competences conferred on them by the Member States through autonomous decision-making and judicial institutions.
>
> The European Communities and the Member States have both concluded the Energy Charter Treaty and are thus internationally responsible for the fulfillment of the obligations contained therein, in accordance with their respective competences.
>
> The Communities and the Member states will, if necessary, *determine among them who is respondent party to arbitration proceedings* initiated by an Investor of another Contracting Party. In such case, upon the request of the Investor, the Communities and the Member States concerned will make such determination with a period of 30 days. [emphasis added]
>
> This is *without prejudice to the right of the investor to initiate proceedings against both* the Communities and their Member States [emphasis added].

See also M Burgstaller, 'European Law and Investment Treaties' (2009) 26 Journal of International Arbitration 181, 207.

the only EU IIA that included provisions on expropriation and extensive remedies through investor-state arbitration indicates the importance of such clauses for EU IIAs that establish a complete investment framework.

As Member States cannot bear international responsibility for violations of FDI provisions, it is more important to devise new mechanisms which can allow the 'responsible' Member State to participate in arbitral proceedings and/or be bound by the outcome of arbitral proceedings to pay compensation, in particular in cases where the EU assumes international responsibility for the conduct of Member States. In the framework of the ECHR, a co-defendant mechanism is proposed, so that the EU will be able to join as co-defendant in proceedings against Member States and Member States join as co-defendants in proceedings against the EU.[100] The devise of a similar mechanism in future EU IIAs would allow Member States to obtain standing in international arbitration in cases where their conduct has led to a violation of EU IIA provisions, while this could be complemented by internal legislation, determining the conditions under which compensation paid to third country investors should be apportioned between the EU and a specific Member State.

In sum, the conclusion of comprehensive EU IIAs in the post-Lisbon era will significantly affect the determination of international responsibility. Even though Member States may still be theoretically considered as internationally responsible in certain cases, it can be expected that the EU will assume responsibility for all violations of EU IIAs, including those resulting from Member State acts. This is also expected even with regard to violations of expropriation provisions by Member States, as the EU can avail itself of the necessary tools to deal with such problems both internally and under international arbitration, and overcome the practical and moral concerns that may arise.

5.2 Relation between EU IIAs and between EU and Member State IIAs

The large number of EU IIAs and its future expansion raises questions regarding their overlap with other EU IIAs and Member State IIAs.[101] Considering, first, the relation between EU IIAs, it is apparent that bilateral and regional EU IIAs have been concluded with different third countries and, therefore, cannot give rise to conflicting international commitments. Nevertheless, problems may arise from the overlap between bilateral and regional or multilateral EU IIAs, namely the

[100] Council of Europe Group on Human Rights, 'Study of Technical and Legal Issues of a Possible EC/EU Accession to the European Convention on Human Rights', Strasbourg, 28 June 2002 DG-II(2002)006 [CDDH(2002)010 Add.2], paras 57–62; European Parliament Resolution of 19 May 2010 on the Institutional Aspects of the Accession of the European Union to the European Convention for the Protection of Human Rights and Fundamental Freedoms, paras 12–13.

[101] Next to the problem of overlapping commitments in IIAs concluded between the same parties, another important aspect of the relation between EU IIAs and Member State IIAs concerns the effect that they have on each other's MFN clause. On the scope of MFN clauses in EU IIAs and BITs and to what extent they cover preferential treatment granted under other IIAs, see Section 3.2.2.4.2.

WTO Agreement and the ECT, which have been concluded to a large extent by the same countries. Secondly, and more importantly, EU IIAs may overlap with IIAs concluded between individual Member States and third countries. For example, foreign investment relations between the EU and its Member States and Chile are not only addressed in the EU-Chile Association Agreement, but also in the 18 BITs that EU Member States have concluded with Chile.[102]

Despite the large number of overlapping foreign investment agreements, in essence there is only limited substantive overlap. As discussed in Chapter 3, existing EU IIAs usually regulate different aspects of foreign investment regulation from Member State BITs, while the WTO Agreement and the ECT cover only some aspects of foreign investment regulation in specific sectors.[103] On the other hand, as discussed in Chapter 6, future EU IIAs that will include comprehensive provisions on foreign investment will gradually substitute Member State BITs.[104]

Nevertheless, to the extent that substantive overlap exists, international law questions arise concerning the validity of these IIAs and their application in case they include conflicting commitments. Incorporating the principle of *lex posterior*, Article 59 VCLT provides that a later treaty terminates an earlier treaty if it covers the same subject matter and the termination of the earlier treaty was the intention of the parties, or the provisions of the later treaty are incompatible with the provisions of the earlier treaty.[105] In cases where the strict conditions of Article 59 VCLT are not met, Article 30 VCLT provides rules to determine the relation between international treaties in cases of partial overlap. More specifically, paragraph 2 recognizes that the successive treaty can specify the relation to a prior treaty so that 'when a treaty specifies that it is subject to, or that it is not to be considered as incompatible with, an earlier or later treaty, the provisions of that other treaty prevail'. In cases where no reference to the earlier treaty is made, paragraph 3 provides that 'the earlier treaty applies only to the extent that its provisions are compatible with those of the latter treaty'.[106] It is important to highlight at this point that there is party identity between EU IIAs and Member State agreements with EU counterparties, since all EU IIAs are mixed agreements, which are equally binding for individual Member States.[107]

Recognizing the overlap and the occurrence of potential conflicts, many EU IIAs include provisions determining their relation to other agreements. Taking into account the existence of divergent provisions determining the relation between IIAs and the different fields of substantive overlap, a systematic analysis requires the separate examination of the relation between bilateral and multilateral EU IIAs and between EU IIAs and Member State BITs.

[102] Chile has concluded BITs with Austria, Belgium, Czech Republic, Denmark, Finland, France, Germany, Greece, Hungary, Italy, Luxembourg, Netherlands, Poland, Portugal, Romania, Spain, Sweden, and the UK. An indicative list of these BITs is available at <http://www.foreign-investment.cl/index.php?option=com_content&view=article&id=220&Itemid=77> (last accessed 30 April 2011).

[103] See Section 3.2. [104] See Section 6.2.3.1.

[105] For an overview of the scope of Art 59 VCLT see Villiger, above n 31, pp 723–9.

[106] For an overview of the scope of Art 30(2) and (3) VCLT see Villiger, above n31, pp 404–6.

[107] See above Section 5.1.2.2.

5.2.1 Relation between bilateral EU IIAs and the WTO Agreement and the ECT

Nearly all existing bilateral EU IIAs are concluded with countries that are either members of the WTO or signatory parties of the ECT or both, while the number of bilateral EU IIAs with other WTO members will increase in the future. More specifically, almost all EMAs[108] the EPA with the CARIFORUM states, and the agreements with Korea, Chile, Mexico, and South Africa are concluded with countries that are members of the WTO. Furthermore, the European Economic Area (EEA) Agreement, almost all SAAs,[109] and the PCAs with Armenia, Georgia, Kyrgyzstan, Moldova, and Ukraine are concluded with countries party to both the WTO and the ECT, while the rest of the PCAs are concluded with countries party to the ECT. Considering that future EU IIAs will gradually substitute Member State BITs the number of EU IIAs concluded with third countries that are WTO members is bound to increase.

5.2.1.1 The relation between EU IIAs and the GATS

In first examining the relation between bilateral EU IIAs and the WTO Agreement, it is crucial to point out that in the field of foreign investment[110] overlapping commitments exist only with regard to the establishment of foreign investment in service sectors. The existence of substantive overlap raises particular concerns relating to the obligation of WTO members to offer most favoured nation (MFN) treatment to all other WTO members, as well as with dispute settlement.

For the purpose of considering conformity with Articles I and V of the General Agreement on Trade in Services (GATS), bilateral EU IIAs make explicit reference to the GATS, using it as a benchmark for further liberalization. They strive to ensure WTO compatibility, so that their substantive provisions do not conflict with the GATS commitments of the parties and conform to the WTO rules on MFN treatment and GATS Article V on economic integration, which lays down an exception to the MFN rule and grants a conditional right for WTO members to enter into an agreement liberalizing trade in services among themselves.[111]

More specifically, as discussed in Chapter 3, many EU IIAs simply reaffirm the parties' GATS commitments, providing for future liberalization of trade in services in conformity with Article V GATS.[112] These EU IIAs do not incorporate any substantive obligations on establishment of foreign investors in service sectors, thus excluding any potential conflict with WTO rules. Turning to the EU

[108] As at 30 April 2011 Algeria, Syria, and Palestine are not yet members of the WTO.

[109] As at 30 April 2011 Serbia and Bosnia/Herzegovina are not yet members of the WTO, but have started accession negotiations.

[110] For an overview of the overlap and compatibility of EU IIAs in general with the WTO Agreement and in particular with regard to trade in goods, see P Hilpold, 'Regional Integration According to Art XXIV GATT. Between Law and Politics' (2003) 7 Max Planck Yearbook of United Nations Law 219; JH Mathis, *Regional Trade Agreements in the GATT/WTO: Art XXIV and the Internal Trade Requirement* (2002).

[111] See Section 3.2.2.4.2.

[112] Eg Arts 29 and 30 of the TDCA with South Africa.

IIAs that include substantive provisions on trade in services, it is important to distinguish the agreements with countries that were not members of the WTO at the time of their conclusion.[113] Building upon the GATS, these agreements in essence extended the application of the EU's GATS commitments to the non-WTO party, ensuring that parallel commitments do not conflict per se. Furthermore, these EU IIAs took into account the possible future accession of the non-member party to the WTO. In order to ensure that their provisions do not infringe WTO rules, they require that on accession to the WTO, treatment accorded thereunder shall not be more favourable than the MFN treatment provided to other WTO members. Some also include a provision on further future liberalization, which should be in conformity with Article V GATS.[114]

Only a handful of EU IIAs include commitments in the field of trade in services that go beyond the multilateral obligations of the parties. Either by adopting a GATS-style approach to establishment in service sectors, such as the agreements with Mexico and Chile, or by regulating establishment uniformly for service and non-service sectors, such as the EEA Agreement, the SAAs, the Free Trade Agreement (FTA) with Korea, and the EPA with the CARIFORUM states, these EU IIAs have a broad sectoral coverage and far-reaching liberalization commitments. They establish, or aim gradually, to achieve economic integration in the field of trade in services in accordance with Article V GATS, thus being compatible with the GATS obligations of the parties. The conformity of these EU IIAs with the GATS obligations of the parties is highlighted in the agreements, which stress that they are in conformity with Article V GATS.[115] All these EU IIAs have been notified to the WTO according to Article V:7 GATS[116] indicating the conviction of the parties that these agreements are compatible with WTO law.

Whether these EU IIAs are actually compatible with Article V GATS would first require a detailed analysis of the commitments included in each of them. However, even if the level of liberalization achieved in each was defined, it would be very difficult to assess whether and to what extent EU IIAs satisfy the conditions of

[113] The agreements with Jordan, Algeria, Ukraine, Moldova, and Kyrgyzstan were concluded prior to the accession of these countries to the WTO.

[114] Eg Art 44 of the PCA with Ukraine provides that 'Treatment granted by either Party to the other hereunder shall, as from the day one month prior to the date of entry into force of the relevant obligations of the GATS, in respect of sectors or measures covered by the GATS, in no case be more favourable than that accorded by such first Party under the provisions of the GATS and this in respect of each service sector, subsector and mode of supply', while Art 40(1) of the Agreement with Jordan provides that 'The Parties undertake to consider development of this title with a view to the establishment of an 'economic integration agreement' as defined in Art V of the General Agreement on Trade in Services (GATS).'

[115] Eg Arts 6 and 78 of the SAA with Albania provide respectively that 'This Agreement shall be fully compatible with and implemented in a manner consistent with the relevant WTO provisions, in particular Art XXIV of the GATT 1994 and Art V of the GATS' and that 'the provisions of [the Title on Establishment and Services] shall be progressively adjusted, notably in the light of requirements arising from Art V of the General Agreement on Trade in Services (GATS)'. Similar provisions are found in the other SAAs, the agreements with Korea, Mexico, Chile, and the CARIFORUM states.

[116] On the notification of EU IIAs under Art V GATS see <http://www.wto.org/english/tratop_e/region_e/region_e.htm> (last accessed 30 April 2011).

Article V, given the lack of clear guidance in the WTO thus far concerning the scope of this provision. However, the fact that Article V grants a great degree of flexibility to the parties regarding the fulfilment of its substantive requirements indicates that these EU IIAs are in all probability compatible with Article V.[117]

In light of the above considerations, it is expected that future EU IIAs with WTO members will take cognizance of the GATS. To the extent that EU IIAs include provisions on the establishment of foreign investment in service sectors, they have to aim either at the liberalization of substantially all trade in services in order to be within the scope of Article V GATS, or merely confirm the existing level of the parties' GATS commitments.

Secondly, the existence of overlapping commitments between the GATS and bilateral EU IIAs raises problems relating to inter-state dispute settlement. The exclusive jurisdiction of WTO Panels to settle all disputes arising from the GATS[118] is threatened by the possibility of initiating a dispute under an EU IIA on the same subject matter. Furthermore, the existence of two dispute settlement systems can lead to forum-shopping, concurrent proceedings, and potentially conflicting decisions.[119] Recognizing these systemic problems, the agreements with Mexico, Chile, Korea, and the CARIFORUM states—which establish a quasi-adjudicative dispute settlement system[120]—attempt to provide solutions.

All three agreements safeguard the exclusive jurisdiction of the WTO system, providing that their dispute settlement system does not apply, when the subject matter of the dispute relates to a WTO obligation.[121] Nevertheless, the dispute settlement system of these EU IIAs can be used for the adjudication of cases relating to obligations equivalent to those existing under the WTO, as this may be necessary for the effective understanding and adjudication of the WTO-plus obligations that exist in bilateral EU IIAs.[122] This possibility does not violate the exclusive jurisdiction of the WTO, as the adjudication of the same matter in both fora is not excluded.

However, the multiplication of dispute settlement mechanisms cannot avoid the potential of forum-shopping and concurrent proceedings. In order to avoid these dangers EU IIAs have followed the example of other Preferential Trade and Investment Agreements and include either a forum exclusivity or a choice of forum

[117] For an analysis of the level of commitments in EU IIAs see M Roy, J Marchetti, and H Lim, Services liberalization in the new generation of Preferential Trade Agreements (PTAs): How much further than the GATS?, WTO Working Paper ERSD-2006–07.

[118] The Dispute Settlement Understanding (DSU) does not provide explicit rules on the obligatory jurisdiction of the WTO system, but the latter is implied in Art 1 DSU, which specifies the coverage of the DSU, Art 3.1 which affirms the adherence of WTO members to the principles of dispute settlement and Art 23 where WTO members accept to settle any disputes according to the rules contained in the DSU.

[119] K Kwak and G Marceau, 'Overlaps and Conflicts of Jurisdiction between the World Trade Organization and Regional Trade Agreements' in Bartels and Ortino (eds), *Regional Trade Agreements and the WTO System* (2006), pp 465–7.

[120] See Section 3.2.5.2.

[121] Art 43.3 of the EU-Mexico Services Agreement, Art 189.4 of the EU-Chile Agreement, Art 222.1 of the EU-CARIFORUM EPA, and Art 14.19(1) of the FTA with Korea.

[122] I Bercero, Dispute Settlement in European Union Free Trade Agreements: Lesson Learned?' in Bartels and Ortino (eds), *Regional Trade Agreements and the WTO System* (2006), p 403.

clause. More specifically, the agreement with Chile provides that the selection of a forum results in the exclusion of the other. This provision guarantees the avoidance of multiple proceedings without violating the exclusive jurisdiction of the WTO, as the EU-Chile agreement explicitly provides that cases relating to the violation of an obligation that is 'equivalent in substance to an obligation under the WTO shall be settled in the WTO, unless the parties otherwise agree'.[123] Nevertheless, this provision may result in the fragmentation of a case in multiple fora, depriving the parties of the opportunity to raise all aspects of a case in a single forum.[124]

A different solution to the problem of multiple proceedings is adopted in the agreements with Mexico, Korea, and the CARIFORUM states, which include a choice of forum clause, so that initiation of proceedings in one forum hinders the parties from raising the same dispute in the other forum until the first proceedings are complete.[125] However, this provision raises greater concerns, as it does not bind the later forum with *res judicata*, potentially leading to conflicting decisions. Furthermore, it is doubtful whether it can actually prevent states from initiating parallel proceedings, as a WTO Panel is not bound to apply this norm in case the proceedings in the WTO are initiated afterwards.[126]

In order to avoid the problems arising from the proliferation of dispute settlement systems, similar clauses could be incorporated in future EU IIAs with regard to inter-state dispute settlement. However, such provisions would be without prejudice to investor-state arbitration, which, dealing with a dispute between a private party and a WTO member, cannot stop or be estopped by the initiation of proceedings under the WTO.

5.2.1.2 The relation between bilateral EU IIAs and the ECT

As mentioned in Chapter 3, the ECT devotes a chapter to foreign investment in the energy sector. In that regard, its provisions overlap partially with bilateral EU IIAs concluded with the members of the Energy Charter. With regard to existing EU IIAs, the overlap concerns in particular capital movements, establishment, and post-establishment treatment of foreign investment, while the scope of overlap will be more substantive with future EU IIAs which will include comprehensive provisions on foreign investment.

Nevertheless, most existing EU IIAs with countries that are members of the Energy Charter make explicit reference to the ECT, determining their relation and the effects that they have on it. All PCAs exclude from their scope of application foreign investment matters regulated in the ECT. They provide that

123 Ibid, pp 403–4. 124 Ibid, p 401.

125 Arts 43.4 of the EU-Mexico Services Agreement, Art 222.2 of the EPA with the CARIFORUM states, and Art 14.19(1) of the FTA with Korea.

126 Kwak and Marceau, above n 119, pp 468–9; Taylor, 'Choice-of-Forum Provisions in Regional Trade Agreements and Their Implications for International Dispute Resolution and International Law' (2008) 3 Global Trade and Customs Journal 27, 33. For a critic of the international economic legal system and suggested solutions see EU Petersmann, 'Justice as Conflict Resolution: Proliferation, Fragmentation and Decentralization of Dispute Settlement in International Trade' (2006) 37 U Pa J Int'l L 280; Taylor, above n 126.

insofar as matters covered by this Agreement are covered by the Energy Charter Treaty and Protocols thereto, such Treaty and Protocols shall upon entry into force apply to such matters but only to the extent that such application is provided for therein.[127]

As a result, these bilateral EU IIAs provide that the ECT is the only applicable IIA with regard to foreign investment in the energy sector. The exclusion of investment in the energy sector from the scope of application of PCAs has been confirmed in practice, as arguments concerning the applicability of PCAs have not been raised publicly in any investment disputes between EU investors and Commonwealth of Independent States (CIS) countries.[128]

In contrast with PCAs, neither the EEA Agreement nor the SAAs make explicit reference to the ECT. SAAs include only a general provision concerning their relation to all other international agreements, providing that they do not affect rights ensured to individuals under existing agreements until they achieve equivalent rights,[129] while the EEA Agreement provides that it prevails over existing bilateral or multilateral agreements between the parties, to the extent that the same subject matter is governed by it.[130]

A similar conflict of laws provision is found in the ECT. Article 16 of the ECT provides that in a particular case the choice between its investment provisions and the investment provisions of a prior or subsequent international agreement depends on the determination of which are more favourable for the investor or the investment. This provision can obtain a particularly important role as regards future EU IIAs, which will be subsequent agreements covering essentially the same subject matter as the ECT.

The application of these provisions with regard to the relation between these IIAs and the ECT raises significant questions, requiring the determination of whether and to what extent they cover the same subject matter and whether they establish equivalent rights for individual investors and/or more favourable treatment for them. Considering that the same questions are also relevant for the determination of the relation between these EU IIAs and the BITs concluded between EU Member States and these countries, the relation between these EU IIAs, on the one hand, and the ECT, on the other, will be addressed below, together with the relation between these EU IIAs and Member State BITs.

5.2.2 The relation between EU IIAs and Member State BITs

In contrast with the GATS and the ECT, most existing EU IIAs do not make explicit references to Member State BITs. Stemming from the conviction of the parties that EU IIAs have a different subject matter than the BITs between Member

[127] Arts 93, 96, 96, 91, 90, 97, 105, 100, and 93 of the PCAs with Armenia, Azerbaijan, Georgia, Kazakhstan, Kyrgyzstan, Moldova, Russia, Ukraine, and Uzbekistan respectively.

[128] For a list of arbitrations under the ECT see <http://www.encharter.org/index.php?id=213> (last accessed 30 April 2011).

[129] Arts 128, 122, 131, 131, and 120 of the SAAs with Albania, Croatia, Montenegro, Serbia, and the Former Yugoslav Republic of Macedonia respectively.

[130] Art 120 EEA Agreement.

States and EU counterparties,[131] existing EU IIAs do not usually directly address the relation between them and BITs. Nevertheless, EU IIAs regulate aspects of foreign investment law that are also regulated under BITs. Even though the vast majority of European BITs do not include establishment provisions, which are the main subject matter of EU IIAs, both sets of agreements cover the areas of capital movements and post-entry treatment of foreign investment.

The overlap between EU IIAs and BITs raises the danger that the application of the provisions of EU IIAs can lead to an infringement of the BITs provisions and vice versa. Using as an example the EU-Chile agreement and the UK-Chile BIT, the potential conflicts between them in the fields of capital movements and post-establishment treatment illustrate the dangers posed. For example, the use of safeguard measures restricting capital movements according to Article 166 of the EU-Chile agreement could lead to a violation of Article 6 of the UK-Chile BIT,[132] which does not allow for any limitations to the free transfer of capital. Furthermore, the limitations on national treatment (NT) provided in Annex X of the EU-Chile agreement relating to the operation of established foreign investments appear to conflict with Article 3 of the UK-Chile BIT which offers unfettered NT to foreign investors in the post-establishment phase.

Despite the lack of explicit references to BITs in most EU IIAs, the latter recognize that they impact on previous agreements between Member States and EU counterparties. A significant number of EU IIAs include provisions determining the extent to which they affect Member States' prior international agreements, either specifically in the field of foreign investment, or in general with regard to all fields covered.

In contrast to existing EU IIAs, the relationship between future EU IIAs and Member State BITs is expected to be more clearly defined. As discussed in Chapter 6, to the extent that future EU IIAs provide a comprehensive framework of foreign investment regulation, they are expected to substitute Member State BITs with EU counterparties. Nevertheless, if certain future EU IIAs retain the structure and focus of existing EU IIAs, their relation to Member State BITs will be determined along similar lines to those pertaining to existing EU IIAs.

5.2.2.1 EU IIAs making explicit reference to Member State BITs

The need to clarify the relation between EU IIAs and Member State BITs, which is more compelling for agreements having extensive foreign investment provisions, has led to the inclusion of relevant provisions in the Agreements with Mexico, Chile, Korea, and the CARIFORUM states. These agreements aim to keep Member State BITs intact from any impact they may have on the latter, reaffirming the position of Member State BITs as the primary international instruments on foreign investment.

131 S Szepesi, *Comparing EU Free Trade Agreements: Investment*, InBrief 6D of European Centre for Development Policy Management (2004), p 5.

132 Above n 102.

More specifically, the EU-Mexico Services Agreement and EU-Chile Agreement subrogate their application to Member State BITs. Confirming and recalling their commitment and obligations arising from existing international agreements, the agreements with Mexico and Chile indicate that international obligations arising under existing agreements between the parties remain valid.[133] Thus, in cases of conflict between these EU IIAs and the BITs with Mexico or Chile, the provisions of the BITs would apply unaltered, and EU IIAs do not affect their application. What is problematic, though, is the reference to existing agreements, as this does not cover future BITs concluded between the parties. Given the lack of explicit or implicit hierarchy in these cases, it is arguable that, similar to the EU IIAs that do not make any reference to Member State international agreements, the general rules of *lex posterior* and *lex specialis* apply.[134] As a result, in cases of conflicting commitments, the later BIT provisions would apply, as they would be more recent and would deal specifically with foreign investment.

The EPA with the CARIFORUM states and the FTA with Korea take a more nuanced approach insofar as the relation to BITs between EU Member States and Korea and the CARIFORUM states is concerned. They provide that nothing in the chapter relating to investment shall be taken to limit the rights of investors of the parties to benefit from any more favourable treatment provided for in any existing or future international agreement relating to investment to which an EU Member State and a signatory CARIFORUM state or Korea are parties.[135] In comparison to the EU-Chile and EU-Mexico Services Agreements, these provisions have a broader coverage, as they also include future agreements. Although they do not explicitly establish primacy for BITs, the agreements with Korea and the CARIFORUM states do not apply if they provide less favourable treatment to foreign investors than other IIAs.

In considering the rights of foreign investors under BITs, the right to initiate investor-state arbitration and demand from the host country that it fulfil its BITs obligations, is the most important investor right which is not guaranteed under these EU IIAs. In that regard, the EPA with the CARIFORUM states and the FTA with Korea respect the procedural rights of foreign investors under BITs and recognize that their provisions do not impose any limitations. With regard to the substantive rights that foreign investors have under BITs, it is again obvious that these EU IIAs do not affect investors' rights under BITs concerning not only expropriation and compensation, but also post-entry treatment of foreign investment. As long as BITs provide for more favourable treatment, any limitations found in the agreements with Korea and the CARIFORUM states do not result in a deterioration of the investors' position. This provision gains particular weight with regard

[133] Art 134 of the EU-Chile Agreement provides that, 'With respect to [the Chapter on capital movements and establishment], the Parties confirm their rights and obligations existing under any bilateral or multilateral agreements to which they are parties'. Art 34 of the EU-Mexico Services Agreement provides that, 'The Community and its Member States, within the scope of their respective competences, and Mexico recall their international commitments with regard to investment, and especially the OECD Codes of Liberalisation and OECD National Treatment Instrument.'

[134] See below Section 5.2.2.3.

[135] Art 71 of the EPA with the CARIFORUM states and Art 7.15 of the FTA with Korea.

to the provisions on investors' behaviour and maintenance of standards. Foreign investors' rights and in particular their right to fair and equal treatment (FET) would not be limited, if a measure was adopted in accordance with the host state's obligations under those EU IIAs' provisions. Even though the enforcement of national laws and the implementation of international environmental, labour, and anti-corruption standards would rarely lead to a violation of the FET standard, it is possible that such measures violate investors' legitimate expectations and, thus, the FET standard, since the adoption of legitimate policy measures is weighed against the legitimate expectations of the investor.[136]

Nevertheless, Article 71 of the EPA with the CARIFORUM states and Article 7.15 of the FTA with Korea apply only with regard to the investment/establishment chapters of these EU IIAs. Hence, they do not cover the provisions on capital movements. In addition, they refer only to the rights of foreign investors under other IIAs and not to the rights of states arising from BITs. Consequently, it is arguable that with regard to these matters the relation between the EPA and the FTA with Korea and Member State BITs is governed by the rules of international law that apply when there is no explicit provision determining the relation between EU IIAs and Member State BITs.

5.2.2.2 *EU IIAs making reference to Member State IIAs in general*

Even though most EU IIAs do not make explicit reference to Member State IIAs, they recognize that they do not arise in a legal vacuum and that they may affect prior agreements on the same subject matter between the parties. In that regard, many EU IIAs aim to safeguard the rights of individuals and private persons deriving from prior international agreements. More specifically, SAAs, PCAs, and the TDCA with South Africa include similar provisions stipulating that they

> shall not, until equivalent rights for individuals and economic operators have been achieved under this agreement, affect rights ensured to them through existing Agreements binding one or more Member States, on the one hand and the [EU counterparty], on the other.[137]

This provision is of paramount importance for recognizing the procedural and substantive rights granted to foreign investors under BITs. Considering that rights of individuals under BITs can be affected only if these agreements establish equivalent rights, the lack of investor-state arbitration as well as of provisions on investment protection in these EU IIAs signify that the latter do not affect investors' rights under BITs. Even in areas of overlap—such as capital movements—EU IIAs do

[136] *Waste Management Inc v United Mexican States* (*Waste Management* case), ICSID Case No ARB(AF)/00/3, Award, 30 April 2004, para 98. On the violation of the FET standard via the adoption of legitimate policy measures see I Tudor-Knoll, 'The Fair and Equitable Treatment Standard and Human Rights Norms' in Dupuy, Francioni, and Petersmann (eds), *Human Rights in International Investment Law and Arbitration* (2009), ch 14.

[137] Arts 128, 122, 131, 131, and 120 of the SAAs with Albania, Croatia, Montenegro, Serbia, and the Former Yugoslav Republic of Macedonia respectively; Art 105 of the TDCA with South Africa; Arts 97, 100, 100, 95, 94, 101, 109, 104, and 97 of the PCAs with Armenia, Azerbaijan, Georgia, Kazakhstan, Kyrgyzstan Moldova, Russia, Ukraine, and Uzbekistan respectively.

not directly grant rights to individuals similar to those established in BITs, so that foreign investors' rights under BITs remain unaffected.

Even though EU IIAs do not directly establish rights for individuals, it could be argued that their provisions grant rights to individuals as long as they have direct effect. Apart from the fact that the direct effect of these provisions in the legal order of both parties is not always clear,[138] it is highly controversial whether such rights are equivalent to BITs' rights, where the option of investor-state arbitration is offered. More importantly, such an interpretation of the requirement to achieve equivalent rights would conflict with the wording of this provision, which clearly provides that equivalent rights for individuals shall be achieved 'thereunder', meaning directly in the provisions of the agreement. This position was also adopted in the *Eastern Sugar* award, where it was ruled that the Europe Agreement with the Czech Republic, which included a similar provision, did not affect investors' rights under the Netherlands-Czech Republic BIT.[139]

Although these EU IIAs safeguard the rights of individuals under BITs, this does not mean that the rights of the states parties to the EU IIAs and BITs remain unaffected. The silence of most EU IIAs on this subject indicates that the rights and obligations of states are determined in accordance with the general rules of public international law that apply when there is no explicit reference to other agreements. This position is further enhanced by the wording of the provision on individual rights in the PCAs. These agreements provide that individual rights remain unaffected 'except in areas falling within Community competence and without prejudice to the obligations of Member States resulting from this Agreement in areas falling within their competence'. This provision makes clear that although individuals' rights remain unaffected, this does not prejudice the obligations of the EU and its Member States in the fields of their respective competences.

5.2.2.3 EU IIAs that do not make reference to Member State BITs

EU IIAs do not provide a complete set of rules determining the relation between them and Member State BITs, leaving unanswered important aspects of this relationship. The relevant provisions in the EU-Mexico and EU-Chile agreements do not cover future agreements, in the EPA with the CARIFORUM states and the FTA with Korea individual rights relating to capital movements, and in the rest of the agreements the rights of states. In addition to these 'gaps', another category of EU IIAs, the Euro-Mediterranean Agreements, do not make any reference at all to Member State agreements. In order to address these deficiencies, it is necessary to resort to the general rules of public international law determining when and to what extent treaties between the same parties have an effect on each other. Considering that EU IIAs overlap only partially with other IIAs, it is clear from the outset that a later EU IIA or BIT cannot result in the termination of the earlier one, in accordance with Article 59 VCLT. However, the application of the later

[138] On the direct effect of EU IIA provisions in the Union legal order see Section 6.1.3.3.

[139] *Eastern Sugar BV v Czech Republic*, ICC Partial Award and Partial Dissenting Opinion, 27 March 2007, paras 145, 154, 157. For a discussion of the case see Burgstaller, above n 99, pp 186–93.

agreement may affect the applicability of the earlier agreement in accordance with Article 30 VCLT.

Under the provisions of Article 30(1) VCLT, it is necessary to determine to what extent EU IIAs and BITs cover the same subject matter and whether their provisions are incompatible. Examining the areas where overlapping and potentially conflicting commitments exist, the provisions on capital movements and transfer of assets are considered. Establishing an obligation to secure free movement/transfer of capital related to foreign investment, subject in some cases to exceptions, it is undisputable that EU IIAs and Member State BITs cover the 'same subject matter', as 'the fulfilment of the obligation under one treaty affects the fulfilment of the obligation of another'.[140] This requirement is satisfied even if a narrow definition of 'same subject matter' is adopted, instead of the above-mentioned broad definition, since both sets of treaties deal with the same subject, namely foreign investment, and provide rules for the same aspect of foreign investment regulation, namely capital movements/transfers.[141] It is noteworthy that despite the fact that BITs grant rights to individuals while EU IIAs grant only rights to states, both sets of treaties deal with the same subject. The determination of the same subject matter depends on the existence of conflicting obligations and not on whether the beneficiary is a state or an individual.[142]

Turning to the question of whether the provisions in EU IIAs are conflicting, a detailed examination of all provisions is required in order to assess whether there is a conflict between them. Avoiding the danger of generalizing, it appears that conflicts, in the sense of incompatibilities that arise when states in complying with one set of norms necessarily violate another, exist only insofar as a BIT does not allow for the exceptions provided in the EU IIA with the specific third country.[143] As a result, applying the *lex posterior* rule incorporated in Article 30 VCLT, it is arguable that the later treaty will apply. For example, a restriction on capital movements imposed by Barbados in accordance with the EPA with the CARIFORUM states conflicts with Article 5 of the Barbados-Germany BIT, which does not provide for limitations to free transfer of capital.[144] In such cases the restriction imposed according to the EPA, which is the later treaty, will apply, as it has validly

[140] Report of the Study Group of the International Law Commission—Finalized by Martti Koskenniemi, *Fragmentation of International Law: Difficulties Arising from the Diversification and Expansion of International Law* (2006) (hereinafter, Report on the Fragmentation of International Law), A/CN.4/L.682, para 254, available at <http://daccessdds.un.org/doc/UNDOC/LTD/G06/610/77/PDF/G0661077.pdf?OpenElement> (last accessed 30 April 2011); see also J Pauwelyn, *Conflict of Norms in Public International Law* (2003), p 365.

[141] In favour of a narrow definition of 'the same subject matter' see C Borgen, 'Resolving Treaty Conflicts' (2005) 37 George Washington International Law Review 573, 603 and references therein; F Paolillo in Corten and Klein (eds), *Les Conventions de Vienne sur le Droit des Traites, Commentaire Article par Article* (2006), p 1263.

[142] E Roucounas, 'Engagements parallèles et contradictoires' (1987) 206 RdC 81, 83.

[143] For a detailed discussion of the scope and application of Art 30 VCLT in intra-EU BITs, which raise similar concerns see A Dimopoulos, 'The Validity and Applicability of International Investment Agreements between EU Member States under EU and International Law' (2011) 48 CMLR 63, 64–6, 73–5.

[144] Agreement on the promotion and protection of investments between Barbados and the Federal Republic of Germany, signed on 2 December 1994 and entered into force on 11 May 2002,

substituted Article 5 of the Barbados-Germany BIT. On the other hand, a limitation on capital movements imposed by Jordan in accordance with the EMA with Jordan would breach the obligation to guarantee free transfer of capital provided in Article 6 of the Jordan-Greece BIT, which was concluded and entered into force after the EMA.[145]

Similar concerns to capital movements also exist with regard to the obligation to provide NT to foreign investors in the post-establishment phase. Conflicting obligations appear in particular when one of the aforementioned EU IIA includes limitations on NT, while Member State BITs provide for unfettered NT. For example, Article 30 in conjunction with Annex V of the EMA with Jordan provides for limitations to NT for Jordanian companies establishing a subsidiary in the EU. Such limitations conflict and, thus, supersede the obligation of the UK to provide NT to all Jordanian investments according to Article 3 of the Jordan-UK BIT, which entered into force before the EMA.[146] On the contrary, the same limitations imposed on Jordanian companies are incompatible with the obligation of Greece to provide unfettered NT to all Jordanian investments according to Article 3 of the Jordan-Greece BIT, which supersedes the provisions of the EMA, as it entered into force at a later date.

Less clear is the relation between the obligation to provide other standards of treatment at the post-establishment phase, such as FET and full protection and security, which exist under most BITs, and the lack of such standards under EU IIAs. Even if it were considered that both sets of treaties have the same subject matter, as they regulate post-entry treatment of foreign investment, this does not necessarily mean that the obligations of the parties in this field conflict and are incompatible. Given that the FET and other standards protect, in essence, the procedural rights of foreign investors and their legitimate expectations, which are also guaranteed indirectly under EU IIAs,[147] it is arguable that these regimes are complementary rather than incompatible. For example, the adoption of a measure restricting beneficial treatment to foreign investors in accordance with Article 224 of the EPA with the CARIFORUM states would rarely violate the FET standard, as a legitimate measure under the general exception clause has to be non-discriminatory and proportionate, thus satisfying the conditions required in order to be FET-compatible.

Finally, consequences may arise with regard to MFN treatment when a BIT between a Member State and a third country is concluded after an EU IIA with the same third county. Apart from the EU law implications that such Member

available at <http://www.unctad.org/sections/dite/iia/docs/bits/germany_barbados.pdf> (last accessed 30 April 2011).

[145] Agreement on the promotion and protection of investments between the Hashemite Kingdom of Jordan and the Hellenic Republic, signed on 21 December 2005 and entered into force on 8 February 2007, available at <http://www.unctad.org/sections/dite/iia/docs/bits/Greece_Jordan.pdf> (last accessed 30 April 2011).

[146] Agreement on the promotion and protection of investments between the Hashemite Kingdom of Jordan and the United Kingdom of Great Britain and Northern Ireland, signed on 10 October 1979 and entered into force on 24 April 1980, available at <http://www.unctad.org/sections/dite/iia/docs/bits/uk_jordan.pdf> (last accessed 30 April 2011).

[147] See Section 3.2.2.4.3.

State action has, since it deviates from Union law,[148] the lack of exact party identity between successive treaties also has effects in terms of international law. More specifically, better standards of treatment under a BIT affect the right of the other parties of the EU IIA to MFN treatment, so that the other EU IIA parties can claim the better treatment provided in the BIT. Consequently, a later BIT between a Member State and a third country triggers the application of the MFN clause found under the EU IIA with the same third country, so that all EU Member States can benefit from the better treatment provided in the later BIT.[149]

5.2.2.4 Future EU and Member State IIAs

Addressing the deficiencies of current EU IIAs, it should not be expected that future EU IIAs will merely introduce new clauses, conditioning their application on compatibility with Member State BITs. On the contrary, the scope of EU exclusive competence over FDI will result in the conclusion of comprehensive EU IIAs, which will explicitly revoke and terminate earlier Member State BITs.[150] However, to the extent that future EU IIAs replicate existing ones, they are expected to establish stronger and clearer connections to Member State BITs. If EU interests in the short/medium term are better served by the conclusion of an EU IIA focusing mainly on admission of foreign investment, the clauses used in the FTA with Korea and the EPA with the CARIFORUM states can be used to safeguard the interests of foreign investors under Member State BITs.

5.3 Conclusions

The emergence of the EU as an international actor in the field of foreign investment raises significant international law concerns, resulting from its nature as an REIO and the fact that foreign investment is a field already covered by Member State BITs. Nonetheless, EU IIAs fit comfortably in the existing regime of international law rules, preserving the need of third parties for legal certainty.

With regard to the EU and Member States' international responsibility for the performance and potential breach of EU IIAs, the recognition of EU exclusive responsibility regarding FDI obligations, and joint and several responsibility regarding non-FDI obligations of EU IIAs, preserves the autonomy of Union law and guarantees legal certainty for third parties, as it allows for the internalization of the difficult question of demarcation between EU and Member States' responsibility in areas of shared competence. This approach respects the international law rules on responsibility of states and international organizations. As regards FDI obligations, Article 63 DARIO allows the internal rules of the international organization to determine the question of responsibility, which is particularly important when Member States act as EU executive organs. As regards non-FDI obligations, capital

[148] See Sections 6.2.2.1 and 6.2.2.3.

[149] See also Section 3.2.2.4.2.

[150] See Section 6.2.3.1.

transfers and FDI in transport services, which remain a field of shared competence after the Lisbon Treaty, they are apportioned to both the EU and its Member States, while both the EU and its Member States are responsible for any wrongful conduct authored by Member State organs. Although the recognition of EU exclusive responsibility regarding FDI obligations and joint and several responsibility regarding non-FDI obligations may lead to practical and moral hazard concerns, specific tools can be devised in order to tackle them efficiently so as to enable EU responsibility for all violations of EU IIAs.

Turning to the relation between EU IIAs and other IIAs, existing EU IIAs recognize that they are only part of a complex network of IIAs and determine sufficiently their relation with other IIAs. Considering that they mainly cover aspects of foreign investment regulation that are not covered under other IIAs, EU IIAs attempt to minimize substantive incompatibilities which may arise. However, to the extent that overlapping commitments exist, EU IIAs aim to avoid potential conflicts, mainly by establishing a hierarchical relation between IIAs. Bilateral EU IIAs respect multilateral EU IIAs and ensure that they do not affect the rights of third parties under multilateral rules. Furthermore, most bilateral EU IIAs concluded in the pre-Lisbon era condition their application to the preservation of Member State BITs. As a result, the potential for conflicting commitments exists only to a limited extent with regard to specific aspects of foreign investment regulation.

It is true that there have not as yet been any cases where the dangers arising from the need for demarcation of EU and Member States' responsibility or the application of conflicting commitments has materialized. There have not been any cases applying the investment provisions of EU IIAs, whereas investment cases between EU Member States or third countries that have concluded BITs and EU IIAs and investors from these countries have always applied BIT law, without reference to EU IIAs. However, the increasing relevance of these questions should not be underestimated. These problems will become more acute under future EU IIAs that will include a comprehensive framework on foreign investment regulation. Indeed, future EU IIAs face not only the challenges to establish EU responsibility for all violations of EU IIAs, those resulting from Member States' acts included, and to eradicate actual and potential conflicts between EU and Member State IIAs, but also to establish stronger and clearer connections between bilateral and multilateral instruments of foreign investment regulation, enhancing the role of the EU as an international actor in foreign investment relations.

6

EU Law Effects of EU Foreign Investment Law

Next to its international law effects, EU foreign investment law has a significant impact within the Union legal order. Recognizing the importance of EU international investment agreements (IIAs) as sources of international law binding on the EU, EU IIAs create Union law obligations as regards the compliance of EU institutions and Member States with them. In that regard, the EU and its Member States have, parallel to their international responsibility, Union law responsibility for the performance of EU IIAs. Specific attention should be paid to the procedural mechanisms and the conditions under which different actors can enforce these obligations, focusing on the scope of judicial review of EU and Member State measures in light of EU IIAs and the creation of individual rights. In addition to their Union law obligations regarding the performance of EU IIAs, EU institutions and, more importantly, Member States have to ensure that their legal framework on foreign investment is in conformity with EU law in general. The latter obligation obtains significant dimensions in light of the regulation of foreign investment in Member State BITs. Examining the relation and compatibility of Member State BITs with EU law, from a Union law point of view, attention is paid to the determination of the specific incompatibilities that arise and how they can be remedied, in particular in light of proposed action. Furthermore, the compatibility of EU IIAs with EU law is considered, paying particular attention to the obligations arising from the application of multilateral EU IIAs, such as the Energy Charter Treaty (ECT), between Member States.

6.1 The Union law obligation and responsibility to perform EU IIAs

EU law recognizes and respects the international commitments arising from agreements concluded by the EU. Article 216(2) TFEU provides that EU international agreements are binding on EU institutions and on Member States. This provision has been interpreted as imposing a Union law obligation on EU institutions and Member States to take all appropriate measures in order to fulfil the EU's international commitments.[1] The fact that not only EU institutions, but also Member States, are equally responsible for respecting the EU's international commitments is further enhanced in Article 4(3) TEU, which articulates the duty of loyal cooperation of the Member States.[2]

6.1.1 The scope of the Union law obligation to perform and comply with the provisions of EU IIAs that are mixed agreements

6.1.1.1 The link with the scope of EU law

Identifying whether the Union law obligation to perform EU international commitments covers the entire content of EU IIAs is crucial, not only for determining the fields where EU institutions are empowered to take action but, more importantly, for defining the fields where Member States have, irrespective of their international law obligation, a Union law obligation to perform EU IIAs. However, the determination of the scope of this Union law obligation of Member States is not straightforward. All existing EU IIAs are mixed agreements, while future EU IIAs will be concluded in all likelihood as mixed agreements also.[3] Hence, the scope and extent of the Union law obligation to perform EU IIAs depends on whether the EU or its Member States are responsible for their implementation. As the European Court has clearly stated, the implementation of a mixed agreement follows the division of powers between the EU and the Member States,[4] so that mixed agreements 'have the same legal status in the [Union] legal order as purely [Union] agreements insofar as the provisions fall within the scope of [Union] competence'.[5]

Determining whether the provisions of EU IIAs fall within the scope of EU competence for the purpose of defining the Union law obligation to perform EU IIAs is crucial. Although Article 207 TFEU establishes exclusive EU competence over foreign direct investment (FDI), which covers an important part of the investment provisions of EU IIAs, there are still many provisions falling under shared competence. Also, at the time of the conclusion of EU IIAs, almost all their investment

[1] See indicatively Case 104/81 *Hauptzollamt Mainz v Kupferberg* [1982] ECR 3641, paras 12–13; Case C-61/94 *Commission* v *Germany* [1996] ECR I-3989, para 52; Case C-13/00 *Commission v Ireland* [2002] ECR I-2943, para 15.

[2] On the obligation of EU institutions and Member States to respect, implement, and apply Union agreements see A Rosas, 'The European Union and mixed agreements' in Dashwood and Hillion (eds), *The General Law of EC External Relations* (2000), pp 211–16; Koutrakos, *EU International Relations Law* (2006), pp 184–5; M Cremona, 'Defending the Community Interest: the Duties of Cooperation and Compliance' in Cremona and de Witte (eds), *EU Foreign Relations Law—Constitutional Fundamentals* (2008), pp 144–52; C Caddous, 'Effects of International Agreements in the EU Legal Order' in Cremona and de Witte (eds), *EU Foreign Relations Law—Constitutional Fundamentals* (2008), pp 292–3.

[3] See Sections 3.1.2.2, 3.2.7, and Conclusions.

[4] Opinion 1/78 [1978] ECR 2151, para 36.

[5] Case C-239/03 *Commission v France (Etang de Berre)* [2004] ECR I-9325, para 25.

provisions fell under concurrent competence, while none of them offered any indication concerning the actor that exercised its (shared) competence. By avoiding ruling directly on the question of whether the EU exercises its (shared) competence in mixed agreements,[6] the Court has gradually adopted an alternative reasoning, albeit directly linked with the notion of competence, in order to determine the limits of the Union law obligation to perform and comply with mixed agreements.

Initially the Court based the existence of a Union law obligation to perform mixed agreements on the existence of EU international responsibility for their performance. The Court has repeatedly emphasized that Member States fulfil a Union law obligation by respecting commitments arising from an EU agreement, as the EU has assumed responsibility for the due performance of the agreement.[7] Considering that mixed agreements have the status of pure EU agreements to the extent that they fall under EU competence,[8] and, hence, the EU bears international responsibility for their performance, the Court seems to consider that the Union law obligation to perform mixed agreements extends to all parts of mixed agreements falling under competence, either exclusive or shared, which the EU has exercised.[9]

However, the Court has gradually taken a more nuanced approach, linking the scope of the Union law obligation to perform mixed agreements with the scope of EU law. In considering the scope of its interpretative jurisdiction, the Court recognized in *Hermes* and in *Dior*,[10] albeit not entirely consistently,[11] a link between the Union law effects of the provisions of mixed agreements with the scope of EU law. The provisions of mixed agreements were considered to create Union law effects, in these cases relating to their interpretation, to the extent that they fell within the scope of EU law and there were EU rules that could be affected by their application and interpretation.[12] Building on these cases, more recently the Court had the opportunity to elaborate further on the link between the scope of EU law and the Union law obligation to perform mixed agreements.[13] Irrespective of the exercise of its competence in a given field, the EU has a broad interest in the performance of the parts of mixed agreements that fall within the scope of EU law, allowing it to

[6] See also Section 5.1.2.2.

[7] *Hauptzollamt Mainz v Kupferberg*, above n 1; Case 12/86 *Demirel v Stadt Schwabisch Gmünd* [1987] ECR 3719. For a review of these cases see I Cheyne, 'Haegeman, Demirel and their progeny' in Dashwood and Hillion (eds), *The General Law of EC External Relations* (2000), pp 20–42.

[8] See above n 2.

[9] P Eeckhout, *External relations of the European Union: legal and constitutional foundations* (2004), p 220.

[10] Case C-53/96 *Hermes International v FHT Marketing* [1998] ECR I-3603; Joined Cases C-300/98 & C-392/98 *Parfums Christian Dior SA v Tuk Consultancy* [2000] ECR I-11307.

[11] For an overview and a critical analysis of these cases see Eeckhout, above n 9, pp 237–43; P Koutrakos, 'The Interpretation of Mixed Agreements under the Preliminary Reference Procedure' (2002) 7 EFA Rev 25; M Karayigit, 'Why and To What Extent a Common Interpretative Position for Mixed Agreements?' (2006) 11 EFA Rev 445.

[12] *Hermes*, above n 10, paras 28, 33. See C Hillion, 'Mixity and Coherence in EU External Relations: The Significance of the "Duty of Cooperation"' in Hillion and Koutrakos (eds), *Mixed Agreements Revisited* (2010), p 97.

[13] *Commission v France (Etang de Berre)*, above n 5, para 25; *Commission v Ireland*, above n 1, paras 16, 18, 19; Case C-431/05 *Merck Genéricos v Merck and Co Inc* [2007] ECR I-7001, paras 34–8.

hold Member States accountable under Union law for the breach of mixed agreement provisions that can affect EU law.[14]

Turning to the determination of the scope of EU law, the jurisprudence of the Court is rather unclear. Although the Court identifies that the Union law obligation for the performance of mixed agreements arises to the extent that the provisions of a mixed agreement cover an area which is covered 'in large measure' by EU legislation,[15] it is controversial when the level of legislative activity is sufficient to bring a provision of a mixed agreement within the scope of EU law.[16] However, in any event the test determining the existence of a Union interest is less strict than that determining competence exclusivity according to the *AETR* principle.[17] Although the existence of EU legislation on the specific subject matter covered by the mixed agreement is not necessary,[18] there must be a body of EU rules of 'sufficient importance' to bring the field within the scope of EU law.

At this point it should be highlighted that the Union law obligation of Member States to perform EU IIAs is not the foundation on which their international responsibility arises. Articles 216(2) TFEU and 4(3) TEU create only internal legal effects, without prejudicing the international responsibility of Member States, which in the case of EU IIAs is premised on different grounds.[19] This is better illustrated in the case of pure Union agreements, where Member States have a Union law obligation to comply with them, but in cases of their violation, it is the EU that incurs international responsibility.[20]

6.1.1.2 Are the investment provisions of EU IIAs within the scope of EU law?

Examining the provisions of EU IIAs on capital movements, it appears that they are covered in large measure under EU rules. The general rules on free movement of capital in the TFEU provide a framework for EU action in the field of capital movements. A similar framework of EU rules covers the area of foreign investment

[14] Cremona, above n 2, pp 147–8, 152–3; P Koutrakos, 'Interpretation of Mixed Agreements' in Hillion and Koutrakos (eds), *Mixed Agreements Revisited* (2010), pp 123–5.

[15] *Commission v France (Etang de Berre)*, above n 5, paras 29–30.

[16] On the debate regarding the scope of EU law after the *Merck* case, where the Court adopted a narrower reading of when an area is covered in large measure by EU legislation see Koutrakos, above n 14, pp 130–5; R Holdgaard, 'Annotation on Case C-431/05 *Merck*' (2008) 45 CMLR 1233.

[17] Cremona, above n 2, p 150.

[18] The judgment of the Court in *Sellafield* (Case C-459/03 *Commission v Ireland (Sellafield)* [2006] ECR I-4635), where it was ruled that 'a finding that there has been a transfer to the [EU] of areas of shared competence is contingent on the existence of [EU] rules within the areas covered by the Convention provisions in issue' is not conflicting with the general rule that specific EU legislation is not required. In that case, the necessity of existing, specific EU rules arose from the wording of the declaration of competence attached to the UNCLOS. The Court makes clear that the 'Declaration of Community competence... specifies the extent and the nature of the areas of competence transferred by the Member States to the Community' (para 99) and that '[a] passage of the Declaration of Community competence makes the transfer of areas of shared competence subject to the existence of Community rules' (para 106).

[19] Koutrakos, above n 2, p 185; P Kuijper and E Paasivirta, 'Further Exploring International Responsibility: The European Community and the ILC's project on responsibility of international organizations' (2004) 1 International Organizations Law Review 111, 134.

[20] See Case C-327/91 *France v Commission* [1994] ECR I-3641.

promotion. Regarding the provisions in EU IIAs that create a specific framework for cooperation on investment promotion, there is an extensive network of secondary EU legislation dealing with development aid and cooperation which focuses, among others, on the promotion of foreign investment.[21]

The same conclusion can be reached with regard to the establishment and post-establishment treatment of foreign investment. Of course, FDI falls after the entry into force of the Lisbon Treaty under exclusive EU competence. But even under the EC Treaty, when it fell under shared competence, there was a plethora of EU law instruments determining the conditions of establishment and post-establishment treatment of third country nationals in many fields, such as in the areas of financial and telecommunication services.[22] These provisions, and in particular the EU law instruments that establish a general framework covering the establishment and provision of services by third country nationals in all fields, are still relevant for determining whether the EU IIA provisions relating to foreign investment in the form of concession contracts fall under the scope of EU law. For example, the Services Directive[23] incorporates rules on treatment and operation of service providers in all service sectors, which also apply to foreign investors. As a result, there is a Union interest in the performance of all EU IIA provisions on admission and operation of foreign investment, whether FDI or not, which lies in the fact that their violation may result in a violation of EU law rules.

Whether expropriation provisions fall under the scope of EU law is more controversial. The examination of the coverage of expropriation provisions under the scope of EU law is crucial not only for EU IIA provisions relating to foreign investment in the form of portfolio investment or concession contracts, but also for FDI, in particular if it were accepted that expropriation is excluded from the scope of Article 207 TFEU. In that respect, the existence of EU competence in these fields[24] indicates first that expropriation provisions are not excluded from the scope of EU law as are the provisions that fall under exclusive Member State competence. However, there is no secondary legislation relating to expropriation of private property.

Nevertheless, it is arguable that expropriation provisions fall within the scope of EU law, creating a Union law obligation for compliance with them, even when they are applied in a purely national context. As discussed, the Court has explicitly provided that EU law protects private property rights from limitations imposed by EU measures, since indirect expropriations resulting from EU measures are subject to EU rules articulated in the Charter of Fundamental Rights and as general principles of law binding on EU institutions and Member States.[25] Consequently, there is a Union law obligation for EU institutions and Member States to perform

[21] See Section 1.3.6. [22] See Section 2.2.2.2.2.

[23] Directive 2006/123/EC of the European Parliament and of the Council of 12 December 2006 on services in the internal market [2006] OJ L376/36.

[24] See Section 2.5.

[25] See Case 4/73 *Nold* [1974] ECR 491; Case C-84/95 *Bosphorus* [1996] ECR I-3953. See also Section 2.5.3.

and comply with the expropriation provisions of an EU IIA, to the extent that an expropriation results from an EU measure.

But even in cases where a limitation of private property rights is the outcome of national measures, there is still a Union law obligation for the Member States to comply with the expropriation provisions of an EU IIA. Even though EU law does not offer sufficient rules in that regard,[26] the EU has an interest in Member States complying with EU IIA provisions on expropriation, as their application and interpretation in cases involving Member State measures can affect the application and interpretation of these provisions in cases involving EU measures. Drawing a parallel to the reasoning of the Court in *Hermes* and *Dior*,[27] the need for consistent application and interpretation of provisions of mixed agreements that can apply both in an EU context and in a purely national context indicates the EU interest and justifies the existence of a Union law obligation to perform and comply with the expropriation provisions of EU IIAs. Even if a strict interpretation of the scope of EU law were adopted, similar to *Merck*,[28] EU IIA provisions on expropriation fall within the scope of EU law, given that there are sufficient internal rules on property rights limitations resulting from EU measures.

In identifying the content of the EU law obligation to perform EU IIAs, it is apparent that it relates primarily to the implementation and application of EU IIA provisions. The proper implementation of investment provisions may require legislative changes, such as abolishing restrictions on capital movements or limitations to market access for foreign investors that exist in current legislation. While such legislative initiatives can be taken by EU institutions, the existence of such limitations in national law instruments indicates that Member State action may be required. As the Court has stated, in cases where EU rules are absent, 'it is for the Member States to lay down the rules which are necessary to give effect in their territory to the provisions of [an] agreement'.[29] However, legislative changes are not always necessary, as the EU and its Member States may already have legislation in place that satisfies the requirements of EU IIAs. Irrespective of the need for implementing legislation, EU institutions and Member States have to apply national and EU law instruments in conformity with the provisions of EU IIAs, giving effect to their content.

6.1.2 The limitations on the existence and exercise of Member State powers in the areas covered by EU IIAs

The obligation to comply with and perform EU IIAs extends beyond their implementation and proper application. Member States have to ensure that their actions do not jeopardize the fulfilment of EU international commitments and respect EU law.[30] This raises particular concerns, first, as regards existing Member State legislation and in particular their BITs, which is addressed in the following section and,

[26] See also below Section 6.3.2.2. [27] *Hermes, Dior*, above n 10.
[28] *Merck*, above n 13. [29] *Demirel v Stadt Schwabisch Gmünd*, above n 7, para 10.
[30] Cremona, above n 2, p 129; Hillion, above n 12, p 106.

secondly, the exercise of Member State competence to regulate the subject matter of EU IIAs in the future. Of course, after the entry into force of the Lisbon Treaty, which introduces exclusive EU competence over FDI, the scope of Member States' powers in the field of foreign investment is significantly curtailed. Nevertheless, in the areas where Member States still hold concurrent competences, their obligation to respect EU IIAs entails limitations to their powers to regulate the same area as in EU IIAs, both in their national legislation and, more importantly, in their BITs.

The identification of the limitations posed on Member State competence in the areas covered by EU IIAs begins first with a determination of whether and to what extent EU IIAs have an *AETR* effect. As discussed, the *AETR* principle renders EU competence in a specific field exclusive, as long as there are EU rules covering that field.[31] When viewing the *AETR* principle from the point of its effects on Member State powers, it results in their pre-emption in a given field, without requiring that national legislation actually conflicts with EU rules.[32]

In examining the *AETR* effect of EU IIAs, it is undisputable that EU legislation implementing the investment provisions of EU IIAs could potentially result in the pre-emption of Member State powers, to the extent that such legislation provides for complete harmonization. However, the implementation of the investment provisions of EU IIAs is left in many cases to the Member States, while implementing legislation may not be necessary when EU IIAs simply bind the existent level of liberalization in each Member State. In such cases, where there is no internal EU legislation, it appears that the *AETR* principle does not apply.

However, it could be argued that *AETR* exclusivity may result directly from the investment provisions of EU IIAs, irrespective of whether there is implementing EU legislation. Although such an expansion of the *AETR* principle has not been recognized by the Court, the nature of the provisions of Union agreements could support the argument that they have *AETR* effect. More specifically, as discussed in Chapter 2, the *AETR* principle comes into effect as long as there are EU rules covering a specific area. Even though the existence of 'EU rules' has been based so far on the existence of secondary EU law instruments, this does not necessarily exclude the provisions of EU international agreements from being considered as EU rules. The fact that they are 'an integral part of Union law', and take priority before secondary EU legislation, indicates that they have a similar legal nature to secondary rules. In addition to the similar legal nature of secondary legislation and EU international commitments, the extension of the scope of application of the *AETR* principle to EU international commitments is strengthened by the purpose of *AETR* exclusivity. The rationale behind *AETR* exclusivity is to 'ensure a uniform and consistent application of the EU rules and the proper functioning of the system which they establish in order to preserve the full effectiveness of EU law'.[33] This objective also

[31] See Section 2.1.2.

[32] R Schütze, 'Supremacy Without Pre-Emption? The Very Slowly Emergent Doctrine of Community Pre-Emption' (2006) 43 CMLR 1023, 1037–8.

[33] Opinion 1/2003 [2006] ECR I-1, para116.

applies to EU international commitments, the consistent application and interpretation of which is crucial for the functioning and effectiveness of EU law.[34]

Even if this position were adopted, this does not mean that the mere existence of investment obligations in EU IIAs leads automatically to the pre-emption of Member State competence. First, as EU IIAs create rules that apply only to specific third countries and their nationals, the investment provisions of EU IIAs lead to exclusive competence in the fields covered therein only with regard to those specific countries. Hence, EU IIAs do not prejudice Member State competence to conclude international agreements in the same field with other countries. Secondly, and most importantly, even with regard to EU counterparties, exclusive EU competence arises only if the other criteria of *AETR* exclusivity are satisfied. EU IIA provisions result in exclusive EU competence only if they result, for example, in complete harmonization of a particular issue.

Even if EU IIAs do not give rise to exclusive EU competence, they impose severe limitations on the freedom of Member States to legislate in the area they cover. To the extent that Member States have competence over foreign investment, the exercise of their power is subject to constraints imposed by EU law.[35] This obligation, which is derived from the duty of loyal cooperation in Article 4(3) TFEU, requires that Member States respect EU law, including EU IIAs, so that the adoption of national legislation and the conclusion of agreements by Member States do not infringe EU law. Hence, Member States are not *a priori* pre-empted from rule-making in an area covered by an EU IIA, but their rules have to be consistent with the EU IIA provisions, as a violation of the Member States' obligation to respect EU international commitments exists only to the extent that there is an actual conflict between EU IIAs and Member State instruments.[36]

The limitations on the existence and exercise of Member State competence resulting from EU IIAs are particularly important with regard to the power of Member States to conclude BITs with third countries. If it is accepted that EU IIAs have an *AETR* effect, Member States cannot legislate in the area covered by EU IIAs, otherwise violating significant EU law obligations. Even if EU IIAs do not have an *AETR* effect, they still limit the power of Member States to conclude BITs, as the latter must be compatible with EU IIAs. Using the example of the Jordan-Greece BIT, which was concluded after the EMA with Jordan, and bearing in mind their conflicting provisions on capital movements,[37] it appears that in any event Greece violated its Union law obligation to respect the EU IIA with Jordan.

The fields where substantive conflicts between EU IIAs and BITs are more likely to occur, as well as the remedies provided in cases of violation of this obligation, are addressed below, when examining the Union law obligations of Member States regarding their BITs.

[34] On the need for consistent application and interpretation of EU international commitments see in particular *Hermes*, above n 10.

[35] J Klabbers, 'Restraints on the Treaty-making Power of Member States Deriving from EU Law: Towards a Framework for Analysis' in Cannizzaro (ed), *The European Union as an Actor in International Relations* (2002), p 175; Cremona, above n 2, pp 129–30; Hillion, above n 12, p 108.

[36] Schütze, above n 32, pp 1037, 1043.

[37] See Section 5.2.2.3.

6.1.3 Enforcing EU IIAs under EU law: review of legality and direct effect of EU IIAs

The purpose of the Union law obligation of EU institutions and Member States to perform and comply with EU IIAs would be severely damaged if it could not be effectively enforced. Reaffirming the central position of the rule of law in the Union legal system, the Court has been very eager to review the legality of EU and Member State acts on the basis of their compatibility with EU international agreements.[38] Recognizing international law norms as an important source of EU law,[39] the Court has extensively applied and interpreted the provisions of Union agreements,[40] in particular in light of the examination of the legality of EU and national measures. Nevertheless, the Court has distinguished international agreements from other sources of EU law, creating additional conditions in order for them to constitute a threshold for the assessment of the legality of EU and Member State acts.

6.1.3.1 The conditions for judicial review

The basic test for reviewing the legality of EU and Member State acts has been formulated by the Court in *International Fruit Company*,[41] subjecting judicial review in light of Union agreements to a two-stage test. The first limb of the test requires that an international agreement is binding on the EU, creating international law obligations, while the second limb requires that the provision of the international agreement, in light of which the legality of an act is assessed, has direct effect. In order to determine the direct effect of a provision of a Union agreement, the Court has imposed two conditions, the first relating to the nature and structure of the Union agreement as a whole, and the second to the nature of the specific provision, which has to be clear, precise, and unconditional.[42] While the first limb of the test has been an issue only rarely—mainly in cases of mixed agreements[43] and agreements concluded only by Member States[44]—the second limb of the test has raised more controversy, both in terms of its content and its consistent use by the Court.

[38] In this section the terms EU international agreements and Union agreements will be used interchangeably, including EU IIAs and other mixed agreements that have the same status as pure Union agreements.

[39] Case 181/73 *Haegeman* [1974] ECR 449; Case C-61/94 *Commission v Germany*, above n 1.

[40] On the interpretation of the provisions of EU IIAs, particularly in light of the similarities in their wording with primary EU law see Section 3.2.2.4.1.

[41] Cases 22–24/72 *International Fruit Company* [1972] ECR 1219, paras 7–8.

[42] The test for determining the direct effect of the provisions of an international agreement comes into play only insofar as the parties have not determined the effects of the international agreement in its text (Case C-149/96 *Portugal v Council* [1999] ECR I-8385, para 34). Since no EU IIA, with the exception of the ECT, which provides that the direct effect of its investment provisions is neither required nor excluded (see below n 73), makes reference to the effects of their provisions in the domestic legal orders of the parties, the direct effect of EU IIA provisions in the Union legal order depends on the criteria of *International Fruit*, as they have been formulated by the Court.

[43] Eg in *Hermes*, above n 10.

[44] Eg in *International Fruit Company*, above n 41, and in Case C-308/06 *Intertanko* [2008] ECR I-4057.

Considering the variety of the available mechanisms for judicial review of EU and Member State acts, the Court of Justice has not consistently applied the second limb of the judicial review test in all cases relating to compatibility with EU international agreements. Depending on the means of action and the legal subject initiating the judicial review process, the Court has distinguished between direct actions relating to the legality of Member State acts according to Article 258 TFEU, direct actions relating to the legality of EU acts according to Article 263 TFEU, and indirect actions where the legality of EU and Member State acts is reviewed under the preliminary reference procedure or under an action for determining the non-contractual liability of the EU. The Court has made a distinction between actions raised by individuals, on the one hand, and EU institutions and Member States, on the other, distinguishing further between actions concerning the legality of EU acts and those concerning the legality of Member State acts.

More specifically, in cases of enforcement actions brought against Member States according to Article 258 TFEU, the Court has based its judicial review on the sole condition that an international agreement is binding on the EU, without examining whether it has direct effect.[45] This approach appears to be correct, as the EU has an interest in compliance with a Union agreement irrespective of whether it produces direct effect, since non-compliance triggers its international responsibility.[46] However, the Court has not taken the same view when Member States request review of the legality of EU acts according to Article 263 TFEU. Even though Member States, equally with EU institutions, are guardians of the Union interest and have a direct interest in the legality of EU acts, since an infringement of a mixed agreement binding on the EU can also lead to their international responsibility,[47] the Court has repeatedly examined whether the conditions for direct effect exist, examining in particular the first limb of the test relating to the nature and structure of the agreement.[48] This jurisprudence illustrates that as long as the creation of individual rights is not an issue, judicial review of EU and Member State acts does not depend on the direct effect of the Union agreement. Nevertheless, the nature and structure of the agreement has become an independent condition for the judicial review of EU acts, while it is not necessary for the judicial review of Member State acts under enforcement proceedings.

The direct effect of Union agreements is required where the creation of individual rights is concerned. The Court has consistently required that both limbs of the *International Fruit* test are satisfied in order to review the legality of EU and Member State acts under Articles 263 and 267 TFEU.[49] Furthermore, direct

[45] *Commission v Germany*, above n 1; *Commission v Ireland*, above n 1.

[46] On the lack of necessity of direct effect in enforcement proceedings and its justification see Eeckhout, above n 9, pp 244–5, 254–5.

[47] P Kuipjer and M Bronckers, 'WTO Law in the European Court of Justice' (2005) 42 CMLR 1313, 1343–51.

[48] *Portugal v Council*, above n 42; Case C-280/93 *Germany v Council* [1994] ECR I-4973; Case C-377/98 *Netherlands v European Parliament and Council* [2001] ECR I-7079.

[49] For recent jurisprudence see Case C-344/04 *R v Department of Transport, ex parte IATA* [2006] ECR I-403, para 39; *Intertanko*, above n 44, paras 44–5. See P Eeckhout, 'Case C-308/06 *The Queen*

effect is also a condition for assessing the lawfulness of an EU act under Article 340 TFEU in order to determine the non-contractual liability of the EU.[50]

As a result, it appears that the test relating to the nature and structure of an agreement has a dual function, serving both as a condition for judicial review and as a condition of direct effect. In its first dimension, the WTO cases suggest that the crucial elements of the nature and structure of a Union agreement are those related to its purposes and objectives, concerning whether a Union agreement creates a legal regime based on reciprocity, where judicial deference is necessary for enabling the political institutions to use any flexibilities granted to them in the agreement. In its second dimension, the nature and structure of an agreement is linked with the creation of individual rights, concerning in particular whether a Union agreement intends to vest individuals with rights and freedoms. Considering that the existence of clear, precise, and unconditional provisions is also a condition for direct effect of secondary EU legislation in national legal orders, the nature and structure of an agreement presents the threshold that distinguishes international norms from secondary EU rules.[51] The double function of the test relating to the nature and structure of a Union agreement has been recently confirmed in the *Intertanko* case,[52] where the Court dealt extensively with the nature and structure of the UNCLOS agreement, looking successively at the questions of the purposes of that agreement and the balance it struck and whether it intended to attach the freedoms and the rights stipulated therein to individuals.

Finally, even if the provisions of a Union agreement do not satisfy the conditions for direct effect, they may still trigger judicial review of EU and Member State acts. Judicial review is first possible under the so-called *Nakajima* principle, where the legality of EU legislation can be assessed in light of the international agreement which it explicitly implements.[53] Secondly, judicial review is possible, as EU and Member State legislation has to be interpreted consistent with the provisions of Union agreements.[54] Hence, the *Nakajima* doctrine and the principle of consistent interpretation present alternative ways for reviewing the legality of national and secondary EU law in light of EU international commitments, leading in many instances to results that do not differ in substance from those that would have been reached if an agreement had direct effect.[55]

6.1.3.2 *The binding nature, the purposes, and the structure of EU IIAs*

In applying the tests for judicial review and direct effect on EU IIAs, it is necessary to distinguish between the different types of EU IIAs and their investment

on the application of Intertanko and others v Secretary of State for Transport, judgment of the Court of Justice (Grand Chamber) of 3 June 2008' (2009) 46 CMLR 2041.

[50] Case T-69/00 *FIAMM v Council and Commission* [2005] ECR II-5393. See also M Cremona, 'External Relations of the EU and the Member States: Competence, Mixed Agreements, International Responsibility, and Effects of International Law', EUI Working Paper No 2006/22, pp 32–3.

[51] Eeckhout, above n 9, pp 313–14. [52] Above n 44.

[53] Case 69/89 *Nakajima All v Council* [1991] ECR I-2069.

[54] *Commission v Germany*, above n 1, para 52; Case C-89/99 *Schieving-Nijstad* [2001] ECR I-5851.

[55] Kuipjer and Bronckers, above n 47, pp 1326, 1328–9.

provisions. Starting with the first limb of the judicial review test, namely whether an agreement is binding on the EU, it is clear that EU IIAs pass this test. As discussed, even when EU IIAs are concluded as mixed agreements, they all create binding obligations on the EU, in particular their investment provisions.[56] Even expropriation provisions affecting expropriation of other forms of foreign investment than FDI, which are only partially covered by EU rules, create binding obligations on the EU, which has to ensure compliance with them.[57] As the initiation of enforcement proceedings requires only the fulfilment of this condition, the primary conclusion can be drawn that the Court can always review the legality of Member State measures in light of the investment provisions of EU IIAs under Article 258 TFEU.

Turning to the nature and structure of EU IIAs, the failure of the WTO[58] and the UNCLOS Agreements to satisfy this condition—which is in sharp contrast with most other agreements examined by the Court—indicates that a closer look at each group of EU IIAs is necessary according to their specific characteristics. Beginning with Stabilisation and Association Agreements (SAAs), it is arguable that, because of their integration purposes, their nature and structure satisfy this condition for judicial review and direct effect. The existence of closer integration purposes, leading ultimately to EU accession, has been repeatedly considered sufficient ground by the Court for offering direct effect to the Europe Agreements (EAs).[59] Bearing in mind the striking resemblances between SAAs and EAs not only in terms of common purposes but also in terms of content, these agreements satisfy the condition for judicial review and direct effect relating to their nature and structure.

The jurisprudence of the Court has been illuminating also with regard to the nature and structure of Partnership and Co-operation Agreements (PCAs) and Euro-Mediterranean Agreements (EMAs). In *Simutenkov*[60] the Court held explicitly that the nature and structure of the PCA with Russia could not prevent its provisions from having direct effect, despite the fact that it did not create an association or aim at future accession to the EU.[61] A similar conclusion was also reached in the *El-Yassini* and *Gattoussi* cases,[62] which recognized that the nature and structure of the Cooperation Agreement with Morocco, which has been already replaced by an EMA, and the EMA with Tunisia, did not impede the provisions of these agreements from having direct effect. Hence, it is not only the establishment of an association

[56] See above Section 6.1.1.2. [57] See Section 5.1.4.

[58] On the nature and structure of the WTO Agreement and its failure to satisfy the conditions for judicial review see *Germany v Council*, above n 48; *Portugal v Council*, above n 42. For a discussion of the topic in the literature see Kuijper and Bronckers, above n 47; F Snyder, 'The Gatekeepers: The European Courts and the WTO' (2003) 40 CMLR 313; Eeckhout, above n 9, pp 301–12.

[59] Eg in Case C-257/99 *Bakoci and Malik* [2001] ECR I-6557; Case C-268/99 *Jany and Others* [2001] ECR-I 8615; Case C-63/99 *Gloszczuk* [2001] ECR I-6369; Case C-327/02 *Panayotova* [2004] ECR I-11055.

[60] Case C-265/03 *Simutenkov* [2005] ECR I-2579.

[61] Ibid, paras 26–8. See also F Jacobs, 'Direct effect and interpretation of international agreements in the recent case law of the European Court of Justice' in Dashwood and Maresceau (eds), *Law and Practice of EU External Relations* (2008), pp 19–21.

[62] Case C-416/96 *El Yassini* [1999] ECR I-1209; Case C-97/05 *Gattoussi* [2006] ECR I-11917.

but also the broader cooperation goals that are sufficient for a Union agreement to have direct effect and fall under the scope of judicial review.[63] The Court clearly recognized that the test relating to the nature and structure of an agreement is not linked with accession and complete integration objectives, indicating that direct effect and judicial review probably depend more on the similarity of the provisions of an agreement with those found in primary EU law and/or pre-accession association agreements and the general purposes that they establish.

The recognition of direct effect in the above-mentioned cases, where the nature and structure of the Union agreement in question was dealt with only secondarily, does not mean that the Court has abandoned this test for judicial review and direct effect.[64] The insistence of the Court in considering the nature and structure of a Union agreement, the denial of direct effect of the UNCLOS Agreement, as well as the more recent jurisprudence of the Court on the WTO Agreement[65] indicate that it is still an important condition for judicial review. As a result, it is necessary to examine more carefully the nature and structure of the agreements with Mexico, Chile, South Africa, Korea, and the CARIFORUM states as well as the ECT. Based on these findings, it is easier to determine whether future EU IIAs containing comprehensive investment provisions similar to BITs, pass this test.

Starting with existing bilateral EU IIAs, it is strongly arguable that their nature and structure are no impediment to their judicial review and direct effect. In first considering the EU-Chile Association Agreement, the establishment of an association between these countries, despite the lack of closer integration or accession purposes, indicates that its provisions are capable of direct effect.[66] A similar conclusion can be reached for the Trade, Development and Cooperation Agreement (TDCA), the Economic Partnership Agreement (EPA), the Free Trade Agreement (FTA) with Korea, and the Global Agreement with Mexico, as

> the fact that [cooperation agreements are] limited to establishing a partnership between the parties, without providing for an association or future accession . . . is not such as to prevent certain provisions from having direct effect. It is clear from the Court's case-law that when an agreement establishes cooperation between the parties, some of the provisions of that agreement may . . . directly govern the legal position of individuals.[67]

Furthermore, the existence of investment provisions in binding instruments adopted by institutions established in these agreements, such as the decision on trade in services and investment adopted by the EU-Mexico Joint Council, does not exclude these provisions from the scope of judicial review and deprive them from direct effect.[68] Moreover, regarding the intention to create individual rights, the Court has explicitly stated that they can govern the legal position of individuals.

[63] Cremona, above n 50, p 31; Jacobs, above n 61, pp 19–21.

[64] Caddous, above n 2, pp 304–5.

[65] See eg *FIAMM*, above n 50; Case T-19/01 *Chiquita* [2005] ECR II-315; Case C-377/02 *Van Parys* [2005] ECR I-1465.

[66] *Gattoussi*, above n 62.

[67] *Simutenkov*, above n 60.

[68] To that effect see the Court decisions in Case C-192/89 *Sevince* [1990] ECR I-3461, paras 14–26 and Case C-277/94 *Taflan-Met and Others* [1996] ECR I- 4085.

More importantly, when considering the purposes of existing bilateral Union agreements, they lack the qualities that, according to the Court, necessitate judicial deference in light of the WTO cases. Unlike the WTO regime, where reciprocity affects the content of the international obligations assumed by the parties, providing leverage to the members' political institutions to conform with their international obligations, existing bilateral EU IIAs go beyond the establishment of reciprocal commitments, where judicial intervention may impede the scope for manoeuvre given to the political institutions of each party. The purposes of these agreements extend beyond mutual liberalization, aiming at creating multilevel integration between the parties. Even though some of them grant flexibility to the parties regarding dispute settlement, which is similar to the WTO Dispute Settlement Understanding (DSU), the objectives of multilevel integration and cooperation indicate that the scope for manoeuvre enjoyed by EU political institutions should be exercised within the confines imposed by the rule of law, irrespective of the political and judicial approaches adopted by EU counterparts.[69] In that regard it is strongly arguable that existing bilateral EU IIAs are able to create individual rights and be the standard for judicial review.

A similar conclusion can be reached with regard to the ECT, the nature and structure of which passes the test for judicial review and creation of individual rights. The ECT differs from the WTO, as its purpose is for the creation of a cooperation framework in the energy field not founded on reciprocity. As the Preamble to the ECT and the principles of the Energy Charter indicate, the main objectives are energy security and efficiency, which are achieved mainly through liberalization measures and cooperation mechanisms. It creates a balance between the divergent interests of the parties including asymmetric obligations for energy-supplying and energy-recipient countries.[70] Even though the Energy Charter emphasizes the role of negotiations for achieving its non-binding objectives, this does not mean that the ECT is based on the 'principle of negotiation' in the sense that the specific obligations assumed by the parties can be amended after negotiations conducted between them. Furthermore, the use of investor-state arbitration as a dispute settlement mechanism indicates that the scope for manoeuvre granted to parties, enabling them to ensure conformity with substantive obligations, is very limited.

Considering now whether the ECT intends to grant rights to individuals, it is suggested that its structure and the content of its provisions have direct bearing on the legal situation of individuals. Considering in particular the investment provisions of the agreement, it is obvious that they contain rules framing rights of individuals, namely foreign investors.[71] The fact that the investment rules are intended to apply directly and immediately to individuals is proven by the reference to investor-state dispute settlement in Article 26 ECT, which provides, among others, that an investor may submit a dispute for resolution 'to the courts or administrative tribunals of

[69] *Kupferberg*, above n 1, paras 19–20.

[70] S Haghighi, *Energy Security: The External Legal Relations of the European Union with Major Oil and Gas Supplying Countries* (2006), pp 192–4.

[71] Haghighi, above n 70, pp 217–18.

the Contracting Party to the dispute'.[72] Even though this provision does not establish an obligation for the contracting parties to give direct effect to the investment provisions of the ECT,[73] it clearly indicates that the intention of the ECT, at least its investment provisions, is to give rights to individuals.

The assessment of the structure and nature of future EU IIAs should rely on similar considerations to those applicable to the ECT. To the extent that they provide for dispute settlement in front of national courts, among other options, they indicate that the nature and purpose of such agreements is favourable to direct effect. In addition, investor-state arbitration does not provide sufficient scope for manoeuvre to political institutions to ensure conformity with the parties' obligations.

Consequently, EU IIAs, with the exception of the WTO Agreement, pass the test relating to their nature and structure. This enables, firstly, judicial review and assessment of the legality of EU and Member State acts under actions initiated by EU institutions and Member States. Secondly, EU IIAs, with the exception of the WTO Agreement, are capable of direct effect to the extent that investment provisions are clear, precise, and unconditional.

6.1.3.3 The nature of the investment provisions of EU IIAs

Having already examined the nature, structure, and purposes of EU IIAs, it is necessary to examine whether their provisions are clear, precise, and unconditional, so that they can give rise to individual rights. This is the case where a 'provision contains a clear and precise obligation which is not subject, in its implementation or effects, to the adoption of any subsequent measure'.[74] This classic direct effect test, which is also relevant for the direct effect of internal EU law, examines whether a provision is sufficiently operational for judicial application.[75] It is without question that an examination of the wording of the investment provisions in each EU IIA is required in order to determine whether individuals can claim their direct application. However, the commonalities between investment provisions relating to certain aspects of foreign investment regulation allow for some general remarks, providing the guidelines for the specific examination of each investment provision.

Starting with provisions relating to the establishment and post-establishment treatment of foreign investors, their language and normative content indicate that they are suitable for direct effect, creating rights for individuals. Such investment provisions are based on the principle of non-discrimination, ranging from qualified MFN treatment to complete Market Access and NT, laying down in clear, precise, and unconditional terms, an obligation for the parties to allow establishment of foreign nationals in a specific field and to treat them in a specific manner. As the Court of Justice has repeatedly found in cases concerning provisions on establishment and

[72] Art 26(2)(a) ECT.

[73] Understanding No 16 provides that 'Art 26(2)(a) should not be interpreted to require a Contracting Party to enact Part III of the Treaty into its domestic law'.

[74] Case C-162/00 *Pokrzeptowicz Meyer* [2002] ECR I-1049, para 19.

[75] Eeckhout, above n 9, p 314.

post-establishment treatment of foreign nationals in EU Member States, an establishment provision 'lays down a precise obligation to produce a specific result and, by its nature, can be relied on by an individual'.[76] The same rationale should be employed for determining the nature of provisions establishing absolute standards of treatment, such as FET, considering that they also lay down a precise obligation which is not subject in its implementation or effects to the adoption of any subsequent measure. Of course, this does not mean that all EU IIA provisions on establishment and post-establishment treatment are capable of producing direct effect. The *Demirel* line of reasoning for denying direct effect[77] is relevant for a number of EU IIAs which include a general 'best efforts' provision and leave the adoption of specific commitments for the future, either through renegotiation of that part of the agreement or by a decision of an institution that they establish.[78]

Next to the establishment and post-establishment treatment provisions, it is arguable that other EU IIA provisions relating to entry and post-entry operation of foreign investment have direct effect. More specifically, the direct effect of provisions on capital movements can be premised on similar grounds that justify the direct effect of the establishment provisions. The provisions on capital movements are based on the principle of non-discrimination, thus creating clear, precise, and unconditional commitments, on which individuals can rely. Furthermore, the provisions relating to the movement of key personnel have direct effect, since they refer to specific types of individuals, defining in detail their rights of entry and type of employment in EU Member States. Considering the eagerness of the Court to grant direct effect to provisions creating specific rights for entry and employment of foreign nationals,[79] albeit in the framework of the free movement of workers, it is arguable that investment provisions on movement of key personnel are similar in that they also lay down in clear and precise terms rights for entry and employment of individuals.

As regards provisions on property protection against expropriation and other political risks, which exist so far only in the ECT but will be a prominent element of future EU IIAs, they can be clear, precise, and unconditional, thus creating individual rights. Taking as an example the expropriation provision of the ECT, it contains a clear and precise obligation to compensate in cases of expropriation, determining in an explicit, albeit broad, manner the conditions under which expropriation is illegal and how compensation is calculated. Furthermore, the expropriation provision of the ECT is unconditional as it does not need further implementation and its application does not require the adoption of additional

[76] *Bakoci and Malik*, above n 59, para 33; See also *Jany and Others*, above n 59; *Gloszczuk* above n 59; Case C-235/99 *Kondova* [2001] ECR I-6427.

[77] *Demirel*, above n 7, para 24; *Taflan Met*, above n 68.

[78] Eg the provisions on establishment in the TDCA with South Africa and the EMA with Egypt, which reaffirm the parties' GATS commitments and include a reference to future negotiations (Arts 29–30), are not clear and unconditional, and thus are incapable of having direct effect.

[79] Case C-171/01 *Wählergruppe Gemeinsam* [2003] ECR I-4301; Case C-275/02 *Ayaz* [2004] ECR I-8765.

measures. Hence, individuals can rely on the expropriation provisions of the ECT and request compensation in cases of expropriation of their property.

Contrary to the investment provisions discussed above, the vast majority of EU IIA provisions on investment promotion are not capable of producing direct effect. Even where such provisions establish legally binding obligations,[80] they only set an objective and a general framework for action, leaving wide discretion to the parties to choose the means and, in most circumstances, the type of action. As a result, the need for further implementation of the investment promotion provisions of EU IIAs indicates that they lack the qualities that would vest them with direct effect.

Finally, it is worth noting that direct effect of the substantive provisions of EU IIAs does not necessarily mean that arbitral awards determining the compatibility of an EU or Member State measure with an EU IIA are also directly effective. As discussed, the enforceability of ICSID awards is subject to the specific rules determined in the ICSID Convention, while other arbitral awards can be enforced under the conditions mentioned in the New York Convention on the Recognition and Enforcement of Arbitral Awards.[81]

Consequently, the investment provisions of EU IIAs are able in most cases to have direct effect, enabling individuals to claim rights based therein and to question national and EU measures that violate those rights. However, even if a provision were found to be deprived of direct effect, which is mainly relevant for the GATS, individuals can still rely on it in order to question the legality of national and EU measures. While the *Nakajima* principle would only be useful in exceptional circumstances, for example if the EU adopted a Directive on movement of key personnel explicitly referring to EU IIAs,[82] the principle of consistent interpretation can be of utmost importance, as it enables individuals to rely on the provisions of an international agreement indirectly in order to determine their rights under national and EU law.

In light of the above, it is necessary to point out that the direct effect of EU IIAs does not affect the jurisdiction of arbitral tribunals. Although EU IIAs have direct effect, this does not entail that the ECJ will substitute investment arbitration. Such concerns lack any basis. Contrary to arbitrations dealing with intra-EU investments, where investment arbitration actually conflicts with the jurisdiction of the Court of Justice, the direct effect of EU IIAs concluded with third countries does not threaten to replace the initiation of dispute settlement proceedings provided in these agreements. On the contrary, the existence of direct effect of future EU IIAs

[80] See eg Art 121 of the EPA with the CARIFORUM states. See also Section 3.2.6.

[81] See Sections 1.3.5 and 2.6.

[82] Such a Directive is expected, as key personnel are excluded from the scope of the proposed Directives on long-term and highly qualified employment of third country nationals (Proposed Directives COM/2007/0638 final, 23 October 2007 and COM/2007/0637 final, 23 October 2007 available at <http://www.libertysecurity.org/IMG/pdf_com2007_0637en01.pdf> and <http://www.libertysecurity.org/IMG/pdf_com2007_0638en01.pdf> (last accessed 10 January 2010)). Arts 3(2)(c) and 3(2)(f) of the proposed Directives provide that third country nationals 'entering a Member State *under commitments contained in an international agreement* facilitating the entry and temporary stay of certain categories of trade and investment-related natural persons' (emphasis added) are excluded from the scope of the Directive as they will be subject to specific rules.

that provide for investor-state arbitration will simply secure an additional forum for foreign investors, who, by choosing to submit their claim in national courts, have the additional guarantee of having their case heard by the Court of Justice in cases where a reference for a preliminary ruling is made by the national court.

6.2 Compatibility of Member State BITs with EU law

In addition to their obligation to respect and perform EU IIAs, the existence and exercise of EU competence over foreign investment creates a broader obligation for Member States to ensure the compatibility of their current legislation and international commitments with EU law. Although a complete examination of the compatibility of Member State rules with EU law also includes an examination of their national legislation in the field of foreign investment, this section is limited to the question of compatibility of Member State BITs with EU law, focusing on the most controversial aspect of existing Member State rules on foreign investment to and from third countries.

Within this framework, the Commission has proposed a Regulation aiming to provide the general framework regarding existing and future Member State BITs, in order to ensure legal certainty until their replacement by EU agreements.[83] However, before examining the suggested proposal regarding the future of Member State BITs, it is important to understand first the doctrinal foundations, which necessitate the authorization and eventual replacement of Member State BITs by EU IIAs.

6.2.1 The legal framework on the compatibility of Member State BITs with EU law

6.2.1.1 BITs concluded after the accession of Member States to the EU

The determination of the compatibility of Member State BITs with EU law arises as a result of the exclusive competence of the EU in the field of foreign investment and the existence of overlapping EU and national rules in areas of shared competence.

6.2.1.1.1 Incompatibilities arising as a result of EU exclusive competence
Starting with the incompatibilities of BITs with EU law resulting from the nature of EU competence in the field, the legality of Member State BITs under EU law

[83] Proposal for a regulation of the European Parliament and of the Council establishing transitional arrangements for bilateral investment agreements between Member States and third countries, Brussels 7.7.2010, COM(2010) 344 (hereinafter, Regulation Proposal); Position of the European Parliament adopted at first reading on 10 May 2011 with a view to the adoption of Regulation (EU) No.../2011 of the European Parliament and of the Council establishing transitional arrangements for bilateral investment agreements between Member States and third countries (EP-PE_TC1-COD(2010)0197) (hereinafter, Parliament Position on Investment Regulation).

depends primarily on whether they cover an area that falls under EU exclusive competence. The pre-emption of Member State powers in fields of exclusive competence suggests that the mere existence of national rules in this field violates the exclusive nature of EU competence, irrespective of whether there is an actual incompatibility between national and EU rules, or even if the EU has not yet exercised its exclusive competence.[84] In that regard, and without prejudice to the application of Article 351 TFEU, the provisions of BITs that cover a field falling under EU exclusive competence are per se incompatible with EU law, requiring specific action from the Member States.

Until the entry into force of the Lisbon Treaty, the cases of outright incompatibility of BITs with EU law were rather minimal, since no provision in the EC Treaty explicitly conferred exclusive competence to the EC in the field of foreign investment and implied exclusivity had arisen only rarely, covering only certain aspects of foreign investment in specific sectors.[85] However, incompatibilities have arisen since the Lisbon Treaty entered into force. The establishment of EU exclusive competence over FDI under Article 207 TFEU indicates first that Member State BITs concluded after the entry into force of the Lisbon Treaty are incompatible with EU law. For example, the BITs that Germany concluded with Iraq and the Republic of Congo in 2010 are per se incompatible with EU law, to the extent they regulate FDI. More importantly, all Member State BITs concluded after the accession of a Member State to the EU are rendered incompatible with EU law, as they infringe on the exclusive nature of EU competence in this field. Taking into account that the new FDI competence comprises not only the entry and promotion of foreign investment, but also investment protection,[86] all substantive and procedural provisions relating to FDI are rendered automatically incompatible with EU law and have to be eradicated, irrespective of whether and when the EU exercises its FDI competence.

In order to avoid direct incompatibility with EU law and to allow Member States to retain their BITs without violating EU law, until they are amended, it has been suggested that Article 351 TFEU applies by analogy to Member State international agreements that were concluded prior to the conversion of EU competence in a given field from shared to exclusive, thus covering post-accession Member State BITs that entered into force prior to the Lisbon Treaty.[87] However, such an expansion of the scope of Article 351 TFEU in order to cover post-accession agreements concluded before EU competence became exclusive in a specific field goes against the narrow scope of Article 351 TFEU.

[84] Joined Opinion of AG Tizzano in the *Open Skies* cases [2002] ECR I-9427, paras 112–14; Opinion of AG Maduro in Case C-205/06 *Commission v Austria* [2009] ECR I-1301 and Case C-249/06 *Commission v Sweden* [2009] ECR I-1335, para 28; Cremona, above n 2, p 129; C Franklin, 'Flexibility vs Legal Certainty: Article 307 EC and Other Issues in the Aftermath of the Open Skies Cases' (2005) 10 EFA Rev 79, 96, 99–100.

[85] See Section 2.2.2.

[86] See Section 2.2.3.1 and Section 2.5.2.

[87] S Johannsen, 'Die Kompetenz der Europäischen Union für ausländische Direktinvestitionen nach dem Vertrag von Lissabon' (2009) 90 Beiträge zum Transnationalen Wirtschaftsrecht 1, 23–6; T Eilmansberger, 'Bilateral Investment Treaties and EU Law' (2009) 46 CMLR 383, 397–8.

Article 351 TFEU has not justified departures from Union rules, in cases where the EU exercised its competence after the conclusion of an international agreement by a Member State.[88] In that regard, Member State BITs are incompatible with EU law to the extent that they regulate FDI. This position is reflected under the current Regulation Proposal, whereby authorizing the renewal of existing Member State BITs, the Commission and the Parliament recognize that they breach EU exclusive competence, so that their authorization is required in order to remain valid under EU law.[89]

6.2.1.1.2 Incompatibilities arising in areas of shared competence

Incompatibilities between Member State BITs and EU law also arise in fields of shared competence. BITs may violate specific EU law rules, including provisions of primary EU law, secondary legislation, and EU international commitments. Without prejudice to Article 351 TFEU, in cases where the application of BIT provisions conflict with EU rules, Member States breach their Union law obligation and have to comply with EU law.[90]

Member State BITs can also lead to a violation of EU rules, even if there is no EU legislation and despite the lack of exclusive competence. An incompatibility between BITs and EU law can arise when they jeopardize the future exercise of EU competence. According to the Court, the fact that the EU has powers

> on a matter which is identical to or connected with that covered by an earlier agreement concluded between a Member State and a third country, reveals an incompatibility with that agreement where, first, the agreement does not contain a provision allowing the Member State concerned to exercise its rights and to fulfil its obligations as a member of the [EU] and, second, there is also no international-law mechanism which makes that possible.[91]

Such incompatibility is premised on the duty of cooperation, which requires that Member States abstain from any measure which could jeopardize the attainment of the objectives of primary EU law. Although the Court based its decision solely on Article 351 TFEU, this provision and in particular its second subparagraph present in essence a clear illustration of the duty of cooperation which applies to all pre- and post-accession agreements.[92]

The broad enunciation of this principle does not mean that the future potential exercise of any EU competence can be jeopardized by the conclusion of an

[88] Case C-170/98 *Commission v Belgium* [1999] ECR I-5493.

[89] Regulation Proposal, recitals 10 and 11; Parliament Position on Investment Regulation, recital 9.

[90] Opinion of AG Maduro, above n 84, paras 25, 27; Case C-55/00 *Gottardo v INPS* [2002] ECR I-413, para 33.

[91] Case C-205/06 *Commission v Austria* [2009] ECR I-1301 and Case C-249/06 *Commission v Sweden* [2009] ECR I-1335, para 37; Case C-118/07 *Commission v Finland* [2009] ECR I-10889, para 31.

[92] Opinion of AG Maduro, above n 84, paras 33–43; P Koutrakos, 'Comment Case C-205/06, *Commission v Austria*, judgment of the Court (Grand Chamber) of 3 March 2009, not yet reported; Case C-249/06, *Commission v Sweden*, judgment of the Court (Grand Chamber) of 3 March 2009, not yet reported' (2009) 46 CMLR 2059, 2060–1.

international agreement by a Member State. Such an interpretation would actually result in severely curtailing Member State powers in fields of shared competence, where Member States can legitimately take action until the EU decides to adopt its own measures.[93] For example, were such a broad reading of the principle that an incompatibility arises to the extent that it jeopardizes the future exercise of EU competence adopted, an all-embracing NT provision of a Member State BIT, even if limited by a negative list, would jeopardize the exercise of EU competence in the future, as it would not allow for the effective adoption of EU measures, which may limit the right of establishment of third country nationals in a specific sector.

Partly recognizing these concerns, the Court emphasized first that its judgments, which concerned compatibility of Member State BITs with the capital movement provisions of primary EU law, do not prejudge the obligations of Member States in other circumstances.[94] In that respect, it could be argued that the enunciation of this principle by the Court should be read narrowly within the particular legal context of capital movement rules, which permit the EU to adopt urgent measures in exceptional circumstances. However, such a narrow reading of this principle appears to conflict with the broad wording adopted by the Court, which refers generally to any area of shared competence, as well as with its underlying rationale, since the duty of cooperation applies in all fields of shared competence.

Nevertheless, the Court offers specific criteria that allow for a narrow reading of its judgments. It should be highlighted that the Court conditions the incompatibility of a Member State's international agreement on the existence of international law rules, both general and specific to that agreement, that enable a Member State to apply and implement any EU rules that may be adopted in the future regarding the same subject matter in relations with the same third country. As the Advocate General clarified in his Opinion, incompatibilities arise only if the international obligations of Member States are liable to

> *de facto* restrict the freedom which the Treaty confers on the [EU] to act in those areas. That will depend on the nature of both the national measures or international obligations and the [EU] competences affected, for example the urgency of the measures to be adopted under such competences.[95]

Based on these statements it is argued that two important conditions must be fulfilled in order for an incompatibility to arise: first, the international commitment entered into by a Member State must be able to restrict de facto the freedom of the EU to act. Hence, an incompatibility arises only if the Member State's international obligation precludes the exercise of EU competence in the sense that *any* measure taken by the EU under the relevant power-conferring provision would be incompatible with the Member State's obligation. In determining when a Member State agreement precludes entirely the adoption of an EU measure, specific attention should be paid to the scope and objectives that Union action serves under a specific

[93] J Klabbers, *Treaty Conflict and the European Union* (2009), pp 184, 190; *Commission v Finland*, above n 91, para 46.

[94] *Commission v Finland*, above n 91, para 49.

[95] Opinion of AG Maduro, above n 84, para 33.

power-conferring provision. Secondly, even in such cases, an incompatibility can be avoided if the Member State avails itself of international law mechanisms that enable it to adjust its international obligation so as not to conflict with future EU measures. Such mechanisms could be found in the Member State's international agreements, such as an exception or renegotiation clause, or in general international law.[96]

In all cases where an incompatibility of Member State BITs with EU law arises, compliance with EU law requires that Member States take all appropriate and available measures in order to eradicate the incompatibility. Considering that compliance with EU law would probably require an amendment or even a denunciation of a Member State's treaty, EU law lacks general rules concerning the appropriate measures that have to be taken. In practice, the Court has provided little guidance, stating that the amendment of Member State agreements within a reasonable time frame has to be pursued first and, only if this is impossible, denunciation is required.[97] Even though this indicates that the principle of proportionality should also be applied with regard to the action required by Member States,[98] it does not offer specific guidance as to the secondary obligations that Member States bear, nor does it deal with the question of whether, when, and under what conditions EU action can or has to be taken in the fields that fall under its exclusive competence.

Regardless of the EU law effects on incompatible BITs, their validity and application as international agreements is not affected. Until Member States denounce or renegotiate an incompatible BIT with the third country at issue, it remains in force and has to be applied. As a result, until an incompatible BIT is amended and to the extent that there is no authorization under EU law permitting such incompatibility,[99] Member States have conflicting obligations, so that if they apply the provisions of the BIT, they infringe EU law.

6.2.1.2 BITs concluded prior to the accession of Member States to the EU

Recognizing that Member States may have international commitments under treaties concluded with third countries, primary EU law includes a specific provision on international agreements concluded prior to the accession to the EU. Article 351 TFEU introduces specific rules regarding Member State international agreements concluded prior to their accession to the EU. Considering that the number of BITs has increased dramatically over the last 15 years, Article 351 TFEU plays only a limited role, concerning mainly the BITs concluded by newly acceded Member States.[100]

[96] See also Koutrakos, above n 92, pp 2067–73, who argues in favour of a similar two-tier test, according to which an incompatibility arises only if a Member State's international agreement undermines the 'practical effectiveness' of EU law, and other alternatives under international law, such as the consistent interpretation of EU rules and Member State international agreements, are not possible.

[97] *Commission v Belgium*, above n 88.

[98] Franklin, above n 84, p 97.

[99] See below Section 6.2.3.

[100] Klabbers, above n 93, pp 212–13.

Article 351 TFEU introduces an exception to the rule that Member States' international agreements have to comply with EU law, as it grandfathers pre-accession agreements between Member States and third countries. This does not mean that incompatibilities found between Member State treaties and EU law are not addressed. Paragraph 2 provides explicitly that if such agreements are incompatible with EU law, Member States have the obligation to take all appropriate measures in order to eliminate the incompatibilities. Hence, Article 351 TFEU differs from the general rules that apply to agreements concluded after EU accession in the sense that the existence of incompatibilities does not infringe EU law per se and Member States can apply their prior agreements. An infringement of EU law exists only if a Member State does not take the appropriate measures to eradicate such incompatibilities.[101]

Even though Article 351 TFEU refers only to incompatibilities, thus covering cases where there is a direct conflict between a Member State BIT and EU rules,[102] it should be interpreted as also covering cases where prior international commitments exist in an area of EU exclusive competence, irrespective of whether there is a direct conflict.[103] In such cases, however, the incompatibility of Member State international agreements with EU law, and thus the obligation to take the appropriate measures to eradicate it, arises at the moment when EU competence becomes exclusive or at the moment of accession, whichever is the later. In that respect, Article 351 TFEU safeguards Member State BITs concluded prior to EU accession, which conflict with the exclusive nature of EU competence over FDI under the Common Commercial Policy (CCP). However, Article 351 TFEU has to be narrowly interpreted, so that it covers only obligations of Member States and not their rights under previous agreements.[104]

As a result, both in cases of pre- and post-accession agreements, the existence of incompatibilities between Member State BITs and EU rules creates the obligation for the Member States to amend a BIT or denunciate it. While Member States do not have to apply conflicting rules simultaneously when Article 351 TFEU applies, this does not mean that they can evade their obligation to conform eventually to EU law and eradicate the incompatibilities.

6.2.2 The fields of substantive incompatibility between BITs and EU law

The existence of many incompatibilities between Member State BITs and EU law has been already acknowledged by EU institutions, Member States, and third countries, which have indicated that the application of Member State BITs can

[101] For an analysis of the mechanism of Art 351 TFEU see Klabbers, above n 93, ch 6; Koutrakos, above n 2, pp 302–4; Cremona, above n 2, pp 131–5; J Klabbers, 'Moribund on the fourth of July? The Court of Justice on prior agreements of the Member States' (2001) 26 EL Rev 187.

[102] So far the case law of the Court of Justice on Art 351 TFEU concerns only incompatibilities with specific EU rules. See Franklin, above n 84, pp 100–2.

[103] To that effect see Opinion of AG Maduro, above n 84, para 28.

[104] Case C-158/91 *Ministere public and Direction du travail et d'emploi v Levy* [1993] ECR I-4287, para 12.

result in a violation of EU rules. During the negotiations preceding the enlargement of Central and East European countries to the EU in 2004, the Commission pointed out the problem of incompatibility between the BITs that these new Member States had concluded with the United States and EU law, resulting in the Commission, the newly acceded Member States, and the United States signing a Memorandum of Understanding (MOU).[105] Aiming to maintain the BITs and to achieve full compliance and implementation of the *acquis* in these Member States, the MOU presented an effort to balance the interests of all parties, without requiring a renegotiation of those Member State BITs with the United States.[106]

The MOU indicated the areas of potential conflict between these BITs and EU law and offered a partial and political solution to the problem of incompatible BITs, mainly by providing for transitional periods and the consistent interpretation of those BITs and EU rules.[107] Considering that its legal nature is questionable, as it does not create legally binding obligations and that it is not subject to judicial review, it presents only the parties' 'best efforts' to find a solution to the problem.[108] In addition, the MOU offered a political solution which covers only eight BITs, excluding not only all other BITs concluded by the newly acceded Member States but also all BITs concluded by the other Member States, prior to and after their accession to the EU.

Unfortunately, EU institutions have not used the opportunity provided under the Regulation Proposal regarding the authorization of Member State BITs to address the substantive areas where incompatibilities between Member State BITs and EU law arise. Opting for vague and ambiguous references to the existence of 'conflicts with Union law',[109] EU institutions decided to disregard the detailed scrutiny of Member State BITs that was undertaken when the MOU with the United States was negotiated.[110] Although a detailed description of all incompatibilities would result in an insurmountable task for the Commission, affecting the flexibility envisaged by the Commission, the Regulation could have been used for broadly sketching the main areas where incompatibilities may arise.

In that respect and using the MOU as a guide, the incompatibilities between BITs and EU law are examined below, following, to a large extent, the categorization of the different aspects of foreign investment regulation.

[105] Memorandum of Understanding (MOU) between the United States, the European Commission, and Acceding and Candidate Countries for accession to the European Union.

[106] Koutrakos, above n 2, pp 321–3.

[107] For an analytical approach to the practical solutions that the MOU offers see A Radu, 'Foreign Investors in the EU—Which "Best Treatment"? Interactions Between Bilateral Investment Treaties and EU Law' (2008) 14 European Law Journal 237; M Burgstaller, 'European Law and Investment Treaties' (2009) 26 Journal of International Arbitration 181, 200–3.

[108] Radu, above n 107, pp 238–9; Koutrakos, above n 2, p 325.

[109] Regulation Proposal, Art 5(1).

[110] On how the flexibility provided in the Regulation Proposal should be used see below Section 6.2.3.

6.2.2.1 Incompatibilities regarding capital movements

The first area where incompatibilities arise is capital movements. In most cases the provisions on free transfer of capital found under all BITs are incompatible with EU law, as they conflict directly with Union rules and jeopardize the potential exercise of EU competence in the field.

As argued above with regard to the relation between EU IIAs and Member State BITs under international law, BITs may provide for the free transfer of funds related to an investment, without allowing any exceptions to this rule, while EU IIAs allow for potential exceptions to capital movements.[111] Such provisions in BITs with countries which have also concluded an EU IIA, directly conflict with the provisions of the EU IIAs, as the application of an exception under the EU IIA would violate the obligation for free transfer under the BIT.

Furthermore, incompatibilities exist not only in BITs concluded with third countries that are parties to an EU IIA, but also in all other BITs that do not provide for exceptions similar to those found under Articles 64, 66, and 75 TFEU. Such provisions would jeopardize the effective exercise of EU competence to adopt restrictive measures with regard to third countries under these articles. Indeed, the absolute scope of the BIT capital transfer provisions would de facto conflict with *any* possible measure that the EU could adopt under these provisions. Secondly, neither the provisions of BITs nor the mechanisms offered by international law, such as suspension of the agreement, could guarantee the practical effectiveness of EU measures adopted under these articles.[112] For example, as AG Maduro advocates, the adoption of safeguard measures under Article 66 TFEU, which are of a temporary nature, would be severely undermined, since

> having to wait for an actual conflict between [EU] legislation and the international obligations to arise before initiating all the necessary steps to eliminate such incompatibility would deprive the [EU] legislation of its effectiveness. It would amount to a restriction on the power that the Treaty confers on the [EU].[113]

Besides, BIT provisions that subject free transfer of capital to national laws or to similar limitations cannot sufficiently cover all possible limitations to capital movements that can be imposed in accordance with EU law.[114]

6.2.2.2 Incompatibilities regarding the admission of foreign investment

As discussed, the vast majority of Member State BITs do not include provisions relating to the admission of foreign investment.[115] Nevertheless, an insignificant number of BITs, and more specifically those concluded between newly acceded Member States and the United States or Canada, extend the scope of the most

[111] See Section 5.2.2.3.

[112] *Commission v Austria* and *Commission v Sweden*, above n 91, paras 38–40 and 39–41 respectively. See also above Section 6.2.1.1.2.

[113] Opinion of AG Maduro, above n 84, para 52.

[114] Ibid, paras 58–61; Case *Commission v Finland*, above n 91, paras 41–2.

[115] See Section 1.3.2.

favoured nation (MFN) and national treatment (NT) obligation to the pre-establishment stage, thus in essence conferring market access rights to foreign investors in all sectors that are not included in the lists annexed to those BITs.

Considering the incompatibility of BITs with EU law regarding admission and establishment of FDI, it is necessary to point out, first, that they conflict with EU exclusive competence over FDI. Incompatibilities arise when a Member State's international agreement falls within the scope of EU exclusive competence, irrespective of whether such competence has been exercised. Nevertheless, considering that BITs covering establishment provisions are almost exclusively post-accession agreements of new Member States, they fall within the scope of Article 351 TFEU.

Turning, secondly, to the existence of incompatibilities regarding BIT provisions on admission of other forms of foreign investment, certain incompatibilities arise, as such BIT provisions may conflict with secondary EU legislation. A number of EU instruments include provisions that limit the right of foreign investors to enter and operate in the internal market. For example, in the field of government procurement secondary legislation imposes limitations on the right of participation of third country nationals. As a result, the NT standard provided for in Member State BITs is incompatible with secondary legislation that imposes such limitations, while the same incompatibility also exists with regard to the MFN standard, insofar as the latter covers the treatment provided to nationals from other EU Member States, which according to EU law is identical to NT.

Avoiding such incompatibilities, these BITs have a Regional Economic Integration Organization (REIO) clause, which excludes from the scope of the MFN the treatment provided to nationals of other EU Member States.[116] Furthermore, the MOU provides, in the form of negative lists, exceptions to the NT requirement, attempting to ensure their compatibility with EU law. Despite the existence of the negative list, which includes the majority of fields where secondary legislation imposes limitations on the right of third country nationals to establish themselves,[117] a negative list cannot always ensure future compatibility with EU law. For example, the aforementioned legislation on government procurement that imposes limitations on the rights of third country nationals entered into force after the signature of the MOU, therefore it is not covered by the negative list annexed to the MOU, thus giving rise to conflicting obligations.[118]

6.2.2.3 Incompatibilities regarding post-establishment treatment

Similar to the BIT provisions on admission of foreign investment, the provisions conferring NT or MFN treatment to foreign investors at the post-establishment stage can be incompatible with EU law in many cases. First of all, such provisions, to the extent that they are applicable to FDI, are incompatible with EU exclusive competence over FDI. Secondly, such BIT provisions are in direct conflict with EU secondary legislation or provisions in EU IIAs imposing restrictions on the

[116] On the scope and extent of the REIO clause and its effects see Section 3.2.2.4.2.

[117] Radu, above n 107, pp 251–2. [118] Ibid.

post-establishment treatment of foreign investors. Even though such restrictions are rather rare, given that most Member States and the EU have concluded the Organisation for Economic Co-Operation and Development (OECD) National Treatment Instrument, there are still limitations affecting the national treatment of foreign investors.[119] In addition, the lack of a REIO clause in a number of Member State BITs, such as in the Denmark-Indonesia BIT,[120] indicates that the MFN provision in these BITs is also in conflict with the limitations on the post-establishment treatment of foreign investors.

Furthermore, even if there is a negative list attached to the NT standard at the post-establishment stage covering limitations found under secondary legislation, the NT provision can still be incompatible with EU law, at the moment when the EU adopts legislation that imposes restrictions on the operation of foreign investors that are not covered under the BIT. For example, in the field of financial services the EU may potentially impose common limitations on the treatment provided to branches of third country financial institutions established in EU Member States. Such legislation would be incompatible with the unfettered NT standard provided in BITs.

Also, the few BITs that have provisions banning performance requirements can be incompatible with EU law. Even though the potential for conflict is limited, given that the EU cannot impose trade-related performance requirements, it is possible that the prohibition of performance requirements in BITs covers requirements beyond the scope of the Agreement on Trade-Related Investment Measures (TRIMs) which may be permitted or even imposed under EU law.[121]

6.2.2.4 Incompatibilities arising from the need for equal treatment of all EU nationals in EU Member States

Incompatibilities between Member State BITs and EU law may arise as a result of the consideration of EU companies established in accordance with Article 54 TFEU as foreign investors. As has already been mentioned, many BITs still use the criterion of ownership and control, next to the criteria of incorporation and effective seat, in order to define the nationality of a foreign investor and whether he or she falls under their scope.[122] On the contrary, Article 54 TFEU confers EU 'nationality' to all firms set up in the EU regardless of whether they are owned or controlled by foreign nationals. More specifically, all firms having their registered office, central administration, or principal place of business in an EU Member State benefit from the application of the non-discrimination rules, and in particular from the application of the NT principle. As EU law prohibits discriminatory measures violating NT, even in fields where no harmonization exists, Member States are obliged to grant non-discriminatory treatment to undertakings established in accordance with Article 54 TFEU.[123] As the element of control is not

[119] Ibid, p 249.
[120] European Commission, Press Release IP/04/618 (10 May 2004).
[121] Eg provisions establishing quotas for agricultural products. [122] See Section 1.2.1.3.
[123] It is only insofar as the treatment of foreign-controlled undertakings is concerned, which are not established in accordance with Art 54 TFEU, such as branches and agencies, that the Member States are free to decide whether to provide non-discriminatory treatment.

included under Article 54 TFEU, the possibility exists that a company can be considered both as a national of an EU Member State and as a foreign investor established in the EU, thus falling under the scope of a Member State BIT.[124]

The fact that a company qualifies both as a third country foreign investor in the EU and as an EU national signifies that it can benefit from the provisions of both regimes, choosing each time the one that fits its interests. Such companies can benefit from the application of EU law, if it offers better treatment to EU nationals than to foreign nationals. Furthermore, and more relevant for the incompatibility of Member State BITs with EU law, they can benefit from the provisions of BITs, which offer companies rights and remedies not available under EU law.

More specifically, BITs offer to foreign investors certain substantive rights that are not found in EU law. Even though EU nationals enjoy MFN and NT under EU law, at least equal to BITs, all BITs offer foreign investors fair and equal treatment (FET) and protection against expropriation; rights which do not exist as such under EU law. Arguably, EU law provides for similar treatment to the FET standard, while EU law guarantees the property rights of EU nationals from interferences resulting from EU action.[125] However, even if it were considered that EU law creates equivalent substantive rights for third country foreign investors/EU nationals,[126] the BIT offers procedural rights that EU law does not. As the tribunal in the *Eastern Sugar* award rightly noted, '[t]he BIT also provides for a special procedural protection in the form of arbitration between the investor and the host state'.[127] The existence of investor-state arbitration is a unique feature of BITs, which is not replicated under EU law. EU nationals do not enjoy a direct right to initiate arbitration proceedings against an EU Member State for the alleged breach of their rights under primary EU law.

The fact that a company can indulge in 'treaty shopping', choosing to exercise its rights either as an EU company or as a foreign investor[128] does not seem to raise incompatibilities with EU law as such. The Union legal order does not prohibit EU nationals from benefitting from rights accrued to them under national or international law that do not exist under EU law. As long as the system of protection of these extra rights respects the primacy and autonomy of EU law, in the sense that it does not extend to determine the rights and obligations of EU nationals under EU law, companies can effectively pursue such additional rights under the relevant legal regime.[129]

[124] See Section 1.2.2.1.2.

[125] L Mola, 'Which Role for the EU in the Development of International Investment Law?', Society of International Economic Law, Online Proceedings Working Paper No 26/08, p 16, available at <http://www.ssrn.com/link/SIEL-Inaugural-Conference.html> (last accessed 1 May 2011). See also Section 2.5.3 and Section 3.2.2.4.3.

[126] Cf *Eastern Sugar BV v Czech Republic*, ICC Partial Award and Partial Dissenting Opinion, 27 March 2007, paras 164, 169, 170; C Soderlund, 'Intra-EU BIT Investment Protection and the EC Treaty' (2007) 24 Journal of International Arbitration 455.

[127] *Eastern Sugar* award, above n 126, para 164.

[128] Radu, above n 107, p 245.

[129] H Wehland, 'Intra-EU Investment Agreements and Arbitration: Is European Community Law an Obstacle?' (2009) 58 ICLQ 297, 310.

Nevertheless, the fact that the BIT between a Member State and a third country provides additional rights and benefits only to certain EU nationals—namely those that are foreign-controlled—breaches the general principle of non-discrimination between EU nationals. Drawing a parallel to the jurisprudence of the Court in the field of tax and social policy law, the principle of non-discrimination requires that where a Member State grants an advantage to some or all of its nationals under a bilateral agreement with a third country it must, on the basis of the equal treatment requirement, extend this advantage to all EU companies.[130] In that respect, the requirement of equal treatment of all EU nationals can be interpreted in the context of BITs in such a way that a Member State has to confer to all EU nationals the rights conferred to foreign-controlled EU nationals under a BIT.

Despite the broad enunciation of the principle of equal treatment, it does not mean that all advantages under bilateral agreements must be extended to all other EU nationals automatically. Elaborating on the principle of equal treatment, the Court has found that exceptions to equal treatment are possible, as long as different treatment is justified.[131] As Cremona points out, 'the principle is one of equal treatment and it may well be that those nationals are not in the same situation with respect to the benefits in question'.[132]

Applying this rule to the benefits accrued to foreign-owned or controlled EU companies under BITs, there does not seem to be any reason justifying why only these EU companies can benefit from investment protection provisions and from investor-state arbitration. First, the principle of reciprocity found in a Member State agreement with a third country does not per se place the EU nationals covered by its provisions in a different situation from other EU nationals. The fact that reciprocal rights apply only to nationals of the two contracting states is the inherent characteristic of Member State international agreements that results in the original difference in treatment and, therefore, it cannot justify the different treatment.[133] Furthermore, as the Court manifestly declared in *Factortame II*,

[130] Case C-307/97 *Saint-Gobain v Finanzamt Aachen-Innenstadt* [1999] ECR I-6161, para 59 and Case C-55/00 *Gottardo v INPS* [2002] ECR I-413 para 32; Cremona, above n 2, pp 136–8; Eilmansberger, above n 87, pp 402–3. Cf Wehland (above n 129, pp 312, 314) who argues that *Saint Gobain* and *Gottardo* do not require equal treatment of EU foreign investors, as in these cases the incriminating advantages were granted by one Member State to its own nationals, and could be extended to other EU nationals without amending the bilateral agreement, while in the case of BITs it is actually the third country that offers the advantageous rights, namely the right to initiate investor-state arbitration, to the nationals of one EU Member State, so that only through amendment of a BIT could the advantage be granted to other EU nationals. However, this argument does not take into account the incriminating advantage that a Member State grants to some of its own nationals, namely those who are foreign-controlled and qualify both as nationals of that Member State under Art 54 TFEU and as foreign investors under the BIT, which makes it possible to initiate arbitration proceedings against their own country.

[131] Case C–376/*03 D v Inspecteur van de Belastingdienst/Particulieren/Ondernemingen buitenland te Heerlen* [2005] ECR I–05821.

[132] Cremona, above n 2, p 138.

[133] Cf *D v Inspecteur van de Belastingdienst*, above n 131, where the justification of different tax treatment was based on the fact that the treaty at issue only applied to residents and nationals of the Member States party to it. The circular logic of the Court where the cause of the difference in treatment was also held to be the reason why the situations were not comparable has been heavily criticized. As AG Bot argued in the *OESF* case (Case C-194/06 *Orange European Smallcap Fund*

a national measure imposing limitations to the freedom of establishment of EU companies based on the nationality of the persons owning or controlling that company is illegal.[134] Hence, the nationality of the person owning or controlling an EU company does not appear to present a legitimate criterion justifying different treatment of EU companies.

Of course, different treatment of EU companies on the basis of their control is possible in cases where primary EU law provides for exceptions to free movement rules, which may provide justification. Considering that the TFEU provides only for limited exceptions, different treatment of foreign-owned or controlled EU companies is possible mainly for reasons of public policy or public security.[135] Even though these exceptions could, under specific circumstances, justify discriminatory treatment against foreign-controlled EU nationals, depriving them of certain EU law benefits, it is difficult to imagine how public security and public policy reasons could justify that foreign-controlled EU legal persons are treated better than EU-controlled legal persons and deprive EU-controlled companies of such benefits.

Finally, it should be added that the incompatibility of BITs with EU law resulting from their coverage of foreign-owned and/or controlled EU investors does not mean that the BIT provisions need to be amended. As the Court emphasized, the Member State that offers preferential treatment only to certain EU nationals has to extend this advantage unilaterally to all other EU nationals.[136] As the *Eastern Sugar* tribunal rightly noted, if a BIT gives rights to certain EU investors that it does not give to other EU nationals, it will be for the latter to claim their equal rights.[137] Hence, unless Member States amend their BITs, excluding from the scope of the definition of foreign investors those that are incorporated in accordance with Article 54 TFEU, they have to provide for investor-state arbitration for all other EU nationals established in their territory.

6.2.2.5 Incompatibilities arising from the need for equal treatment of all EU nationals in third countries

The principle of equal treatment of EU nationals also has another dimension which leads to incompatibilities of Member State BITs with EU law. The Court has clearly declared in the *Open Skies* cases[138] that equal treatment not only concerns

[2008] ECR I-3447) 'In so far as the rule established in *D*, thus appears to constitute an exception to the principle of non-discrimination, it must in my view be interpreted strictly' (para 103). See also A Cordewener and E Reimer, 'The Future of Most-Favoured-Nation Treatment in EC Tax Law—Did the ECJ Pull the Emergency Brake without Real Need?—Part 2' (2006) 5 European Taxation 291, 293–4; J Schuch, 'Critical notes on the European Court of Justice's decision on most-favoured-nation treatment under tax treaties (2006) *EC Tax Review* 6, 8. Cf Wehland, above n 129, pp 316–17.

134 Case C-221/89 *Factortame II* [1991] ECR I-3905, paras 29–33.

135 MOU Annex G.

136 *Gottardo v INPS*, above n 130, para 34.

137 *Eastern Sugar* award, above n 126, para 170.

138 Case C-466/98 *Commission v UK* [2002] ECR I-9427; Case C-467/98 *Commission v Denmark* [2002] ECR I-9519; Case C-468/98 *Commission v Sweden* [2002] ECR I-9575; Case C-469/98 *Commission v Finland* [2002] ECR I-9627; Case C-471/98 *Commission v Belgium* [2002] ECR

the advantages that a Member State grants to its own nationals, but also the advantages that a third country is offering to the nationals of a specific Member State via a bilateral agreement. In such cases, the bilateral agreement between a Member State and a third country conflicts with EU law, because a Member State allows a third country to discriminate against other EU nationals.[139]

Applying the *Open Skies* reasoning on Member State BITs, it is obvious that the latter are incompatible with EU law. BITs not only offer advantages to foreign investors established in an EU Member State, but they also offer the same advantages to the nationals of that Member State established in the third country. However, other EU nationals do not enjoy the same advantages in the third country as the nationals of that Member State, in particular the right to investor-state arbitration. As there are no grounds that could justify different treatment of other EU nationals,[140] the principle of equal treatment necessitates that they are accorded the same treatment in the third country. Therefore, all BITs of Member States with any third country are incompatible with EU law, as their definition of foreign investor covers only the nationals of that Member State and excludes other EU nationals.[141]

Contrary to the incompatibilities raised by unequal treatment of EU nationals in a Member State, this incompatibility cannot be resolved through the adoption of unilateral measures from the Member State that breached EU law, as it is the third country that has to extend the advantages to other EU nationals. In that regard, an amendment of all Member State BITs is required and Member States have to convince third countries to extend the beneficiaries of the BIT rights to all other EU nationals.

6.2.3 The transition from Member State BITs to EU IIAs

It is obvious that all Member State BITs are to a certain extent incompatible with EU law and have to be renegotiated in order to ensure compatibility. In addition to the incompatibilities resulting from EU exclusive competence on FDI, the degree and extent of incompatibility of each BIT needs to be assessed individually, given

I-9681; Case C-472/98 *Commission v Luxemburg* [2002] ECR I-9741; Case C-975/98 *Commission v Austria* [2002] ECR I-9797; Case C-976/98 *Commission v Germany* [2002] ECR I-9855.

139 Cremona, above n 2, pp 138–9; N Lavranos, 'Case Notes on the *Open Skies* cases' (2003) 30 LIEI 81, 89.

140 See above Section 6.2.2.4.

141 Cf Wehland (above n 129, pp 314–15) who argues that such an expansive reading of the *Open Skies* cases would actually strip Member States of their external competences and that, in the case of foreign investment, the non-extension of the benefits of investor-state arbitration to all EU nationals would not affect their competitive position in the internal market as in the field of transport. Considering that EU law can impose a variety of limitations on the exercise of the external competences of Member States, the argument that Member State powers are considerably restricted in the field of foreign investment in comparison to air transport does not appear to have substantial merit. In addition, arguing that the advantages offered by a BIT to only certain EU nationals does not affect competitive conditions in the internal market disregards the role of BITs as investment determinants. If an EU national intends to invest in a specific third country, the existence of BITs between that third country and only a few Member States can severely affect her decision to set up a primary establishment in a Member State that has concluded a BIT.

the different provisions that each agreement incorporates. In that respect, the existence of more than 1,200 BITs concluded by Member States with third countries indicates the significant body of international treaties that need to be thoroughly examined for incompatibilities with EU law. Nevertheless, this is not the first time the EU has been faced with such a challenge. The introduction of EU exclusive competences, such as in the areas of trade, air transport, and freedom, security, and justice have raised concerns in the past regarding the transition from a national to an EU policy framework.[142] For example, the renegotiation and conclusion of the new Lugano Convention[143] by the EU alone, which replaced the old Lugano Convention concluded between European Free Trade Association (EFTA) countries and EU Member States, is an illustrative example of how a Union agreement replaces Member State agreements in a field of exclusive competence.[144] Building on past experiences, the EU and its Member States can use similar methods in order to replace existing Member State agreements by new agreements, promoting legal certainty and guaranteeing the advantages accrued to EU and third country investors under the existing network of BITs.

As a result, EU institutions are currently in the process of introducing secondary legislation that will set the foundations for a smooth transition from Member States' investment policies to EU investment policy. More specifically, the Commission has proposed a Regulation aiming to provide the general framework regarding existing and future Member State BITs, in order to ensure legal certainty until their replacement by EU IIAs.

6.2.3.1 The long-term objective of replacing Member State BITs with EU IIAs

In light of the broad incompatibilities between Member State BITs and EU law, the long-term objective of the EU is to replace Member State BITs with EU IIAs. Indeed, a comprehensive EU investment policy would be unattainable, were Member State BITs kept intact beyond a transitional period. This long-term objective, which presents the main rationale behind the proposed Regulation on transitional arrangements for Member State BITs, is explicitly recognized by EU institutions.[145] Indeed, the Parliament emphasizes the 'transitional validity of bilateral investment agreements concluded by Member States', as the 'Commission shall take the necessary steps towards a progressive replacement of all existing agreements'.[146]

[142] For an overview on the transition from national to EU policy in the fields of trade, air transport, and freedom, security, and justice see A Lykotrafiti, 'Consolidation and rationalization in the transatlantic air transport market—prospects and challenges for competition and consumer welfare' TILEC Discussion Paper 2011–33, pp 13–25; M Cremona, 'Member States as Trustees of the Community Interest: Participating in International Agreements on Behalf of the European Community', EUI Working Paper LAW 2009/17, pp 16–18.

[143] Convention on jurisdiction and the recognition and enforcement of judgments in civil and commercial matters [2009] OJ L147/5.

[144] The exclusive character of EU competence to conclude the Lugano Convention was recognized by the Court in Opinion 1/2003 ([2006] ECR I-1).

[145] Regulation Proposal, recital 4.

[146] Parliament Position on Investment Regulation, recitals 4 and 5.

Within this policy framework, the authorization of existing and future Member State BITs presents only a transitional measure which shall not impede the development of future EU investment policy.[147] Guaranteeing the transitional nature of the authorization mechanism, the Regulation Proposal grants power to the Commission to withdraw authorization of existing BITs and deny authorization for the conclusion of new or amended BITs by Member States, if they affect the development of the EU investment policy.[148] More specifically, the Commission will be allowed to block Member State BITs if they present a (serious) obstacle to the conclusion of future EU IIAs. Without elaborating further on how these provisions should be interpreted, it is obvious that the initiation of negotiations of an EU IIA with a third country covering the same subject matter as a Member State BIT will result in the latter's termination.[149] This position is reinforced by the suggested addition to Article 6(1) of the explicit statement that 'The authorization provided... shall be withdrawn where the Union has already ratified an agreement with the same third country related to investment negotiated by the Commission.' Moreover, recognizing that Member States may deploy their powers in the Council to delay the implementation of EU investment policy, the Regulation Proposal provides another innovative mechanism that can contribute to the speedier and more efficient implementation of EU investment policy. It grants the power to the Commission to withdraw authorization of Member State BITs if the Council delays for more than a year in authorizing the opening of EU negotiations on investment with a specific third country.[150]

As a result, the replacement of Member State BITs by EU IIAs remains a long-term objective of the EU. Despite suggestions to limit the duration of the authorization, they have not so far been reflected in the text of the Regulation Proposal. Such policy orientation recognizes that the substitution of Member State BITs by EU IIAs would necessarily imply tremendous coordination and require substantial resources in order to be completed.[151] Besides, it may be politically difficult, as it would require Member States to convince third states to renegotiate their agreements with the EU, thus losing their negotiating leverage. Nevertheless, the authorization of existing Member State BITs and the potential for their amendment need not result in a lengthy transitional period as in the field of trade, where the transitional arrangements under Council Decision 69/494/EEC[152] lasted for more than 30 years.[153] Following the main

[147] Ibid, recital 8.

[148] Ibid, Arts 5(1)(b), 6(1)(b) and (c), 9(1)(d), and 11(3).

[149] S Woolcock and J Kleinheisterkamp, 'The EU approach to international investment policy after the Lisbon Treaty', Study Directorate General for External Policies of the Union (October 2010), p 64.

[150] Regulation Proposal, Art 6(1)(c). See Woolcock and Kleinheisterkamp, above n 149, p 65.

[151] European Parliament Resolution of 6 April 2011 on the future European international investment policy (2010/2203IINI)), para 16.

[152] Council Decision 69/494/EEC on the progressive standardisation of agreements concerning commercial relations between Member States and third countries and on the negotiation of Community agreements (16 December 1969), OJ L326 (29 December 1969), pp 39–42.

[153] Until 2001 the Council issued regulations that authorized Member States to renew certain bilateral trade agreements with third countries. Recognizing the benefits arising from the substantive scope of such agreements, the Commission was eager to propose their renewal as long as there

rationale behind the development of EU trade policy, namely that it followed the degree of internal integration,[154] it would suggest that a shorter transition period for EU investment policy is feasible and desirable. The introduction of EU investment policy comes during a different era, where the foundations of EU integration and the general characteristics of the role of the EU as an international actor are well established.

In that respect, granting review and authorization powers to the Commission instead of the Council, as well as recognition of the delay in the Council to authorize opening EU negotiations on investment with a specific third country as a valid ground for withdrawal of authorization of Member State BITs, can contribute to the speedier and more efficient implementation of EU investment policy.[155] In addition, drawing inspiration from the recent enlargement experience, the accomplishment of this task by the Commission and the Member States is not insurmountable. Recording and grouping the Member States' investment agreements as well as prioritizing their renegotiation could be well planned and executed by the EU and its Member States. In that respect, the prioritization of EU negotiating partners which the Commission proposes[156] can boost the gradual substitution of Member State BITs more efficiently. Finally, the EU can also draw some insights from other mechanisms used previously during the transition from national to Community policies. The Commission could insist, for example, on the inclusion in every new or amended Member State BIT of a clause that would provide that any future renegotiation of a Member State BIT would be undertaken by the EU (in addition to the contracting Member State), which could assist in faster recognition of the EU as an international actor in the field of foreign investment.

6.2.3.2 Authorizing existing and future Member State BITs

Although Member State BITs should be gradually substituted by EU IIAs, existing Member State BITs should be preserved until their replacement by EU IIAs. An immediate denunciation of Member State BITs would result in a deterioration of the competitive position of EU investors, as they would not be able to claim protection and favourable treatment under existing BITs. Such an extension of the right of Member States to retain their BITs does not violate EU law, as the Court has recognized that in areas of EU competence Member States can be given permission to keep their bilateral agreements in force until they are replaced by EU agreements.[157] Within this framework, the proposed regulation determines the

were no similar or conflicting rules established at the EU or international level. For a detailed analysis of the transition from national to EU trade policy see A Dimopoulos, 'The development of EU trade and investment policies: drawing lessons from past experiences' in Sauvant and Ortino (eds), *Yearbook on International Investment Law and Policy 2010–2011* (forthcoming 2011).

[154] See Section 4.1.1.1.1.

[155] Cf Woolcock and Kleinheisterkamp, above n 149, p 67, who argue that the mechanism proposed 'does not really contribute to enhancing legal certainty but could be seen as an instrument to give the Commission more leverage in its relation with Member States that are reluctant to change or give up their BITs'.

[156] Investment Policy Communication, pp 6–7. See also Section 4.1.1.3.

[157] Case 41/76 *Donckerwolcke* [1976] ECR 1921.

conditions under which Member States can retain their existing BITs and conclude new ones in the future. Ensuring legal certainty and promoting the interests of foreign investors, the Regulation Proposal envisages a 'conditional authorization' system, which recognizes the international law validity of existing and future Member State BITs, as long as they respect the primacy of EU law and the gradual development of EU investment policy.

More specifically, the authorization to maintain in force existing BITs is subject to notification to the Commission. Article 2 obliges Member States to notify all their BITs to the Commission, which are then granted authorization according to Article 3.[158] However, the Regulation Proposal envisages the right of the Commission to withdraw authorization if Member State BITs conflict with EU law or impede the conclusion or overlap with EU IIAs. While the second ground for withdrawing authorization is related to the future development of a comprehensive EU investment policy, which has already been discussed, the first ground aims to incorporate the principle of primacy of EU law.[159]

Nevertheless, the proposed transitional regime undermines legal certainty. As the proposed Regulation empowers the Commission to request that Member States terminate their BITs or renegotiate them if it finds a conflict with Union law,[160] the future of Member State BITs seems dubious, which in turn will affect investors who rely on BITs when planning and executing their investments. Taking into consideration the substantive conflicts between EU law and Member State BITs, which were highlighted in the previous sections, Member States would have to renegotiate all their BITs including new provisions that would (a) provide exceptions to free transfer rules allowing for EU action, (b) include a REIO exception to the MFN treatment of foreign investors, (c) exclude from the definition of foreign investors those who are established in the EU in accordance with Article 54 TFEU or eliminate control as a criterion of corporate nationality, and (d) include in the definition of foreign investors nationals of other EU Member States. Bearing in mind that the introduction of such significant amendments in all Member State BITs would affect a significant number of BITs and would be very difficult to achieve, at least in the short term, the option of terminating Member State BITs when they conflict with EU law seems to run contrary

[158] Despite the initial Commission proposal to subject initial authorization for the continuation of Member State BITs on their review for compatibility with substantive EU law as well as on the development of EU investment policy, the Parliament suggested granting authorization automatically, without requiring review of all notified agreements, so that Member State BITs *may* be reviewed by the Commission. In light of the large number of existing Member State BITs, a mandatory review of all notified BITs could actually distract the Commission from its primary purpose, which should be to develop the new EU investment policy and negotiate and conclude EU IIAs.

[159] See above Section 6.2.1.1.1.

[160] In recognition of the fact that Member States may be required or may find necessary to amend or modify investment agreements, in particular to bring them in compliance with Treaty obligations, this proposal also establishes a framework and conditions to empower Member States to enter into negotiations with a third country with a view to modifying an existing bilateral agreement relating to investment. (Proposed Regulation, Explanatory Memorandum, p 1)

to the purpose of ensuring high standards of protection for EU investors during the transitional period.[161]

Addressing this concern, the Regulation Proposal allows the amendment and renegotiation of Member State BITs. Subjecting the amendment of existing Member State BITs to authorization and close scrutiny by the Commission,[162] this mechanism enables Member States to adapt their BITs in cases where their authorization is withdrawn because of incompatibilities with EU law. The renegotiation of the Open Skies agreements presents a useful and successful example, where a mandate was given by the Council for the renegotiation of the Open Skies agreements by Member States,[163] under which Member States bore an obligation to ensure that the substantive provisions of the renegotiated agreements were compatible with EU law and such compatibility was supervised and authorized by EU institutions.[164] Hence, this additional mechanism attempts to address the need for continuity of Member State BITs, as their duration can be prolonged until their replacement by EU agreements, without leaving a gap in the event that they have to be terminated.[165]

However, the option of renegotiating Member State BITs that are incompatible with EU law would rather prolong legal uncertainty; Member States could contest the existence of incompatibilities, ultimately leading to a determination of incompatibility by the Court of Justice, an option that existed and could have been used at least since 2004, when the Commission and the Member States identified the existence of incompatibilities when they negotiated the MOU with the United States.[166] As a result, the whole purpose of promoting a political solution regarding the fate of Member State BITs and guarantee legal certainty is severely undermined given the contested nature and results of the review of compatibility of Member State agreements. Resolving the problem, the 'authorization system' incorporated in the Regulation Proposal should have been complemented by a 'replacement system', whereby Member State BITs need only be terminated once

[161] On the difficulties that Member States would face, if they have to renegotiate their BIT provisions only on capital transfer, see E Denza, 'Bilateral investment treaties and EU rules on free transfer: comment on Commission v Austria, Commission v Sweden and Commission v Finland' (2010) 35 EL Rev 263, 269–72.

[162] Art 6(2) allows the renegotiation of incompatible Member State BITs, which should then be conducted in accordance with Arts 9, 10, and 11. These provisions guarantee that the negotiating mandate given to the Member State complies with EU law and does not affect pending EU IIAs, ensuring at the same time an active role for the Commission as regards the subject and conduct of the negotiations with the third country. Indeed, the role of EU institutions, and in particular the Commission, in the renegotiation of Member State BITs, as guaranteeing compatibility with EU law and directing Member States has been explicitly emphasized by the Court. See Cases *Commission v Austria* and *Commission v Sweden*, above n 91, para 44; *Commission v Finland*, above n 91, para 35; Koutrakos, above n 92, pp 2073–5.

[163] Council Regulation 847/2004/EC on the Negotiation and Implementation of Air Service Agreements between Member States and Third Countries [2004] OJ L/157/7.

[164] On the substantive and procedural rules relating to the renegotiation of Open Skies agreements see Cremona, above n 2, pp 140–1.

[165] Regulation, Proposal, Explanatory Memorandum, p 2.

[166] Even though the Commission initiated proceedings against Austria, Sweden, and Finland in 2006 concerning the compatibility of their BITs with EU law, they related only to incompatibilities in the area of capital movements, without touching on the other incompatibilities which arose.

the EU has concluded and ratified an IIA with a particular country. Ensuring that incompatible BITs would not outlive a long transitional period, the Regulation Proposal could have insisted on additional measures that would speed up the negotiation and conclusion of new EU IIAs.

In addition to the authorization of existing Member State BITs, the Regulation Proposal envisages the conclusion of new BITs by Member States, under the authorization and close supervision of the Commission.[167] However, this mechanism should be viewed with scepticism. The authorization of Member States to conclude new international agreements in areas of EU exclusive competence on behalf of the EU has been used very rarely, mainly in order to substitute for the lack of international standing of the EU under specific international legal frameworks. Member States were authorized to conclude international agreements only where it was impossible for the EU to participate.[168] However, there is no legal or external political impediment for the conclusion of investment agreements by the EU. On the contrary, the conclusion of new BITs by Member States could impact negatively on the establishment of EU investment policy, as it would deprive a major incentive for Member States to cooperate with the Commission and jointly conclude new agreements.[169]

Finally, it is worth pointing out that the Regulation Proposal incorporates specific obligations regarding the conduct of Member States under existing and future BITs, in particular under dispute settlement proceedings. Violations of BIT provisions can be the result of the application and implementation of EU legislation by a Member State. The existence of Energy Charter Treaty (ECT) arbitrations against EU Member States, where the application of EU state aid and environmental law rules resulted in the alleged violation of investment rules, illustrates that a Member State can bear international responsibility under an IIA for applying, in a specific case, EU law that does not violate BIT provisions per se.[170] It is easy to imagine numerous scenarios under which the fulfilment of the Member States' obligations under the EU Treaties or the exercise of the rights granted to them thereunder can

[167] Arts 8–12 of the Regulation Proposal.

[168] Eg agreements concluded under the aegis of the UN, such as the International Labour Organization or the International Maritime Organization, where only states are entitled to participate in agreements. See Cremona, above n 142, pp 1–3.

[169] Addressing indirectly these concerns, the Parliament suggested the inclusion of a new paragraph 4 to Art 9 of the Regulation, which grants discretion to the Commission to deny authorization for negotiating a new BIT, if a majority of Member States indicate their interest to amend or conclude a BIT with a specific third country. Although this provision contributes to the speedier replacement of Member State BITs by EU IIAs, it relies on the willingness of Member States to substitute their own BITs, which in essence contradicts their stated aim to renegotiate their own BITs.

[170] *Electrabel SA v Republic of Hungary*, ICSID Case No ARB07/19; *AES Summit Generation Ltd and AES-Tisza Erőmű Kft v Republic of Hungary*, ICSID Case No ARB/07/22, Award, 23 September 2010; *Vattenfall AB v Germany*, ICSID Case No ARB/09/06 (withdrawn). A similar situation where adherence to EU law state aid rules has been challenged under investment arbitration is the *Micula* case (*Micula v Romania*, ICSID Case No ARB/05/20, Decision on Jurisdiction and Admissibility, 24 September 2008), where the tribunal did not mention the potential conflict between the Sweden-Romania BIT provisions and EU law.

lead in a specific case to a violation of Member State BIT provisions.[171] Addressing these concerns, the Regulation Proposal imposes an obligation on Member States to inform the Commission and cooperate fully with EU institutions, which may imply in certain situations that the Commission participates in the procedure.[172] Nevertheless, although the engagement of the EU in dispute settlement would allow the Commission to defend its position, the lack of parallel or supplementary EU international responsibility, in cases where a breach of a Member State BIT results from an EU action, would not discharge Member States from their international responsibility for EU acts, which will only be effectively achieved when Member State BITs are replaced by EU IIAs.

Consequently, the Regulation Proposal represents an important step towards addressing the future of Member State BITs. Although the transitional nature of the authorization mechanism is emphasized, a long transitional period, characterized by legal battles and uncertainty regarding the compatibility of Member State BITs with EU law seems inescapable. Considering that most BITs include a clause that extends their application for a specific period after termination,[173] which entails that BITs will continue to create international law effects for a long period, EU institutions should promote immediately the replacement of Member State BITs by EU IIAs.

6.3 Compatibility of EU IIAs with EU law

An important aspect of the EU law effects of EU IIAs concerns the obligations they impose on EU institutions and Member States under the prism of their compatibility with EU law. Next to the obligation to respect and comply with EU IIAs—which concerns mainly their implementation and the conformity of Member States' international commitments and national law with EU IIAs—EU IIAs give rise to another EU law obligation relating to their overall conformity with primary EU law. In that regard, EU institutions and Member States have to ensure that EU IIAs and their application are compatible with EU law and respect its primacy and autonomy.

[171] For a detailed description of potential situations where the application of EU law may lead to a violation of BITs see Eilmansberger, above n 87, pp 413–20.

[172] Art 13(2) of the Regulation Proposal.

[173] Eg Art 13 of the Austria-Chile BIT provides

> This Agreement shall remain in force for a period of ten years. Thereafter it shall remain in force indefinitely, unless one of the Contracting Parties gives one year's written notice of termination to the other Contracting Party through diplomatic channels. In respect of investments made prior to the date of receipt of the notice of termination of this Agreement, the provisions of Arts 1 to 12 of this Agreement *shall remain in force for a further period of ten years* from that date on. (Emphasis added).

6.3.1 The obligation of EU institutions to respect the primacy of EU law

First, by considering in brief the obligation of EU institutions to ensure that EU IIAs do not result in a violation of the primacy and autonomy of primary EU law, they have to ensure that both the conclusion and the substantive content of EU IIAs meet the requirements and limitations imposed by the founding Treaties. The conclusion of EU IIAs has to meet the procedural requirements for the conclusion of international agreements by the EU, a matter inextricably linked with the use of the proper legal basis.[174] Further, EU IIAs have to respect the objectives and limitations provided in primary EU law that concern the substantive content of EU IIA provisions, such as those proscribed in Articles 63 to 66 and 75 TFEU concerning limitations to free movement of capital to and from third countries.[175]

Nevertheless, if a future EU IIA is incompatible with primary EU law, EU institutions bear the responsibility to bring them into conformity with it. This may require their renegotiation, amendment, or termination, not only when their incompatibility concerns substantive deviations from primary EU law, but also in some cases when procedural rules have been violated.[176] However, it should be highlighted that where a Union agreement is found to be incompatible with primary EU law, the annulment declared by the Court concerns only the decision adopting this agreement and does not affect its validity in terms of international law, so that the agreement continues producing international law effects irrespective of its position as a matter of internal EU law.[177]

6.3.2 The obligation of Member States to respect the primacy and autonomy of EU law

The obligation of Member States to respect the primacy and preserve the autonomy of Union law differs from the obligation of EU institutions, as it concerns primarily the impact of EU IIAs on the relations between Member States, as a matter of EU law. More specifically, Member States have to ensure that the application of an EU IIA in the relations between them should be conducted in a manner that cannot affect Union law. This obligation arises only in multilateral EU IIAs that are concluded in the form of a mixed agreement; Member States undertake international commitments towards the other parties to the agreement, including not only third countries but also the other Member States. Such multilateral agreements create international

[174] See Section 3.1.2.1.

[175] See Sections 3.2.1.3, 3.2.2.7, and 3.2.7.

[176] Compare, eg, the aftermath of the *Energy Star Agreement* (Case C-281/01 *Commission v Council* [2002] ECR I-12049) and the *Rotterdam Convention* cases (Case C-94/03 *Commission v Council* [2006] ECR I-1), where the nullification of the act concluding the international agreement did not lead to renegotiation of the agreement but to the use of a different legal basis for its conclusion, with the *PNR cases* (Joined Cases C-317/04 & C-318/04 *European Parliament v Council (PNR)* [2006] ECR I-4721), where the agreement was terminated and a new agreement was negotiated. See P Koutrakos, 'Legal Basis and Delimitation of Competence in EU External Relations' in Cremona and de Witte (eds), *EU Foreign Relations Law—Constitutional Fundamentals* (2008), ch 7.

[177] Case *France v Commission*, above n 20, paras 13–17; See also Eeckhout, above n 9, pp 244–5.

law obligations between Member States to perform the agreement.[178] As a result, the WTO Agreement and the ECT are the only EU IIAs which affect the relations between Member States and give rise to potential problems, affecting the obligation of Member States to preserve the autonomy of Union law.

The potentially negative effects of the application of multilateral mixed agreements in relations between Member States have been recognized in practice and have given rise to judicial proceedings. A number of multilateral mixed agreements include disconnection clauses, namely provisions that exclude the application of the agreement from intra-EU relations to the extent that EU law covers their subject matter. Such clauses ensure the primacy of EU law in the relations between Member States and guarantee its autonomy.[179] The scope and extent of the obligation of Member States to respect the primacy and autonomy of EU law when applying a multilateral mixed agreement in the relations between them was the main subject of the *Sellafield* case,[180] which exemplifies a way in which a Member State can violate this obligation. Considering whether the initiation of proceedings under the United Nations Convention on the Law of the Sea (UNCLOS) violated the exclusive jurisdiction of the Court according to Article 344 TFEU, the Court found that, to the extent that the EU had exercised its external competence, which coincided in this case with the scope of EU law in the field, the primacy and autonomy of EU law were violated by the application of the UNCLOS provisions in the relations between Member States and their determination by another dispute settlement body.[181]

The same result would be reached if an examination of a potential violation of the principles of primacy and autonomy of EU law was not based on whether the EU exercised its external competence, but rather on the scope of EU law. As Cremona points out, the question

> to what extent the [EU] exercised its non-exclusive competence... should not bear on the issue of protection of the autonomy of the [Union] legal order... the real issue is rather that a dispute under the agreement gave rise to issues within the scope of [EU] law... It is the existence of this body of law which calls into play Article [344 TFEU] (which refers, it will be recalled, to 'the interpretation or application of this Treaty').[182]

It is worth noting that Article 344 TFEU is violated irrespective of whether there is an actual conflict of the provisions of the multilateral agreement with EU law, since Article 344 TFEU establishes the exclusive jurisdiction of the European Court of Justice (ECJ) over matters of EU law.

[178] A Rosas, 'Mixed Union—Mixed Agreements' in Koskenniemi (ed), *International Law Aspects of the European Union* (1998), p 142.

[179] On disconnection clauses see M Cremona, 'Disconnection Clauses in EU Law and Practice' in Hillion and Koutrakos (eds), *Mixed Agreements Revisited* (2010), pp 160–186; J Klabbers, 'Safeguarding the Organizational *Acquis*: The EU's External Practice' (2007) 4 International Organizations Law Review 57.

[180] *Sellafield* case, above n 18.

[181] For an overview of the facts and the result of the case see N Lavranos, 'The MOX Plant judgment of the ECJ: How exclusive is the jurisdiction of the ECJ?' (2006) 15 European Environmental Law Review 291.

[182] Cremona, above n 2, p 151; Koutrakos, above n 14, pp 128–9.

Considering now the scope of EU law, it should be perceived similarly to Article 216(2) TFEU, which provides the obligation of Member States to respect and comply with EU IIAs, as both obligations of Member States serve the same goals, namely to protect the supremacy and autonomy of EU law. In that respect, Member States violate their obligation to ensure the primacy and autonomy of EU law to the extent that they apply in their relations *inter se* the provisions of multilateral mixed agreements that are covered 'in large measure' by primary EU law provisions and secondary legislation.

6.3.2.1 The application of the GATS in disputes between Member States

So far there has not been any case where the application of the General Agreement on Trade in Services (GATS) by one Member State was contested in the WTO by another Member State. In fact, most cases concerning the application of the GATS by the EU and its Member States have been directed against the EU, while there has not been any final report in cases launched against individual EU Member States.[183] However, it is worth examining briefly how the direct application of the GATS and the initiation of a WTO complaint by an EU Member State against another EU Member State would violate their obligation to respect the primacy and autonomy of EU law.

The repercussions of the *Sellafield* litigation for the application of the provisions of the GATS in relations between Member States are apparent. If a Member State initiated a WTO complaint against another Member State, alleging the failure of the latter to apply the provisions of the GATS, it would infringe the provisions of Article 344 TFEU and Article 4(3) TFEU. Adopting the competence-based approach of the Court for determining whether there is a violation of Article 344 TFEU, it would be necessary to determine whether and to what extent the EU has exercised its competence in the field of trade in services. Although the Court seems to favour the position that at the time of the conclusion of the WTO Agreements the EU exercised its competence only with regard to the adoption of commitments under Mode 1 of the GATS,[184] the recognition of EU competence over the entire content of the GATS after the Nice amendments to the CCP[185] and the explicit recognition of exclusive EU powers in the area of trade in services after Lisbon, indicates that the initiation of WTO proceedings by one Member State against another would violate Article 344 TFEU.

Adopting the broader approach based on the scope of EU law, it becomes clearer why such a WTO complaint would violate the obligation of a Member State to respect the supremacy and autonomy of EU law. Trade in services between Member States is the subject of the freedom of establishment and the freedom to provide services, so that, even if the WTO rules covered trade in services between Member States, the application of the GATS in relations between them would clearly violate the provisions of the TFEU.

[183] In the field of trade in goods, the Court indicated since its early jurisprudence that the application of multilateral agreements by Member States in their relations *inter se* is incompatible with primary EU law: Case 10/61 *Commission v Italy* [1962] ECR 1.

[184] Opinion 1/2008 [2009] ECR I-11129, para 119.

[185] Ibid, para 124.

6.3.2.2 The application of the ECT in disputes between Member States

Contrary to the GATS, the investment provisions of the ECT are consistently applied in relations between Member States and have so far led to a number of investor-state disputes between EU investors against another EU Member State, which are arbitrated on the basis of the ECT provisions.[186] The application of the ECT in the relations between EU Member States raises concerns regarding the Union law obligation of the parties to respect the primacy and autonomy of EU law. Even though the international law validity of the ECT and the obligations of its Member States towards all other signatory parties under international law are not affected,[187] it is necessary to examine whether its application and adjudication by investment tribunals breaches the Union law obligation of Member States to safeguard the primacy and autonomy of EU law. This is also important because the compatibility of the ECT, insofar as it is applied in relations between Member States, with EU law, also has a significant impact on its international law applicability.[188]

A first important distinction from the *Sellafield* case is that the settlement of investment disputes under the ECT may involve private parties, as foreign investors can initiate proceedings against a host state. In that regard, Article 344 TFEU does not appear to be violated, as it explicitly imposes an obligation only on Member States to safeguard the jurisdiction of the Court and is not directly binding on private individuals.[189] Hence, even though interstate dispute settlement under the ECT would be covered under Article 344 TFEU, investor-state arbitration remains outside the protective scope of this provision.

However, this does not mean that investor-state arbitration cannot lead to a violation of the primacy and autonomy of EU law. As the Court has repeatedly emphasized, the exclusive jurisdiction of the Court is based on Article 19(1) TEU (which replaced Art 220 TEC).[190] This provision safeguards the autonomy of EU law by establishing the Court of Justice as the exclusive and ultimate judicial mechanism with the right to apply and interpret EU law.[191] Although the Court has accepted that submission to third party adjudication of a Union agreement may be possible under certain conditions, it has explicitly recognized that situations when a third court could offer a binding interpretation of EU rules without

[186] See above n 170. For an overview of these cases see Burgstaller, above n 107, pp 211–12.

[187] C Tietje, 'The Applicability of the Energy Charter Treaty in ICSID Arbitration of EU Nationals v EU Member States' (2008) 78 Beiträge zum Transnationalen Wirtschaftsrecht 1.

[188] For a detailed analysis of the international law applicability of the ECT in relations between Member States, see A Dimopoulos, 'The Validity and Applicability of International Investment Agreements between EU Member States under EU and International Law' (2011) 48 CMLR 63, 69–77.

[189] Soderlund, above n 126, p 459; Von der Groeben and Schwartze, *EU-EG Vertrag, Kommentar* (2004), Art 292 EGV, pp 1486–7.

[190] Opinion 1/91 (*EEA Agreement*) [1991] ECR I-6079, para 35; Opinion 1/00 (*Common Aviation Area*) [2002] ECR I-3493, paras 11 and 12.

[191] Von der Groeben and Schwartze, above n 189, Art 220 EGV, pp 310–12.

the possibility of review by the ECJ conflicted with its exclusive jurisdiction under Article 220 TEC (now Art 19(1) TEU).[192]

Before examining whether an investment tribunal under the ECT could rule on issues of EU law, it is important to see whether such arbitration awards are binding and subject to review by the ECJ. Starting with investor-state arbitration conducted under the auspices of the International Centre for Settlement of Investment Disputes (ICSID), this self-contained regime, which ensures that ICSID awards are valid and can be enforced bypassing national and international rules on the enforcement of arbitral awards,[193] indicates that ICSID awards offer binding awards that fall outside the scope of judicial review by the Court of Justice.[194] Similar issues are also raised by ad hoc arbitration, which is an alternative to ICSID arbitration according to the ECT,[195] as it can take place and be enforced outside the territory of EU Member States, thus circumventing any scrutiny by Member State courts and eventually the Court of Justice.[196] As a result, the provisional conclusion can be drawn that, to the extent that investor-state arbitration deals with issues falling within the scope of EU law, it violates the autonomy of EU law, as it evades the exclusive jurisdiction of the Court to apply and interpret EU law.

Considering now whether and to what extent an arbitral tribunal deals with issues that fall within the scope of EU law, it is necessary to examine each of the substantive provisions of the ECT. Starting with Articles 10, 11, and 14 ECT which deal with the promotion, establishment, and treatment of foreign investors as well as movement of capital and key personnel, these provisions regulate matters that fall directly within the scope of EU law. The establishment and treatment of EU investors in another EU Member State as well as capital movements are the subject of the freedoms of capital, establishment, and provision of services. It is worth noting that, even if primary EU law does not offer the FET standard to EU nationals established in another Member State as such, it covers 'in large measure' the treatment of EU nationals in the post-establishment phase, offering equiva-

192 Opinion 1/91, above n 190. See also Section 2.6.

193 R Dolzer and C Schreuer, *Principles of International Investment Law* (2008), pp 279, 287–9.

194 Eilmansberger, above n 87, pp 427–8; Tietje, above n 187, pp 16–17.

195 Art 26(5) ECT.

196 Although the Court has accepted that arbitral tribunals can determine issues of EU law, (Case 102/81 *Nordsee v Reederei Mond* [1982] ECR 1095; Case C-126/97 *Eco-Swiss v Benetton* [1999] ECR I-3055; Case C-168/05 *Mostaza Claro v Centro Movil Milenium* [2006] ECR I-10421), it has emphasized the public policy nature of EU law which renders arbitral awards subject to review by courts regarding the application of EU law (see S Prechal and N Shelkoplyas, 'National procedures, public policy and EC Law. From Van Schijndel to Eco Swiss and beyond' (2004) 5 European Review of Private Law 589). The need to ensure uniform interpretation of EU law provisions, irrespective of the circumstances in which they are applied (*Eco-Swiss*, para 40), requires that arbitral awards dealing with questions of EU law have to be open to examination by national courts and thus by the Court of Justice. This rationale, which has been accepted with regard to private commercial arbitration applying competition and consumer protection law, becomes clearer in investment arbitration, due to the public law nature of investor-state arbitration. This raises questions about the compatibility of Member States' actions with EU law. See also SW Schill, 'Crafting the international economic order: The public function of Investment Treaty arbitration and its significance for the role of the arbitrator' (2010) 23 Leiden Journal of International Law 401.

lent standards of protection.[197] Hence, if an EU investor could require compliance with the standards provided in Articles 10, 11, and 14 ECT from another Member State in an investor-state arbitration, this would directly affect the applicability of the fundamental freedoms, thus resulting in a breach of the primacy and autonomy of EU law.

It is more contestable whether the protection of the property rights of EU nationals in another Member State against political risk and expropriation fall within the scope of EU law, as guaranteed under Articles 12 and 13 ECT. EU law does not offer a system guaranteeing the property rights of EU nationals in another Member State. On the one hand, the Charter of Fundamental Rights, as well as earlier case law of the Court explicitly recognizes that EU law protects private property rights from limitations imposed by EU measures,[198] thus covering partly the protection of the property rights of EU nationals in another Member State. On the other hand, with regard to limitations imposed by Member States, the Court has only ruled that national law on property protection shall be applied in a non-discriminatory manner.[199] In that regard, it is arguable that EU law does not yet offer equivalent rules, or 'sufficiently important' rules regarding the protection of property of EU nationals who are investors in another Member State. Even though there are some EU rules on the subject, they are only 'procedural' as they do not offer substantive protection of property rights. As a result, the initiation of investor-state arbitration requiring protection based on Articles 12 and 13 ECT does not infringe the primacy and autonomy of EU law, since it is not covered in large measure by the existing EU rules on the matter.

Nevertheless, not every challenge of national measures is compatible with EU law. Considering that national measures may be taken in order to apply and/or implement EU law,[200] the violation of the property protection provisions of the ECT can, first, be the result of a national measure applying EU legislation breaching the ECT. In such cases, the protection of private property rights falls within the scope of EU law, as the violation results indirectly from EU measures. Secondly, a national measure may violate the expropriation provisions of the ECT, if it applies and/or implements 'wrongly' correct EU legislation. As EU law provides remedies for the incorrect application and/or implementation of Union rules,[201] the protection of individual rights, including property rights, is covered by Union rules.[202] However, the link to the scope of Union law is less clear in cases where EU legislation grants discretion to the Member States

[197] Cf the *Eastern Sugar* award, which considers that EU law deals only with capital movements and does not offer FET to EU nationals who are foreign investors in another EU Member State (above n 126, paras 161–5). Considering the substantive overlap of intra-EU BITs and primary EU law the tribunal erred in not taking into account the scope of the other fundamental freedoms as well as the scope of property protection in primary EU law. Burgstaller, above n 107, pp 190–1.

[198] Above n 25.

[199] Case 182/83 *Fearon* [1984] ECR 3677. For a more detailed analysis see Section 2.5.3.

[200] See also Section 5.1.3.2.

[201] On the remedies provided to individuals for wrongful application and implementation of EU rules by Member States, see P Craig and G de Búrca, *EU Law: Text, Cases, and Materials* (2008), ch 9.

[202] Case 44/79 *Hauer v Land Rheinland-Pfalz* [1979] ECR 3727.

concerning the application and implementation of EU rules. The violation of the ECT expropriation provisions may result from a national measure adopted within the limits and in conformity with the margin of discretion granted to the Member States. Although in such cases the national measure falls outside the scope of EU law, it is arguable that its challenge under investor-state arbitration proceedings infringes the primacy and autonomy of EU law. As long as the legality of such national measures under EU law, namely whether it was actually adopted within the margin of discretion granted to Member States, has not been determined by EU courts, the examination of their legality under the ECT would inevitably prejudice any future examination of this EU law question, thus the primacy and autonomy of EU law.

As a result, the ECT provision on investor-state arbitration violates the principle of autonomy of EU law when the subject matter of the arbitration concerns the admission and treatment of foreign investors as well as the protection of their property rights against EU or national measures applying or implementing EU law. However, when the subject of arbitration is property protection against purely national measures, there is no incompatibility with EU law.

The lack of a direct obligation on individuals to respect the primacy and autonomy of EU law indicates that investor-state arbitration cannot be successfully halted, as in the *Sellafield* case. As a result, the obligation of Member States to respect the primacy and autonomy of EU law indicates that an amendment of the ECT is required, so that either through the insertion of a disconnection clause or through a limitation of the right of EU investors to initiate investor-state arbitration against other EU Member States, the application of the ECT in the relations between Member States does not affect the primacy and autonomy of the Union legal order.

6.3.3 Do investment tribunals have an obligation to respect the primacy and autonomy of EU law?

The initiation of investment disputes by EU nationals against another EU Member State under the ECT, which can threaten the primacy and autonomy of EU law, brings forward the broader problems arising from the potential consideration of EU law issues by investment tribunals. The application of the ECT in intra-EU investment disputes presents only one scenario under which investment tribunals have to deal with EU law. EU law questions regarding the compatibility of Member State BITs with EU law or the legality of Member State measures in light of EU law can also be considered by investment tribunals, as the validity, application, and interpretation of BITs may depend on the determination of EU law. The *Eastern Sugar* case is an illustrative example, as the compatibility of the Dutch-Czech BIT with EU law was necessary for the determination of the validity of the BIT, while the legality of the Czech sugar regime in light of the EU sugar regime was relevant for the determination of whether there was a breach of the BIT provisions by the Czech Republic.[203]

[203] *Eastern Sugar* award, above n 126, paras 118, 222–42.

In such situations the problem which arises is that while the determination of EU law questions by arbitral tribunals may violate, from a Union law perspective, the exclusive jurisdiction of the ECJ and, thus, the autonomy of EU law,[204] EU law falls, from an international law perspective, within the ambit of the applicable law to the investment dispute. Whether EU law is viewed as a subsystem of international law or as the national law in force in the contracting party concerned,[205] it falls within the mandate of arbitral tribunals, which have to consider it in order to determine whether there is a violation of BIT provisions.

Resolving this problem, it is necessary to distinguish first the consideration of EU law questions, such as the compatibility of BITs or of Member States' national measures with EU law by investment tribunals from the actual scrutiny of Member State measures that apply or implement EU law in light of BIT provisions. In the second case it is, of course, problematic that the application and implementation of EU legislation by a Member State can result in the violation of BIT provisions; however, such scrutiny of Member State measures does not violate the exclusive jurisdiction of the ECJ, as investment tribunals apply only BIT law.[206] In that respect, the question of the compatibility of a Member State measure with EU law, which can arise under any BIT between a Member State and a third country,[207] does not threaten the autonomy of EU law, to the extent that this question is examined in order to assist the interpretation of BIT provisions and the investment award does not bind the ECJ.

Secondly, as regards the compatibility of BITs with EU law, which affects the international law applicability of the IIA,[208] neither EU law nor international investment law offers a clear cut solution. On the one hand, the determination of this question by an arbitral tribunal clearly violates the exclusive jurisdiction of the ECJ. On the other hand, the obligation to respect the primacy and autonomy of EU law is not binding on arbitral tribunals, which do not have the option to submit a reference for a preliminary ruling under Article 267 TFEU.[209] Besides, an arbitral tribunal is bound by arbitration rules to apply the law which is applicable to the dispute, including international law.

Of course, the problem of whether, when, and to what extent a dispute settlement organ established under a special legal regime can decide on issues falling under another 'self contained' regime of international law is not unique to investment tribunals and EU law.[210] Without entering into a detailed analysis of the

[204] *AES v Hungary*, above n 170, para 7.6.6. See above Section 6.3.2.

[205] On the debate of the role of EU law within international law see Chapter 5, nn 4 and 5.

[206] See also Burgstaller, above n 107, p 191.

[207] Wehland, above n 129, pp 300–3.

[208] Dimopoulos, above n 188, pp 67–8.

[209] Art 267 TFEU requires that a reference for a preliminary ruling can be raised only by 'any court or tribunal of a Member State', which has been interpreted as excluding arbitral tribunals (Case 102/81 *Nordsee* [1982] ECR 1095, paras 10–12).

[210] On the potential conflicts and possible solutions for competing jurisdictions of various international law fora see indicatively Y Shany, *The Competing jurisdiction of International courts and tribunals* (2003); C Brown, *A Common Law of International Adjudication* (2007); N Lavranos, 'On the Need to Regulate Competing Jurisdictions Between International Courts and Tribunals', EUI Working Paper MWP No 2009/14.

existing examples in international law and the solutions that have been proposed, it could be argued that the significant degree of differentiation of EU law from general international law combined with the exclusive jurisdiction of the ECJ, which is a public court, point towards the need for the exercise of self-restraint and deference on the part of arbitral tribunals regarding the compatibility of EU or Member State IIAs with EU law.[211] Certainly, a denial by arbitral tribunals to rule on questions of EU law, requesting private investors to initiate proceedings under national courts and, eventually, the ECJ may lead to delays which conflict with the legitimate goals of investment arbitration. Nevertheless, investment tribunals should abstain from determining such core questions of EU law, recognizing that investment arbitration is not the most appropriate or best equipped forum to provide the correct answers.

6.4 Conclusions

EU IIAs and, in general, EU foreign investment regulation generate a number of obligations for EU institutions and Member States having significant and far-reaching implications for EU and national legislation. Their obligation to comply with and respect EU international commitments in the field of foreign investment presents more than just a reflection of the international law obligation to respect and comply with EU IIAs. In conjunction with the obligation to respect the primacy and autonomy of EU law, EU institutions and, more importantly, Member States have to ensure that they implement EU IIAs consistently not only with EU international commitments but also with primary EU law, paying particular attention to existing norms in fields covered by EU foreign investment rules.

The determination of the scope and content of these obligations depends on the scope of EU law in the field of foreign investment. Foreign investment is a field where, typically, EU competence has been to a large extent shared with the Member States and has been regulated in mixed agreements, thus blurring the determination of the Union law obligations of the EU and its Member States. Departing from the complex competence-based definition of the scope of the above-described Union law obligations, the scope of EU law provides a clear and sound criterion for determining whether and when EU institutions and Member States have to take measures in order to conform to EU international obligations and EU law.

The definition of the scope of EU law rests on simple and precise criteria that do not attempt to speculate on the actual exercise of EU shared competence, which is a question that the political actors have left unanswered. Indisputably, the Union law obligations to comply with EU IIAs and respect the primacy and autonomy of EU law cover fields of EU exclusive competence, either explicit, as in Article 207

[211] On the need for judicial self-restraint and deference by investment tribunals see EU Petersmann, 'Constitutional Theories of International Economic Adjudication and Investor-State Arbitration' in Dupuy, Francioni, and Petersmann (eds), *Human Rights in International Investment Law and Arbitration* (2009), pp 137, 164–86.

TFEU, or implied by virtue of the *AETR* principle, which fall under the scope of EU law. However, the scope of EU law extends beyond exclusive competence, covering fields where there is EU legislation, albeit not capable of creating exclusive competence, that can be affected *in concreto* by measures adopted by Member States or EU institutions. Finally, even with regard to the fields of shared competence where there is no EU legislation, they may still fall within the scope of EU law, insofar as the future exercise of EU competence can be compromised or prejudiced.

Determining the scope of EU law and, thus, the EU law obligations arising from EU IIAs and EU foreign investment regulation in general, it becomes apparent that it covers the entirety of foreign investment matters. Even though expropriation is only regulated in the ECT, it is necessary to highlight again that expropriation provisions fall within the scope of EU law, creating a Union law obligation for EU institutions and Member States to respect them and comply with them and enabling the Court of Justice to enforce and interpret them, even if a violation of expropriation provisions is the result of national measures and the claim is raised by an individual investor.

In addition, it is necessary to highlight that, reaffirming the central position of the rule of law in the Union legal order, EU IIAs are subject to judicial review and have direct effect. Following the largely positive attitude of the Court of Justice towards judicial review and direct effect of Union agreements, it is suggested that investment provisions in EU IIAs can be the threshold for scrutiny of national and EU measures, creating direct rights for individuals, who are the main beneficiaries of investment provisions and the ultimate guardians of the preservation of the rule of law in the Union legal system.

Finally, the most significant implication of the Union law obligations arising from EU foreign investment regulation concerns the legality of Member State BITs. Member State BITs are incompatible with EU law, not only because they conflict with the EU's exclusive competence over FDI, but also because they conflict with substantive obligations provided under EU law and, more importantly, the principle of equal treatment. Eradicating these inconsistencies, the Lisbon Treaty provided an excellent opportunity to bring these inconsistencies to the surface and establish a framework for the amendment and renegotiation of all Member State BITs with third countries. Under the Regulation Proposal concerning transitional arrangements for Member State BITs, EU institutions firmly declare their desire to replace Member State BITs with EU IIAs in the long term, while preserving them until such replacement takes place, thus guaranteeing the rights of foreign investors. Although the Regulation Proposal poses threats to legal certainty and may result in the initiation of a long and contestable transitional period, it solidifies the new enhanced role of the EU as an international actor in the field of foreign investment, which will ultimately result in the conclusion of comprehensive EU IIAs with third countries.

Conclusions

Building a comprehensive EU common investment policy

It is undeniable that the EU is an emerging global actor in the field of international regulation of foreign investment. The EU has gradually established its presence in the international sphere, questioning the exclusive role of Member States in the area of foreign investment. Recognizing and exercising its competence, the EU has gradually acquired the dynamic to become a leading international actor in the field of foreign investment by developing a common investment policy. The establishment of a common investment policy that covers the entire spectrum of foreign investment regulation bears significant consequences not only for the re-determination of the role of the EU and its Member States as international actors, but also for the development of international norms on foreign investment, as the EU appears to view international regulation of foreign investment through a different prism than other international actors.

The foundations for the development of a common investment policy are already established. First and foremost, the EU is vested with competence to take external action in the entire field of foreign investment. Although the founding Treaties do not provide a single legal basis for foreign investment, a number of provisions, among which Article 207 TFEU is the most important, confer powers on the EU to regulate the different forms and the different aspects of foreign investment.

More specifically, EU competence on admission and post-admission treatment and operation of foreign investment is clearer and less ambiguous. As was analytically addressed in Chapter 2, Article 63 TFEU, which provides for liberalization of capital movements to and from third countries, covers portfolio investment and the transfer of assets related to foreign direct investment (FDI). Article 207 TFEU confers powers to the EU to regulate the conditions of initial establishment and post-establishment treatment and operation of FDI and foreign investment in the form of concession contracts in service sectors. In addition to Article 207 TFEU, the provisions on establishment and services confer implied powers to the EU with regard to the post-establishment treatment of FDI in the transport sector, foreign-controlled

FDI established in the EU and the operation of foreign investment in the form of concession contracts in non-service sectors. Of course, EU competence over admission and operation of foreign investment is not entirely exclusive. On the one hand, Article 207 TFEU confers exclusive powers to the EU to regulate FDI and foreign investment in the form of service contracts. However, Articles 63, 49, and 56 TFEU establish shared competence, while the criteria of *AETR* exclusivity are not satisfied with regard to most economic activities. Nevertheless, the existence of shared competence with the Member States does not entail that the EU cannot exercise its powers to the fullest extent covering the entirety of regulatory issues concerning admission and operation of foreign investment.

More problematic is the justification of EU competence to regulate protection of foreign investment against expropriation. Article 345 TFEU, which preserves the property ownership system of the Member States, presents a significant obstacle in affirming EU competence. However, this provision has been interpreted very narrowly, reserving only for the Member States the power to decide if and when an expropriation occurs and not the conditions under which such expropriation takes place. The latter, which is the subject of foreign investment regulation, does not fall under the scope of Article 345 TFEU. On the contrary, the EU is vested with competence to determine the conditions for the legality of expropriation and compensation based on Articles 207 and 114, 115, and 352 TFEU. In fact, EU law already has rules to determine restrictions to property rights resulting from EU measures which can amount to indirect expropriation. Furthermore, the EU also has the powers to harmonize Member State law on restrictions to property rights that amount to expropriation, which result from national measures. The power to harmonize rules on the exercise of property rights has already been used in the field of intellectual property (IP) rights, indicating that harmonization of rules on property restrictions that amount to expropriation can be considered necessary for the attainment of the objectives of the internal market. In addition, the fact that the internal power for harmonization has not been used thus far does not imply that external competence does not exist, as this would negate the foundations of the principle of parallelism which determines the scope of EU external competence. Hence, it is obvious that the EU has the legal powers to develop a common investment policy that covers all aspects of foreign investment.

The existence and, to a large extent, exclusive nature of EU competence in the field of foreign investment is of course indispensable for creating a common investment policy, but it is not the only prerequisite. The exercise of EU competence is actually what brings a common investment policy to life, indicating its characteristics and how it integrates into the world of international investment agreements (IIAs) and international regulation of foreign investment. In that respect, the existing EU IIAs present a valuable indicator of the current role that the EU holds in the international arena, which will be complemented in the future by comprehensive EU IIAs.

So far, the EU has concluded a considerable number of international agreements including provisions related to foreign investment. Although the number of EU IIAs is smaller than the number of IIAs concluded by most states, they confirm the presence of the EU as an international actor. EU current investment policy is better reflected in bilateral EU IIAs, which, unlike the General Agreement on Trade in Services (GATS) and the Energy Charter Treaty (ECT), which are also binding on the EU, present many common characteristics that are distinct from traditional Bilateral Investment Treaties (BITs) and other IIAs.

As discussed in Chapter 3, the overwhelming majority of existing EU IIAs deal with admission and post-admission operation and treatment of foreign investment. Unlike BITs, existing EU IIAs have so far excluded property protection against expropriation and investor-state dispute settlement from their scope. But even with regard to admission and operation of foreign investment they differentiate significantly from BITs: regulation of post-admission treatment depends on the existence of provisions on admission, FDI is regulated separately from other forms of foreign investment, and finally, EU IIAs lack absolute standards of treatment, such as fair and equal treatment, providing only for most favoured nation and national treatment, which are in fact applied and interpreted differently than the same standards used in BITs. Explaining these differences, the influence exerted by the EU internal market provisions and the GATS on the scope and content of EU IIAs acquires enormous significance. However, EU IIAs do more than merely replicate primary EU law or the GATS provisions, as they have sufficient original elements that can justify their characterization as an innovative model for international regulation of foreign investment.

Covering the main handicap of existing EU IIAs, EU institutions have demonstrated their willingness to include investment protection and investor-state arbitration in future EU IIAs, thus establishing a comprehensive common investment policy. Nevertheless, it is still unclear whether future EU IIAs will merely replicate existing Member State BITs or whether they will introduce a new type of IIA, combining elements of existing Union agreements with improved BIT-based provisions. In any event, drafting new EU IIAs requires particular care in order to take into account and respect the specific limitations provided under primary EU law, in particular as regards the fair and equitable treatment and protection of property rights of foreign investors.

The challenges concerning the content of future EU IIAs are directly linked with the regulatory aims that EU investment policy is pursuing. The analysis provided in Chapter 4 illustrates that the emphasis placed on admission and operation of foreign investment is linked with the pursuance of the goals of liberalization, market access, and competitiveness as the main objectives of EU investment policy. Adhering to these objectives, the EU seems to prioritize the demand for increasing investment flows, addressing the role of regulation of admission of foreign investment, in particular in the field of services, as a major economic determinant of foreign investment. In addition to liberalization and competitiveness, EU investment policy appears also to focus on the more 'neglected' goals of international regulation of foreign investment. Based on the objectives ascribed in primary EU law, the EU attempts to link foreign investment with development and broader public policy considerations. For example, under current EU IIAs it establishes a network of provisions, such as those on investors' behaviour, maintenance of standards, and investment promotion, which draw away from the obscurity that characterizes development and public policy concerns in most BITs.

However, development considerations seem to be overlooked in the plans for future EU investment policy. Although the Commission recognizes the need to balance investors' rights with public policy considerations and enhance coherence with other EU external relations policies, these objectives are not reflected in the suggestions regarding the substantive obligations provided in future EU IIAs. On the contrary, the Parliament takes an audacious stance, proposing the inclusion of innovative provisions, such as on Corporate Social Responsibility.

Setting up the EU investment policy presents a unique opportunity to render the EU a pioneer in international investment law. It rests in the hands of EU and Member State policy makers to decide whether the EU will alter international investment law, proposing a regulatory framework that, on the one hand, preserves the protection of foreign investors and enhances their investment opportunities and, on the other, addresses the host states' public policy concerns, or whether the EU will merely replicate existing EU IIAs and Member State BITs, thereby adding to the current dichotomy and the proliferation of norms of international investment law.

In addition to political obstacles, the formation of a common investment policy encounters further problems that arise from the international presence of the EU. Given that Member States have so far been the main international actors in the field of foreign investment, a common investment policy places important restrictions on the powers of Member States to conclude IIAs in the future, affecting also the existing BITs and IIAs concluded by Member States. As regards the conclusion of future agreements, Member States are prohibited from taking any external action where EU competence is rendered exclusive. But even to the extent that EU powers are not exclusive, Member States still bear the obligation to respect and abide by EU law in the conclusion of their IIAs.

The latter obligation imposed on Member States also has significant consequences for their current BITs and their compatibility with EU law. Chapter 6 has clearly demonstrated that all Member State BITs are incompatible with EU law. In addition to their incompatibilities regarding capital transfer provisions, which have been confirmed by the Court in the *Commission v Austria*, *Commission v Sweden*, and *Commission v Finland* cases, the BIT provisions on expropriation and investor-state arbitration breach the principle of equal treatment of EU nationals in all EU Member States and in third countries. In the first case, BITs grant the specific advantages only to certain EU nationals, namely those incorporated in a Member State according to Article 54 TFEU, but are foreign-controlled and, in the second case, they exclude other EU nationals from the advantages granted though a bilateral agreement with a third country.

As a result, the creation of a common investment policy requires the replacement of all Member State BITs by EU IIAs, materializing the role of the EU as an international actor. Recognizing, however, the importance of existing Member State BITs for securing investors' interests in the EU and in third countries, EU institutions have decided to authorize their maintenance and allow Member States to conclude new ones, under close cooperation with the Commission. Although this interim solution is necessary, it entails great dangers, as it can result in a prolonged transitional period, which would only add to legal uncertainty and ultimately affect investors' confidence regarding the applicable legal regime. Mitigating the threat of prolonged legal battles on the extent of inconsistencies of Member State BITs with EU law, EU institutions and Member States should realize their common interests, implementing the mandate of the new investment policy together by initiating negotiations for future EU IIAs and replacing existing Member State BITs.

At this stage it has to be pointed out that the EU law incompatibilities of Member State BITs do not affect their international law validity, so that they are still applicable until they are renegotiated. Nevertheless, the international law status of Member State BITs is affected by the exercise of EU competence through the conclusion of EU IIAs. As noted in Chapter 5, most EU IIAs preserve the integrity of Member State BITs, indicating that in the fields where there is substantive overlap, such as capital transfers, the Member State BITs prevail. Nevertheless, a few gaps exist, questioning the applicability of both EU IIA and Member State BITs provisions. In order to avoid similar problems in the future, EU institutions have declared that the conclusion of future EU IIAs will be combined with the termination of Member State BITs.

Similar problems also arise with regard to EU law compatibility of multilateral EU IIAs, and in particular the ECT, to the extent that they are applied in relations between EU Member States. Raising questions that are also pertinent for the validity and EU law compatibility of BITs between EU Member States, the application of the ECT by an EU investor in another EU Member State breaches the autonomy of Union law. It brings outside the scope of the jurisdiction of the Court of Justice issues that fall within the ambit of EU law, which covers almost the entire scope of the investment provisions of the ECT regarding its application in intra-EU relations. Given, of course, that EU law cannot oblige individuals to refrain from initiating investor-state arbitration, urgent action is needed in order to eliminate the potential threat of arbitral tribunals being outside the system of EU law deciding vital questions of EU law.

Finally, the international presence of the EU raises concerns regarding the international law responsibility of the EU and its Member States in cases of violation of the obligations included in EU and Member State IIAs. Although the EU can be held internationally responsible for the acts of its organs violating its international commitments, problems arise regarding the responsibility of the EU for wrongful conduct of Member States insofar as Member States can be found responsible under BITs for applying and implementing EU law. The ILC Draft Articles on the international responsibility of international organizations indicate that the EU can be held responsible for the conduct of Member State acts that violate the commitments undertaken by the EU under EU IIAs. The broad recognition of EU responsibility for Member State acts raises, however, practical and moral concerns, as Member States may act in violation of their obligations under EU IIAs, knowing that responsibility for their acts will eventually be assumed by the EU. This danger, which will be more acute under future EU IIAs which will include expropriation provisions, should not necessarily lead to a limitation of EU international responsibility. Apart from the fact that EU law provides certain tools for minimizing these negative effects, as it enables the EU to bring infringement proceedings and, thus, 'transfer' responsibility to the 'responsible' Member State, the EU can devise internal procedural mechanisms for ultimately rendering responsible the violating Member State. As for Member States' responsibility under BITs for applying and implementing EU law, this scenario illustrates the necessity for renegotiating the existing BITs, in order to engage the EU in dispute settlement proceedings where EU measures result in a violation of international investment law rules.

In light of these observations, the creation of a common investment policy is a fact, setting strong foundations for the presence of the EU in the field of international regulation of foreign investment. However, the political reality will affect the breadth and strength of any future EU common investment policy. Although the assumption of all powers in the field of foreign investment by the EU is possible, the ambiguity regarding the scope of EU competence over expropriation and the existence of shared competence over portfolio investment and investment in the form of concession contracts after the Lisbon Treaty allow the Member States to retain certain powers in the field. In that respect, the conclusion of comprehensive EU IIAs may take the form of mixed agreements, to the extent that Member States oppose and question the exercise of the EU's shared competence.

Indeed, the renegotiation of Member State BITs and the conclusion of future EU IIAs as mixed agreements would satisfy all actors, as it would allow Member States to retain a significant role in foreign investment policy and would enable the EU institutions to form, together with the Member States, a strong and complete common investment policy. Indeed, mixity has been successfully used so far in the framework of the WTO for creating a common policy on trade in services, enabling the EU to set the framework for common action and the Member States to retain their flexibilities. In addition, as the analysis in Chapters 5 and 6 illustrates, the use of mixity in current EU IIAs does not create unsolvable legal concerns regarding the determination of the international and the EU law rights and obligations of the EU and its Member States.

Does an EU common investment policy better serve the regulatory interests of the stakeholders involved?

The gradual creation of an EU common investment policy and the increased presence of the EU as an international actor in the field of foreign investment are viewed with scepticism and reservation by a significant number of policy makers, academics, and practising lawyers both in Europe and around the world.[1] In addition to raising the legal concerns regarding EU competence and the legal effects that an

[1] Eg a study conducted in December 2008 among government advisers, lawyers, and academics indicated that almost two-thirds were opposed to the EU exclusively undertaking the field of intra-EU investments. See <http://www.lovells.com/Lovells/MediaCentre/PressReleases/68+oppose+ECJ+role+as+sole+arbiter+in+investment+disputes.htm> (last accessed 1 May 2011).

increased EU international presence will bring, practical and policy considerations are equally important, questioning whether the creation of an EU common investment policy will benefit the actors and stakeholders involved.[2] In light of these considerations, it is submitted that the creation of a comprehensive and fully integrated EU common investment policy better serves the regulatory interests of the EU, its Member States, third countries, and finally foreign investors.

Starting with the benefits that the EU will reap from the creation of a common investment policy, the strengthening of its powers and the firm establishment of its international role in the area of foreign investment are rather obvious. However, the increase of centralized powers is not an end in itself. The creation of a common investment policy can, first, contribute significantly to the attainment of the objectives of the internal market. The conclusion of EU-wide IIAs ensures equal opportunities for all European investors who wish to invest in third countries, minimizing the distortions on competition that result from the existence of benefits for only certain EU nationals arising from the conclusion of BITs between certain Member States and third countries. Furthermore, a common investment policy can enhance competitiveness in the internal market, eradicating the influence that the existence of a BIT between a Member State and a third country may exert on the choice of third country investors to establish themselves in that specific Member State rather than in another.

Next to the internal market objectives, the creation of an EU common investment policy can contribute significantly to the pursuance of EU external relations objectives. The attainment of market access and better competitive opportunities for European investors abroad can be more easily achieved through a common EU investment policy, which can offer a complete framework of rights and guarantees for European investors. Ending the division between promotion and protection of foreign investment, a comprehensive, single package on foreign investment can be more easily negotiated, accommodating the divergent regulatory interests of the EU and its counterparties, thus providing more benefits for European investors.[3] In addition, a common investment policy would advance the broader external relations goals of the EU, and more importantly its development objectives. It would provide the opportunity for the EU to fulfil its development rhetoric and introduce development and public policy considerations in a field of international economic relations where they are largely missing and obscure. Given the influence that the EU can exert on third countries as a large, single negotiating bloc, attainment of

[2] See also S Woolcock and J Kleinheisterkamp, 'The EU approach to international investment policy after the Lisbon Treaty', Study Directorate General for External Policies of the Union (October 2010), pp 13–15.

[3] Eg Mexico and Chile insisted on including in their respective EU IIAs a separate investment chapter in line with that existing in other regional trade agreements (J Reiter, 'The EU-Mexico Free Trade Agreement: Assessing the EU approach to regulatory issues' in Sampson and Woolcock (eds), *Regionalism, Multilateralism and Economic Integration* (2003), p 90). Were this proposal accepted, the EU IIAs would offer more advantages to all European investors, while they may have provided an opportunity for the EU and its Member States to achieve better concessions in the field of market access, in which they were primarily interested.

these objectives would probably be better served than if individual Member States were left as single international actors.

The creation of a common investment policy could be equally beneficial for individual Member States. Of course, the transfer of powers to the EU presents a loss for their sovereignty. However, this does not mean that Member States will not be able to preserve and promote their individual regulatory interests in the field of foreign investment. On the contrary, the assumption of powers in the field of foreign investment by the EU can better serve the regulatory interests of Member States. It will first benefit Member States, in particular the smaller ones, which have not concluded IIAs with third countries,[4] while the conclusion of IIAs at the EU level can lead to the achievement of more regulatory goals as a result of the greater negotiating power and influence that the EU can exert on third countries in comparison to most small and medium-sized Member States.

The achievement of Member States' regulatory goals through a common investment policy depends ultimately on their endorsement by the EU, raising concerns that individual Member States' concerns may be neglected by EU policy makers and that Member States lose flexibility in determining their specific objectives. Responding to this argument, one has to bear in mind that it is ultimately the Member States that will determine the orientation of a common investment policy, setting the priorities and the flexibilities for negotiations, allowing at the same time for the concerns of each Member State to be incorporated. As described in Chapter 3, the conclusion of EU IIAs will have to be made on a variety of legal bases, including Article 207 TFEU and Article 217 TFEU, which, with regard to foreign investment, require unanimity for decision making in the Council and the consent of the Parliament. In addition, Member States can substantially influence the orientation of EU IIAs in case the latter are negotiated and concluded as mixed agreements.

Of particular merit is the concern that the centralization of foreign investment powers in Brussels may actually prove inefficient, at least in comparison to the pursuance of investment policy objectives by some Member States. Indeed, the vast transfer of powers to the EU can lead to delays in decision making and legal uncertainty. The divergent views of the Commission and the Parliament on the objectives of EU investment policy illustrate these difficulties, as the lack of a common position in the EU affects its negotiating leverage. However, the existing political difficulties in agreeing a common agenda should not be exaggerated. As in every other EU policy field, the formation of policy orientation is subject to the complicated structure of European politics without, however, leading to dead-ends affecting the implementation of policies. Also, EU investment policy

[4] There are striking differences on the number of BITs concluded by Member States with third countries. As at 1 June 2011 the number of BITs with third countries each Member State had concluded were: Germany 124, the UK 94, France 91, Italy 88, the Netherlands 87, Belgium 79, Luxembourg 79, Czech Republic 70, Spain 65, Romania 63, Sweden 59, Finland 58, Austria 52, Bulgaria 47, Denmark 44, Poland 39, Portugal 39, Hungary 37, Slovakia 32, Greece 31, Lithuania 30, Latvia 23, Slovenia 18, Cyprus 14, Estonia 12, Malta 8, and Ireland 0. For a detailed list of each Member State's BITs see UNCTAD, Country-Specific Lists of BITs, available at <http://www.unctad.org/Templates/Page.asp?intItemID=2344&lang=1> (last accessed 1 June 2011).

as an autonomous field is still nascent, thus time is needed to form the basis of EU policy. In that respect, the success of EU investment policy depends on the willingness of all institutional actors to cooperate closely.

The delays in decision making resulting in legal uncertainty are particularly acute as regards the fate of Member State BITs and the rights secured therein. In that respect, the current Regulation Proposal on transitional arrangements regarding Member State BITs indicate the willingness of the EU to secure the rights of foreign investors, clarify the conditions under which Member State BITs will be terminated, and promote their replacement by EU IIAs. Nevertheless, the development of EU investment policy should avoid a long transitional period, as this would only prolong legal uncertainty. In that respect, the commitment of sufficient resources by the EU and its Member States could mitigate the effects of a long and uncertain transition.

The smooth transition from Member State BITs to EU IIAs is actually a central regulatory concern of third countries. The creation of a common investment policy has to contribute to legal certainty, which requires a clear determination of the role of the EU and its Member States in the field of foreign investment, in order to ensure the rights of third country investors and to avoid multiple and conflicting obligations towards the EU, its Member States, and their nationals. As mentioned, the EU can be held internationally responsible for the violation of its obligations under EU IIAs that result from either its own or Member State acts, thus securing the rights of third countries and their nationals. Furthermore, the direct effect of the provisions of EU IIAs in the EU could be conceived as threatening jurisdictional and procedural prerogatives, namely the right to initiate investor-state arbitration, which third countries provide to their investors under the existing BITs concluded with Member States. As argued in Chapter 6, such concerns lack any basis, as the existence of direct effect for future EU IIAs that provide for investor-state arbitration will simply secure an additional forum for foreign investors, who, by choosing to submit their claim to national courts, have the additional guarantee of having their case heard by the Court of Justice when a reference for a preliminary ruling is made by the national court.

In addition to their procedural regulatory interests, third countries are also affected by the substantive orientation of an EU common investment policy. In that respect, the current orientation of EU IIAs appears to raise significant regulatory concerns for a large group of third countries, namely developing countries. The provisions on investment promotion and the recognition of the development aspects of foreign investment regulation in existing EU IIAs take into consideration the increasing regulatory concerns of developing countries over the development impact of international investment regulation. Even if the development orientation and effects of existing and future EU IIAs are questioned by third countries, the mere fact that the EU puts the development aspect of foreign investment regulation on the negotiating agenda can assist developing countries in forming, expressing, and ultimately turning into legally binding provisions their own positions regarding the development aspects of foreign investment regulation.

The emphasis on development and public policy considerations could be perceived as conflicting with the regulatory interests of third countries that aim to secure stronger protection standards for their nationals who wish to invest in an EU Member State. As these regulatory concerns affect both third country investors in the EU and EU investors abroad, they are examined in light of the regulatory interests of foreign investors.

The explicit recognition of specific public policy exceptions to the rights of foreign investors in existing EU IIAs and the suggestions to include more stringent standards in future EU IIAs could be viewed as threatening the guarantees that foreign investors enjoy under BITs. Indeed, the abstract language used in most BITs with regard to when and under what circumstances public policy considerations justify exceptions to the rights of foreign investors and the ambiguity that follows the determination of the normative content of the principle of fair and equal treatment have so far led to arbitral awards that protect and guarantee foreign investors in controversial cases.[5]

Within this framework, a future EU common investment policy that focuses on development and public policy concerns can contribute to the existing debates regarding the reformulation of current BIT provisions. The clarification of legal guarantees which foreign investors enjoy under BITs can be beneficial for them in the long term, as more and more countries question the necessity of concluding and being bound by BITs.[6] A situation where developing countries group together and question the necessity for concluding or renewing their BITs, similar to their reaction in the 1970s that led to the UN resolutions on a New International Economic Order is not unimaginable. In that respect, the introduction of development concerns by the EU and its Member States in the international debate on the scope and orientation of foreign investment regulation can contribute to regaining the trust of developing countries in the existing system and lead to informed changes. In addition, the creation of a strong EU common investment policy can benefit foreign investors to the extent that it addresses their regulatory interests in achieving market openness and competitiveness. Bearing in mind that market access commitments gain importance as regulatory determinants of foreign investment, the emphasis placed on admission of foreign investment by current EU IIAs can significantly serve the interests of foreign investors, as argued in Chapter 4.

As a result, the creation of an EU common investment policy has the potential to advance the regulatory interests of all relevant stakeholders. However, the centralization of policy making in the field of foreign investment does not guarantee as such that it will be beneficial for home and host states and foreign investors. It is the specific scope and content of the common investment policy

[5] See Chapter 1, nn 30 and 31.

[6] A number of Latin American countries, such as Bolivia, Ecuador, Venezuela, and Argentina, have denounced or threatened to denounce the ICSID Convention and to review and renegotiate their BITs with third countries, indicating their dissatisfaction with the current developments in international investment law. See eg E Gaillard, 'Anti-Arbitration Trends in Latin America' (2008) New York Law Journal, 5 June; I Vincentelli, 'The Uncertain Future of ICSID in Latin America', Independent Research Paper, University of Miami Law School, 2008.

that will determine its positive or negative effects. EU institutions and Member States will face a number of challenges in order to set up a common investment policy, particularly when establishing the formula for future EU IIAs that will take into account the requirements of primary EU law and the peculiarities regarding the international law position of the EU and its Member States, as well as securing the smooth transition from Member State BITs to EU-wide IIAs. But more importantly, policy makers will have to set out the specific objectives of an EU common investment policy, incorporating them in future EU IIAs. In that respect, EU investment policy should be based on clear and strong foundations, identifying both the orientation and substantive content of EU investment policy and also the proper method of cooperation with Member States. Considering the boost to EU competitiveness that a complete EU investment policy will bring in light of EU internal economic integration, EU investment policy can be successful only if it is well planned and properly implemented.

Bibliography

Acconci, P (2004), 'Determining the Internationally Relevant Link between a State and a Corporate Investor–Recent Trends concerning the Application of the Genuine Link Test', 5 Journal of World Investment and Trade 139

——(2008), 'Most-Favoured-Nation Treatment' in Muchlinski, Ortino, and Schreuer (eds), *Oxford Handbook of International Investment Law* (Oxford: Oxford University Press)

Adede, A (1983), 'The Minimum Standards in a World of Disputes' in MacDonald and Johnston (eds), *The Structure and Process of International Law* (The Hague; Boston; Lancaster: Martinus Nijhoff)

Agmon, T (2003), 'Who gets what: the MNE, the national state and the distributional effects of globalization', 34 Journal of International Business Studies 416

Aisbett, E (2007), 'Bilateral Investment Treaties and Foreign Direct Investment: Correlation versus Causation', MPRA Paper No 225

Aldrich, G (1996), *The jurisprudence of the Iran-US Claims tribunal* (Oxford: Clarendon Press)

Alexandrov, S (2004), 'Application of the MFN-clause in investment treaties: Replies to two questions', 1 Transnational Dispute Management 1

Amerasinghe, CF (1964), *State Responsibility for Injuries to Aliens* (Oxford: Clarendon Press)

Andreeva, Y (2008), 'Salvaging or Sinking the Investment? *MHS v Malaysia* revisited', 7 Law and Practice of International Courts and Tribunals 161

Antoniadis, A (2010), 'The EU's implied competence to conclude international agreements after the Reform Treaty Reformed enough?' in Laursen (ed), *The EU in the Global Political Economy* (Brussels: PIE Peter Lang)

Arnull, A (2000), 'Left to its own Devices? Opinion 2/94 and the Protection of Fundamental Rights in the European Union' in Dashwood and Hillion (eds), *The general law of EC external relations* (London: Sweet & Maxwell)

—— et al (2006), *Wyatt and Dashwood's European Union Law* (London: Sweet & Maxwell)

Arrowsmith, S (2005), *The Law of Public and Utilities Procurement* (London: Sweet & Maxwell)

Arts, K (2003), 'ACP-EU relations in a new era: The Cotonou Agreement', 40 Common Market Law Review 95

——(2004), 'EU Development Cooperation: From Model to Symbol' in Arts and Dickson (eds), *EU Development Cooperation: From Model to Symbol* (Manchester; New York: Manchester University Press)

Arup, C (2008), 'Services and Investment in Free Trade Agreements: Liberalization, Regulation and Law' in Buckley, Lo, and Boulle (eds), *Challenges to Multilateral Trade The Impact of Bilateral, Preferential and Regional Agreements* (Alphen aan den Rijn: Kluwer Law International)

Babarinde, O and Faber, G (2004), 'From Lomé to Cotonou: Business as usual?', 9 European Foreign Affairs Review 27

Barnard, C (2001), 'Fitting the Remaining Pieces into the Goods and Persons Jigsaw', 26 European Law Review 35

——(2010), *The Substantive Law of the EU: The Four Freedoms* (Oxford: Oxford University Press)

—— and Deakin, S (2002), 'Market Access and regulatory competition' in Barnard and Scott (eds), *The Law of the Single European Market: Unpacking the Premises* (Oxford: Hart Publishing)

Bartels, L (2005), *Human Rights Conditionality in the EU's International Agreements* (New York: Oxford University Press)

—— (2007), 'The Trade and Development Policy of the European Union', 18 European Journal of International Law 715

——and Baudenbacher, C (2005), 'The EFTA Court Ten Years on' in Baudenbacher, Tresselt, and Örlygsson (eds), *The EFTA Court Ten Years On* (Oxford; Portland: Hart Publishing)

Bencheneb, A (2000), 'Sur l'évolution de la notion d'investissement' in Kahn and Leben (eds), *Souveraineté étatique et marches internationaux a la fin du 20eme siècle, Mélanges en l'honneur de Ph Kahn* (Paris: Litec)

Bende-Nabende, A (2002), *Globalisation, FDI, Regional Integration* (Aldershot; Burlington: Ashgate)

Benyon, F (2010), *Direct Investment, National Champions and EU Treaty Freedoms* (Oxford; Portland: Hart Publishing)

Bercero, IG (2006), 'Dispute Settlement in European Union Free Trade Agreements: Lesson Learned?' in Bartels and Ortino (eds), *Regional Trade Agreements and the WTO System* (Oxford: Oxford University Press)

Bezborodov, S (2007), 'Freedom of Establishment in the EC Economic Partnership Agreements: in Search of its Direct Effect on Direct Taxation', 35 International Tax Review 658

Bhagwati J and Panagariya, A (1996), 'Preferential Trade Areas and Multilateralism; Strangers, Friends, or Foes?' in Bhagwati and Panagariya (eds), *The Economics of Preferential Trade Agreements* (Washington, DC: AEI Press; College Park: Center for International Economics, University of Maryland)

Billiet, S (2005), 'The EC and WTO Dispute Settlement: the Initiation of Trade Disputes by the EC', 10 European Foreign Affairs Review 203

Bieber, R (2002), 'Democratic Control of International Relations of the European Union' in Cannizzaro (ed), *The European Union as an actor in international relations* (Hague; London: Kluwer Law International)

Bishop, R Crawford, J, and Reisman, W (2005), *Foreign Investment disputes: Cases, materials and commentary* (The Hague: Kluwer Law International)

Björklund, M (2001), 'Responsibility in the EC for mixed agreements—Should Non-Member Countries care?', 70 Nordic Journal of International Law 373

Blanch, J, Moody, A, and Lawn, N (2008), 'Access to dispute resolution mechanisms under Article 26 of the Energy Charter Treaty' in Coop and Ribeiro (eds), *Investment Protection and the Energy Charter Treaty* (Huntington, NY: JurisNet)

Bleckmann, A (1983), 'The Mixed Agreements of the EEC in Public International Law' in O'Keefe and Schermers (eds), *Mixed Agreements* (Deventer; Boston: Kluwer Law)

Borgen, C (2005), 'Resolving Treaty Conflicts', 37 George Washington International Law Review 573

Bosse-Platiére, I (2002), 'Le Parlement européen et les relations extérieures de la Communauté européenne après le Traite de Nice', 39 Revue Trimestrielle de Droit Europeen 527

Bourgeois, J (1995), 'The EC in the WTO and Advisory Opinion 1/94: An Echternach Procession', 32 Common Market Law Review 763

—— (1999), 'External Relations Powers of the European Community', 22 Fordham International Law Journal 149

Brandtner, B (1992), 'The "Drama" of the EEA: Comments on Opinions 1/91 and 1/92', 3 European Journal of International Law 309

Brewer, T and Young, S (1998), 'Investment issues at the WTO: the architecture of rules and the settlement of Disputes', 1 *Journal of International Economic Law* 457

—— (1998) *The Multilateral Investment System and Multinational Enterprises* (Oxford: Oxford University Press)

Brown, C (2007), *A Common Law of International Adjudication* (Oxford: Oxford University Press)

Brownlie, I (2008), *Principles of Public International Law* (Oxford: Oxford University Press)

Bungenberg, M (2011), 'The Division of Competences Between the EU and its Member States in the Area of Investment Policies' in Bungeberg Griebel and Hindelang (eds), *International Investment Law and EU Law*, European Yearbook of International Economic Law Special Issue

Burgstaller, M (2006), 'Nationality of Corporate Investors and International Claims against the Investor's Own State', 7 Journal of World Investment and Trade 857

—— (2009), 'European Law and Investment Treaties', 26 Journal of International Arbitration 181

——, Cabral, P, and Cunha, P (2000), 'Presumed Innocent: Companies and the exercise of the Right of Establishment under Community Law', 25 European Law Review 157

Caddous, C (2008), 'Effects of International Agreements in the EU Legal Order' in Cremona and de Witte (eds), *EU Foreign Relations Law - Constitutional Fundamentals* (Oxford; Portland: Hart Publishing)

Cardwell, P and French, D (2010), 'Liberalizing Investment in the CARIFORUM-EU Economic Partnership Agreement: EU Priorities, Regional Agendas and Developmental Hegemony' in Cordonier-Segger, Gehring, and Newcombe (eds), *Sustainable Development in World Investment Law* (Alphen aan den Rijn: Kluwer Law International)

Ceyssens, J (2005), 'Towards a common foreign investment policy?—Foreign investment in the European constitution', 32 Legal Issues of Economic Integration 259

Chanda, R (2001), 'Movement of natural persons and the GATS', 24 World Economy 631

Cheyne, I (2000), 'Haegeman, Demirel and their progeny' in Dashwood and Hillion (eds), *The General Law of EC External Relations* (London: Sweet & Maxwell)

Civello, P (1999), 'The TRIMS Agreement: A failed attempt at Investment Liberalization', 8 Minnesota Journal of World Trade 97

Coban, A (2004), *Protection of Property rights within the European Convention of Human Rights* (Aldershot; Burlington: Ashgate)

Conze, A (1987), *Die Völkerrechtliche Haftung der Europäischen Gemeinschaft* (Baden-Baden: Nomos)

Cordewener, A and Reimer, E (2006), 'The Future of Most-Favoured-Nation Treatment in EC Tax Law—Did the ECJ Pull the Emergency Brake without Real Need?'—Part 2', 5 European Taxation 291

Cordonier-Segger, MC and Khalfan, A (2004), *Sustainable Development Law: Principles, Practices and Prospects* (Oxford: Oxford University Press)

Correa, C and Kumar, N (2003), *Protecting foreign investment: implications of a WTO regime and policy options* (London; New York: Zed Books/New Delhi: Academic Foundation)

Cosbey, A et al (2004), *Investment and Sustainable Development: A Guide to the Use and Potential of International Investment Agreements* (Winnipeg, International Institute for Sustainable Development)

Cossy, M (2008), 'Some thoughts on the concept of "likeness" in the GATS' in Panizzon, Pohl, and Sauve (eds), *GATS and the Regulation of International Trade in Services* (Cambridge: Cambridge University Press)

Cottier, T, Delimatsis, P, and Diebold, N (2008), 'Article XIV GATS' in Wolfrum, Stoll, and Feinäugle (eds), *WTO—Trade in Services* (Leiden; Boston: Martinus Nijhoff)

Cottier, T and Mavroidis, P (eds) (2000), *Regulatory Barriers and the Principle of Non-Discrimination in World Trade Law* (Ann Arbor, MI: University of Michigan Press)

—— and Molinuevo, M (2008), 'Article V GATS' in Wofrum, Stoll, and Feinäugle (eds), *WTO Trade in Services* (Leiden; Boston: Martinus Nijhoff)

Craig, P and de Búrca, G (2008) *EU Law: Texts, Cases, and Materials* (Oxford: Oxford University Press)

Cremona, M (1996), 'Human Rights and Democracy Clauses in the EC's Trade Agreements' in Emiliou and O'Keefe (eds), *The European Union and World Trade Law* (Chichester; New York: Wiley)

—— (2000), 'Flexible Models: External Policy and the European Economic Constitution' in de Búrca and Scott (eds), *Constitutional Change in the EU From Uniformity to Flexibility?* (Oxford: Hart Publishing)

—— (2000), 'Variable Geometry and the Setting of Membership Conditionalities: an EU Perspective' in Clapham, Mills, Morner, and Sidiropoulos (eds), *Regional Integration in Southern Africa: Comparative International Experiences* (Johannesburg: South African Institute of International Affairs)

—— (2001), 'A Policy of Bits and Pieces? The Common Commercial Policy after Nice', 4 Cambridge Yearbook of European Legal Studies 61

—— (2001), 'Neutrality or Discrimination? The WTO, the EU and External Trade' in de Búrca and Scott (eds), *The EU and the WTO Legal and Constitutional Issues* (Oxford; Portland: Hart Publishing)

—— (2002), 'The External Dimension of the Internal Market' in Barnard and Scott (eds), *The Law of the Single European Market* (Oxford: Hart Publishing)

—— (2003), 'The Draft Constitutional Treaty: External Relations and External Action', 40 Common Market Law Review 1348

—— (2003), *Values in the EU Constitution: The External Dimension*, Workshop on Values in the EU Constitution, EUI, Florence

—— (2004), 'The Union as a Global Actor: Roles, Models and Identities', 41 Common Market Law Review 553

—— (2006), 'A constitutional basis for Effective External Action? An assessment of the provisions on EU External Action in the Constitutional Treaty', EUI Working Paper 2006/30

—— (2006), 'External Relations of the EU and the Member States: Competence, Mixed Agreements, International Responsibility, and Effects of International Law', EUI Working Paper No 2006/22

—— (2008), 'Coherence through Law: What difference will the Treaty of Lisbon Make', 3 Hamburg Review of Social Sciences 11

—— (2008), 'Defending the Community Interest: the Duties of Cooperation and Compliance' in Cremona and de Witte (eds), *EU Foreign Relations Law - Constitutional Fundamentals* (Oxford; Portland: Hart Publishing)

—— (2008), 'Defining Competence in EU External Relations: Lessons from the Treaty Reform Process' in Dashwood and Maresceau (eds), *Law and Practice of EU External Relations* (Cambridge: Cambridge University Press)
—— (2009), 'Extending the Reach of the AETR Principle: Comment on *Commission v Greece* (C-45/07)', 34 European Law Review 754
—— (2009), 'Member States as Trustees of the Community Interest: Participating in International Agreements on Behalf of the European Community', EUI Working Paper LAW 2009/17
—— (2010), 'Balancing Union and Member State interests: Opinion 1/2008, choice of legal basis and the common commercial policy under the Treaty of Lisbon', 35 European Law Review 678
—— (2010), 'Disconnection Clauses in EU Law and Practice' in Hillion and Koutrakos (eds), *Mixed Agreements Revisited* (Oxford; Portland: Hart Publishing)
—— (2011), 'External relations and external competence of the European Union: The emergence of an integrated policy' in Craig and de Búrca (eds), *The Evolution of EU Law* (Oxford: Oxford University Press)
Dashwood, A (2000), 'The Attribution of External Relations Competence' in Dashwood and Hillion (eds), *The general law of EC external relations* (London: Sweet & Maxwell)
—— (2004), 'The Relationship between the Member States European Union/European Community', 11 Common Market Law Review 355
—— (2010), 'Mixity in the era of the Treaty of Lisbon' in Hillion and Koutrakos (eds), *Mixed Agreements Revisited* (Oxford; Portland: Hart Publishing)
Davies, A (2008), 'One Step Forward Two Steps Back? The *Viking* and *Laval* Cases in the ECJ', 37 Industrial Law Journal 126
Davies, G (2003), *Nationality Discrimination in the European Internal Market* (The Hague; London: Kluwer Law International)
de Búrca, G (2002), 'Unpacking the concept of discrimination in EC and international trade law' in Barnard and Scott (eds), *The Law of the Single European Market: Unpacking the Premises* (Oxford: Hart Publishing)
—— and Scott J (eds) (2000), *Constitutional Change in the EU From Uniformity to Flexibility?* (Oxford: Hart Publishing)
de la Rochére, J (2002), 'EMU: Constitutional Aspects and External Representation', 19 Yearbook of European Law 427
de Walsche, A (2005), 'La procédure de conclusion des accords internationaux' in Dony and Louis (eds), *Commentaire J Mégret 12 - Relations extérieures* (Brussels: Ed de l'Université de Bruxelles)
de Schutter, O (2006), 'The Challenge of Imposing Human Rights Norms on Corporate Actors' in de Schutter (ed), *Transnational Corporations and Human Rights* (Oxford; Portland: Hart Publishing)
de Witte, B (2000), 'Institutional Principles: A Special Category of General Principles of EC Law' in Bernitz and Nergelius (eds), *General Principles of European Community Law* (The Hague; London: Kluwer Law International)
de Witte, B, Hanf, D and Vos, E (eds) (2001), *The Many Faces of Differentiation in EU Law* (Antwerp; Oxford; New York: Intersentia)
Delaume, G (1966), 'Convention on the Settlement of Investment Disputes Between States and Nationals of Other States', 1 International Lawyer 64
Delimatsis, P (2007), 'Due Process and "Good" Regulation Embedded in the GATS-Disciplining Regulatory Behaviour in Services through Article VI GATS', 10 Journal of International Economic Law 13

Delimatsis, P and Molinuevo, M (2008), 'Article XVI GATS' in Wolfrum, Stoll, and Feinäugle (eds), *WTO Trade in Services* (Leiden; Boston: Martinus Nijhoff)

Denza, E (2010), 'Bilateral investment treaties and EU rules on free transfer: comment on Commission v Austria, Commission v Sweden and Commission v Finland', 35 European Law Review 263, 269–272

di Mascio, N and Pauwelyn, J (2008), 'Non-discrimination in Trade and Investment Treaties: Worlds Apart or Two Sides of the Same Coin?', 102 American Journal of International Law 48

Dicke, DC (1990), 'Public International Law and a New International Economic Order' in Sarcevic and van Houtte (eds), *Legal Issues in International Trade* (London; Boston: Graham and Trotman)

Dimopoulos, A (2011), 'The development of EU trade and investment policies: Drawing lessons from past experiences' in Sauvant and Ortino (eds), *Yearbook on International Investment Law and Policy 2010–2011* (Oxford: Oxford University Press, forthcoming)

—— (2011), 'The Validity and Applicability of International Investment Agreements between EU Member states under EU and International Law', 48 Common Market Law Review 63

Dischendorfer, M (2002), 'Implementation and Legal Effects of the WTO Agreement on Government Procurement in the European Community', thesis, University of Vienna

Dolzer, R and Myers, T (2004), 'After *Tecmed*: Most-Favoured-Nation Clauses in Investment Protection Agreements', 19 ICSID Review—Foreign Investment Law Journal 49

—— and Schreuer, C (2008), *Principles of International Investment Law* (Oxford: Oxford University Press)

—— and Stevens, M (1995), *Bilateral Investment Treaties* (The Hague; Boston: Martinus Nijhoff)

Dunning, J and Lundan, S (2008), *Multinational Enterprises and the Global Economy* (Cheltenham: Edward Elgar)

Dupuy, P, Francioni, F, and Petersmann, EU (eds) (2009), *Human Rights in International Law and Arbitration* (Oxford: Oxford University Press)

Echandi, R (2006), 'A new generation of international investment agreements in the Americas: impact of investor state dispute settlement over investment rulemaking', Fourth Annual Conference of the Euro-Latin Study Network on Integration and Trade (ELSNIT)

Eeckhout, P (2004), *External relations of the European Union: legal and constitutional foundations* (Oxford: Oxford University Press)

—— (2006), 'The EU and its Member States in the WTO—Issues of Responsibility' in Bartels and Ortino (eds), *Regional Trade Agreements and the WTO System* (Oxford: Oxford University Press)

—— (2009), 'Case C-308/06 *The Queen on the application of Intertanko and others v Secretary of State for Transport*, judgment of the Court of Justice (Grand Chamber) of 3 June 2008', 46 Common Market Law Review 2041

Eilmansberger, T (2009), 'Bilateral Investment Treaties and EU Law', 46 Common Market Law Review 383

Elkins, Z, Guzman, A, and Simmons, B (2008), 'Competing for Capital: The Diffusion of Bilateral Investment Treaties, 1960–2000', University of Illinois Law Review 265

Emch, A (2008), 'News from Luxembourg—Is the New EU Investment Law Taking Shape?', 9 Journal of World Investment and Trade 497

Endicott, M (2005), 'The Definition of Investment in ICSID Arbitration: Development Lessons for the WTO?' in Gehring and Cordonier-Segger (eds), *Sustainable Development in World Trade Law* (The Hague: Kluwer Law International)

Energy Charter Secretariat (2004), *The Energy Charter Treaty and Related Documents* (Brussels: Energy Charter Secretariat)
European Investment Bank (2007), *Investment Facility Annual Report* (Luxembourg: European Investment Bank)
Eurostat (2008), *European Union Foreign Direct Investment Yearbook 2008* (Luxembourg: Office for Official Publications of the European Communities)
Faber, G (2005), 'Economic Partnership Agreements and Regional Integration' in Babarinde and Faber (eds), *The European Union and Developing Countries: The Cotonou Agreement* (Leiden; Boston: Martinus Nijhoff)
Falsafi, A (2008), 'Regional Trade and Investment Agreements: Liberalizing Investment in a Preferential Climate', 36 Syracuse Journal International Law 43
Fares, S (2003), 'Current Payments and Capital Movements in the EU-Mediterranean Association Agreements', 30 Legal Issues of Economic Integration 15
Fierro, E (2003), *The EU's Approach to Human Rights Conditionality in Practice* (The Hague; London: Martinus Nijhoff)
Fietta, S (2005), 'Most Favoured Nation Treatment and Dispute Resolution under Bilateral Investment Treaties: a Turning Point?', 8 International Arbitration Law Review 131
Fink, C and Jansen, M (2009), 'Services Provisions in Regional Trade Agreements: stumbling blocks or building blocks for multilateral liberalization' in Baldwin and Low (eds), *Multilateralizing Regionalism: Challenges for the Global Trading System* (Cambridge: Cambridge University Press)
Footer, M (1998), 'The EU and the WTO Global Trading System' in Laurent and Maresceau (eds), *The State of the European Union: Deepening and Widening* (Boulder, CO; London: Lynne Riener)
Franklin, C (2005), 'Flexibility vs Legal Certainty: Article 307 EC and Other Issues in the Aftermath of the Open Skies Cases', 10 European Foreign Affairs Review 79
Frenz, W (2004), *Handbuch Europarecht: Europäische Grundfreiheiten* (Berlin: Springer)
Friedland, P (2008), 'The scope of Most Favored Nation treatment under the Energy Charter Treaty' in Coop and Ribeiro (eds), *Investment Protection and the Energy Charter Treaty* (Huntington, NY: JurisNet)
Gaillard, E (1999), 'Chronique des sentences arbitrales', 126 Journal du Droit International 273
—— (2008), 'Anti-Arbitration Trends in Latin America', New York Law Journal, 5 June
—— and Banifatemi, Y (2003), 'The meaning of "and" in Article 42(1) Second sentence of the Washington Convention: The role of international Law in the ICSID Choice of Law process', 18 ICSID Review—Foreign Investment Law Journal 375
Gauttier, P (2004), 'Horizontal Coherence and the External Competences of the European Union', 10 European Law Journal 23
Gavin, B (2003), 'Trade and Investment in Wider Europe: EU Neighborhood Policy for Enhanced Regional Integration', 4 Journal of World Investment and Trade 893
Gehring, M and Cordonier-Segger, MC (2005), *Sustainable Development in World Trade Law* (The Hague: Kluwer Law International)
Geiger, R (1998), 'The Multilateral Agreement on Investment', 31 Cornell Journal of International Law 467
Geiger, T and Kennedy, D (eds) (1996), *Regional Trade Blocs, Multilateralism, and the GATT: Complementary Paths to Free Trade?* (London: Pinter)
Glania, G and Matthes, J (2005), *Multilateralism or Regionalism? Trade Policy Options for the European Union* (Brussels: Centre for European Policy Studies)

Globerman, S and Shapiro, D (2008), 'Outward FDI and the economic performance of emerging markets' in Sauvant, Mendoza, and Ince (eds), *The Rise of TNCs from Emerging Markets: Threat or Opportunity?* (Cheltenham: Edward Elgar)

Gomez-Palacio, I and Muchlinski, P (2008), 'Admission and Establishment' in Muchlinski, Ortino, and Schreuer (eds), *Oxford Handbook of International Investment Law* (Oxford: Oxford University Press)

Görs, B (2005), *Internationales Investitionsrecht* (Frankfurt am Main: Recht und Wirtschaft)

Govaere, I (2010), 'Beware of the Trojan Horse: Dispute Settlement in (Mixed) Agreements and the Autonomy of the EU Legal Order' in Hillion and Koutrakos (eds), *Mixed Agreements Revisited* (Oxford; Portland: Hart Publishing)

Grierson-Weiler, T and Laird, I (2008), 'Standards of Treatment' in Muchlinski, Ortino, and Schreuer (eds), *Oxford Handbook of International Investment Law* (Oxford: Oxford University Press)

Griffith-Jones, S (1998), *Global Capital Flows* (Basingstoke: Macmillan)

Griller, S and Weidel, B (2002), *External Economic Relations and Foreign Policy in the European Union* (Vienna; New York: Springer)

Gugler, P and Chaisse, J (2008), 'Foreign Investment Issues and WTO Law—Dealing with Fragmentation while waiting for a Multilateral Framework' in Chaisse (ed), *Essays on the Future of the World Trade Organization*, vol I (Geneva: Editions interuniversitaires suisses (Edis))

——(2009), *Sovereign Wealth Funds in the European Union: General Trust Despite Concerns*, NCCR Working Paper 2009/4

Guohua, Y, Mercurio, B, and Yongjie, L (2005), *WTO Dispute Settlement Understanding: A Detailed Interpretation* (The Hague: Kluwer Law International)

Guzman, A (1998), 'Why LDCs Sign Treaties That Hurt Them: Explaining the Popularity of Bilateral Investment Treaties', 38 Virginia Journal of International Law 667

Haghighi, S (2007), *Energy Security The external legal relations of the European Union with major oil and gas supplying countries* (Oxford; Portland: Hart Publishing)

Handoll, J (2006), *Capital, Payments and Money Laundering in the European Union* (Richmond: Richmond Law and Tax)

Hanf, D and Dengler, P (2004), 'Accords d'Association', 1 College of Europe Research Paper in Law 1

Heliskoski, J (1999), 'Joint Competence of the European Community and its Member States and the Dispute Settlement Practice of the World Trade Organization, 2 Cambridge Yearbook of European Legal Studies 61

——(2001), *Mixed agreements as a technique for Organizing the International Relations of the European Community and its Member States* (Hague; Boston: Kluwer Law International)

Hemetsberger, W, et al (2006), *European Banking and Financial Services Law* (Alphen aan den Rijn: Kluwer Law International)

Hermann, C (2002), 'Common Commercial Policy after Nice: Sisyphus would have done a better job', 39 Common Market Law Review 7

—— (2002), 'Monetary Sovereignty over the Euro and External Relations of the Euro Area: Competences, Procedures and Practice', 7 European Foreign Affairs Review 1

—— (2010), 'Die Zukunft der mitgliedstaatlichen Investitionspolitik nach dem Vertrag von Lissabon' 77 Europäische Zeitschrift für Wirtschaftsrecht 207

Hilf, M (1995), 'The ECJ's Opinion 1/94 on the WTO, No Surprise but Wise?', 6 European Journal of International Law 245

Hillion, C (2008), 'Tous pour un, un pour tous! Coherence in the External Relations of the European Union' in Cremona (ed), *New Developments in EU External Relations* (Oxford: Oxford University Press)

—— (2010), 'Mixity and Coherence in EU External Relations: The significance of the "Duty of Cooperation"' in Hillion and Eeckhout (eds), *Mixed Agreements Revisited* (Oxford; Portland: Hart Publishing)
Hilpold, P (2003), 'Regional Integration According to Article XXIV GATT Between Law and Politics', 7 Max Planck Yearbook of United Nations Law 219
Hilson, C (1999), 'Discrimination in Community Free Movement', 24 European Law Review 445
Hindelang, S (2007), 'The EC Treaty's freedom of capital movement as an instrument of international investment law?' in Reinisch and Knahr (eds), *International Investment Law and Context* (Utrecht: Eleven International Publishing)
—— (2009), *The Free Movement of Capital and Foreign Direct Investment: the scope of protection in EU Law* (Oxford: Oxford University Press)
—— and Maydell, N (2011), 'The EU's Common Investment Policy—Connecting the Dots' in Bungeberg, Griebel, and Hindelang (eds), *International Investment Law and EU Law* (European Yearbook of International Economic Law Special Issue)
Hjelmborg, S, Jakobsen, P, and Poulsen, S (2006), *Public Procurement Law—the EU Directive on Public Contracts* (Copenhagen: DJØF Publishing)
Ho, J (2010), 'The meaning of "Investment" in ICSID arbitrations', 26 Arbitration International 633
Hoekman, B and Newfarmer, R (2005), 'Preferential Trade Agreements, Investment Disciplines and Investment Flows', 5 Journal of World Trade 949
—— and Özden, C (2009), 'The Euro-Mediterranean Partnership: Trade in Services - An alternative to Migration?', World Bank Policy Research Working Paper 5049
Hoffmeister, F (2007), 'Outsider or Frontrunner? Recent Developments Under International and European Law on the Status of the European Union in International Organizations and Treaty Bodies', 44 European Foreign Affairs Review 41
—— (2010), 'Curse or Blessing? Mixed Agreements in the Recent Practice of the European Union and its Member States' in Hillion and Koutrakos (eds), *Mixed Agreements Revisited* (Oxford; Portland: Hart Publishing)
—— (2010), 'Litigating against the European Union and Its Member States—Who Responds under the ILC's Draft Articles on International Responsibility of International Organizations?', 21 European Journal of International Law 723
Holden, P (2003), 'The European Community's MEDA Aid Programme: A strategic instrument of civilian power?', 8 European Foreign Affairs Review 347
Holdgaard, R (2003), 'The European Community's Implied External Competence after the Open Skies cases', 8 European Foreign Affairs Review 365
—— (2008), 'Annotation on Case C-431/05 *Merck*', 45 Common Market Law Review 1233
Horng, DC (2003), 'The Human Rights Clause in the European Union's External Trade and Development Agreements', 9 European Law Journal 677
Hossain K (ed) (1980), *Legal Aspects of the New International Economic Order*
International Monetary Fund (2001), *Global Portfolio Investment Survey* (Washington DC: IMF)
—— (2001), *World Economic Outlook 2001: The Information Technology Revolution* (Washington DC: IMF)
Jacobs, F (2008), 'Direct effect and interpretation of international agreements in the recent case law of the European Court of Justice' in Dashwood and Maresceau (eds), *Law and Practice of EU External Relations* (Cambridge: Cambridge University Press)
Jarass, H (2002), 'A Unified Approach to the Fundamental Freedoms' in Andenas and Roth (eds), *Services and Free Movement in EU Law* (Oxford: Oxford University Press)

Johannsen, S (2009), 'Die Kompetenz der Europäischen Union für Ausländische Direktinvestitionen nach dem Vertrag von Lissabon', 90 Beiträge zum Transnationalen Wirtschaftsrecht 1

Kahai, S (2004), 'The Role of Foreign Direct Investment and its Determinants' in Kehal (ed), *Foreign Investment in Developing Countries* (New York: Palgrave Macmillan)

Karayigit, M (2006), 'Why and To What Extent a Common Interpretative Position for Mixed Agreements?', 11 European Foreign Affairs Review 445

Karl, J (2002), 'On the way to Multilateral Investment Rules: Some Recent Policy Issues', 17 ICSID Review—Foreign Investment Law Journal 293

—— (2004), 'The Competence for Foreign Direct Investment', 5 Journal of World Investment and Trade 413

Karli, M (2008), 'Assessing the Development Friendliness of Dispute Settlement Mechanisms in the Economic Partnership Agreements', Occasional Paper European Studies Centre, University of Oxford

Kehal, H (2004), *Foreign Investment in Developing Countries* (New York: Palgrave Macmillan)

Kelley, G (2001), 'Multilateral Investment Treaties: A Balanced Approach to Multinational Corporations', 39 Columbia Journal of Transnational Law 483

Kennedy, K (2003), 'A WTO Agreement on Investment: A Solution in search of a problem?', 24 University of Pennsylvania Journal of International Law 77

Kenneth, T (2000), *Competing for Capital: Europe and North America in a Global Era* (Washington DC: Georgetown University Press)

Kentin, E (2002), 'Prospects for Rules on Investment in the new WTO Round', 29 Legal Issues of Economic Integration 61

Kiekebeld, B and Smit, D (2007), 'Freedom of establishment and free movement of capital in Association Agreements and direct taxation', 35 International Tax Review 216

Kingreen, T (1999), *Die Struktur der Grundfreiheiten des Europäischen Gemeinschaftsrechts* (Berlin: Duncker and Humblot)

Klamert, M and Maydell, N (2008), 'Lost in Exclusivity: Implied Non-exclusive External Competences in Community Law', 13 European Foreign Affairs Review 493

Klabbers, J (2001), 'Moribund on the fourth of July? The Court of Justice on prior agreements of the Member States', 26 European Law Review 187

—— (2002), *An Introduction to International Institutional Law* (Cambridge: Cambridge University Press)

—— (2002), 'Restraints on the Treaty-making power of Member States Deriving from EU Law: Towards a Framework for Analysis' in E Cannizzaro (ed), *The European Union as an Actor in International Relations* (Hague; London: Kluwer Law International)

—— (2007), 'Safeguarding the Organizational *Acquis*: The EU's External Practice', 4 International Organizations Law Review 57

—— (2009), *Treaty Conflict and the European Union* (Cambridge: Cambridge University Press)

Klein, P (1998), *La responsabilité des organisations internationales dans les ordres juridiques internes et en droit des gens* (Brussels: Bruylant)

Kokko, A (2002), 'FDI and the structure of home country production' in Bora (ed), *Foreign Direct Investment* (London; New York: Routledge)

Koulen, M (2001), 'Foreign Investment in the WTO' in Nieuwenhuys and Brus (ed), *Multilateral Regulation on Investment* (The Hague; Boston: Kluwer Law International)

Koutrakos, P (2002), 'The Interpretation of Mixed Agreements Under the Preliminary Reference Procedure', 7 European Foreign Affairs Review 25

—— (2006), *EU International Relations Law* (Oxford; Portland: Hart Publishing)

—— (2008), 'Legal Basis and Delimitation of Competence in EU External Relations' in Cremona and de Witte (eds), *EU Foreign Relations Law—Constitutional Fundamentals* (Oxford; Portland: Hart Publishing)

—— (2009), 'Comment Case C-205/06, *Commission v Austria*, judgment of the Court (Grand Chamber) of 3 March 2009, not yet reported; Case C-249/06, *Commission v Sweden*, judgment of the Court (Grand Chamber) of 3 March 2009, not yet reported', 46 Common Market Law Review 2059

—— (2010), 'Interpretation of Mixed Agreements' in Hillion and Eeckhout (eds), *Mixed Agreements Revisited* (Oxford; Portland: Hart Publishing)

Kovar, R (1988), 'Nationalisations—privatisations et droit communautaire' in Scwartze (ed), *Discretionary Powers of the Member States in the Field of Economic Policies and their Limits under the EEC Treaty* (Baden-Baden: Nomos)

Krajewski, M (2005), 'External Trade Law and the Constitutional Treaty: Towards a federal and more democratic common Commercial Policy?', 42 Common Market Law Review 91

—— (2008), 'Article VI GATS' in Wolfrum, Stoll, and Feinäugle (eds), *WTO Trade in Services* (Leiden; Boston: Martinus Nijhoff)

—— (2011), 'The Reform of the Common Commercial Policy' in Biondi and Eeckhout (eds), *European Union Law after the Treaty of Lisbon* (forthcoming)

Krenzler, HG and Pitschas, C (2001), 'Progress or Stagnation? The Common Commercial Policy After Nice', 6 European Foreign Affairs Review 291

Kuijper, P (2010), 'International Responsibility for EU Mixed Agreements' in Hillion and Koutrakos (eds), *Mixed Agreements Revisited* (Oxford; Portland: Hart Publishing)

——and Bronckers, M (2005), 'WTO Law in the European Court of Justice', 42 Common Market Law Review 1313

—— and Paasivirta, E (2004), 'Further Exploring International Responsibility: The European Community and the ILC's project on responsibility of international organizations', 1 International Organizations Law Review 111

Kwak, K and Marceau, G (2006), 'Overlaps and Conflicts of Jurisdiction between the World Trade Organization and Regional Trade Agreements' in Bartels and Ortino (eds), *Regional Trade Agreements and the WTO System* (Oxford: Oxford University Press)

Lachmann, P (1984), 'International Legal Personality of the EC: Capacity and Competence', 10 Legal Issues of Economic Integration 5

Lastra, R-M (2006), *Legal Foundations of International Monetary Stability* (Oxford: Oxford University Press)

Lavranos, N (2003), 'Case Notes on the Open Skies cases', 30 Legal Issues of Economic Integration 81

—— (2006), 'The MOX Plant judgment of the ECJ: How exclusive is the jurisdiction of the ECJ?', 15 European Environmental Law Review 291

—— (2009), 'On the Need to Regulate Competing Jurisdictions Between International Courts and Tribunals', EUI Working Paper MWP No 2009/14

Leal Arcas, R (2009), 'EU Relations with China and Russia: How to Approach New Superpowers in Trade Matters', 4 Journal of International Commercial Law and Technology 1

Leben, C (1999), 'L'évolution du droit international des Investissments' in *Un accord multilatéral sur l'investissement: d'un forum de négociation à l'autre*, 10 Journée d'études de la SFDI 1

Leino, P (2005), 'European Universalism? The EU and Human Rights Conditionality', 24 Yearbook of European Law 329

Lenaerts, K and de Smijter, E (2000), 'The European Union as an Actor Under International Law', 19 Yearbook of European Law 95

Liberti, F (2008), The European Union and the South Mediterranean Partners: *L'Union pour la Méditerranée*, a French Attempt to Refocus the EU Engagement toward the South' in Delocour and Tulmets (eds), *Pioneer Europe? Testing EU Foreign Policy in the Neighbourhood* (Baden-Baden: Nomos)

Lipsey, R (2004), 'Home and host country effects of FDI' in Baldwin and Winters (eds), *Challenges to Globalization* (Chicago, IL: University of Chicago Press)

Lipson, C (1985), *Standing Guard, Protecting Foreign Capital in the Nineteenth and Twentieth Centuries* (Berkeley, CA: University of California Press)

Lloyd, PJ and MacLaren, D (2006), 'The EU's New Trade Strategy and Regionalisation in the World Economy', 61 Aussenwirtschaft 423

Loewendahl, H (2001), 'A framework for FDI promotion', 10 Transnational Corporations 1

Louri, V (2002), 'Undertaking as a jurisdictional element for the application of EC competition rules', 29 Legal Issues of Economic Integration 143

Lykotrafiti, A (2011), 'Consolidation and rationalization in the transatlantic air transport market-prospects and challenges for competition and consumer welfare', TILEC Discussion Paper 2011–33

MacLean, R and Volpi, B (2000), *EU Trade Barrier Regulation: Tackling Unfair Foreign Trade Practices* (Bembridge: Palladian Law Publishers)

Macleod I, et al (1996), *The external relations of the European Communities* (Oxford: Clarendon Press/Oxford University Press)

Malik, M (2010), *Recent developments in international investment agreements: Negotiations and Disputes* (Winnipeg, International Institute for Sustainable Development)

Manciaux, S (2005), *Investissements étrangers et arbitrage entre Etats et ressortissants d'autres Etats: 25 années d'activité du CIRDI* (Paris: Litec)

Marin Duran, G (2008), 'Development-based differentiation in the European Community's external trade policy: selected issues under Community and International Trade Law', EUI thesis, Florence

—— and Morgera, E (2006), 'Towards Environmental Integration in EC External Relations? A comparative analysis of selected Association Agreements', 6 Yearbook of European Environmental Law 179

Martenczuk, B (2002), 'Cooperation with Developing Countries and Other Third Countries: Elements of a Community Foreign Policy' in Griller and Weidel (eds), *External Economic Relations and Foreign Policy in the European Union*, (Vienna; New York: Springer)

Mathis, JH (2002), *Regional Trade Agreements in the GATT/WTO Article XXIV and the Internal Trade Requirement* (The Hague: TMC Asser Press; Norwell: Kluwer Law International)

Mavroidis, P (2001), 'Transatlantic Regulatory Cooperation: Exclusive Club or "Open Regionalism"' in Bermann, Herdegan, and Lindseth (eds), *Transatlantic Regulatory Cooperation: Legal Problems and Political Prospects* (Oxford: Oxford University Press)

—— (2007), *Trade in Goods: an analysis of international trade agreements* (Oxford: Oxford University Press)

McLeay, F (2006), 'Corporate Codes of Conduct and the Human Rights Accountability of Transnational Corporations: a Small Piece of a Larger Puzzle' in de Schutter (ed), *Transnational Corporations and Human Rights* (Oxford; Portland: Hart Publishing)

Mestmäcker, J (2007), *EG-Wettbewerbsrecht: Kommentar*, Band I (Munich: Beck)

Mola, L (2008), 'Which Role for the EU in the Development of International Investment Law?', Society of International Economic Law, Online Proceedings Working Paper No 26/08

Moran, T (2005), *Does Foreign Investment promote development?* (Washington DC: Institute for International Economics)

—— (2006), *Harnessing Foreign Direct Investment for Development: Policies for Developed and Developing Countries* (Washington DC: Brookings Institution Press)

—— (2008), 'What policies should developing country governments adopt toward outward FDI? Lessons from the experience of developed countries' in Sauvant, Mendoza, and Ince (eds), *The Rise of TNCs from Emerging Markets: Threat or Opportunity?* (Cheltenham: Edward Elgar)

More, G (1999), 'The principle of Equal Treatment: From Market Unifier to Fundamental Right?' in Craig and de Búrca (eds), *The Evolution of EU Law* (Oxford: Oxford University Press)

Müller, D (2000), 'L'investissement etranger: tentative d'une identification' in Daillier (ed), *Droit de l'économie internationale* (Paris: Pedone)

Müller, J (2000), *Kapitalverkehrsfreiheit in der Europäischen Union Bedeutung, Inhalt und Umfang, Weiterentwicklung, Auswirkung auf Völkerrecht und Nationales Recht* (Berlin: Duncker and Humblot)

Müller-Graff, P-C (2008), 'The Common Commercial Policy Enhanced by the Reform Treaty of Lisbon?' in Dashwood and Maresceau (eds), *Law and Practice of EU External Relations* (Cambridge: Cambridge University Press)

Neframi, E (2002), 'International Responsibility of the European Community and of the Member States Under Mixed Agreements' in Cannizzaro (ed), *The European Union as an Actor in International Relations* (Hague; London: Kluwer Law International)

Norberg, S et al (1993), *EEA Law: A Commentary on the EEA Agreement* (Stockholm: Fritzes)

Noyes, J and Smith, B (1988), 'State Responsibility and the Principle of Joint and Several Liability', 13 Yale Journal of International Law 225

Nutall, S (2005), 'Coherence and Consistency' in Hill and Smith (eds), *International Relations and the European Union* (Oxford: Oxford University Press)

Nwobike, J (2006), 'The Emerging Trade Regime under the Cotonou Agreement: Its Human Rights Implications', 40 Journal of World Trade 291

OECD (2002), *'Forty Years' Experience with the OECD Code of Liberalisation of Capital Movements* (Paris: OECD)

—— (2004), *The REIO Exception in MFN Treatment Clauses* (Paris: OECD)

O'Keefe, D (2000), 'Exclusive, Concurrent and Shared Competence' in Dashwood and Hillion (eds), *The general law of EC external relations* (London: Sweet & Maxwell)

O'Keefe, D and Twomey, P (eds) (1994), *Legal Issues of the Maastricht Treaty* (London; New York: Chancery Law Publishing)

Oman, C (2000), *Policy Competition for Foreign Direct Investment: A Study of Competition Among Governments to Attract FDI* (Paris: OECD)

Ortino, F (2004), *Basic Legal Instruments for the Liberalization of Trade: a comparative analysis of EC and WTO Law* (Oxford; Portland: Hart Publishing)

—— (2005), 'From Non-Discrimination to Reasonableness: A Paradigm Shift in International Economic Law?', Jean Monnet Working Papers 1/2005, NYU School of Law

—— (2008), 'The Principle of Non-Discrimination and its Exceptions in GATS: Selected Legal Issues' in Alexander and Andenas (eds), *The World Trade Organization and Trade in Services* (Leiden; Boston: Martinus Nijhoff)

—— (2009), 'Non-Discriminatory Treatment in Investment Disputes' in Dupuy, Francioni, and Petersmann (eds), *Human Rights in International Investment Law and Investor-State Arbitration* (Oxford: Oxford University Press)

Palmeter, D and Mavroidis, P (2004), *Dispute Settlement in the World Trade Organization* (New York: Cambridge University Press)

Paolillo, F in Corten and Klein (eds) (2006), *Les Conventions de Vienne sur le Droit des Traites, Commentaire Article par Article* (Brussels: Bruylant)

Parra, A (1993), 'Principles Governing Foreign Investment, as Reflected in National Investment Codes' in Shihata (ed), *Legal treatment of Foreign Investment: The World Bank Guidelines* (Dordrecht; Boston: Martinus Nijhoff)

Passos R (2010), 'Mixed Agreements from the Perspective of the European Parliament' in Hillion and Koutrakos (eds), *Mixed Agreements Revisited* (Oxford; Portland: Hart Publishing)

Pauwelyn, J (2008), 'The unbearable lightness of likeness' in Panizzon, Pohl, and Sauve (eds), *GATS and the Regulation of International Trade in Services* (Cambridge: Cambridge University Press)

Peers, S (1999), 'Constitutional Principles and International Trade', 24 European Law Review 185

—— (2000), 'EC Frameworks of International Relations: Co-operation, Partnership and Association' in Dashwood and Hillion (eds), *The general law of EC external relations* (London: Sweet & Maxwell)

—— (2000), 'Fragmentation or Evasion in the Community's Development Policy? The Impact of Portugal v Council' in Dashwood, and Hillion (eds), *The General Law of EC External Relations* (London: Sweet & Maxwell)

—— (2002), 'Free Movement of capital: Learning Lessons or Slipping on Split Milk?' in Barnard and Scott (eds), *The Law of the Single European Market* (Oxford: Hart Publishing)

—— (2006), *EU Justice and Home Affairs Law* (Oxford: Oxford University Press)

Pernice, I (1979), *Grundrechtsgehalte im Europäischen Gemeinschaftsrecht* (Baden-Baden: Nomos)

Petersmann, EU (2004), *The WTO Dispute Settlement System 1995–2003* (The Hague; New York: Kluwer Law International)

—— (2006), Justice as Conflict Resolution: Proliferation, Fragmentation and Decentralization of Dispute Settlement in International Trade, 37 University of Pennsylvania Journal of International Economic Law 280

—— (2009), 'Constitutional Theories of International Economic Adjudication and Investor-State Arbitration' in Dupuy, Francioni, and Petersmann (eds), *Human Rights in International Investment Law and Arbitration* (Oxford: Oxford University Press)

Peterson, L and Gray, K (2005), *International Human Rights in Bilateral Investment Treaties and in Investment Treaty Arbitration* (Winnipeg, International Institute for Sustainable Development)

Petrov, R (2008), 'Exporting the *Acquis Communautaire* into the Legal Systems of Third Countries', 13 European Foreign Affairs Review 33

Pinsolle, P (2007), 'The Dispute Resolution Provisions of the Energy Charter Treaty', 10 International Arbitration Law Review 74
Poli, S (2007), 'The EC's Implementation of the WTO Ruling in the Biotech Dispute', 32 European Law Review 705
Pollan, T (2006), *Legal Framework for the Admission of FDI* (Utrecht: Eleven International Publishing)
Prechal, S and Shelkoplyas, N (2004), 'National procedures, public policy and EC Law From Van Schijndel to Eco Swiss and beyond', 5 European Review of Private Law 589
Radu, A (2008), 'Foreign Investors in the EU—Which "Best Treatment"? Interactions Between Bilateral Investment Treaties and EU Law', 14 European Law Journal 237
Reiter, J (2003), 'The EU-Mexico Free Trade Agreement: Assessing the EU approach to regulatory issues' in Sampson and Woolcock (eds), *Regionalism, Multilateralism and Economic Integration* (Tokyo; New York: United Nations University Press)
Reiterer, M (2009), 'From the (French) Mediterranean Union to the (European) Barcelona Process: The "Union for the Mediterranean" as part of the European Neighbourhood Policy', 14 European Foreign Affairs Review 313
Riegel, R (1979), 'Die Einwirkung des Europäischen Gemeinschaftsrechts auf die Eigentumsordnung der Mitgliedstaaten', 25 Recht der Internationalen Wirtschaft 744
Rigaux, A and Simon, D in Corten and Klein (eds) (2006), *Les Conventions de Vienne sur le Droit des Traites, Commentaire Article par Article* (Brussels: Bruylant)
Ritter, C (2004), 'The New Technology Transfer Block Exemption under EC Competition Law', 31 Legal Issues of Economic Integration 161
Rittstieg, H (1982), Grundgesetz und Eigentumsordnung', 35 Neue Jurisitische Wochenschrift 721
Robles, ER (2006), 'Political and Quasi-Adjudicative Dispute Settlement Models in European Union Free Trade Agreements', WTO Economic and Research Statistics Division, Staff Working Paper ERSD-2006–09
Rosas, A (1998), 'Mixed Union—Mixed Agreements' in Koskenniemi (ed), *International Law Aspects of the European Union* (The Hague; Boston: Kluwer Law International)
—— (2000), 'The European Union and Mixed Agreements' in Dashwood and Hillion (eds), *The general law of EC external relations* (London: Sweet & Maxwell)
——(2001), 'Human Rights in the External Trade Policy of the European Union' in *World Trade and the Protection of Human Rights Human Rights in Face of Global Economic Challenges* (Brussels: Bruylant)
——(2003), 'International Dispute Settlement: EU Practices and Procedures', 46 German Yearbook of International Law 284
Roucounas, E (1987), Engagements parallèles et contradictoires, 206 Recueil de Cours 81
Roy, M, Marchetti, J, and Lim, H (2006), 'Services liberalization in the new generation of Preferential Trade Agreements (PTAs): How much further than the GATS?', WTO Working Paper ERSD-2006–07
Rubins, N (2004), 'The Notion of Investment in International Investment Arbitration' in Horn (ed), *Arbitrating Foreign Investment Disputes* (The Hague: Kluwer Law International)
Sacerdoti, G (1989), 'Barcelona Traction Revisited: Foreign-owned and Controlled Companies in International Law' in Dinstein (ed), *International Law at a Time of Perplexity: Essays in Honor of Shabtai Rosenne* (Dordrecht; Boston: Martinus Nijhoff)
Sachs, L and Sauvant, K (eds) (2009), *The Impact of Bilateral Investment and Double Taxation Treaties on Foreign Direct Investment Flows* (New York: Oxford University Press)

Salacuse, J (2004), 'Towards a Global treaty on Foreign Investment: the Search for a Grand Bargain' in Horn (ed), *Arbitrating foreign Investment Disputes* (The Hague: Kluwer Law International)

—— and Sullivan, N (2005), 'Do BITs really work: an evaluation of bilateral investment treaties and their grand bargain', 46 Harvard International Law Journal 67

Sauvant K (ed) (2008), *Appeal Mechanisms in International Investment Disputes* (New York: Oxford University Press)

—— and Weber, S (2005), *International Investment Agreements: Key Issues Volume III* (New York; Geneva: United Nations Publications)

Sauve, P and Ward, N (2009), 'Services and Investment in the EC-CARIFORUM Economic Partnership Agreement Innovation in Rule Design and Implications for Africa', ECIPE

Scharf, D (2008), 'Die Kapitalverkehrsfreiheit gegenüber Drittstaaten', 76 Beiträge zum Transnationalen Wirtschaftsrecht 1

Schill, SW (2010), 'Crafting the international economic order: The public function of Investment Treaty arbitration and its significance for the role of the arbitrator', 23 Leiden Journal of International Law 401

Schokkaert, J (2002), 'European Conventional Practice of Protection of Investments Abroad', 3 Journal of World Investment and Trade 615

—— and Heckscher, Y (2009), 'Protected Investors Nationality', 10 Journal of World Investment and Trade 699

Schott, J (2004), 'Free Trade Agreements: Boon or Bane of the World Trading System?' in Schott (ed), *Free Trade Agreements: US Strategies and Priorities* (Washington DC: Institute for International Economics)

Schreuer, C (2001), *The ICSID Convention: A commentary* (Cambridge: Cambridge University Press)

—— (2006), 'The Concept of Expropriation under the ECT and other Investment Protection Treaties' in Ribeiro (ed), *Investment Arbitration and the Energy Charter Treaty* (Huntington, NY: JurisNet)

—— (2008), 'Fair and Equitable Treatment (FET): interactions with other standards' in Coop and Ribeiro (eds), *Investment Protection and the Energy Charter Treaty* (Huntington, NY: JurisNet)

Schrijver, N and Weiss, F (2004), *International Law and Sustainable Development* (Leiden; Boston: Martinus Nijhoff)

Schuch, J (2006), 'Critical notes on the European Court of Justice's decision on most-favoured-nation treatment under tax treaties, 15 EC Tax Review 6

Schütze, R (2006), 'Supremacy Without Pre-Emption? The Very Slowly Emergent Doctrine of Community Pre-Emption', 43 Common Market Law Review 1023

—— (2008), 'Lisbon and the federal order of competences: a prospective analysis', 33 European Law Review 709

Scott, J (2002), 'Mandatory or Imperative Requirements in the EU and the WTO' in Barnard and Scott (eds), *The Law of the Single European Market: Unpacking the Premises* (Oxford: Hart Publishing)

Sermet, L (1998), *The European Convention on Human Rights and Property Rights* (Strasbourg: Council of Europe Publishing)

Shan, W (2001), 'Towards a common European Community policy on investment issues', 2 Journal of World Investment and Trade 603

—— (2005), *The legal framework of EU-China investment relations* (Oxford; Portland: Hart Publishing)

Shany, Y (2003), *The Competing jurisdiction of International courts and tribunals* (Oxford: Oxford University Press)

—— (2005), 'Contract Claims vs Treaty Claims: Mapping Conflicts between ICSID Decisions on Multisourced Investment Claims', 99 American Journal of International Law 835

Shihata, I (1988), *Multilateral Investment Guarantee Agency and foreign investment* (Dordrecht: Martinus Nijhoff)

—— (1994), 'Recent Trends Relating to Entry of Foreign Investment', 9 ICSID Review—Foreign Investment Law Journal 47

Sideek, M (1999), *European Community Law on the Free Movement of Capital and the EMU* (The Hague; Boston: Kluwer Law International)

Sinclair, I (1984), *The Vienna Convention on the Law of the Treaties* (Manchester; Dover: Manchester University Press)

Smith, M and Woolcock, S (1999), 'European Commercial Policy: A Leadership Role in the New Millennium?', 4 European Foreign Affairs Review 439

Snyder, F (2003), 'The Gatekeepers: The European Courts and the WTO', 40 Common Market Law Review 313

Soderlund, C (2007), 'Intra-EU BIT Investment Protection and the EC Treaty', 24 Journal of International Arbitration 455

Sornarajah, M (2000) *Settlement of Investment Disputes* (The Hague; Boston: Kluwer Law International)

—— (2010), *The International Law on Foreign Investment* (Cambridge: Cambridge University Press)

Staker, C (1990), 'Diplomatic Protection of Private Business Companies', 61 British Yearbook of International Law 155

Steinberger, E (2006), 'The WTO Treaty as a Mixed Agreement: Problems with the EC's and the EC Member States' Membership of the WTO', 17 European Journal of International Law 843

Stephenson, SM (2000), 'GATS and Regional Integration' in Sauve and Stern (eds), *GATS 2000—New Directions in Services Liberalization* (Washington DC: Brookings Institution)

Szepesi, S (2004), *Comparing EU Free Trade Agreements: Investment*, InBrief 6D of European Centre for Development Policy Management (Maastricht: ECDPM)

Taylor, R (2008), 'Choice-of-Forum Provisions in Regional Trade Agreements and Their Implications for International Dispute Resolution and International Law', 3 Global Trade and Customs Journal 27

te Velde, D and Bilal, S (2005), 'Foreign Direct Investment in the Cotonou Agreement: Building on Private Sector Initiatives' in Babarinde and Faber (eds), *The European Union and Developing Countries The Cotonou Agreement* (Leiden; Boston: Martinus Nijhoff)

Thallinger, G (2007), 'From Apology to Utopia: EU-ACP Economic Partnership Agreements Oscillating between WTO Conformity and Sustainability', 12 European Foreign Affairs Review 499

Thym, D (2008), 'Parliamentary Involvement in European International Relations' in Cremona and de Witte (eds), *EU Foreign Relations Law: Constitutional Fundamentals* (Oxford; Portland: Hart Publishing)

Tietje, C (1997), 'The Concept of Coherence in the Treaty on European Union and the Common Foreign and Security Policy', 2 European Foreign Affairs Review 211

—— (2008), 'The Applicability of the Energy Charter Treaty in ICSID Arbitration of EU Nationals v EU Member States', 78 Beiträge zum Transnationalen Wirtschaftsrecht 1

—— (2009), 'Die Außenwirtschaftsverfassung der EU nach dem Vertrag von Lissabon', 83 Beiträge zum Transnationalen Wirtschaftsrecht 1

Tobin, J and Rose-Ackerman, S (2003), 'Foreign direct investment and the business environment in developing countries: The impact of bilateral investment treaties', Yale Law School Center for Law, Economics and Public Policy Research Paper No 293

Tomuschat, C (2002), 'The International Responsibility of the European Union' in E Cannizzaro (ed), *The European Union as an Actor in International Relations* (The Hague; London: Kluwer Law International)

Torrent, R (2007), 'Derecho comunitario e Inversiones extranjeras directas: Libre circulacion de los capitales vs Regulacion no discriminatoria del establecimiento De la golden share a los nuevos Open Skies', 22 Revista Espanola de Derecho Europeo 283

Trebilcock, M and Howse, R (2005), *The Regulation of International Trade* (London: Routledge)

Tridimas, T (2000), The WTO and OECD Opinions' in Dashwood and Hillion (eds), *The general law of EC external relations* (London: Sweet & Maxwell)

—— (2006), *The General Principles of EU Law* (Oxford: Oxford University Press)

Tudor-Knoll, I (2009), 'The Fair and Equitable Treatment Standard and Human Rights Norms' in Dupuy, Francioni, and Petersmann (eds), *Human Rights in International Investment Law and Arbitration* (Oxford: Oxford University Press)

Tudor, I (2008), *The Fair and Equitable Treatment Standard in the International Law of Foreign Investment* (Oxford: Oxford University Press)

Tupman, M and Broches, A (1966), 'The Convention on the Settlement of Investment Disputes: Some observations on Jurisdiction', 5 Columbia Journal of Transnational Law 268

—— (1986), 'Case Studies in the Jurisdiction of the International Centre for Investment Disputes', 35 International and Comparative Law Quarterly 816

UNCTAD (1998), *World Investment Report 1998: Trends and Determinants* (New York; Geneva: United Nations Publications)

—— (1999), *Admission and Establishment* (New York; Geneva: United Nations Publications)

—— (1999), *World Investment Report 1999: FDI and the Challenge of Development* (New York; Geneva: United Nations Publications)

—— (2002), *World Investment Report 2002: Transnational Corporations and Export Competitiveness* (New York; Geneva: United Nations Publications)

—— (2003), *FDI and Performance Requirements: New Evidence from Selected Countries* (New York; Geneva: United Nations Publications)

—— (2003), *Investment and Technology Policies for Competitiveness: Review of Successful Country Experiences* (New York; Geneva: United Nations Publications)

—— (2003), *World Investment Report 2003: FDI Policies for Development: National and International Perspectives* (New York; Geneva: United Nations Publications)

—— (2004), *World Investment Report 2004: The Shift Towards Services* (New York; Geneva: United Nations Publications)

—— (2005), *Economic Development in Africa, Rethinking the Role of Foreign Direct Investment* (New York; Geneva: United Nations Publications)

—— (2006), *World Investment Report 2006: FDI from Developing and Transition Economies: Implications for Development* (New York; Geneva: United Nations Publications)

—— (2008), *Investment Promotion Provisions in International Investment Agreements* (New York; Geneva: United Nations Publications)

—— (2008), *World Investment Report 2008: Transnational Corporations and the Infrastructure Challenge* (New York; Geneva: United Nations Publications)

—— (2009), *World Investment Report 2009: Transnational Corporations, Agricultural Production and Development* (New York; Geneva: United Nations Publications)

—— (2010), *World Investment Report 2010: Investing in a Low-carbon Economy* (New York; Geneva: United Nations Publications)

Usher, J (2006), 'Monetary Movements and the Internal Market' in Nic Shuibhne (ed), *Regulating the Internal Market* (Cheltenham; Northampton, MA: Edward Elgar)

—— (2008), 'The Evolution of the Free Movement of Capital', 31 Fordham International Law Journal 1533

van den Hende, L (2001), 'Free Movement of Services and the Right of Establishment in a Pan-Euro-Mediterranean Economic Area: Between EU Membership and the GATS' in Maresceau and Lannon (eds), *The EU's Enlargement and Mediterranean Strategies* (Basingstoke; New York: Palgrave)

—— and Smith, H (2008), 'GATS Article XVI and National Regulatory Sovereignty: What lessons to Draw from *US-Gambling?*' in Alexander and Andenas (eds), *The World Trade Organization and Trade in Services* (Leiden; Boston: Martinus Nijhoff)

Vandenberghe, J (2008), 'On Carrots and Sticks: The Social Dimension of EU Trade Policy', 13 European Foreign Affairs Review 561

Villiger, M (2009), *Commentary on the 1969 Vienna Convention on the Law of Treaties* (Leiden; Boston: Martinus Nijhoff)

Vincentelli, I (2008), 'The Uncertain Future of ICSID in Latin America', Independent Research Paper, University of Miami Law School

von der Groeben, A and Schwartze, I (2004), *EU-EG Vertrag Kommentar* (Baden-Baden: Nomos)

von Milczewski, C (1994), *Der Grundrechtliche Schutz des Eigentums im Europäischen Gemeinschaftsrecht* (Frankfurt am Main; New York: Peter Lang)

Walden, I and Angel, J (2005), *Telecommunications Law and Regulation* (Oxford: Oxford University Press)

Wälde, T (2001), 'The Energy Charter Treaty' in Redgwell (ed), *Energy Law in Europe* (Oxford: Oxford University Press)

—— (2004), 'Investment Arbitration under the Energy Charter Treaty: An Overview of Selected Key Issues based on Recent Litigation Experience' in Horn (ed), *Arbitrating Foreign Investment Disputes* (The Hague: Kluwer Law International)

Weatherill, S (2006), 'Supply of and demand for internal market regulation: strategies, preferences and interpretation' in Nic Shuibhne (ed), *Regulating the Internal Market* (Cheltenham; Northampton, MA: Edward Elgar)

Wehland, H (2009), 'Intra-EU Investment Agreements and Arbitration: Is European Community Law an Obstacle?', 58 International and Comparative Law Quarterly 297

Wessel, R (2000), 'The Inside Looking Out: Consistency and Delimitation in EU External Relations', 37 Common Market Law Review 1135

White, G (1992), 'The New International Economic Order: Principles and Trends' in Fox (ed), *International Economic Law and Developing States: An Introduction* (London: British Institute of International and Comparative Law)

Williams, R (2005), 'Community Development Cooperation Law, Sustainable Development, and the Convention on Europe—From Dislocation to Consistency?', 4 Oxford Yearbook of European Environmental Law 303

Wimmer, A (1996), 'The Impact of the General Agreement on Trade in Services on the OECD Multilateral Agreement on Investment', 19 World Competition 109

Woods, L (2004), *Free Movement of Goods and Services Within the European Community* (Aldershot; Burlington, VT: Ashgate)

Woolcock, S (2007), 'European Union Policy Towards Free Trade Agreements', ECIPE Working Paper No 3/2007

——and Kleinheisterkamp, J (2010), 'The EU approach to international investment policy after the Lisbon Treaty', Study Directorate General for External Policies of the Union (Strasbourg: European Parliament)

Wouters, J (2001), 'Constitutional Limits of Differentiation: the Principle of Equality' in de Witte, Hanf, and Vos (eds), *The Many Faces of Differentiation in EU Law* (Antwerp; Oxford; New York: Intersentia)

——and Coppens, D (2008), 'GATS and Domestic Regulation: Balancing the Right to Regulate and Trade Liberalization' in Alexander and Andenas (eds), *The World Trade Organization and Trade in Services* (Leiden; Boston: Martinus Nijhoff)

——and De Meester, B (2008), 'The European Union's External Relations after the Lisbon Treaty' in Griller and Ziller (eds), *The Lisbon Treaty: EU Constitutionalism without a Constitutional Treaty?* (Vienna; New York: Springer)

WTO Trade in Services Division (2005), *A handbook on the GATS agreement* (Cambridge: Cambridge University Press)

Yala, F (2005), 'The Notion of Investment in ICSID Case Law: A Drifting Jurisdictional Requirement?', 22 Journal of International Arbitration 105

Young, AR (2007), 'Trade Politics Ain't What it Used to Be: The EU in the Doha Round', 45 Journal of Common Market Studies 789

Zagel, G (2005), 'Article 300 TEC' in Herzog, Campbell, and Zagel (eds), *Smit and Herzog Law of the European Union, A Commentary* (New York: Matthew Bender)

Index

The manufacturer's authorised representative in the EU for product safety is Oxford University Press España S.A. of El Parque Empresarial San Fernando de Henares, Avenida de Castilla, 2 - 28830 Madrid (www.oup.es/en or product.safety@oup.com). OUP España S.A. also acts as importer into Spain of products made by the manufacturer.

Printed and bound by CPI Group (UK) Ltd, Croydon, CR0 4YY

14/09/2026

02216305-0015